SAMUEL N. C. LIEU

MANICHAEISM

IN THE LATER ROMAN EMPIRE
AND MEDIEVAL CHINA
A HISTORICAL SURVEY

WITH A FOREWORD BY MARY BOYCE

D0769166

MANCHESTER UNIVERSITY PRESS

Copyright © S. N. C. Lieu 1985

Published by Manchester University Press
Oxford Road, Manchester M13 9PL
and 51 Washington Street, Dover,
New Hampshire 03820, USA

The author and publishers are grateful to the trustees of The British
Academy for a subvention towards the production of this volume

British Library cataloguing in publication data
Lieu, Samuel N. C.
　Manichaeism in the later Roman Empire
　and medieval China, a historical survey
　1. Manichaeism—History
　I. Title
　299'.932　　BT1410

Library of Congress cataloging in publication data
Lieu, Samuel N. C.
　Manichaeism in the later Roman Empire and medieval China.
　Bibliography: p. 314
　1. Manichaeism—Rome—History.　2. Manichaeism—China—History.
　3. Rome—Religion.　4. China—Religion.
　I. Title.
　BT1410.L47)　1984　　299'.932　　84-26093

ISBN 0-7190-1088-8 cased only

Printed in Great Britain
at the Alden Press, Oxford

CONTENTS

FOREWORD

The many striking discoveries of Manichaean documents made this century have shed new light on this remarkable faith; and the time was clearly ripe for a fresh synthesis, with a reconsideration of earlier known data from the Roman world. In treating these data together with the largely unfamiliar Chinese material, Dr Lieu has been able to offer penetrating insights, with both contrasts and parallels. For the west he has drawn on a wealth of primary sources, in Syriac, Greek and Latin, to trace the success and ultimate eclipse of this gentle, much persecuted, missionary religion. In the Mediterranean lands its growth was bound up with that of the proliferating early Christian sects; and the reader is accordingly presented with a lucid analysis of rival doctrines and communities. Dr Lieu perceives the strongest influences on the formation of Mani's own beliefs to be Jewish apocalyptic, Christianity and Marcionism; and in arguing this he gives a concise summary of the prophet's own teachings, thus making his book accessible to students of religion in general, as well as to specialists in Manichaeism. After considering the earliest days of the faith, he traces its spread during the relatively tolerant times of the pagan Roman emperors, under whom it suffered chiefly on political grounds (because of its links with Rome's enemy, Persia); and then under Christian rulers down to the time of St Augustine. A process of civil excommunication, he demonstrates, began with Theodosius in the fourth century; and there followed not only serious theological debates, mixed with unscrupulous polemic, but also harsh persecution. By the sixth century, anathematised, vilified as a defilement, its leaders beheaded, their followers exiled, impoverished, or also slain, Manichaeism was extinguished and, with its books destroyed, left only its name to the Christian world, as a term of abuse for dualisms generally.

Dr Lieu then turns eastward, following the Silk Road with Sogdian merchants and missionaries, to trace how the religion found a foothold in China, where, according to tradition, it arrived in the latter

part of the seventh century. Again working from primary sources, Dr
Lieu shows how in China hostility to Manichaeism arose mainly from
national pride and fear of a threat by this foreign, ascetic teaching to
social order; and how nevertheless a small Manichaean community
managed to establish itself and survive, taking on protectively now
the outer guise of Buddhism, now that of Taoism. Under the Sung its
members, living mostly in the south, were among those classed as
'vegetarian demon-worshippers', who were persecuted for being
socially disruptive. Tolerance was extended to them subsequently by
the Mongols; and it was not until sometime after 1600 that Manichaeism disappeared from China, and so from the earth. Its existence
there for over 800 years is recorded by a growing number of documents; and these, Dr Lieu shows, testify to the remarkable fidelity of
the little Chinese community to the teachings of the 'prophet of
Light'. China also possesses the only Manichaean temple to survive
anywhere in the world.

The Chinese evidence, in one instance entirely new, has hitherto
been largely inaccessible to most western scholars; and its evaluation
is clearly difficult, because of the nature of the sources and the need
for a scholarly understanding of the historical and cultural background
over centuries. Dr Lieu's learned and judicious treatment is therefore
an important and very welcome contribution to Manichaean studies.
His book has also wide interest through his analysis of the different
forces at work in two great empires, with the complex interaction on
the destiny of an other-worldly religion of politics, diplomacy, war,
trade and national feeling, as well as rival systems of belief. That
Manichaeism withstood so many pressures for generations in such
different environments, and, as Dr Lieu stresses, without benefit of
state support, military conquest or an ethnic base, makes it truly a
religion worthy of study.

Despite the impressive scope of this work, there is one area where
the writer could wish that Dr Lieu had felt able to go back a little
further in time. In treating the much-debated question of the formative influences on Mani, he wholly dismisses, in the light of new
Coptic evidence, the possibility of an Iranian component; but Jewish
apocalyptic, Christianity and Marcionism all arguably themselves
owed great debts to Zoroastrianism, whose doctrines had been known
in the eastern Mediterranean lands for centuries, and which was still a
living presence in Anatolia in Marcion's lifetime. It is possible, therefore, to see Iran as a powerful contributor to Mani's theology at one
remove – which presumably aided his own missionary work in that
land. Dr Lieu may justly consider, however, that in covering with
exemplary clarity and thoroughness a period of over 1,300 years, in
geographical areas stretching from Spain to the coasts of China, he has

contributed richly enough already, and can properly leave such remoter analyses to others who may choose to labour further in this field.

Mary Boyce

ACKNOWLEDGEMENT

Ever since the discovery of genuine Manichaean texts from Tun-huang and Turfan at the beginning of this century, the study of Manichaeism has been an interdisciplinary one, drawing together classicists, orientalists, theologians and historians. A trans-cultural survey of the history of Manichaeism therefore requires no justification. Mani, the founder of the religion had intended that it should be preached in every part of the known world. Any attempt, therefore, at a missionary history of Manichaeism must inevitably involve the crossing of the boundaries of established academic disciplines. I have based my research, as far as I am able, on a study of the original sources in Greek, Latin, Syriac and Chinese. Since I have no first-hand knowledge of the sources in Sogdian, Uighur and Arabic, the history of the sect in Muslim Iraq and in the Uighur Kingdom of Qočo can only be sketched in outline. However, although the main focus of the book is on the history of the sect in the later Roman empire and China (from late T'ang to early Ming), I have provided the readers with what I hope is an adequate introduction to the principal tenets of Mani's teaching and the main facts about his life. The successful decipherment of the *Cologne Mani Codex* which contains accounts of the formative years of Mani's life has brought about revolutionary changes to the study of Manichaeism and most standard introductory works or articles in reference books are now seriously in need of revision. A great deal of new material on the history of the sect has also come to light through the continuing publication of Manichaean texts from Turfan and from archaeological finds in China. This work endeavours to show how this material has broadened and deepened our knowledge of the missionary history of this extraordinary gnostic world religion.

This book grew out of a doctoral dissertation in Literae Humaniores for the University of Oxford which was completed in 1981. I am greatly indebted to my three supervisors who at various stages offered me indispensable help and guidance. Professor Peter R. L. Brown has consistently nurtured my interest in the interdisciplinary study of history. His own signal contributions to the study of Manichaeism and the age of Augustine have been a constant source of illumination. Dr Sebastian Brock introduced me to the complex world of early Syriac Christianity. His immense learning on the subject was an invaluable asset to me and his willingness to find time to deal with my problems, no matter how trivial, was examplary. Professor P. van der Loon undertook the arduous task of checking and improving my translations from Chinese sources and saved me from innumerable careless errors. He also kindly drew my attention to a hitherto unnoticed passage in the Taoist Canon on Manichaeism in south China which provides some interesting new information.

Professor Mary Boyce acted as my unofficial external supervisor on the Iranian aspects of the work and I am grateful to her for taking the trouble to read and comment on substantial parts of the work. I have learned much from her about the history and culture of Sassanian Iran as well as Manichaeism. Professor Hans-Joachim Klimkeit has been a constant source of encouragement and advice. I would like to thank him in particular for his translation into English of a Manichaean historical text in Uighur. Similarly, I would like to express my sincere gratitude to Dr and Mrs G. Stroumsa for supplying me with a translation from the Arabic of a section of the *Annales* of Eutychius which deals with Manichaeism in Roman Egypt. To my colleague, Mr Charles Morgan, I owe a special debt for the many hours we spent wrestling with the tortuous Greek of Titus of Bostra. The staff of the Inter-Library Loans division of the University Library of Warwick have been indefatigable in securing loans of obscure oriental texts from both British and foreign libraries. Without their help, the work would have certainly taken much longer to accomplish. Mrs Janet Bailey, our Joint School Secretary, kindly undertook to type a substantial part of the final draft of my polyglottal manuscript, and I am greatly indebted to her skill and patience.

The original research for this work was greatly facilitated by my election to a junior research fellowship at Wolfson College, Oxford, which provided me with a stimulating academic environment for two years (1974–6). Two of the College's senior fellows, Sir Ronald Syme and the late Sir John Addis both took considerable interest in my work and imparted freely of their considerable learning and mature judgement. It is indeed sad that the work was not completed before Sir John's sudden death in 1983.

Many fellow Manichaean scholars have kept my knowledge of the subject up to date by generously sending me their publications. I am particularly grateful to regular communications from Professors Asmussen, Boyce, Henrichs, Klimkeit, Koenen and Ries, and from Drs Coyle, Sundermann, Stroumsa and Zieme. Mr Lin Wu-shu not only sent me his own works on Manichaeism but those of other Chinese scholars and has kindly translated two of my earlier articles on the subject into Chinese for publication in the People's Republic of China.

My wife Judith has shared with me many of the joys and excitements of my research. Despite pressures of motherhood and her own academic work, she has found time to be my most valuable help and critic. Her loving care has sustained me throughout the writing of the book and has made the experience of it immensely enjoyable. My parents too gave me much encouragement and support, and to my father especially I owe my love for the study of history.

The publication of this book has been made possible by a generous grant from the British Academy. I would also like to thank the Research and Innovation Fund of Warwick University for a further subvention towards the cost of publication and the Spalding Trust for a grant towards the cost of preparing the final manuscript.

The Nuffield Foundation deserves to be mentioned although it has not directly funded the research for this book. It has generously supported my research into two related areas: Romano-Persian relations and the comparative study of Byzantine and Chinese (Buddhist) hagiography. Both these projects yielded much useful background information for this book and I would like to thank the many scholars who have assisted me with them, especially Mrs Marna Morgan, Mrs Doris Dance and my wife Dr Judith Lieu. Much of the book was written during our three happy years of residence at Queen's College, Birmingham, and we both owe much to the friendship of its staff and students as well as its excellent library facilities.

University of Warwick

IBERIA

ARMENIA

Artaxata

Amida

Gonzak

Edessa
OSPHOENE
Nisibis

Antioch

ATROPATENE

Carrhae

Chaboras

Callinicum

Hatra
ADIABENE
(Bet Garmai)

SYRIA COELE Circesium
Palmyra

Arbela

Karkā de Bēt Selōk

Dura
Europos

Ecbatana

SYRIA PALESTINA

ASSURISTAN
(Bet Aramaie)

Holwan

Alexandria

Bostra

Ctesiphon

Bet
Lapat

Gaza
Jerusalem

Seleucia

Tigris

Leontopolis
Eleutheropolis
Ziph

ARABIA

Babylon

Medinet
Medi

BABYLONIA

(Kashkar)

SUSIANA

Oxyrhynchos

Euphrates

MESENE
(Maisan)

Hermopolis
Magna

Ailat

Ferat

Lycopolis

Hypselis

EGYPT

Berenice

0   Miles   250

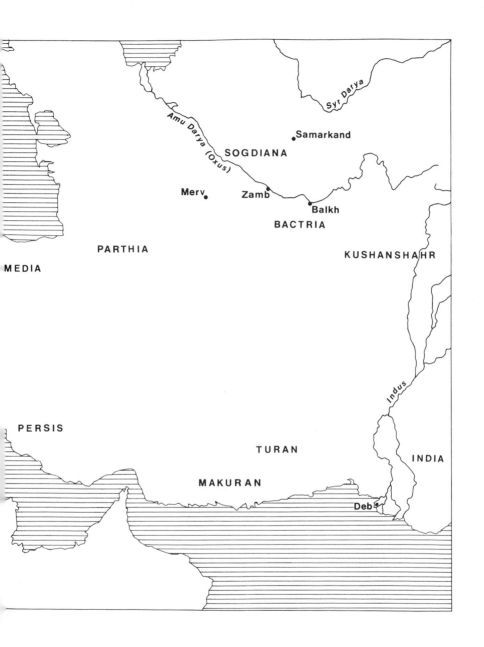

The Near East in the time of Mani

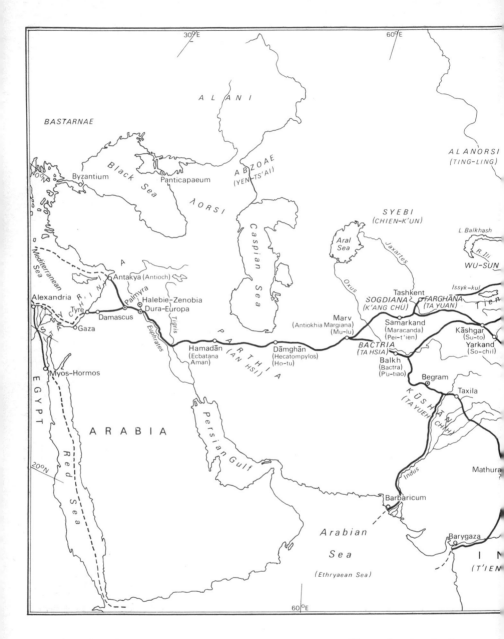

The Silk Road from China to the Roman Orient (from the *Cambridge History of Iran*)

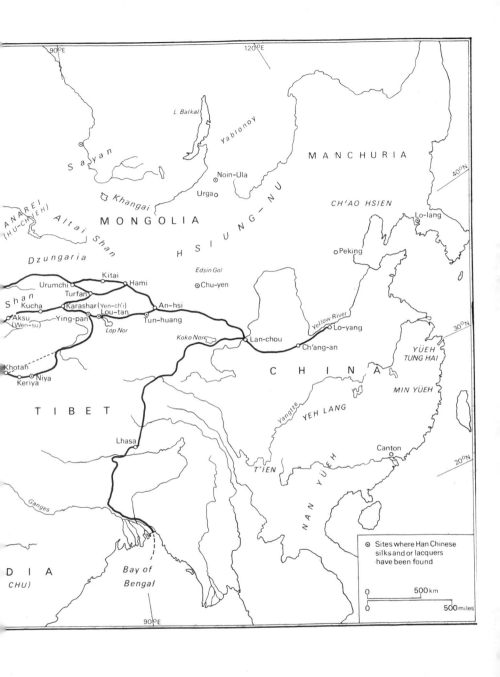

90°E 120°E

L. Balkal

S a y a n

Yablonoy

MANCHURIA

40°N

Noin-Ula

Khangai

Urga

CH'AO HSIEN

MONGOLIA

Lo-lang

ANAREI
(HU-CH'IEH)

Altai Shan

Dzungaria

H S I U N G - N U

Peking

Edsin Gol

Chu-yen

Kitai

S h a n

Urumchi   Hami

Turfan

Kucha   Karashar (Yen-ch'i)

Aksu   Lou-tan

(Wen-su) Ying-pan

An-hsi

Yellow River

Lo-yang

30°N

Lop Nor

Tun-huang

Koko Nor

Lan-chou

Khotan

Niya

Keriya

Ch'ang-an

C H I N A

YÜEH
TUNG HAI

T I B E T

MIN YÜEH

Yangtze   YEH LANG

Lhasa

Ganges

T'IEN

20°N

Canton

N A N   Y Ü E H

D I A
(CHU)

Bay of
Bengal

⊙ Sites where Han Chinese
silks and or lacquers
have been found

0   500 km

0   500 miles

90°E

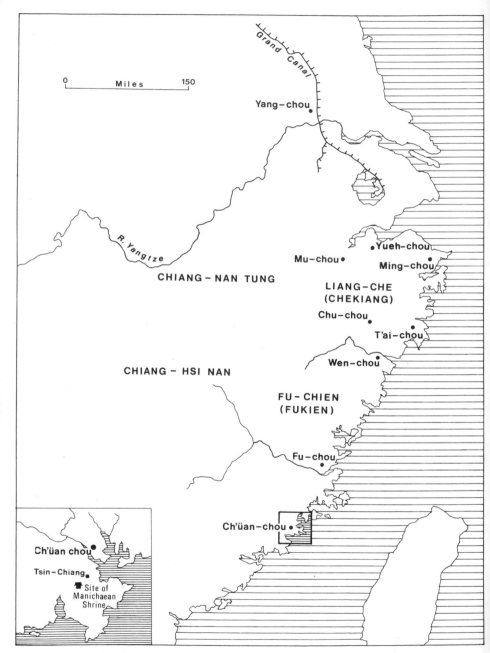

South China, showing place names mentioned in chapter VII

CHAPTER I

THE GNOSIS OF MANI

(1)   MESOPOTAMIA IN THE LATE
             PARTHIAN PERIOD

The social and political history of Mesopotamia, the Land of the Two
Rivers, in the pre-Islamic period is characterised by periodic changes
of hegemony.[1] The cycle of ancient empires which earned the region
the epithet of the 'cradle of civilisation' was completed by the coming
to power of the Persians under Cyrus the Great (559–529 BC). In its
heyday the Achaemenid Empire held complete sway over the Near
East from the foothills of the Hindu Kush to the straits of the Bosporus
and the sandy wastes of Libya. This first ever world empire was
brought abruptly to an end by the brilliant victories of Alexander of
Macedon, especially his defeat of Darius at Gaugamela (331 BC)
which gave him control of Mesopotamia and Iran.[2] After his death
Greek political domination and cultural influence were maintained in
the region by the Seleucids who, after the treaty of 278 BC with
Macedon, were confirmed in their possession of the eastern provinces
of Alexander's empire.[3] Seleucus I Nicator (c. 358–281 BC) founded a
new and important city on the right bank of the Tigris some ninety
miles north-east of the ancient city of Babylon.[4] Throughout the
Hellenistic period, the city of Seleucia was a thriving outpost of Greek
culture as well as being a prosperous river port and the administrative
capital of the eastern half of the Seleucid empire.[5] Although Greek
culture in Mesopotamia was largely an urban affair and enjoyed
mainly by the upper echelons of society, it contributed to the region's
cosmopolitan outlook and laid the foundations for further diffusion of
ideas and cultural influences, especially those of a religious nature,
from the more Hellenised regions of the Near East such as Syria,
Palestine, Asia Minor and Egypt.

The Parthians who became overlords of Mesopotamia in c. 141 BC
were determined to preserve the social and economic structure of the
region and to this end they openly expressed their admiration for

Greek culture, especially in the fields of art and architecture.[6] Documents and inscriptions of this period found in Dura Europos, Susa and Avrōmān show that Greek remained in use as an administrative language in former Greek colonies of Mesopotamia and the adjacent parts of Iran.[7] The importance of the Greek communities and their culture within the Parthian empire was clearly recognised by the Arsacids who chose to strike coins with legends in a debased Greek alphabet which displayed among others the title of 'Philhellenos'.[8] The propaganda value of Parthian cultural policy towards the Greeks in the Near East, however, diminished rapidly as the Greeks of Europe and Asia Minor found a new champion of Hellenism in the emergent power of Rome. The initial conflict between the Roman and Parthian empires witnessed the complete defeat of Crassus near Carrhae in 53 BC and the severe mauling of Mark Antony's legions in Media seventeen years later.[9] The victories brought Parthian control to Upper Mesopotamia and for much of the early decades of our era Rome remained on the defensive. The disaster which befell Crassus served as a salutary warning against ill-conceived ventures across the Euphrates.

Within Mesopotamia, the metropolis of Seleucia was little affected by the change of hegemony. The city was not stormed and suffered nothing more serious than verbal reprimands from the Parthians when her inhabitants were accused of aiding the Seleucids and later the Romans.[10] She was even spared from having a Parthian garrison as the Arsacids appreciated her strategic and economic importance by establishing their winter capital at the former Greek settlement of Ctesiphon on the opposite bank of the river. From there, they could enjoy the cultural life and the economic benefits which the Greek city had to offer. A much quoted example of the popularity of Greek culture among the Parthian royals is that it was in the middle of a performance of Euripides's *Bacchae* at the court that the severed head of the defeated Crassus was brought on stage as part of the mutilated limbs of Pentheus.[11] The city minted its own coins and retained its political institutions into the first century AD. According to Tacitus, Seleucia still possessed a senate of three hundred citizens, chosen for their wealth and wisdom as late as the last years of Tiberius (Augustus from 14–31 AD). Tacitus's remark that when the senate and the people were at one they were united in their contempt for the Parthians and when they were at odds with each other they played the Parthians to their advantage testifies to the level of autonomy which the city enjoyed despite the closeness of the Parthian capital.[12] Greek culture continued to flourish in former Hellenistic foundations in Parthian held Mesopotamia and they might have even attracted Greek immigrants from adjacent parts of the Roman empire.[13]

For most of the first century AD, Armenia and the upper reaches of the Euphrates rather than Mesopotamia was the scene of military confrontation between Rome and Parthia.[14] Trajan's annexation of Arabia and the Nabataean kingdoms in 105, of Armenia in 114, and his lightning invasion of Mesopotamia resulted in a major southward shift of Rome's eastern frontiers.[15] By means of a well co-ordinated two-pronged attack, Trajan threw the Parthian defences in Mesopotamia completely off-balance.[16] His capture of Ctesiphon and his eventual arrival at the head of the Persian Gulf showed the vulnerability of this important region of the Parthian empire to a determined Roman thrust down the Euphrates. Although Rome soon withdrew from Babylonia, her control over Upper Mesopotamia was now much firmer. Under the Antonines, Ctesiphon was once more raided by Roman forces, but of much greater strategic significance was the absorption of the kingdom of Osrhoene centred round the city of Edessa (ancient and modern Urfa) which became a Roman province after the successful eastern campaigns of Lucius Verus in 163–6.[17] At the same time, Nisibis with its surrounding territory of Mygdonia became a Roman city and was later rewarded with the title of *colonia* by Septimius Severus.[18] Edessa also became a *colonia* before 213/4 as indicated by a dated Syriac manuscript from Dura Europos.[19] The latter, itself an important Hellenistic foundation, passed into Roman control in 165 and became one of Rome's line of watch-posts on the Euphrates which kept open both the important trade route to Palmyra and the invasion route to the Parthian capital.[20] This gradual extension of Roman power into Upper Mesopotamia gave Rome several vantage points from which she could launch attacks against Parthian held Babylonia and the Trans-Tigritanian territories. The brief flag-showing campaign of Septimius Severus in 197/8 led once more to the flight of the Parthian court from Ctesiphon, and the ease with which this phase of the campaign was concluded provides ample proof of the superior position which Rome now enjoyed on the Euphrates frontier.[21] His son Caracalla, who desired to emulate the exploits of Alexander the Great, was in the midst of an expedition against Parthian held Trans-Tigritanian territories when he fell to the dagger of an assassin at Carrhae. His praetorian prefect, Opelius Macrinus, who contrived his murder, was forced to take the field against the Parthian king Artbanua V near Nisibis after failing to negotiate a peaceful withdrawal of the Roman forces. The ensuing battle was a long drawn out affair with crippling losses to both sides. Artabanus finally agreed to disengage after learning that his arch-enemy Caracalla was in fact dead.[22]

Artabanus's pyrrhic victory at Nisibis was only the beginning of a series of disasters for the Parthians. Frequent defeat by the Romans had not enhanced the reputation of the Arsacid dynasty. The intercontinental trade in silk and other exotics from which the Parthians derived considerable profit could hardly escape from the adverse effects of military set-backs along the frontier. Moreover, the Parthians were regarded by the Persians with natural hostility and the liberal outlook of their cultural and religious policies might well have offened the more conservative elements of Iranian society. Thus, when a rebellion broke out *c.* 216 in the province of Fars (Persis) under the leadership of a Persian nobleman called Ardashīr, intent on avenging the wrongs suffered by the Iranian people since the defeat of Darius III at the hands of Alexander of Macedon, many rallied to his cause.[23] After conquering the neighbouring principalities one by one he finally challenged Artabanus to battle on the plain of Hormizdagān. The result was a resounding victory for the rebels. According to al-Ṭabarī, the Arab historian who chronicled the rise of the new dynasty, Ardashīr came out of his own lines to kill Artabanus with his own hands.[24] In the same battle, his son Shapur also distinguished himself in valour. On that day (28 April, 224?)[25] the title of Shahanshah (king of kings) passed to Ardashīr and a new Persian dynasty, that of the Sassanians (named after his grandfather Sasan who was a superintendent of a fire temple at Istachr) was inaugurated.

Ardashīr followed the example of his Parthian predecessors in establishing a major administrative centre near to the city of Seleucia. The latter had now been eclipsed in importance by Ctesiphon. It had ceased to be a river port because some time towards the end of the first century, the Tigris changed its course after a violent storm. Instead of flowing between the Hellenistic city and a hillock called Coche, the Tigris carved a new channel to the east of the hillock leaving a dry valley between it and Seleucia.[26] It seems that by the time of the invasion of Septimius Severus in 197/8, both Hellenistic Seleucia and the ancient city of Babylon were sparsely populated ruins.[27] However, the geographical advantages once enjoyed by Seleucia were appreciated by Ardashir who founded a royal city bearing his name, Veh-Ardashīr, between the Tigris and Seleucia with its fort on the Coche.[28] The new city enjoyed a river frontage and together with Ctesiphon it formed a new conurbation which although sometimes still called Seleucia-Ctesiphon was more commonly referred to as the 'Twin Cities' (Syr.: *mdynt' trtyhyn*, Ar.: *al-Madaïn*). It was the most important of all urban centres in the Sassanian empire, yet, it was not the permanent venue of the court. The Sassanians made extensive use of provincial capitals like Hamadan, Istachr, Bishapur etc. as centres of imperial administration, a custom so well known that it is even mentioned in the Chinese dynastic history of the Wei (220–64, compiled in the sixth century).[29] The picture we sometimes get of the

Sassanian empire as a highly articulated bureaucracy centred on the Twin- Cities and foreshadowing the Umayid caliphate with its administrative tentacles emanating from Baghdad was a later development brought about by the reforms of Chosroes I Anūshīrvān (531–79).[30]

The years immediately after Hormizdagān saw the conquest of the eastern territories of the Parthians by Ardashīr. Abrashahr, Merv, Balch, Chwārizim came under his suzerainty and he also received the submission of rulers from territories further east: Kūshānshāhr, Makrān and Tūrān.[31] Having settled the affairs in the east to his satisfaction, Ardashīr turned his attention to his western frontiers and began to make forays across the Tigris which because of earlier Roman victories had become the boundary between the two empires instead of the Euphrates. He was of the opinion that the entire mainland facing Europe contained by the Aegean Sea and the Propontis Gulf belonged to him by ancestral right since he claimed to be a direct descendant of the Achaemenids.[32] A contemporary Roman historian, Dio Cassius, speaks of a general lack of discipline and widespread demoralisation among the Roman troops in Mesopotamia, and large numbers of them went over to the enemy.[33] In reality, Ardashir's gains in the west were limited. He captured Carrhae and Nisibis and advanced into Cappadocia but his left flank was exposed to attack by forces from the semi-independent Arab kingdom of Hatra on the Tigris which had remained loyal to the Parthians.[34] Its garrison was now augmented by detachments of Roman troops as indicated by Latin military inscriptions found among the ruins of the city.[35] Hatra which had earlier defied the triumphant armies of Trajan and Septimius Severus held out for nearly a decade. It succumbed in the end to Shāpūr, son of Ardashir, and then only through treachery and after a siege which lasted four years.[36]

(2)   THE TEACHINGS OF MANI

[When I was four and] twenty years old, in the year in which Dariadaxir [i.e. Ardashīr], the King of Persia, subjected the city of Hatra, and in which Sapores [i.e. Shāpūr], his son assumed the mighty diadem, in the month of Pharmuthi on the [eight] day according to the moon [i.e. 18/19 April, 240], the most blessed Lord had compassion on me and called me to his grace and [immediately] sent to me [from there] my Syzygos [i.e. divine twin] ... He remembered and passed on all the noble counsels which came from our Father and from the Good Right which is from the beginning.[37]

The speaker of these words and the claimant to the special divine revelation they implied was Mani, a native of Babylonia, who founded ◄

a world religion at the time when the political fortunes of the Sassanian dynasty were in the ascendant. The religion which bears his name, Manichaeism, not only found followers within Mesopotamia but also in the adjacent parts of the Roman empire and Iran within the lifetime of the founder (216–76). In the century which followed his death, the religion achieved amazing missionary success in the Roman empire and came to be attacked at first as a subversive foreign religion and later as one of the most pernicious forms of Christian heresy. Although it was largely wiped out by severe persecution in the fifth and sixth centuries, it left a legacy of fear and hatred among medieval churchmen both in the Latin west and the Greek east. The term 'Manichaean' was used by church leaders to stigmatise the teachings of a number of Christian heretics such as the Messalians, the Paulicians and the Bogomils in Byzantium and the Paterenes and the Cathars or Albegensians in the west who had in common the view that the human body is intrinsically evil and therefore cannot be the creation of a good God. In the east, Manichaeism had established a firm base in eastern Iran by the end of the fourth century and from there it would eventually be conveyed even further eastwards along the Silk Road to Bactria, Tochara and the Tarim Basin. In the eighth century it became the state religion of the Uighur Turks, one of the main military powers on the northern frontiers of China. Under their patronage the religion enjoyed greater diffusion in China. After the eclipse of the first Uighur empire in the ninth century, the religion continued to thrive in the Tarim Basin until the rise of Genghis Khan. In China it also survived as a secret religion in the southern coastal regions and traces of it can be found in the province of Fukien as late as the sixteenth century. The geographical spread of Manichaeism over the Eurasian landmass rivals that of Islam and Christianity and its success is all the more remarkable in that it was achieved without military conquest and enforced conversions or the accompaniment of more advanced technology.

The principal elements of Mani's teaching are contained in a canon of seven works which he wrote in the Aramaic dialect of southern Mesopotamia. They are: (1) *The Living Gospel*, (2) *The Treasure of Life*, (3) *The Pragmateia*, (4) *The Book of Mysteries*, (5) *The Book of the Giants*, (6) *The Letters*, (7) *Psalms and Prayers*.[38] In addition, he made a summary of the main points of his teaching in Middle Persian which he presented to Shapur I, with whom he had a particularly cordial relationship. This work, the *Šābuhragān*, was so important that one sometimes finds it listed in the canon in place of *Psalms and Prayers*.[39] None of these works have survived in a complete form, but a considerable number of citations from them can be found in the writings of Church Fathers and in Syriac and Arabic writers who used them to demonstrate the absurdity of Mani's teaching. Fortunately we are now no longer entirely reliant on these polemical writers for information on Mani's teaching and the text of his works. The extant corpus of genuine Manichaean texts has grown considerably since the end of the last century. From 1904–14, in four expeditions to Central Asia, German archaeologists led by Professors Albert von Le Coq and A. Grünwedel brought back to Berlin from sites of ruined Manichaean monasteries at Turfan in Sinkiang (China) several thousand fragments of Manichaean texts. These once constituted handsomely bound and beautifully illuminated manuscript codices but had been mutilated by zealous Islamic conquerors in the fourteenth century. The texts are written in a number of Central Asian languages but Middle Persian, Parthian, Sogdian and Uighur predominate.[40] In 1905 came the news of the discovery of a large hoard of manuscripts, mostly Chinese Buddhist texts, by Aurel Stein in the Temple of the Thousand Buddhas at Tun-huang. Among them were three Manichaean texts in Chinese as well as a long confessional for the Manichaean Hearers in Uighur.[41]

The west too made its contributions to this growing body of Manichaean texts. A Latin Manichaean manuscript was found in a cave near Tebessa (Theveste) in Algeria in 1918.[42] More significantly, a sizeable collection of Manichaean codices in Coptic was shown to Professor Carl Schmidt in 1930 by Egyptian dealers in Cairo and their place of origin was eventually traced to Medinet Medi in the Fayoum near the former Hellenistic military settlement of Narmouthis. The find, totalling some two thousand leaves contained: (1) *The Letters of Mani*, (2) *The PsalmBook*, (3) *The Kephalaia*, (4) *Commentary on the Living Gospel*, (5) a historical work which gave a life of Mani and the early history of the sect, (6) *The Homilies*, (7) some unidentifiable leaves.[43] Part of this find was acquired by the Chester Beatty collection in London (now Dublin) but the greater part of it went to the Prussian Academy in Berlin. The *Letters* and the historical work which were housed in Berlin were unfortunately lost in the chaotic aftermath of the second world war before they could be properly examined and studied.[44]

These newly discovered texts have greatly enriched our knowledge of Manichaeism, although they have not yielded a canon of Mani's writings. The loss of the *Letters* from Berlin has deprived us of possessing a canonical work in entirety. However, the texts from Turfan have so far yielded a number of fragments from the canonical works, especially from the *Book of the Giants* and the quasi canonical *Šābuhragān*.[45] No doubt when it is fully published, the *Commentary on the Living Gospel* in Coptic will shed a great deal of light on the text of the *Living Gospel* itself.[46] On the other hand, the new texts, even if most of them are not of canonical status, are genuine writings of the sect and touch upon many fundamental aspects of its doctrines and history. The *Kephalaia*, for instance, purports to be a record of Mani's discourses with his inner circle of disciples and is listed by Epiphanius as one of the most important works of the sect.[47] The *Psalm-Book* has furnished us with one of the finest anthologies of Manichaean poetry and the *Homilies* contain much new information on the early history of the sect. These genuine Manichaean writings allow us to reconstruct many important aspects of the original teaching of Mani without fear of misrepresentation by the sect's enemies. Surprisingly these texts have shown that some of the polemicists, especially Augustine and Theodore bar Kōnī, have been remarkably accurate in their presentation of Mani's teaching.

'Everyone who wishes to join the sect', states a Chinese Manichaean handbook, 'must know that Light and Darkness are principles, each in their own right and that their natures are completely distinct. If he does not perceive this how will he be able to practise the religion? Next he must be enlightened on the 'Three Moments': (1) The Former Time, (2) The Present Time, (3) The Future Time.' The work goes on to summarise the events which take place in these periods as follows:

In the Former Time, there are yet no heavens or earths, there exists only Light and Darkness. The nature of Light is wisdom, that of Darkness is folly. In all their motion and rest they are completely opposed to each other.

In the Present Time, Darkness invades Light and gives rein to its passions to chase (the Light) away. Light in turn enters Darkness and is deputed with pledges to push back this 'Great Calamity'. It [i.e. the Light] detests its departure from its original body and pleads to leave the 'fiery abode'. One must therefore wear out the [physical] body in order to save the [luminous] nature [?]. This is what the holy doctrine explicitly states and if the truth is fashioned from falsehood, who would dare listen to the commandments? One must therefore be critical and search for the cause of deliverance.

In the Future Time, the things which we teach and preach on come to an end and truth and falsehood return to their roots. Light once more belongs to the Great Light and Darkness returns to the Ultimate Darkness. The Two Principles return to their normal state and give up and return to each other (what they have received from each other).[48]

Within this framework then of the 'Three Moments', a cosmic drama involving the two primordial principles, Light and Darkness, unfolds itself. This drama is central to Mani's teaching as it explains how the enlightened souls of men which are of divine origin came to be clothed in the body of matter which is evil. Our sources on the detailed outworking of this drama are exceedingly rich but one testimony which is regarded to be of exceptional value is a collection of extracts from an unknown Manichaean work preserved in the *Book of Scholia* of Theodore bar Kōnī, Nestorian Bishop of Kashkar (al-Wāsiṭ) in Bēt Ārāmāiē in the eighth century.[49] As the extracts are in Syriac, they are the closest extant source we have to the original writings of Mani in the Aramaic of Babylonia. Many of the names of the deities and demons as well as technical terms found in the extracts are probably the very ones which Mani himself used. The authenticity of these extracts has been borne out by comparison with similar passages in genuine Manichaean writings, especially those in Coptic. The latter of course are fundamental to the reconstruction of the details but important too are extracts from another unnamed Manichaean work, probably the *Book of the Giants*, cited by Severus, the Monophysite patriarch of Antioch (c. 465–538) in one of his *Cathedral Homilies*. Originally delivered in Greek, the homilies have not survived in that language and have come down to us in a number of Syriac translations of which those by Jacob of Edessa (c. 640–708)[50] and Paul of Callinicum[51] (Bishop of Edessa from 510) are the most easily available.

In the first of the three scenes of this cosmic drama, i.e., the Former Time, there existed before the creation of heaven and earth, two principles (Syr.: *kynyn*) one good and the other evil. The good principle dwells in the Region of Light (Syr.: *'tr' dnwhr'*) and he is called the Father of Greatness (Syr.: *'b' drbwt'*).[52] (In the version preserved by Severus, the good principle is represented by the Tree of Life (Syr.: *'yln' dḥy'*) which occupies the regions of east, west and north.)[53] The Father of Greatness possesses a four fold majesty which according to eastern sources consists of Divinity, Light, Power and Wisdom (Pth.: *bg, rwsn, zwr, jyryft*).[54] Hence in Greek sources he is known as the 'Four Faced (τετραπρόσωπος) Father of Greatness'.[55] Besides him, the Region, or Kingdom, of Light is inhabited by twelve Aeons arranged about his flower crowned throne in groups of four each.[56] From them come the Aeons of Aeons to the number of 144.[57] These are all hypostases of the Father and together they dwell in the 'unbegotten air' of the 'unbegotten land'.[58] Acting as the Father's consort is the Great Spirit who instils life into the Kingdom. This idyllic land of light is depicted by a Manichaean psalmist as follows:

> The Kingdom of Light consisted of five Greatnesses,
> these are the Father and his twelve Aeons
> and the Aeons of the Aeons, the Living Air,
> the Land of Light; the Great Spirit blows in them
> and feeds them with its Light.[59]

The Kingdom of Light is composed of five elements (στοιχεῖα), air, wind, light, water and fire (ἀήρ, ἄνεμος, φῶς, ὕδωρ, πῦρ) and has also five 'dwellings' (Syr.: *škynt'*) which are intelligence, knowledge, reason, thought and deliberation (Syr.: *hwn', md't, r'yn', mhsbt', tr'yt'*).[60] With attributes such as these it is not surprising to learn from the *Fihrist* of al-Nadim that the spiritual qualities of the Kingdom of Light are love, faith, fidelity, benevolence and wisdom.[61] In the Severan version of the cosmology, the Tree of Life is adorned with all that is beautiful and is filled and clad with all good things. It stands fast and does not vacillate in its nature.[62]

The evil principle in its primordial manifestation is the exact antithesis of the good. Its realm is the infernal mirror image of the Kingdom of Light. Instead of being bedecked with flowers and luxuriating in life-giving air, the kingdom of Darkness has a lunar landscape: cut up by deep gulfs, abysses, pits, quagmires, dikes, fens and pools. It is also smothered by smoke, the 'poison of death'.[63] It too consists of five worlds (*'lymyn*) which are caverns and in them are five types of devilish creatures: the world of Smoke (*tnn'*) is inhabited by bipeds, Fire (*nwr'*) by quadrapeds, Wind (*rwh'*) by flying things, Water (*my'*) by swimming things and Darkness (*ḥswk'*) by reptiles.[64] The Kingdom of Darkness is not even united under one ruler but each of its sub-world has its own archon in the form of an animal – demon, lion, eagle, fish and dragon.[65] The term 'Prince of Darkness' (*ml'k ḥšwk'*) is a collective designation for these five evil archons.[66] Hence in some sources he is described as a monster which had the head of a lion, the body of a dragon, the wings of a bird, the tail of a great fish and the feet of a beast of burden.[67] The term πεντάμορφος (in five shapes) is aptly used to describe this collective pesronification of evil by the neo-Platonist Simplicius.[68] However, the Prince is also the archon of the bipeds in the world of Smoke. In the same way that the Father of Light is one of the five Greatnesses of the Kingdom of Light, the Prince of Darkness is part and parcel of his realm and yet provides it with its mind and source (Lat.: *mens et origo*).[69] The inhabitants of the five worlds of Darkness are divided into two sexes and they are overcome by lust and desire. The smoke which is the 'poison of death' rises from a pit whose bottom seethes with turbid mud covered over with a layer of dust, the receptacles of the elements of Fire, the heavy and dismal elements of the Wind, of the elements of Turbid Water.[70]

Out of the five worlds or caverns spring five trees which together constitute the Tree of Death (*'yln' dmwt'*), the symbol of Matter (*hwl'* = ὑλή). It is as unlike the Tree of Life as a king and a pig. The one, says Mani, moves in a royal palace in chambers fitting for him. The other wallows in dirt, feeds on filth and takes pleasure in it and is like a snake creeping round its den. Among its many branches are war and cruelty and they are strangers to peace, filled with every wickedness, and never have good fruits. Its relationship with its branches and fruits is a classic example of a 'house divided against itself' for the Tree of Death stands in opposition to its fruits and the fruits in opposition to the tree. They are not at one with him who produced them but they all produce the maggot (Syr. *ss'* = σής) for their own destruction.[71] Each of the individual parts also seek to destroy what is near by. As the psalmist puts it:

> But the Kingdom of Darkness consists of five store-
> houses [ταμεῖον], which are Smoke and Fire and
> Wind and Water and Darkness; their Counsel
> Creeping in them and inciting [?] them to
> make war with one another.[72]

The two realms, though contiguous, are separate and distinct in this first period of cosmic history. Theoretically their spheres of influence do not overlap. The Kingdom of Light extends to the north, east and west while that of Darkness expands southwards and downwards. On the other hand Darkness does drive a wedge through the realm of Light and Darkness being unregulated passion is in a constant state of agitation or 'random motion' (ἄτακτος κίνησις), a term used by the Manichaeans in Roman Egypt, with its various warring factions verging to spill outside its boundaries.[73] The whole realm is permeated with the Instinct (Gk. & Copt.: ἐνθύμησις) of Death rather than the Spirit of Life.[74]

By a fortuitous combination of 'random motions', some demons (i.e. bipeds) came within sight of the upper regions and were captivated by what they saw. They desired to mingle with the Light and soon a full-scale invasion was launched with devils of all shapes and sizes and even incorporeal and intangible ones taking part. The entire mass of Darkness, or Matter which it symbolises, was now thoroughly aroused and ascended with its winds, its turbid waters, its phantoms and princes and powers all seeking to enter into the Kingdom of Light. This major incursion of Darkness into Light resulting from a minor border incident marks the beginning of the second epoch, i.e. the Present Moment, of Mani's cosmological drama.[75]

The Kingdom of Light was panic-stricken. Its five dwellings were intended for quiet and peace, not war. Some other instrument had to be found to oppose this invasion. The Father of Greatness therefore was compelled to face the enemy 'by himself' (Syr.: *bnpšy*, or' by his own soul'), namely by means of new emanations or hypostases of himself. These emanations or, more precisely, evocations, become the good gods of the Manichaean system, but they are essentially parts of the Father, consubstantial with him, and evoked for performing certain specific tasks. They are not his generations as Mani consistently avoids the use of words which suggest sexual procreation when describing the Kingdom of Light. The first of these evocations is the Mother of Life (Syr.: *'m' dhy'*) who in turn evoked the Primal Man (*'nš' qdmy'*) who evoked as his five sons, Air, Wind, Light, Water and Fire, i.e. the five constituent elements of the Kingdom of Light and the wholesome opposites of the five worlds of Darkness. These five Light Elements are also sometimes designated as the 'Maiden' who is the soul of the Father. The Primal Man wore these Elements as his armour and set forth to battle guided by an angel called Nachashbat who came to meet him with a victor's crown and shone the light before him.[76]

The Prince of Darkness was delighted with seeing this delegation from the Kingdom of Light. 'What I sought far off', he congratulated himself, 'I have found close by.'[77] He armed himself with his own five infernal powers and joined in battle for a long time with the powers of Light. In the end, he mastered the Primal Man and laid him down to a drugged sleep while his five powers swallowed some of the Light Elements which formed the armour of the Primal Man.[78] Little did he know that he had fallen into a well-laid trap. The Father is like a good general who, when taken by surprise, is willing to sacrifice part of his forces in order to save his main forces for a battle on more favourable terms.[79] Or,

> Like unto a shepherd that shall see a lion coming to
> destroy his sheep-fold: for he uses guile and takes
> a lamb and sets it as a snare that he may catch him
> by it [i.e. the lamb]; for by a single lamb he saves his
> sheep-fold. After these things he heals the lamb that
> has been wounded by the lion.[80]

In fact the psalmist sees the surrender of the Light Elements to the powers of Darkness as a central part of the strategy:

> He [i.e. the Primal Man] held her [i.e. the Maiden's]
> power fast, he spread her over them like
> nets over fishes, he made her rain down upon them
> like purified clouds of water, she thrust herself
> within them like piercing lightning. She crept
> in their
> inward parts, she bound them all, they not knowing
> it.[81]

Through their concupiscence and desire for the Light, the evil archons had now trapped portions of the Light Element within them but it was they who were ensnared. As a Chinese Manichaean treatise on cosmogony puts it: 'The five classes of demons clung to the five Light Elements as flies cling to honey, like birds caught by bird lime or like fishes which have swallowed the hook'.[82] The fact that they were now satisfied meant that the invasion was at an end but they had also

part which is slightly defiled, over a thousand stars. As for the part of Light which is heavily defiled, a more complicated arrangement is necessary for its redemption. The Living Spirit first formed three wheels (Syr.: '*gn*') which are made of wind, water and fire. To operate them he evoked a third series of deities led by the Third Messenger (Syr.: '*yzgd*'). The latter evoked in turn the Maiden of Light or the Twelve Maidens (Syr.: *trt*'*sr*' *btwlt*'), each corresponding to a sign of the zodiac. The Third Messenger and the Maiden of Light then induced the enchained archons to release the Light which they had swallowed by exploiting their lustful nature. They appeared to them naked in the sun and the moon respectively, he to the female archons and she to the male archons. Excited by the sight of the beautiful Maiden, the male archons ejaculated the Light within their bodies which fell to earth as seeds. The Sin (*ḥtyt*') which activates the archons like a yeasted portion (*mnt*') in bread-dough (*lyš*') also tried to mingle with the Light Particles as they left the archons. However, the Third Messenger concealed himself and was able to separate the Light from Sin. The latter fell back upon the archons but they did not take it up, like a man who feels disgust at his own vomit (*tywb*). Sin then fell upon the earth and the part of it which fell into water became a fearful beast (*ḥywt*' *snyt*') which resembles the Prince of Darkness. One of the deities of the Second Evocation, Adamas of Light, was sent out against it and he slew it with a lance (Syr.: *dwrty*' = δοϱάτιον).The part of Sin which fell on dry ground became five trees and from them were derived all other forms of plant-life.[94]

The female archons, made pregnant by their own nature (*mn kynhyn*) were also overcome by desire when they beheld the naked form of the Third Messenger. In their state of agitation they miscarried and their foetuses ('*wly*') too fell on the ground. They not only survived their premature birth but also devoured the buds of the trees and therefore assimilated part of the Light contained in them. Since they were descended originally from the demonic animals in the Kingdom of Darkness and seized by concupiscence, these abortions copulated and gave birth to the innumerable species of animals as we know them, and they are rated by Mani as lower in the hierarchy of values than vegetables. So the Light which was not yet saved was transferred to the earth, but scattered and bound in plants and, to a lesser extent, in the bodies of animals.[95]

Another important deity of the Third Evocation is the Column of Glory (Syr.: '*ṣtwn swbh*) whose visible appearance is the Milky Way.[96] When the three wheels are set in motion by the Messenger, the Light Particles or souls are drawn up, refined and sublimated and at the same time conveyed along the Milky Way from the moon to the sun. The two stellar bodies are both receiving stations for the Light

Particles as well as vessels ('lp') for their conveyance.[97] The periodic
waxing and waning of the sun and the moon are therefore caused by
the migration of these Light Particles. From the sun the Light Particles
eventually go to a New Earth which was created by the Great Builder.
This New Earth or Paradise ruled by the Primal Man is not the same as
the Kingdom of Light but is made of the same substance. Its main
function is to be a home for the deities which have been evoked and
the Light which they have redeemed so that the Kingdom of Light may
stay aloof from the turmoil.[98]

Seeing that the universe now constructed by the Great Builder and
set in motion by the Third Messenger would eventually redeem all the
captured Light Particles or souls from there, the Prince of Darkness
(i.e. Matter) devised a plan of counter attack. He engendered two
demons, Ashqalun ('šqlwn) or Saclas (Aramaic for 'fool') the male
demon, and Namrael (nmr'yl) or Nebroel (nbr'yl), the female demon,
and used them to undermine the redemptive process. Saclas, knowing
that the abortions (yht') lusted after the image of the Third Messenger,
persuaded them to hand over their offspring to him, promising them
that he would produce for them an image of that deity. He devoured
the male offspring of the abortions and handed the female ones to
Nebroel for her to eat. The two devils then copulated and Nebroel gave
birth in succession to a son, Adam ('dm) and a daughter, Eve (hw').
Thus created, Adam was a microcosm, an exact miniature of the
universe (macrocosm) since both possessed a mixture of Light and
Matter.[99] 'Like a goldsmith', says the Chinese treatise from Tun-
huang, 'who copies the shape of an elephant and inscribes it inside a
ring without adding or subtracting anything from its exact appearance, so also is the human world.'[100] As the microcosm, man was
designed to perpetuate the confinement of the soul in body through
lust and procreation from generation to generation. The archons had
so fashioned him that they intended to rule the world through him.[101]

Created by the demonic powers Adam was senseless and weighed
down by his infernal flesh and completely unaware that within him
were Light Particles which belonged to the Kingdom of Light. When
the five angels or hypostases of the Father of Greatness (i.e. intelligence, knowledge, reason, thought and deliberation) perceived
that the Light of the Father has been despoiled and made captive in the
bodies of Adam and Eve, they implored the Third Messenger, the
Mother of Life, the Primal Man and the Spirit of Life to send someone
to free Adam from his servitude to Matter and to teach him the
knowledge of righteousness. So they sent Jesus of Light (Syr.: yšw'
zywn') who found Adam sunk in a deep sleep. He woke him and took
hold of him and stirred him to life. He also drove away from Adam the
deceiving demon (dyw' mt'yn') and fettered the great archontess

('rkwntwt' sgy't'). Above all he showed him the Father in the heights and his own self (i.e. his soul: npsw) which is cast down before the teeth of wild beasts, devoured by dogs, mingled with and imprisoned in everything that exists, shackled in the corruption (zhwmwt') of darkness. Jesus raised him and made him eat of the Tree of Life ('yln hya). Adam then glanced upward and wept and uttered a tragic and pathetic lament: 'Woe, woe to the maker (gbwl) of my body and to the one who has held my soul in bondage and the rebels (mrwd') who have enslaved me'.[102]

This momentary realisation made clear to Adam the divine origins of his soul and the wretched state of his body but Jesus warned Adam of the danger of lust and the need to restrain himself from having intercourse with Eve. Adam obeyed him but the male archon had intercourse with Eve his daughter and she gave birth to Cain. Cain in turn had intercourse with his mother who then gave birth to Abel. One incestuous relationship follows another as both Cain and Abel married each other's daughters which they had through Eve. This mishmash of family ties was further complicated by the intervention of a demon who caused Abel's wife to give birth to two children. Abel logically assumed that this was the work of Cain and implicated him before Eve. He incurred his brother's wrath and was killed by him. The archon (called al-Sindīd in Arabic) then taught Eve how to entice Adam with magic so that he would break his vow of chastity. This she succeeded in doing and she later gave birth to a boy child. Because Adam had more Light Particles in him than Eve, this, his first child with Eve, was regarded by the archon al-Sindīd as a stranger whom he desired to kill. However Adam nursed him and implored the Father of Greatness, the Mother of Life and the Living Spirit to come to his aid. They duly answered his prayer by sending him a Crown of Splendour and the demons were thus repelled. Adam later called the child Seth (Arabic: Shātil) and nourished him with the milk of the lotus. Al-Sindīd once more used Eve to ensnare Adam and she again was successful but Adam was reproached by his son Seth who told him to go to the East with him, to the Light and Wisdom of God. Adam followed his advice and because of it he was able to enter the Kingdom of Light after his death while Eve and her offspring went to hell.[103]

Sometime after the creation of mankind, the archons who were chained to the firmament and guarded over by the King of Honour rebelled and were recaptured. Two hundred of them, however, escaped to the earth where they perpetrated all kinds of evil deeds and revealed the mysteries of heaven to men. Rebellion and ruin then came about on the earth. On account of this, four archangels, Raphael, Michael, Gabriel and Istrael, were ordered to descend to earth to apprehend them. The demons or giants (Gk. and Copt.: ἐγρήγοροι = Aramiac:

Nephīlīm in Enochic literature) assumed the shape of man and hid themselves. However they were singled out and after a fierce battle were recaptured and placed in a prison of thirty-six towns which had been prepared for them by the Living Spirit. Their sons, the progeny of the giants and human beings, were destroyed on earth.[104]

Jesus of Light is the first of a series of redemptive figures in Manichaeism who was entrusted with a special revelation. His redemptive role is carried out for mankind in future by the Great Nous (intelligence) who is his emanation. It is from the Nous that the true religious leaders are derived as he is the father of all apostles and he enters the world through their teaching. He adorns the soul (i.e. the five Light Elements: air, wind, light, water and fire) with his own five limbs or sons who are the hypostases of the five attributes of the Kingdom of Light (i.e. intelligence, knowledge, reason, thought and deliberation). In due course they engender the five virtues: love, faith, contentment, patience and wisdom, which enable the soul to withstand the attack of the flesh and to combat the rebellious tendencies of sin. The Nous imparts knowledge of the divine origin of the soul and with this knowledge comes the possibility of redemption.[105] The earthly embodiment of this divine intelligence is a line of perfect men: Seth, Noah, Abraham, Shēm, Enosh, Nikotheos, Enoch and after them the founders of true religions, the Buddha, Zoroaster and Jesus the Messiah. Its final and most complete manifestation is Mani, whose teaching was imparted to him directly by Jesus of Light.[106]

The awakening of the soul by the Nous as we have noted, does not imply immediate deliverance – hence the tragic cry of Adam. Matter seeks to submerge the soul in a state of drunken sleep so that it can re-enslave it to its body. A constant battle therefore is fought between the 'New Man' and the 'Old Man', terms which Mani borrowed from St Paul (Cor. 3: 9–10 and especially Eph. 4: 22–4).[107] Being Light itself, the soul can only sin through forgetting its divine origin. As the Chinese Manichaean *Treatise* from Tun-huang explains:

Sometimes the Old Man [Chin.: *ku-jen*, lit.: a deceased person] and the New Wise Man [*hsin-chih-jen*] come into conflict with each other. This is similar to when at the beginning the Demon of Greed [*t'an-mo*] disturbed and invaded the Realm of Light. This has the following distinguishing signs: His actions will lack compassion and he will be quick to anger. It follows that he will despoil the pure spiritual body of the Light-Nature [*ming-hsing*]. The Guest Nature [*k'e-hsing*] which dwells temporarily in him will also be damaged. However, if he had taken the necessary steps to protect his memory and his vigilance, he will be able to oppose and expel spite and hatred and properly practise compassion. The spiritual body of the Light-Nature will revert to purity. The temporarily resident Guest-Nature will be released from all dangers and, bouncing with joy, it will make a ceremonious gesture of thanks and depart.[108]

In this inner struggle, the New Man (i.e. the soul), being purely good, is, like the Kingdom of Light, entirely devoid of destructive weapons and therefore defenceless. His only source of succour is the Nous which in practical terms means the message of Mani and the Manichaean church, the one being the special envoy, the other the earthly manifestation of the Nous.[109] Through the teaching of Mani, the Enlightener (Gk. & Copt.: Φωστήρ) or the Apostle of Light (Pth.: frystgrwšn) and the observance of the precepts of the Manichaean church, the soul will remain in possession of the vital knowledge and should he 'forget', the Church will be at hand to remind him of it.[110] Thus, sin from the Manichaean point of view, is not an act of one's own volition but a temporary loss of consciousness by the soul and atonement for it is contrition, confession and a renewal of awareness of the soul's divine origins. The ultimate sin, for which there is no repentance, is the refusal to accept the special knowledge imparted by the Nous about the primordial existence of the two principles.[111]

The long-term imprisonment of Light by Matter in the physical universe has important practical consequences for those who had been illumined by the Nous. It is their duty to be instruments for the liberation of this Light. To do this requires both a conscious effort for virtue by the individual as well as the avoidance of any action which might harm the Light or prolong its captivity. The Manichaeans are therefore enjoined to observe the 'Five Commandments' and the 'Three Seals'. The 'Five Commandments' as listed in the *Psalm-Book* are as follows:

> This is the honour of the Paraclete-Spirit; the honour
> of Fasting, Prayer and Almsgiving; the honour of the commandment
> that we lie not; the honour of the commandment that
> we kill not, the honour of the commandment that
> we eat no flesh; the honour of the commandment that
> we make ourselves pure; the honour of the commandment of
> blessed Poverty; the honour of Humility and Kindliness.[112]

The 'Three Seals' are according to Augustine, those of 'mouth, hands and breast' (*signacula oris, manuum et sinus*).[113] Eastern Manichaean documents speak of 'mouth, hands and thoughts' (Pth.: *dst, rwmb 'wd 'ndyšyšn*).[114] The 'Seal of the Mouth' forbids blasphemous speech, the eating of meat and the drinking of wine. Meat contains less Light than plants because animals feed off the plants and some of this Light which they have ingested escape through their bodies. The unclean dregs which remain become flesh through sexual intercourse.[115] Wine is designated the 'bile of the Prince of Darkness' because its intoxicating effect induces forgetfulness of the divine message.[116] A fragment of a Manichaean text in Middle Persian lists among the sins and harms of wine and drunkenness: unconsciousness, sickness, regret, contentiousness, fear (through falling), strife and punishment.[117] The 'Seal of the Hands' enjoins the believer not to perform any task which might hurt the Light Particles which are held captive in Matter. This Light is a deity because it is part of the Father of Greatness. In eastern Manichaeism, the sum total of this captive Light is represented by the Living Self (Pth.: grywjywndgyg) and in the west by the Suffering Jesus (Jesus patibilis) who is suspended on the Light-Cross (crux luminis) which is present in all plants as well as the soil and the rocks. To spare this suffering deity from further injustices, Manichaeans are forbidden to till the soil, or to pluck fruit, or to harvest any plant or to kill any animal no matter how small. They are not even allowed to walk on ground which has been planted in case they might step on a plant and hurt the Light Particles within them.[118] Bathing is also forbidden as the act of ablution defiles the water.[119] The 'Seal of the Breast' applies to the carnal sins and by it the Manichaeans are forbidden to partake in sexual intercourse which is regarded as an imitation of demonic fornication and results in the procreation of Matter and thus the further enslavement of the Light.[120]

Taken to its logical conclusion, strict observance of these Manichaean ethical precepts would result in starvation and the eventual extinction of the human race. That they could be fully observed only by a select number of believers was accepted by Mani and constitutes a fundamental part of his teaching. The membership of the Manichaean church is divided into two basic classes, the Elect and the Hearers (or Catechumens). The Elect are the chosen few and they provided the leadership of the Church. The Manichaean ecclesiastical hierarchy is further subdivided as follows: (1) the Leader who is the successor of Mani; (2) twelve Apostles; (3) seventy-two Bishops; (4) 360 Elders. These four grades, together with the general body of the Elect and the Hearers, are attested both in eastern and western Manichaean sources, e.g.:

Latin	Greek	Middle Persian	Chinese
princeps	ἀρχηγός	s'r'r	yen-mo
magistri	διδασκάλοι	hmwc'g'n	mu-she
episcopi	ἐπισκοι	'spsg'n	sa-po-sa
presbyteri	πρεσβύτεροι	m'ns'r'r'n(or mhystg'n)	mo-hsi-hsi-te
electi	ἐκλέκτοι	wcydg'n (or 'rd'w'n)	a-lo-han
auditores	ἀκροάτοι	nyws'g'n	nou-sha-an[121]

The Elect, because of their keeping of the 'Three Seals' and the commandments of purity, are the earthly agents for the release of the captive Light. This is achieved through their digestive systems as they refine the Light Particles in the food which they eat and release them through their belches.[122] Hence they are scorned by their enemies as men who were not in need of salvation as they saw themselves as 'saviours of God' (*salvatores dei*).[123] At meal times the Elect would say a prayer which will absolve them from the responsibility of procuring the food.[124] The meals themselves are a form of sacrament and are generally referred to as the Eucharist by Manichaeans in the west.[125] The Hearers too play their part in the process of redemption through what is called 'Soul Service' (Pe. & Pth.: *rw'ng'n*), i.e., by the caring of the Elect through alms-giving and the preparation of the food for their redemptive meals.[126] Manichaean texts stress that the role of the Hearer is an honourable one. Like the two sisters, Mary and Martha, in the New Testament, the two classes, Elect and Hearer, both perform important and complementary tasks for the rescue of Light.[127] The Hearers are not required to observe the same strict commandments as the Elect. They are allowed to marry or to have mistresses but are advised to avoid procreation.[128] They are also permitted to possess property and wealth. The Manichaean church was unashamed of its efforts to befriend the rich and the powerful. After all, Jesus told his disciples to make friends with the 'Mammon of Iniquity' (Luke 16:9).[129]

The Manichaean scheme of individual salvation also differentiates between the Elect and the Hearer. At death, the soul of the Elect returns direct to the Kingdom of Light and is received with great honour. The soul of the Hearer however, has to remain on earth and by a series of reincarnations in the luminous bodies of fruits and finally in the body of the Elect it too will return to the Kingdom of Light. How soon this final liberation is achieved depends on how devoted the Hearer has been to the service of the Elect. The souls of those who have not been awakened by the Nous are reincarnated in the souls of beasts and are punished with eternal damnation.[130]

The last act of the cosmic drama, the Future Moment, is, as the term suggests, an eschatological event. When the liberation of Light has attained near-completion, a great war will break out since by then what remains on earth will be primarily Matter and dominated by sin and strife. This will be presaged by the second coming of Jesus as the Great King. He will set up his judgement seat in the middle of the world and separate the righteous from the sinners. The Hearers, placed on the right of Jesus, will receive the victory while the sinners, placed on the left will be cast into hell. The Elect will be transformed into angels. After this Jesus will give a sign to the Column of Glory and the

Five Sons of the Living Spirit who are holding up the universe to leave their posts. The entire universe will then collapse and a Great Fire will break out which will burn for 1,468 years. The Instinct of Life will take the form of the 'Last Statue' and gather up all the remaining Light- Particles and ascend to the Kingdom of Light. At the same time, the Prince of Darkness and his followers will withdraw into a great pit prepared for them in which they will be shut in by a great stone. The three-fold drama will have run its full course and the two principles, Light and Darkness, will once more be distinct and separate entities.[131]

Mani did not intend his teaching on cosmogony and ethics to be the basis of philosophical inquiry or metaphysical speculation. It was not the product of his own intellect but a divine revelation which he had received from the Nous. The truth of his teaching was therefore not susceptible to human proof but was authenticated by his claim to be an apostle of Jesus Christ and the Paraclete which Jesus had promised to send to his disciples. 'The truth and the secrets of which I have spoken', says Mani in his letter to his followers in Edessa, 'as well as the laying on of hands which is mine, I did not receive from men or bodies of flesh, but also not from the reading of books.'[132] His certainty of the divine nature of his teaching is even more emphatically stated in the prologue of his *Living Gospel*:

I, Mani, Apostle of Jesus Christ through the will of God, the Father of Truth, from whom I also came into being. He lives and abides for all eternity. Before everything, he is and he remains after everything. Everything which has happened and will happen is established through his might. From him I came and I am also from his will. And from him all that is true was revealed to me and I am from [his] truth. I saw [the truth of eternity which he revealed]. And I revealed the truth to my companions; I preached peace to the children of peace; I proclaimed hope to the immortal generation; I chose the Elect and showed the path leading to the height to those who go up according to this truth. I have proclaimed hope and revealed this revelation; and have written this immortal Gospel, in which I have put down these pre-eminent mysteries and disclosed in it the greatest works, the greatest and most majestic forms of the most powerful works of [pre-eminence]. And these things which he revealed, I have made known to [those who live] from the most true vision which I have seen and from the most glorious revelation which was revealed to me.[133]

Mani's claim to have received his special teaching by divine revelation means that the word 'myth' which is so often used to designate Mani's cosmogonic drama never enters into the sect's own evangelistic vocabulary. Every part of his teaching on the origins and the present day workings of the universe is intended to be literally understood and supposed to be scientifically accurate. Similarly the myriads of deities and demons involved in the cosmic drama are meant to be historical and not fictional characters. This total acceptance of the Manichaean gnosis is essential for the believer's redemption as it demands his participation in a special lifestyle which has a salvific function and which is only meaningful within a literal understanding of the cosmogonic drama. If Mani's explanation of the function of the planetary bodies as vehicles for the conveyance of liberated Light Particles was at variance with the teaching of the astronomers, the Manichaeans would argue that it was the astronomers who were deluded and ignorant of the definitive truth. Manichaeism, therefore, was a easy target for polemics in the later Roman empire because, if viewed narrowly as a philosophical system, it was full of fantastic assertions and riddled with contradictions and illogicalities glossed over by a primitive literalism and buttressed by the appeal to Mani's apostolic claims. The sixth century neo-Platonist Simplicius justifiably voiced his disquiet over the sect's complete rejection of the allegorical method in its understanding of the cosmogonic drama:

They [sc. the Manichaeans] mention certain pillars, but they do not take them to mean (those) 'which hold heaven and earth together' as they do not think it right to understand any of the things they say allegorically, but those which are made of solid stone and carved, as one of their wise men informed me. (They also mention) twelve doors and one of them opens each hour. They also show a marvellous excess of ingenuity in explaining the cause of eclipses. They say that when the evil [archons] who are chained in creation cause upheaval and disorder by their own movements, their Light Particles inside them throw up some sort of veil so as not to share in their excitement. Eclipses are therefore caused by the interposition of this veil ... Why do I quote their views at length? For they fabricate certain marvels which are not worthy to be called myths. However, they do not use them as myths nor do they think that they have any other meaning but believe that all the things which they say are true.[134]

This literalism made Manichaeism a static religion. We can see from the records of Mani's lectures assembled by his students that as a teacher he was more concerned with further elaboration of his complex myth and fitting the details into neat numerological, horological or astrological schemes than to explore the philosophical implications of his gnosis.[135] No wonder one convert, Augustine, eventually had to admit that he could make no progress in the religion.[136] On the other hand, because Manichaeism was based on a cosmic drama which is largely unrelated to human history and certainly not to the history of a particular people, it lends itself to evangelism across cultural boundaries. This was particularly effective in relation to polytheistic systems as Manichaean missionaries readily assimilated local deities and demons with those of their own pantheon. Their literal interpretation of the myth also set strict limits to these cultural adaptations and ensured a high degree of doctrinal uniformity among the far-flung communities of the sect.

CHAPTER II

THE APOSTLE OF JESUS CHRIST

(1) JUDAEO-CHRISTIANITY IN MESOPOTAMIA IN THE SECOND CENTURY

Under the late Parthians, southern Mesopotamia or Babylonia was not the major centre of Persian culture and religion as one would expect from its being an important part of the Parthian empire. The use of the Parthian language and the practice of Zoroastrianism which the Parthians like their Sassanian successors, seldom imposed on non-Iranians, rarely extended outside the ruling class. In the field of religion, Babylonia had a long established reputation for particularism. Under the Achaemenids, the temple of Bel, for which the city of Babylon was justifiably famous, was used as a sanctuary and a focus of nationalist aspirations when the city rose against Darius I (499 BC).[1] Other Babylonian temples continued their role as centres of social and economic as well as religious activities into the early Hellenistic period.[2] Eclipsed by the foundations first of Seleucia and then of Ctesiphon, the city of Babylon fell into decay and its ruins were quarried for building material by the time of Trajan's invasion in 115. Although the Chaldaean religion with its emphasis on astrology and mathematics which the city had come to symbolise had gone into an irreversible decline along with the city, the worship of ancient Semitic gods like Bel, Nergal and Atargatis was still prevalent in Mesopotamia.

The presence of a large and prosperous Jewish community which had found a congenial home in their former land of capitivity contributed to the cosmopolitan outlook of Babylonia under the Parthians. Important Jewish communities could also be found in the Roman controlled cities of Upper Mesopotamia like Edessa and Nisibis.[3] East of the Tigris, the religion was well established in the Kingdom of Adiabene where the ruling house was converted to it in the first century AD.[4] Jews from Mesopotamia are mentioned in the Acts of the Apostles (2:9) as present in the crowd which heard the

Apostle Peter speak on the day of Pentecost in Jerusalem. It was for the benefit of these less Hellenised Jews that Josephus produced the first draft of his *Bellum Judaicum* in Aramaic.[5] Under the later Sassanians, the Rabbinic academies of Babylonia would achieve great literary fame through the compilation of the Talmud.

The Jewish communities in the chief cities of both Roman- and Parthian-held Mesopotamia undoubtedly prepared the ground for the introduction of Christianity to lands east of the Euphrates. We learn from the legendary account of the conversion of the city of Eddessa, the *Doctrina Addai*, that when Addai, one of the seventy apostles of Christ, came to Edessa at the bidding of Judas Thomas, he stayed at the home of a certain Tobias whose father was a Jew from Palestine. Among Addai's first converts to Christianity were Jewish merchants who specialised in the silk trade.[6] We may infer from this legend that the pioneering work of disseminating the Christian faith in Mesopotamia was undertaken by speakers of Aramaic, the *lingua franca* of much of the Near East. The publication in Syriac, a dialect of Aramaic, of Tatian's *Diatessarōn*, a harmony of the four gospels, sometime in the second half of the second century must have greatly facilitated the spread of Christianity outside the Greek-speaking parts of the Syrian Orient.[7] The Greek version of it might have also been popular in the more Hellenised cities and colonies, as a small fragment of it was found among the ruins of Dura Europos.[8] It is not improoabable that the work was originally published in a diglottal (Gk. & Syr.) format, given the widespread knowledge of Greek among the educated classes in the former Hellenistic cities. In a region where parchment was still preferred, an epitome like that of Tatian would have distinct advantage in terms of cost over four separate gospels and it might well have been the principal gospel text which many Christian communities in Mesopotamia possessed towards the end of the second century.

The evangelisation of Mesopotamia was an untidy affair comprising small individual ventures in particular localities. Edessa, as is well known, claimed to have received the gospel from the apostle Addai (or Thaddaeus) as a result of a personal exchange of letters between Abgar, its king, and Jesus before his crucifixion.[9] We learn from a local chronicle that there was a Christian church in Edessa by the beginning of the third century as the building was damaged by the flood waters of the river Daisan in 205.[10] However, the same document makes no mention of the evangelisation of the city by Addai. Further to the east, the Christian community at Arbela in Adiabene harboured the legend that their first bishop, Mar Paqida, was personally ordained by the same Addai who brought the Gospel to Edessa and that the church there was founded before the end of the first century.[11] Similarly, the

Christians of Karkā de Bēt Selōk in Bēt Garmai also maintained that the gospel was first brought to their city by Addai and his disciple Mari and that the congregation was later swelled by refugees from the Roman empire during the persecutions of Hadrian.[12] The metropolis of Seleucia boasted of a church founded by Mari on the Kōḥē in the Apostolic period.[13] In short, where contemporary evidence is lacking legends abound, but most of them are no earlier than the fourth century and in the case of Arbela, the extant history of the church there in the Parthian and Sassanian periods may have been a more recent forgery.[14] The legends were made into history when important sees in Mesopotamia felt the need to lay claim to apostolic origin.

From sources other than these foundation legends we learn that among the first Aramaic-speaking Christian groups to be established in Mesopotamia were those who had preserved certain observances of the Mosaic laws including circumcision and the observance of the Sabbath. They also rejected certain scriptures of the early church including the letters of Paul, and placed great emphasis on the redemptive role of baptism. One leading exponent of this Judaising Christianity was Elchasaios whose teaching came to the notice of the Roman church during the pontificate of Callistus (217–22) when a controversy arose as to whether, and with what limitations, forgiveness might be bestowed on grievous post-baptismal sin.[15] Alcibiades, a native of Apamea in Syria, had brought a book to Rome which announced a novel method of forgiveness of sin by submitting the culprit to a new baptism with a special formula.[16] The book also prescribed other formulae for such misadventures as being bitten by a mad dog or a serpent or afflicted by an illness.[17] The book had been obtained from the Seres (= silk merchants?) and its contents were originally revealed to a righteous man called Elchasaios, whose name means 'hidden power', in the third year of Trajan (100/1) by an angel of gigantic proportions who was accompanied by a female of equal size. The angel is the Son of God and the female is the Holy Spirit – a representation which points to the Aramaic origin of the work.[18] A further pointer to the Jewish origins of Elchasaios is his making Jerusalem the centre of the world's devotion, and the faithful were exhorted to pray not merely facing the east but towards Jerusalem.[19]

Evidence from extant citations of the 'Book of Elchasaios' suggests that the sect had followers in Mesopotamia and the adjacent parts of Iran. A passage from it preserved by Epiphanius speaks of a Jew called Phineas, a descendant of the famous Phineas in Numbers 25: 7–8, who worshipped Artemis in Susa and so escaped death and destruction in the time of Darius.[20] By contrast the Phineas from whom he was descended was a champion of the Jewish faith and killed with his own hands an Israelite who took a Midianite woman into his household.

The more compromising attitude of his descendant towards pagan deities may well imply a measure of support for the Parthians by the Jews and Judaising Christians of Babylonia. Some of the Jews would have been refugees from the destruction of Jerusalem by the legions of Titus and Vespasian in 70 AD. They might have also resented the attempts by the Romans to wrest the profitable silk trade from their hands in Mesopotamia.[21] In another fragment of the 'Book of Elchasaios', the calendrical number of three is deemed inauspicious because it was in the third year after Trajan had subjected the Parthians (113–16) that a conflict would flare up among the impious angels of the north.[22]

The 'Book of Elchasaios' enjoins a legalistic way of life which entails circumcision and the observance of Sabbath, but sacrifice and the sacerdotal actions associated with it are prohibited.[23] The superiority of the forgiveness of sin by ablution over the fire of sacrifice is based on the belief that water is more acceptable to God than fire.[24] Elchasaios also confesses Christ in name and says that he was a great king but he was a man like every other man, nor was this the first occasion that he was born of a virgin for he had been born and continues to be reborn many times and undergoes transformations as he moves from body to body. This idea, according to Hippolytus, Elchasaios borrowed from the Pythagoreans.[25] From another heresiologist, Epiphanius, we learn that Elchasaios regards Adam as the first of these incarnations.[26] He made use of texts from every part of the Old Testament and the Gospels but rejected completely the writings of Paul.[27] The church historian Eusebius records a propagandist advance by the sect into Caesarea in Palestine in 247 but it met with little success and soon disappeared.[28] However, Eusebius might have underestimated their achievements as Epiphanius testifies that in his own time (i.e. fifth century), the Elchasiates could still be found in the country of Perea at the other side of the Dead Sea and in the lands of the Moabites, the Ituraeans and the Nabataeans.[29]

(2)   MANI AND THE ELCHASAITES

A frequent feature of the Christian sects which flourished in Mesopotamia at the end of the second century was asceticism. Tatian, the compiler of the *Diatessarōn*, was also a leading figure in the so-called Encratite movement which advocated abstention from meat, wine and sexual intercourse, as well as the rejection of worldly possessions.[30] Since asceticism was not commonly encountered among devotees of pagan Semitic cults or Zoroastrianism, it might have been a distinguishing characteristic of the Judaeo-Christian sects. Some of their followers might have been drawn to them initially by their ascetical practices rather than by the esoteric teaching on which the practices were based.

One such convert was Patīk (Gk. & Lat.: Patticius, Arab.: Futtuq), a resident of the Twin Cities (i.e. Seleucia-Ctesiphon), who joined a baptising sect through responding to a call to ascetical living. A native of Hamadan (Ecbatana), his wife Maryam was related to the ten ruling house of the Arsacids. One day while he was worshipping in a temple of idols, someone spoke to him in a loud voice, admonishing him not to eat meat nor to drink wine nor to marry. This happened to him a number of times in the next few days. He was duly won over by the persistence of the caller and joined a sect known in later Arabic sources as the Mughtasilah (i.e. those who baptise themselves). Its members lived in some villages in the environs of Dastumīsān, a place between al-Wāsiṭ and al-Baṣrah. His wife was pregnant when he decided to join the sect and in due course she gave birth to their son Mani on 14 April, 216. When the child was four years old, his father sent for him so that he could be brought up with him according to the rule of his sect.[31] Patik may have been a devotee of Zoroastrianism even though he worshipped in a temple of idols rather than a fire temple. Or, he might have been a devotee of the cult of Bel or Atagartis or of more than one cult. The region round the Twin Cities seemed to have been a fruitful recruiting ground for the Mughtasilah, as one of Patīk's fellow sectarians by the name of Aianos came from Coche, the hilly ground between Seleucia and Ctesiphon on which the Sassanian royal city of Veh-Ardashir would later be built.[32]

Mani remained with his father in the sect of the Mughtasilah until the age of twenty-four or twenty-five when he broke away from it and formed his own sect together with his father and a handful of fellow baptists. Until recently our only reliable source of information on the childhood and adolescence of Mani has been the relevant chapters of a long article in Arabic on Mani and his teaching in the *Fihrist* (i.e., *Catalogue*) of al-Nadim first published in Baghdad in 988. It is from this article that we come to know of Mani's parentage and his connection with the Mughtasilah. The latter is also alluded to by Theodore bar Kōnī:

Some say that he [sc. Mani] was called Ḳurḳabios [Syr.: qwrqbyws] and at first he was a devotee of the doctrine of purification [hrsys dmnqd'] because he was bought by the sect. His place of birth was Abrūmia and his father was Patīk (ptyq). The Pure Ones, who called themselves the White Force [hyl' hwr'] [or: White Garment (hl' hwr')] could not tolerate him and expelled him from their midst. They nicknamed him the 'Vase of Evil' [m'n' dbyst'] and because of this he was called Mani (m'ny).[33]

Unfortunately Theodore does not seem to give much credence to this account and goes on to give us a more common polemical version of Mani's life which originated in the Roman Empire in the fourth century.[34] Al-Nadim, on the other hand informs us in a separate article on the Mughtasilah, whom he also calls the Ṣābat al-Baṭa'ih (i.e. the Sabians of the marshlands), that their head was known as al-Ḥasiḥ and it was he who instituted their sect.[35] The identification of this al-Hasiḥ with Elchasaios has long been accepted by scholars but the implication that the Mughtasilah were the Elchasaites of the Christian heresiologies was treated with considerable scepticism.[36] Part of al-Nadim's description of the Mughtasilah seems to fit the Mandaeans, a gnostic batpising sect which can still be found in small numbers of isolated communities in the marshes of southern Iraq.[37] Not surprisingly, some scholars maintained that the Mughtasilah were proto-Mandaeans and the Mandaean origins of Manichaeism could be demonstrated by stylistic and thematic similarities between Mandaean hymns and the Coptic Manichaean psalms from Medinet Medi.[38] However, accurate information on the presence of Mandaeans in southern Iraq only goes back to the Islamic period, and the fact that the modern Mandaeans are actively anti-Christian throws doubt on a direct relationship between them and the Manichaeans who revered their founder as an 'Apostle of Jesus Christ'.

This state of academic agnosticism and uncertainty over the exact identity of the Mughtasilah came to an end in 1970 with the announcement by two German scholars, Professors Albert Henrichs and Ludwig Koenen, of the successful decipherment of a tiny Greek codex in the papyrus collection of the University of Cologne (P.colon.inv.nr.4780). The *Codex Manichaicus Coloniensis* (*CMC* for short) as the document is now called by scholars, is the smallest papyrus codex yet discovered. Its pages measure only 4.5 cm. × 3.5 cm. and the writing on them is 3.5 cm. × 2.5 cm. Despite its minute format, the Manichaean scribes, at least four in number, managed to copy an average of twenty-three lines of Greek immaculately onto each page.[39] To the editors of this delicate and difficult text, Professors Henrichs and Koenen, as well as to its conservator, Dr Anton Fackelmann of Vienna, all Manichaean scholars owe a considerable debt of gratitude.

The codex bears the title 'On the genesis of his (sc. Mani's) body' (περὶ τῆς γέννης τοῦ σώματος αὐτοῦ) and may have constituted the first part of a history of the early Manichaean church. Such a work was discovered at Medinet Medi but is now sadly among those Coptic codices which had not been returned to Berlin after the end of the second world war, and the work had not been properly examined before its untimely loss.[40] The extant pages of the *CMC* (and some 190 pages have been conserved and published) have as their main theme the story of Mani's sojourn among the 'baptists' and his earliest missionary journeys after his final break with the sect at the age of twenty-four or twenty-five. It is not the work of one author but comprises excerpts (at least nineteen in number) from the writings of Mani's closest disciples and followers which contain biographical details or autobiographical statements concerning this period of Mani's life. Among the names of the Manichaean authors preserved are Salmaios the Ascetic, Baraies the Teacher, Timotheos, Abiesus the Teacher, Innaios the brother of Zabed, Za [cheas?], Kustaios the Son of the Treasure of Life and Ana the brother of the disciple Zacheas. The style is eclectic, as one would expect from an anthology, but in most of the excerpts the autobiographical format is retained.[41] It seems from the number of different authors represented in the collection that Mani viewed his own calling and the supramundane nature of the revelation which he had received as fundamental to the authenticity and authority of his teaching. He must have therefore spoken frequently, repetitively and at length about himself and his supernatural experiences.

The new text dispels any suggestion that the sect in which Mani grew up were the predecessors of the modern Mandaeans of southern Iraq. The baptising sect to which Patīk gave his allegiance were Judaising Christians who acknowledged Elchasaios ('Αλχασαῖος) as their founder (ἀρχηγός).[42] Entry into such a sect for a gentile like Patik might have involved circumcision and being educated in the Mosaic law.[43] The members were vegetarians and were given to working in the fields. It appears that individual members were allocated their own lands to cultivate, as the *CMC* at one point describes two of Mani's friends as 'of the adjacent fields' (πλησιόχωροι).[44] The young Mani had to assist in the harvesting of fruit and vegetables and the gathering of firewood.[45] The sedentary and agrarian outlook of the sect reminds us more of the Qumran sectarians than the more peripatetic form of Christian asceticism which became popular in the Syrian Orient in the fourth century.[46] The fact that Mani was taken into the sect at the age of four brings to mind the Essenes who, according to Josephus, while eschewing marriage yet picked out male children of other people and moulded them according to their rules.[47] A similar practice among the Mughtasilah may explain why Mani joined the sect at such a tender age and why Theodore bar Kōni alleged that Mani was bought by the sect as a slave. The members of the sect observed the Jewish Sabbath which in the *CMC* is referred to as the 'Rest of the Hands' (ἀνάπαυσις τῶν χειρῶν), a term which anticipates the 'Seal of the Hands' of the Manichaean Elect.[48] Since the *CMC* mentions no woman in connection with the sect we may assume that it is an all

male community. This calls into question Epiphanius's remark that
Elchasaios detested virginity and compelled people to marry.[49] On the
other hand the *CMC* confirms Origen's claim that Elchasaios rejected
the writings of the Apostle Paul.[50] For Mani's fellow 'baptists' to have
read Paul was tantamount to having gone over to the 'Greeks' and
thereby becoming an enemy of the sect.[51] Among the scriptures of the
sect were Jewish apocalyptic writings and the *Diatessarōn* of Tatian.[52]
The main cultic practices of the sect included the Eucharist which
they celebrated with unleavened bread and water, and regular
ablutions which the members performed on themselves for the
remission of sins and on their food according to their rules of purity.[53]
This concern with physical cleanliness was not unrelated to their
belief in the resurrection of the body which they conceived of as a
'resting of the garment' (ἀνάπαυσις τοῦ ἐνδύματος).[54]

Mani remained a member of the Mughtasilah until the age of
twenty-four or twenty-five when he broke away from it amidst much
bitter controversy and mutual recrimination between him and its
leaders. The final confrontation which led to Mani's involuntary
departure is vivdly and dramatically recounted in the *CMC* but the
hagiographical style of the work allows us to see only one side of the
picture. Furthermore since the *CMC* was compiled for the edification
of the Manichaean faithful, both Mani and Elchasaios, whose original
teachings Mani claimed to have upheld in the dispute, are therefore
portrayed as champions of doctrines and practices which were at
the heart of the fully-fledged Manichaean church. This constant
retrospection has to be borne in mind as we come to examine this
Manichaean version of Mani's intellectual and spiritual developments
during his formative years among the Mughtasilah.

Mani told his disciples that since his youth he had come under
special divine protection and instruction. He claimed to have been
protected through the might of the angels and of the powers of
holiness which were entrusted with his safe-keeping. They also
brought him up by means of visions and signs which were at first short
and brief such as he could bear. One of these angels was his Syzygos
(companion), i.e. his divine twin or *alter ego* who, according to his
later teaching, is an emanation of the Jesus of Light who in turn is an
emanation of the Nous.[55] An intimate relationship grew up between
Mani and his Syzygos, one which he would later celebrate in poetry:

> . . . piously . . . and him
> and I obtained him as my own property.
> I believed him
> and that he belongs to me
> and that he is a good and useful counsellor.
> I recognised him

and understood that I am he
from whom I was separated.
I have borne witness
that I myself am he
and am unshaken . . .[55a]

Since Elchasaios, the founder of the sect, claimed to have received the special revelation which lay at the heart of his esoteric teaching, the apocalyptic tradition was clearly not only a living one among his followers in the time of Mani but also a binding one.[56] The *CMC* supported the uniqueness and the authenticity of Mani's visionary experience with quotations from the 'Apocalypses' of Adam, of Seth, of Enosh, of Shem and of Enoch. All these works are now lost to us and the quotation from the 'Apocalypse of Enoch' is not paralleled in the extant Greek or Ethiopic versions of the *Book of Enoch*.[57] Jewish apocalyptic writings undoubtedly exerted considerable influence on the spiritual development of the young Mani. We learn from the first discourse in the *Kephalaia* that Mani regarded Seth (or Sethel), the son of Adam, as the first of a line of special prophets from the Father. He was followed by Enosh, Enoch and Shem. After them came Buddha, Zoroaster, Jesus and Paul. After Paul, mankind was gradually led astray into sin until the time when there appeared again a just man who belonged to the 'kingdom'. Together with another righteous person they gave strength to the church. Their names have unfortunately not been preserved because the text is extremely fragmentary at this point. After they had ascended to the Land of Light, the church again degenerated and became like a tree which was deprived of its fruits. It was then that Mani's apostleship began, as he was the Paraclete of Truth who was promised by Christ to this last generation.[58] Although Manichaeism later became well known for its anti-Jewish stance on many doctrinal issues, it could not fully obliterate its Jewish origins. The *Book of Giants*, one of the seven canonical scriptures of the Manichaeans and Iranian fragments from Turfan, can be shown to be based on a similar work in Enochic literature which has survived in a number of Aramaic fragments from Qumran.[59] A total of six copies of the Aramaic version of the proto-Manichaean *Book of Giants* have now been identified, which points to the popularity the work would have enjoyed among the Qumran sectarians.[60] The same might have been true of the work among the Elchasaites of Babylonia.

The divine secrets and instructions which Mani received ran counter to some of the accepted doctrines and cultic practices of his sect. One of the first areas of controversy between the enlightened Mani and his fellow 'baptists' was the legitimacy of harvesting. Since the community was vegetarian and derived its subsistence entirely from agriculture, the matter was not without cogency. According to the *CMC* the young Mani did not collect vegetables from the fields but asked for them as a form of alms (ἐν μέρει εὐσεβείας).[61] The Manichaean Elect, as we have already noted, do not take any part in the procurement of food but rely instead on the alms-giving of the Hearers because the act of harvesting and the preparation of the food would damage the Light Particles embodied in the plants. Thus when Mani was forcibly taken by one of his fellow 'baptists' to pick dates, the palm spoke to the 'baptist' and warned him that if he did not stop inflicting pain on it he would die as a murderer.[62] On another occasion when one of the leaders compelled him to perform agricultural work, a similar miracle occured. Blood oozed from the places where the plants had been hurt by the blows of the sickle. They also cried out with a human voice because of the blows they received.[63]

The *CMC* depicts Mani as leading a dream-like existence among the 'baptists'. In the words of Baraies, one of Mani's later disciples:

He was like a lamb dwelling in an alien flock or similar to a bird living with other birds who do not speak the same language. For throughout all that time he lived always in their midst with wisdom and skill without any of them knowing who he was or what he had received and what had been revealed to him. Rather they treated him according to his bodily significance.[64]

Mani came to speak of himself as 'the only one' (μονήρης) or 'the only begotten one' (μονογενής), terms which readily remind us of the Syriac *yhydy'* (a person who lives singly) which is fundamental to the vocabulary of early Syrian asceticism, as it denotes one's singleness by not having family ties.[65] In Mani's case it also indicates his singleness of mind and his self-induced sense of isolation which was brought about by his belief that he alone possessed the true doctrine as taught by Elchasaios, the founder of the sect.

Mani's self-isolation and his occasional disagreement and confrontation with his co-religionists were his tutelage for a destiny which was yet to be fully revealed. When he reached the age of manhood the decisive revelation came in a typically dramatic fashion:

In this way he [i.e. his Syzygos] called me and chose me and drew me and separated me from their midst. He drew [me to the divine] side . . . [and revealed to me] who I am and my body, in what way I came and how my coming into this world happened, and who I have become among those who are most distinguished in pre-eminence, and how I was born into this fleshly body, or through what woman I was brought to birth and delivered according to this flesh, and from whom I was begotten [in love (?)] . . . and who is my Father in the height or in what way I was separated from him and was sent according to His will and what command and instruction He gave to me before I was clothed with this organ and before I fell into error in this loathsome flesh and before I put on this intoxication and its habits, and who [he is] who is [my ever wakeful Syzygos] . . . secrets and the [visions,] and the pre-eminence of

my Father, and concerning myself, who I am, and who then is my closely
fitting Syzygos; moreover, concerning my soul, which is the soul of all worlds,
what it itself is or how it came to be. He also revealed to me in addition to
these things the boundless heights and unsearchable depths, he showed [me]
... [66]

In another context Mani told his disciples that what the Syzygos
revealed to him were the fundamental teachings of the Manichaean
sect on cosmogony, ethics, ecclesiastical organisation and the
apostleship of Mani:

He revealed to me the mystery of light and of darkness, the mystery of the
destruction [?], of the fight and the war and the great . . . the battle which
darkness stirred up . . . [Afterwards?] he also revealed to me how the light has
. . . darkness in consequence of its mingling and how this world was
established. He also enlightened me as to how the ships were made firm so
that [the gods] of light might let themselves down in them, to purify the light
from Creation, [to cast] the dregs and the refuse into the abyss; the mystery of
the creation of Adam, the first man. He also taught me the mystery of the tree
of knowledge from which Adam ate, [through which] his eyes were opened.
Also about the mystery of the apostles who were sent into the world [in order
that they] might choose the churches; the mystery of the Elect [and their]
commandments; the mystery of the Catechumens, their helpers, and [their]
commandments; the mystery of the sinners and their works and the
punishment which awaits them. In this way everything that has happened and
will happen was revealed to me by the Paraclete . . . [67]

Emboldened and enlightened by this all-embracing revelation, Mani
was no longer prepared to hide the doctrinal differences which existed
between him and his fellow baptists. His relationship with the leaders
of the sect was soured by his rejection of the special favours
which one of them wanted to lavish upon him.[68] The breaking point
came when he challenged his co-religionists on the validity of ritual
ablutions and the liturgical purification of their food. The arguments
he adduced are given ample coverage in one of the best preserved
sections of the *CMC*:

When I [perceived] their thoughts I said to [them] mildly, 'There is [no value]
in [this] ritual washing with which you cleanse your food. For this body is
defiled and is formed by a defiled moulding. Consider how when someone
purifies his food and then partakes of it after it has been ritually washed, it is
apparent that from it come blood, bile, burps and shameful excrement and the
foulness of the body. If he restrains his mouth for a few days from this food,
immediately it is clear that all these shameful and loathsome dis[charges] will
cease and be wanting [in the] body. But if he then partakes [again of food in
the] same way they abound in the body again, thus showing that they flow
from the food itself. It someone partakes of food that has been ritually washed
and purified and [then] partakes of that which has not been cleansed, it is plain

that the beauty and power of the body are shown to be the same (in both cases). Similarly the foulness and excrement from both are seen not to differ at all. Therefore that which has been ritually washed, which (the body) [casts] out and discharges [is] no more notable than the other which is un[washed].

'And the way you ritually wash yourselves in water every day, this also has no value. For if you have once been cleansed and purified why do you ritually wash yourselves again every day? From this it is evident that you become loathsome (to yourselves) every day, and because of the foulness you ritually wash yourself before you can be purified. There it is clearly very plain that all defilement [is] from the body. Behold you [yourselves] are clothed in it.'[69]

Mani clearly drew no distinction between evil in the moral sense with physical defilement and dirt. The body is a producer of dirt because it is inherently evil and defiled and the food which it partakes is composed of matter and therefore can not be purified merely by washing. True purity on the other hand can only be achieved through special knowledge: 'However, the purity which was spoken about is the purity through knowledge [γνῶσις] [it is] the separation of Light from Darkness, of death from life, and of living waters from turbid ones.'[70]

The 'baptists' in Mani's eyes had gone too far in separating evil from defilement and had turned ablution into an act of bodily purification with no moral or spiritual significance: 'You have turned away from it and have begun to bathe and have adhered to the purification of the body which is utterly defiled and fashioned from impurity, through it [i.e. the impurity] it [i.e. the body] coagulates and is built up and comes to exist.'[71]

Mani's forthright exposé of the errors of the sect won him a few friends but many more enemies; the latter were led by Sita whose affection for him he had earlier rejected.[72] To show that his ideas were not entirely the products of his own imagination Mani told them stories about Elchasaios, the founder of their rule: how when he was going to bathe in water, an image of a man appeared from the spring and rebuked him for defiling the water and when this happened to him a second time he gave up bathing in water; how when he ploughed the soil objected to being exploited by him and how he found his disciples baking and when the loaf spoke to him he forbade them to bake again.[73] 'Consider those famous men of your Rule', concluded Mani in his own defence, 'who had seen these visions and were moved by them and preached about them to others. I achieve all that I have learned from them.'[74]

The leaders of the sect who constituted its *sanhedrin* (συνέδριον) were predictably incensed by Mani's words and the manner in which he annulled their arguments in the debate. They seized him and rained blows on him and such was their rage that they would have killed him had not his father Patīk, who was a well-regarded member of the sect, beseeched them not to commit sacrilege.[75] When he was finally left ot himself Mani fell into deep despair as he contemplated on his future in the sect. Now that all his closest friends had become his most vociferous enemies where should he go? If those who shared so much in common would not listen to the revelations and commandments which he had received how would he fare before kings and princes?[76] At this precise moment his Syzygos appeared to him and his words of encouragement and commissioning for world evangelism form a rhetorical counterpart to Mani's intense self-introspection which was focused narrowly on himself and his sect:

You were not sent only to this Rule, but to every people and [school] of learning and to every city and region; for [this] Hope will be made manifest and preached by you in every clime and [zone] of the world and many [men] will receive your word. Go from here and travel about. For I will be with you as your helper and protector at every place where you will preach everything which I have revealed to you. Therefore do not grieve and feel distressed.[77]

After receiving further words of encouragement from his divine *alter ego*, Mani made the final break with the baptists and travelled to Ctesiphon. He was later joined by two fellow baptists, Simeon and Abizachias, who were among the few who supported Mani's stand against the leaders and regarded him as the 'True Prophet' – a figure which the sect believed had previously appeared in Adam and then through reincarnation in the prophets, Christ and Elchasaios.[78] Patīk, who thought something untoward had happened to his son, came looking for him and was at first distressed by the fact that his son had no intention of returning to the baptist sect. However, after he came to realise the divine nature of the revelation which he had received he too became one of his disciples.[79]

(3)   GNOSTIC AND OTHER CHRISTIAN INFLUENCES ON MANI

Mani's claim to have received his esoteric knowledge through special revelation means that he would admit to no terrestrial influences on the formation of his teaching. However, a valuable clue to one human influence on his thinking is offered by the accusation by his opponents that he had 'eaten Greek bread.'[80] Given the intensely theological nature and the strong antinomian flavour of the controversy between Mani and 'baptist' leaders, paganism was hardly the issue at stake. Rather, the accusation was directed at Mani's contacts with the writings of Paul, the apostle of the gentiles. The Elchasaites were not the sole representatives of Christianity in Babylonia. On the opposite end of the theological spectrum to Judaising Christianity was the hyper-Paulinism of Marcion whose teaching also found fruitful soil in Syria and Mesopotamia. Son of a wealthy shipwright of Sinope, a city in Pontus on the shore of the Black Sea, Marcion (d. c. 160) created a major division in the Christian church in the Roman empire in the second century by asserting that the God of whom the Law and the Prophets speak is not the Father of our Lord Jesus Christ for he is the creator of evil things and takes delight in wars.[81] Jesus came from the Father, who was high above the Creator-God of the Old Testament. He therefore rejected the authority of the Old Testament not because it was untrue but because its contents were unethical and sub-Christian. He also rejected such parts of the New Testament which show approval of the Old or bring Christ into any sort of relationship with the God who made the world. To demonstrate the incompatibility between the Law and the Gospels, Marcion contrasted passages from the two Testaments in his work entitled *Antitheses*.[82] Of the Gospels he accepted only that of Luke but even then he exised from it all mention of Christ's genealogy and nativity for to admit his human birth would have made him subject of the creator of the world. Accordingly Marcion would own no birth at all and his version of Luke began with an edited introduction which contains no account of the nativity, no genealogy, no mention of Christ's baptism and temptation nor that of his preaching from the Book of Isaiah at Nazareth.[83] Besides this specially edited version of Luke, Marcion's canon of scriptures contained ten epistles of Paul, a collection which he entitled the *Apostolicon*.[84] Even these epistles were edited by the removal of places in which the Old Testament is cited in support of Christian doctrines.

Marcion's teaching not only created a division within the church, it also led to the foundation of a new church with its own identity and structure. It also played a major part in evangelism. Epiphanius says that even in his own day (i.e. the late fourth century) Marcionite communities could still be found in Rome, Palestine, Arabia, Syria, Cyprus, the Thebaid (Upper Egypt) and even in Persia.[85] The same success is witnessed to by the biography of the much travelled Abercius Marcellus, bishop of Hierapolis in Phrygia (d. c. 200) composed in the fourth century. It speaks of the churches around Antioch and Apamaea in Syria as being much disturbed by the heresy of Marcion.[86] During the Great Persecution of the fourth century, a Christian from Eleutheropolis found himself yoked to a Marcionite bishop on the same martyr's pyre.[87] However, if the sect suffered along with the rest of the Church under the tetrarchy, it also shared the benefits of the Constantinian religious peace. An inscription from

Deir-Ali near Damascus speaks of the erection of a Marcionite 'synagogue' in the village of Lebaba in 318/9.[88] The ubiquity of Marcionite communities in Syria and Palestine may also be inferred from the warning of Cyril of Jerusalem that the faithful must be careful not to step into a Marcionite church by mistake.[89] How easily Marcionites could be taken as Christians, especially by pagans, in areas where Marcionism had strong support is well illustrated by a remark in the story of the conversion of Mar Aba, the future Catholicos of the Christian church in Persia in the sixth century. Prior to his conversion, Mar Aba was an important Persian official, perhaps a Zoroastrian as he was well-versed in Persian literature. One day, while about to cross the Tigris on his way to his native village in Bēt Garmai, he was offended by the sight of a Christian holy man in his habit and he arrogantly ordered him to be ejected from the ferry together with his baggage. The ferry was then rocked by a storm midstream and the violent winds did not abate until the holy man was readmitted on board. Struck by his distinctive dress, Mar Aba wondered if the holy man was a Jew or a Marcionite. At this point in the Syriac text of Mar Aba's life, the biographer makes an interesting editorial comment: 'for he [Mar Aba] called a Christian a Marcionite [mrqywn'] following the local custom'.[90] The numerical strength of the Marcionities in that region must have once been considerable for the title of their sect to be used coterminously with that of the orthodox (i.e. Nestorian) Christians. The strength of Marcionism in Persian-held Mesopotamia is also amply attested in the writings of the Syriac Fathers beginning with Aphraat in the fourth century and it was explicitly condemned by the Catholicos Simeon bar Sabba'e who suffered martyrdom under Shāpūr II (c. 339).[91]

Marcion's influence on Mani is both profound and pervasive even though the latter did not deign to acknowledge it. In differentiating the stranger-God, the Father of Jesus Christ, from the creator of the visible world, Marcion led the way in dissociating the supreme Godhead from creation and especially from its pain and suffering. This implied dualism between God and creation would in due course be mythologised by Mani in his epic on the two realms. Mani's understanding of the salvific role and nature of the historical Jesus strongly resembles that of Marcion and proceeds from the same theological framework. The Jesus of the Manichaeans was never truly born and it was only a semblance or phantasm of him which was crucified. The Manichaeans went some way to acknowledge the source of their Christology when they used the term 'the god of Marcion' ('wy yzd 'y mrkywn) to denote the malevolent creator-god who brought forth the Jesus who was seized and slain by the Jews, in a polemical poem against other religions in Middle Persian.[92] The arguments adduced by the Manichaeans against the authority of the Old Testament are often the same as the Marcionites, such as the Gospel metaphors of the new patch on old clothes or new wine in old bottles.[93] One disciple of Mani, by the name of Addai (Lat.: Adimantus), would even model the format of his anti-Old Testament work on the *Antitheses* of Marcion by juxtaposing apparently conflicting verses from the two Testaments.[94] The missionary success of the Marcionite movement might have influenced Mani's thinking on ecclesiastical organisation. The Manichaean division of the believers into Elect and Hearer might have its origins in the Marcionite church which only received into full membership those who eschew marriage but permitted the catechumen to partake in the Eucharist and the general life of the church.[95] As we have seen, there were Marcionite bishops, which points to a structured ecclesiastical hierarchy. This too might have influenced Mani in his formulation of a clear pyramidal system for the leadership of his church. Mani's desire to ensure that his church possessed a canon of his writings might have stemmed from the success he saw of the Marcionites in perpetuating Marcion's teaching through his specially edited collection of scripture texts (viz. the *Apostolicon*). This stood in contrast to the tendency among Judaising Christians like the Ebionites to liberally remove from their scriptures passages concerning sacrifice or instances of anthropomorphism through their teaching on 'false pericopai'.[96]

Mani's debt to Marcion is most clearly apparent in his high regard for the apostle Paul. He saw his own controversy with the 'baptists' as a Pauline reaction against Jewish legalism. Furthermore, he regarded himself as an apostle of Christ through the revelations he received from his divine twin in the same way that Paul, though never a personal witness of Christ's teaching and miracles was nevertheless an apostle through his Damascus road experience. Mani's close identification with Paul is shown in his use of a distinctly Pauline formula at the beginning of his letters.[97] His description of his call in the *CMC* is couched in the style of Paul:

When my father showed favour to me and treated me with pity and solicitude, he sent from there my all unfailing Syzygos, the complete fruit of immortality, so that he might ransom and redeem me from the erros of those of the Rule. He came to [me and] brought to me [the] noblest hope, the [redemption] of immortality, true instructions and the laying on of hands from my Father. He came and chose me in preference to others and separated me, drawing me away from the midst of those of that Rule in which I was brought up.[98]

Baraies, one of the witnesses in the *CMC*, also cites from Paul's epistles to the Galatians and the Corinthians where Paul alluded to his calling, as authentication of Mani's apostleship as he too shared the same visionary experiences as Paul.[99] This veneration of Paul would remain a distinguishing feature of Manichaeism. After Augustine had broken away from the sect, a Roman Manichaean called Secundinus would write to him to persuade him to return to the fold and become the 'Paul of our time' who would lead a revival of true Christianity against the Jewish superstition of the Christians.[100]

Marcionism counted many enemies in the Roman Church: Irenaeus, Hippolytus, Epiphanius, [Adamantius] and above all Tertullian – to name but a few. Mesopotamia also produced an early polemicist against Marcion in the person of Bardaiṣan of Edessa (c. 154–222). Philosopher, poet, courtier, astrologer, historian, sportsman, Christian evangelist and man of fashion, Bardaiṣan was undoubtedly the most original and colourful figure at Edessa in the last days of the Abgar dynasty.[101] Although little of his writings has survived, his reputation as a polemicist against Marcion is not in doubt, as we learn from Hippolytus that a Syrian Marcionite by the name of Prepon was impelled to reply to Bardaiṣan's anti-Marcion dialogues.[102] It seems clear that the Marcionites and the followers of Bardaiṣan were keen rivals in Edessa and both sects might have played an important part in the evangelisation of the city, since the Edessan Chronicle gives the date of Marcion's apostasy and that of Bardaiṣan's birth but makes no mention of the coming of Addai or of the consecration in Antioch (end of the second century?) of Palut, whose followers later became the orthodox party in Edessa.[103]

Only one major work of the school of Bardaiṣan, the Book of the Laws of Nations (Syr.: ktb' dnmws' d'trwt') has come down to us.[104] It is cast in the form of a dialogue and has an anti-Marcionite tone even though the arch-enemy is not explicitly named. Awida, one of the interlocutors, provokes an answer from Bardaiṣan with the question: 'If God is one, as you say he is, and if he is the creator of men . . . why did he not so create men that they should not be able to do wrong, but should always do what is right?'[105] Bardaiṣan in his reply makes clear the Marcionite position of his opponent by asking him in turn why he thought God is not one or that he is one and does not desire men's conduct to be just and good.[106] He clearly disapproves of Marcion's concept of two gods, a good one and a just one. He then proceeds to point out that the behaviour of certain animals are conditioned by the laws of nature. Serpents and scorpions will hurt those who have given them no provocation; while sheep will not attempt to return evil for evil, and lions and tigers will hurt those who only hurt them.[107] These three may be called evil, good and just respectively. Men on the other hand are not so morally determined, as they are endowed with free will (ḥ'rwt') which makes them greater than the angels who also possesses it.[108] Bardaiṣan also rejects the view of the Chaldaeans which he once held, that the influence of the stars determines all the fortunes of men. Instead he steers a middle way between a complete denial of Fate which implies that all bodily defects and human calamities are fortuitous and the view that all sufferings are forms of divine punishment. Men are subject to nature (kyn') in things of the body, but they are also subject to fate (ḥlq') which sometimes helps and sometimes disorders the work of nature. Yet fate does not have complete control over events because men's free will can override fate and the planets themselves possess a certain degree of liberty.[109] In order to demonstrate further the workings of free will, the work goes on to give a long list of the special laws and customs which prevail in different tribes and nations.[110] The anti-Marcionite tendency of this work seems to have been acknowledged by the fourth-century biographer of Abercius. The latter might even have met Bardaiṣan himself as he is said to have met a certain rich and noble person called Barchasanes in his eastern travels. The biography contains a dialogue which is clearly modelled on the Book of the Laws of Nations and the opponent of Abercius is suitably named Euxenianos.[111]

Bardaiṣan's antipathy to the Marcionites was also a reflection of the position he held in Edessan society. Having been educated with the then reigning monarch, he was well connected at court.[112] A generous patron of the arts, he gave his son Harmonius the best education then available in sending him to Athens, the foremost seat of learning in the Roman Empire, where he became as fluent in Greek as in Syriac. He lived up to the Greek meaning of his name by becoming a musician of some reputation and set his father's verses to catchy tunes.[113] According to Bardaiṣan's enemies, these songs made him highly popular among the rich and powerful and he came to be protected by them as if 'by a strong wall'.[114] He also enjoyed the national sport of hunting and his skills in archery were proverbial.[115] The followers of Marcion, on the other hand, were fervent in their denunciation of worldly pleasures. Because of their belief in the evil nature of material creation they seem to have lacked any form of gaiety. Ephraim, a famous leader of the church in Edessa in the fourth century, would contrast them as follows: 'He (the Devil) adorns Bardaiṣan with (costly) attire and precious stones while he clothes Marcion in sack-cloth to darken the Sons of Light'.[116] And, 'In the caverns of Bardaiṣan are heard hymns and songs – for he saw that the youth hankered after amusements, so he made them dissolute through the singing of his psalms. Marcion fasted like a serpent and showed by means of a mass of words, the serpent in his audience.'[117]

Bardaiṣan's greater openness to the good things of life than the

Marcionites also stems from a more positive view of the origins of man and the material world. He taught that at the beginning the world was composed of five Entities or Elements (*'yty'*), viz. fire, wind, water, light and darkness. Each was situated at its own point of the compass, Light (east), Wind (west), Fire (south), Water (north), and Darkness (below), and the Lord of all high above them. At some moment in time the first four of the Entities were thrown against each other and Darkness ventured to come up from the depths to mingle with them. They fled before it and sought help from the Lord. At the sound of commotion, the Word (*m'mr'*) of the Lord who was Christ (*msyḥ'*) duly removed the intruder and threw him back into the depths where he naturally belonged. The purified Entities were reordered according to the mystery of the Cross (*r'z' dṣlyb'*). Out of the mixture which had come into being through the mingling of Darkness with the Entities, Christ created the world.[118] Thus the universe as envisaged by Bardaiṣan was not created *ex nihilo* and the creator was not the originator of its constituent matter but its moulder or arranger. The mixture itself would be gradually purified through conception and birth – a view which would have horrified the Marcionites since they condemned marriage and a married man who was received as a catechumen would not be admitted to baptism until he agreed to separate from his wife.[119] However, Bardaiṣan would not go as far as to believe in the resurrection of the body. For him Christ's redemption was only applicable to souls since the body is made of impure matter.

As a religious movement, the school of Bardaiṣan was much more localised than that of Marcion. When the Abgar dynasty came to an end in 216, Bardaiṣan travelled north in Armenia which was then still ruled by a Parthian royal house related to the Abgars. The armenian historian Moses Khorenats'i speaks of Bardaiṣan's sojourn in that country as being devoted to historical research and evangelism.[120] In Edessa his sect later broke up into several factions, each paying more emphasis on certain aspects of his teaching. They continued to thrive until the time of Bishop Rabbula (bishop from 412–35) when they were subjected to forced conversion *en masse* to orthodoxy.[121] Some of the works of the school were translated into Greek. An accurate account by Bardaiṣan on the food habits of Hindu priests and Buddhist monks of India was preserved by Porphyry.[122] Substantial extracts of the Greek version of the *Book of the Laws of Nations* are cited in the *Praeparatio Evangelica* of Eusebius, who did not regard Bardaiṣan as a dangerous heretic since he later recanted most of his errors.[123] The pseudo-Clementine *Recognitiones*, originally composed in Greek but now only extant in Latin translation, also contain quotations from this best known work of the School.[124] A southward and later eastward diffusion of the sect is hinted at by the *Fihrist* of al-Nadim:

In former times the adherents of Ibn Daysān were in the regions of al-Batā'iḥ
(i.e. the relatively inaccessible swamps of the lower Tigris and Euphrates
between al-Wāsiṭ and al-Baṣrah) and even in China and Khurasan there are
scattered communities of them, although no point of union or place of worship
belonging to them is known.[125]

We do not know the precise date of this subsequent migration of
the sect. It may be that like the Nestorians of Edessa in the fifth century, they were first driven across the frontier into Persian-held
Mesopotamia by their ecclesiastical opponents in Osrhoene and with
the advent of Islam two centuries later they moved along with the
Nestorians into Central Asia.[126]

There is not the slightest doubt that Mani was familiar with the
teaching of Bardaiṣan. We learn from al-Nadim's summary of the
contents of the now lost *Book of the Mysteries* that the first part of
this canonical work of Mani was devoted to a discussion of the
teaching of the Daysāniyūn.[127] Furthermore, the title of the work
itself was borrowed from one of similar name by Bardaiṣan.[128] The
influence of Bardaiṣan's teaching is most strongly felt in Mani's
cosmogony. The orderly arrangement of the elements in the universe
prior to the disruption which led to the creation of matter as taught by
Bardaiṣan was most probably the main inspiration behind Mani's
own view of a primordial confrontation between two realms
possessing symmetrical sets of elements with antithetical qualities.
Mani also followed Bardaiṣan in depicting darkness as an active,
invading and contaminating force and not merely as the absence of
light. In both systems, the visible universe was created out of
elements which had been corrupted by darkness and therefore required
purification. So many points of resemblance can be noted between the
teaching of Mani and those of Marcion and Bardaiṣan that Ephraim,
one of the leading Christian opponents of all three systems in Edessa,
saw Manichaeism as essentially a combination the basic teachings of
the two older heresies, and the ground therefore had already been
tilled for its dissemination. 'Marcion had separated his sheep', says
Ephraim and 'Mani fell upon them and led them away.'[129] Similarly,
'Because he [sc. Mani] was unable to find another entrance, he entered
though unwillingly the door which Bardaiṣan had opened.'[130]
Although Ephraim might have exaggerated the similarity between
Mani and the teachings of the two earlier heretics in order to denigrate
his originality, he was essentially correct in seeing them as major
formative elements of Mani's system. The eventual diffusion of
Manichaeism in the Roman empire also finds its most natural
explanation in the eastward extension of Judaeo-Christianity instead
of the 'mirage oriental' which captured the imagination of many
Romans of the third century and which facilitated the spread of cults
like those of Isis and of Mithras.[131]

However, central to Mani's teaching is an epic battle between the realms of light and darkness, a fearful tale of greed, lust, fornication and even cannibalism which has no part in the teaching of Marcion and is infinitely more elaborate and dramatic than Bardaiṣan's metaphysical speculation on the creation of matter out of a disruption of an orderly arrangement of elements. Our search for the originating influences on Mani's teaching must necessarily take us beyond the teachings of Marcion and Bardaiṣan to a wider religious and philosophical movement which had also established roots in Mesopotamia by the end of the second century. The exponents of this teaching are termed gnostics (from γνῶσις, knowledge) by their opponents who regarded them as heretics. However, the Christian church was not their only enemy as their teaching was opposed by some pagan philosophers, especially the great neo-Platonist Plotinus of Lycopolis in the third century.[132] There was never a gnostic church in the same way that one could discern the movement of Marcion as a distinctive ecclesiastical entity. Instead we have a profusion of different gnostic schools, systems and sects which were named by their opponents after their particular leaders, symbols, Biblical or mythological figures or even animals which they held to be sacred to their cult. This great diversity is reflected in their doctrines, which makes it difficult for one to generalise about the movement. Irenaeus of Lugdunum (Lyon), one of its staunchest critics in the early church, found that it was impossible to obtain consistent statements on the same doctrinal issues from different members of the same gnostic sect.[133] Such apparent confusion is the consequence of a distinguishing feature of the movement, namely that salvation is achieved through receiving a special and often esoteric knowledge which was granted to a chosen few. Hence, this knowledge is not purely intellectual speculation but is based on revelation. The various gnostic sects claimed to have a revelation of their own which was essentially secret and they maintained traditions and literature which were also closely guarded.

Central to most gnostic systems is the belief in a primordial dualism between God and Matter. God is entirely transcendant and wholly good. He is also unknowable and unfathomable. Matter is conceived as opposed to God and as something uncreated by him and independent of him. Evil is nearly always inherent in matter in the manner of a physical quality. The metaphysical opposition between God and Matter is also correlated with the ethical opposition of good and evil. Like Marcion, most gnostics therefore regarded the Old Testament, especially the account of creation, as non-essential to salvation and such portions of it they retained were often interpreted allegorically. The special knowledge of the different sects takes many forms and guises but, in essence, it imparts to the recipient the realisation that the imperfect world in which he finds himself is not the work of a just and loving God but of a fallen angel or emanation of God, whom the gnostics called the Demiurge, after Plato's Craftsman, if he was sole creator, or Archons if there were more than one. Man's fleshly nature, which is the seat of evil, is not the conscious creation of God in his own image but an accidental product of concupiscence and desire. However, within man's sinful body is his soul, which contains seeds of divine consciousness. They have been imparted to man by a divine Spirit or Mind (Nous) but they are incarcerated, manacled and drugged to sleep by the desires of the flesh.

If the material world then is intrinsically evil and the transcendant realm of God entirely good, how can one explain the presence of a divine portion in man? Much of the esoteric teaching of the gnostics is devoted to an explication of this problem. Among the various answers offered by the sects, the most common ones assume either a primordial mixing of the elements of good and evil or that the physical world was created as the result of the fall of a divine being. The Redeemer in most gnostic systems is a semi-divine being whose main function was the imparting of a special esoteric knowledge. Christ, who was regarded by some gnostics as one of these messengers, was never truly man, and his suffering on the Cross was in appearance only. One gnostic school teaches that it was Simon of Cyrene who was really crucfied while Jesus, who had changed places with him, stood at a distance and mocked.[134]

Individual salvation for the gnostic entailed the awakening of the sleep-walking soul by a 'Call' from the divine messenger. From this moment onwards, the gnostic knew the distinction between his present situation and the divine origin of his soul. Hitherto he had been held back from this knowledge by ignorance and desire. The function of the special knowledge is to provide answers to such basic questions of human existence as 'Who are we? What has become of us? Where are we or where have we been placed? Where do we go from here? From what are we redeemed? What is birth and what is rebirth?'[135] The answer in most gnostic systems takes the form of a two-fold revelation. The first comprises a cosmic myth which explains how this imperfect world came to be created. The second is a myth of redemption which assures him that although he is clothed in evil and defilement, there is a part of the divine in him which has remained unharmed in the process of creation. It is sufficient therefore to awaken the divine spark which is always present in us or given to us by the divine intelligence (Nous) for us to be reunited with the supreme deity with whom we are consubstantial.

Thus enlightened, some gnostics believed that the only true life was that of the spirit and thus became rigorous ascetics, endeavouring to withdraw more completely from the material world. Others were accused by the church Fathers of extreme libertinism, since they believed that as people who had escaped from the control of the flesh through their special knowledge they could indulge in carnal desires without harmful consequences. Just as gold, when submerged in filth, loses not its beauty but preserves its own nature, so some gnostics were alleged to have maintained that spiritual substance could never come under the power of corruption.[136] Not surprisingly, they were accused of gross immorality and even of condoning the practice of abortion as a means of preventing the perpetual enslavement of the soul by the human body through procreation.

Foremost among the gnostic teachers of the second century was Valentinus, an Egyptian of the Phrebonitic nome, whose disciples claimed that he had been taught by Theodas, whom they said was a pupil of St Paul but is otherwise unknown.[137] He lived in Rome from about 136 to 165 and had harboured hopes of being made bishop on account of his intellectual force and eloquence. Naturally disappointed when he was passed over, he withdrew to Cyprus where he founded his own sect.[138] The insinuation that he became a heretic because of his failure to become bishop is a well-tried motif in polemical writings; the same is also said of Bardaiṣan and later of Mani.[139]

Valentinus had a large following and several of his leading disciples later founded schools of their own. Though he was known to have been a prolific writer, little has survived of his writings. The *Gospel of Truth*, a meditative and speculative work on the gnostic Jesus which was recovered in a Coptic version from Nag Hammadi, is generally regarded to have been written by him on the basis of a reference to a work of the same title by Irenaeus as a fabrication of his school. Otherwise we are largely dependent on polemical writings against the teachings of his principal pupils for our knowledge of the main tenets of Valentinus, especially on the subject of cosmogony. The church Fathers themselves repeatedly stress the doctrinal divergencies of the individual teachers of the school. Not surprisingly, there are many disagreements and discrepancies in detail between the main patristic representations of his teaching on cosmogony, so many in fact that attempts to harmonise them can only result in confusion.

According to one version of his teaching, the heavenly world, the Pleroma, consists of twenty-eight aeons (worlds or ages) which are arranged in *Syzygiai* (pairs).[140] They are the hypostasised attributes of the Monad or Father and emanated from him because he did not love solitude and had the power of generation. When the youngest of these emanations, Sophia (wisdom), discovered that the Father could generate without a partner, she desired to imitate him. Since she

was begotten and born after many others, she did not have the power
of the unbegotten one. 'For', says Valentinus, 'in the ungenerated, all
things exist simultaneously. But among generated things, it is the
female who projects the substance, while the male gives form to the
substance which the female has projected.'[141] Consequently Sophia
brought forth that of which she was capable, an abortion (ἔκτρωμα)
'without form and void'. This caused great consternation among the
other Aeons of the Pleroma, and the Father, paying heed to their
entreaty, sent them to her aid. Two new Aeons, Christos and the Holy
Spirit were brought forth by the Syzygia, Nous (intelligence) and
Aletheia (truth). This new Syzygia separated the abortion of Sophia
from the Aeons, thus removing the cause of the alarm. They drew her
with them within the Pleroma, which was thereupon closed by the
emanation from the Father of yet another Aeon, the Cross (Σταυρός)
which marks the limit of the Aeons (also called Boundary: ''Ορος).
Outside this boundary remained Sophia's abortion whom Christos
and the Holy Spirit had fashioned into an Aeon as perfect as any
within the Pleroma. She, like her mother, is also called Sophia but is
generally distinguished from her as the Sophia Without (ἡ Σοφία ἔξω).
On completing their tasks, Christos and the Holy Spirit returned to
the Syzygia of their origin, Aletheia and Nous. The thirty Aeons of the
Pleroma now determined to present a common progeny to the Father
as their joint fruit so that he might be proof of their unity, agreement
and peace. This 'Common Fruit of the Pleroma' was Jesus.

The Sophia Without was greatly distressed by the departure of the
Aeons who had given her shape. 'And she mourned and was grief
stricken when she considered who it was that had given her shape,
who the Holy Spirit was, whither he had gone, who had hindered them
from being together, and who had begrudged her that fair and blessed
vision.'[142] Thoroughly depressed, she turned herself to fervent
pleading with the one who had left her. Christos, who was inside the
Pleroma, and the other Aeons took pity on her and sent forth the
'Common Fruit of the Pleroma', i.e. Jesus, who entered into a
partnership with her and relieved her of the four main passions which
were besetting her, namely fear (φόβος), grief (λύπη), perplexity
(ἀπορία), and entreaty (δέησις), and turned them into hypostases. The
fear he made into a psychic essence (ψυχικὴ οὐσία), the grief into a
material (ὑλικὴ) one, perplexity into a demonic (δαιμόνος) while
entreaty and the supplication for ascent were made into repentance
(μετάνοια) and the power of the psychic substance, which is called 'the
right' (δεξιά).[143]

From the psychic substance came the Demiurge (δημιουργὸς) or
Creator. He presided over the psychic sphere, below this is the cosmos
and lowest of all, the chaos of unformed matter. The souls of men

proceed from the Demiurge, but he is controlled, unbeknown to himself, by his mother Sophia Without, and as a result of this two-fold influence certain souls are 'pneumatic' (spiritual), others 'psychic', and the rest, given wholly to the element of matter and the devilish essence in which they are incarnated, are 'hylic'. The law and the prophets likewise came from the Demiurge. The 'psychic' soul has in the words of Paul, 'a veil upon his heart' (2 Cor. 3:15) which blinds it to the higher world of the spirits. For the redemption of souls and rectifying the creation, Jesus the 'New Man' was born through Mary the Virgin. He cured the suffering of the souls just as Christos had healed the Sophia Without the Pleroma. The 'pneumatic' souls, because they belong to the higher sphere by their nature require only the moulding influence of the espteric knowledge (gnosis) imparted by Jesus. Once they have ascended to the Pleroma they will unite with angelic beings. 'Psychic' souls who constitute the majority of the church have to make up, with the aid of Jesus, their deficiencies by faith and good works and they will be raised to the Middle Sphere, the heaven of the Sophia Without the Pleroma. Thus, in each of three worlds, Pleroma, Middle Sphere and Cosmos, a saviour was required. Sophia is saved by Christ, her offspring by Jesus and the souls which stem from the Demiurge by Jesus, the son of Mary. According to another witness of Valentinus's teaching, when the process of perfecting the 'psychic' souls had run its course, the fire that is hidden in the world will blaze and burn: when it has consumed all matter it will be consumed with it and pass into non-existence.[144]

Among the followers of Valentinus in the east, some church Fathers counted Bardaiṣan of Edessa. However, reliable Syrian writers are mostly silent on this issue. Bardaiṣan's teaching on free will and the creation of the world out of the mixture of Darkness with other elements has little in common with the complex cosmology of Valentinus and his school with its many distinctive technical phrases, like the Pleroma, Sophia, Aeons, Syzygia etc.[145] Eusebius compromised by saying that Bardaiṣan had once been a devotee of Valentinus's teaching but after having abjured it and refuted a great deal of the heretic's fiction, he had now come over to the more correct doctrine. Nevertheless he was never completely free from the filth of that ancient heresy.[146]

There is no denying that the teaching of Valentinus found receptive soil in Mesopotamia even if its influence on Bardaiṣan can not be proved. Valentinians were condemned along with Marcionites by Aphraat who lived in Persian-held Mesopotamia in the early part of the fourth century.[147] The sect at Edessa found an unlikely champion in the person of Julian the Apostate, who, in a famous letter (c. 362) ordered the confiscation of the property of the Arians of the city for their part in the persecution of the Valentinians; 'in order that they, having become poor, may show self-control and may not be deprived of the heavenly kingdom'.[148] Ephraim, who came to Edessa after the death of Julian and the cession of Nisibis by Jovian in 363, bemoaned the fact that the followers of Valentinus (wlntynws) stole the sheep from the Christian flock.[149] Towards the end of the fourth century (388) at Callinicum (ar-Rakka), a town of considerable military and commercial importance in Euphratensia, some Christian monks, provoked by an interruption of their procession when they were celebrating the Feast of the Maccabees (1 August), set fire to a chapel which belonged to the Valentinians.[150] This came shortly after a similar incident in the same town saw the destruction of a Jewish synagogue by the Christians.[151] The sect seemed to have lost much of its influence by that date. In the fifth century, Theodoret of Cyr in Syria described Valentinianism as belonging to the past, one of the 'former heresies' which he knew only through the writings of earlier heresiologists.[152]

The fortunes of the Valentinians, the most readily identifiable group of gnostics, show clearly that gnosticism occupied an important place in the early diffusion of Judaeo-Christianity in Syria and Mesopotamia. Its influence on Manichaeism is immanent, so much so that Manichaeism must be regarded as a form of gnosticism. The Manichaean myth also seeks to answer basic questions of human existence, especially how souls which are of divine origin came to be incarcerated in human bodies which are evil. Many of the mythological details in the Manichaean cosmic drama are also encountered in gnosticism, such as Archons, Aeons, Syzygos, Abortions, Demiurge etc. The Manichaean demon Saklas is often encountered in the gnostic texts from Nag Hammadi.[153] The deity, the Custodian of Splendour (Syr.: ṣpt zyw', Gk.: φεγγοκάτοχος), also strikes one as an adaptation of a gnostic divine figure δοξοκράτωρ, a ruler of great glories who is found in the untitled text of the *Codex Brucianus* and who also calls to mind the Doxomedon-aeon in the Gospel of the Egyptians from Nag Hammadi.[154] The episode in the Manichaean myth which depicts the seduction of the archons by hermaphrodite-deities has strong parallels in the untitled text (commonly referred to as *On the Origin of the World*) in one of the gnostic codices from Nag Hammadi.[155] The Manichaean belief that the suffering Jesus is crucified in every rock and tree is also paralleled by a *logion* in the gnostic *Gospel of Thomas*.[156] The term 'Cross of Light' can be linked to gnostic writings as it is discussed at length in the *Acts of John*.[157] The Valentinian division of mankind into the *Pneumatikoi*, the *Psychikoi* and the *Hylikoi* (or *Sōmatikoi*) was also accepted by Mani and is discussed in one of his discourses in the *Kephalaia*.[158]

Whether this gnostic influence came to Mani via the same channels
as the teachings of Marcion or Bardaiṣan or whether it was an integral
part of his Judaising Christian upbringing among the Elchasaites is
hard to determine. We know from a Manichaean fragment in Middle
Persian that Mani counted the gnostic apocalyptist Nikotheos among
the prophets of mankind, along with those more commonly
encountered in Manichaean writings – Shēm, Enosh and Enoch.[159]
The Apocalypse which bears his name is mentioned by Porphyry as
one of the many gnostic revelations which were popular in the
lifetime of the great neo-Platonist Plotinus (205–69/70).[160] The work
is also cited in the untitled text in the *Codex Brucianus*.[161] A great
admirer of this work was the early fourth-century Greek alchemist,
Zosimus of Panopolis, who cites the work in his little treatise on the
letter Omega. In his speculation on the first man, Zosimus tells us
that only Nikotheos knows his real name. But his common name is
Phōs ($\varphi\dot\omega\varsigma$, poetic word for 'man') which is clearly a play on the word
phōs ($\varphi\tilde\omega\varsigma$, i.e. 'light'). This Phōs was beguiled by Fate to clothe
himself with their Adam and thus became their slave. Jesus Christ
appeared to Adam and bore him up to the place where the Phōtes
('men' or 'Light Particles') originally lived. Through feigned suffering
Jesus was able to redeem these 'men' or 'Light Particles', and, until
the end of the world this Jesus returns regularly to his own people and
counsels them secretly through their minds to get rid of their Adam.[162]
Nikotheos could have been a Graeco-Egyptian like Valentinus and
Zosimus whose work would have come to Mani through translation
into Syriac, or he could have been a Judaising Christian like Elchasaios
whose work was later translated into Greek from Aramaic like the
Book of Elchasaios. However, the pun on the word *phōs* is so Greek
that it could hardly have been first thought of in Aramaic.

One gnostic text with which Mani appears to be familiar is a long
poem called the 'Hymn of the Pearl' or the 'Hymn of the Soul' by
modern scholars. The poem is found in the apocryphal Acts of Judas
Thomas and although we possess them in both Greek and Syriac
versions, most scholars would accept the Syriac as the original.
However, the only complete Syriac version was partially revised
according to later and more orthodox teachings.[163] Their provenance is
indubitably Mesopotamian and the hymn itself, which is probably
older than the Acts, centres on a Parthian royal family which had sent
a son to Egypt via Mesene (Syr.: *myšn*) to redeem a pearl which was
guarded by a fierce dragon. They equipped him with a cargo (*mwbl'*) of
five treasures: gold, silver, chalcedony, agate and diamond but they had
to make him take off the (robe) of glory (Syr.: *zhy(w)t'*) or precious
vestment (Gk.: $\dot\eta$ $\dot\epsilon\sigma\theta\dot\eta\varsigma$ $\delta\iota\dot\alpha\lambda\iota\theta\varsigma$) which they had wrought for him. They
made a pact with him that should he bring back the pearl he would be
reclothed in his heavenly vestment. Two messengers accompanied

him for the first part of the journey and they travelled to Egypt via
Mesene, i.e. the southernmost part of Mesopotamia, Babylonia and
Sarbug (Mabbogh, i.e. Hierapolis in Syria (?)). He went into Egypt
alone as a stranger (Syr.: *nwkry'*). In order not to be insulted as a
foreigner, he unwisely put on the garb of the Egyptians and partook of
their food, which caused him to forget that he was a son of kings and
the purpose of his mission, as well as drugging him to sleep.
Mercuifully, his heavenly parents perceived his distressful condition
and they wrote a letter, signed by all the other kings and princes of
Parthia to remind him of his royal origins, the purpose of his journey
and the reward which awaited him at home. To prevent it from falling
into the hands of wicked people and demons, the letter was sent direct
to the prince:

> It flew in the likeness of an eagle,
> the king of all birds;
> It flew and alighted beside me,
> And became nothing but speech.
> At its voice and the sound of its rustling,
> I started and arose from my sleep.
> I took it up and kissed it,
> And loosed its seal [and] read;
> And according to what was traced on my heart
> Were the words of my letter written.
> I remembered that I was a son of kings,
> And my free soul [*h'rwt'*] longed for its natural state [*kyn'*].
> I remembered the pearl,
> For which I had been sent to Egypt.[164]

Thus awakened, the prince duly lulled the dragon to sleep and
snatched the pearl. His mission accomplished, he stripped off the
filthy and unclean garb of the Egyptians. The letter, his awakener
(*m'yrnwt'*), guided him back to his royal home. He received from his
parents the robe of glory which he had left behind and suddenly
realised that the garment was a mirror (*mhzyt'*) of himself:

> I saw it all in my whole self,
> Moreover I faced my whole self in [facing] it,
> For we were two in distinction
> And yet again one in one likeness.[165]

Not only was it exquisitely wrought and expensively adorned, it was
also quivering with life:

> Again I saw that all over it
> The motions of knowledge [*yd't'*] were stirring,
> And as if to speak
> I saw it also making ready.[166]

The robe was none other than his divine *alter ego* which had grown with his deeds and had been perfected by his toils. He wrapped it round himeslf and was duly reunited with his royal parents amidst much rejoicing.[167]

The poem is a gnostic parable based probably upon a pre-Christian romance and is commonly interpreted as the sending of a Redeemer from his heavenly home, who there forgets both his origin and mission until aroused by a divine message. Thereupon he performs the task assigned to him and returns to the upper regions where he is reunited with his heavenly *alter ego*.[168] The motif of a redeemer who himself requires redemption is a central theme in the Manichaean cosmogonic myth. Traces of direct literary influence of this hymn can be found in a number of Manichaean psalms and allusions to it can also be seen in Manichaean parable texts.[168a] Its use of the symbol of the garments is of particular interest in view of the importance given to the imagery of the 'robe of glory' by later Syriac Christian writers.[169] Adam and Eve were clothed in 'robes of glory' before the Fall and at his baptism Christ, the Second Adam, deposited his 'robe of glory' in the waters of Jordan. It is therefore at the baptismal font that the believer retrieves this divine garment. As Ephraim puts it succinctly: 'Our body became Your garment, Your Spirit became our robe'.[170] In this merging of the First and Second Adam, we see the continuum of symbolism which reaches back to the hymn, where the prince reunites with his divine *alter ego* through putting back on his robe.

Mani was a visionary, a poet, an artist and a missionary. The diverse influences which we have tried to identify are skilfully woven by him into a system which has a startling originality. His claim to be an apostle of Jesus Christ and the earthly twin of the Paraclete gives a cogency and a finality to his teaching which differs from the other gnostic systems. The Manichaean 'myth' formed the basis of an elaborate ecclesiastical organisation which allowed the religion to outlive all its gnostic predecessors by many centuries. The basic teaching was accurately transmitted from the original Syriac into the main ancient languages of Europe and Central Asia. There is probably less divergence in the Coptic and Chinese versions of the Manichaean 'myth' than in the two main accounts, both in Greek, of the system of Valentinus. Mani was undoubtedly a syncretist but his religious background was predominantly Judaeo-Christian, as is revealed by the newly discovered texts. The view once commonly held of him fusing together elements of Christianity, Zoroastrianism and Buddhism to create a world religion which was all things to all men must now be decisively abandoned. As we shall see, the Zoroastrian and Buddhist elements were acquired in the course of mission and were not fundamental to Manichaeism. The study of Manichaean origins underlines the diverse and heterodox nature of early Syriac Christianity and the extent to which it was subjected to both Judaising and gnosticising influences.

(4) MANI'S FIRST MISSIONARY JOURNEYS

Mani and his few companions do not appear to have stayed long in Ctesiphon. They soon took to the road and became itinerant preachers and miracle workers. The last extant portion of the *CMC* furnishes us with a number of episodes from these early missionary activities covering a period of perhaps several months. The text is very fragmentary and it is hazardous to reconstruct from a few legible place names a full itinerary. The mention of the Medes and Gonzak on p. 121 seems to indicate that Mani's first missionary journey was in a north easterly direction. Gonzak was the seat of the summer palace of the Sassanian kings and Mani's purpose for visiting it might well have been to try to obtain from Ardashīr the necessary permission to preach his new religion. However, Ardashīr was noted, even in Greek sources, for being a devotee of Zoroastrianism. Although the more tolerant Shāpūr had become co-regent, the Sassanian court was probably still impervious to new ideas in matters of religion.[171] The *CMC* does not hint at such a political purpose for Mani's visit to Gonzak. He demonstrated his skills there by healing the daughter of an important person who was stricken by convulsions. When Mani was asked by the grateful father what he would like for reward, he repiled that he would not want any of his most plentiful and most excellent treasures but: '[Offer] me only the girl [?] who is the most modest of [her] sisters'.[172] This was granted and we may assume that the young girl was taken into the sect following the custom which first brought Mani among the Elchasaites.

The party then travelled through mountainous country and was startled by the appearance of a shaggy and hairy hermit. He recognised Mani as a prophet and duly received from him the teaching about the Rest (of the Hands), the commandments and the worship (προσκύνησις) of the Luminaries (i.e. the sun and the moon). The hermit departed from Mani and became a herald of Mani's gospel.[173] The next episode sees Mani in more exalted circles:

I went to a little known area which was some distance from the Cities [i.e. Veh-Ardashir and Ctesiphon] but even so there were in it a great number of people and many cities. Just as I arrived in the area, the orb of the day [i.e. the sun] rose and the king of that country went hunting . . . Then indeed my most reputable guide and most trusty companion (*syzygos*) stood beside me and said to me ... I stood before the king and his nobles. Seeing me the king and his nobles were stirred and marvelled. And I [thought] ... towards them ... and when I approached nearer them the king and his nobles dismounted from their horses, and standing in front of him I did obeisance ... I expounded the wisdom and the commandments before him and explained everything to him. [And in the few days] I spent there he sat before me with his nobles and I revealed to them the distinction between the two natures ... [he treated me like a brother (?)] and received favourably everything that he heard from me. After the fulfilment in me of this most glorious task, suddenly while the king was sitting there and his nobles in like manner in front of him, [listening to me] [my] most reputable guide (i.e. his Syzygos) descended from above ... to me ... The king and his nobles marvelled ... The king was strengthened in the wisdom and was nurtured in the knowledge and the faith. His nobles were similarly fulfilled in the faith. The king also accepted in good cheer all the injunctions which I imparted to him ... and since then this sanctity (i.e. Mani's religion) was spread over that area.[174]

We know from sources in Coptic that Mani spent the last years of Ardashir's reign travelling and preaching in India and the mention of the port of Farat on the Persian Gulf on p. 140 of the Codex may well indicate his place of departure.[175] Further mention of the port in connection with merchants and ships travelling to India on p. 144 seems to point to the beginning of Mani's missionary journey to India which took place during his first or second year as a missionary.

In addition to the *CMC* we possess as an important source for the earliest missionary journeys of Mani and his disciples a considerable number of Turfan fragments in Middle Persian, Parthian and Sogdian. These fragments probably constituted a version or versions of the Acts of Mani and the Manichaean apostles and as a literary genre they, like the missionary episodes of the *CMC*, show a strong resemblance to Christian apocryphal Acts of the Apostles in that they highlight the miraculous and the successful conversions of important personages, kings, princes and nobles. Though these examples of Manichaean hagiography present a history of the early years of the sect seen exclusively through the ideals and aspirations of the sect, they do nevertheless offer the modern scholar much valuable material on Mani's missionary methods as well as enabling us to trace the itinerary of Mani's own travels and those of his disciples.

At the time of Mani's visit to India, the regions of Tūrān, Makrān, Pārdān, parts of India and the Kūshānshāhr up to Pashkibur were, according to the Great Inscription of Shapur, parts of the Ēranshahr.[176] However, for much of the Parthian period, they constituted an important part of the Kūshān empire and did not come under Persian control until their annexation by Ardashir.[177] Under the Kūshān kings, Buddhism had made considerable impact on the cultural and religious outlook of these regions. Thus, Mani, after having landed at Deb, one

of the most important ports on the Indus Delta well into the Middle
Ages, found himself having to explain the uniqueness of his new
religion to people   who were not versed in Judaeo-Christianity.
According to a Parthian Manichaean text reconstructed from a number
of fragments, Mani visited an *ardaw* (righteous person?) with the Shah
of Tūrān and demonstrated his skills at levitation by conducting, in
mid-air, a metaphysical discussion with the *ardaw*. The Shah was so
impressed by this supernatural feat and the profundity of the dialogue
that he came to regard Mani as the Buddha himself and he and his
nobles were converted to his religion.[178]

One wonders how much a Syrian from Babylonia would have
known about Buddhism and the skills of levitation before setting foot
in India. Mani might have read about Buddhist monks in the writings
of Bardaiṣan, who professed to have met a deputation of them on their
way to the Roman emperor and might have learned something about
their food habits.[179] Moreover it seems clear that the purpose of
Mani's visit to India was not merely to imbibe the wisdom of the
Orient but to export his newly received revealtion. Admittedly the
Coptic *Kephalaia* mentions the Buddha and Aurentes (= Sanskrit:
arhan or *arhat*, Chin: *A-lo-han*, the highest type or ideal saintly man in
Hīnayāna Buddhism) in connection with India, but they are passing
references and it is hazardous to argue from them that Mani had a deep
knowledge of Buddhism.[180]

The great Arab scholar of the eleventh century, al-Bīrūnī (d. 1048) in
his survey of Indian history, thought and culture, asserts that when
Mani was exiled from the Persian empire, he came to India where he
learned the doctrine of metempsychosis from the Hindus and
transferred it to his own system. He also cites from the *Book of
Mysteries*, one of the canonical works of Mani in which we find Mani
being asked by his student about the fate of the souls of those who did
not receive the truth. To this Mani replied that they would be
punished, in contrast to the followers of Bardaiṣan who believes that
the soul could be purified through the body.[181] Since the doctrine of
samsara (birth-death, i.e. birth and rebirth) is of fundamental
importance to Buddhism, it is not surprising that scholars have come
to regard the similar Manichaean concept of *metaggismos* (i.e. rebirth
in other forms of life) as of Indian or Buddhist origin.[182] This, they
argue, may explain why one of the most implacable opponents of
Manichaeism, Ephraim of Nisibis, accused Mani of having imported
the teaching of the Hindus.[183] However we must question whether
Ephraim had a thorough enough grasp of Buddhism to qualify him to
make a valid assessment of Buddhist influence on Manichaeism
beyond certain superficial resemblances. Moreover he exhibits a
tendency to apply ethnic labels as terms of opprobrium to enemies of

Rome or of the true faith. In one of his poems against Julian, he claims
the success of the Romans under Constantius II to hold Nisibis against
Shāpūr II as a victory of Christianity over the Magians of Persia, the
Chaldaeans of Babylon and the sorcerers (*hrš'*) of India.[184] Even if
Mani did derive the concept of metempsychosis from the Indians it
only represents a small part of his teaching. Extant Manichaean
writings in western languages exhibit virtually no knowledge of
Buddhist scriptures. In the east where Manichaeism flourished
alongside Buddhism, the eastern Manichaeans rarely handled
Buddhist scriptures with the same confidence and felicity as their co-
religionists in the West did with Christian scriptures.[185] Manichaean
borrowings from Buddhism, as we shall see, are mainly external and
limited to stock phrases, legends, artistic motifs, literary formats and
monastic organisation.

Had the real purpose of his journey, like that of the famous Chinese
pilgrim Hsüan-tsang of the T'ang period, been to learn about
Buddhism he would have taken the trouble to learn Sanskrit and
would have have travelled southwards or eastwards from Deb to the
main centres of Buddhism instead of heading back to Mesene overland
via Tūrān. From another Parthian fragment we learn that when he
reached Rēv-Ardashīr in the province of Pars, he sent Patticius and
another of his earliest disciples, Innaios, to Deb to continue his work
there.[186] Among the titles of Mani's works which have been preserved
for us by al-Nadim is a 'Letter to India (a long one)' which indicates
that as a result of his visit and that of his disciples, Manichaean
communities were established in India. Considering the fact that
Mani's first missionary journey did not last longer than two years, it is
more likely that he assumed the mantle of a wandering preacher than
the *kasāya* of a novice monk. Two recently published fragments of
Manichaean missionary history show Mani teaching in a province in
India or eastern Iran in which Buddhism was practised. There a certain
Gwndyš, apparently the wisest of the listeners, bombarded Mani with
weighty academic questions ranging from which was the oldest script
to the nature of the world. Gwndyš was so impressed by Mani's
answers that he was impelled to declare that in truth Mani was the
Buddha (*bwt*) and Apostle (*fryštg*).[187] If this incident did take place in
India and was indicative of Mani's activities there, we can be certain
that he did not spend his time sitting at the feet of great Buddhist
teachers.

The Manichaeans were proud of their connection with India. The
Apostle Thomas, the harbinger of Christianity to India, therefore
came to occupy a place of importance in the catalogue of Manichaean
saints borrowed from the apocryphal Acts.[187a] However, the subsequent history of the Manichaean communities in India is still

little known. The missionaries no doubt benefited from active
maritime trade between India and the Persian Gulf, but Syrian
Christians came to dominate this route as the century wore on.[188] In
the fifth century the trade from Farat was conducted under the
watchful eye of the local Nestorian bishop and this would have made
it difficult for Manichaeans to obtain passage to India on board
merchant vessels.[189] Christian sources of a later period say that the
heretics came to India when there was an hiatus in the leadership of
the Christian community.[190] Thus, had the normal vigilance been
maintained, Manichaeans would have had little opportunity of
gaining entry into these tightly-knit communities of expatriate
Christians who clung tenaciously to their faith amidst a sea of other
religions.

A recurrent theme in Manichaean accounts of their own early
missionary activities is the conversion of important personages:
kings, nobles and princes. The fact that Manichaeism throughout its
history enjoyed little support from the powers-that-be must have emphasised the need felt by its followers to show that at one time they
had friends among the highest in the land. Undoubtedly it was the
policy of Mani and that of his earliest disciples to bring the religion to
the attention of powerful and influential people in the hope of winning
their support for its propagation. Although the outcome of such royal
encounters was open to exaggeration, it seems that Mani was clearly
not without success. In a fragment of Manichaean missionary history
which belongs to Mani's earliest travels we find him converting to his
religion Mihrshāh, the Lord of Mesene (Mēsūn-Khwadāy), by giving
him a foretaste of the Paradise of Light.[191] More significant still for the
propagation of his religion in the Iranian parts of the empire was his
friendship with Pērōz, the brother of Shāpūr who was then the
governor of Khurāsān. Through him, Mani was eventually admitted to
the presence of Shāpūr who had now succeeded his father as
Shahanshah. According to a Manichaean tradition preserved by al-
Nadim, Shāpūr originally intended to slay Mani but when he saw light
emanating from Mani's shoulders, he fell down in awe of him and
became well-disposed towards him and his religion.[192] He gave Mani
written permision for him and his disciples to travel and preach
anywhere in his empire.[193] In Manichaean literature, considerable
capital is made of Shāpūr's apparent friendliness to Mani. He was
admitted to Shāpūr's entourage (comitatus) and Shāpūr discoursed
with him so frequently that his exasperated students once suggested to
him that there should be two Manis instead of one.[194]

Scholars have speculated that the motives behind Shāpūr's amicable
relationship with Mani were political since the new religion, because
of its syncretistic nature, offered him greater advantages for his impe-

rialistic designs than Zoroastrianism.[195] However, if Shapur did intend to use Manichaeism as a form of propaganda either for furthering Sassanian designs in neighbouring empires or for bringing about greater unity among the diverse parts of his great empire, this was never openly acknowledged. On his great inscription at Kaaba of Zoroaster, Shāpūr depicts himself as a champion and devotee of Zoroastrianism.[196] Recent research has also shown that Sassanian, i.e. Zoroastrian, religious propaganda enjoyed some success in Armenia, Georgia and (Caucasian) Albania, obviating the argument that Zoroastrianism did not lend itself readily to political ends.[196a] Mani's encounter with Shāpūr must be viewed against his general missionary strategy.[197] As a non-Iranian, he needed support from the highest authority to gain access to the heartland of traditional Iran. He was referred to by Shāpūr and his successors as 'the doctor from the land of Babylon' and it was on the charge of being an inept physician that he was later executed by Vahrām. Mani's relationship with the Sassanian monarchs was that of patron and client rather than king and prophet.[198] As Mani himself declared before Vahrām: 'Always have I done good to you and your family. And many and numerous were your servants whom I have freed of demons and witches ... And many were those who came unto death, and I have received them'.[199] He was the first of the many Syrian Christians who found favour at court because of their skills as doctors and exorcists.[200] His standing with Shāpūr and his son Hormizd probably had little to do with the nature of his teaching or his desire to found a universal church.

Mani spent several years in Shāpūr's entourage, first in Ctesiphon and then travelling with the Sassanian court throughout Persis and Parthia. He even visited Adiabene and other territories bordering on the Roman empire.[201] According to a Greek source, Mani accompanied Shapur on his campaigns against the Roman empire.[202] He may even have been at the scene of the capture of Valerian in 260. However, we do not know the exact year in which Mani entered Shapur's service, and he could have partaken in the Shahanshah's earlier campaigns. It is a strange irony that in the ranks of the Roman army which took part in Gordian's abortive campaign to regain Mesopotamia in 244 was Plotinus of Lycopolis whose later philosophical teaching was to lay the ground for the refutation of Mani's religious system by both Christian theologians and pagan philosophers in the Roman empire.[203]

CHAPTER III

MISSION AND THE
MANICHAEAN CHURCH

(1)   MANI'S VIEW OF MISSION

The Sassanian empire under Shapur embraced a number of different cultures and religious. Mani's extensive travels in the domains of the Shahanshah took him to countries which had their own distinctive religions. In India and Turan he would have encountered Hindu, Brahmin and Buddhist monks, in Mesopotamia, Christian bishops and congregations from the eastern provinces of the Roman empire, and in Persia and Media he would have entered upon the heartland of Zoroastrianism. What struck him most were the apparent cultural and geographical delimitations of these three historic religions. Although Christianity was beginning to spread throughout the Persian Empire and Buddhism had already won an important foothold in China, yet, to Mani, Jesus was the prophet of the Jews, Buddha was the prophet of the Indians and Zoroaster was the prophet of the Persians. He believed that the true church would embrace all humanity and he therefore used the apparent 'parochialism' of these earlier prophecies as a foil against which to set his own revelation to greater advantage. In the preface of the *Šābuhragān*, a work which he dedicated to Shapur, he says:

Wisdom and deeds have always from time to time been brought to mankind by the messengers of God. So in one age they have been brought by the messenger called Buddha, to India, in another by Zaradust to Persia, in another by Jesus to the West. Thereupon this revelation has come down and this prophecy has appeared in the form of myself, Mani, the envoy of the true God in the Land of Babylon.[1]

His revelation therefore, which was definite and final, would also transcend cultural and national barriers which had hitherto bedevilled the earlier revelations. In order to prove the veracity of his special revelation, it was imperative that Manichaean mission should be directed towards more than one country or culture. In a far-reaching declaration of world evangelisation which is attested both in Coptic and Middle Persian, Mani says:

He who has his Church in the West, he and his Church have not reached the East: the choice of him who has chosen his Church in the East has not come to the West ... But my hope, mine will go towards the West, and she will go also towards the East. And they shall hear the voice of her message in all languages, and shall proclaim her in all cities. My Church is superior in this first point to previous churches, for these previous churches were chosen in particular countries and in particular cities. My Church, mine shall spread in all cities and my Gospel shall touch every country.[2]

Mani's zeal for world mission is undoubtedly a reaction against the isolationist outlook of the Elchasaites who would not even allow their members to read Paul for fear of their 'going to the Greeks'. However it was from Elchasaites that Mani derived the concept of the cyclical reappearance of the true prophet and he broadened the list of former appearances to include Buddha and Zoroaster in order to substantiate his own claims to be a universal prophet.[3] The *Act of Thomas*, which played a significant part in the formation of Mani's views on cosmogony, may have also awoken him to the missionary possibilities outside Mesopotamia, especially in India and Egypt.[4]

Mani was very conscious of the fact that he had founded his church at the crossroads of east and west. To some extent, this was a reflection of the position of the Persian empire as the middle kingdom between the European powers of Greece and Rome and the Asiatic empires of India and China. The Sassanians regarded themselves as rulers of 'Iran and non-Iran' and the latter was interpreted freely to suit their political designs. The *Farsnameh* says that in the throne room of Chosroes Anūshīrvān were three vacant seats kept for the kings of Rome, China and the Khazars (i.e. the Turks) should they come to pay homage to the Shahanshah.[5] Hence, when Mani spoke of earthly powers in one of his discourses, he reminded his disciples of the four-fold division of the world into the empires of Persia, Rome, the Axumites (i.e. Ethiopia) and Silis (i.e. China).[6] This broad view of the known world can also be found in the *Book of the Laws of Countries* of the school of Bardaiṣan in which accounts are given of the distinctive characteristics of parts of the Roman empire as well as regions as far as Bactria and China.[7] As Syrian Christianity expanded eastwards, it too acquired a more cosmopolitan outlook. In a medieval Nestorian commentary on the lectionary, the coming of the Anti-Christ is not merely a Judaeo-Hellenic phenomenon. To the Greeks he would appear as Zeus or Hermes, to the Jews as the Messiah, to the Magians as Pesiotan,[8] to the Indians as Brahm and Buddha, to the Chaldaeans as Bel, to the Turks as Tangri, and to the Chinese as 'Bagour' (Pth.: bgpwhr, 'son of God' = Chin.: t'ien-tzu (son of Heaven).[10]

It was Mani's awareness of the potential extent of his mission field which enabled Manichaeism to become a world religion during his own lifetime. Mission was a driving force behind the religion from its very inception. Mani's understanding of his own role as a missionary seems to have been modelled on Paul. As Heinrich Schaeder puts it succinctly: '[Mani] was as much a missionary as a religious leader. His entire life's work, his travels, his writings were mission; we must conclude from his style that (the Apostle) Paul stood before him as his model even if we have not got the evidence for this.'[11] The CMC has now shown beyond doubt that his imitatio Pauli was both conscious and deliberate.[12]

Like Paul he undertook extensive missionary journeys, mostly within the Sassanian empire. Later sources even credited him with having visited lands as far east as China.[13] He appointed his disciples both to consolidate the work which he had begun and to open up entirely new fields for mission. An indefatigable correspondent, he remained in contact with disciples and Manichaean communities in far-flung corners of the known world, as attested by the long surviving list of the recipients of his letters.[14] As we have seen, he even prefaced his letters with a pseudo-Pauline greeting.[15] As a Christian bishop of the fourth century sardonically remarks: 'There are even times when he, though himself a barbarian by race and by intellect, writes as the Apostle of Christ who wrote to those who are barbarians by race'.[16] Consciously trying to surpass the previous apostles in their missionary endeavour, he was anxious that his 'Hope' should reach the east as well as the west, the northern climes as well as the southern, as no other apostle has achieved this before him.[17] The uniqueness of his revelation, therefore, was to be proved by its spectacular missionary successes.

The Manichaean Elect was called to a lifetime of travel and evangelism. He was permitted only to possess enough food for one day and a single garment for one year.[18] The restriction on the amount of food which he could carry may have originated in Mani's dispute with the Elchasaites, among whom it was stipulated that each one had to bake his own unleavened bread for the celebration of their liturgical meals. Mani believed that this was in direct contradiction to the actual teaching of Elchasaios and supported his argument with an appeal to Jesus's instruction to his disciples not to carry more than their immediate requirements on their journeys, which according to Mani, specifically forbids the carrying of baking equipment.[19] In the course of time the Manichaeans developed an elaborate cell structure which allowed the Elect to travel relatively unencumbered from one community to the next. As we shall see, these cells (*conventus*) would become the target of restrictive legislations both in Rome and China.[20]

One class of Manichaean priests in the east had the significant title of *xrwhxw'n* (or *xrwhw'n*), i.e. a 'Call-caller', and Mani describes himself as having been led out of Babylon in order to cry out a cry (*xrws'n xrws*) to the world.[21] Even in transliterating the title *xrwhxw'n* into Chinese, the Manichaeans endeavoured to retain some of the original significance of the term by choosing three characters which all have something to do with the emission of sound: *Hu-lu-huan* (i.e. call, grunt and summon) and the *Compendium* defines their task as specialising in 'commendation and persuasion'.[22] The concept of 'the Call' (Syr.: *qry'*, Pe.: *myzdgt'c*, Pth.: *xrwstg*, Chin.: *huan*), occupies an important place in Mani's soteriology.[23] The sleep-walking soul of the fallen man comes to life again when he is awakened by this messenger God of 'the Call' and responds to it through the messenger God of 'the Answer'.[24] Manichaean mission-aries, therefore, were the earthly agents of this divine 'Call'. The importance of their task warranted a special exemption from the normal Manichaean prohibition of excessive travelling, which was believed to be injurious to the Light Particles in the ground. Mani likens an Elect who travels for the sake of his divine mission to a doctor who heals rather than exacerbates the condition of the captive 'Cross of Light' which lies in his path.[25] A similar analogy can be found in the Chinese *Treatise* in which the *tien-na-wu* (= Per.: *dyn'wr*, a devout member of the sect) is compared to a king who does not reside permanently in one abode but travels with his entourage, fully equipped to subdue the fierce animals and jealous enemies which they may encounter.[26]

(2)   THE FIRST MANICHAEAN
                       MISSIONS TO THE WEST

The spread of Manichaeism from southern Mesopotamia to the adjacent provinces of the Roman empire was part of a well-orchestrated effort by Mani to demonstrate the veracity of his revelation through its universal recognition. We have seen in Mani's own visit to India and in his sending of Patīk and Innaios to consolidate the work which he had begun there that mission was an integral part of the church from its very beginning. Mani's visit to Adiabene and the regions bordering onto the Roman empire must have opened him to the missionary opportunities within and without the Sassanian empire. From Seleucia (i.e. Veh-Ardashīr) Mani sent out a succession of missions both across the frontier into the Roman Empire and also to the eastern parts of the Eranshahr. These were spearheaded by some of his most able and devoted disciples. Among those who went to Rome were Adda, Patīk the teacher (Sogd: *mwz-''k'*), not to be confused with Mani's father, Patīk the house-steward, Gabryab, Pappos, Thomas and Akouas.[27] Adda also took part in 260/1 in a mission to Karkā de Bēt Selōk, a former Hellenistic settlement named after Selecucus Nicator on the Little Zab, a tributary of the Tigris, in Bēt Garmai.[28] The main task of evangelising the eastern parts of the Sassanian empire fell to Mar Ammo, the apostle of the east.

Of these missionary journeys, that of Adda and Patīk to the Roman empire is by far the best documented. The account is preserved in a number of fragments of Manichaean missionary history in all three of the main dialects of Middle Iranian.[29] One version begins with Mani exhorting Adda and Patīk to familiarise themselves with his writings.[30] From a shorter version we learn that they were given four instructions (*'bdys*) and certain 'writings of Light' (*nbyg'n rwsn'n*).[31] The shorter version also adds that they were accompanied by a scribe (*dbyr*) whose task undoubtedly was to assist in the diffusion of Mani's writings.[32] Adda, who had the title of Bishop (*'spsg*), was one of Mani's intimate circle of disciples. In the Chinese treatise he figures as in inspired pupil who posed a profound question to his master on the nature of man's carnal nature which occasioned a long discourse from Mani in reply.[33]

The party ventured into territories under Roman control (*hrwm*) and soon got involved in debates with religious leaders.[34] These debates were to follow the Manichaeans wherever they went in the Roman empire. As we shall see, the Christians in the Roman empire would later allege that Mani himself crossed the frontier to engage in debate with a Christian bishop, and was duly put to shame by him.[35] However, according to the Manichaean sources, Adda emerged triumphat in similar encounters, having been fortified by the writings of Mani.[36] Thereupon Mani instructed Adda to remain where he was and to 'collect a store like a merchant'.[37] Mani also sent him three more scribes together with a copy of his 'Living Gospel'.[38] Adda remained where he was told and worked diligently for the faith with considerable success. In the words of the Middle Persian account he 'founded many monasteries (*m'nyst'n'n*), chose many Elect and Hearers, composed writings and made wisdom his weapon'.[39]

Adda enjoys the dubious reputation of being an important Manichaean author in the writings of later Christian polemicists. Heraclianus, the bishop of Chalcedon, whose long work against the Manichaeans has come down to us as a single citation in Photius's *Bibliotheca*, tells us that Adda's works were often taken for Mani's own writings. Hence, Diodorus of Tarsus who thought he was directing his treatise, which is now lost, against the 'Living Gospel' of

Mani, was in fact attacking a work of Adda called 'Modius'.[40] The unusual choice of the title reminds us of the practice of giving fanciful names to written works, especially lexicons and anthologies, in late antiquity. Bardaiṣan, for instance, composed a work called 'Domnus' and both the meaning and significance of the title still evade modern scholars.[41] The word 'modius' itself most readily calls to mind Christ's command not to hide a light under a bushel (μόδιος; cf. Matthew 5:15; Mark 4:21 and Luke 11:33).[42] This oddly titled work may therefore have as its subject the struggle between light and darkness, a central theme of Manichaean cosmogony.[43] It is worth pointing out, though, that the word σκεῦος is used instead of μόδιος for a similar metaphor in Luke 8:16 and the Syriac for σκεῦος is m'n' which sounds very similar to the name 'Mani'. The proximity of these two words occasioned for Mani the derogatory title of the 'Vase of Perdition' (m'n' dbyst') from his Syriac speaking enemies which is echoed by the phrase 'vas Anti-christi' in the Latin version of the Acta Archelai.[44] The Greek and Latin versions of his name, Μανιχαῖος and Manichaeus, may have come from the Syriac *mny hy' (the living Mani) which would have sounded similar to m'n' hy' (the vessel of life).[45] It is therefore possible that Adda wrote a work entitled 'Mani' or 'The Vessel (of Life)' which in the course of translation had been corrupted, perhaps deliberately, into 'Modios' – to slight its content. A modius is, in Dupont-Somer's words, 'un objet utile mais vulgaire' and certainly not an elegant vessel (m'n').[46]

Adda probably based his own writings on the books and letters which he had received from Mani, adapting them for a Christian Roman readership which had a different Biblical tradition from that of Mani. His works circulated in the west under a Hellenised version of his name: 'Αδείμαντος, Latin: 'Adimantus Manichaei discipulus'.[47] Augustine devoted an entire polemical treatise against a work of this Adimantus. From it we learn that Adda tried to demonstrate the apparent contradiction between the Old and New Testaments by juxtaposing verses from one with the other. The method which the adopts is undoubtedly borrowed from Marcion's Antitheses which was refuted by Tertullian.[48] It is not improbable that Adda was a Marcionite prior to his joining the new sect of Mani.

(3)   THE POLITICAL AND CULTURAL
         BACKGROUND OF THE EARLIEST
      MANICHAEAN MISSIONS TO THE WEST

The passage of Manichaeism from Mesopotamia to the eastern provinces of the Roman empire was considerably aided by the fact that Rome and Persia enjoyed a relatively open frontier in the third century. As the rivers Euphrates and Tigris flow in a south-easterly direction and as the line of transhumance lies diagonally across them, it was impossible for the Romans to construct a static system of defence, along the lines of Hadrian's wall, in Europe.[49] The eastern *limes* was, strictly as the word implies, a system of roads which enables the swift movement of troops, especially of mounted cohorts, from one outpost to another. The fulcrum of this defensive system was not in Mesopotamia itself but lay several hundred miles to the north-west in the metropolis of Antioch-on-the-Orontes in Syria with her famous armament factories.[50] Roads radiated from her to the frontier regions of Syria. Mesopotamia and Arabia. The basis of this communicaton network was laid down by the Hellenistic kings and Roman engineers made further additions to it, linking the more important centres of population with each other as well as with Antioch. On the map, the frontier was in the form of an arc of cities and colonies stretching from Nisibis in the north-east to Bostra in Provincia Arabia, passing through Edessa, Carrhae, Emesa and Damascus. To the south of this line lay the disputed territories between the two empires. At the height of her power in the second century, Rome was able to establish military outposts like Singara, Circesium and Dura Europos further to the south of this line forming an outer line of defence with its flanks guarded by the semi-independent kingdoms of Palmyra and Hatra. The loss of Hatra to a determined attack by Shāpūr and the revolt of Zenobia at Palmyra led to the abandonment of the outlying Roman settlements and the establishment of a line of defence further to the north.[51]

War between Rome and Persia in Mesopotamia in the third century was a highly mobile affair as attack was the best form of defence in a region which possessed no natural boundaries. The task of Roman garrisons in outposts like Dura Europos was not to hold out against an invasion force indefinitely but to delay the advance of the enemy so as to give the emperor time to muster and equip an expeditionary force at Antioch. In the wars between Rome and Parthia in the High Empire, sieges and counter sieges were rare as Edessa and Hatra were the only cities which had the necessary fortification to withstand determined assaults. The Hellenistic fortifications of Dura Europos, for instance, proved completely inadequate against the skilled engineers of Shāpūr I. It was only after the decision by later Roman emperors like Contantius to turn frontier towns like Amida and Bezabde into formidable fortresses that war between Rome and Persia became one of attrition.[53] Even then, as late as 505, we find Byzantine generals complaining to the Emperor Anastasius that their troops suffered undue hardship from having to operate in regions with few well-populated and defended sites near the border. Consequently the army was reluctant to advance for fear of its supply lines being severed.[54]

In the third century, the outcome of wars in Mesopotamia was generally decided by open battle. Shāpūr I, after his epic victory over Valerian 'beyond Harran and Edessa'[55] found that the entire eastern half of the Roman empire lay at his mercy. He entered Antioch against little resistance and even ravaged the towns of southern Cappadocia.[56] Very few Roman towns south of the Orontes escaped mention on his Great Inscription at the Kaaba of Zoroaster which lists all the places he conquered from the Romans.[57] His success was to be repeated in the sixth century by Chosroes Anūshīrvān against the much stronger frontier defences of Justinian.[58] The efficient road system no doubt played an important part in the swift advance of the Sassanian army. The Syrian desert was no impenetrable barrier and was difficult to defend as watch-posts could easily be bypassed as shown by the near disastrous ploy by the Persians to invade Osrhoene in 354 via Batnae when the town was occupied with its famous trade fair.[59] Arab guides were often able to find a way through for the invading army even along a well defended section of the frontier.[60]

The political frontier between the two powers, fixed by the arbitrariness of war and diplomacy was therefore not an effective cultural divided and we should not allow it to obscure from us the degree of cultural homogeneity on both sides of it. Although Greek was the language of *haute culture*, and administration for territories under Roman rule and Middle Persian was beginning to replace the 'Imperial Aramaic' of the Achaemenids as the administrative language of the Sassanian Empire, Aramaic remained the *lingua franca* from Antioch to Charax Spasinou. The fact that Mani's own native tongue was a dialect of Aramaic akin to Syriac means that his writings could be easily understood by Aramaic speakers in the Roman empire. As far as we know, all the seven canonical works of the Manichaean church were written in Aramaic but the semi-canonical work, the *Šābuhragān*, was in Middle Persian.[61] It is very likely that Mani had this work written or translated for him for the specific purpose of presenting a summary of this teaching to the Shahanshah.[62] Little is heard of this work in the West even though a considerable number of fragments of it in the original (?) Middle Persian are among the manuscripts from Turfan and there are also citations from it in later Arabic works.[63] The fact that an important work of the Manichaeans was not circulated in a western language seems to imply that Middle Persian presented more problems than Aramaic or Syriac to the Manichaean translators in the Roman empire.

Many of the Roman captives resettled in the Persian empire, mainly to undertake construction work for the Shahanshah, were from Antioch and among them were a large number of Christians including

Demetrianus, their bishop. The exiled diocese soon established churches and monasteries in their land of captivity, giving orthodox Christianity a lasting foothold in Persia.[64] These newcomers, many of whom were Greek speaking, were referred to in Sassanian inscriptions as *klystyd'n* (= Syr.: *krstyn'*) as distinct from the *n'sl'y* (= Syr: *nzry'*) who were the native Aramaic-speaking Christians.[65] These new Christian communities with their strong ties with their places of origin were the ideal stepping-stones for Manichaean mission to the Roman empire. Their members would more easily grasp the message of one who called himself the 'Apostle of Christ' than their Zoroastrian or pagan neighbours. It is worth noting that an early Manichaean mission led by Adda and Abzakyā (the latter was probably Mani's former neighbour in the baptist sect) went to Karkā de Bēt Selōk, a predominantly Christian community which traced its Christian origins to the apostle Addai and exiles from the Hadrianic persecutions.[66] The missionaries seem to have met with success as Manichaeans were accused of having taken part in the persecutions of the Christians there under the later Sassanians.[67] However, it was also in these Christian communities with their more hierarchically structured religious life that the Manichaeans received their first baptism of fire. As we have seen, Adda was involved in disputations and debates with religious leaders from the beginning of his missionary journeys. In a Christian polemical work, Mani is depicted as having taken part in a debate with Archelaus, the Bishop of Carchar, a city of Mesopotamia which has commonly been identified as Carrhae (Harran).[68] Cross-frontier debates would later become so popular that in John of Ephesus's *Lives of Eastern Saints* we encounter the figure of Simeon the Persian debator, who was a professional refuter of Nestorians and Zoroastrians.[69] Among his contemporaries was Paul the Persian who debated with the Manichaean Photeinos at the instigation of Justinian.[70] Since the Christian church in Persia had virtually no political power, to disgrace the Manichaeans publicly in debates was her most effective means of combating the sect. Hence the Manichaeans in Persian-held Mesopotamia had first to avoid the Christian bishops before taking shelter from the Magian priests or the Marzbāns (provincial governors).[71]

According to Epiphanius of Salamis, the first person to bring Manichaeism to his home town of Eleutheropolis in Palestine was a veteran from Mesopotamia by the name of Akouas, hence the sect was known as the Akouanitans in that town.[72] Akouas is almost certainly to be identified with Mar Zaku in Iranian sources.[73] Epiphanius dates his activities to the reign of Aurelian (273–4) which would suggest that he was among Mani's second generation of disciples whom Mani sent to consolidate the work of Adda and Patik in the eastern provinces of the Roman empire.[74] He may have been one of the prisoners of war who came in touch with the religion during his enforced stay in the Persian empire. However his military background should not mislead us into thinking that the Roman army was an important factor for the diffusion of Manichaeism as it was for Mithraism in the High Empire.[75] Manichaeism did not become the religion of the soldiers in the same way that Mithra virtually became a military mascot, for the simple reason that Manichaeism was explicit on its prohibition of killing.[76] The fact that Mar Zaku was held in high regard by the Manichaeans in the east means that he was an important disciple of Mani and not merely an ordinary soldier who came into contact with the new religion while stationed in Mesopotamia and subsequently brought it home on retirement from active service. Furthermore the designation of *veteranus* might have been a reference to his senior position in the Manichaean hierarchy and therefore has no military significance.[76a]

(4)   COMMERCE AND MISSION

The factors which made the defence of Mesopotamia a nightmare for the Roman emperors worked in favour of those who traded between the two empires. Silk from China was the most famous item of this cross-frontier trade but it also included precious metal, spices and other luxury goods. The so-called 'Silk Road' (*Via Serica*) began at Ch'ang-an (the Σῆρα Μετροπόλις of Ptolemy) and followed the oasis route through the Tarim Basin. After traversing the Pamirs, it kept a southerly course through Transoxania and Parthia until it reached Seleucia-Ctesipon. From there the silk was taken by caravans to Antioch in Syria or to Egypt via the Red Sea ports. As the steppe-like conditions of the Hungar Plain to the north of the Caspian Sea are inimical to commercial activities, the main artery of the silk trade ran through Persia which meant that Rome had no independent supply of silk and could only obtain it by trading with Persia.[77]

It was in Persia's interest to foster this trade with the Romans. As she lay astride its main channel she could use the trade as an economic weapon against the Romans by regulating its prices and the volume of its flow.[78] As she herself was a high consumer of silk, re-exporting raw silk at an inflated price to the Romans was a means of maintaining her balance of trade. A Chinese source, the *History of the Later Han Dynasty (Hou Han-shu)* says that as the Persians greatly profited from being the middle-men in this trade, they were reluctant to see the Romans establishing direct trading relationships with China.[79] This commercial link between Rome and Persia was so important that it regularly featured in treaties between the two powers. Even after a debilitating war between the two states such as the one which ended in 297, the Shahanshah Narses allowed himself to be persuaded by Sicorius, the envoy of Galerius and Diocletian, to reopen the trade across the frontier through Nisibis.[80]

This trade in luxury goods between the two empires was almost entirely in the hands of Syrians, Palmyrenes and Jews. The cities from which they came, such as Palmyra, Edessa, Nisibis and Artaxata, acquired both fame and wealth from their commercial activities. The role of Syriac and Aramaic speakers in the commercial life of the Near East throughout the classical period is amply attested by both literary and archaeological evidence as Palmyrene inscriptions have been found as far east as Merv.[81] The author of the *Expositio totius mundi et gentium*, a late Roman manual on geography and commerce, who was probably himself a Syrian, mentions the acuteness of the inhabitants of Edessa and Nisibis in trade and hunting.[82] 'Buying from the Persians, they sell to the Romans and then sell back to the Persians what they purchase from the Romans with the exception of bronze and iron as it is not legal to trade in such items with the enemies'.[83] They would travel with their goods probably as far east as the foot of the Pamirs. An outstanding landmark of this inter-continental trade was the Stone Tower (Λίθινος Πύργος *Turris lapidea*) which was well known to Roman writers and mediaeval cartographers as 'a station and refuge for travellers'.[84] At this point or in the nearby cities, their goods would be exchanged with the silk which had been brought there by caravans using the oasis-route through the Tarim Basin.

As a mercantile race, the Syrians often equated their spiritual endeavours with their commercial activities. In Syriac Christianity, the motif of the merchant (*tgr'*) had long been used to express apostolic functions. A missionary was often compared with a merchant seeking a pearl which is Christ or trading with talents. A Syrian hymn-writer of the fourth century, the so-called 'Cyrillona', embroidered Christ's exhortation to his disciples, 'Let not your heart be troubled', with the charge:

> Travel well-girt like merchants,
> that we may gain the world.
> Convert men to me,
> fill creation with teaching.[85]

This close association between mission and commerce is frequently alluded to in Manichaean literature as well as in Christian writings against the sect. We have seen that Mani's missionary command to Adda was to remain where he was in the Roman empire 'like a merchant who gathers a store'. In the *Kephalaia*, the Manichaean apostle is compared to a merchant who returns with his ships double laden with merchandise.[86] Although there is no firm evidence to show that men like Adda were actually merchants by profession, it is probable that they travelled to Roman-held territories along established trade routes in the company of merchants. Since the religion enjoins its adherents, especially if they were Elect, to refrain from all agricultural labour, its appeal to the peasantry, as distinct from landlords, would have been limited. Augustine tells us that the Manichaeans while denouncing farmers as murderers, condoned the practice of usury.[87] One may infer from this that the Manichaeans preferred trade to agriculture, a preference which may have originated from the early association of the sect with merchants and commerce. Augustine himself, according to his biographer Possidius, actually converted a Manichaean by the name of Firmus, who was a merchant, through a particularly moving Sunday sermon.[88]

In the minds of most Romans, the merchant was the archetypal conveyor of strange and esoteric ideas and stories because of his frequent visits to foreign lands. In the Christian literature against the Manichaeans, the figure of a merchant, appropriately named Scythianus, looms large in the genesis of the sect. He was a Saracen who 'exchanged' pernicious ideas as well as merchandise and his books were later inherited by Mani.[89] Epiphanius in his 'definitive' history of the sect introduced this person to us with a vivid description of his commercial activities:

This Scythianus was brought up in the language of the Greeks in the aforesaid places [i.e. somewhere between Palestine and Arabia] and in the discipline of their writings. At the same time he became skillful in the vain tenets of the world. He made frequent visits to the lands of India for commercial purposes and did much trade. Loaded with earthly goods, he would travel via the Thebaid. For there are several ports on the coast of the Red Sea dotted along the edges of Roman Empire. One of them is at Ailat which is mentioned in the Holy Scriptures. Every three years, the ship of Solomon visited it bringing home gold and ivory, spices, peacocks etc. Another port is at Castle-on-the-Beach and yet another is further up at the place called Berenice and it is through so-called Berenice that one reaches the Thebaid. Goods from India are distributed from there either to the Thebaid or to Alexandria, the latter via the Rive of Gold, by which I mean the Nile (or Geon as it is called in the Scriptures) and then taken to the whole land of Egypt and on to Pelusium. Such is the way people from India travel by sea to other countries and trade with Rome.[90]

This description of the maritime trade via the Red Sea ports is borne out in detail by the so-called *Periplus of the Erythraean Sea*, a well known manual for merchant mariners.[91] The Romans had traded with India since the end of the first century but this trade took on increased

significance at the end of the third century as the overland trade with
China was interrupted by war and subjected to growing governmental
interference. Political instability in east Turkestan also caused China
to export increasing amounts of silk via India and Ceylon. The Red Sea
ports were ideally situated to handled this trade with India. The
Sassanians also developed their own trade with India from the ports on
the Persian Gulf.[92] In the following century, the Persians gained a
virtual monopoly of this trade leaving their competitors like the
Byzantines and the Himyarities trailing at a distance.[93] As we have
seen, one of the earliest Manichaean missionaries to have used this
trade route for the purpose of mission was Mani himself.

The growing importance of Rome's maritime connection with the
Orient is also hinted at by Ammianus's remark that the silk which he
saw at the September fair at Batnae came there from the East 'by land
and sea'. The decline in importance of the overland route may also
account for the fact that Ammianus's description of Central Asia is
heavily dependent on earlier geographical works, especially that of
Ptolemy, implying that little new information about the East was
filtering through to the Roman empire via the Silk Road.[94] In the
subsequent centuries, if Seres or Σηρική was mentioned at all, it was
to conjure up Pliny's picture of it being a land unaffected by war or
strife. This myth was even used by Christian writers, who in their
polemics against gnostics and Manichaeans, cited the Seres (or the
people of Sin) as a race untouched by original sin, in order to disprove
their opponents' belief that sin was present at creation and is therefore
unavoidable.[95]

Rome's trade with the orient via both land and sea was an important
factor in the westware diffusion of Manichaeism. The merchant was
an ideal missionary because he was usually conversant in several
languages, which was necessary for his occupation. Syrian merchants
were often used for this reason as envoys to Persia by the Roman
emperors. Bilingualism was therefore a prominent feature of the
cultural life in Syriac or Aramaic speaking parts of the Roman empire.
We learn from the *Itineranium Egeriae* that Christian congregations
in Jerusalem spoke a mixture of Greek and Syriac (Aramaic) and
sermons would normally be translated into Syriac if they were
delivered in Greek.[96] As orthodox Christianity began to make strong
in roads into the Syriac speaking regions in the fourth century, Greek-
speaking churchmen began to take more interest in the religious
affairs of these parts and translations from Syriac works became more
common. In citing the famous correspondence between Jesus and
Abgar, Eusebius mentions the fact that the texts were found among
the royal archives of Edessa.[97] It is highly probable that they were
available to him in Greek translation. According to Sozomen, the

hymns and theological works of Ephraim of Nisibis were held in such high regard throughout Christendom that they were translated into Greek during the saint's lifetime and translations were still being made at the time of Sozomen. What Sozomen found to be most amazing about the translations was that they preserved so much of their original force that Ephraim's works were no less admired in Greek than when read in Syriac.[98]

A merchant who traded with the Orient via Berenice like Scythianus and travelled through the Thebaid would probably know Coptic in addition to Greek and Syriac. Epiphanius gives Hypseles as the city in which Scythianus found his wife, which would have been a Coptic (especially sub-Achmimic) speaking area and the Manichaean codices recovered from Medinet Medi, as it happens, are written in that language, even though their place of discovery was in the Fayum.[99] The translation of Manichaean scriptures from Syriac into Coptic must have been done through Greek and in the CMC we have precisely the required intermediary.[100] However, it has been pointed out by Allberry that the passage of Manichaean technical terms through Greek would have caused perplexity if the translators into Coptic did not have access to Syriac originals.[101] Hence if the translators themselves were not trilingual, it is likely that they would have been helped by their Elect who were polyglots like Scythianus.

An important stopping-place for traders who travelled to the Roman empire from southern Mesopotamia in the third century was Palmyra or Tadmōr. Situated on one of the main routes which linked Antioch with the Euphrates, it was, as Pliny says, the first cause of concern for both the Romans and the Persians at any outbreak of hostility.[102] The city derived its wealth from trade and the importance of the merchant to its civic life is attested by large numbers of inscriptions and monuments dedicated to or by caravan leaders.[103] In the second half of the third century, its reputation was further enhanced by the successful raid by her forces under Septimius Odenathus against the southern flank of Shāpūr I, culminating in a brief siege of Ctesisphon. As reward for stabilising the political situation in the east after the victory of Shāpūr over Valerian in 259/60, Odenathus received from the Romans the title of *restitutor totius Orientis* (= Aramaic: *MTQNN' DY MDNH' KLH*).[104] Before 271 he had also adopted the more grandiose title of 'King of Kings' (*MLK MLK'*) as epigraphical evidence indicates. It is quite possible that Adda was for a while active as a missionary in this mercantile and strategically important city. An important convert who was brought to the faith by Adda was Nafšā. According to two recently published fragments of Manichaean missionary history in Sogdian, this Nafšā was cured of an illness by invoking the name of Jesus and the laying on of hands by Adda.

Thereupon she became a believer and many other people were confirmed in their faith as a result of her miraculous healing. The sister of Nafšā was Queen (Sogd: *xwt'ynh*) Taδī whose husband held the title of Caesar (*kysr*), and she too appears to have been greatly impressed by Adda. The rest of the text is too fragmentary for us to reconstruct a continuous narrative.[105] Since Septimus Odenatus or his son Vaballathus were the only rulers in this period within the orbit of early Manichaean mission to have held the title of Caesar, it seems highly possible that it was at Palmyra that Nafšā was converted and her sister Taδī was none other than the redoubtable Zenobia who murdered her imperial husband in 267. The term 'Queen of Tādmor' (i.e. Palmyra) is also attested in Coptic Manichaean texts, which further strengthens the link between Manichaeism and Palmyra.[106]

The dissemination of Manichaean literature played an important part in the diffusion of the religion. We have seen that professional scribes and portrait painters were included among the early missionary journeys for this purpose.[107] It was not uncommon for scribes to travel with caravans or official embassies. The inscriptions in Middle Iranian on the walls of the synagogue at Dura were the work of such professional scribes (*dbyr'n*) who accompanied visiting Iranian dignitaries.[108] The Manichaean scribes adopted an Aramaic script which is attested in Palmyrene inscriptions as the official script of the sect and used it for works in Syriac as well as Iranian and other central Asian languages as the religion spread eastwards. In the hands of these artists, the Palmyrene script became a very elegant book hand and Manichaean books were works of art.[109] Aramaic incantation texts in this script have been found as far south as Nippur, near where Mani had spent his boyhood and adolescence among the Elchasaites, which implies that its use was not limited to Palmyra.[110] However, the choice of a script which was well known to merchants who travelled from southern Mesopotamia to Palmyra re-emphasises the link between commerce and the diffusion of Manichaeism.

Iranian Manichaean sources say that Adda eventually reached Alexandria in the course of his travels. But he was not the first Manichaean missionary to reach Egypt for we are told by Alexander, a neo-Plantonic philosopher from Lycopolis, that the first Manichaean missionary to Egypt was called Pappos.[111] His name is also known to us in a list of Manichaean saints in the *Psalm-Book*.[112] He was a close friend of Mani and was regarded as a 'brother' by his master. He was the recipient of a letter of Mani and was also mentioned in a letter addressed to another disciple.[113] The unfortunate loss at the end of the second world war of the letters of Mani in Coptic sadly prevents us from knowing more about his activities and those of many other disciples.

Adda's missionary activities present a number of chronological problems. The only journey of his for which we have a firm date is his visit to Karkā de Bēt Selōk which according to the local acts of the Christian martyrs took place in the twentieth year of the reign of Shāpūr (260/1). As Odenathus did not become a major political figure until his defeat of Shapur in the same year which earned him his titles from Rome, we may assume that it was after 260 that he was generally acclaimed as Caesar or Imperator. Given these chronological land-marks, two solutions seem possible. The first solution presupposes that the mission of Adda and Patīk the Teacher to the eastern parts of the Roman empire was sent sometime after 244, the year of Philip the Arab's temporary truce with Shāpūr which would have seen more stable conditions along the frontier.[114] Patīk returned within a year as clearly stated by the sources. Adda remained where he was as enjoined by Mani. He then visited Alexandria and on his return to Seleucia he stopped at Palmyra where the conversion of Nafšā took place sometime after 260. He left shortly afterwards and rejoined Mani, and was almost immediately sent out again with Abzakyā to Bēt Garmai. The second solution rests on the assumption that Adda's visit to Bēt Garmai took place before his journey to the west. Since Odenathus was alive until 267, the mission to the Roman empire could have taken place anytime between 261 and 267. It is only logical that Adda should have had some missionary experience in Mesopotamia before departing for the Roman empire.[115] This would allow Adda to spend a longer period of time in Palmyra and may also explain his visit to Alexandria, as Egypt was captured and briefly held by one of Zenobia's generals in 269. Or, Adda might have remained in Palmyra until the city's final subjection by Emperor Aurelian in 273.

With the decline of Palmyra, the main trade route between Rome and Persia shifted northwards to Edessa and Nisibis. We know from Manichaean sources that the religion was established in Edessa in Mani's life time as the Manichaean community there was the recipient of a letter from Mani, an excerpt of which is preserved in the CMC and its title is also known to us from the list of Mani's letters preserved by al-Nadim.[118] Edessa may have also provided the stepping-stone for the entry of the religion into Armenia. The cities of southern Armenia had important cultural and commercial links with the Roman cities of Upper Mesopotamia, especially with Edessa and Nisibis. The ties between Edessa and Armenia were particularly strong. In Armenian tradition, the Abgar of Edessa who was alleged to have corresponded with Jesus was the then ruler of Armenia.[119] Artashat (Artaxata), the royal city of Armenia, also shared in the benefits of a general northward shift of the main trade route. In an edict of Honorius and Theodosius II (c. 408 or 409) we find it designated along with Callinicum and Nisibis as the only approved venues of commercial exchange between Roman and Persian merchants.[120] Since Tiridates I was officially crowned by Nero as King of Armenia in 66, the kingdom had been ruled more or less continuously by a minor branch of the Arsacids.[121] She therefore generally sided with the Parthians in their conflicts with Rome. The coming to power of the Sassanians in Iran and Mesopotamia caused the Arsacids of Armenia to become implacable enemies of the Persian empire. Ardashīr attempted to invade Armenia after his victory at Hormizdagan but was thwarted by the then Armenian Arsacid ruler Chosroes I (sometimes called Tiridates II) who offered stiff resistance.[122] However, Chosroes was murdered at the contrivance of the Sassanians sometime before 244 and Shāpūr I's victorious campaigns of 244 and 256 forestalled any effective Roman intervention in Armenia. A Sassanian viceroy governed Armenia until the reign of Vahrām II (277–94) when Diocletian exploited the Persian preoccupation with the invasion of Mesopotamia by Carus to install Tiridates III, the fugitive son of the Khosroes I, on the throne of Armenia in 286.[123] The Arsacid restoration was consolidated by the victory of Diocletian and Galerius over Narses in 297/8.[124] It was during the reign of Tiridates III (286–330) that Armenia became the first state in the world to adopt Christianity on a durable basis and the process of Christianisation was centred on the figure of St Gregory the Illuminator who was consecrated bishop in 302 by Leontius, the archbishop of Caesarea in Cappadocia.[128]

The task of bringing Manichaeism to Armenia was entrusted to a disciple called Gabryab (Gk.: Γαβριάβιος) whose missionary activities in the Armenian city of (E)revan (Sogd.: ryβ'n) are known to us in a recently published fragment of Manichaean missionary history in Sogdian.[125] As in so many of these missionary accounts, the story of the conversion took place at court and it centres on the miraculous healing of a young girl who was in the throes of a fatal illness. Of particular interest is that at the court of the King of (E)revan, the opponents of Manichaeism were said to have been Christians (trs'kt). The fragment begins with a challenge from Gabryab to the King to turn from the Christian religion (trs'k'n δynyh) to the religion of the Lord Mar Mani if he was able to cure the sick girl. He then reminded the Christians that Christ was a great wonder-worker who had cured the lame and the cripple from their sufferings and had even raised the dead to life. If they were his true disciples they would be able to do the same. The Christians admitted their inability to cure the maiden and handed her over to Gabryab. On the fourteenth day of the month he and his helpers persisted in prayer and praise. Towards the evening, as Jesus appeared (in the form of the full moon?), Gabryab implored his help. Gabryab then took oil and water and blessed them in the name of the Father and of the Son and of the Holy Spirit and commanded the maiden to rub in the oil and to sprinkle the water over her. She was immediately cleansed from the defilement of her illness. When morning came he prayed to the Sun God and again took oil and water and blessed them and gave them to the maiden. She was entirely set free from her illness and any further needs. Gabryab duly inducted the King and his wife, the mother of the maiden, into the community of the Hearers (Sogd.: nγ-'ws'ky'kh) by anointing them with oil, and commanded them to turn from heresy, idolatry and demon-worship. After he had elected many men to the priesthood and converted many from their heresy, he went to another region to preach. On the day on which the crucifixion of Christ was commemorated with fasting, the Christians pressed the King of (E)revan to come to their church and he agreed. Gabryab hastily returned when he got wind of this and although the fragment ends at this point we may assume that he was successful in winning him back to the teaching of Mani. We know from al-Nadim's list of the titles of Mani's letters that Armenia was the destination of one of them and it might have been occasioned by the success of Gabryab's mission.[126]

The subjugation of Armenia by Shapur I might have provided Manichaeism with opportunities for evangelism in that country. If Gabryab's main opponents in Armenia were indeed Christians, we must assume that Christianity had considerable influence in the vassal princedoms of Armenia before the time of Gregory the Illuminator. It is important to note too in this typical Manichaean wonder-story that Manichaeism vied with Christianity for the conversion of a local grandee. Gabryab proved through his greater skill as a healer that he was the true follower of Christ while those who called themselves Christians were not. In their missionary endeavours in the west, the Manichaeans owed a considerable debt to the expansion and diffusion of Christianity, as it prepared the ground for receiving the revelations of a new apostle of Jesus Christ.

There may even have been a Manichaean mission to Georgia, as a number of fragments of Manichaean missionary history in Parthian and Uighur speak of the conversion of Hbz', the Waručān-Šāh. We know of a wlwc'n MLK' from the Middle Persian version of the Great Inscription of Shapur I (= Pth.: Wyršn) and its equivalent in the Greek version in 'Iβερία.[127] Unfortunately, the state of the fragments is so poor that no meaningful reconstruction of the story is possible. It appears that Hbz' saw the figure of the apostle and was so struck by it that he fell on his face and became unconscious. Whether Mani himself or one of his disciples like Adda or Gabryab was the chief missioner in the story we cannot be certain but whoever he was he

'overcame the teachings of the other religions by their own evil'.[128]
There seems to be a reference to water ('b?) in one of the Parthian
fragments and the Uighur fragment speaks of all the lame, the blind,
the wounded, all those with dislocated hips, all those infected by
worms or scabies were cured of their various ailments by drinking
from a special water at the gate of a temple. Within that temple sat a
naked man whose arms and legs were shackled with heavy chains.[129]
The fragment breaks off at this point but we may assume from the
general tenor of such stories and that of the apocryphal Christian Acts
of Apostles on which they are based, that we have here the beginning
of an account of an exorcism.

(5)   THE EASTWARD SPREAD OF MANICHAEISM AND THE DEATH OF MANI

In his travels in the eastern parts of the Sassanian empire prior to his
important meeting with Shāpūr, Mani must have seen for himself the
opportunities for propagating his religion in the heartland of Iran and
Central Asia. It was indeed fortunate that he won the friendship of
Pērōz, the governor of Khurāsān whose territories comprised the
gateway to the east. The permission which he obtained from Shapur to
preach anywhere within his domains meant that Mani could begin to
conduct missionary activities in the eastern parts of the empire which
were less influenced by Judaeo-Christianity.

In his disciple Mar Ammo, Mani had someone ideally equipped for
the task of evangelising the east.[130] He not only knew the language and
was familiar with the Parthian script which was different from that of
Middle Persian, but he also knew many members of the Parthian
aristocracy.[131] Besides being accompanied by several scribes and a
book-illuminator, among his travel companions to the 'upper lands'
('brshr) was a prince by the name of Ardavān.[132] He was evidently a
member of the deposed house of the Arsacids and his status was
undoubtedly indicative of the type of people Mani hoped to convert in
the north-eastern parts of the Sassanian empire.[133] Mar Ammo's
mission was highly successful. In the words of a Sogdian fragment,
'he ordained numerous kings and rulers, grandees and noblemen,
queens and ladies, princes and princesses. He fully exposed the
Buddhaship of the Prophet of Light. He completed and fulfilled all
orders and injunctions that had been given him by Mani'.[134] In another
fragment, this time in Middle Persian, we find Mani being visited by a
nobleman from 'the upper lands' by the name of Dāryāv, together with
two brothers, when he was in Rev-Ardashīr in the province of Fars.[135]
We later find one of Dāryāv's two brothers, by the name of Chusrō,

working as a missionary in Khurāsān.[136] These three noblemen were probably converts sent back by Mar Ammo to Mani for further missionary training or they were missionaries in their own right also working in 'the upper countries'.

The Sassanians were as successful militarily in the east as they were against the Roman empire. By the time of Shāpūr I, the kingdoms of Kūshān, Tūrān and Makūrān had theoretically been brought under the direct suzerainty of the Shahanshah, in addition to the lands of the former Parthian dynasty. In fact, these newly acquired territories still enjoyed a substantial degree of independence and they provided Mani with more opportunities for mission than lands over which the Sassanians had more direct control. The *Drang nach Osten* of his religion was Mani's main concern in the last years of his life. His patron Shāpūr died c. 272 in Bishapur and Mani wasted no time in approaching his successor Hormizd, from whom he secured a reconfirmation of the status of his religion in the Persian empire.[137] However, time was running out for Mani as the Zoroastrian priests were gaining in influence at court.

The reign of Hormizd lasted for only a year. The new Shahanshah, Vahrām I (273-6) did not share his two predecessors' enthusiasm for the 'Doctor of Babylon'. Unlike Shāpūr who seemed to have adopted a genuinely tolerant stance in matters of religion, Vahrām was under the sway of Kirdir the Chief Mobed. The latter was not the Zoroastrian equivalent of a pope and the exact function of his ecclesiastical position is still a mystery.[138] What is clear, however, from his inscriptions at Sar Mašhad and on the Kaaba of Zoroaster, is his desire to keep all the other religions of the empire within very strict limits.[139] He regarded the Manichaeans as heretics since in the course of their missionary activities they had assimilated some Zoroastrian concepts and names of deities into their system. As the *Denkart* emphasises: 'The most dangerous enemy of religion is the heretic who betrays the stronghold from within'.[140] Manichaeism, with a hierarchical organisation which was to rival that of the Christian church in the Roman empire, was a serious stumbling block to Kirdir's plans for reform. Moreover, Mani's success in winning converts in client kingdoms like Armenia and former Parthian strongholds like Khurāsān made his religion a divisive factor at a time when Vahram was trying to bring these states under closer control in the face of renewed conflict against the Romans.[141]

The exact sequence of events in the last period of Mani's life is difficult to reconstruct because of the very fragmentary nature of the evidence. It seems that he travelled to Mesene with the intention of seeking help from its ruling house as one of Mani's earliest converts was Mihrsāh, the Mēsūn-Khwadāy. However, according to a Parthian

Manichaean fragment which has recently come to light, Mani was shocked to discover that the palace of the Mesun-Šāh (Parth.: *myšwn š'h* = *myšwn xwd'y*(?)) had been destroyed. We find him later in a Manichaean 'monastery' (*m'nyst'n*) in Hormizd-Ardashīr (modern Ahwāz), the capital city of Chuzistan.[142] He might have hoped to go from there to Kūshān where he would be among friends but he was explicitly forbidden to do so by imperial order. Mani returned to Ctesiphon and there gathering together several disciples decided to meet Vahrām at Bet-Lāphāt to see if he could regain from the new Shahanshah the toleration which had been accorded to him by Shāpūr and Hormizd. His sense of mission and of pastoral care for his flock remained undiminished even during this most serious crisis of this life. He managed to visit the Manichaean community at Gaukhaï on his way from Ctesiphon to Bēt Lāphāt.[143] The outcome of his encounter with Vahrām was not unexpected as Mani was clearly prepared for martyrdom when he arrived at the court. After a perfunctory interview with Vahrām he was thrown into jail where he later died of torture.[144]

The death of Mani was followed by a general persecution of Manichaeans, especially those in 'the Low Country'. Al-Nadim says that the Manichaeans did not stop fleeing eastwards until they had crossed the River Oxus where Manichaean missionaries had remained active.[145] In a Parthian fragment is preserved the text of a letter addressed to Mar Ammo at Zamb (modern Kerki) on the left bank of the Upper Oxus.[146] The sender was an *archegos*, probably Mar Sīsin (Gk. & Lat.: Sisinnios) who had succeeded Mani was the head of the sect in Mesopotamia after in interregnum of five years.[147] Writing from Merv, he promised Mar Ammo that he would be sending him more books of the Lord Mani and some more helpers.[148]

Mar Sīsin was the leader of the sect for ten years (c. 276–86) and he also suffered martyrdom in a renewed outbreak of persecution against the sect under Vahrām II (276–93).[149] This occasioned another exodus of Manichaeans from Mesopotamia. Many of them came to settle in the eastern parts of the Roman empire bringing with them bitter memories of the recent persecutions against the sect, as manifested in their writings which have survived in Coptic translation.[150] They seem to have managed to find a patron in the person of King Amarō who was almost certainly the then ruler of Hira, a Bedouin kingdom strategically situated on the edge of desert to the north of the great swamp of the lower Euphrates.[151] He wrote several letters on behalf of the Manichaeans to his overlord Narses seeking an end to the persecution. The letters mention a certain Innaios who was perhaps their courier,[152] probably the same person as Mani's earlier envoy to India who had now succeeded Mar Sīsin as *archegos*.[153] The exchange of letters brought about an audience between Narses and Innaios which led to an end of persecution. However, under his successor Hormizd II, the Zoroastrian priests once again clamoured for the extirpation of the sect and persecution was renewed.[154] The favour shown to the sect by the Lakhmids of Hira must have provided the Manichaeans with vitally needed shelter from persecutions and enabled some of them to enter the Roman empire via the caravan routes.

The history of Manichaeism in Mesopotamia for the remainder of the Sassanian period is still a largely unexplored field of study. The relevant material which is scattered in the numerous acts of Christian martyrs and the pronouncements of the major councils of the Nestorian church, has not been assembled. Furthermore, the term Manichaeans was applied to the followers of Mazdak, an Iranian social revolutionary of the fifth century, and, after the Islamic conquest, to the Sabians of Harran. One is, therefore, never entirely certain of the true identity of sects or individuals attacked as *mnyny'* in Syriac sources. Accounts of widespread persecution of Manichaeans under Kawad and the earlier years of Chosroes Anūshīrvān are particularly suspect given what is known of the persecution of Mazdakites in the same period. Similarly grotesque descriptions of the crimes of the Manichaeans which include among others human sacrifice, the use of the victim's skulls for divination, ritual use of human foetuses etc., must be treated with caution as very similar charges were also made against the Sabians of Harran.[155]

The Syriac acts of Christian martyrs furnish us with tit-bits of local information on the survival of Manichaeism in Mesopotamia and Iran and the acts of the martyrs of Karkā de Bēt Selōk are of particular interest. As we recall, Manichaeism was first brought to this city in Bēt Garmai by Adda and Abzakyā in the twentieth year of the reign of Shāpūr I (i.e. 260/1). The acts imply that the Christian community there was sufficiently impervious to the heresy and that Manichaeism found its followers mainly among descendants of Iranian settlers. They figured as the *vilain de la pièce* who had the ears of the Sassanian authorities in the persecution of the Christians under Shapur II:

And in his days [i.e. the episcopate of Ma'na] there arose a persecution of Christians and the church was destroyed, for fury broke out among the inhabitants of Karkā and some of them became destroyers of the church of their town. And, a persecution arose in Karkā – not only with murders, but also with plundering of possessions, and with shackles and bitter blows, to such an extent that the Daughters of the Covenant [*bnt qym'*], who had taken vows of chastity, who had come from the royal residence [i.e. Seleucia-Ctesiphon] because of the persecution which was in the church and who were

living in our town, were slandered by the Manichaeans to the Paigansalar
[*pygn slr*, lit.: general of the infantry, i.e. police-chief]; and the bloodthirsty
villain ordered that they should be killed outside the town, at a place called
Hora. And after the crowning of these saints a fig-tree sprang up out of their
blood at the place where they were crowned and this tree and a healing effect
on all who took refuge to it. But when the Manichaeans saw the miracle which
was performed by that same fig-tree they cut it down and burned that place
with fire. God however, whose mercy can not be put to shame had them
overcome by the disease of elephantiasis [*k'b' d'ry'*] which made them so sick
that they disappeared completely from the town.[156]

It is in fact unusual to find Manichaeans exempted from a general
persecution of Christians in Sassanian Mesopotamia. In the acts of
Aitallāhā who was martyred under Shapur II (*c.* 379), we find the
Sassanian authorities trying to use the willingness of a Manichaean to
abjure his faith under torture to induce the Christian holy man to
recant. The Manichaean satisfied the authorities that his conversion
was genuine by killing some ants, since it was understood by the
authorities that Manichaeans would not exterminate what they themselves called the 'Living Spirit' (*npš' ḥyt'*). However, the readiness
of the Manichaean to renounce his faith only proved to the Christian
holy man the truth of his own and rekindled his desire to see his
cause triumph through his own suffering.[157]

The Christians in the Sassanian empire tried to ensure that any
relaxation of imperial attitude towards the Christian church would
not be applied to heretics like the Manichaeans. After 'Aqwālāhā, the
bishop of Karkā de Bēt Selōk, had succeeded in healing the daughter of
Vahrām V who suffered convulsions caused by an unclean spirit (*c.*
420), he asked the Shahanshah to put an end to the destruction of
Christian churches and that those which had been destroyed should be
rebuilt. Once the Shahanshah had acceded to his request, he
immediately set about removing the two most troublesome thorns
(*spy'*) of his time, the teachings of Mani and Zradhurst (Mazdakites?).
The plague of elephantiasis evidently had not removed the curse of
Mani entirely from the city in the time of Shapur II. 'Aqwālāhā's
successors Bar Ḥadbšabba, Aḥsnāya and Sābōr Brāz continued his good
work, especially Sābōr Brāz who purged and cleaned out the weeds of
Mani from the fields of Karkā and made pure vessels (*m'n' dky'*) out of
the immigrant families who were noted for their heresies. Despite the
conscientious efforts of these church leaders, the heresy of Mani
persisted in Karkā until the time of Chosroes Anūshīrvān.[158]

The decisive victory of the Arabs over the Persians at Qadisiya in
April 637 heralded the beginning of another major epoch in the history
of Mesopotamia. The initial tolerance of the Arabs gave a brief respite
from persecution to the Manichaeans and some even returned from

Khurāsān to Mesopotamia. The seat of the *archegos* of the sect remained in the Twin Cities throughout the Sassanian period but the real strength of the sect now lay in the lands east of the River Oxus (Āmū Daryā). The authority of the *archegos* was acknowledged by all Manichaean communities which had remained in contact with Mesopotamia until those who were beyond the Oxus formed a new sect under the leadership of Sād-Ōhrmizd and styled themselves the Dēnāwars (the pure ones, Arab.: *Dīnāwwarīyah*) in the course of the sixth century.[159] The schism was not healed until the period of Mihr as *archegos* (end of the seventh century) when a man of great wealth, called Zād Hurmuz, joined the sect. With the help of the secretary of the governor of Iraq, he made the religion important once more in the Twin Cities and brought about a reconciliation between the *archegos* and the Dēnāwars. Mihr was succeeded as *archegos* by Zād Hurmuz who was in turn succeeded by Miqlās.[160] The sect had evidently relaxed some of its rules concerning social relationship (Arab.: *wisallat*) under the leadership of Mihr and efforts by Miqlās to tighten them precipitated yet another division of the sect into two parties, the *Mihrijja* and the *Miqlāsijja*. This was temporarily papered over under the leadership of Abū Hilāl al-Dayhūri who came from Africa. Among the charges brought against the *Mihrijja* by the *Miqlāsijja* was the assertion that the governor of Iraq had provided Mihr with a mule for transport and bestowed upon him a silver seal and embroidered garments – luxuries which were strictly proscribed by the sect.[161]

The 'Abbasid dynasty which imposed its authority upon the Islamic empire in 750 was much less tolerant in the field of religion than the Umayids whose power they had usurped. Manichaeans were persecuted as *zanādika* (sing.: *zindīk*), a term borrowed from the Iranian vocabulary of the Sassanian administration which was originally used to label someone who introduced a new gloss or an allegorical interpretation into the Zoroastrian scriptures. Though the offical definition of a *zindīk* as a dualist ascetic would fit all those who were brought up as Manichaeans and Muslim apostates to Manichaeism, the term came to be loosely applied to any heresy which might imperil the Islamic state. It was alleged that individuals, after undergoing a superficial conversion, had retained their former Manichaean convictions and were even working for this religion in order to destroy Islam. The catalogue of their crimes included dualism, ritual fornication, incest, the consumption of alcohol, and sodomy. They were accused also as idolators, a pertinent charge when one considers the importance of the artistic representation of the cosmogonic drama to the Manichaeans. Persecution of the *zanādika* was particularly severe in the years 783–7. At the Twin Cities, the seat of the *archegos* (Arab.: *imam*) and the venue of an important

Manichaean community, large numbers were arrested on suspicion
of being *zanādika* and paraded through the streets under the eyes of the
populace. The suspected were often put in chains and escorted to the
capital city of Baghdad. Led before an inquisitor or the sovereign
himself, the accused would first be subjected to a detailed interrogation on their beliefs. If they were adjudged to be *zanādika*, they
would be invited to repent and if they abjured their error they would be
released on passing certain tests which sought to confirm the
genuineness of their recantation. The most common ones involved
the penitents being asked to spit on a portrait of Mani and to eat a bird.
Those who refused to repent suffered death by decapitation and their
severed heads were placed on gibbets.[162] Despite the persecutions, the Manichaean community in Iraq remained influential and
in the nineth century it produced an important theologian in the
person of Abū 'Īsā al-Warrāq whose writings on Manichaeism, now
lost, were the source of al-Nadim's excellent entry on the religion in
his *Fihrist*, published in Baghdad in 988.[163]

The Manichaeans were not much in evidence after the Caliphate of
al-Muqtadir (908–32). 'For after that', says al-Nadim, 'they feared for
their lives and clung to Khurāsān. Any one of them who remained kept
his identity secret as he moved about in this region [i.e. Iraq].' About
five hundred of them assembled at Samarkand but the ruler of
Khurāsān came to know of their movement and wanted to kill them.
Fortunately Manichaeism had by then become the state religion of the
Uighur Turks who had established the capital of their Second Empire
at Qočo (modern Turfan) on the other side of the Pamirs. The Khaghan
of the Turks interceded on behalf of the Manichaeans and threatened
to kill all the Muslims in his kingdom as reprisal. So the ruler of
Khurāsān left them alone except for exacting tribute from them. al-
Nadim claims to have personally known some three hundred *zanādika*
(not all necessarily Manichaeans) in the time of the Caliph Mu'izz al-
Dawlah (945–67). However, at the time of compiling his *Fihrist* (c.
987–8) there were no more than five left among his friends.[165]

The refugees from the 'Abbasid persecutions in the 'Low Country'
were not always received with open arms by their co-religionists in
Central Asia who now could luxuriate in the privileges and wealth
bestowed upon them by the Uighur Khaghans. Of particular interest to
the tension caused by these new arrivals from the West are two letters
written in Sogdian in the Berlin Turfan collection which were first
reported by Henning in 1936 and have only just recently been
published by Sundermann. They are letters of complaint from a now
unknown Manichaean community addressed to a Manichaean leader,
perhaps the head of the Diocese of the East who resided at Qočo. The
author of these letters was greatly annoyed by certain damnable

innovations to and deviations from the established rules of the sect for which certain neighbouring communities or members of their own communities had been responsible. An *Electa* of the offending party was seen digging the earth with a mattock as well as plucking herbs and cutting wood. This group apparently practised bleeding for curative purposes and had the audacity to wash the surgical instruments (?) in springwater. The members were accused of having introduced "filthy and vulgar Syrian customs and skills" (a reference to their medical expertise?) and were regarded as a source of strife and contention. At the heart of the problem was the old antagonism between the followers of Mihr and Miqlās on social relationships. The dissenters were *Mihrijja* (*myhry'nd*) and their hosts were *Miqlāsijja* (*mkl'syktyy*). The precise date of the letters is uncertain and may be later than 880, when there was theoretically a state of truce between the two parties, which shows that the issues which led to the schism were still cogent to the more conservative communities in Central Asia.[166]

A more detailed survey of the history of Manichaeism in Mesopotamia after the death of Mani lies outside the scope of this present study and must be left to scholars who are competent Arabists. The few remarks made so far on the subject are merely intended to alert the reader to the fact that Manichaeism did not simply disappear from Mesopotamia as a result of the Sassanian persecutions after the death of Mani. The excellent material on the doctrines and history of the sect preserved by Arab writers such as al-Bīrūnī and al-Nadim bear witness to its continued influence on the cultural life of the land of its origins and its survival amidst periodic persecutions by the 'Abbasids until the tenth century – a story which certainly merits telling in full.

(6)   MANICHAEISM IN THE ROMAN EMPIRE
AFTER THE DEATH OF MANI

By the time of Mani's death in 276, his religion was already well established in the eastern parts of the Roman empire through the missionary work of disciples like Adda, Patīk the Teacher, Gabryab, Pappos, Thomas and Akouas. One of the earliest sure indications of the sect's presence in Egypt by the end of the third century is a circular letter, probably issued from the chancery of the Bishop Theonas of Alexandria, warning the faithful against being deceived by the 'madness of the Manichaeans'.[167] To this letter, which has survived on papyrus, we shall return in due course. The teaching of the sect also came under attack by the neo-Platonist, Alexander of Lycopolis, who was particularly irked by its unscientific character and the literalism with which the Manichaeans interpreted Mani's teaching on cosmogony.[168] The discovery of genuine Manichaean texts in Coptic at Medinet Medi and in Greek at Lycopolis shows beyond doubt that Egypt was an important centre of Manichaeism in the fourth and fifth centuries.[169] From Egypt, the religion spread swiftly along the Mediterranean coast to Roman North Africa and it had clearly gained sufficient followers for it to be considered a major nuisance by the authorities at the turn of the century. The proconsul of Africa himself wrote to Emperor Diocletian giving him a detailed account of the sect's activities in areas within his jurisdiction. On the basis of this report, the emperor would in 302 issue the first public edict against the sect.[170]

From bases in the cities along the eastern frontier, the Manichaeans took their religion into Syria and Asia Minor and thence the Balkans and Italy. An inscription on a fourth-century (?) tombstone found in 1906 to the south of the Basilica Urbana in Salona on the Dalmatian coast shows that a certain *Manichaea*, a Παρθένος (= *Electa*) by the name of Bassa who came originally from Lydia, had been active in the region.[171] The same cemetery has also yielded funerary inscriptions which indicate that some of the Christian leaders of Salona came from the frontier city of Nisibis, already an important centre of Christianity when Abercius Marcellus visisted it before the end of the second century.[172] It appears that the church at Salona had close connections with Christian communities along the eastern frontier and the Manichaeans might have exploited the link for their own ends. The presence of Manichaeism in the Balkans in the fourth century is further confirmed by the story of Sarapion the Sindonite in the *Historia Lausiaca* of Palladius. On a visit to Greece, this Egyptian holy man heard that a leading citizen of Lacedaemon (i.e. Sparta) was a Manichaean although a virtuous person in other aspects. Sarapion sold himself to his family as a slave and within two years was able to deliver him and his household from the bondage of the heresy.[173]

According to an uncorroborated piece of information provided by the sixth-century Greek chronographer, John Malalas, the first Manichaean missionary to arrive at Rome was called Bundos and he came during the reign of Diocletian. This Bundos broke away from the received doctrines of the sect and taught that the Good God triumphed over the Evil One. He eventually returned to disseminate his teaching in Persia where the doctrine of the Manichaeans, according to Malalas, was known as 'that of Daristhenes' which apparently means that the Good (God).[174] The term strongly resembles the name Daristhenos which appears in Malalas's *Chronographia* as the surname of the Shahanshah Kawad who supported the Mazdakites.[175] Like most Byzantine historians, Malalas calls Mazdakites 'Manicheans' and it is not improbable that he had confused or conflated two traditions, one concerning the arrival of Manichaeism in the city of Rome and the other the origins of the Mazdakite movement. The date of Bundos's mission seems reliable enough as the Manichaeans in Rome first came under papal ban during the pontificate of Miltiades (311–14).[176]

Spain and Gaul also had active trading links with the east, especially with Egypt. At Nitria, Palladius met two brothers whose later father was a *spanodromos*, a merchant who regularly made the 'Spanish run'.[177] However, our evidence on the diffusion and later the persecution of Manichaeism in Spain is completely obscured by the Priscillianist controversy as Priscillian and his supporters were castigated as Manichaeans by their enemies. The validity of the charge will be examined in another chapter. However, it is worth mentioning at this stage that the missionary success of the Manichaeans had galvanised the church into frantic attempts to counter its spread, and especially the diffusion of its literature, by means of polemics. These anti-Manichaean works which were also highly popular, tended to simplify Manichaean doctrines and create the impression that the main tenets of the sect were dualism, asceticism and astrology. Soon orthodox-minded churchmen began to detect 'Manichaean' traits among the more ascetical members of the Christian church. The ecumenical structure of the church provided efficient channels for the dissemination of anti-Manichaean literature. They were popular because they were probably more readily available to church leaders than genuine Manichaean literature as the sect was renowned for its secretiveness. The dissemination of anti-Manichaean literature kept pace with the diffusion of Manichaeism itself in the fourth century and in the case of Spain, it might have even outstripped it. A good example of uncritical use of anti-Manichaean literature in the context of the Priscillianist controversy is provided by Filastrius of Brescia. He wrote a handbook of heresies in Latin between 380 and 390 and for the section on Manichaeism he used a Greek anti-Manichaean work, the *Acta Archelai* (see below, pp. 97–100), as his source. But as soon as he had finished citing it he stated categorically that these criminals (*latrones*) were once everywhere but were now said to be in hiding in Spain and the Five Provinces (i.e. Novempopuli, Aquitanica, Narbonensis, Viennensis and Alpes Maritimae) and were holding many captive by deceit.[177] Elsewhere in the same work he says that there were many ascetics in Gaul and Spain who were in fact followers of the pernicious teaching of the gnostics and Manichaeans.[178] Augustine, who used Filastrius's work as one of the two main sources for his own *De Haeresibus*, took the second of the two references as directed against the followers of Priscillian.[179] If the latter were genuinely Manichaeans, Filaster would hardly have needed to resort to using a Greek anti-Manichaean work as his main source on the history and teaching of Manichaeism.

Manichaean missionaries showed exemplary zeal in the translation of the literature of the sect. As we have seen, the bilingualism of Syria and Upper Mesopotamia (i.e. Greek and Syriac) enabled Manichaean literature to become available in Greek. From Greek the texts were translated into Coptic and Latin. Syrian merchants who traded via the Thebaid using the port of Berenice would have some knowledge of Coptic. The discovery of Syriac fragments in Manichaean script at Oxyhrynchus shows that the earliest Manichaean communities were Syrian implantations but names like Jmnoute, Pshai, and Apa Panai in the Coptic *Psalm-Book* attest to the Egyptian origin of some of the sect's earliest martyrs and followers in Egypt.[180] As in Syria, bilingualism was a common social phenomenon in the Nile Valley. Hieracas of Leontopolis, an extreme ascetic who preached that asceticism was essential for salvation, was fluent in both Greek and Coptic and could compose psalms in the latter.[181] We learn from the *Sancti Pachomii vita prima graeca* that when a Greek-speaking lector came from Alexandria to join the monastic community of Pachomius, the holy man made him live with a bilingual monk from who he could learn 'the language of the Thebaid'.[182]

The first Latin translations of Manichaean texts must have been made by the end of the third century since the religion had already gained a foothold in Africa Proconsularis after Diocletian's edict of 302.[183] Although the majority of the extant fragments of Manichaean works in Latin belong to the *Treasure of Life* and an important letter of Mani commonly known as the '*Epistula fundamenti*', we can be certain that many other Manichaean texts were available in Latin.[184] Felix the Manichaean *doctor* who debated with Augustine had a corpus of Manichaeans works consisting of five *auctores* of which the *Epistula fundamenti* was one.[185] The *Decretum Gelasianum* (5th century) condemns as apocryphal a work entitled *Liber de Ogia nomine gigante etc.* which strikes one as the Latin translation of either the Manichaean or the Jewish pseudpigraphal *Book of the Giants*.[186] The North African Manichaeans also had in Latin the anti-Old Testament work of Adimantus which was probably translated from Greek as a Greek version of it is mentioned by <Zacharias Mitylene>.[187] Among other Manichaean works in Latin which Augustine was able to consult were those dealing with astrology. We are not told whether these were those dealing with astrology. We are not told whether these were parts of Manichaean canonical works or separate treatises but the fact that Augustine says that they were by Mani suggests that they were canonical or semi-canonical, like the discourses in the *Kephalaia* which are purported to be the *ipsissima verba* of Mani's lectures. Augustine adds that there was a great deal of this material.[188] The Manichaean books were copied by zealous or duty-bound Hearers on expensive parchment and cased in handsome binding. Their Latin style was judged to be elegant by as severe a literary critic as Augustine.[189] The Biblical quotations in the extant examples of Latin Manichaean texts are closer to the Old Latin than the Vulgate, which is natural, given a late third-century date for the translation of the Manichaean texts. Some of the Gospel quotations in them exhibit a number of peculiarities which point, even at this distance, to the original use of the *Diatessarōn* by Mani.[190]

Some of the Manichaean psalms in Coptic from Medinet Medi have repetitive and mnemonic refrains, e.g.:

> We are men of rest: let no man add toil to us.
> It is Jesus that we seek, on whom we have modelled ourselves.
> Let no man.
> Our loins are girded, out witness is in our hand.
> Let no man.
> We knocked at the door, the door was opened to us, we went
> in with the Bridegroom.
> Let no man.
> We were numbered in the number of the virgins in whose lamps
> oil was found.
> Let no man.
> We were numbered in the number of the Right, we passed from
> the number of the Left.
> Let no man.
> [etc.][191]

This responsorial form is most noticeable in a group of psalms entitled 'Psalmoi Sarakōtōn' and it is from one of these psalms that our example is taken. If the word *sarakōte* does mean 'wanderers' as some scholars have suggested, we have here the continuity of the Syrian tradition of wandering monks, *'ksn'* (from Gk.: ξένος)[192] The format of the psalms would have been appropriate to small groups of wandering preachers. The Manichaeans might have adopted an existing literary genre and some of the 'Psalmoi Sarakōtōn' which do not touch on Manichaean doctrine might have been purely Christian in origin.[193]

The growing popularity of pilgrimage in the Roman empire in the fourth century would have also affected the diffusion of Manichaeism. The travels of a *sanctimonialis* like Egeria would have taken her through many cities and towns in Palestine, Syria and Osrhoene which by the fourth century would have harboured sizeable Manichaean communities.[194] Although the apocryphal Gospels and

Acts of Apostles which the Manichaeans used liberally to support
their teaching were also important to the cult of martyrs, the
Manichaeans themselves, according to one of their leaders, frowned
upon the practice of paying homage to the shrines of martyrs as they
regarded it as a Christian version of pagan sacrifice.[195] Moreover, it is
worth emphasising that Manichaeism was a secretive religion and was
not merely a body of doctrines but also a highly regulated way of life.
Thus a pilgrim on a brief visit to a city like Edessa, unless he actually
joined the sect there, would not normally come away knowing a great
deal about it. Nor would we expect portions of Manichaean scriptures
or isolated aspects of Mani's teaching to be circulated like relics. On
the other hand, the growing popularity of pilgrimage would have
improved the travelling facilities in the later empire, especially in the
provision of hostels.[196] It might not have been pure coincidence that
the only genuine Manichaean text in Latin which had so far come to
light was discovered in a cave near Tabessa (Theveste) which in the
Byzantine period was a favourite stopping place for pilgrims.[197] Once
Manichaeism became established in a region, its own network of cells
would have provided accomodation for their itinerant teachers.

CHAPTER IV

THE STATE, THE CHURCH AND MANICHAEISM (302-83)

(1)   THE SERPENT FROM PERSIA

In the course of a routine visit to Egypt in 302, Diocletian received a disturbing report from Amnius Anicius Julianus, the proconsul of Africa, concerning the activities of the Manichaeans in areas within his jurisdiction.[1] Evangelistic sects of whatever religious persuasion were no longer a novelty in the Roman empire but what deeply worried Diocletian was that this new fangled cult of the Manichaeans was Persian in origin. It was generally known in Egypt that their founder Mani was once a member of the entourage of Shapur I in whose hands the Roman army had suffered some of her worst defeats in the east since the ill-fated expedition of Crassus.[2] There was no doubt in the mind of the Roman emperor that these Manichaeans were a Persian fifth column, seeking to pervert the morals of the Roman empire and by so doing to undermine its resolve to maintain its unending contest with Persia for the hegemony of the Near East. Although the empires were now at peace, Rome could not afford to relax her vigilance. It was during times of peace in particular, Diocletian felt, that the common folks were more prone to fall prey to the doctrines of wicked men because of excessive idleness (otia maxima).[3] In his rescript, which had the force of an imperial edict, Diocletian warned Julianus of the danger of overlooking this potential threat to the moral welfare and the security of the Empire:

We have heard that the Manichaeans, concerning whom your Carefulness [sollertia tua] has written to our Serenity [serenitas nostra], have set up new and hitherto unheard of sects in opposition to the older creeds so that they might cast out the doctrines vouchsafed to us in the past by divine favour for the benefit of their own depraved doctrine. They have sprung forth very recently like new and unexpected monstrosities among the race of the Persians – a nation still hostile to us – and have made their way into our empire, where they are committing many outrages, disturbing the tranquility of the people and even inflicting grave damage to the civic communities [civitates]: our fear is that with the passage of time, they will endeavour, as usually happens, to infect the modest and tranquil Roman people of an innocent nature with the damnable customs [consuetudines] and the perverse laws [leges] of the Persians as with the poison of a malignant serpent.[4]

Having read through what Julianus had written about this religion, Diocletian came to the conclusion that their doctrines and their activities were 'carefully devised and thought out contrivances of obvious malefactors [maleficii]'.[5] He therefore decreed what he believed to be suitable and effective punishments for these miscreants. The leaders of the sect (auctores ac principes) were ordered to be burnt, along with their abominable scriptures. Their followers would be punished according to the dual-penalty system of the late empire. Those of a lower social standing would be executed while those of the official rank (honorati aut cuiuslibet dignitatis vel maioris personae) would be sent to the quarries of Phaeno and Proconnesus. The mines of Phaeno in Arabia, as we learn from Eusebius, were a frequent destination of Christians during the Great Persecution. In both cases, the property of the accused would be confiscated and added to the imperial treasury.[6]

The Persian connection of the sect, then, was the chief cause of concern for Diocletian. War psychology clearly still conditioned the emperor's mind when the rescript to Julianus was issued.[7] Rome had not fared well in her clashes with a revitalised Persia, and Galerius's victory in 298 was the first after a long series of Roman defeats at the hands of the early Sassanian Emperors.[8] What Diocletian might not have known was that the Manichaeans who flocked into the Roman empire at the turn of the third century were mostly Syrians escaping from persecution in the 'Low Countries' by the Sassanian officials. Thus it is hard to believe, as Diocletian's rescript implies, that they were agents provocateurs working hand in glove with the Persian high command. The fear was therefore more imaginary than real but the Persian connection was stressed in the rescript because it made the sect sound more foreign and dangerous and therefore more deserving of severe punishment.[9]

The Romans did not have any inherent antagonism towards foreign religions. As the empire expanded, a great many Greek and Egyptian cults were absorbed into her religious life with the help of the occasional prohibition against excessive indulgence in them.[10] The second and third centuries were the golden age of oriental cults in the Roman empire. The worship of Isis and Serapis was common in many Mediterranean cities. Mithraism, which enjoyed particular popularity among soldiers, claimed to have originated in Persia. It was attacked as a foreign religion in the Roman empire mostly by the church Fathers.[11] Judaism and Christianity, however, were treated differently by the state because of their exclusivism and their evangelistic tendencies. Diocletian, judging from the prologue of his edict against Manichaeans, seemed to regard proselytising as an enemy of social tranquillity (*quies*) because people joined the sect not out of genuine interest but because their minds had been perverted by selfish and immoral men.[12] The same principle underlies the proscription of new religions which were in force at the time of Diocletian's edict:

'Those who introduce new sects or religions unknown to reason by which the minds of men were perverted should be punished. Those who are of high status shall be exiled while those who are of low status shall be executed.'[13]

Diocletian might have been afraid that a proselytising creed like Manichaeism would cause dissension in the empire because it demanded from its converts the whole-hearted obedience which was the state's due. The same fear had earlier been expressed by Dio Cassius, historian and senator of the third century, to Emperor Severus through the advice of Maecenas to Augustus in his *History*. According to Maecenas, it was necessary to compel the subjects of the empire to worship the gods of Rome not only because they deserved to be worshipped but because those who substituted new gods for old would persuade others to accept different laws and customs (ἀλλοτριονομεῖν), from which sprang conspiracies and rebellions which would be injurious to the empire.[14]

An air of patriotic conservatism therefore permeates Diocletian's rescript: 'It is indeed highly criminal to alter those things which have been stated and defined since ancient times and still hold their status and have the right to go on holding it.'[15] Diocletian, who found it difficult to tolerate marriage customs within the Roman empire which did not conform to Roman practices, did not hesitate to lash out against those who were importing 'Persian customs' (*leges Persarum*).[16] This response has been attributed by many scholars to his staunch conservatism.[17] Behind the mask of his conservatively-worded edicts, however, lurks an utterly revolutionary mind which, according to the contemporary Christian writer Lactantius, had wrought more changes for the Roman empire than any of his predecessors.[18] Diocletian strove with remorseless energy for greater unity and uniformity within the empire. 'Disciplina' was his watchword for the day as the maintenance of public order was essential for the successful outcome of his reforms. Complete obedience was demanded from his subjects and one way of expressing their loyalty to the state was to participate in the cult of emperor worship which Diocletian had revived and vigorously enforced.[19] The Christian church had expanded considerably during the third century and Diocletian could not fail to see an impending conflict of loyalties on a scale hitherto unknown to the empire. His attempt to regulate the customs and religions of the empire by administrative means was epitomised by the so-called 'Great Persecution' of the Christian church which began shortly after the edict against the Manichaeans was issued and continued sporadically until the accession of Constantine.

The edict of Diocletian against the Manichaeans therefore has to be seen in relation to his administrative reforms, especially his regulation of religious practices within the empire, in addition to Romano-Persian relations. However, there was undoubtedly a general hardening of Roman attitude towards foreign influences. Under the High Empire, Persia was seen by many Romans as the guardian of the wisdom of the Orient and it was also the gateway to the exotic customs and mystical philosophies of India. Even at the end of the third century, the desire to imbibe the teachings of the Persians and Indians could motivate Plotinus to partake in Gordian's abortive expedition against Shāpūr I.[20] A mystery religion like Mithraism, which many scholars now regard as Roman in origin, acquired many Persian trappings in order to increase its esoteric appeal.[21] The revival of Persia as an agressive military power under the Sassanians put an end to such romantic notions about the east and the conversion of the empire to Christianity erected new barriers between the two states. The once fluid frontier in Mesopotamia was now more clearly defined. Jovian's handing over of Nisibis to Shapur II in 363 was an important step in the formation of more discernible boundary between the two states and had the immediate effect of cutting the Syriac-speaking region into two; placing its two principal cities, Edessa and Nisibis, in opposing spheres of influence.[22] Commercial contacts also came under stricter regulation. A law of Honorius (408 or 9) stipulates that trade between the two empires can only be carried out through three cities on the frontier, Nisibis, Callinicum and Artaxata. It also takes elaborate measures to forestall espionage by merchants.[23] The Syriac *Doctrina Addai*, which most scholars regard as later than Eusebius, seems to reflect this new state of affairs along the frontier when it tells us that the Persians who desired to hear the apostle Addai had to travel to Edessa in the guise of merchants.[24]

The fact that Mani was a subject of the King of Kings meant that Persia came to be seen as the theological as well as the political enemy of the Christian Roman empire.[25] The religious gulf between the two empires was further widened by the corresponding popularity of Nestorianism in Persian-held Mesopotamia and of Monophysitism in Roman Syria and Upper Mesopotamia. Writing in the sixth century, John of Ephesus, himself a Monophysite, would speak of Persia as a land of heresies because Mani had taught there and that the Persians were keen inquirers and therefore more prone to error. He also tells us that the school of Persians in Edessa was immersed in the doctrines of Bardaiṣan and Marcion which is clearly a way of slighting the school for its Nestorianism rather than for its actual devotion to the teaching of these heresiarchs.[26] This feeling was reciprocated by the Christians in Persia who in the Nestorian synod of 612 claimed that Manichaeism originated in the Roman empire and was later grafted into Persia, a land which had hitherto not known any heresies.[27]

(2)   FROM CONSTANTINE TO JOVIAN

The strong words of Diocletian's anti-Manichaean rescript of 302 and the harsh penalty it prescribes might have had the effect of temporarily halting the steady advance of Manichaeism in parts of the empire blessed with efficient imperial administrators. A few Manichaean martyrs might have been produced here and there and a few more might have been added to the roll of honour during the Great Persecution when Manichaeans along with Marcionites were probably hounded by officials who could not distinguish between the various Christian sects. Constantine's victory over his rival Maxentius at the battle of Milvian Bridge (28 October 312) heralded the arrival of a new age in church and state relations. The Edict of Milan which was issued early in the next year granted toleration for all religions equally. Diocletian's edict of 302 against the Manichaeans was probably annulled along with the ones against the Christians promulgated a year later at the beginning of the Great Persecution. The anti-Manichaean edict, however, was not entirely forgotten, as it would in due course be alluded to by the Christian emperors when they legislated against the sect as a heresy.[28] It is also mentioned by an anonymous commentator on the Pauline espitles, commonly called Ambrosiaster, who, in warning the faithfully against door to door Manichaean evangelists, reminds them that the sect had once been banned. He even gave the original wording of the edict a subtle twist to bring it into line with the new conditions of a Christian empire by referring to it as a 'heresy (haeresis) from Persia'.[29]

The ending of the Great Persecution against the Christian church brought relief to the various heretical sects as well as the church in general. The Marcionites at Lebaba, as we have seen, openly advertised their place of worship in the village. Similarly, the friends of Bassa, the Manichaean *Electa* from Lydia who died at Salona, made no attempt to hide her sect and her rank on her tombstone. They were clearly not in fear of being tracked down as associates of a persecuted sect.[30] Once the church had resumed its missionary activities among the pagans, the Manichaeans could profit on the side lines. The process of Christianisation also brought about a keen interest in theology and asceticism among all classes of Roman society. Manichaeism, which gave a prominent place to Jesus in its doctrines and psalmody as well as being uncompromisingly ascetic, readily assimilated itself into the new religious scene and gave the impression to the imperial authorities of being one of the many sects which constituted the Christian church.

In the first half of the fourth century, the foremost theological debating point in the Christian church was the doctrine of Arius who postulated that God the Son was created from a different but similar substance to God the Father and was therefore inferior. The Manichaean view of Jesus as an emanation of the Father of Greatness stood surprisingly close to the principle of consubstantiality (ὁμοούσιος) as laid down by the First Ecumenical Council of Nicaea in 325 against Arius. As Epiphanius says, 'We [i.e. the orthodox] use the same language as they [i.e. the Manichaeans] do, that the Good Off-spring of the Good Father, Light of Light, God of God, True God of True God came to us in order to save us.'[31] Similarly Arius himself pointed out in one of his letters preserved by Epiphanius that the Nicene position of the Son and the Father as being 'of one substance' was verging on the Manichaean.[32]

The official documents of this period which have come down to us make no mention of Manichaeism, nor was the sect condemned by name in any of the ecumenical councils. We learn from Ammianus Marcellinus that Constantine sent one of his polylingual officers, Strategius Musonianus (who might have been a Syriac-speaker) to investigate the Manichaeans and other sects.[33] The fact that we possess no anti-Manichaean legislation issued by Constantine seems to imply that he was content merely to believe that their Christological stance conformed with the Nicene creed. The official tolerance of the sect may also be deduced from the high rank of one of its better known converts, Sebastianus, who rose to the office of *magister peditum (Orientis)* in 378. One of the most distinguished soldiers of the fourth century, he served with distinction under several emperors from Julian onwards and died along with the Emperor Valens at Hadrianople in 378.[34] He was so popular with his troops that at the death of Gratian in 375 there was genuine fear that they might proclaim him emperor.[35] While he was *dux* of Egypt (*c.* 356–8) he sided with the Arian Bishop George of Alexandria and expelled the adherents of the pronouncements of Nicaea from their churches. Athanasius, the staunchest opponent of Arianism repeatedly claimed that he was maltreated by Sebastianus whom he alleged to have been a Manichaean.[36] This allegation is also found in the church histories of Theodoret and

Sozomen who probably drew their material from Athanansius's own writings.[37] It may seem odd to us that a religion which prohibits the taking of any form of animal life should appeal to a professional soldier. On the other hand, as we shall see, Manichaeism later became the state religion of the Uighurs in Central Asia who were at one time the most effective mercenary force of the late T'ang government of China. Before we congratulate the Manichaeans for winning such an important convert we need to be reminded that the exploits of Sebastianus were also well documented by contemporary pagan authors like Libanius, Ammianus and Eunapius and none of them mention his devotion to Manichaeism.[38] It may be that Manichaeans in Egypt, as they did elsewhere, had the reputation of being cruel because they would refuse alms to those who were not of their sect.[39] Athanasius might have labelled Sebastianus a Manichaean because of the cruel manner in which he was treated by him and his troops.

While the state took no drastic steps to suppress Manichaeism, individual church leaders kept alive a verbal battle against the sect. One of the earliest examples of these personal initiatives was a circular letter issued probably from the chancellery of Bishop Theonas of Alexandria and dated on paleographical grounds to the end of the third century, now in the papyrus collection of the John Rylands University Library of Manchester.[41] The surviving portion of the letter warns the faithful against being persuaded by the Manichaean argument that marriage is inherently evil.[42] Their 'apology for the bread' (ἀπολογία πρὸς τὸν ἄρτον), by which the Elect endeavoured to exempt himself from the guilt of procuring food, was 'the work of a man possessed by madness'.[43] The faithful were advised to be on guard against those who penetrated into houses with deceiving words, and especially against women whom the Manichaeans called the Elect. They were honoured because their menstrual blood was required for the abominable rites of the sect.[44]

Since Mani claimed that he was apostle of Jesus Christ and the Paraclete whom Jesus promised to send to his disciples, a popular and effective form of counter-propaganda was to present him as the antithesis of a 'man of God'. The fourth century witnessed an upsurge of popular interest in the lives of saints, martyrs and ascetics. The natural corollary to this in the propaganda war against the Manichaeans was a biography of Mani which depicts his life and character in terms diametrically opposed to those used in the popular lives of saints. This work, entitled the *Acta Archelai*, was completed no later than 340 and was first composed in Greek.[45] This original version has not survived but an important section of it has been preserved by Epiphanius in his *Panarion*.[46] It proved to be a popular work and was quickly translated into Latin, in which language alone it survives in entirely.[47] We possess a quotation from it in Coptic[48] and from the use of some its contents by later Syriac writers, we may assume that it was translated into that language as well.[49] Most scholars no longer accept the view first put forward by St Jerome that the *Acta* was first composed in Syriac.[50] The Syriac writers of the fourth century seem to be unaware of it and the parallels in later Syriac writers give the impression of having been translated from the Greek.[51]

The *Acta* depicts Mani as the inheritor of erroneous teaching from a line of pseudo-prophets. The first of these was Scythianus who, as we have already mentioned, traded with Egypt and took as his wife a certain captive from the Upper Thebiad. One version of the story preserved by Epiphanius describes her as a prostitute – an attempt no doubt to make him resemble more closely Simon Magus the arch-heretic whose mistress Helen, according to Irenaeus, was also a prostitute.[52] This Scythianus imbibed the esoteric teaching of the Egyptians and had a disciple called Terebinthos who wrote for him four books entitled the *Book of the Mysteries*, the *Kephalaia*, the *Gospel* and the *Treasures*. Scythianus died while on a visit to Judaea and Terebinthos went on to Babylonia. There he gave a fanciful account of himself claiming that he was born of a virgin and was reared in the mountains by an angel and his real name was Buddas. Though replete with all the knowledge of the Egyptians, Terebinthos was worsted in debates with pagan priests and took himself to lodgings with a widow to get away from his inquisitors. He was cast down from the roof of his house while performing some magical rites and died. His effects, especially his books, passed into the possession of his landlady. The latter took as a child slave a boy of seven called Cubricus and instructed him from these books and also gave him his freedom. She died when he was twelve years old and left him all her possessions.[53]

This Cubricus acquired great erudition and much perverse learning from these books. He took up his residence in the royal city of the king of Persia and changed his name to Mani. He gathered a group of disciples round him and with their help he revised the contents of the books he had inherited and passed them off as his own. Later, at the age of sixty, he sent them to disseminate his teaching in different parts of the world. While they were away, the son of the Persian king fell seriously ill and his father offered a large reward to anyone who could cure him. Mani decided to take a big gamble and presented himself to the king as the one who could cure his son. He was well received but his skill did not match his claims; the boy died in his hands and he was thrown into jail.[54]

The anti-hagiographical nature of this assertion is clear, as Mani was celebrated as a great physician in Manichaean literature. Moreover, it has been pointed out that the story appears to have been a polemical counterpart of the achievements of a certain Christian saint called Cyriacus, martyred under Maximinus, which are recorded in the *Gesta* of Pope Marcellus in the Roman martyrology (feast day 16 January). This Cyriacus was a healer of such distinction that his services were called upon by Emperor Diocletian, whose daughter Artemia was possessed by a demon which claimed that its powers could only be nullified by Cyriacus. This he succeeded in doing and Diocletian rewarded him with a mansion and befriended him. Later his reputation reached the Persian King Shapur (*sic.*) whose daughter Jobia was also possessed by a demon and he sent an ambassador to Diocletian to request the sending to him of Cyriacus. The latter duly travelled to Persia with two companions Largus (feast day 16 March) and Smaragdus (3 August). He was again successful in curing his royal patient but this time he declined the rich presents which the Persian king wanted to give him.[55] In contrast, Mani offered his services in the hope of receiving the large reward promised by the king.[56] The date of the Cyriacus legend is uncertain; it might have influenced the formulation of the account of Mani's life in the *Acta Archelai* but it might also have been a further development of the church's anti-Manichaean propaganda in that we find the antitheses of Mani's negative qualities being given a hagiographical expression in the life of an individual saint.

While Mani was in jail, he was visited by his disciples who had returned from their missionary journeys to tell him of the difficulties which they encountered in disseminating his teaching, especially in lands which held the name of the Christians in high esteem. Mani berated them for being men of straw and sent them back to purchase Christian writings with small sums of money. On receiving these works he singled out of them passages which appear to support his views and claimed that his teaching was the same as that of Christ. He also bestowed upon himself the title of the Paraclete and recommissioned his disciples to disseminate this Christianised form of his erroneous teaching. When the king of Persia came to hear of his subversive activities in jail he decided to put him to death. Forewarned of the king's intentions in a dream, Mani bribed the jailer and escaped across the frontier into the Roman empire to Castle of Arabion (*castellum Arabionis*).[57] There he came to know of a leading citizen of the city of Carchar (Carrhae?), a Christian by the name of Marcellus who was much admired for his philanthropy.[58] Mani attempted to convert him by letter via a special courier but Marcellus was unmoved and Mani decided to pay him a personal visit and arrived in the city in weird and colourful costumes.[59] Waiting to attack his doctrines was Archelaus, the bishop of the city, but, knowing his zeal, Marcellus duly arranged a formal debate between the two so as to avoid a public harangue.[60] As expected, Mani was outpointed by the Christian in every round and he left the city in disgrace. He was afterwards re-arrested and put to death in the most cruel manner at the order of the Persian king who held him responsible for his own son's death and for the execution of the jailer who had allowed his escape.[61]

This polemical version of Mani's life was such welcome counter-propaganda to the miracle-filled biographies of Mani disseminated by the sect as exemplified by the *CMC*, that it immediately became the main source on the early history of Manichaeism for church historians, chronographers and heresiologists. The fact that Eusebius did not use this material in his *Historia Ecclesiastica* while his continuators, namely Socrates and Theodoret both show familiarity with it may help us to fix approximately the date of the work.[62] It is interesting to note that Augustine, who used the works of Epiphanius and Filastrius as sources for his own handbook of heresies, did not make any reference to this polemical version of Mani's life despite the fact that the two earlier heresiologists both cited from it.[63] Having been a Manichaean Hearer for nine years, Augustine probably knew too well the falsity of this polemical version. Despite the lack of his endorsement the Latin version of the *Acta* enjoyed a wide circulation in the Middle Ages, as evidenced by the considerable number of manuscripts made in France later than the ninth century – an indication, no doubt, of its use by the French church against the Albegensians.[64]

One of the first church leaders of the fourth century to make use of *Acta Archelai* in a pastoral context was Cyril of Jerusalem (c. 315–86, bishop from c. 349). He devoted one of his catechetical lectures, delivered around 350 as instructions in Lent and Eastertide to the catechumens who were baptised on Holy Saturday, to the dangers of heresies, especially of Manichaeism. He gave a long paraphrase from the *Acta Archelai* and acknowledged his source.[65] He also warned them against accepting too readily the repentance of those who had turned from Manichaeism. The genuineness of their denial of Manichaeism had to be ascertained before they could be trusted.[66] Although there was no mention yet of set abjuration formulas, it appears that catechumens who had formerly been Manichaeans had to renounce Mani publicly before they could be baptised.

The reason for the lack of any direct action against Manichaeism by the church beyond verbal assaults is not difficult to find. The sect could hardly be regarded as a major threat to the unity of the church compared with the Arian heresy which had followers in most parts of the empire and especially in the eastern provinces or the Donatist schism which was seriously affecting the church in Africa. The fear of a pagan revival and with it a reversion to the status of affairs before the Edict of Milan was far more real than a Manichaean takeover. The short reign of Julian (360–3) was a most unwelcome confirmation to the church of her vulnerability to external pressures and internal disunity. Julian was fully aware of this when he recalled the supporters of Nicaea and the Donatist bishops who had been exiled by pro-Arian Constantius II.[67] This plunged the church into turmoil and Julian's apparent indifference towards pagans who had taken the law into their own hands and exacted vengeance on Christian leaders who had despoiled pagan shrines with the connivance of the state certainly did not help matters. When George, the Arian patriarch of Alexandria, was lynched by a pagan mob in 362, the citizens of Alexandria received nothing more severe than 'exhortation and words – the mildest medicine' from Julian.[68] Some bishops might have therefore been compelled by the new circumstances to mobilise their congregations to defend themselves against occasional attacks by pagans and to maintain internal unity. Once mobilised, such forces were hard to control and, as we have mentioned earlier, the Valentinians in Edessa fell victim to this type of sectarian warfare.[69] In Bostra in Arabia, the Christians fell in behind their bishop Titus in resisting the re-introduction of paganism. This prompted Julian to issue an edict forbidding anyone to follow the lead of clergymen in riots, to be seduced by them to take up stones for street fighting or to disobey magistrates.[70] Julian's attempt to dislodge Titus from his see was entirely unsuccessful as he remained bishop of Bostra till c. 371.[71]

Besides his determined stand against the policies of Julian, Titus of Bostra also acquired a reputation as a skilled refuter of Manichaean doctrines. This he did in a work consisting of four books but until recently only the first two books and the first six chapters of the third have survived in the original Greek and the entire work is available only in a Syriac translation made within half a century of the completion of the Greek.[72] Thanks to a new Athos manuscript containing both the anti-Manichaean works of Titus and Serapion of Thmuis, we now possess a further twenty-three sections of the third book in Greek.[73] The work is best known for its resolute attempt to discredit the easy answer which the Manichaeans gave to the problem of evil through postulating the existence of an uncreated evil principle. Titus's main thesis is that man is born neither good nor bad but fair. He acquires goodness through education and training. From birth he is imbued with the knowledge of good and evil. Consequently he has the 'power of reflection' (ἐνθύμησις) on the moral outcome of his actions and can therefore come to the right decisions beforehand. For Titus, evil is not an active force, it is the product of sin which has no power to invade goodness. The real answer to the problem of evil lies in positive living and a willingness to endure natural disasters and physical hardships which Titus saw as part of the process of refinement which ultimately is beneficial to man.[74]

The death of Julian at the hands of the Persians and the desire of his successor to effect a swift and peaceful withdrawal of the Roman expeditionary force led to a major cession of Roman territories to Persia.[75] The loss of Nisibis with its surrounding territory of Mygdonia was particularly grievous as it deprived Rome of easy access to the Tigris. The city had withstood three attempts to capture it by Shāpūr II during the reign of Constantius.[76] The local hero of the first siege was undoubtedly Jacob, the bishop of the city who with the assistance of a novitiate called Ephraim offered continuous prayers for deliverance and exhorted the troops when the defences were in dangers of being breached.[77] Jacob passed away in the fullness of his fame and did not witness the humiliating surrender of the city to the Persians without a struggle. The terms of the treaty of 363 provided for the safe withdrawal of the Christian population to the west. Among those who left Nisibis was Ephraim. After a brief period of wandering, he found a permanent home in Edessa where he became a famous teacher and an active adviser to the church leaders of the city although he never rose to the rank of bishop. At his death (June 373) he was buried without pomp at the cemetery 'of the foreigners'.[78]

Ephraim was one of the most important theologians of the early Syriac church as well as being an outstanding literary figure. A number of his works are devoted to the refutation of heretical sects which he found to have been well supported in Edessa.[79] The main targets of his polemics were the followers of Marcion, Bardaiṣan and Mani but he also took occasional swipes at Valentinians and Arians. The ecclesiastical scence at Edessa was clearly one of great diversity. Ephraim was appalled by the fact that the name 'Christian' was not applied by all to those who confessed what Ephraim regarded as orthodoxy. The latter were named Palutians after a certain Palut in the same way that heretical sects were named after their founders. The identity of this Palut was much more difficult to establish than that of the heresiarchs. Ephraim maintained that he was a pupil of Paul but the *Doctrina Addai* claims that he was a local convert and was appointed deacon in Edessa by Addai.[80] In short the Christians with whom Ephraim identified himself were regarded in Edessa as a sect among other sects and were certainly not seen by all as members of the mother church. 'They again call us "Palutians" ', as Ephraim remonstrated in one of his poems, 'this we quite decisively reject and disown. Cursed be those who let themselves be called by the name of Palut instead of by the name of Christ.'[81]

The refutation of Mani's cosmology is the main subject of a series of discourses which he addressed to a certain Hypatius who is otherwise unknown.[82] The discourses also seek to refute the teachings of Marcion and Bardaiṣan but these older heresies received less attention perhaps because at the time of writing, Manichaeism was the more serious threat. His method was to attack Mani's system piecemeal and nowhere does he allow his opponent to present his case in full. The cosmology of Mani is basically a human drama projected onto the cosmic level. Its main supports are psychological and emotional rather than metaphysical. Once the critic focuses on individual aspects of the myth, its epical and dramatic qualities are immediately lost and one is left with a mass of details which run counter to human observation and common sense. Shadows, as Ephraim points out, flee before the Light, therefore it is absurd to imagine Darkness, which is absence of light, ever being able to invade Light. If the natures of Light and Darkness are distinct in every respect, how can they mingle with each other? That the five Light Elements (Syr.: *zywn'*) could become food for the Sons of Darkness shows that the 'essence' (*'ytwt'*) of Light is akin to Darkness.[83] Once the individual parts of the myth are found to have no metaphysical or scientific basis, the polemicist simply allows the edifice to crumble in the reader's mind. To add poignancy to his arguments, Ephraim also made scathing remarks on the holy idleness of the Manichaean *Electae* (*zdyqt'*)[84] and the occasional reminder that Mani, the heresiarch, came to a sad end: 'And they did well who skinned the lying Mani, who said that Darkness was skinned, though it has neither hide nor sheath-skin.'[85]

When Ephraim perceived that the teaching of Bardaiṣan owed some of its popular appeal to the elegance of the sect's hymns and the rhythm of their melodies, he decided to take a leaf out of his enemies's book by mastering the metre of Harmonius and composed poems in it which are in accordance of the doctrines of the church. 'From that period', says the church historian Sozomen, 'the Syrians sang the odes of Ephraim according to the law of the ode established by Harmonius.' The value of using hymns for polemical purposes was generally recognised.[85a] Augustine who wrote an Abecedarian psalm against the Donatists explains in his *Rectractationes* that his purpose is to 'bring the facts of the Donatist affair to the attention of the humble masses and of the ignorant and unlettered and to fix the matter in their memories as much as we can'.[86] Since the Manichaeans themselves put great emphasis on hymns and the sect in Edessa would have possessed the Syrian original of many of the hymns composed by Mani and his earliest disciples, it was vitally important for the church leaders to provide their own flock with hymns which not only defined their own doctrinal position but also derided that of the Manichaeans. Among the surviving works of Ephraim is a collection of fifty-six hymns against the heresies, and as in the discourses to Hypatius, they attack all three of the main heretical groups in Edessa.

The hymns against the heretics show that as a polemicist Ephraim is not devoid of wit even if they give free rein to his virulence and sarcasm. He shows for instance how by literary sleight of hand one could deride the teachings of the three heresiarchs by puns on their names:

Who has (so aptly) named Bardaiṣan after the (River) Daiṣan? Satan has drowned more people in him than in the Daiṣan and his flood-water overflows its banks and brings forth tares and thistles. [Satan] has polished [mrq] Marcion [Mrqywn] so brightly that he may rust. He sharpened him so that he might blunt his intellect with blasphemy. Mani [Mny] is a garment [m'n'] which corrupts those who wear it.[87]

Mani's name in Greek lends itself to puns even more readily than in the Syriac. 'It was truly provident', remarks Epiphanius, 'that he should have adopted this name.'[88] The resemblance between Μανῆς and the word for 'raving' μανείς, especially in their respective genitive forms: Μανέτος and μανέντος, is uncanny and was mercilessly exploited by his enemies. It was to avoid being called disciples of a mad man that the Manichaeans, as we learn from Augustine, doubled the letter n in his name Manichaeus to make him sound like the 'pourer of Manna'.[89] This altered form is found in Greek and Coptic Manichaean texts which seems to confirm Augustine's remark.[90] The play on Mani = maniac was so well known that the following stanza which is directed against the writings of the heresiarchs may well contain a reference to it:

Your Lord will exalt you, O faithful Church! For you are not concealing the book of the insane Marcion, nor the writings of the mad Mani [šny' Mny], nor the Book of the Horrible Mysteries [spr r'zwhy sny'] of Bardaiṣan. The Two Testaments of the King and his Son are placed in your Ark.[91]

The brevity of the hymns did not allow for lengthy refutation of Manichaean doctrines and Ephraim resorted to condemnation of individual aspects or particular deities of the cosmogonic myth:

Let us give advice to the disciples of Mani and let us heal their wounds. For they arouse the anger of the Holy One by saying thunder and lightning are the unrestrained sounds made by the archon when he catches sight of the Virgin [btwlt']. At the sound of thunder their hearts should have been shattered with fright, but instead of giving you praise they provoke you greatly to anger.

As in his *Discourses to Hypatius*, Ephraim does not hesitate to remind the Manichaeans in the hymns that their course was doomed because of what befell their founder:

Mani has marshalled the woes which our Lord has pronounced. He has denied his creator and reviled the Holy One. He has raged against Moses and the Prophets and called them by every bad name and was contemptuous of them. Because he has refused the help of his own doctor, he has been shattered without pity. Having received his due ruin and died, he bequeathed it to his sons.[93]

Shortly after the death of the Emperor Julian, the Manichaeans in Palestine won the sympathy of Libanius, the famous rhetor of Antioch and one of the most influential pagans of his day. In 364 he wrote to Priscianus, Consularis (?) of Palestina Prima, to seek protection from him for a harmless group of people who were being harassed:

Those who worship the sun without blood [sacrifices] and honour it as a god of the Second Grade [προσηγορίᾳ δευτέρᾳ] and chastise their appetites and reckon the Last Day as gain are very dispersed in the land but few in numbers anywhere. They harm no one but are harassed by some people. I wish that those of them who live in Palestine may have your authority for protection and be free from anxiety and that those who wish to harm them will not be allowed to do so.[94]

Judging from the number of letters which Priscianus received from Libanius, the two were on such excellent terms that there is some ground for assuming the request was not made in vain.[95] That such a request could have been made at all shows that the sect was not officially banned and it suffered mainly from those who persecuted them on their own initiative or at the goading of local church leaders. Libanius's sympathy for the sect must not be seen as an indication of a revival of oriental cults under Julian. The division of paganism into 'Roman' (or 'ancestral') and 'oriental' can not meaningfully be applied to the religious situation of the fourth century.[96] The victory of Christianity had, if anything, helped to close the ranks of paganism and transformed it into a religion, albeit syncretistic, which was more comparable to Christianity. Libanius's plea for toleration of Manichaeism was made in the same spirit as his defence of the rights of pagans and Jews in Antioch which were increasingly being ignored by officials.[97]

Given the strength of Arianism in this period, it is not surprising that the followers of the Council of Nicaea did not have a complete monoploy in the campaign against Manichaeism. Aetius, one of the most highly regarded Arian theologians, was according to Philostorgius, a great enemy of heretics. When a Manichaean teacher called Aphthonius began to acquire a great fame for his eloquence, Aetius challenged him to public debate in Alexandria and undertook the journey there from Antioch. After a few regular discussions, Aphthonius was cast from his pinnacle of fame and reduced to deep shame. He took his unexpected defeat so badly that he fell ill and died a week later.[98]

The Arians also contributed to the war of words against the Manichaeans. We learn from Photius that the semi-Arian George of Laodicea (bishop from *c.* 335) was the author of an anti-Manichaean work but it has not survived.[99] Photius also tells us that a Manichaean called Agapius polemised against the heretical teaching of Eunomius.[100] Since Photius does not identify this Eunomius, we may assume that he was the Arian bishop of Cyzicus in Mysia from 360 and a distinguished pupil of Aetius whom we have just mentioned. As for Agapius our knowledge of his teaching is derived almost entirely from Photius who had read one of his works which, according to him, contains 23 fables (λογύδρια) and 102 other sections 'in all of which he shows himself feigning the name that belongs to the Christians but none is proved such an enemy of Christ by those very works'.[101] His name also appears in Byzantine abjuration formulas in which he is anathematised as a disciple of Mani along with one of his works entitled the *Heptalogue*.[102] If this was his principal work then it might have been the one which Photius had consulted. In his summary of its contents, the patriarch does not explicitly condemn Agapius as a Manichaean although he does think that the work has some value for the refutation and the shaming of those who were devoted to Manichaeism.[103] The teaching of Agapius on good and evil as summarised by Photius is uncompromisingly dualist:

He lays down and affirms every principle contrary to the Christians. He establishes against God for evermore a wicked, self-subsisting principle, which sometimes he calls nature, sometimes matter and sometimes Satan and the Devil and the ruler of the world and God of This Age, and by countless other names. He maintains that men stumble by necessity and against their will, and that the body belongs to the evil portion but the soul to the divine and (alas what madness!) is of one substance with God. And he mocks the Old Testament (Oh the impiety!) to the evil principle which stands opposed to God. In his telling of fantastic tales he also says that the tree in Paradise is Christ whom he professes with his lips to honour, but whom by his deeds and beliefs he blasphemes more than words can tell.[104]

So far, his views are close to the Manichaean position as understood by most Christian polemicists. His belief that Christ was the tree in Paradise was also attributed to the Manichaeans in the *Acta Archelai*. Like the Manichaean Elect he abstained from meat, wine and sexual relationships. He worshipped air as a god, celebrating it as a pillar and as a man which reminds us of the Manichaean belief, again expressed in the *Acta Archelai*, that the Column of Glory is also called the Perfect

Man (ἀ<ν>ήρ or Air ἀήρ).[105] He speaks of the sun and the moon as gods and announces them as consubstantial with God. He abominated fire and earth and attributed them to the evil portion. His use of the Christian scriptures was highly selective and he relied upon apocryphal works like the *Acts of the Twelve Apostles*, especially those of Andrew. He borrowed liberally from the writings of pagan philosophers such as Plato and subscribed to the transmigration of souls which would release to God the souls of those who have advanced to the height of virtue and present to fire and darkness those who have reached the ultimate of evil.[106]

What we do not know is whether Agapius confessed in his book that he was a Manichaean or whether he was declared such by his opponents. The claim that he was a disciple of Mani was made only in Byzantine sources and was not mentioned in the abjuration formula of <Zacharias Mitylene> or the handbook on the abjuration of heresies by the Presbyter Timothy of Constantinople.[107] In both these sixth-century works Agapius is mentioned only as the author of the *Heptalogue*. His teaching undoubtedly fits the popular definition of Manichaeism in that it is strongly dualist, it believes in the evil nature of the body, rejects the Old Testament, makes use of apocryphal scriptures and pagan writings, and believes in the transmigration of souls. On the other hand he honours and preaches the body of Christ and Christ crucified, and the Cross and baptism and entombment of Christ and the resurrection of the dead which are not Manichaean. Though he wages a truceless war against the ever-Virgin Mary, says Photius, he nevertheless speaks of her as the mother of Christ.[108] Moreover, nowhere in the summary does Photius say that Agapius honoured Mani as the Paraclete or that he was familiar with genuine Manichaean literature or that he was an Elect member of the sect.

Agapius's work was dedicated to a lady by the name of Urania who was referred to as a 'fellow-philosopher' (συμφιλόσοφος).[109] This designation may indicate that they were both members of that wing of the Roman intelligentsia which tried to combine Christianity with pagan philosophy. It comprised men of wealth and leisure who were drawn together by common intellectual interests. Augustine, for instance, was once member of a circle of amateur philosphers who met regularly to discuss the views of the neo-Platonists as transmitted into Latin by Marius Victorinus.[110] There were probably many more such groups in the cities of the empire in the fourth century when the relative tolerant atmosphere allowed them to combine their Christian beliefs with a genuine interest in pagan philosophy, alchemy and hermeticism. Participants of this *salon-culture* might have also practised asceticism for a variety of reasons, philosophical and theological. The Christian Sybillines might have come from such groups as well as collections of utterances which combined pagan oracles with Jewish and Christian prophecies.[111] Gnostic writings with their pseudo-philosophical air might have found some readers in such circles. A closed system like Manichaeism, however, which was based entirely on the apodictic utterances of its founder prophet and which did not lend itself to allegorical interpretation might have had less appeal.

To such an intellectual circle might have belonged a certain Aristocritus, the author of a work entitled *Theosophia*, who was condemned as a Manichaean in the abjuration text of <Zachrias Mitylene> and in Byzantine formulae. He apparently tried to demonstrate in his work that

Judaism, Paganism and Christianity and Manichaeism are one and the same doctrine, striving through it as far as he is able, [to do] nothing else than to make all men Manichaeans. For in this work he also makes Zarades a god, appearing, so he says, like Manichaeus among the Persians and he says that he is the sun and our Lord Jesus Christ. Although he gives the appearance of attacking Mani as evil in order to deceive and ensnare those who are trapped by the book of his 'Divine Madness and Folly' – a more suitable title for his work.[112]

It is hard to believe that any genuine Manichaean would go to the extent of attacking the person of Mani in order to disguise his Manichaean views. The *Theosophia* of Aristocritus has been suggested as the source of an extant collection of pagan and Jewish oracles and prophecies known to scholars as the *Theosophy of Tübingen*.[113] However, this work shows no clear Manichaean influence. It may be that because Aristocritus was a syncretist who tried to show that all religions are the same and, like the compiler of the *Theosophy of Tübingen*, he drew his inspiration from a variety of religious traditions, he was condemned as a Manichaean as the religion of Mani was generally regarded as syncretistic by its opponents.

A genuine syncretist like the famous alchemist of the early fourth century, Zosimus of Panopolis, who cited Hermes, Zoroaster and the Gnostic Nikotheos among his diverse authorities, seemed far from enthusiastic about the new prophet from Persia. In his short treatise on the letter Omega, he envisages an eschatological struggle that involves opposition from a mimic deity (ὁ ἀντίμιμος δαίμων), preceded by a forerunner from Persia telling fictitious and erroneous tales and leading men on about fate. His name, according to Zosimus who wanted to give his readers a brain-teaser, has nine letters if the diphthong in it is counted as two letters as in the word 'Fate' (εἱμαρμένη).[114] Mani's name in Greek, which has nine letters (Μανιχαῖος) and a diphthong (-αῖ), would have readily come to the minds of many fourth-century readers as a solution to the puzzle.[115]

(3)   SORCERY AND HERESY

Among the Romans, Persia had a reputation as the homeland of magic. It was from the Magians, i.e. the priests of Zoroastrianism, according to Origen, that the word 'magic' was originally derived.[116] Mani's cosmogony abounds in astrological details and he demonstrates in one of his extant discourses that he has a strong amateur interest in astrology.[117] It is logical therefore, that Manichaeism and magic were closely linked in popular thinking. Procopius would say in the same breath that Peter Barsymes, an important official under Justinian, was interested in 'sorcerers and evil spirits' and was 'strongly fascinated by the so-called Manichaeans'.[118] The quite numerous Manichaean astrological and magical texts would have certainly gone some way to satisfy his curiosity.

With its emphasis on astrology and with Persia as its native land, it is not surprising that Manichaeism was considered by Diocletian as a pernicious form of sorcery. He was convinced that its followers were sorcerers (maleficii), injuring the Roman people with the poisonous spells of their perverse laws and customs, and punished them as such.[119] The penalties he prescribed were in accordance with those normally meted out to sorcerers. Contemporary laws condemned magicians to death by burning. Sooth-sayers (haruspices) who operated privately rather than as part of the public sacrifices, were to be interdicted by fire and water (i.e. exile) if convicted, and their property would be confiscated.[120] The two forms of execution, beheading and burning, were to remain common to convictions for both sorcery and Manichaeism in the Byzantine empire.[121]

Two forms of magic were distinguished in pagan Rome. The more dangerous form was the use of spells as a form of poison to cause physical harm to one's opponents (veneficium), while the other was sooth-saying (haruspicina). Whereas the former had been prohibited since the time of the Republic, the latter became part of the pagan state-cult. The inability of the magister haruspicum to read the entrails of the sacrificed animal was one of the excuses which Diocletian and his colleagues used to launch the Great Persecution. The presence of Christians at the sacrifices was blamed for the unwillingness of the gods to disclose the future.[122]

Under the Christian emperors, the harmful use of magic continued to be proscribed but the consultation of oracles was at first preserved. Constantine forbade the holding of sacrifices at night in secret recesses.[123] His law was later repealed by the pagan usurper Magnentius whose reign lasted for a mere three years.[124] Christianity was itself once a secret religion but now that it was practised openly and was becoming a dominant social and religious force in the empire, it wanted all other religious observances to be brought into the open. The residual pockets of unquantifiable, and, in the popular imagination, often demonic forces must therefore be ferreted out.[125] The secretive nature of the Manichaean sect inevitably gave rise to accusations of obscene magical practices. The author of *P. Rylands Greek 469*, as we have noted, warned the faithful of his diocese that the Manichaeans took the menstrual blood of their *electae* for sacramental use.[126] We know from Roman magical papyri that menstrual blood was indeed used for magical purposes at that time.[127] However, the fact that Epiphanius later made an identical accusation against the Barbelognostics of Alexandria seems to imply that it was a fairly standard charge of immorality which the church authorities would hurl at more than one heretical sect.[128]

Constantine's immediate successors were men who, with the exception of Julian, lived in perpetual fear of usurpation and plots against their lives. The pages of Ammianus's history for the reigns of Constantius II and Valens (c. 320–70) are cluttered with instances of sorcery accusations.[129] The charges were mainly against individuals who consulted oracles and soothsayers.[130] Thus a person could be charged with treason for something as innocuous as trying to find out by means of divination the sex of his offspring before birth.[131] The accusation of sorcery was an easy one to make as it is a moot point whether a person consulted soothsayers for his own benefit or to another person's detriment. Since the emperors themselves most probably believed in the efficacy of the black arts they proscribed, they wanted no meddling with their own stars or life-lines.[132] Thus the unfortune Theodorus who discovered that the would-be successor of Emperor Valens had a name beginning with the letters Θ, E, O, Δ, had to pay dearly for his curiosity as every one thought that he was the destined candidate.[133] In due course Valens was succeeded by Theodosius whose name shared the same first four letters with that of Theodorus. Though the story is told with the hlep of hindsight, it nevertheless gives us some idea of how seriously the emperors felt themselves threatened by occultic or demonic forces in the fourth century.

The only surviving anti-Manichaean edict issued between the edict of Diocletian and the legistlations of Theodosius was clearly actuated more by fear of the harm such a secretive group of people could do to the moral welfare of the state than by intolerance of its heretical doctrines. Valentinian's edict of 372, the first law against the Manichaeans by a Christian emperor, was aimed at the Manichaean conventicle rather than at the tenets of the sect.[134] Both Valentinian and Gratian were noted for their toleration to heretics in general. According to Socrates, Gratian in 379 declared a general amnesty for all heretics with the exception of Eunomians, Photinians and Manichaeans. We learn from other legislations of the period that it was quite common for sorcerers to be excluded from Easter amnesties for heretics.[135]

Gratian's edict of toleration, which was issued while he was in Sirmium, did not, however, endear him to the church leaders. On his return journey to Trier he stopped at Milan and Ambrose, the bishop of that city, might have made clear to him the dangers of such an act of tolerance to the unity of the church. The outcome of his stay at Milan was a vaguely-worded rescript in which he formally abrogated his edict of toleration and declared that all heresies must forever cease and all persons should abstain from the meeting places of a doctrine already condemned.[136] This sudden about-turn from the policy of religious neutrality which he had inherited from his father and had hitherto scrupulously observed gives us some hint of the pressure which must have been brought to bear on the young emperor by the Bishop of Milan.

Meanwhile, the cause of orthodoxy in the empire received a great boost from the appointment in 379 of Theodosius as Augustus of the eastern empire. A pious, a almost fanatical Christian, he was brought up in the western provinces where Arianism was universally abhorred. He fell seriously ill in 380 while he was at Thessalonica and fearing that he was at death's door, he received baptism from the bishop of the city who was a follower of the faith of Nicaea.[137] After his recovery, he devoted himself to the extirpation of heresies from the empire. To this end he issued on 28 February 380 his famous edict 'Cunctos populos' which he addressed to the citizens of Constantinople from Thessalonica. In it he decreed that any Christian sect whose teaching did not conform to that of the Catholic church as defined by the pope and the bishop of Alexandria would be denied the right of assembly. Such demented and insane heretics would be punished by secular authorities, in addition to being smitten by divine vengeance.[138] After his triumphal entry into the new Rome on 24 November 380, he immediately handed over all the city's Arian churches to the Catholics.[139] On 10 January 381 he issued an edict which denied the heretics any place of celebrating their mysteries or any opportunity for exhibiting their demented obstinacy. All who did not accept the Nicene faith were forbidden to approach the thresholds of the churches, or to hold their illegal assemblies within the cities.[140]

The main target of the early anti-heretical legislations of Theodosius was of course the Arians. The turn of the Manichaeans came in the next year when they found themselves the object of a comprehensive edict issued on 8 May 381 which branded them with *infamia* and deprived them of their right of testation and of living

under Roman law. The property bequested by a Manichaean would be
confiscated by the imperial authorities.[141] The power of taking and of
bequeathing legacies, *testamenti factio*, was a fundamental right of
Roman citizens. In general only slaves, persons *alieni iuris* as long as
they were under paternal power, persons below the age of puberty,
lunatics, spendthrifts and women did not enjoy this right. Since the
time of Hadrian, women were permitted to make a testament with the
consent of their guardians.[142] The edict also states that its rule (*forma*)
should prevail not only for the future but also for the past. It goes on to
explain that while the force of imperial edicts normally applied to
matters about to follow and not to completed matters, the obstinacy
which the Manichaeans had shown in holding their illicit and profane
assemblies had compelled the emperors to make the severity of the
statute not so much as an example of a law to be established but as of a
law to be vindicated.[143] In other words, the edict was intended to be a
constitutional anomaly as it was an example of a retroactive law
which runs counter to the general character of Roman law and
contrary to a later statute of Theodosius (27 February 393) which
forbids any prosecution for past deeds and declares that all con-
situtions establish regulations for the future.[144] The Manichaeans
were further denied the right to plead that the lapse of time has
debarred legal action, a right which was defended by Constantine in a
fragmentary law on papyrus which rules that those who can prove
possession of property for forty years need no title to offset a suit for
recovery.[145] Finally the Manichaeans were also forbidden by the law of
381 to establish their 'sepulchres [*sepulcra*] of their funeral mysteries'
in towns and cities or to disguise their sects under the names of
ascetical groups.[146]

The same punishment of intestability had earlier, six days to be
exact, been inflicted on Christians who had become pagans.[147] In
the third of the legislations of Theodosius which touch upon
Manichaeism (21 May 383), those who 'crossed over' (*transisse*) to
'Judaean rites or Manichaean infamy' were condemned in the same
way and both types of apostates were denied the right to make an
elective will.[148] The Roman state, in meting out the same penalties to
those who became Manichaeans with those who apostasised to
Judaism and paganism, placed Manichaeism in a different category
from heresies within the main body of the church like Donatism and
Arianism. She acknowledged the fact that Manichaeans were not like
the gnostic heretics of the second century who infiltrated the
Christian communities and sought to destroy them from within.
Manichaeans formed an exclusive community and strove to convert
both pagan and Christian Romans to their religion. This made them
rivals and competitors of the church with respect to her own

missionary efforts in the fourth century. What the church feared most in a Christian becoming Manichaean was the possibility that entry into the sect involved the denial of Christ.[149] Mani was alleged in a Byzantine source to have said that he was more 'humane' than Christ to his followers who denied him before men. He would 'receive back with joy those who for the sake of their own safety lied to the officials and denied his faith'.[150] This would allow for repeated conversion to Manichaeism and hence repeated denials of Christ. Therefore someone who turned to Manichaeism was seen not only to have been defiled by a heresy but to have virtually become an apostate. The fact that Manichaeism was generally associated with magical acts and obscene rites might have also reinforced the non-Christian or pagan nature of the sect. The same feeling is expressed in one of the so-called Canons of Gregory of Nyssa which says that those who lapse without compulsion, so as to deny Christ, or become Jews, idolators, Manichaeans or infidels of any sort may not be admitted to communion till their hour of death.[151] In the mind of Theodosius, Christianity and citizenship were coterminous and anyone who denied Christ automatically made himself an outlaw of the Christian Roman society.

An even more sternly worded edict against the Manichaeans was issued by Theodosius (31 March 382) in which the recipient, Florus, the praetorian prefect, was told to establish special courts for the trial of Manichaeans and receive informers (*indices*) and denouncers (*denuntiatores*) without the odium of delation.[152] It was a well-held principle of Roman Law that frivolous or baseless accusations put forward by anonymous *indices* should be discouraged and all accusation should be conducted by formal delation in which an unsuccessful delator was liable to an action for *calumnia*.[153] Constantine laid down in a law of 313 certain regulations concerning informers and threatened those who broke them with the death penalty and this was reaffirmed by a later law of 319 (?).[154] Sycophancy was detested by all under the High Empire, especially if the intention of the informer was to obtain a part of the confiscated property of the accused for reward after a successful prosecution.[155] No wonder that one of the salutations with which the late Roman senate greeted the emperors was 'suppressors of informers, suppressors of chicanery! (repeated twenty-eight times)'.[156] However, Constantine himself made an exception of his own ruling by decreeing in 319 that denouncers of soothsayers (*haruspices*) would not incur the odium of delation but would be considered for reward.[157] Hence Theodosius's edict of 382 was not unprecedented in its provision for encouraging citizens to inform on those suspected of malpractices in secret places. The provision also highlights the most intractable problem which the

Roman government faced in her campaign against the Manichaeans, namely, the lack of reliable information on the identity of their leaders and the whereabouts of their meeting places and safe houses.

Gratian fell victim to usurpation in 383 and was replaced as Augustus of the western empire by Magnus Maximus, an officer of Spanish birth who was elevated to the purple by his troops. He held his court at Trier – 'Trevericus imperator' as he was called by Gregory of Tour,[158] and it was there in the summer of 386, that Priscillian, the leading figure of an ascetical movement in Spain, was tried and put to death with a number of followers on the charges of Manichaeism and sorcery.[159] After the event, Maximus wrote to Pope Siricius justifying his action by his avowed desire to see the Catholic faith continue steadfastly unimpaired and inviolable through the removal of dissension and heresies. He referred to the victims as 'Manichaeans' who had admitted during the trial to having committed crimes which would cause him enormous embarrassment to report in detail to His Holiness.[160] The charge that the movement of Priscillian was indelibily linked to Manichaeism was accepted by most contemporary writers. Filastrius concluded his section on Manichaeism in his handbook on heresies with the remark that the sect had many followers in Spain and Gaul, referring no doubt to the Priscillianists.[161] Similarly Augustine, who came to know of the movement through Orosius, an ardent campaigner against the sect, described Priscillianism as a mixture of gnosticism and Manichaeism.[162]

The discovery in 1885 of genuine writings by Priscillian himself or by one of his closest followers in a codex in the Würzburg Cathedral which might have once belonged to St Bilihild, the abbess of Altmunster at Mainz, has cast serious doubts on the validity of the charge that Priscillian was a Manichaean or a crypto-Manichaean.[163] He was uncompromisingly ascetic in his teaching and his belief in the soul as of *divinum genus* seems to imply acceptance of a distinction between flesh and body.[164] However his asceticism and his dualism were not based on the writings of Mani but on his own eccentric interpretation of the Bible and his avid reading of apocryphal Christian literature. His opponents listed among the apocryphal writings held sacred by the sect the *Acts of Thomas, The Acts of Andrew, The Acts of John, The Acts of Paul, The Acts of Peter* and the *Memoria Apostolorum*.[165] Priscillian held that the enlightened believer who has attained the plenitude of grace could legitimately and beneficially use these apocryphal writings as his spiritual gifts would allow him to distinguish what in them was erroneous or heretical.[166] The Manichaeans shared Priscillian's regard for the apocryphal Christian literature. They held the Acts of Peter, Paul, John, Thomas and

Andrew as an additional canon as they lent support to their ideas of celibacy.[167]

The charge that Priscillian was a Manichaean was first publicly made against him and his followers by their opponent Hydatius, bishop of Merida and Metropolitan of Lusitania who obtained a rescript from the Emperor Gratian condemning in general terms 'pseudo-episcopos et Manichaeos'.[168] Priscillian and his followers were forced into exile and he composed an apologetic work addressed to his fellow bishops in which he repudiates every kind of heresy and especially Manichaeism. 'Let him be anathema who does not denounce Mani and his works and his doctrines and his principles. Let us persecute categorically their abominations with the sword and let us send them to the Lower Regions or that which is worse than hell and ever wakeful torment where "the fire does not die out nor the worm perish" '.[169] He also anathematises those who offer cultic acts to demons with strange names like Saclas, Nebroel, Samael, Belzebuth, Nashbodeus, Belial, etc.[170] The male and female demons, Saclas and Nebroel, as we recall, were responsible in the Manichaean myth for the creation of Adam and Eve.[171] In another tractate which is an appeal to Pope Damasus, the author condemns Manichaeans not only as heretics but also as sorcerers and idolators who are slaves to the invincible sun and moon.[172] Although Priscillian was rebuffed by Ambrose and the Pope Damasus, he managed to secure a repeal of the rescript by greasing the palm of Gratian's *magister officiorum* and the charges against him were dropped for the time being.[173]

Priscillian's opponents were able to exploit the accession of Maximus to their full advantage. By playing on his desire to conciliate himself to the Gallic bishops and the papacy as a champion of orthodoxy as well as his need for income from confiscations to pay his troops, they renewed their charge of heresy against Priscillian.[174] The latter, along with a number of supporters, were duly summoned to Trier. Under torture Priscillian himself confessed that he had studied obscene doctrines, had held conventicles of depraved women by night and had been accustomed to pray naked.[175] This was readily construed by his inquisitors as his devotion to Manichaeism and sorcery (*maleficium*) – a capital offence. Priscillian evidently had a genuine interest in astrology. In a fragment of his works preserved by Orosius he asserts that human souls and bodies are subject to the influence of the stars. Orosius goes on in his resumé of Priscillian's teaching to say that he believes that the twelve signs of the zodiac correspond to the various parts of the body and of the soul and are connected with the names of the twelve patriarchs.[176] The assigning of the body to the zodiac was in accordance with the astrological practice of the late antiquity and it was also used by Mani in one of his *Kephalaia*.[177] To the authorities the charges of Manichaeism and sorcery went hand in hand and Priscillian's passionate disavowal of Manichaeism was nullified by his interest in magic. Some of his extreme ascetical practices might have also been seen by his opponents as bordering on Manichaeism or the occult. The contemporary anti-Manichaean laws could therefore be easily brought to bear on the Priscillianists since they were directed not so much against Manichaeism as a heresy but against the Manichaean conventicle as a venue of obscene and immoral practices under the guise of asceticism. Priscillianism, which had a number of features in common with Manichaeism as popularly conceived, thus became one of the first main victims of the anti-Manichaean legislation even though neither side in the controversy could demonstrate any real knowledge of Manichaeism, and what Priscillian knew he anathematised.

CHAPTER V

'INGENS FABULA ET LONGUM MENDACIUM' –AUGUSTINE AND MANICHAEISM

And so I fell among men who were arrogant in their madness, exceedingly carnal and loquacious; on whose lips were the snares of the Devil which were smeared with a birdlime compunded out of a mixture of the syllables of Your name and of the Lord Jesus Christ and of the Holy Spirit our Paraclete of Comforter. These names were forever on their lips, in as much as they were the rattling noise of the tongue as their hearts were devoid of any truth whatsoever. They kept on saying 'Truth, Truth'; and they bombarded me incessantly with these words, yet Truth was never in them but falsehood which they uttered not only about You who are the real Truth but also about the elements of this world which was Your creation.[1]

This insalubrious and well known introduction to the Manichaeans in the *Confessions* does not of course reflect Augustine's actual impression of the sect when he became a Hearer at the age of nineteen. Born in Thagaste (Souk-Ahras, Alegeria) in 354, the most celebrated convert (and later apostate) of Manichaeism was in the last year of his university course at Carthage when he was drawn to the teaching of Mani by a quest for philosophical truth. The story of his involvement with the sect has been the subject of many fine biographies and need not be retold here. However, in his writings, Augustine offers his readers a number of reasons for joining the sect which are of considerable interest to historians of Manichaeism. His writings are also by far the most important source of information on the history of the sect in the western empire during his lifetime. Although the material which Augustine provides is of a highly personal nature, the reasons he gives for joining the sect are sometimes echoed in the anti-Manichaean writings of earlier polemicists like Alexander of Lycopolis, Titus of Bostra, Ephraim and Epiphanius. An examination of some of them will throw much light on the missionary tactics and techniques of the Manichaeans as well as the underlying causes for the extraordinarily wide diffusion of the sect in the later Roman empire.

(1)   THE CRITICAL APPEAL OF MANICHAEISM

Prior to his conversion to Manichaeism, the young Augustine, like many of his university friends, had his eye on a legal or adminsitrative career. His reading of Cicero's *Hortensius*, a work which is now lost to us, turned his mind from worldly achievements which he had now come to see as transient and ephemeral to a quest for true wisdom. Being only moderately competent in the language of Plato and Aristotle, Augustine's search for wisdom among the great philosophical writings of the past was strictly circumscribed. Furthermore, his upbringing in the hands of a devoutly Christian mother also conditioned him to seek a form of philosophy which was not entirely pagan in origin and outlook nor irreconcilable with Christianity. He turned first to the Christian scriptures for inspiration. But, like Jerome, he found the bland and uncouth style of the pre-Vulgate Latin versions of the Bible unworthy of comparison to the eloquent pages of Cicero and Quintililan.[3] Given the sophisticated nature of Augustine's quest for wisdom it may strike us as odd that he should have succumbed to what he would eventually denounce as nothing more than a 'great fable and a long lie (*ingens fabula et longum mendacium*)'.[4] For nine years he would accept such fabulous teachings of the sect as figs which wept when plucked, but from which a Manichaean Elect could release angels and even little bits of God as he groaned and belched in his prayer after his meal.[5]

Augustine did not suspend his critical faculties when he became a Manichaean Hearer. Looking back on it some twenty years later he would tell his friend Honoratus whom he had converted to Manichaeism and who had remained a Manichaean, that what attracted him most was the Manichaean claim to subject faith to the critique of pure reason. 'What else induced me for nearly nine years to reject the religion which had been instilled in me by my parents and to follow these men and to be a diligent Hearer than their claim that we have put faith before reason; whereas they themselves commanded no one to believe until the truth has first been discussed and then explained?'[6] The religion of his mother Monica appeared as little more than superstition reinforced by parental authority when exposed to the apparent critical light of Manichaeism. 'A childish supersitition', as he explains to another friend, Theodorus, 'has prevented me from a searching investigation ... and as soon as I was more resolute, I discarded the darkness and satisfied myself more with men that taught than in those who demanded obedience, having myself encountered persons (i.e. Manichaeans) to whom the very light, seen by their eyes, apparently was an object of the highest and even divine veneration.'[7]

Augustine was not the only philosophically minded person to fall for the pseudo-intellectualism of the Manichaeans. Alexander of Lycopolis, an Egyptian neo-Platonist and the author of a refutation of Manichaeism, was amazed that some of his fellow philosophers should have fallen for a system which could not withstand any serious philosophical investigation and which relied on the apodictic utterances of its founder to substantiate the literal truth of its outrageous myths. A full exposé of Mani's cosmogonic myth, Alexander believes, would clearly demonstrate its manifold short-comings and inconsistencies.[8] However, a straightforward presentation of the myth was probably not what the Manichaean missionaries would have used as an opening gambit when addressing a sophisticated and educated audience. The Manichaeans were more likely to begin by directing their arguments at the imperfections of the other religions (although they contained kernels of religious truth which would find their complete fulfillment in the gnosis of Mani). The Manichaean missionaries in the Roman empire were noted for their zeal as door-to-door Gospel-peddlers and skilled debaters. This featured in their own hagiography. Adda, the first important Manichaean missionary to the Roman empire was commemorated by the historians of the sect for his skills in making wisdom his weapon' and for his success in putting other 'dogmas' (Per.: qyš'n) under subjection.[9] It was not surprising therefore that the author of the polemical Acta Archelai should have chosen a public disputation in which Mani himself was humbled by a Christian bishop as his main theme. The same critical acumen, however, was not applied by the sect to Mani's own revelation as the acceptance of its verity was by special knowledge and insight. 'They were more clever and quick witted', as Augustine points out to Honoratus, 'in refuting others than firm and sure in proof of what is their own ... They argued at great length and extensively and vigorously against the errors of the simple people, which I have since learned to be a easy task for someone moderately educated. If on the other hand they were to teach us anything, we necessarily retained it, judging that we have so far come across nothing in which we were compelled to acquiesce.'[10]

Faustus of Milevis (now Mila) in Numidia, the outstanding Manichaean teacher when Augustine was a Hearer, epitomised the combative and critical spirit of the Manichaeans. A convert from paganism, he came from a poor family and his high social standing later in life shows the opportunities for advancement which the sect could offer to men of talent and ambition. His reputation extended well beyond North Africa, as he was equally well known to the Manichaeans in Rome. It appears that he was regularly invited by this or that Manichaean community to give courses of evangelistic addresses or conduct open debates. He had a penchant for large crowds and sharp questions and was also adept in dealing with doubting Thomases within the sect like Augustine. His long-awaited visit to Carthage in 383 was held out to Augustine as 'a gift from heaven' as he would most certainly be able to solve all the problems which were unsettling him.[11]

Besides Augustine's recollections of him in his *Confessions*, we are fortunate in possessing substantial extracts of a work which he wrote in defence of Manichaeism which later became the subject of a lengthy refutation by Augustine.[12] In these extracts we are brought starkly face to face with his aggressive method of disputation. Some of his arguments might have been standard ammunition for Manichaean missionaries and Augustine himself might have argued along similar lines when he was chalking up victories as a champion debator for the Manichaeans. The debates in which Faustus excelled were not inter-faith dialogues where Christians and Manichaeans would exchange their views on major theological issues. Since the contents of Manichaean canonical scriptures were known probably only to the Elect, to cite them in debates before an audience which was unfamiliar with them would have cut very little ice. However, as Mani styled himself the apostle of Jesus Christ and his gospel embraced the teaching of Christ as correctly understood and purged of superstitions, the champions of Manichaeism therefore could take the battle to the Christians and base their arguments solely on Christian scriptures. Not a single citation from a Manichaean source can be found in the extant fragments of Faustus's 'Apologia'. The same reluctance to use Manichaean scriptures in debates was shown by Fortunatus, a local Manichaean agent in Carthage who disputed in public with Augustine in 392. They featured in Augustine's debate with the Manichaean *doctor* Felix in 404 largely because Felix wanted to prove that his confiscated Manichaean tomes contained no error and Augustine should return them to him.[13] Faustus's defence of Manichaeism, as far as the fragments show, was conducted in the form of an attack on the misue of the Christian scriptures by the Catholics. The inherent weaknesses of Mani's teaching, so often exposed by Christian polemicists, received no reply from Faustus whose only concern in the 'Apologia' was to show that the Catholics were semi-Christians because they were completely uncritical in their use of the Bible and had signally failed to separate the truth of Christ from the superstition of the Jews and the lies which the church had perpetuated about Christ. In short, if the Christian scriptures were properly interpreted and purged of fraudulent interpolations, they would be found to be in harmony with the message of Mani.

The acceptance of the Jewish scriptures as the Old Covenant by the Christians afforded the Manichaeans – and especially Faustus – with an obvious target. The Manichaeans saw themselves as Christians of the New Convenant only and saw no relevance in much of the Jewish scriptures. To them the two Testaments were mutually contradictory and by retaining the Old, the Catholics had ignored the warning of Christ and had put 'a piece of new cloth onto an old garment'. In doing so they had returned the Church to the bondage of circumcision.[14] In his attack on the Catholic retention of the Old Testament, Faustus saw himself as the inheritor of the mantle of the Manichaean apostle Adimantus (i.e. Adda) whom he considered to be the greatest teacher of the Manichaean church after Mani.[15] As we have seen, Adda/Adimantus was a skilled debater and the author of a work against the Old Testament which was based on the *Antitheses* of Marcion.

Many of the Manichaean objections to the retention of the Old Testament had a familiar ring about them; they were not the first nor will they be the last to make them. The lives of the Old Testament patriarchs and some of the prophets, especially their sexual mores, were seen as flagrant violation of the moral precepts of the New. Abraham not only consorted with a mistress, he even gave his wife for the gratification of foreign kings. Lot committed incest and Isaac followed Abraham's example in calling his wife his sister so that he might gain a shameful livelihood through her. David coveted the wife of one of his generals and Solomon was polygamous. Hosea married a prostitute at the command of God, and Moses was a murderer.[16] The list is endless and the only conclusion one could draw from it, says Faustus, was that these stories were false or that the patriarchs had really sinned and the crime in either case was equally detestable. He would therefore like to leave to the Jews their own property and content himself with the 'bright inheritance of the kingdom of heaven'.[17]

The Catholics would argue that the Old Testament had to be retained because the Mosaic laws were fundamental to the moral precepts of a Christian society. Furthermore, since the Old Testament was seen to have prophesied the coming of Christ, it was needed as proof of his divinity and Christ himself had forbidden his disciples to reject the law and prophets when he claimed not to have come to destroy but to fulfill them (Matt. 5:17). In his reply Faustus could point with ample justification to the Catholics's own ambivalent attitude towards the Mosaic laws and their very selective use of the prophecies:

Why then since you believe the Old Testament, do you not believe all that is found in any part of it? For you only excerpt from it the prophecies which point to the future coming of a king of the Jews because you think he is Jesus, together with a few other precepts of common civility such as Thou shalt not kill, Thou shalt not commit adultery; and all the rest you pass over and consider it to be what Paul thought as 'dung' (cf. Philem. 3:8).[18]

Faustus did not hesitate to point out to the Catholics that they had undermined their own defence of the Old Testament in their disregard of its more distinctively Jewish precepts:

> I reject circumcision as disgraceful and if I mistake not, so do you; I reject the Rest of the Sabbath as superfluous, and I believe you do the same. I reject sacrifices as idolatory, and I am in no doubt that you do the same. I do not only abstain from pork and pork is not the only flesh you consume. I regard all flesh as unclean. In both cases, the Old Testament has been overthrown by both of us.[19]

Faustus's criticism of the Old Testament did not, however, go back as far as Enoch and Seth. To these righteous men who had received special commandments delivered by angels of the highest rank may be attributed the only laws worthy of observance, and the general moral decline only set in after Abraham. The exemptions were necessary as Seth featured prominently in gnostic writings as the recipient of unique revelations and both Enoch and Seth were regarded by Mani as part of a chain of revealers which finally terminated with him.[20] As we have seen, his *Book of the Giants* was closely modelled on a similar work in the Enochic literature which had grown up in the inter-Testamental period.[21]

As for the argument that the Old Testament must be kept because it foretold the coming of Christ, Faustus replied that he could find no such prophecies in the Old Testament and it was assuredly the sign of a week faith which required proofs and testimonies.[22] In any case, how could these so-called prophecies be of relevance to those 'Gentile Christians' like himself who had been converted from paganism and had not been brought up under Judaism and whose first religious teachers were pagan poets? Would it not be fairer if the utterances of the Sibyl or the Hermetic Corpus should also have foretold the coming of Christ?[23] Furthermore, some of the sayings of the Old Testament, far from being prophecies about Christ, could only be seen as curses or maledictions against him. For instance, 'Cursed is everyone that hangeth on a tree'. (Deut. 21:23). If the verse did refer to Christ – and Paul himself thought it did (Gal. 3:20) – then Moses who uttered the curse must have either been a sinner or not divinely inspired. Moses had also said that everyone who raiseth not a seed in Israel is cursed (Deut. 25:5–10) and could this not be construed as a curse against Christ who did not have any offspring?[24]

Christ's claim that he came not to destroy the law but to fulfil it (Matt. 5:17) was seen by many as the surest defence of the authority of the Old Testament. Faustus, however, was not one to be deterred by it even if he could not dismiss it on moral grounds. The authenticity of the claim, he believed, could be undermined by source criticism. The *logion* is part of the Sermon on the Mount in the Gospel of Matthew but why was it not recorded by the other evangelists, especially when Matthew was not a witness to the discourse since he was converted only after the sermon had been delivered?[25]

It is not without reason that we never give ear to the scriptures without critical judgement since there are such discrepancies and contradictions, but, by examining everything and comparing one passage with another, we note carefully what could or could not have been said by Christ. For your predecessors have made many interpolations in the words of our Lord, which now appear under His name though they disagree with His doctrine. Furthermore, it has frequently enough been proved by us that these writings are not by Him or His disciples, but were compiled long after their departure out of rumours and conjectures by some unknown Semi-Jews who could not agree among themselves and all were published by them under the names of the Apostles of the Lord or of those who were considered the followers of the Apostles so that they could deceitfully claim that the Apostles had written these errors and lies themselves.[26]

If the gospel generally attributed to Matthew was indeed the work of Matthew, why then did he not use the first person when he described his own conversion (9:19)? Thus, the authenticity of Christ's claim that he came to fulfil rather than to destroy the law and prophets can be refuted on two counts: Matthew was not a personal witness when Christ actually said it and secondly he was not the author of the gospel which bears his name because he did not describe himself in the first person.[27]

Faustus's method of criticism as illustrated above may seem like academic sleight of hand. Yet his passionate rejection of the Old Testament as essential to a 'true' Christian faith would have found him some admirers among those pagans who regarded the Old Testament as a major obstacle to their conversion to Christianity. Among Augustine's friends who were converted to Manichaeism whom we know by name, Nebridius and Honoratus both joined the sect directly from paganism and there were probably many like them who preferred a purified form of Christianity as preached by Manichaeans like Faustus to Catholic Christianity, which they were persuaded to regard as a Jewish error.[28] If Christ's claim was indeed genuine, Faustus argued, then one would need to become a Jew first before one could become a Christian, just as a vessel in order to be filled full must not be empty, but partly filled already. For someone who had not been prepared for the reception of Christianity through the observation of the Sabbath, circumcision, sacrifices, food taboos, baptism, the feast of the unleavened bread etc., would the intimations of Christ's coming in the Sibylline books and the pagan poets (e.g. Virgil's *Eclogae* 1, 6) not be more relevant than the so-called prophecies in the Old Testament?[29] What Faustus and those pagans who shared his position might not have realised was that the Sibylline books dealing with the character of the Messiah and his coming (i.e. Books 6 and 8) were in fact Christian forgeries.[30] In winning pagans to its ranks, Manichaeism takes its place among the various Christian sects of the fourth century which all played a part in the eventual eradication of paganism from the empire. The general openness of the pagans to conversion to some form of Christianity at a time of inexorable religious change was undoubtedly a major factor in the missionary success of Manichaeism. Mark the Deacon (ordained *c.* 397), close companion and biographer of Porphyry, Bishop of Gaza, who has given us an account of a visit by a *Manichaea* Julia to Gaza (*c.* 401–2) in the *vita*, confirms the view that Manichaeism had a special appeal to those recently converted from paganism as those of his flock whom he felt to have been most at risk were the neophytes who were not yet strong in their Christian faith.[31]

The Manichaeans were also eager to stress their tenuous links with pagan myths and philosophical systems. Since the pagans did not have an absolute view of truth like the Christians, the Manichaeans could afford to draw analogies between their teaching on cosmogony and Graeco-Roman mythology without the fear of compromising the uniqueness of Mani's revelation. 'For they say about Hermes in Egypt', says Ephraim, 'and about Plato among the Greeks, and about Jesus who appeared in Judaea, that 'they are Heralds of that Good One to the world'. The Manichaeans borrowed freely from Greek philosophical vocabulary in their translation of Manichaean writings and a Greek neo-Platonist took exception to their use of the word $\H{\upsilon}\lambda\eta$ to designate the Evil Principle, for they used it neither in the Platonic sense of 'all receiving' (*Timaeus* 51a7), 'mother' (*ibid.* 50d3) and 'nurse' (*ibid.* 49a6), namely that which becomes everything when it has received quality and shape, nor in the Aristotelian sense as the element in relation to which form and privation occur. (*Physica* 190b17–191a22 etc.), but as $\H{\alpha}\tau\alpha\kappa\tau\sigma\varsigma$ $\kappa\acute{\iota}\nu\eta\sigma\iota\varsigma$ ('random motion').[33] Alexander then goes on to demonstrate that 'random motion' was an absurd concept for no motion or change was entirely random. Moreover, the term as used by Plato (*Tim.* 30b) indicates the primordial state of chaos which existed before the creation of matter. It was therefore ridiculous to assert that this 'random motion' could invade the Realm of Light. Furthermore, since matter itself could not produce any motion, it could not elevate itself to the upper regions to invade the Realm of Light save by the collusion of God himself, which appeared to Alexander to be nonsensical.[34] However, Plutarch had in the second century AD used the same phrase in his essay on Egyptian myths (*De Iside et Osiride*) to describe the kind of cosmic chaos which was the cause of human suffering.[35] The Manichaeans, though they might have borrowed the phrase from Plato, were probably not using it in a narrowly Platonic sense but as a general designation of an active cause of evil in the world which has a philosophical ring about it.[36]

We also learn from Alexander that those Manichaeans who were schooled in Greek literature reminded the pagans of their own mythological tradition. They compared the dismemberment of Dionysius by the Titans to the dividing up of the divine power into matter. They also alluded to the battle of the giants as told in Greek poetry to prove that the Greeks were not altogether ignorant of aspects of the Manichaean cosmogonic myth.[37] However, for a pagan intellectual like Alexander of Lycopolis the eagerness of the Manichaeans to draw analogies with Greek mythology only showed that their own myths were in the same vein as those which spoke of the castration of Uranus or the scheming against Kronos by his sons. Whereas the Greek mythographers intended their tales to be understood allegorically, the Manichaeans took their account of a war between matter and God as nothing other than an actual event.[38]

To show that there was no real similarity between the teaching of Mani and that of Hermes Trismegistos, the reputed author of sundry philosophical, religious, astrological and alchemical texts from the Roman period known to scholars as the *Hermetica*, Ephraim made superficial comparison between the two:

For Hermes taught that there was a Bowl [Syr.: '*gn*'], filled with whatever it was filled with, and that there are Souls excited by desire, and they come down beside it, and, when they have come close to it, in it and by reason of it they forget their own place. Now Mani teaches that the Darkness made an assault on Light and desired it, while Hermes teaches that the Souls desired the Bowl; and this is a little more probable, even though both are lying, . . .[39]

One of the Hermetic discourses in a collection known as the Poimandres is indeed devoted to the doctrine of the Bowl (κρατήρ). God, according to Hermes, had imparted the faculty of speech to all mankind when man was first created but he did not give them all Mind (νοῦς). Instead he filled a great bowl with Mind and sent it down to earth and dispatched a herald to go before it with the command to proclaim these words to men: 'Plunge yourself into this bowl if you can, you who believe that you shall ascend to him who sent the bowl down and you who recognise for what purpose you have been created.' Those who paid heed to the proclamation and received this baptism of the intellect partook in a special knowledge (*gnosis*) and became perfect men. Those who did not follow the command became *logikoi* because they had not acquired this additional intellect and were therefore ignorant of the purpose for which they were made nor who made them.[40] Ephraim's choice of this example from the Hermetic corpus might not have been made at random. One does not associate Ephraim with a detailed knowledge of such pagan works. It is quite possible that the analogy was drawn by the Manichaeans, or even by Mani himself, to show that the desire which Darkness conceived for Light was similar to the desire of the souls for the Bowl in the teaching of Hermes. It is worth pointing out that the Hermetic teaching on the Bowl was known to the alchemist Zosimus of Panopolis who shared Mani's admiration of the gnostic teacher Nikotheos.[41]

Augustine grew up at a time when the fortunes of paganism were distinctly on the wane. Although the last ditch battles like Symmachus's famous defence of the Altar of Victory against its removal by Theodosius I were yet to be fought, we can nevertheless discern from the writings of the Emperor Julian and Libanius that the decline was verging on the irreversible.[42] Athens was fast becoming the only important centre of pagan learning in the empire but the findings of her neo-Platonic schools built on a solid tradition of Greek philosophy would have been inaccessible to someone like Augustine who was primarily a Latin speaker. As society itself was becoming Christian at every level it was unthinkable for Augustine who had come from a Christian background to opt for a purely pagan form of wisdom. Manichaeism which, by the time of Augustine, had become actively anti-pagan and anti-Jewish, would not have been seen by Augustine as an exotic oriental cult like Mithraism but a higher and purer form of Christianity. The name of Christ was not only omnipresent on the lips of the Manichaeans, their Christ was also the personification of the Mind, who was not a degraded, suffering saviour but a gnostic redeemer who imparted special wisdom to those who had been initiated into the faith.

The Jesus of the Manichaeans differed considerably in his soteriological role from the Jesus of Catholic Christianity. Jesus in Manichaeism possessed three separate identities: (1) Jesus of Light, (2) Jesus the Messiah and (3) Jesus *patibilis*. The three conceptions were not always kept distinct by the Manichaeans in controversies, although they were clearly discernible in the genuine writings of the sect.[43] The Jesus of Light, as we have seen, was the guardian angel of Mani and the Syzygos was one of his emanations. His primary role was as supreme revealer and guide and it was he who woke Adam from his slumber and revealed to him the divine origins of his soul and its painful captivity by the body and mixture with matter.[44] Jesus the Messiah was a historical being who was the prophet of the Jews and the forerunner of Mani. However, the Manichaeans believed that he was wholly divine. He never experienced human birth as the notions of physical conception and birth filled the Manichaeans with horror and the Christian doctrine of virgin birth was regarded as equally obscene. Since he was the light of the world, where was this light, they asked, when he was in the womb of the Virgin?[45] Jesus the Messiash was truly born at his baptism as it was on that occasion that the Father openly acknowledged his sonship. The suffering, death and resurrection of this Jesus were in appearance only as they had no salvific value but were an *exemplum* of the suffering and eventual deliverance of the human soul and a prefiguration of Mani's own martyrdom. The pain suffered by the imprisoned Light Particles in the whole of the visible universe, on the other hand, was real and immanent. This was symbolised by the 'mystic placing of the Cross whereby the wounds of the passion of our souls are set forth'.[46] On this mystical Cross of Light was suspended the Suffering Jesus (*Jesus patibilis*), who was 'the life and slavation of Man'.[47] This *mystica cruxificio* was present in every tree, herb, fruit, vegetable and even stones and the soil.[48] This constant and universal suffering of the captive soul is exquisitely expressed in one of the Coptic Manichaean psalms:

> The strangers with whom I mixed, me they know not;
> they tasted my sweetness, they desired to keep me with them.
> I am life to them, but they were death to me;
> I bore up beneath them, they wore me as a garment upon them.
> I am in everything, I bear the skies, I am the foundation,
> I support the earths, I am the Light that sines forth,
> that gives joy to souls.
> I am the life of the world: I am the milk that is in all trees:
> I am the sweet water that is beneath the sons of Matter.[49]

Augustine did not fail to distinguish the Jesus of the Catholic Christians from that of the Manichaeans merely because he was drawn to the sect by its frequent use of the name of Christ. In one of his later polemical works, he gives us a very precise definition of the triple usage of the name of Christ by the Manichaeans:

Again, tell us how many Christs you say there are. Is there one whom you call the suffering one whom the earth conceives and brings forth by the power of the Holy Spirit, and another crucified by the Jews under Pontius Pilate, and a third who is divided between the sun and the moon?[50]

One may assume that Augustine fully accepted the Manichaean view of Jesus when he became a Hearer and it was the Catholics, he believed who had failed to arrive at a correct understanding of the nature and role of Christ through their uncritical use of the scriptures. He might have even gone as far as some extreme Manichaeans who asserted that the Jesus of the Christians who suffered death on the cross was in fact Satan. In a fragment of Mani's *Epistula fundamenti*, preserved only by Evodius, Mani is alleged to have said that the Enemy (i.e. Satan) who hoped to have crucified that same Redeemer, the Father of Righteousness, was himself crucified; for at that time, appearance and reality were distinct.[51] Augustine's mother, Monica, was certainly not deceived by the Christian elements of her son's new found religion into thinking that he had returned from his studies at Carthage an ardent Christian. She was so horrified by the change that had come over him that for the first and only time in her life she forbade him to live under the same roof as her. She changed her mind only after she had received a special vision and had visited an aged bishop who comforted her with the famous words that 'it is impossible for the son of such tears to be lost'.[52]

The extreme docetic Christological position of the Manichaeans was, as one would expect, a major bone of contention between their leaders and Catholic theologians. The Manichaeans were out on a limb with regard to the other Christian sects in the Christological debates of the fourth century. Not even the most determined enemies of Arius would assert that Christ was an emanation of the Father and that he was never truly born of the Virgin as did the Manichaeans, who maintained a clear distinction between the son of Mary and Jesus the Messiah.[53] To substantiate this extreme view in a theological debate by arguing only from Christian scriptures might seem to have been an impossible task but Faustus was not one to be overawed. His defence of the Manichaean position in the '*Apologia*' was conducted with considerable rhetorical skill, although the enormity of the task did stretch the power of dialectics of this self-educated grammarian to its extreme limit of endurance. Frequently he had to resort to the use of syllogisms to put his opponent into positions in which not to agree with him would mean giving consent to worse error.

'Do you believe that Jesus was born of Mary?', his opponents would ask. Faustus's immediate response was to which Jesus (or Joshua) was his opponent referring since there were several persons with that name in the Bible – an opening gambit which might unsettle some of the opposition since not every one would have been aware that the name of Jesus (i.e. Joshua) was not unique in the scriptures (*cf.* Exodus 23:11, Haggai 1:1 etc.). If the answer was Jesus the Son of God (Mark 1:1), Faustus would ask on what authority did he claim that the Son of God was born of Mary. The reply would most likley to have been 'the Gospel of Matthew' which would give Faustus the opportunity to show off his skills as a Biblical critic. Firstly, the genealogy of Jesus at the beginning of the Gospel is entitled 'The Book of the generations of Jesus Christ, the son of David etc.', and no mention is made in it to his being the Son of God. In fact Matthew only designated Jesus as the Son of God at his baptism, and, if taken literally, his witness contradicted the Catholic creed which said that Jesus the Son of God was born of the Virgin Mary. The attack could be taken one stage further. Jesus could only have been the son of David if he had been begotten by Joseph who carried the seed of David. Since, according to the creed, Jesus was born of a virgin, he could not have been the son of David, and still less the Son of God.[54] Though he clamoured against interpolations and false accretions in the scriptures, Faustus was not averse to borrowing material from apocryphal gospels when it suited his argument to do so. Was it not generally known that Mary's father was Joachim who was a priest and therefore of the tribe of Levi? Why was he not included in Matthew's genealogy unless the inclusion of a Levi would invalidate the claim that Jesus was of the house of Judah?[55] The parentage of Mary is known to us only in the apocryphal gospels and especially the *Protevangelium of James* from which the later and more popular *Evangelium de nativitate Mariae* derived most of its material. Extant versions of these apocryphal works give Joachim and Anna as Mary's parents but nowhere do we find any mention of Joachim being a priest and therefore a member of the tribe of Levi. Faustus might have inferred this from the fact that Elizabeth, Mary's kinswoman, was the wife of a priest (Luke 1:5 and 36). In short, Jesus, the Son of God, could not have been born of Mary because Matthew did not say so in these exact words nor was he of the house of David because the Virgin Birth would have prevented him from carrying the seed of Joseph, and Mary herself was not of the house of David because her father was a Levite.[56]

Although the Manichaeans believed that Jesus the Messiah was not born in a human fashion, they did believe that he died even if his death was in similitude. To prove this Faustus drew attention to the view commonly held by both Jews and Christians that Elijah did not die. Both views – that Jesus could die without having been born and that Elijah, though he was born did not die – run counter to the laws of nature. The first belief seemed to be more plausible since more power was vested in Jesus than in Elijah and this could be demonstrated by the number and the nature of the miracles he performed.[57] 'According to our belief', he says 'it is no more true that Jesus died (although he was not born) than that Elijah was immortal.'[58] Faustus was at his best in verbal fencing when he could turn a charge back against the challenger. 'Believe me', he retorted at the person who tried to argue that if Jesus had suffered, He must have been born, 'it is not advantageous for you to inquire into the natural consequences of these things, or else your own faith will be at risk.'[59] Since the Christians believed that Jesus could be born without being begotten, why could

He not also suffer without being born? If the Christians were to reply that the Virgin Birth was possible because with God nothing is impossible, then they had no right to deny the Manichaeans the right to say that Christ could have suffered without having been born. 'In short', Faustus concludes, 'we hold that he suffered in appearance and did not really die; you believe in an actual birth and conception in the womb (without coition). If it is not so, you have only to acknowledge that the birth too was a delusion and our whole dispute will be at an end.'[60] Faustus's reliance on syllogism is all too apparent in his method of argument and is justifiably parodied by Augustine: 'I do not know whether I should call his argument very fraudulent or very stupid. Yet, Faustus was not a fool. On this basis I rather think that he wished to throw a cloud over the less attentive reader than that he did not see what he was saying . . .'.[61] On the other hand, Augustine shows in his reply to Faustus that the Christians themselves were not entirely innocent of tailoring a scriptural text to suit their argument. The Manichaeans like the gnostics used 2 Cor. 4:4: 'The God of this world has blinded the minds of them that believe not . . .' to argue for the existence of a malevolent deity opposed to God.[62] Most Catholics, according to Augustine, punctuated the verse in such a way that it incorporated some words from the previous clause and reads: '. . . in whom God has blinded the minds of the unbelievers of this world'.[63] This rewording is completely impossible in the original Greek and is very forced in Latin.

To a young man 'made proud and garrulous by the disputes of learned men at school'[64] and who also had in mind a career of lifelong debate as a lawyer or rhetor, the apparent skills of the Manichaeans in controversies and their pseudo-intellectualism were no mean attractions. Once Augustine became involved with the sect, he was made to dispute on its behalf and Augustine would later see this as an encouragement to find out more about the tenets of the sect in order that he might further triumph in arguments:

I was almost always perniciously victorious in arguing with Christians who though not well educated, defended their own faith as well as they could. By a quick succession of disputes my youthful zeal was inflamed, and by its own impulse recklessly verged upon the spirit of stubborness. Since I had begun this type of disputing only after hearing these people, whatever I picked up by my own wits or by reading I attributed most willingly to their teaching alone. And so from their preaching, I grew in my desire for such contests, and from success in such contests, my love for these people grew daily. This was how it happened that by some strange process, I came to regard whatever they said was true, not because I knew it to be true but because I wished it to be so. So it came about that I for such a long time followed men who preferred a sleek straw to the living soul, though I did so gradually and cautiously.[65]

Augustine was drawn to Manichaeism as much by its aggressive evangelistic medium as by its message. Since the central teaching and the canonical works of Mani were shrouded by the elect in an aura of mystery, a novice like Augustine would have to commit himself wholeheartedly to the sect in order to catch further glimpses of the wisdom which he so fervently desired. 'Though I did not agree with them', as he reminisced on his time as a Hearer to his friend Theodorus, 'I neverthless thought that they were concealing something vitally important in these veils which they would reveal some time in the future.'[66]

The Manichaean attack on the Old Testament particularly impressed Augustine. He was then accustomed to measuring all the behaviour of mankind by his own moral standards and was therefore disturbed by the loose sexual mores and the apparent cruelty of the patriarchs. 'You know well', he says to Honoratus, 'the Manichaeans by their censures of the Catholic faith and especially by their destructive criticism of the Old Testament affect the unlearned, who do not quite know how these things are to be understood . . . Because some of these things offend ignorant and unwary minds – the great majority – they can be popularly attacked.'[67] Not many had the power to defend the criticisms in an equally popular way and the few who did probably shunned public controversy and its attendant publicity. Moreover, the defence could not be conducted in the same flamboyant and self-confident manner in which the attack was made. Although the church had faced the same problem earlier with the Marcionites, no ready replies were generally at hand. Augustine, in his attempt to win back Honoratus had to draw on the latest theories of Biblical interpretation:

The Old Testament Scripture to those who diligently desired to know it, is handed down with a four-fold sense – historical, aetiological, analogical and allegorical. Do not think me clumsy in using Greek terms . . . as you will notice that among us Latins, there are no words in common use to express these ideas. If I were to attempt a translation of them I might have been clumsier. If I were to use circumlocutions, I shall be less speedy in my exposition . . .[68]

To us Augustine sounds little different from modern theologians who cannot argue their case without resorting to German theological terms like *Heilsgeschicte* and *Sitz im Leben* etc. One can see why in the context of a disputation before a theologically untrained audience, the swift and hard-hitting arguments of the Manichaeans were the more persuasive and popular. The Old Testament was a topic which Augustine would studiously avoid in his debates with Manichaean leaders after his conversion.

The publication in *c.* 398 of the *Confessions* made famous
Augustine's experience as a Manichaean Hearer and the popularity of
the work was undoubtedly a major media set-back for the sect. Some
time in 405/6, Augustine received a letter from a Manichaean Hearer
from the city of Rome called Secundinus who claimed to have known
Augustine by sight although Augustine had no recollection of him.
With transparent obsequiousness and in a highly affected style,
Secundinus endeavoured in the letter to persuade Augustine to stop
his attack on the sect – not to be the 'lance which pierced the side of
Christ', and to return to the Manichaean fold.[69] Augustine's erstwhile
disdain for the implied morality of some of the Old Testament
patriarchs was the Achilles's heel which Secundinus sought to exploit:

How dearly I wished that on leaving the Manichaeans, you would have sought
the Academy where you could have commented on the wars of the Romans in
which they are always victorious. What lofty themes and illustratious matters
you would have found there. But, no, morally chaste that you are and replete
with modesty and moderation, you went instead to the Jews, a people who
were barbarians in their morals, when you mingled fables with precepts and
invoked: '[take] a prostitute [for your] wife', and 'get children of her
wantonness; for like a prostitute this land is unfaithful to the Lord' [Hosea
1:2]; and 'Do not wash your hands after coition' [?]; and, 'Put your hand under
my thigh' [Gen. 24:2 and 47:29], and 'Kill and eat' [Acts 10:13] and 'Be fruitful
and multiply' [Gen. 1:28]. Did the lions in the pit please you more than those
which were caged [*cf.* Dan. 6:16]? Or, did the sterility of Sarah grieve you,
although a vendor of her modesty existed in her husband who pretended that
she was his sister [*cf.* Gen. 16:1]? Or, was it possible that after the combat
between Dares and Entelles [*cf.* Virgil, *Aeneid* 5, 362 ff.] you wished to spectate
at the contest of Jacob himself [*cf.* Gen. 32:23–33]? Have you decided to look
intently at the number of Amorites [*cf.* Joshua 10:5] or the variety [*pancarpus*]
in Noah's Ark [*cf.* Gen. 7:7–17]? I knew you always have hated these things. I
knew you always loved great things which forsake the earth and seek the
heights, which mortify the flesh and enliven the souls. Therefore who is he
who has changed your mind all out of a sudden?[70]

If only Augustine could see the error of his ways and devote his
undoubted literary and theological talents to the service of
Manichaeism, hinted Secundinus, he could 'revive Paul in our times,
who though he was a doctor of the laws of the Jews, received the grace
of apostleship from the Lord and looked down upon what he once
thought precious as dung as that he could shine forth for Christ'.[71] The
appeal fell on deaf ears. Augustine was too experienced a polemicist
against the Manichaeans by then to be unduly worried by such
predictable arguments. However, Secundinus must have thought that
the depth of feeling against the morality of the Old Testament
patriarchs among most Christians and pagans was such that it was
worth trying to rekindle those same feelings which he knew from the

Confessions to have played a part in Augustine's turning to the Manichaeans.

(2)   THE SECTARIAN APPEAL OF MANICHAEISM

A second reason which Augustine gave for his continued involvement with the Manichaeans was their apparent cordiality which 'inexplicably and suddenly, by a certain false appearance of goodness, wrapped many times round my neck as a sinuous cord'.[72] The organisation of the Manichaean sect into small cells grouped round a small number of the Elect would have given its members a greater sense of belonging than the established church. As someone who put great emphasis on genuine friendship, Augustine found in the Manichaeans a ready-made intimate circle of serious-minded friends, quite unlike those fellow students whom he called the 'wreckers' (*eversores*).[73] On his return to Thagaste in 375 at the end of his studies at Carthage, his desire for similar friendship turned him into an ardent Manichaean evangelist. He won over a number of his boyhood friends among whom were Honoratus, Nebridius, Cornelius and even his patron Romanianus.[74] The wealth and hospitality of the latter enabled Augustine and his Manichaean friends to meet regularly to discuss philosophical and religious issues.[75] However, his stay in his native city was of brief duration as he was frustrated by the lack of career opportunities and he might have also felt the loneliness of being a young pioneering missionary. His return to Carthage immediately brought him back to his former Manichaean friends. Looking back on the years in which he taught rhetoric at Carthage, the initmate and genuine companionship of his friends, many of whom were Manichaeans, stood out vividly in his memory as it had meant more to him than the teaching of the sect:

What revived and refreshed me most was the comfort I found in other friends, with whom I went on loving the things I loved instead of You. And this was one huge fable and one long lie. By its adulterous caressing, my mind which was 'itching in the ears' [2 Tim. 4:3] was corrupted. But that fable did not die within me although one of my friends had died [reference to a friend whom he converted to Manichaeism but who later received Christian baptism before his death]. [The reason is that] there were other things which fully captivated my mind: to discuss and banter, to do kindnesses to each other, to read books with sweet phrases together, to trifle together and to be earnest together, sometimes to disagree but without rancour as if a man disagrees with himself and to find through these rare disagreements that our many agreements had been made all the more sweet, to teach each other, to long for those who were absent with impatience and to receive those joyously on their return – these and similar expressions of feeling proceeded from the heart of the lover and the loved through the mouth, the tongue and the eyes, and a thousand ingratiating gestures – as if to set ablaze our minds with tinder-wood and to make one out of many.[76]

As a Hearer, Augustine was unlikely to have had free and regular access to the canonical works of Mani. Nor was he permitted to participate in certain rites which were reserved for the Elect. He admitted in his debate with the Manichaean Fortunatus that he was ignorant of what forms of worship the Elect held among themselves.[77] The Coptic Manichaean texts from Medinet Medi, especially the *Psalm-Book*, give the impression that the liturgical life of the Manichaean Hearer was devoted mainly to prayer, confessions, the singing of hymns which was devoted mainly to prayer, confessions, the singing of hymns which were sometimes responsorial or antiphonal as well as listening to the accounts of the achievements and martyrdoms of the sect's earlier heroes and reported versions of Mani's discourses to his close circle of disciples on specific points of Manichaean theology. The Manichaean hymns in the *Psalm-Book*, most which were originally composed in Syriac, are among the largest and oldest collection of religious songs known to us and predate the works of great Christian hymn writers like Prudentius and Venantius Fortunatus by more than a century. Their high literary qualities and their undoubtedly sensual appeal were further enriched by a wealth of apposite and striking religious symbols fundamental to Syriac Christianity.[78] The hymns were a particularly effective means of conveying aspects of Manichaean theology to Hearers who did not have access to the canonical works of Mani. It has been shown that the extant fragments of the *Epistula fundamenti* bear many close verbal parallels to a Coptic Manichaean psalm in the Medinet Medi collection, so much so that the psalm is very probably a liturgical version of the *Epistula*.[79] Because of their rhythms and their tunes, hymns were also easier to remember than plain texts. In Augustine's refutation of the 'Apologia' of Faustus, he could paraphrase from memory the main part of a Manichaean hymn called the 'Song of the Lovers' (*Amatorium canticum*) which gives a detailed description of the Kingdom of Light and the five Sons of the Living Spirit:

Do you recall your 'Song of the Lovers' in which you describe the supreme reigning monarch, forever sceptre-bearing, crowned with flowers and possessing a fiery countenance? . . . As you follow the song, you add [to the list of gods] Twelve Aeons [*duodecim saecula*] clothed in flowers and full of song, throwing their flowers at the Father's face. Whereupon you profess that he was surrounded by these twelve great so-called gods, three of them in each part of the four region . . . Carry on then with what you are singing and watch out, if you can, for the shame of your idolatry. The doctrine of the

deceiving demons has invited you to the imaginery dwellings of the angels
where the wholesome breeze blows and to fields which abound in sweet scent
and to seas and rivers which flows forever with sweet nectar . . . Have you ever
come face to face with the reigning, sceptre-bearing monarch bedecked with
floral crowns and surrounded by the armies of gods and the great Custodian of
Splendour [splenditenens] with six faces and expressions and is radiant with
light; and another – the King of Honour [rex honoris] surrounded by cohorts of
angels; and another – the heroic and belligerent Adamas who carries a spear in
his right hand and a brazen shield in the left; and another – the King of Glory
[gloriosus rex] who propels three wheels, those of fire, water and wind; and
Atlas, chief of all carrying the world on his shoulders, down on one knee and
supporting it with both arms? Have you seen all these and thousands of other
portents face to face or has the doctrine of the deceiving demons been sung to
you through the lips of the deceived although you are not aware of it?[80]

The mythological details conveyed by the song are very similar to
those found in two fragmentary Coptic Manichaean psalms which
touch on the same subject:

> O rest of the universe, we glorify thee,
> Father of Greatness. Glorious King.
> Sun that is in his Aeons. Crowned potentate . . .
> His 12 princes Garland of renown of the Father.
> His 12 strong walls. His 12 henchmen.
> His 12 Aeons. The Aeons of the Aeons.
> Householders of the Land of Light. The air of our city.
> Light of the blessed. Manna of the Lord of Light . . .
> Habitation of the blessed. Fountain that gushes greatness.
> Trees of fragrance. Fountain filled with life.
> All the holy mountains. Fields that are green with life.
> Dew of ambrosia . . .[81]

> The Splenditenens in the height of the heavens,
> who is between them that wander [?] and them that are fixed.
> The tenth who . . . who suspends the universe guarding the universe.
> The King of Honour, the strong God, who is in the seventh heaven,
> judging the demons, the creatures of the abyss [?].
> We sing to him, we glorify him.
> The Adamas of Light unsubdued who treads upon
> the earth's trembling foundation [?] . . .
> that is laid [?] in the midst of the world.
> The King of Glory, the holy counsel,
> who turns [?] in the abyss [?]
> the three wheels, that of the winds, that of the water and
> that of the living fire, the armour of our Father, the First Man.
> The Omophoros [i.e. Atlas], the great burden-carrier,
> who treads upon the . . . with the soles of his feet,
> supporting the earths with his hands,
> carrying the burden of the creations.[82]

The spiritual life of the Manichaeans in whose company Augustine spent nine years of his adulthood was not as Christocentric as one would expect from their frequent use of the name of Christ in their liturgy. The supreme martyr of the sect was Mani, the Apostle of the Jesus of Light, and, unlike Jesus the Messiah who feigned death, the suffering of Mani was real and worthy of the highest form of commemoration. Augustine recalled that when he was a Hearer he noted that the paschal feast of the Lord was celebrated generally with no real interest, though sometime there were a few languid worshippers. No special vigils or fasts were prescribed for it. On the other hand, the Feast of the Bēma which commemorated the death of Mani was a very special occasion at which the members would erect a platform (bēma) of five steps, covered with precious cloth and placed conspicuously so as to face the worshippers. Augustine and his fellow Hearers used to devote themselves with all the more ardour to the Feast of the Bēma since it took the place of the paschal feast which was once dear to him.[83] The Feast of the Bēma provided the occasion for the singing hymns and the reading or chanting of passages from Mani's writings.

The Manichaean Hearer was never allowed to take a back seat in the religious life of the community. From the moment he joined the sect he was involved in the cosmic design for the redemption of the captured Light Particles through his service to the Elect. According to the *Fragmenta Tebestina*, a North African Manichaean work, the Hearer would be exalted before the Judgement Seat for the assistance (*auxilium*) he had rendered to the Elect.[84] For nine years, Augustine looked upon his service to the Elect, especially the provision of food, as a necessary purgation of his vanity occasioned by his worldly success. He carried food to the Elect in the belief 'that out of the workhouses [*officina*] of their paunches [*aqualiculi*] angels and gods would be forged for their liberation'.[85] This service was not only vital to the welfare of the Elect, it was an important reminder to the Hearer of the difference in status between the two classes of believers and emphasised the soteriological role of the Elect. Even after he had begun to doubt the truth of some aspects of the religion, Augustine remained tied to the sect out of his sense of duty far longer than he would have wished. 'These things I did follow and I performed them with my friends who were deceived by me and with me.'[86]

Besides tending to the alimentary needs of the Elect, the Hearers were also expected to provide them with shelter and devote part of their wealth, if they were men of means, to their upkeep. A story is told in the *Verba Seniorum*, a collection of sayings of the Egyptian Fathers, of how a Christian ascetic once welcomed an itinerant Manichaean preacher so warmly that the latter concluded from his reception that the Christian was a 'true servant of God' and was thus converted. The story was aimed probably at discrediting Manichaean hospitality, a cardinal virtue among the sect.[87] A rich Roman Manichaean Hearer by the name of Constantius went out of his way to provide shelter for all the Elect he could find in the city of Rome in the hope that they would form a model Manichaean community but the project fell to pieces because of internal bickering, although the Hearer was exemplary in his own ascetical endeavours.[88] The Hearers were also expected to give a child or a relative or a member of their family to the sect. The precedence for this, as we have seen, was established by Mani who, in his missionary travels took from a man whose daughter he had cured one of his other daughters in lieu of payment. It is interesting to note that the bishop to whom Monica turned for solace after she had learnt of Augustine's disposition towards the Manichaeans was once a member of the sect because he had been given to it by his mother.[89]

The empire-wide network of Manichaean cells stood Augustine in good stead when he arrived in Rome to start a new career in the latter part of 397. His acquaintance with Faustus who was well known in Italy made sure of a warm reception from the co-religionists in the capital city. His first circle of friends were almost exclusively Manichaeans and he was surprised to find that there were many of them in the city. He lodged with an ardent Manichaean Hearer, probably the same Constantius who later tried to establish a hostel for the Elect. When he fell into a serious illness, it was his Manichaean host who helped him to recuperate.[90] The encouragement and friendship he received from the Manichaeans helped him to remain strong in his faith, for even when he was at death's door he would not consider Christian baptism as some of his friends had done.[91] His connection with the sect also paid him rich dividends in terms of his future career. When the chair of rhetoric at Milan fell vacant, his Manichaean friends secured an interview for him with Q. Aurelius Symmachus, the prefect of the city who duly recommended him for the post.[92] Being one of the last great champions of paganism, Symmachus was all too aware of the political possibilities of the appointment since the western emperor was more often in Milan than in Rome. A Manichaean rhetor might have therefore been preferable to a Catholic one. The city already had one of the most ardent champions of Christian orthodoxy and religious uniformity in Ambrose, her bishop.

The sect evidently still enjoyed the support of the rich and the powerful in the capital despite the anti-Manichaean legislations. As we have mentioned, a Manichaean Hearer even had the courage to found a Manichaean monastery in his house and gathered together all the vagrant Manichaean Elect in the city.[93] Such a gathering would have provided the authorities the opportunity to bag most of the Elect in Rome at one fell swoop. Yet the project failed because of internal dissention and not because of external pressures and persecution. There was little in Augustine's writings covering the period 373–c. 388 which suggests that Manichaeans were systematically persecuted in Africa and Italy. Although he speaks of his participation in the activities of the sect as matter of secrecy (occulte), yet, to a youth who, by his own later admission, 'hated security and a path without snares',[94] the fact that the Manichaeans were liable to persecution might have proved an attraction, especially if the laws against them were not stringently applied. The authorities clearly did not try to track down the Manichaeans systematically but acted entirely on the information of informers and accusers. The fear of being denounced to the authorities though, was real and it was this, according to Augustine, which deprived the Elect of effective control over the more wayward members as they could turn informers by way of revenge.[95] However, in the later empire, court cases were costly and lengthy affairs and they might even involve the parties travelling to the imperial court as Augustine's patron Romanianus had to do.[96] Thus, for the irate brother of a virgin who was seduced by a Manichaean Elect who taught in the 'quarter of fig-sellers' (ficariorum vicum), to arrange for the miscreant to be expelled from church and soundly beaten was probably a more effective way of settling the score. The Manichaean could hardly hope to have his grievance redressed by the imperial authorities.[97]

The Manichaean Elect were certainly not house-bound refugees. They travelled in groups and attended the theatre and a few were even seen at the baths – a flagrant violation of the Manichaean prohibition of bathing.[98] Faustus boasted of having addressed large audiences, one of which prevented Augustine from bringing to Faustus his most pressing intellectual problems at their first meeting.[99] The trial and execution of Priscillian in 386 for Manichaeism and magic might have stirred Messianus, the proconsul of Africa, into taking some action against the Manichaeans. Petilianus, Augustine's Donatist opponent in later years, would insinuate that this was the cause of Augustine's visit to Italy. In fact, Augustine was in Rome by 384 and he delivered a new year panegyric before the Consul Bauto in 385.[100] Faustus, on the other hand, was sentenced by Messianus along with others to exile for being a Manichaean. Augustine would later see it as a sign of the gentleness of the Christian times that Faustus was given such a light sentence. Even then, Faustus tried to make himself a martyr although he was soon released because of an imperial amnesty.[101] According to the Chronicle of Hydatius, Arcadius celebrated his quinquennalia in 387 and we may assume that Faustus' exile lasted for no more than a year.[102]

(3)   THE AESTHETIC APPEAL OF THE SECT

Since Mani had intended that the unique revelation which he had received from his divine Twin should be literally understood, he made an actual pictorial representation of his complex teaching on cosmogony both to guard against allegorical interpretation and to serve as a visual aid for the missionaries. 'So also Mani painted in colours on a scroll', bemoaned Ephraim, ' . . . the likeness of the wickedness which he created out of his mind . . . as he said, 'I have written them in books and pictured them in colours; let him who hears them in words also see them in an image, and let him who is unable to learn them from words learn them from pictures.'[103] This picture-book (Gk./Copt.: εἴκων Pe./Pth.: 'rdhng, Chin.: Ta-men-ho-i t'u) was held in the highest regard by the Manichaeans and was provided with a commentary (Pth.: 'rdhng wyfr's), of which several fragments have survived.[104] Art and calligraphy therefore played an important part in the dissemination of the religion. We may recall that Adda and Patīk were accompanied by scribes (Pe.: dbyr'n) on their missionary journey to the Roman empire and among those who went with Mar Ammo to the east were scribes and a miniature painter or book illuminator (Pe.: nbyg'n-ng'r).[105] We also learn from a letter to Mar Ammo from Sisinnios that duplicate copies of the 'Picture Book' were being made at Khorasan.[106] In the Islamic period, the artistic achievements of the Manichaeans received much comment as the pictorial representation of religious figures and motifs was a source of doctrinal controversy. Mani was denigrated as the leader of the 'Chinese school of painters'.[107] Later traditions maintain that he spent a year in a cave before he emerged with his completed 'Picture Book' which astonished everyone who saw it and which Mani claimed to have brought from heaven as proof of his prophetic mission.[108] His artistic skills reached legendary proportions. It was said that he could draw a line on a piece of silk in such a way that if one pulled out a single thread, the entire line would disappear.[109]

Extant fragments of Manichaean manuscripts from Turfan show that the Manichaean scribes in the east took the utmost care to make sure that the script was readable and the text was arranged in neat columns. Some of the manuscripts were also painstakingly and exquistitely illuminated. The work was executed by the Hearers and the pious attitude which they adopted towards it is shown by a Manichaean prayer and confessional book in which a monk was required to ask for forgiveness for having neglected the art of writing.[110] The calligraphy of the Manichaean scribes was of such a high standard that it won the grudging admiration of the sect's enemies. 'I wish the zānadika were not so keen to spend good money on clean white paper and glossy black ink and did not hold calligraphy in such high esteem or incite calligraphers to be so competitive', remarked an Islamic man of letters, 'For truly, no paper I have ever seen is to be compared with the paper of their books and no calligraphy with that employed in them.'[111]

Manichaean texts from the west also show a high standard of penmanship although they were less lavishly illustrated. According to Augustine, the Manichaeans boasted of their numerous and valuable manuscripts, the finely ornamented bindings of their codices and the time, effort and cost which went into their production.[112] They, too, were the work of the Hearers as the priest who comforted Monica, and who, as we have mentioned, was given by his mother as a child to the Manichaeans not only had read her scriptures but had also copied them. He later left the sect after he had convinced himself, without anyone to argue with him, that the teaching of the sect had to be avoided.[113] Like their colleagues in the east, the Manichaean scribes in the Roman empire were also experts in miniaturised writing. The scribes who executed the *CMC* managed to copy twenty-three lines to a page and the text face measured only 3.5 × 2.5 cm. This skill was highly necessary in the west as Manichaean texts were a primary target in the legislations against the sect and small format could help to escape detection.[114]

The aesthetic qualities of the sect seem not to have made a strong impression on Augustine. His reasons for joining the sect belonged primarily to the realm of the intellect. However, there might have been many who were drawn to the sect because of what it had to offer in the realm of the senses. The charm of the Manichaean hymns and the visual beauty of their texts might have helped many to form a good first impression. Mani's 'Picture Book', as Ephraim hinted, was a great asset to the missionaries when addressing a mainly illiterate audience. In his refutation of the *Epistula fundamenti*, Augustine himself used the illustration of four pieces of bread, three white and one black, to explain the Manichaean concept of the Realm of Light extending outwards in three directions and the Realm of Darkness extending downwards.[115] He might have learned this illustration from the Manichaeans who used it as a visual aid in their presentation of Mani's cosmogonic myth.

(4)   MANICHAEISM AND ASTROLOGY

The career of a teacher of rhetoric, so well illustrated by that of Libanius of Antioch, was of a highly competitive nature. His reputation and his ability to attract students rested on his success in literary competitions. In the course of his career as a rhetor, Libanius was accused on more than one occasion of achieving his success and his popularity be means of magic. The methods he was alleged to have employed included the murdering of innocent people so as to use their skulls for the purpose of divination.[116] It was probably taken for granted by many that the rhetors, like the charioteers in the later empire, because their livelihood depended on winning competitions, would dabble occasionally in occultic arts to achieve their goals. During his time as a Hearer, Augustine was once offered the service of a *haruspex* after he had decided to enter a poetry competition to be recited on the stage. He asked how much Augustine would pay him to be assured of winning the competition. This would involve the killing of an animal by the *haruspex* for the examination of its entrails. Being a Manichaean Augustine rejected the offer haughtily: 'Even if the victor's garland was of immortal gold, I would not suffer a fly to be killed to ensure my gaining it.'[117] The Manichaeans's total refusal to perform blood sacrifices, as we have mentioned earlier, had been considered by Libanius as a point in their favour in his plea for a measure of toleration for the sect. Towards astrology, Augustine was much less inhibited and by his own admission he was a devotee of the subject. He was therefore pleased to discover that Mani had written a great deal on the subject.[118] The Manichaeans, as we have noted, had by then acquired considerable reputation, or notoriety, as astrologers. The Manichaean cosmogonic system abounds in astrological details and in one of his extant discourses, Mani showed off his knowledge of astrology to his students by using the signs of the zodiac to denote the positions of the five regions of the Kingdom of Darkness.[119] Astrology, as scholars of comparative religions have observed, is often a neces-sary complement of religious systems in which dualism or *karma* (the concept of ethical causation in Buddhism) disposes of the problem of theodicy on a cognitive level but not on a psychological level. To say that evil is external and therefore uncontrollable, as did the Manichaeans, can leave people feeling powerless to influence their fate or luck. Astrology gives at least some premonition of the next onslaught of evil.[120] Thus Julia the *Manichaea*, whose visit to Gaza (c. 397) was recorded by Mark the Deacon, talked about 'horoscopes, fate and the stars, so that man may sin without fear as the comission of sin is not in us but in the stars.'[121]

Augustine's infatuation with astrology might have sparked off an initial interest in Manichaesism but in the long run it also provided him with the first of his series of disappointments with the sect. As his knowledge of pagan astrology increased, Augustine began to notice a disquieting number of discrepancies between the scientific study of the planetary bodies and Mani's revelation on the working of the universe. Augustine could find no rational explanation of solstices or of eclipses in Manichaean writings. 'What I was commanded to believe in these writings', he later remarked, 'did not correspond with those rational explanations using numbers nor with the discoveries made by my own eyes.'[122] Mani's explanation for the behaviour of the planetary bodies had similarly vexed Alexander of Lycopolis. 'If only they [i.e. the Manichaeans] had graced the doors of the astronomers, even occasionally', he says 'they would not have been in this plight nor would they have been ignorant of the fact that the moon, which according to some does not possess its own light, is illumined by the sun and that its appearances are controlled by its distances from the sun, and that it becomes full when it is at a hundred and eighty degrees away from the sun and that it is in conjuncftion whenever it is situated in the same degree as the sun.'[123] Furthermore, Augustine might have found, as a modern expert on ancient astrology has called to our attention, that Mani was very amateurish in his use of accepted astrological concepts and practices. In the discourse on the symbols of the zodiac which we have mentioned, he uses them to denote a number of cosmogonic details and themes in a manner which might have been frowned upon by pagan astrologers who considered themselves as the true heirs of the Chaldaeans.[124] Mani claims that the twelve symbols were twelve archons taken from the five worlds of darkness and fastened to the firmament – two per world (?):

From the world of Smoke:	Gemini and Sagittarius.
From the world of Fire:	Aries and Leo.
From the world of Wind:	Taurus, Aquarius and Libra.
From the world of Water:	Cancer, Virgo and Pisces.
From the world of Darkness:	Capricorn and Scorpio.[125]

He then reveals that the twelve zodiac symbols are divided and arranged into four parts, each one triangular, in four different positions and are fastened on the revolving sphere. This is an accepted form of division and is also found in the writings of the great Roman astronomer Ptolemy:[126]

	Symbols	(Position according to Ptolemy)
First triangle	Aries, Leo, Sagittarius	(north-west)
Second triangle	Taurus, Virgo, Capricorn	(south-east)
Third triangle	Gemini, Libra, Aquarius	(north-east)
Fourth triangle	Cancer, Scorpio, Pisces	(south-west)

The four triangles are further related to four types of disasters:

When the part belonging to Aries, Leo and Sagittarius is robbed by the overseer standing over it and making demands of it and the pathway guides on it, then hardship strikes all four-footed creatures. But when [the part of] Taurus, Virgo and Capricorn is being robbed, then immediately [hardship] arises among herbs, gourds, and all fruit of trees. But when the part of Scorpio, Pisces and Cancer is robbed then is a lack of water on earth and then is famine in all places. When the part of Gemini, Libra and Aquarius is robbed, loss and decrease are manifest under the seal of humanity in all places.[127]

The four categories of disasters bring to mind the first four trumpet-blowing angels in the Book of the Revelations (8:8–12) and the use of the symbols of the zodiac to designate disasters also has parallels in pagan astrological literature. However, the sudden switch by Mani of their use from the spatial to the temporal would strike many as illogical and the Trigon was normally regarded as a favourable symbol.[128]

(5)   THE ASCETICAL APPEAL OF MANICHAEISM

The Manichaeans, as Augustine explains, had two tricks to catch the unwary. One was finding fault with the scriptures they misunderstood or wished to be misunderstood, and the other was making a show of chastity and of notable abstinence.[129] The diffusion of Manichaeism coincided with the Christianisation of the empire and an important feature of the latter was the increasing popularity of the practice of asceticism. Since the Manichaean Elect was called to a life of chastity, vegetarianism and poverty, they saw themselves as the true followers of Christ. This is clealry expressed by a Coptic Manichaean psalm which echoes a number of Biblical injunctions:

> I am a holy Continent [ἐγκρατής] one. [Response:]   My.
> I have purified my God by my tongue . . .   My.
> I prayed, I sang, I gave alms.   My.
> I served all the holy ones.   My.
> I clothed thy orphans.   My.
> I closed not my door in the face of the holy.   My.
> I fed the hungry, I gave drink to the thirsty.   My.
> I left father and mother and brother and sister.   My.
> I became a stranger for thy name's sake.   My.
> I took my cross. I followed thee.   My.
> I left the things of the body for the things of the Spirit.   My.
> I despised the glory of the world,   My.
> because of the glory that passes not away.   My.[130]

The Manichaeans regarded the asceticism of their Elect as the real gospel of Christ. They argued that a clear distinction should be made between the dogma of the church and the gospel of Christ. It was the church which formulated doctrines such as the Incarnation and the Virgin Birth and framed them as essential articles of faith while Christ himself never made such statements. For a Manichaean Elect like Faustus, the gospel was the actual, verifiable words of Christ and especially his commandments. Since he followed the lifestyle of a Manichaean elect how could he not be a true follower of the gospel since he was an embodiment of the beatitudes pronounced by Christ:

Do you accept the Gospel? – You ask me whether I accept it when it is clear to me that I accept it because I observe what it commands. Or shall I ask you whether you accept it even though there seems to be no indication of acceptance of the Gospel? I have left father and mother, wife, children and whatever else that is commanded by the Gospel [Matt. 19:29] and you ask whether I accept the Gospel? Unless you are still ignorant of what it is that is called the Gospel. For it is nothing other than the commandments of Christ. I have rejected silver and gold and have ceased to keep even copper in my waistband. I am content with my daily food, carrying nothing for that of tomorrow, unsolicitous as to how my stomach is to be filled or my body covered [Matt. 10:9 ff and 6:25 ff.] and you ask me if I accept the Gospel? You see in me those Beatitudes of Christ [Matt. 5:3 ff.] which make up the Gospel; and you ask whether I accept it? You see me poor, you see me meek, you see me peace-loving, one pure in heart, enduring of suffering, accepting hunger, thirst, and suffering persecutions and hatred for righteousness's sake and you doubt if I accept the Gospel?[131]

Since Manichaean asceticism bore so many pratical resemblances to its Christian counterpart, the Manichaeans were not unjustified in thinking that their version was superior since it was demanded of all Elect and was *sine qua non* of full salvation. In Mesopotamia, the ascetic endeavours of the Manichaeans clearly made a strong impression on some of the Christians (i.e. the Palutians) as Ephraim constantly warned them against admiring the Manichaeans as exemplary Christians. As he says in his *Prose Refutations*: 'for their works are similar to our works, as their fasting is similar to our fasting, but their faith is not similar to our faith'.[132] The women-folk seemed to Ephraim to be particularly at risk because they were easily impressed by the false sanctimonious acts of the Manichaeans: 'And also today he [the demon] seduces the simple women through diverse pretenses: he catches one by fasting, the other by sackcloth and leguminous plants.'[133] It was the Devil, Ephraim warned, that had given Mani a pale complexion in order to deceive the unwary.[134] The faithful must learn to judge them not by the outward filth of their garments but by the inward filth of their doctrines.[135]

Egypt, the other major centre of asceticism and monasticism in the late empire, also afforded Manichaeans with special opportunities to assert their claims as superior Christians on the grounds of the self-abnegating lifestyle of their Elect. We learn from a later Christian Arabic source, the *Annales* of Patriarch Eutychius (Said ibn Batriq) that Manichaeism found many followers among the ranks of the clergy and the monks. They were divided into two classes on the issue of food. The Samakini (i.e. Hearers, from *samoun*) were permitted to eat fish while those of the Sadikini (i.e. the Elect, from Syr.: *zdyqt'*) refused all contact with meat.[136] The Manichaeans also clearly put forward their rejection of marriage as obediance to scriptural command and cited Paul [1 Cor. 7:1 ff.] in support of their claim.[137] Didymus the Blind, a famous ascetic and exegete found it necessary to explain to the Manichaeans that it was not wrong for a Christian to marry but it was wrong for an ascetic to do so as he had submitted himself to a different code. A Manichaean then tried to ensnare him with sophism by asking him what he thought to be the 'will of Jesus', hoping that the holy man would say something like 'Not to marry' and he could then denigrate the Patriarchs by pointing out that they married. However, Didymus told him that the 'will of Jesus' was to do the work of Abraham and believe in Moses. The Manichaean then accused him of muddling the issues like confusing a pugilist with a tragedian. Didymus concluded the discussion by stating that he had not confused the issues and he considered himself an honest adjudicator.[138]

The editors of the *CMC* have drawn our attention to the fact that in the Codex, Mani's father Patik (Patticius) is consistently referred to as a house-steward ($oἰϰοδεσπότης$) although he is not known to have held any important rank among the baptists.[139] The title or office which calls to mind the Middle Persian term *mānsārār* (head of house) seems to suggest monastic functions and is strikingly similar to the word $oἰϰιαϰὸς$ in Christian usage. This, together with the fact that Adda was credited with the foundation of communities (Pe./Pth.: *m'nyst'n'n*) and that he travelled as far as Egypt, have led to the suggestion that Manichaeism might have played some part in the early history of monasticism in Egypt. Adda's foundations would have predated the earliest Christian cenobitic communities by nearly half a century and might have provided monastic founding-fathers like Pachomius with some sort of model.[140]

We know pitifully little about the organisation of the earliest Manichaean communities in the Roman empire, certainly not enough to effect an adequate comparison with that of Pachomian monasteries. Manichaean asceticism was seen as a dangerous perversion of an exalted form of Christian living and we are unlikely to find Christian authors admitting to Manichaeism as a formative influence to the growth of asceticism and monasticism in Egypt. Athanasius in his *Life of Antony* made the point that this great Christian ascetic studiously avoided contacts with the Manichaeans during his sojourn in the desert. Athanasius might have felt it necessary to mention this so that Antony's ascetic endeavours would not be construed as a form of Manichaeism.[141]

Asceticism was not the preserve of orthodox Christians in fourth-century Egypt. Dedication to a particular lifestyle could bring together men from a wide theological spectrum. This may explain why an Egyptian ascetic by the name of Hieracas came to be associated with Manichaeism. According to Epiphanius, who devoted a chapter of his handbook on heresies to the Hieracites immediately following that on the Manichaeans, Hierax or Hieracas was a native of Leontopolis. He was fluent in both Greek and Coptic and practised the art of calligraphy. He denied the resurrection of the body because of its evil nature. He utterly rejected marriage and taught that children who died before the use of reason could not inherit the kingdom of heaven as they had not proven their worth in the strike.[142] Once an ascetic like Hieracas had narrowed Christianity to ascetical practices, he might have had no qualms about using gnostic, or even Manichaean writings, to support his extreme position. In fact some scholars have suggested that Hieracas might have been the author of the tractate 'The Gospel of Truth' in the gnostic codices discovered at Nag Hammadi.[143] In Byzantine sources, Hieracas was generally regarded as a leading exegete and commentator of Manichaean scriptures.[144]

Early ascetic communities in Egypt might have therefore included members who had first been drawn to asceticism from a variety of theological backgrounds and they might have continued to draw their ascetical inspiration from works which were later regarded as heretical. As orthopraxy gave way to orthodoxy in the Theodoasin era, they were forced to readjust. According to Eutychius, the Patriarch Timothy of Alexandria (patriarch from 380–85) was so alarmed by the extent of Manichaean infiltration into the ranks of the clergy and monastics that he instituted food-tests by allowing monks to eat meat on Sundays and thereby singling out the Manichaeans among them.[145] The more unorthodox reading matter of the ascetics now had to be concealed. This may explain why in both the Nag Hammadi and Medinet Medi finds, the gnostic and Manichaean books were found in sizeable collections rather than as individual works. The material used in the manufacture of the cartonnage of the gnostic codices from Nag Hammadi shows strong connections between the collection and the Pachomian monasteries found in the same region.[146]

Organised asceticism had not yet taken root in North Africa when Augustine was a Hearer and the Manichaeans therefore had few rivals in their claim to be true Christians through their ostentatious acts of self-denial. Alypius, one of Augustine's coverts who had some unfortunate sexual experience in his youth and had developed an abhorrence for it, was particularly attracted by the Manichaean views on chastity.[147] Cornelius, another one of Augustine's friends, was, on the contrary, a well-known womaniser and he joined the sect to curb his desires. Years later Augustine, writing to him on the occasion of the death of his wife made the comment that when they were both involved in the sect, Cornelius tried to rein his passions with a finely-tempered will but after a short time he fell back more basely than before.[148] Himself an admirer of the call to the asectical life, Augustine was deeply aware that his cohabitation with his mistress and his all too apparent worldly ambitions were preventing him from attaining it. The division of the Manichaean sect into two classes offered an escape-route to his conscience as it allowed him to live according to his acquired habits and at the same time through his service to the Elect he was assured of a part of the cosmic redemptive process through their pure living. Augustine was by no means a voluptuary and his self-confessed moral shortcomings have to be judged against his high standards. The Manichaean doctrine of man as a mixture of good and evil offered him much consolation as it assured him that no matter how much he sinned, there always remained in him a good part (soul, nature or substance, whatever one chooses to call it) which was untarnished by evil. This facility to abnegate the responsibility to sin was the umbilical cord which held him to the sect after he had begun to reject intellectually some of its tenets. 'For I still thought that it is not us who sin but some kind of alien nature in us which sins. It gratified my pride to think that I beyond blame, and when I had done something evil, not to confess I had done it . . . but instead I liked to excuse myself and accuse something which existed within me and yet was not really I.'[149] This must not be construed as Augustine's licence for moral laxity. He valued it because it offered him with a theological safety valve when he was beset by his own sense of failure.

Egyptian asceticism began to find an increasing number of admirers and imitators in the west as accounts of the heroic self-mortification of the Desert Fathers came to be known and translated into Latin. Augustine was profoundly affected by the tale of the two members of the secret police (*agentes in rebus*) who, after having read the *Life of Antony* by Athanasius in the Latin translation of Evagrius, decided to leave their comfortable posts in Trier to become monks.[150] The ascetical call seems to have particularly appealed to women of noble birth in the city of Rome. One such was Marcella, who listened to the teaching of Athanasius when he was in Rome (c. 343). When she became a widow, she refused to marry again and opened her house on the Aventine to any who would devote themselves to prayer and

study.[151] Inevitably most of her circle were well-born and well-heeled
ladies like herself and prominent among them was Paula who was
connected through birth and marriage to some of the most
distinguished Roman families.[152] We learn, however, from Jerome
who was much involved with these two saintly ladies, that there were
many women who practised asceticism because it was a fashionable
thing to do and when they saw someone pale or sad they would
disdainfully call her a 'wretch', a 'nun' (monacha) or a 'Manichaean'.
Rightly so, remarked Jerome since such ladies regarded fasting itself as
a form of heresy![153]

This heightening of interest in ascetisicm in the west gave the
Manichaeans a golden opportunity to present themselves as a higher
class of Christians. Women seemed to have been particularly
vulnerable to their propaganda. A special word of warning to them was
given by an anonymous commentator on the Pauline epistles, now
commonly called 'Ambrosiaister' who wrote probably in Rome, in the
370s. When he came to the verses in II Timothy (3:6–7) which warn
the faithful against those who make their way into households and
capture weak women who were burdened by sin, he saw the need to
stress the proclivity of the Manichaeans to exploit 'feminine
weaknesses':

Although this would fit all heretics as they [all] inveigle themselves into
houses and charm women with persuasive and crafty words so that through
them they might deceive the men in the fashion of the Devil their father who
defrauds Adam through Eve, it matches the Manichaeans above all others.
None are so ruthless, so deceitful, so enticing than those whose practice it is to
cultivate one idea and declare another, say one thing in private and another in
public. Although they uphold saintly living, they lead a life of gross immorality with the support of their own rule. Although they praise compassion they are found to be harsh towards each other. They preach that
the world is to be despised while taking care of their personal advancement.
They boastfully vaunt that they are strict in their fasting though they are all
well weighed down, because it is only by some trickery that they appear pale
so that they may deceive (other people). The Apostle had prophesised this
especially about them who, as it is well known, were not then in existence just
as neither were the Arians. The Emperor Diocletian makes this quite sure by
his edict in which he says: 'This impure and sordid *heresy* which has recently
arrived from Persia . . .'. They seek out women who always want to hear
something for sheer novelty and persuade them through what they like to hear
to do foul and illicit things. For the women are desirous to learn though they
do not possess the power of discrimination. This is what is meant by 'always
willing to listen but not having the knowledge of the truth'.(2 Tim. 3:7)[154]

Christian and Manichaean asceticism differed so little at a practical,
as distinct from doctrinal, level that some Christians began to warn

against the prevalent exaggerated estimate of asceticism. One who did so was Jovinian who had been a monk but came to the conclusion that the harsh ascetical regimen which he endured was unprofitable. He left his monastery and became a *bon vivant* in Rome.[155] He attacked the more ascetic-minded Christians as 'Manichaeans' because of their rejection of marriage and their refusal to eat food which God created for use. He taught that virgins and widows and married women were all equal before God and that although Mary was a virgin when she conceived Christ she did not remain one after his birth.[156] This was aimed particularly against monks who held the perpetual virginity of Mary as a reason for their own glorification of celibacy. The defenders of asceticism were scandalised, and a group of them denounced him to Pope Siricius and succeeded in having him banned from the capital. Jovinian then took himself with his chief adherents to Milan. Ambrose, forwarned by Siricius, convoked a small council of bishops of Upper Italy in 393 and saw to it that Jovinian was convicted of 'Manichaean' errors because of the denial of the perpetual virginity of Mary, which was seen as an attack on the Virgin Birth itself.[157] An imperial edict of 389 which ordered the expulsion of Manichaeans from cities was duly invoked against the 'Christian Epicurus'. In his letter to Siricius on the affair, Ambrose commended some of his presbyters for their zeal in exposing and expelling the Manichaeans. The affair might have occasioned a crack-down on the genuine Manichaeans in Milan.[158] The charge that Jovinian was a Manichaean is one of the flimsiest on record. Unlike Priscillian, much of what he stood for was entirely antithetical to the teaching of Mani. His successful conviction of a heresy which he abhorred shows how easily the charge of Manichaeism could be brought to bear on a variety of heresies deemed worthy of severe condemnation.

(6)   THE DUALISTIC APPEAL OF MANICHAEISM

A problem inherent in a monotheistic religious system like Judaism or Christianity is that of the origin of evil. Christianity sought the answer in human volition and free will. However, this ethical solution of the problem does not always satisfy those who are troubled by it on an experiential level and who view evil as an aggressive power, not merely the result of human frailty and indiscipline. For them the Manichaean teaching of an invasion of good by the forces of evil which are co-existent and co-eternal with good must have symbolised on a cosmic scale the Pauline dilemma: 'For the good that I would, I do not: but the evil which I would not, that I do'. (Romans 7:19). In his debate with Augustine, the Manichaean Fortunatus would later quote from Paul's epistle to the Galatians to support the Manichaean view that man does not have complete control over his actions, however good his intentions were: 'It is plain from this that the good soul is seen to sin, ... and not of its own accord, but following the way in which "the flesh lusteth against the spirit and the spirit against the flesh and that which you wish not, that you do".'[159]

For a philosophically-minded young man from a Christian background like Augustine, the problem of the origin of evil, or theodicy as the issue is termed by scholars of religions, could be an acute one since Christianity affirms that there is only one God and he is a God of goodness and love. 'Where then is evil, and whence does it come and how did it break in here?', Augustine was wont to ask himself,

What is its root, what is its seed? Or does it not exist at all? Why then do we fear and shun what does not exist? ... What is its source then, for God is good and has made all these things good? Indeed He is the greater and highest good and it is He who made all the lesser goods; but both the Creator and the created things are all good. Whence then is evil?[160]

In affirming that evil had an independent existence and is co-eternal with God, the Manichaeans provided a ready answer to the problem of theodicy and their belief that good and evil are intermingled helped to explain sin and moral failings as a result of the conflict of light and darkness in each individual.

The Manichaean solution to the problem of evil was a successful by-product of Mani's teaching – a by-product because as far as we can tell from extant evidence, Mani did not seem to have shown any serious interest in it at a philosophical level. Instead he gave us many vivid descriptions of the Prince of Darkness in his kingdom.[161] However, because the Roman empire was becoming increasingly Christian and therefore monotheistic, the problem of theodicy was all the more cogent. The Manichaean missionaries were quick to exploit this and they were adept in bringing the problem to the notice of their potential converts even if they had not wrestled with it like Augustine. The Manichaeans, as Augustine remarked were so obsessed by the problem of evil that they found evil everywhere.[162] Similarly, Titus of Bostra informs us that the Manichaeans whom he met were wont to ask the question 'Whence evil if it is not derived from some sort of principle?' From the manner in which Titus fashioned his reply it is possible for us to discern some of the questions which the Manichaeans would have raised with their listeners in order to guide them to belief in evil as a pre-existent principle: If it is God's will that man should do good why was he not created perfect and hence incapable of sinning? Why is there injustice in the world and why are some poor and some rich? Why should the innocent suffer? Why are there wars in which thousands fall in a short space of time? What causes natural disasters like earthquakes, pestilence and famine which cannot easily be attributed to human greed and self-will?, etc.[163] The Manichaean view of evil was not merely confined to acts of deliberate malevolence or natural catastrophes. Anything which could inconvenience a congenial existence was seen as evil. The Kingdom of Light, according to a Manichaean fragment in Parthian, was not only free from trickery, turmoil, pillage and sin but also from heat and cold, hunger and thirst, sickness and old age.[164]

With such a broad definition of evil, the Manichaeans could easily present it as an active force to both the uneducated masses as well as the intellectuals. In one of Augustine's homilies, we have an excellent illustration of how a Manichaean preacher could capitalise on a mundane situation to make a theological point on the evil nature of creation. A Catholic was once greatly troubled by flies and confessed to a Manichaean who chanced upon him that he could not tolerate flies and hated them exceedingly. The Manichaean asked him, 'Who made them?'. Since he was suffering intensely from the flies, the Catholic dared not say, 'God made them', even though as a Catholic this was expected of him. The Manichaean, who was clearly working through a stock of prepared questions, immediately asked, 'If God did not make them, who made them?'. 'To tell you the truth, I believe that the Devil made the flies.' The Manichaean came out with another prepared question, 'If the Devil made the flies, as you seem to me to be saying since you are thinking more along the right lines, who made the bee which is slightly larger than the fly?'. The bemused Catholic had little choice but to admit that the Devil also made the bee. From the bee the Manichaean led him to the locust, from the locust to the lizard and from the lizard to the bird, sheep, cow, elephant and finally man. He even managed to persuade him that it was the Devil who made man. 'Poor fellow', remarked Augustine, 'being troubled with flies he had himself become a fly as the name Beelzebub means "Lord of the Flies".'[165]

Compared with the Greek east which was much more strongly affected by gnosticism in the second and third centuries, the Latin west was much more susceptible to the dualist solution of the Manichaean to the problem of evil. Whereas Greek philosophers and church Fathers could call upon an impressive tradition of anti-gnostic writings by Clement of Alexandria, Irenaeus and Plotinus among others to formulate their reply to the Manichaean challenge, the Latin west was much less well endowed. Tertullian's attack on Marcion was directed mainly against his misuse of the Christian scriptures. On the

problem of evil, Tertullian resorted to the traditional Christian
response of evil as the result of human volition.[156] In fact, there was
no major Christian writer in Latin on the problem of evil before
Augustine. The only significant Latin anti-Manichaean work
composed in the fourth century was a tract attributed to Marius
Victorinus and addressed to an educated Roman Manichaean called
Justinus.[157] However, Augustine did not seem to know of the work
although he was familiar with the philosophical writings of Marius
Victorinus. The first sign of an intellectual counter-attack on
Manichaeism in North Africa appeared with a certain Elpidius who,
according to Augustine caused him some disquiet when he was a
Manichaean Hearer, for he produced texts in his sermons in Carthage
to which the Manichaeans could make only feeble reflies.[158] One of
Augustine's Manichaean friends, Nebridius, also came up with a
question which Augustine found hard to answer: 'What would the
amassed ranks of the powers of darkness do if the Father refused to do
battle with them? If he was afraid then he was capable of violation but
if he was invincible he had no cause to fight.'[159] Augustine would in
due course employ this argument with considerable effect in his
debate with the Manichaean leaders Fortunatus and Felix after his
conversion.

(7)   EPILOGUE: AUGUSTINE'S BREAK
               WITH THE MANICHAEANS

Milan provided Augustine with the venue for his decisive break with
the sect. He mentions no generous Manichaean hosts there to greet
him which may indicate that the sect was not as well organised in
Milan as in Rome. He was accompanied there by Alypius, formerly
one of his pupils whom he had converted to Manichaeism. Two other
Manichaean friends from Africa joined them, Nebridius and
Augustine's patron Romanianus. The latter had travelled to Milan, the
preferred residence of later Roman emperors, to pursue a legal suit.
This reconstituted circle of old friends was no longer a small
Manichaean cell. As we have mentioned, Nebridius had become
hostile to Manichaeism. They certainly did not prevent Augustine
from attending the lectures and sermons of Ambrose, who, in his
capacity as the bishop of the city had warmly received him when he
first arrived. At first contemptuous of the subject matter of Ambrose's
sermons Augustine listened to him as a professional rhetorician.
However, by means of the allegorical method, Ambrose presented the
Christian scriputres to him in a manner which he found intellectually
stimulating. He had earlier been led by the Manichaeans to think that
they had to be literally understood like the writings of Mani. When his

mother Monica arrived at Milan after a hazardous journey from Africa in the spring of 385, Augustine had sufficiently moved away from the doctrines of Mani to be able to admit to her that though he was not yet a Catholic, he was no longer a Manichaean.[170]

Augustine's celebrated convesion to Catholic Christianity in the garden of his house in August 386 was still a year away and much water still has to flow under the bridge between his determination to leave the Manichaeans and his bapitsm by Ambrose on Easter Day 387. The events of this important period of Augustine's life belong more properly to a biography of Augustine than a study of his experience as a Manichaean. It will suffice to say that Augustine's intellectual horizon was considerably broadened in this period through his reading of the works of neo-Platonists, especially those of Plotinus rendered into Latin by Marius Victorinus. The neo-Platonist view of God as the source of all being released him from the anthropomorphism of the Old Testament and the picture of a good but desperately vulnerable Father of Greatness of the Manichaeans. His perennial worry about the origins of evil was also ameliorated by the neo-Platonist view that matter is not the creation of a hostile power but the outflow of a creative divine source emenating from the First Principle. As a beam of light fades into darkness, so, matter has degenerated owing to its distance from the original into non-existence or evil. Hence, evil is not an active power but merely the privation of good which is inherent in all forms of existence. Augustine would later formulate what he learned from the neo-Platonists into a formidable set of arguments against the Manichaeans on the problem of evil. His own solution ultimately became the majority report of the Catholic church on this very important problem for much of the Middle Ages.[171]

Nevertheless, the teachings of the neo-Platonists did not turn Augustine into a Christian. The last stepping stone to conversion was provided by the Christian ascetical movement which was at last taking root in the Latin west. Augustine came to see that the ideals of the Christian ascetics matched those of the Manichaeans in their stringency but they were not based on a negative view of creation but on obedience and were practised solely for the unfettered contemplation of God. He might have still remained in contact with Constantius, his former Manichaean host in Rome and what he heard about the latter's failure to found a hostel for the Manichaean Elect would not have encouraged him to renew his attachment to the sect. In Milan, however, he had encountered communities of true Christian saints which were presided over by men of learning and moral integrity and the members of which lived in charity, sanctity and liberty.[172]

CHAPTER VI

'THE MOST PERSECUTED OF HERESIES'

Petrus Siculus, hist. Manich 33

(1)   THE BISHOPS AND THE MANICHAEANS

Augustine was made *presbyter* in the diocese of Hippo Regius (modern Boñ, Tunisia) in 391, four years after his conversion in Milan. The Theodosian edicts against the Manichaeans were clearly not rigorously enforced in that city as a local Manichaean *presbyter* by the name of Fortunatus had gained a considerable following and led a 'pleasant existence' (*delectaret habitare*).[1] In other words, his day to day needs as a Manichaean Elect were clearly met in abundance by his many devoted followers. The amnesty of 387 which might have ended Faustus's brief exile was probably seen by imperial officials as being still in force and hence no active step was taken to expel Fortunatus. His popularity, however, caused consternation not only among local Catholics but also among Donatists. Both parties urged Augustine, who was in the process of establishing his reputation as an anti-Manichaean polemicist, to challenge him to open debate. Fortunatus, who had known Augustine as a Manichaean, reluctantly agreed to take part.[2] A flat refusal would have undoubtedly been seen by many as a sign of defeat. The debate, which lasted two days (28 and 29 August 392), was held in the Baths of Sossius before a large crowd which included some who wer genuinely interested in the issues to be debated and many more who were merely curious.[3]

Fortunatus at first wanted to make the morality of the Manichaeans the central issue of the debate, hoping no doubt for an opportunity to extol the virtues of the Elect. Augustine maintained that since he did not know enough about what went on in the prayer meetings of the Elect, they must debate on doctrinal issues. Fortunatus then declared that God is incorruptible, perspicuous, unapproachable, ungraspable, impassible. He inahbits his own eternal light and nothing corruptible could proceed from him.[4] This assertion of the purity of God was intended to form the basis of the argument that evil could not have come from him and must therefore be an external force and co-eternal with God. Augustine could hardly have expected a better opening to the debate from his opponent. To him the incorruptibility of God did not only mean that he was incapable of doing anyone any harm but also that he himself could in no way be corrupted or injured. Thus the origin of evil and the cause of sin formed the main theme of the debate. Fortunatus had completely underestimated his opposition and was much more interested in parading passages of Christian scriptures which seemed to him to argue for a self-existent and external source of evil than in answering Augustine's questions. As a result they often spoke at cross purposes to each other.[5] However, in the second session of the debate Augustine confronted his opponent repeatedly with variations of the same question: 'Why did God have to send forth his soul (i.e. the Primal Man and his Light Elements) if he was incorruptible (i.e. if he could suffer no harm)?'.[6] To this Fortunatus could find no satisfactory answer. By exalting the moral superiority and purity of the Father of Greatness, Fortunatus had turned him into the God of the Christians and the charge that a God who felt so threatened by Darkness that he needed to send a part of himself to appease his adversary could not have been omnipotent was difficult to counter. In the end, Fortunatus declared that he would refer the said arguments to his superiors. He probably sensed from his performance in the debate that his good life in Hippo was coming to an end and that in Augustine he had a skilled, pugnacious and persistent opponent. He quietly left the town and nothing more was heard of him.[7]

However, unless a Manichaean Elect was actually converted and made to anathematise Mani and his teaching, his voluntary or compulsory departure from a city acutally helped the religion to spread. Accustomed to the peripatetic life, the Elect simply moved elsewhere to set up a new cell and begin afresh. Round about 397, the city of Gaza in Palestine was visited by a Manichaean *Electa* called Julia who came originally from Antioch. She might have been expelled from Antioch and had come to find a new start at Gaza. Mark the Deacon who recorded the visit in his *Life of Porphyry*, the Bishop of Gaza, alleged that she bewitched many by her crafty teaching and especially by generous gifts of money.[8] The city of Gaza had been a stronghold of paganism and was favoured by Julian the Apostate in its rivalry with Constantia, is predominantly Christian neighbour. Porphyry had the unenviable task of having to reassert Christianity in Gaza after the reign of Julian and the many new converts from paganism who were not yet strong in their Christian faith provided Julia with rich pickings.[9] Her activities were duly brought to the attention of Porphyry and he summoned her before him. After some preliminary questioning in which she readily confessed to being a Manichaean, the bishop urged her to desist from her beliefs.

Undaunted, Julia demanded that her case should be given a full hearing. Porphyry took this as a challenge to public disputation and told her to appear before him the next day. She duly appeared at the appointed time with four of her companions, two men and two women. Mark describes them as 'meek' and 'pale' which may indicate the effects of frequent fasting on their physiognomy and the extent to which their lives were dominated and regulated by their *Electa*. The debate was recordced by a deacon who was skilled in the shorthand of Ennomus and Mark later published it as a separate work from the *Life of Porphyry*. We no longer possess this work, which is a great pity as according to the *vita* Julia began the debate by making a long and passionate defence of the tenets of her sect. Porphyry was so angered by what he heard that he called upon God to muzzle her tongue. She was instantly struck dumb and died. The sad story of Julia and that of Aphthonius, the Egyptian Manichaean teacher who met the same fate as a result of his debate with Aetius give us some indication of the kind of psychological pressure which could be brought to bear on the Manichaeans in public debates. Deprived of their *Electa*, Julia's followers were like sheep without a shepherd. Porphyry caused them all to anathematise Mani and, after instructing them as catechumens, he received them into the church.[10]

The Manichaeans in Palestine, as Libanius had mentioned in his letter to Priscianus, were found in many places but in small numbers everywhere. The geographical distribution of the sect would have caused considerable problem to the town-based secular authorities in the enforcement of the anti-Manichaean legislations. The wandering Christian ascetic therefore played his part in mopping up small communities of Manichaeans founded by missionaries like Akouas and Julia. Before becoming a famous abbot in Jerusalem, the monk Euthymius (377–473) was accustomed to taking long walks with a few companions in the desert regions west of the Dead Sea. According to his *vita* by Cyril of Scythopolis, on one of these journeys which he undertook sometime before 411, he cured the son of the headman ($\pi\varrho\omega\tauo\varkappa\omega\mu\acute{\eta}\tau\eta\varsigma$) of the village of Aristoboulias at Ziph who was afflicted by an evil spirit. When the news of this miraculous cure got about, the grateful villagers of Aristoboulias built a small monastery for Euthymius and his companions and saw to their needs. We learn from Cyril that some of the Zipheans who had formerly accepted the doctrine of Mani were so inspired by the teaching of Euthymius that they apostasised from the heresy, and, after they had anatnematised Mani, were instructed in the catholic and apostolic faith by the holy man and received the baptism.[11]

An imperial edict of 383 had given the faculty to 'bring charges (*facultas accusandi*) against the Manichaeans by common consent to those who observed the right religion'.[12] This could be interpreted by some Romans as an incitement to anti-Manichaean pogroms. As the crime involved was of a theological nature, the role of the holy man as prosecutor, inquisitor or demagogue would have been of paramount importance. An auto-hagiographical story told by an Egyptian ascetic called Copres to the anonymous author of the *Historia monachorum in Aegypto*, a collection of monk-lives modelled on the *Historia Lausiaca* of Palladius which was published in Greek *c.* 390 and later translated into Latin by Rufinus, shows us how Copres's ability to incite the crowds gave him the decisive edge in his confrontation with a Manichaean preacher:

> On one occasion I went down to the city [i.e. Hermopolis Magna] and there I found a certain Manichaean who was leading the people astray. As I was unable to make him change his mind by debating with him in public, I said to the crowd of listeners, 'Light a large fire in the streets and both of us shall enter the flames, and whichever one of remains unhurt, he shall be the one with the true faith? When the fire had been lit, the crowd dragged us both together to the edge of the flames. But the Manichaean said, 'Let each of us go in by himself and you should be the first one since you suggested it'. Then, having made upon myself the sign of the Cross in the name of Christ, I went into the fire. The flames parted asunder this way and that and did not harm me for the half hour which I spent in the fire. At the sight of this miracle, the crowd made a loud acclamation and compelled the Manichaean to go into the fire. But he dragged his feet as he was frightened and the crowd took hold of him and pushed him into the middle of the fire. He suffered serious burns all over his body and the crowd expelled him from the city in disgrace shouting, 'The deceiver should be burnt alive.' As for me, the crowd carried me with them to the church, ascribing praises to God as they went.[13]

A later version of the story given in Syriac by Anan-Isho says that the Manichaean was entirely consumed by the fire.[14] This pertinent difference may indicate the popular expectation of the outcome of such encounters at a later period.

To return to North Africa, the gap in the leadership of the sect created by the voluntary departure of Fortunatus was eventually filled by Felix who styled himself *doctor* (= *magister*?, i.e. Pe.: *hmwc'g*). He might have come to Hippo after having been made to leave another city. The ability of the Manichaean cells to regroup and re-emerge once the authorities had relaxed their vigilance might have prompted the passing of the sternly worded edict of 399 which not only subjected Manichaeans to severe punishments but also warned that those who maintained Manichaeans in their homes with 'damnable provisions' would be visited by the 'sting of the law'.[15] Some time before 404, the imperial authorities in Hippo confiscated from Felix a set of Manichaean works consisting of five *auctores*.[16] He might have been denounced to them by an informer. Among the undated letters of Augustine is one addressed to an unnamed Manichaean who Augustine regarded as the successor of Fortunatus. Some of Augustines's brethren had engaged him in conversation and he made clear to them that he was not afraid to die since death to him was merely the separation of the good from the evil. In his letter Augustine warned him of the death which he was bringing upon himself by his blasphemous assertions about God. He also challenged him with the same question which had baffled Fortunatus, namely, what need was there for the soul to suffer when God was omnipotent; and if he could not come up with an adequate answer he should leave Hippo.[17]

The recipient of this letter might well have been Felix, as the action he took to recover his books was entirely in accordance with his professed willingness to die. He went before the curator of the city and offered himself to be burnt along with his books if anything of evil could be found in them.[18] This histrionic gesture echoes the call of Copres to a trial by fire between him and the Manichaean which we have just cited and Felix might well have read the story in the Latin translation of the *Historia monachorum* by Rufinus. Augustine took his declaration as a challenge to public debate and Felix duly appeared before Augustine the next day. However, the debate between the two, which was also recorded by stenographers, was not to be an exact rerun of the public spectacle in the Bath of Sossius nearly a dozen years ago. In the intervening time, Augustine had succeeded Valerius as bishop of Hippo Regius and the debate with Felix was held in the cathedral before a small and select audience.[19] This arrangement, according to Augustine, was made to assuage his opponent's fear of crowds. The debate was also held in two sessions with an adjournment of three days at the request of Felix as one of his major complaints at the start of the debate was that he had not been given adequate time to formulate proper answers to Augustine's prepared questions.[20] As soon as the debate was rejoined he complained about his lack of access to his books which were under the public seal and placed before Augustine. He was duly allowed to use the books but Augustine turned down his request for a further adjournment of two days to allow him to study them on the grounds that Felix was hardly a debutant in the teaching of Mani.[21] Felix had shown considerable unease from the start of the first debate. Despite his clamour for martyrdom, he seemed to have been overawed by Augustine's authority as a bishop and he felt too that Augustine was more of an inquisitor acting on behalf of the authorities than an equal partner in a genuine debate. 'For I can scarcely go against your power. For the bishop's position is wonderfully powerful. Nor can I contravene the laws of the Emperors',[22] was the much quoted excuse which he gave to

Augustine as tried to deflect one of the latter's many barbed questions.

The debate covered a wide range of topics including the apostleship of Mani, his teaching on cosmogony, free will, the origins of the soul and the passibility of God. Unlike Fortunatus who was a master in creating diversions whenever he found himself confronted with a topic he did not wish to discuss, Felix actually endeavoured to answer Augustine's questions. This proved to be his undoing as Augustine pursued him relentlessly with the question on whether God could be corrupted – the same question which Fortunatus evaded finally by his voluntary departure from Hippo.[23] Both Manichaean leaders were too Christian in their understanding of God's supremacy and omnipotence to admit that he was fearful of an attack by the powers of evil. In the second session of the debate, Augustine was able to manoeuvre Felix into a position in which not to anathematise Mani would mean giving assent to a worse error of Christian doctrine:

Augustine: The error which affirms that God is corruptible, should it or should it not be anathematised?

Felix: Say that again?

Aug.: The error which affirms that God is corruptible should it or should it not be anathematised?

Fel.: One needs to ask if this is what it says.

Aug.: I have asked you this: He who affirms that is corruptible, should he or should he not be anathematised?

Fel.: He who affirms that God is corruptible or not – is this what you are throwing at me?

Aug.: This is what I am asking.

Fel.: You say 'God is corruptible' but not what you have previously said that he has given a part of himself to his adversaries.

Aug.: I am asking you again to answer my question: He who affirms that God is corruptible, shoule he or should he not be anathematised?

Fel.: Very much so.

Aug.: He who says that the nature and the substance of God are corruptible should he or should he not be anathematised?

Fel.: I do not understand what you are saying.

Aug.: What I say can be understood by anyone who does not pretend not to understand: He who affirms that the nature and substance of God, that is, that thing itself whatever it is that is God, is corruptible, should he or should he not be anathematised?

Fel.: Indeed he should be anathematised if this could be proved to be true.

Aug.: I have not yet said to you that Manichaeus affirms that the nature of God is corruptible but I have said that he who says this should be anathematised.

Fel.: And I have said yes to it.[24]

The debate ended on a triumphal note for Augustine. Felix gave in completely and since the option of leaving the city was not open to him because of what he had promised, he was entirely at the mercy of

Augustine. Instead of insisting that Felix should be burnt with his books he made him anathematise Mani and to sign a simple formula of abjuration:

I, Felix, who was a believer of Mani, now anathematise him and his doctrine and the spirit and the seducer which was in him. He has said that God has mixed a part of himself with the tribe of darkness and liberated it in such an abominable manner that he transformed his powers into female [demons] with respect to male [demons] and into male [demons] with respect to female demons so that he would in due course fasten what remains of a part of him in the globe of darkness forever. I anathematise these and other blasphemies of Mani.[25]

We learn from Possidius's biography of Augustine that Felix was in due course converted to Catholicism.[26]

Standard formulas for the abjuration of Mani and Manichaeism came to be drawn up before the end of the fifth century for those converted from the heresy to Catholicism. One of the best known extant examples of such a formula is entitled the *Commonitorium sancti Augustini*.[27] It is not mentioned in the index of Augustine's writings compiled by Possidius and most scholars regard its link with Augustine as purely a pious attribution. Its compilers might have used his anti-Manichaean works as his source. It was composed before 526 because a slightly expanded version of it was used by a certain Prosper in Lyon to abjure the heresy in that year.[27a]

The bishops played a crucial role in the enforcement of the laws against the Manichaeans as the Roman government did not have a large professional constabulary. It had not proved itself adequate against the Christians in the Great Persecution and was unlikely to fare better against the more elusive Manichaeans. In a constitution of Honorius and Theodosius II we find the task of executing the laws against the Manichaeans and Donatists being assigned to specific members of the secret service (*agentes in rebus*).[28] That this supplementary force was necessary seems to imply that the normal machinery for enforcing the laws in the provinces were insufficient. Furthermore, as barbarian attacks began to disrupt the existing system of provincial government, the task of combating heretics must have fallen heavily on the shoulders of church leaders. The bishop's involvement was in any case unavoidable as he alone would have sufficient knowledge of the heretical doctrines concerned to substantiate a charge against a person accused of heresy or a group of heretical assembly. An official like the Tribune Ursus who detected and arrested a group of Manichaeans in a church sometime between 421 and 428 could deal with accusations of immorality against the sect by summoning a midwife to examine one of them who was a sort of nun (*sanctimonialis*) and claimed to be a virgin.[28a] However, it was unlikely that the entire trial could have been conducted in the absence of a trained theologian. It is interesting to learn from the episcopal acts which Quodvultdeus sent to Augustine from Carthage that when some Manichaeans were discovered there some time before 428, they were taken to the church for questioning rather than to the headquarters of the imperial administrator or the city council.[29] A bishop would have certainly been needed to press home the charge of heresy and if the accused were prepared to recant it would be his task to ascertain the genuineness of their abjuration. If he was satisfied, then he alone had the authority to issue them with a certificate in the form of a letter which would protect them from then on from being inconvenienced by the anti-heretical laws.[30] Moreover, if the penitent had been an Elect, it was the duty of the bishop to oversee his rehabilitation. As the *Commonitorium* explains:

The letter however must not be given readily to their Elect who say they have been converted to the Catholic faith, even if they themselves have anathematised the same heresy according to the above formula, but they must remain with the servants of God, either clerics or laity, in a monastery or a guest-house for strangers [xenodochium], until it appears that they are completely free of that superstition itself. And then, either let them be baptised, if they have not been baptised, or let them be reconciled, if they have received the status of penitence. And, when they have received the letter, let them not move quickly elsewhere and heedless in themselves on account of the same document. They must be questioned if they know of any [other Manichaeans] so that they also may themselves be healed and thus be admitted to [the Catholic church].[31]

The bishop would have also been responsible for extracting from those who wished to abjure Manichaeism information concerning the identity of the other members of their respective cells. For a Manichaean Hearer who was a man of property, the inability to make an effective will which would result from his conviction could be a considerable inconvenience. The upper classes of the later empire were particularly dependent upon their status to protect their wealth by litigation and a penalty like *infamia* which involved the denial of testamentary rights could involve their heirs in long and costly court cases.[32] In a brief document first published by Baronius in 1740 and which has since then often been wrongly associated with the *acta* of the debate between Felix and Augustine, we have the signed statement of a certain ex-Manichaean called Cresconius who rejoiced in his conversion by denouncing his co-religionists in Hippo and Tipasa to the authorities before his 'departure':

I, Cresconius, one of the Manichaeans, have written [this] because if I should depart before the proceedings have been signed, so I should be considered [i.e. as a Manichaean] as if I had not anathematised Mani. Happy in my conversion from Manichaeism[*Felix conversus ex Manichaeis*] I have said – God being my witness – that I have confessed the whole truth about which I know, that in the region of Caesarea, Maria, and Lampadia, the wife of Mercurius the money-changer [*argentarius*] are Manichaeans and I have prayed together with them before the Elect Eucharistus. Caesarea and her daughter Lucilla, Candidus who live in Tipasa, Victorinus, Hispana, Simplicianus and the father of Antoninus, Paulus and his sister who are at Hippo, these I have known to be Manichaeans through Maria and Lampadia. This much I know. So if I could be shown to know more than I have said, I confess myself condemned.[33]

Augustine and Porphyry were not the only two bishops which the Manichaeans had to fear in the first half of the fourth century. Rabbula became bishop of Edessa in 412 and until his death in 435, he waged a tireless campaign against the various heretical sects of that city. The position of the orthodox in Edessa had clearly improved as a result of the anti-heretical legislations of the Theodosian era. Unlike Ephraim who was only a deacon and had to reply on his literary skills to restrain the spread of the teachings of Mani, Marcion and Bardaisan, Rabbula the Bishop could play a much more active role in ridding the city of these heresies. His tally of victories is commemorated in his panegyric-like *vita* in Syriac:

Just as in the days of old, Hoshua [*ysw'*] the son of Nun and [later, King] Josias [*ywsy'*] found the land of Caanan firmly planted with every thorn of paganism, likewise he [i.e. Rabbula] found the entire region of Urhai [i.e. Edessa] solid with every briar of sin. The wicked teaching of Bardaisan flourished in particular in Urhai until it was vanquished and uprooted by him. For, through his cunning and the sweetness of his songs, this accursed Bardaisan had once drawn all the leading people of the city to himself, so that by them he might be protected as by strong walls. For this idiot supposed in his error and in his deception of his followers that by the transient power of the patrons he would be able to make his error firmly established. However, this skilled cultivator of the soil of the heart [i.e. Rabbula] endeavoured not only to attack the tares [*zyzn'*] and to leave the wheat to grow undisturbed which is an easy task, but he also strove to convert the tares into wheat by his wisdom which is truly necessary. Thus, instead of the powerful sound of the trumpets of Joshua and his companions which thundered against the walls of Jericho and brought them down and which annihilated the men and consecrated their possessions to the Lord, this victorious field commander [*rb ḥyl'*] of Jesus Christ through his peaceful and loving voice destroyed the meeting places of the heretics in the power of his God without encountering any opposition and transferred their entire possessions to his church so that he could utilise their building-stones for its improvement. To the followers of this sect [i.e. the Bardaisanites] however, he bestowed great care. He taught them gently and brought them into subjection through his mildness and converted them to the imperturbable truth of the Apostlic Church in which they renounced and abjured their error. He (also) baptised thousands of Jews and myriads of heretics into Christ during the period of his episcopate . . .

Even with an abundance of words I can not show how great his zeal was in caring for the Marcionites. This purulent cancer of the heresy of Marcion he also healed with the solicitude of the great physician [i.e. Christ] and the help of God. For while he handled them with tolerance and long suffering, God sent fear into their hearts in the presence of the holy Rabbula and they faithfully accepted his truth so that they abjured their false teaching. Similarly, through his divine wisdom, he brought the Manichaeans to more composed understanding and more prudent judgement. Therefore they made their confession as he desired. And, they believed in the truth, allowing themselves to be baptised into Christ and to be added to his people.[34]

The stress which the hagiographer put on the mildness of Rabbula in his dealing with the heretics was very necessary as his real character was probably quite the opposite. 'The Tyrant of our city' was the sobriquet by which he was referred to in a letter of Ibas, one of his presbyters, to Mari, a leader of the Church in Persia.[35]

The cellular structure of the sect lent itself to survival as individual units could easily go underground when threatened. As far as we know the Manichaeans did not possess distinctive church buildings like those of the Marcionites in the Roman empire. They met in the form of house-groups, hence an edict of Valentinian I in 372 calls for the confiscation of 'houses and dwelling places' (domus et habitacula) which had been used as meeting places by the Manichaeans.[36] A law of 428 made the owner of the caretaker (procurator) of a house liable to severe fines if it was used by heretics as a meeting place.[37] The large number of houses which had been declared 'derelict' (caducus) as a result of imperial confiscations at the end of the third century might have offered ideal shelter for Manichaean conventicles.[38]

A Manichaean Hearer led a normal life when he was not ministering to the needs of the Elect. As long as he was discreet in his contacts with them he could avoid drawing undue attention to himself from the authorities, especially if the local bishop was not observant or vigilant. Some time after 395, Augustine wrote a letter to Deuterius, a bishop of Mauretania, saying that he had come to know of a certain sub-deacon of that province, a certain Victorinus from Malliana, who had been a Hearer for many years although outwardly he remained a Christian cleric. To aid Deuterius to detect such crypto-Manichaeans, Augustine listed some of the main beliefs and practices of the sect. This Victorinus was an enthusiastic teacher of Manichaeism and probably used his position in the church as cover for his heretical activities. He was betrayed by his pupils who had gained his confidence. He had come to Augustine to ask him to lead him back to the Catholic faith. However, Augustine was so infuriated by this misuse of the clerical status that he expelled Victorinus from the city and recommended to Deuterius that he should not be believed if he should seek an opportunity for repentance unless he was willing to denounce all the Manichaeans he knew in the whole province.[39]

The swift collapse of Roman rule in North Africa before the invading Vandals in 429–30 brought temporary relief to the persecuted heretics and schismatics. Many Romans fled across the seas to Italy and among them were Manichaeans. They helped to swell the ranks of their co-religionists in Rome and, as we shall see, brought a sharp response from Pope Leo I. The Vandal rulers adopted Arianism but once they were firmly established in North Africa, they too became embroiled in her ecclesiastical problems. We learn from Victor Vitensis, our main source on the history of the church in Africa under the Vandals, that they issued at least one law against the Donatists, using as a model a law of the former Roman emperors.[40] They also made occasional demonstrations of the sincerity of their faith to the Catholics by persecuting Manichaeans. Among those whom they rounded up, some were burnt and the rest exiled across the seas. One stalwart Manichaean *monachus*, according to Victor, was found to have the words: 'Mani, the Apostle of Jesus Christ' inscribed appropriately on his thigh. Hunneric, the Vandal king was also greatly embarrassed when he discovered that many of those whom he had arrested as Manichaeans turned out to be Arian clerics.[40a] The Manichaeans somehow managed to survive both the Vandal rule and the Roman reconquest under Justinian which brought with it a reassertion of Catholic authority. North Africa remained in the eyes of the ecclesiastical authorities a hot-bed of heretics and schismatics. As late as 724 Pope Gregory II would still warn against the ordination of Africans who had fled to Italy from the Islamic invaders because many of them were either still Manichaeans or former heretics who had been rebaptised.[41] The Islamic conquest also reunited the Manichaeans in North Africa with their brethren in Mesopotamia. In the time of Abu Ja'far al-*Mansur* (754–75), as we have already noted, a Manichaean from North Africa, Abu *Hilal* al-Dayhuri became the Imam (i.e. *archegos*) of the sect at the Twin-Cities, the traditional seat of the supreme head of the Manichaean church.[42] However, as we do not know whether he was a member of the sect in Africa or an African who became a Manichaean in Iraq, his appointment to the highest office of the sect gives us no clear indication of the sect's strength in North Africa in the eighth century.

(2)   THE POPES AND THE MANICHAEANS

The presence of a considerable number of Manichaeans in the city of Rome became a source of concern to the papacy as early as the pontificate of Miltiades (*sedit* 311–14).[43] From the end of the fourth century onwards, the popes played an increasingly active part in the suppression of the heresy in the metropolis and in Italy. Siricius (*sedit* 384–99) sent those Manichaeans he had discovered into exile and ordered that those who were converted from the sect to be sent into monasteries and not to be admitted to communion till at the point of death.[44] His successor Anastasius (*sedit* 399–401) decreed that he could not ordain any cleric from overseas (*transmarinum*) unless he was certified by five bishops because Manichaeans were detected in Rome at that time.[45] The association of foreign clerics with Manichaeans hints at the strong link between the Manichaeans in Italy and their co-religionists in North Africa which is so clearly evident in Augustine's writings. Another pope who might have taken some form of action against the Manichaeans was Celestine I (*sedit* 422–32) as a law of Theodosius II and Valentinian III published in 425 commands the banning of the Manichaeans from the city of Rome along with heretics, schismatics and astrologers since they had withdrawn themselves from the venerable pope's communion. The same emperors however granted a truce of twenty days to the aforesaid heretics and 'unless they returned to the unity of communion they would be tormented by the solitude which they preferred' after they had been expelled as far as the hundredth milestone of the city.[46]

The conquest of Roman Africa by the Vandals occasioned a steady re-emigration of Roman settlers to Italy. As we have seen, Manichaeans were among those exiled by Hunneric in 477 but many of them might have fled earlier to escape from the fighting and helped to swell the ranks of the sect in the metropolis. Shortly after he had ascended to the throne of St Peter, Leo I (*sedit* 440–61) received a report which informed him of certain rites which were celebrated by the Manichaeans. Leo considered them to be sufficiently scandalous from what he had read to institute a full inquiry. A commission was convoked in late 443 which comprised church leaders as well a sprinkling of leading members of the Roman senate. A number of Manichaean Elect of both sexes were summoned before it and after interrogation they confessed to hideous crimes involving ceremonial intercourse between a youth and girl of ten arranged by a Manichaean bishop.[47] The findings of Leo's court duly prompted the emperors to issue in June 445 an edict which gives prominence to the investigations of 'the court of the most blessed Pope Leo in the presence of the most honourable Senate'. It ordered the arrest of Manichaeans and their subjection to penalties for those who had committed sacrilege. Adherence to the sect was declared a public crime and the opportunity to accuse its followers was given to anyone who wished to do so without the hazard of delation.[48] In one of his sermons Leo urged the faithful to inform on the hiding places of the Manichaeans to their priests for to inform on such enemies of God was not only an act of piety but also a means of grace in the last judgement.[49] He also wrote to the bishops of Italy urging them to be extra vigilant for Manichaean infiltration and a copy of the edict of 445 was also sent to them as a pastoral letter.[50] In another sermon, he suggested that the faithful should be on the look out at Eucharist for those who did not consume the elements, as the Manichaeans would avoid the wine.[51]

Leo's campaign against Manichaeans did not stop at securing the passage of an imperial edict against the sect. According to Prosper of Aquitaine, he also dragged many of them out of their hiding places and compelled them to abjure their error in public. He also confiscated a large number of their books which he ordered to be burnt. To Prosper, the zeal of Leo was divinely inspired 'as it greatly profited not only the city of Rome but also the whole world since from the confessions of those [Manichaeans] captured in the city it was discovered who were their teachers [doctores], bishops and presbyters and in which provinces and cities they lived. Many clerics in the eastern parts [of the Empire] imitated the industry of the Apostolic Bishop.'[52] One eastern cleric who wrote to congratulate Leo for the zeal which he had displayed against the Manichaeans was the famous church historian Theodoret of Cyr.[53] He might have benefited from the information about the sect which was extracted by Leo's inquisitors in his effort to combat the sect in his own diocese.

The persecutions in Rome forced some of the Manichaeans to flee from the capital. One who sought refuge in Asturica in Spain c. 445 was Pascentius. Unfortunately, Turribus, the bishop of Asturica, was an avowed enemy of the followers of Priscillian whom he called Manichaeans and he had earlier discovered and expelled many of them from the city. Pascentius thence fled to Emeritia (Merida) but to his dismay, Antoninus, the local bishop, had earlier been sent the records of Turribius's investigations at Asturica and was therefore alerted to possible fugitive Manichaeans from the north. Pascentius was duly arrested, tried and expelled from Lusitania. The vigorous condemnation of Manichaeism by both sides in the Priscillian controversy had thrown a cordon sanitaire around Spain and southern Gaul and rendered them impervious to infiltration by genuine Manichaeans like Pascentius.[54]

In convoking a special court to investigate the misdemeanours of the Manichaeans in which laymen of the highest social standing sat next to the clerics, Leo was acting entirely within his rights although at first sight he seems to have usurped the judicial powers of the state. As early as 376, Gratian had decreed that matters pertaining to the observance of religion should be heard by the synod of the local diocese and the interpretation of this law in the *Codex Theodosianus* says specifically that matters of contention should be terminated by a trial when the diocesan priests had been convoked by a bishop.[55] Furthermore, in 425, Theodosius II and Valentinian III commanded that bishops following the heretical teachings of Pelagius and Caelestius should be assembled by Patroclus, the bishop of Arles, and unless they were corrected within twenty days from the time of assembly, they would be expelled from the districts of Gaul. The judicial machinery for convicting heretics and compelling them to renounce their error in a specially convoked court was therefore already available to bishops.[56] The laws which Leo tried to enforce were those of the state rather than those of the church. He might have enforced them with an enthusiasm which had not been anticipated by the imperial legislators but his position was very different from that of a medieval pope who possessed his own judicial machinery.

The invasion of the western Roman empire by the Goths inevitably slowed down the pace of persecution of heretics. In a letter on Manichaeans and Priscillianists addressed to Turribius of Asturica (July 447), Leo I regretted that the execution of the laws of spiritual correction had to be suspended in some provinces because of the inroads of the barbarians.[57] Like the Vandals, the Goths who became the masters of the western empire were Arians and the anti-heretical laws of the late Roman emperors were suspended. The most important law code of the Visigoths, the *Breviarium Alarici*, does not repeat the harsh edicts against pagans and heretics found in the *Codex Theodosianus* on which it is based.[58] However, the campaign against Manichaeism was sustained by the papacy and mentions of detection and expulsion of Manichaeans occur so regularly in accounts of fifth century popes in the *Liber Pontificalis* that they give the impression of being a hagiographical motif. Under Gelasius (*sedit* 492–6), the Manichaeans who were discovered in the city of Rome were deported and their books were burnt before the doors of the Basilica of St Mary.[59] Symmachus (*sedit* 498–514) who was insultingly referred to as a Manichaean by the Byzantine Emperor Anastasius because of his objection to the latter's upholding of the *Henoticon*, an edict granting limited toleration to the Monophysites, demonstrated the fallacious-ness of the charge by ferreting out Manichaeans from their hiding places in Rome, sending them into exile and burning their books and images before the Basilica of Constantine.[60] His successor, Hormisdas (*sedit* 514–23) subjected the Manichacans he discovered to investigation under torture (*cum examinatione plagarum*) as well as condemning them to exile and burning their books.[61] Besides these mentions of papal activities against the sect, we know little about

Manichaeism in Italy under the Ostrogoths. The systematic destruction of their books and the exile of their leaders by Leo and his successors gave the sect little chance of recovery in the early Middle Ages.

(3)   MANICHAEISM IN EARLY BYZANTIUM

By the end of the fith century, the Arian controversy had given way to a more localised but equally passionate dispute on the nature of Christ between the followers of Cyril of Alexandria and Nestorius. The followers of Cyril who came to be called Monophysites held the view of Christ having one nature which is both divine and human. Their position could easily be tarred by their opponents as 'Manichaean' since the Manichaeans were insistent on Christ never having had a true human existence. Thus, Eutyches, an extreme Monophysite, was reinstated to his see at the Council of Ephesus in 431 after he had condemned Mani, Valentinus, Apollinarius, Nestorius and all those who say that the flesh of our Lord and God Jesus Christ came down from heaven.[62] However, this disavowal of Mani was never seen by his opponents as adequate and the Eutychians were nicknamed 'Manichaeans' by Severus of Antioch who adhered to a less extreme Monophysite position.[63] Julian of Halicarnassus was another Monophysite who was labelled a Manichaean by Severus because he reckoned the voluntary saving passion of Christ to be a phantasm.[64] Since Severus has shown in one of his cathedral homilies that he had a first hand knowledge of Manichaean literature,[65] the readiness with which he stigmatised his extreme Monophysite opponents as 'Manichaeans' on Christological issues is all the more transparent. However Severus himself was accused by Antiochene monks of being a Manichaean in the synod of 536 for not believing that Mary was the mother of God.[66] In short the term was used as an epithet of opprobrium in early Byzantum with little theological definition. The Emperor Anastasius was habitually called a 'heretic and Manichaean' by Macedonius (patriarch of Constantinople 496–571) because of his upholding of the *Henotikon* of Zeno.[67] It might have been in reaction to this accusation that he issued a particularly harsh decree against the Manichaeans, inflicting on them the death penalty for the first time.[68]

   The desire to conform Monophysites to Manichaeans led to a greater interest being shown by polemicists in Manichaean Christology, especially on its docetism. One of the most detailed treatments of the Manichaean view of Jesus the Messiah (i.e. the historical Jesus) outside the writings of Augustine is to be found in the newly discovered formula for the abjuration of Manichaeism which was very probably compiled by Zacharias of Mitylene:

I anathematise those who do not confess that He [i.e. Jesus] through the holy mother of God and ever virgin Mary, a descendant of David, was incarnate in flesh, flesh which is human and consubstantial with us, and was perfectly made man and was born from her. He was not ashamed to dwell for nine months in her womb which He [i.e. God] had fashioned in an undefiled manner . . . in order that He [i.e. Jesus] should not be thought of as a figment of fantasy and not real by appearing suddenly and without being conceived and born of a woman. For this reason it is written that until His thirtieth year, prior to His baptism, He lived among men and was thus baptised by John, the most holy forerunner and Baptist in the River Jordan and testimony was borne to him by the Heavenly Father, the only good and true God, that He was His Son . . . and the very one who was baptised and not someone else in whom God was well pleased. I anathematise therefore those who think any different from these [statements] and say that while the one who was born of Mary, the one whom they call 'Jesus the Begotten', was baptised and whom they fabulously maintain to have been immersed, it was another one who came out of the water and was witnessed to by His Father and whom they call 'Christ Jesus the Unbegotten' and entitle the 'Luminous' who appeared in the likness of man. They fabulously maintain that while the former was from the evil principle, the other was from the good. I anathematise those who say that our Lord Jesus Christ suffered in appearance and that there was one (Jesus) who was on the cross and another who could not be held by the Jews and who laughed because someone else was hung on the cross. [69]

A remarkably similar statement on Manichaean Christology is found in a letter attributed to the Patriarch Acacius of Constantinople (sedit 471–89) and was addressed to Peter the Fuller, a hard-line Monophysite who was three times patriarch of Antioch (471, 475–7 and 485–8). The Monophysite position on the person of Christ, as far as the author of the letter could see, differed little from that of the Manichaeans:

The Manichaeans, like you, wholly denying the Only Begotten Son of God and His birth from a Virgin, said that the Holy Spirit, who came down from Heaven, in the shape of a dove in the River Jordan, took a body from the water, and conversed among men, and was nailed to the cross, and underwent death for us. [70]

The desire of the followers of the pronouncements of the Council of Chalcedon to use Manichaeism as a negative standard to judge the Christology of their Monophysite opponents may account for the appearance in early Byzantium of short excerpts from certain letters of Mani to his disciples which emphasise the extreme docetic position of the Manichaeans. One which is from a letter addressed to Addas reads:

The Galileans affirm that Christ has two natures but we pour rude laughter on them. For they do not know that the substance of light is not mixed with another matter but is pure, and cannot be united with another substance even

if it gives the impression that it is joined to it. The title of 'Christ' is a name
which is loosely applied and does not give any indication of form and being.
But the Highest Light, remaining one with his own, revealed himself as a body
among earthly bodies, being completely one and the same nature.[71]

The fact that another one of these excerpts is addressed to Scythianus,
one of the forerunners of Mani in the fictional *Acta Archelai* and who
is unattested in genuine Manichaean works, should set us on guard
against accepting the excerpts as genuine.[72] Of the five excerpts we
possess, four come from the anti-Monophysite writings of Justinian
and Eulogius and they all affirm that Christ had 'one nature' ($\mu\iota\alpha$
$\varphi\upsilon\sigma\iota\varsigma$) – hardly a term which Mani himself would have used.[73] These
excerpts are not our only examples of adapted or apocryphal
Manichaean literature which came to the surface in theological
disputes. Towards the end of his life, Augustine entered into a vigorous polemical battle with Julian, the Pelagian bishop of Eclanum
who had the effrontery to call him a 'Manichaean'. In his rejoinder
to Augustine, a work in eight books addressed to a fellow Pelagian
called Florus, Julian reproduced a letter of Mani addressed to a Persian
lady called Menoch which he claimed to have acquired via
Constantinople.[74] The letter reads in part like a Manichaean commentary on certain Pauline passages which are shown to support the
view that concupiscense existed as a permanent force of evil.[75]
Augustine was quick to deny its genuineness. The Manichaeans'
readiness to turn to Paul might have triggered off alarm bells in
Augustine as twenty years ago the Roman Manichaean Secundinus
had appealed to him to return to the Manichaean fold where his
undoubted intellectual gifts would enable him to become the St Paul
of their time and rescue Christianity from Jewish ignorance.[76]

In 527, Flavius Justinianus was crowned co-emperor with the ageing
Justin I in Constantinople. His accession to the throne marked the
beginning of a determined campaign against heretics as well as pagans,
Jews and Samaritans. In a tersely-worded edict issued in the same
year, the two emperors delivered a blistering attack on the Manichaeans forbidding them to appear anywhere as they defiled anything
that came into contact with them. If they were caught in the company
of others they would be subjected to capital punishment.[77]

The publication of the edict seemed to have brought a heroic gesture
from a Manichaean as we learn from the prologue of an anti-
Manichaean work of Zacharias Mitylene:

Refutation [*antirrēsis*] of Zacharias, Bishop of Mitylene, arguing against the
fallacy of a Manichaean and establishing the truth of the one and only principle
which he composed while he was still a *scholasticus* and advocate of the
greatest tribunal of the hyparchs and employed by the Count of Patrimony

when Justinian, our most pious emperor promulgated a decree against the most impious Manichaeans. For at that time, some of them, when the decree against them was promulgated in Constantinople, threw such a pamphlet into the bookshop [βιβλιοπρατείον] situated in the palace and departed. Thereupon the bookseller looked for someone who would refute this Manichaean pamphlet, and finding Zacharias who later became bishop of Mitylene, he gave it to him asking him to compose a refutation [antirresis] of it. For he knew him from the seven chapters, or Anathemas, composed by him against them [the Manichaeans], to be a specialist in the refutation of such fallacies. Accepting it, he refuted it as follows.[78]

Zacharias was also the author of the biography of Severus, the Monophysite bishop of Antioch, and in it we also find someone being given a heretical pamphlet to refute by a bookseller. The similarity between the two stories seems to suggest that in the case of the prologue to the anti-Manichaean work we are dealing with a literary *topos* which contrives to give a greater sense of cogency to a piece of polemical writing.[79] The author's choice of the publication of the edict of 527 as the cause of this bold but desperate reaction shows the serious impact of the law on the Manichaean community in Constantinople.

Not long after the enactment of the edict of 527, a public debate was held by imperial command between a Manichaean leader called Photeinos and a Christian called Paul the Persian.[80] This Paul might have been the same person as Paul of Nisibis who was described by Junilius Africanus, the *quaestor* of the sacred palace, as a Persian by race, who had been educated in the famous theological school of Nisibis where 'the divine law was taught by the public masters in the same systematic manner as in our profane studies of grammar and rhetoric'.[81] At the request of a certain African bishop, Primasius, Junilius translated an introduction to the scriptures bvy this Paul into Latin.[82] The date usually given for this translation is sometime between 541 and 548/9 because Primasius was among the African bishops who visited Constantinople in 551 in connection with the affair of the Three Chapters.[83] We also know of a Paul who became head of the school of Nisibis after Mar Aba had been elevated to *Catholicos* at Seleucia-Ctesiphon. He was later (after 540) appointed to the see of Nisibis and held it until 571.[84] To add to this we know of a Paul the Persian from Bar Hebraeus who was celebrated for his knowledge both of ecclesiastical science and pagan philosophy and was the author of an introduction to Aristotelian logic. He then aspired to become metropolitan of Persis (Fars) but was unsuccessful and decided to become a convert to Zoroastrianism.[85] On the other hand, 'Abdiso' in his catalogue of ecclesiastical writers names Paul of Nisibis as the author of a *Commentary of Scripture* and a *Disputation against the Caesar* (i.e. Justinian).[86] There has been much speculation on how these various Pauls from Persia could be narrowed down to one or two persons.[87] Justinian's appointee for the debate with Photeinos might have been the same Paul as the one whose work on scriptures was translated by Junilius and he might have even been the one mentioned by Bar Hebraeus who later apostasised to Zoroastrianism. He was unlikely, though, to have been the same person as Paul of Nisibis who debated with Justinian, as such an encounter would have most probably taken place after the signing of a more permanent peace treaty between Byzantium and Persia in 562.[88]

The debate between Paul the Persian and Photeinos the Manichaean in 527 was presided by the Prefect Theodore (Teganistes) and was in three sessions, spread over a number of days. The first debate concerned the creation of souls and in his arguments Paul the Persian showed a thorough knowledge of classical Greek philosophy.[89] Photeinos opened the debate by asking whether the human soul which both the Christian and the Manichaean would agree as being rational and intellectual comes from a divine substance. The Christian made the careful reply that he distinguished between the 'whence' ($\pi\delta\theta\epsilon\nu$) and the 'from what' ($\xi\kappa\ \tau\iota\nu\sigma$) and then steered the Manichaean into a position of admitting that the souls are derived from an object.[90] The Manichaean argued vehemently that souls could not have been created out of things that do not exist since anything created out of nothing will eventually dissolve into nothing. The Christian replied that this fear would have been legitimate if not for the fact that creation was the result of divine will and is sustained by divine power.[91] He then proceeded to attack the Manichaean view that human souls are made of divine substance by arguing that divine substance is indivisible and without sin. Therefore it is absurd to think that it can be divided into souls which are capable of sinning.[92] Like Augustine, Paul the Persian saw evil as the capacity to sin and since the Manichaean could not bring himself to confess that the human soul is entirely without sin, his belief that souls are of divine origin was seriously impaired:

Christian: God is entirely without sin or is He in some way sinful?
Manichaean: God is entirely without sin.
Ch.: And the same with the soul? Or, is it in some way sinful?
The Manichaean could find no reply to this and after a period of silence, the
    Christian said: Since you are silent and eyeing everything with suspicion,
    God must therefore be entirely without sin and the soul not entirely without
    sin. Hence, the soul is not of divine substance.
Manich.: This general conclusion can not be inferred directly from what has
    passed between us so far.
Ch.: Show me that it is as you say.

Manich.: I am bound in chains and I can not.

Ch.: The body may be bound but the soul is not fettered by chains. According to you the soul is uplifted by the humiliation and suffering of the body since the latter is evil by nature. Therefore you should discourse in chains rather than without them for the body will be brought low by them while the soul will be uplifted by the same.

Manich.: If the officials will render me assistance, I shall continue to debate. Since I am no receiving help from anyone I shall remain silent.

Ch.: Are you a teacher (διδάσκαλος) of the Manichaeans?

Manich.: I confess I am.

Ch.: Is it for the sake of truth that Manichaean teachers suffer, or would you answer some other way?

Manich.: For the sake of truth, I think.

Ch.: Did the Blessed Apostle Paul have the help of officials when he was cast into jail, or, did he neglect his own teaching because he did not have this help?

The Manichaean fell silent at this point and offered no reply.[93]

The fact that the Manichaean was in chains shows that the debate was even more one-sided than Augustine's disputations with Fortunatus and Felix. Paul the Persian was officially appointed by Justinian and since his function was primarily as an inquisitor, he could afford to be cynical. The second and third sessions of the debate dealt with more conventional topics of dualism and the authority of the Old Testament.[94] However the entire debate was conducted on a higher philosophical level than Augustine's verbal contests with the Manichaean leaders of Hippo. Both the Christian and the Manichaean seem conversant with Aristotelian concepts concerning the soul. If the inquisitor was ideed the same Paul who, according to Bar Hebraeus, wrote an introduction to Aristotelian logic in Syriac and later apostasised to Zoroastrianism, he would have been a formidable and unscrupulous intellectual opponent for any heretic.

The harsh pronouncements by Justin and Justinian on the Manichaeans were not empty threats. According to Malalas, many Manichaeans were put to death by Justinian and among them was the wife of a certain patrician by the name of Erythrius.[95] However, we learn from John of Nikiu that this Erythrius was known as a disciple of Masedes (i.e. Mazdak) and we may assume that his wife was also a follower of his teaching.[95a] It seems unlikely that some sort of alliance could have been forged between Manichaeans and Mazdakites in the early Byzantine empire simply because both sects were exiled from Persia. What we witness here is another example of the confusion of names which has bedevilled the detailed study of Manichaeism in the sixth century. Some Mazdakites might have managed to escape to the Byzantine empire from the persecution of Kawad. Furthermore, according to Bar Hebraeus, another religious group which escaped from Persia into Armenia and hence to Syria at this time were the Messalians [mlywny'] an ascetical sect which he regarded as a branch of the Manichaeans. They occupied monasteries and held mixed nocturnal meetings, where, after having put out the light, the men took hold of any woman present, even another man's mother or sister.[96] It is worth noting that a similarly-worded accusation against the Manichaeans found its way into a post-ninth-century Greek abjuration formula. It anathematises those who have intercourse with their sister, mother-in-law or daughter-in-law and those who ostensibly gather for a feast (i.e. the Feast of the Bēma) in spring and who after much drunken revelry turn out the light and submit themselves to debauchery without regard to sex, kinship or age.[97]

The severe censure of Manichaeism in the edict of 527 was reinforced by other legal enactments in the next few years after Justinian had become sole emperor. One of them confirms the ineffectiveness of wills made by Manichaeans and the illegality of their gifts made during their lifetime.[98] Another law of this period stresses the enormity of the crime of false conversion from Manichaeism and decrees the death penalty for those who had relapsed and had secretly rejoined the sect. It also calls for the burning of Manichaean books and a diligent search for Manichaeans who held imperial office. In the increasingly bureaucratic society of early Byzantium, to be debarred from holding imperial office would have been a serious stumbling block to any form of social advancement. Justinian, like his predecessors, was anxious that the Manichaeans should give up their faith voluntarily. The same edict of 527 (?) makes clear in its preamble that these drastic measures were prescribed only after due warnings and adequate provisions for amnesty had been given to the heretics by the imperial authorities.[99]

The state also seems to have been more effective in religious coercion in early Byzantium than in the last century of Roman rule in the west. Justinian did not hesitate to threaten bishops with removal from office if they did not make sure that the provincial governors performed their duties in the enforcement of laws against heretics and pagans. Even the patriarch of Constantinople was told in no uncertain terms to co-operate with imperial authorities by informing on officials who had been lax.[100]

The role of the clergy in early Byzantium seems to have been ancilliary to that of imperial administration in the campaign against heresy. The laws make clear that if instances of laxity among secular officials were discovered, the duty of the clergy was not to take the law into their own hands but to inform the provincial governor.[101] As trained theologians, the clergy were still needed by the state to ascertain whether someone professed a heresy but their judicial role was kept within bounds. The debate between Photeinos the Manichaean and Paul and Persian which was held in Constantinople in 527 was conducted under the supervision of an imperial official. Paul himself was a nominee of the emperors Justin and Justinian and his personal role in combating the heresy was therefore more subdued than that of Augustine in the west, who less than a century earlier had held forth on his own initiative from his *cathedra* on behalf of the faithful of Hippo against the Manichaean 'foreigners' (*peregrini*).[102]

The sect was so remorselessly persecuted by Justinian that it became extinct in Byzantium in the course of the sixth century. The term 'Manichaean' nevertheless remained as an epithet of opprobrium for many more centuries and was used by Byzantine churchmen to castigate novel heretical sects like the Paulicians and the Bogomils whose doctines manifested dualist or gnostic traits. The refutation of Manichaean dualism also became a standard form of rhetorical training for the theologians. The anti-Manichaean works of Byzantine theologians like John of Caesarea, John of Damascus, Photius and 'John the Orthodox' are statements of orthodoxy *vis à vis* Manichaean dualism as popularly conceived.[103] They are certainly not systematic refutations of Mani's teaching based on first-hand knowledge of Manichaean works. The same lack of interest in the genuine teaching of Manichaeism was shown of Peter of Sicily, one of the first heresiologists to pin the label of 'Manichaeans' on the Paulicians of Armenia. He based his knowledge of Manichaeism almost exclusively on the historical sections of the *Acta Archelai* as summarised by Cyril of Jerusalem.[104] Had the Paulicians been genuine descendants of the Manichaeans, they might have possessed some authentic Manichaean texts which could have provided Peter with more accurate information on the early history of the sect. As we shall see, the remnants of the sect who survived in Ch'üan-ch'ou in South China until sixteenth century had a reasonable knowledge of the history of the diffusion of the sect and possessed genuine Manichaean works.[105]

In the eighth and ninth centuries, the Iconoclasts of Byzantium were branded as Manichaeans by their opponents. When one considers the Manichaeans' veneration of their images and paintings, the charge seems highly inappropriate.[106] As we have noted, the genuine followers of Mani at that time in Muslim Iraq who preferred conversion to execution were required by the 'Abbasid authorities to spit on an image of Mani as a form of abjuration.[107] The frequent and mostly inaccurate use of the term 'Manichaean' was typical of the Byzantine practice of understanding new problems in the light of the old. The laws against heretics too became fossilised. The Justinianic laws against Manichaeans were retained by Byzantine emperors for use against hersies in general and in particular against those sects like the

Paulicians and Bogomils on whom the charge of Manichaeism could more easily be made to stick. As Manichaeans were the only heretics to be regularly threatened with the death penalty in the laws of the late fifth and sixth centuries, the charge of Manichaeism was the ultimate political weapon in theological controversies.[108]

The Byzantine emperors spoke of their body politic as 'our Christian state' (ἡ ἡμῶν τῶν Χριστιανῶν πολιτεία). Membership of this 'koinonia' or community was confined to those who subscribed to the orthodox faith. Racial or cultural differences did not form the same barrier as did heresy. Thus, the Arabs were no part of this koinonia not merely because they were of the Semitic race and speakers of a different language but because they were followers of a Christian heresy.[109] In this theocracy, Jews, pagans, Manichaeans and heretics were second-class citizens as a result of the process of civil excommunication which had begun since Theodosius. The position of a Manichaean in the Byzantine empire was not that of a peregrinus of the Roman empire, as he could not even claim the protection of ius gentium, but that of a 'rightless citizen', resembling a prisoner of war (dediticius).[110]

In the Byzantine empire, apart from those who were born Jews or Samaritans, most citizens would have been brought up as Christians. As the missionary situation began to wane, adherence to any form of heresy could therefore be regarded as apostasy. The myth grew that Mani himself was an apostate. He was once a good Christian, an active warrior who defended the true faith against Jews and pagans. He apostasised only after his disciples had failed to gain the recognition which he thought they deserved.[111] Since Christianity in Byzantium meant orthodox Christianity, heresy was non-Christian and Manichaeism, which had its origins in enemy territory and had hitherto existed on the fringe of Christianity, became the embodiment of the Byzantine concept of heresy. Hence, a Byzantine scholiast on Basilica XXI, 1, 45 defines that sect as follows:

> The disciples of the Mad [Μανέντος] Persian [i.e. Mani] introduce two prin-ciples and two gods, the one good and the other one evil. They disregard every form of religious observance which they attribute to the evil deity and irreve-rently empty it of any significance. They possess certain gospels with they attributed to Philip and Thomas. They worship the sun, the moon, together with the stars and assert that the Incarnation was illusory.[112]

Such a definition is formulated in the light of the Byzantine church's experience of heresies in general rather than the genuine teachings of Mani. Hence it magnifies those aspects of heresy which the church found to be particularly pernicious, namely, sorcery, dualism, docetism and iconoclasm. This flexible use of the term 'Manichaean' coupled with the draconian penalties against the sect accounted for the extraordinary survival of the anti-Manichaean laws in the Byzantine law codes. The majority of the laws against heretics in the *Basilica* are repetitions of Justinianic laws against Manichaeans.[113] In the *Hexabiblos* of Constantine Harmenopoulos, a summary of Justinianic laws compiled in the fourteenth century, the only laws against the heretics to be cited are those against the Manichaeans showing that 'heresy' and 'Manichaeism' were virtually inter-changeable concepts in Byzantium.[114] It is not unamusing to read in the *Hexabiblos* that the penalties against the Manichaeans were still applicable to the Donatists in the fourteenth century, since North Africa, the home of Donatism, had been ruled by the Arabs for almost seven hundred years.[115]

Becoming a 'Manichaean' in Byzantium, therefore, was like deserting one's own country to become a citizen of a 'theological' Persia, perpetually at war with the Romans. The *Hexabiblos* aptly describes the process by which a Christian became a heretic as rebellion (ἀποστάντες).[116] Judging from the severity of the punishment inflicted on the Manichaeans *vis à vis* that of the Jews, the Byzantine government feared heresy more than armed rebellion. The Jews actually resisted the efforts of the Christian emperors at forced conversion and on one ocassion even massacred an entire Christian community.[117] However, the emperors safeguarded carefully the special position of the Jews. Though they made them second-class citizens, they ensured their survivals as a community in order that they might serve as a living testimony to the Christian interpretation of the scriptures and to the victory of the Catholic Church.[118] Those emperors who ordered the wholesale conversion of Jews at the point of death made use of special legislations (*novellae*) rather than altering the statutes in the law codes.[119] While armed rebellion was committed against the majesty of the emperor, apostasy was against the majesty of God. As Mommsen has reminded us, the Christian church was not identical with the Christian state. Delicts against the Christian religion were considered offences against the true majesty of God from whom all earthly majesties are derived.[120] Thus heresy, the principal form of *laesa religio* in the Christian empire was not regarded in exactly the same light as *laesa majestas* which covered both rebellions against the state and delicts against the state cult in the pagan empire. In the exceptionally harsh penalties against the Manichaeans, we have arrived at the conceptual gulf which separates the majesty of this world from the majesty on high which we associate with the Middle Ages and have discovered that the values of the pagan antiquity were becoming incomprehensible to the medieval mind.[121]

CHAPTER VII

FROM MESOPOTAMIA
TO CH'ANG-AN

(1)   MANICHAEISM IN TRANSOXANIA
(FOURTH TO SEVENTH CENTURIES AD)

In Manichaean tradition, the entry of the religion into the lands east of
the Oxus was symbolised by an encounter between Mar Ammo, the
disciple of the east, and the spirit Bagard who guarded the frontier.
The real identity of this spirit was perhaps the goddess Ardvaxš who
was associated with rivers, especially the Oxus.[1] She stopped Mar
Ammo at the frontier and refused him entry. While Mar Ammo
remained there fasting and praying for two days, Mani appeared to him
and told him to read aloud to the spirit the chapter entitled 'The
collecting of the gates' (hrwbysn 'y dr'n) from his *Treasure of Life*.
When the spirit reappeared she asked him for the purpose of his
visit and when she heard that he had come to teach that one should
abstain from wine, flesh and women, she informed him that there was
no shortage of men like him in the lands where she ruled. Mar Ammo
then read to her 'The collecting of the gates' as Mani had instructed
and on hearing it she realised that Mar Ammo was not merely a 'man
of religion' (dynd'r) but a 'true bringer of religion' (dyn'wr 'y r'st) who
had no equal. Since he had been received by her, the gate of the whole
east was now opened for him.[2] It appears from a very fragmentary text
of Manichaean missionary history that Mani himself had encountered
this frontier spirit on one of his missionary journeys and that after
their meeting he proceeded to a city and introduced himself to the
local king as a 'Doctor from Babylon'.[3] We may assume that he won
the king's approval and favour after performing his usual repertoire of
miraculous healings.

Like the story of Mani's conversion of the Tūrān-Šāh, the account of
Mar Ammo's encounter with Bagard bears the marks of being a
product of the Manichaean communities in the east. As a result of the
missionary work of Mar Ammo and his helpers like Zurvandad and
Chusrō, Manichaeism had come to be well established in Transoxania

in Mani's lifetime. In the course of the sixth century the Manichaeans in the east began to challenge the authority of the *archegos* in Babylonia and this led to a schism.[4] The leader of the eastern section was probably Mar Šād-Ohrmizd whose year of death (c. 600) was used, in addition to that of Mani, by the Manichaeans in Central Asia to date a hymn book in Middle Persian.[5] The Manichaeans in the east called themselves 'The True (or Pure) Ones' (*Dīnāwwarīyah*, hence Chinese: *tien-na-wu*). They looked back to Mar Ammo as the 'historical' founder of the sect and the point of the story about Bagard lies precisely in Mar Ammo being called '*dēnāwar ī rāst*' (bringer of the true faith). Having cut off their ties with the homeland of the sect, the Dēnāwars turned their attention to the evangelisation of the lands east of the Oxus and eventually took the religion to China. At the time of the Muslim conquest of Central Asia, the 'Eastern Diocese' (*xwr's'n p'ygws*) of the Manichaean church had extended its influence over a vast area and was impressivley organised into monasteries and assemblics with its *archegos* probably at Qočo (Kao-ch'ang), under whom were heads of monasteries, prayer masters, preachers, hymnodists and scribes as well as lay brothers and sisters.[6]

The lands which lie north-east of the River Oxus (Amu-Darja) were known to the Greeks as Sogdiana, a region familiar to classical scholars through Alexander's victories there against Persian princes who imagined that they were safe within their impregnable fortresses.[7] The Greek victories led to a dispersion of Sogdians who soon established a string of colonies from Merv to the western frontier of China.[8] At the time when Mar Ammo and other Manichaean missionaries were active in Transoxania, Sogdian traders had already established a reputation as the principal conveyor of goods, especially silk, between China and the lands to the west of the Pamirs. The importance of the merchant in Sogdian society was reflected by their social position. Whereas in Sassanian Persia, the merchants were grouped together with other common folk to form the last of the four social classes, in Sogdiana they formed a class of their own (*γw'k-ry*) in between the aristocracy ('*'ztk'r*) and the artisans (*k'ry-k'r*).[9] The Chinese had begun to export silk on a commercial basis to the west since the first century AD. The Sogdians, with their net-work of trading colonies were quick to benefit from this lucrative trade. The Chinese needed in return war horses for their cavalry in order to counter the highly successful Hsiung-nu horsemen. The home of the 'blood horses', a term which the Chinese gave to a particular type of stallion, was situated north-east of the Pamirs in the region of Ferghana and Tochara.[10] The Sogdians, who had connections on both sides of the Pāmirs, were the ideal middlemen for exchanging Chinese silk for war-horses. Thus, given Sogdiana's regular contacts with

China, it is commonly assumed that once the Manichaean missionaries had established a bridgehead on the Oxus, their religion would have soon found its way to the Far East.

However, we have to wait for three centuries before the Middle Kingdom would hear of the teaching of Mo-mo-ni. With the conquest of north China first by the Hsiung-nu and then by the Tobas and other Turkic tribes, the once vigorous trade along the Silk Road came to a standstill. The confused political situation was not conducive to trade and the despondence of the merchants is clearly borne out by a letter from a Sogdian merchant to a colleague in Samarkand which was probably never delivered. Writing from a Sogidan trading community near Tun-huang (Ptolemy's Θρόανα), Nanai-vandak's letter was, in his own words, 'a tale of debt and woes'.[11] The 'Huns' had captured Lo-yang (*Sarag* in Sogdian), the eastern capital of China and had laid waste to Yeh (*$^eNgap^a$*) and the important commercial city of Hsien-yang (*$^aKhumdan$*). The emperor had fled from his capital and the countryside was stricken by war and famine. Nanai-vandak could see no future in doing business with China. In fact, he had not heard from his agents 'inside' for nearly three years. One agent got back to report to him that the Indians and Sogdians in Lo-yang had all died of hunger.[12]

To add to the confusion, Sogdiana itself became the victim of invasion by barbarian tribes towards the end of the third century. Chinese sources say that the land was conquered by the Hsiung-nu who killed her king.[13] Whether they were the same Hsiung-nu who had earlier invaded North China is still a matter of doubt as the Chinese, like the Sogdians and Indians, tended to use the term 'Hsiung-nu' or 'Hun' indiscriminately to describe very different tribes of nomadic people.[14] In the fourth century, Sogdiana was probably ruled by the Chionitae, whose king Grumbates was an ally of the Persian king Shapur II at the siege of Amida against the Romans in 359 AD.[15] In the fifth and sixth centuries, Sogdiana was associated with the Hephthalites or White Huns, who in 484 annihilated a Persian army led against them by Pērōz.[16] How the Hephthalites supplanted the Chionitae is obscure. It is possible that the Hephthalites were not new invaders but members of a loose confederation of tribes who had gradually risen to a position of leadership.[17] Their dominion lay astride the main trade routes west of the Pāmirs. Recent discoveries of Sassanian coins in China of this period bearing Hephthalite counter-marks attest to their hold over east–west commerce.[18] Chinese sources also mention a diminution in trade and political contacts between China and the countries of Transoxania. The *History of the Wei* (*Wei-shu*) says that many merchants from Su-te (i.e. Sogdiana) used to come and sell their ware in the land of Liang (i.e. modern Kan-su). However, when the region was conquered by the Toba rulers of the Wei dynasty of north China, all the Sogdian merchants there were taken captive. The king of Sogdiana sent an emissary asking to be allowed to ransom the prisoners. The Wei emperor ordained that the request be granted. 'Since then', says the *Wei-shu*, 'no envoy has come from them to offer tribute.'[19] The *History of the Sung* (*Sung shu*) also adds that in the Ta-ming period (547–64), Su-te sent a tribute mission to China to present lions and 'blood horses' from Ferghana to the throne. However, bandits deprived them of their horses before they could reach China.[20]

Recent archaeological discoveries have modified somewhat the once commonly held view of a complete cessation in east–west trade in the sixth century. The number of Sassanian coins which have so far been discovered in China is considerable and they could not have all come from Hephthalite tributes.[21] We hear of the occasional tribute from Persia during the fourth and fifth centuries in Chinese literary sources and the envoys might have come together with Hephthalite emissaries at times when the two states were not at war such as during the early years of the reign of Shahanshah Kawad (488–531), who secured his throne with Hephthalite help.[22] Nevertheless, the trade across the Pāmirs was probably conducted by tinkers rather than regular caravans. The body of one such itinerant trader who died of natural causes while travelling through inner Mongolia was not even buried, showing that he had no travelling companions. His cargo of Sassanian and Byzantine silverware was still beside his corpse when it was discovered by workmen in a gully near Huhehot. A *solidus* of Leo I (457–74) helps to set the date of his journey across Central Asia.[23]

Despite the curtailment of east–west trade, the Tarim Basin remained a hive of commercial activity in the fifth century, since China maintained a vigorous overland trade with India, especially in silk. This route was opened at the turn of the millenium when the Sakas were in control of the lands on both sides of the Pāmirs.[24] It also makes use of the oasis towns of the Tarim Basin but instead of traversing the Pāmirs to Merv and Balch as does the *Via Serica*, it turns south to the Ganges Valley before reaching Tochara and Ferghana. Ideal as a highway for the diffusion of Buddhism, Indian monks travelled on it to north China and Chinese pilgrims later used it to go to India in search of Buddhist scriptures. We begin to hear of foreign monks active in the propagation of Buddhism in China from the second century onwards and the link between trade and mission is best exemplified in the person of K'ang Seng-hui, a Sogdian Buddhist priest, whose parents, according to his biography in the *Lives of Eminent Monks* (*Kao-seng-chuan*) by Hui-chiao, traded as far south in China as the Gulf of Tonkin.[25] Since the first century AD the Tarim

Basin itself had become an important centre of Buddhism and acted as a cultural bridge between China and India as well as other centres of Buddhism in Central Asia. Chinese pilgrims would spend time there learning Sanskrit and Pali before they proceeded south to India. Or they would simply try to collect 'simplified' texts of Buddhist sutras from multilingual monks in places like Kutcha who could translate for them into Chinese or Sogidan.[28] Similarly, Indian monks like the famous Fo-t'u-teng would probably have received their basic training in Chinese in the same centres of Buddhist learning.[27] The Tarim Basin was therefore a zone of cultural transition for China as Mesopotamia was for the Roman empire. Once Manichaeism had gained a foothold in the oasis towns of east Turkestan, its passage to China was made considerably easier by the common Buddhist culture which existed between the Tarim Basin and the centres of Buddhism in China.

Many of the Sogdians who resided in the Tarim Basin became Buddhists and they were responsible for spreading the religion westwards to Samarkand and Merv. They also brought the religion to the Turks who were in the process of building a powerful empire in Central Asia in the course of the sixth century. The bilingual inscription at Bugut is a fine testimony to the position both of the Sogdians and the Buddhist religion in the court of the Khaghan. The monument was erected for a Turkish prince but the inscription was in Sanskrit and Sogdian. Ironically, the Sogidan scribe betrayed his own Iranian origin and his Zoroastrian conviction by his choice of religious terms. This mixture of faiths and languages points to the Sogdians as the main civilising influence of the nomadic tribes of Central Asia.[28] They were carriers of culture and religion as well as of goods.

The principal city of Transoxania was Samarkand, and in Chinese sources, Sogdians were generally regarded as the men from Samarkand or Buchara. As the Sogdians were later responsible for bringing Manichaeism to China, it is sometimes assumed that Manichaeism lay dormant in Sogdiana from the fourth to the sixth century when the Silk Road was re-opened. This, however, is not borne out by the sources. Chinese pilgrims occasionally visited Sogdiana during this period and they brought back the picture of a country which was overwhelmingly Zoroastrian in its religious affiliation. According to the *Account of the Western Barbarians* (*Hsi-fan chi*) by Wei Chieh (written soon after 605, *ap. T'ung-tien*) the Zoroastrianism of Samarkand was rich in local rites and rituals:

[The people of Samarkand] customarily worship the God of Heaven with great seriousness. They say that the son of God died in the seventh month of the year and his bones were not recovered. Hence every year when it comes to that month those who worship the God will wear layers of black clothes, go barefooted, beat their breasts and shed tears in great profusion. Three to five hundred men and women will scatter themselves in the nearby fields seeking the bones of the heavenly child. This will go on for seven days. Outside the city walls there is a separate community of over two hundred households who specialise in funerary matters. There is also a separate building in which dogs are kept. Whenever a person dies [members of this community] will go and collect the corpse and place it inside this building and order the dogs to devour it. When the flesh has been entirely devoured, they will bury all the bones but no coffin is used for the burial.[29]

As far as we can tell from our sources, Manichaeism was strongest in the regions south of Samarkand, in what was formerly part of the Kūshān empire, from the fourth to the sixth centuries. The discovery of Manichaean texts in Bactrian and 'Tocharian B', albeit in very fragmentary form, helps to locate the sect to the regions around Balch which was known to the Greeks as Bactria and Ta-hsia to the Chinese.[30] It was situated on the southern trade route between Iran and the Pāmirs. The northern route passes through Merv and it may seem surprising that Merv was not an important centre of Manichaeism in these centuries although missionaries like Mar Ammo were active there earlier. The almost complete absence of later Manichaean activities in Merv from written sources may indicate the effectiveness of Sassanian persecutions, both Zoroastrian and Christian, which had driven the sect further to the south-east.[31] Bactria also came under the suzerainty of the Hephthalites in this period but there was considerably more evidence of Buddhism in this region as distinct from Samarkand which was noted in Chinese sources as a particularly unfriendly place to Buddhist pilgrims.[32] Scholars may argue about the exact policy of her former Kūshān kings towards Buddhism but there is no doubt that the religion commanded a sizeable following in Bactria and Tochara with or without imperial patronage.[33] This is perhaps why Mar Ammo was told by the spirit Bagard at the gates of Khurāsān that he was not needed there as other holy men were there, by whom were probably meant Buddhist monks, who also preached abstinence.

It was during this period of eastward expansion that Manichaeism assimilated many features of Buddhism. A strong Buddhist presence is therefore necessary to help us to locate the whereabouts of the sect before its expansion into China in the seventh century. The use of Buddhist terms is particularly frequent in Manichaean writings in Parthian, which also indicates the depth of Buddhist influence in eastern Iran.[34] Bamiyan, one of the most famous centres of early Buddhism, though more Indian than Persian in its art and culture, was now part of the Ēranshahr through the Sassanian conquest of the Kūshān empire. The discovery of the remains of a Buddhist *stūpa* in the Merv oasis and a Sanskrit manuscript of thin palm leaves containing a commentary on a very early Buddhist sūtra gives us an indication of the westward extension of Buddhism.[35] Although scholars are now less certain about tracing the origins of the Buddhist cult of Amitābha, the Buddha of Light, to Iran, there is no denying that one of its earliest and most celebrated missionaries to China was the monk An Shih-kao, who was reputed to be a Parthian of noble birth.[36] In the same way as their co-religionists in the west used apocryphal Christian gospels and acts to support and illustrate their teachings, the Manichaeans in central Asia made use of the life of the Buddha as a teaching aid, especially on ascetical matters. It was through the Manichaeans in the role of literary intermediaries that the *Life of the Buddha* came to the west via New Persian and Georgian to become the famous medieval saintly legend of Barlaam and Iosaphat whose joint feast day is celebrated in the Roman martyrology on 27 November.[37] When the famous Chinese Buddhist pilgrim Hsüan-tsang passed through Bactria and Tocharistan, he heard that in nearby Persia was a heresy (*wai-tao*) called Ti-na-pa (i.e. *Dīnāwwarīyah*).[38] Since we know that he did not actually visit Persia, he must have learnt about this from Buddhist monks who had more to do with the sect. In its long sojourn in Bactria and Tocharistan, Manichaeism had not only assimilated into its system many Buddhist terms and practices but had also earned the status of a heresy in Buddhist eyes.

(2)   MANICHAEISM AS THE RELIGION
           OF THE 'WESTERN BARBARIANS'

The story of how the Silk Road was reopened in the sixth century is told by the Greek historian Menander the Protector who had a particular interest in Byzantium's relationship with eastern peoples. In the sixth century, the Sassanians made an alliance with the Turks to avenge the indignity which they had suffered at the hands of the Hephthalites. This was tantamount to an invitation to a joint invasion of Transoxania which the Turks eagerly accepted. For the Sassanians, their eventual victory was sweet revenge for the defeat of Pērōz in 484 but more importantly they appeared to have finally overcome the problems of conducting long-distance campaigns which had earlier limited their wars with Rome to a series of hit and run raids. The lessons they learned would in due course be applied with great advantage in their war with Byzantium under Chosroes Parwez.[39] As for the Turks, the destruction of the Hephthalites elevated them to a dominant position in Central Asia.

For the first time since the end of the Kūshān empire, the lands on both sides of the Pamirs came under the same rule and the Sogdians in the court of the Khaghan were the first to see the commercial possibilities of this new political situation. They urged the Khaghan to send a trade mission to the Persian court. Sizabulos, the Turkish Khaghan, agreed to this and the delegation was led by a Sogdian merchant called Maniach.[40] Many scholars have seized upon this name as an indication of his religious affiliation, as the name, if it was derived from Syriac, can mean 'Mani is my brother'.[41] However, this interpretation of the name is highly tentative. Moreover, the practice of adding the suffix -ach to a name to make it mean someone's brother is not often attested in Syriac. The Parthian word for a brother is br'd and in Sogdian it is br't. The 'Mani' part of his name could have come from the Buddhist Sanskrit term for a jewel. It is interesting to note that the word Μανιάκης is defined as a 'torque' in the 'Suidas' (a lexicon).[42] Nor must we forget that in the Alexiad of Anna Comnena we find a Kuman chieftain called Maniach and there is no evidence that he belonged to the sect of the Manichaeans.[43] Similarly, one of the most famous Byzantine generals of Anna's time was George Maniakēs.[44] In short, there is no ground for us to argue that Maniach was a Manichaean from the first four letters of his name.

The plan to sell raw silk to Persia was not well received at the court of the Shahanshah. It was pointed out to Chosroes Anūshīrvān by a Hephthalite in his service that Persia was able to produce silk herself and could rely on imports, presumably from India by sea, to supplement home production. The Persians needed little encouragement to decline the Sogdian offer as they saw in the Turks a potential menace as great as had been the Hephthalites. Poison was administered to the Sogdian envoys at a reception and Manich was fortunate to escape alive with a few companions. He later led a delegation to the court of the Byzantine emperor Justin II. As the most convenient route between Transoxania and Constantinople lay through Persian territory, he and his companions had to take the more arduous route via the Caucasus.[45] The Byzantine court proved to be more receptive to their proposals and Justin sent an envoy to the court of the Khaghan. A military and commercial treaty was concluded between the Turks and the Romans permitting the Sogdians to sell silk direct to the Roman empire.[46] Although it only lasted for eight years it marked a return to more regular trade and diplomatic relationship between Europe and Central Asia. It was undoubtedly through Byzantine envoys to the Turks that the Greek historian Theophylact Simocatta came to know of a place in the east called Taugast, the Turkish name for China. His description of that country is probably the most detailed and accurate account of China in a western language prior to the publication of Marco Polo's Il Milione.[47] The significance of the treaty for the resumption of east–west relations is also shown by the fact that the first of the very few genuine Byzantine coins to be unearthed in China is a *solidus* of Justin II.[48]

Events both in China and Persia also stimulated contact between the two empires. Firstly, China was reunited at first under the Ṣui and then the T'ang Dynasty after several centuries of divided rule and Chinese influence was once more felt in the Tarim Basin. The Chinese also kept the Turks at bay through a series of brilliant campaigns against them under the generalship of Emperor T'ai-tsung of the T'ang dynasty (reigned 627–50). Secondly, with the Crescent looming large on the western horizon, the rulers of Persia and Transoxania turned to China for military assistance against the forces of Islam. According to Chinese sources, the last Sassanian emperor, Yazdegird III (632–51) sent envoys to China requesting direct military intervention to hold back the Arabs but the T'ang government felt that the distances involved were too great for intervention to be effective.[49] As the Arabs pushed relentlessly into Central Asia after the collapse of the Sassanian dynasty, the Chinese were forced to take belated action. A Chinese army under the leadership of a Korean general was sent west of the Pāmirs but it was disastrously defeated on the banks of the River Talas in 751.[50] With the overthrow of the Sassanian dynasty, many Persians fled to east Turkestan and China. Some, like Pērōz, the son of Yazdegird, won fame as mercenaries and condottieri in the service of the T'ang government. Pērōz himself was briefly put in control of a Persian government in exile in Seistan by the Chinese and he later died in China.[51] The tombstone of the wife (or daughter?) of one such Persian *condottiero* inscribed in both Middle Persian and Chinese was discovered at Sian (i.e. Ch'ang-an in T'ang times) in 1955 which shows that he was an officer of an elite corps, the *Shen-ts'e chün*.[52] The Arab conquest also brought about another influx of Manichaeans into Central Asia from the Land of the Two Rivers The Arab rulers were at first tolerant of other religions, and some Manichaeans even returned to Mesopotamia from Khurāsān. After the caliphate of al-Muqtadir (908–32), the Manichaeans had to go into hiding once more and they 'clung to Khurāsān'.[53] These newcomers to Central Asia brought with them practices which alarmed their more conservative co-religionists who were already well established there.[54]

The Sogdians were the principal beneficiaries of this upsurge in trade and diplomatic contact between China and Persia. As caravaneers and traders par excellence, they were instrumental in forging the close ties between China and the west. Samarkand became the boom-town of Transoxania as new trade routes veered north after having crossed the Pamirs and continued on to Byzantium through the Caucasus. Sogdians also exploited successfully the T'ien-shan route which traverses inner Mongolia and Kirghizia. Samarkand was well

situated to be the first major stop on this route which left the Chinese
frontier at Tun-huang and turned north at Turfan into Mongolia
instead of entering the Tarim Basin.[55] From Samarkand, the goods
travelled north as well as west and the presence of Sogdian colonies in
the Crimea and the Caspian Sea shows the extent of their commercial
interest.[56]

We do not possess any fragments of Manichaean history which give
the story of the later eastward expansion of the sect into Sogdian
speaking areas. As far as we know from non-Manichaean sources the
rulers of Samarkand were not sympathetic to the sect. Al-Nadim tells
us that when some Manichaeans fled there from persecutions in the
tenth century, the ruler of Khurāsān wanted to put them all to death.
It was fortunate for the Manichaeans that by then, the neighbouring
king of the Uighurs at Qočo was a Manichaean and he threatened to
kill all the Muslims in his kingdom if any harm should befall the
Manichaeans in Samarkand.[57] Another sign that Manichaeism was not
prevalent in the regions around Samarkand is that the excavations at
Panjikent, an important artistic centre of pre-Islamic Sogdiana, have
so far revealed no traces of Manichaean art as we know it from Qočo
and Turfan.[58] The Sogdian documents recovered from Mount Mugh,
the site of one of the last Iranian strongholds against Muslim invaders
in Sogdiana, are written in the cursive Buddhist script rather than the
squarish Manichaean *Estrangela*.[59]

It was among the Sogdians who traded from oasis to oasis in the
Tarim Basin that Manichaeism found its most ardent followers. They
were the ones who served the business interests of the Turks in their
capacity as traders and advisers. As a Chinese general of the Sui
dynasty remarked, 'The Turks themselves are simple-minded and
short-sighted and dissension can easily be roused among them.
Unfortunately, many Sogdians live among them who are cunning and
insidious; they teach and instruct the Turks.'[60] It is hard to give an
exact date for the beginning of Manichaean missions among sogdian
merchants but the resumption of trade in the sixth century was an
important factor in the eastward spread of the religion. The Turks
often sent tributes of horses to the Chinese court and these horses
were procured by the Sogdians who would thus come into contact
with Manichaean communities in Tocharistan and Bactria. The
Sogdian language came to be used by the Manichaeans alongside
Parthian and Middle Persian for their religious literature in the course
of the sixth and seventh centuries.[61] The spread of Manichaeism was
tied to the trade routes also because the Elect, hemmed in by a host of
taboos, required the constant service of their Hearers. The strict
Manichaean Elect would probably even refuse the luxury of being
transported by an animal which means that they could not travel at

will in the Tarim Basin and their movements would be limited to going from one merchant compound to the next.[62] The association between merchant and Manichaean was so close that in most of the oasis towns the two must have been synonymous.[63] Among the many titles which the eastern Manichaeans gave to one of their leading saints (either Mani or Mar Zaku) in a poetic fragment in Parthian is the 'Greatest Caravan Leader'.[64]

Manichaean priests probably played more than a spiritual role in a mercantile society. Those of a junior rank might have undertaken scribal duties and their hymnodists, as depicted on some Manichaean miniatures, might have performed as musicians and entertainers. Since the priests were normally more sedentary than the caravans, they would have been useful in gathering information for the merchant Hearers *en passant*. As they were ministered to by merchants of different caravans, the priests who prayed and fasted in the merchant compounds would have picked up the latest word on commodity prices, current exchanges rates and news of families back home. In short, they would have information on topics which are contained in the letters in Sogdian which Nanai-vandak and his friends wrote home from Tun-huang in the fourth century.[65] While not attending to the spiritual needs of the merchants, the priests might have served as consultant astrologers to the local courts. In a Saka document of the seventh century we find many calendar details which are clearly Manichaean liturgical terms. This suggests that in the small Saka kingdom at Maralbashi there existed a community of Manichaeans in that period with close contacts with the aristocracy through their skills as astrologers and diviners.[66] In 719 we find Tēs, the King of Cazanistan and Tocharistan sending a *Mōzak* (Mu-che), i.e. a Manichaean priest of the highest rank (= *magister* in Latin sources) as envoy to the T'ang court. He was immensely learned and was particularly well-versed in astrology. Chinese sources say that there was no question which he could not answer. The King specially requested that the *Mōzak* should be allowed to have his own chapel and that the emperor of China should see to his special needs.[67]

The first converts to Manichaeism within China itself were probably Turks and their Sogdian camp-followers who had settled in China after surrendering themselves to the Chinese in the fronteir wars of the sixth and seventh centuries. These residental communities of foreigners were an important link between the Chinese and the more peripatetic caravaneers and traders. Many of their members were multilingual and served as interpreters in business transactions.[68] Living in a more strongly Chinese environment than the oasis towns from which they had come, they would have been more fluent in Chinese than the merchants and were therefore invaluable as translators of literary works. Sogdians in particular were sought after for their skills in translation as they would probably know Khotanese Saka, a language into which many important Indian Buddhist texts have been translated. We even find a Sogdian Christian monk by the name of Adam collaborating in the translation of a Buddhist work into Chinese.[69] Foreign communities in the frontier regions would also have provided hospitality to visitors from the west and helped them to adjust to the new surroundings before they continued their journey into China.[70]

The Manichaeans in China preserved the tradition that the spread of the religion in the Middle Kingdom was inaugurated by the arrival of a *Mōzak* during the reign of the Emperor Kao-tsung of the T'ang Dynasty (650–83). We do not know whether he came solely as missionary or in some official capacity like the *Mōzak* whom Tēs sent to the Chinese court in 719. It would not have taken him long to realise that the Chinese government was trying to bring all foreign religions, including Buddhism, under closer state control. Therefore, when his outstanding pupil, Mihr-Ormuzd (Mi-we-mo-ssu), who held the rank of *Aftādān* (*Fu-to-tan* = *episcopus*), first came to China he presented himself to the royal court where he was granted an audience by Empress Wu (684–704).[71] We learn from a later Buddhist source that he presented a Manichaean work entitled the *Sūtra of the Two Principles* (*Erh-tsung ching*) to the throne which was to become the most popular Manichaean work in China.[72] It is quite possible that Mihr-Ormuzd also initiated the translation of other Manichaean texts into Chinese as one of the characters used in a surviving Manichaean work from Tun-huang was specially created by Empress Wu in 689 and abolished in 705.[73]

(3)   MANICHAEISM IN T'ANG CHINA
         (SEVENTH–NINTH CENTURIES AD)

According to a Chinese Manichaean tradition, Empress Wu Tse-t'ien showed pleasure in what Mihr-Ormuzd had to tell her about his religion and asked him to explain his scriptures to her. The Buddhist monks at her court understandably showed signs of jealousy and calumnated him.[74] Empress Wu herself was a great patroness of the Hua-yen school of Buddhism. Since the Confucian system did not allow for a woman to be head of the state, she had to ransack Buddhist scriptures for the theoretical basis of her rule. In doing so she granted patronage to those Buddhists who would support her claim but also alienated many others.[75] She brought about so many changes that her successors looked back on her reign as a kind of Dark Age. When the short-lived Chou Dynasty which she had inaugurated was abolished in 705 and the T'ang reinstated, temples built after that date were ordered to bear the words 'Chung-hsing', which mean 'restoration'.[76]

With this reaction against the policies of the Empress Wu, it was unlikely that the Manichaeans would receive from the restored T'ang Dynasty the official permission to practise their faith in China which the Nestorians had enjoyed since 632. In 721 serious disturbances broke out among foreign communities in the Six Prefectures and the Chinese government was impelled to keep a closer eye on foreigners in China.[77] To limit the spread of Manichaeism among the indigenous population would help to isolate the foreigners and prevent any co-operation between them and local dissidents. The emperor might also have been urged by political and religious leaders alike to take action against a sect which was actively 'barbarising' Chinese society. A Manichaean priest was duly ordered in 731 to provide the court with a translation of a summary of the doctrines and practices of the sect. A copy of this document has survived and is now commonly known to modern scholars as the *Compendium*.[78] The next year saw the passing of the first imperial edict on the subject of Manichaeism, limiting its practice to foreigners in China:

The doctrine of Mo-mo-ni [= Mar Mani, i.e. Manichaeism] is basically a perverse belief [hsieh-chien] and fraudulently assumes to be [a school of] Buddhism and will therefore mislead the masses. It deserves to be strictly prohibited. However since it is the indigenous religion of the Western Barbarians [hsi-hu] and other [foreigners], its followers will not be punished if they practise it among themselves.[79]

The purpose of this edict was evidently to ban any missionary work by Manichaeans among the local Chinese population. Manichaeism came to China at a time when there was an unprecedented amount of contact between China and the west via Central Asia. The exiled Sassanian court and its followers brought with them Zoroastrianism, and Syrian refugees also introduced Nestorian Christianity. The Persians gained a reputation as conjurors and astrologers *extra-ordinaires*. In the Persian Market in Ch'ang-an the crowds marvelled at the sight of foreign conjurers plunging knives into their bellies and yet remaining inhurt.[80] The Persians also brought to China a more sophisticated calendar which was greatly prized by the Chinese astrologers.[81] The Manichaeans themselves might have been largely responsible for the dissemination in China of a foreign almanac known as the *Almanac of the Seven Luminaries* (*Ch'i-yao-li*) as they required it to work out the important day of Mihr on which they commemorated the death of their founder Mani with the Feast of Bēma.[82] Portions of this work have survived among the manuscripts of

Tun-huang. They show us that the day of Mihr (mi) is particularly auspicious and could be made even more so by the wearing of white dress and the riding of white horses.[83] White, was of course the prescribed colour of ceremonial garments among the Manichaeans.

Zoroastrianism was practised in China almost exclusively by expatriate Iranians. It was not an evangelistic religion and seems to have made little or no attempt to win Chinese followers as we do not possess any Zoroastrian writings in Chinese translation. The Chinese respected it although they found its practices, such as exposing their dead, barbaric and obscene.[84] It is worth mentioning that in the billingual inscription from Sian which we have been already mentioned, the Chinese text says that the deceased lady was the wife (ch'i) of the Persian mercenary commander while the Middle Persian text says she was his daughter (BRTH = dwxt). This difference in wording might have been deliberately contrived by the dedicator of the tombstone to conceal the Persian custom of incestuous marriage.[85] Zoroastrianism died out in China with the expulsion of foreign religions in 845.

Unlike the Zoroastrians who saw themselves as temporary refugees in China, the Nestorians seemed prepared for a longer sojourn in the Middle Kingdom. They formally requested permission from the Chinese court to practise their religion in China and were duly granted it in 638. Having endured repeated persecutions in Sassanian Persia, the Nestorians knew the importance of imperial patronage and were obsequiously grateful for every small token of generosity from the royal house.[87] In 745, they managed to have the title of their religion authorized as 'Ta-ch'in' (i.e. east Roman) so that their temples would not be confused with those of the Zoroastrians.[88] They undertook some missionary work, as there are a number of Nestorian texts in Chinese from the T'ang period among the Tun-huang manuscripts. Some of these are composed in a colloquial style which seems to imply that the Syrian Nestorian priests did not have the help of educated native collaborators in the work of translation and that they themselves did not have a proper grounding in literary Chinese.[89] The missionery success of Nestorianism, however, was limited as we know of few sites of Nestorian churches in T'ang China outside the capital cities of Ch'ang-an and Lo-yang. The religion was expelled along with Zoroastrianism in 845 and for several centuries was largely extinct in China. There is the well known story of al-Nadim which tells of his meeting with a Nestorian monk from Najran in Arabia who had made a special journey in 980 to inquire into the fate of the Christian church in China. To his dismay, he did not meet with one Christian in the whole of China.[90] Nestorianism was re-introduced into China in the thirteenth century by the Mongols, as a significant number of the

Kublai Khan's followers were Nestorians. The religion then became even more closely associated with foreigners than it was under the T'ang and was expelled a century later along with the Mongols.

As foreign religions in China, these three new arrivals from Iran were greatly overshadowed by Buddhism. After a long and difficult period of assimilation spanning some five centuries, Buddhism had by now become an important religious force in China even eclipsing Taoism in popularity and, in the mid-T'ang period, it was the object of considerable royal patronage. The fact that Manichaeism was attacked in the edict of 732 for pretending to be a school of Buddhism may reflect the jealousy of the Buddhist monks of its missionary success and the strength of Buddhist influence at court. However, Buddhism still had its fair share of enemies in China although most Chinese had come to regard it as one of the 'Three (ancestral) Teachings' (San-chiao) the others being Confucianism and Taoism. An outspoken critic of Buddhism in this period was Han Yü (786–824) who based his attack on its foreigness and the fact that it was not known in China at the time of the sages (551–c. 233 BC). In his famous memorial submitted on the occasion of the ceremonious transfer of a relic bone of the Buddha in 819, he gives full vent to his xenophobia:

The Buddha was a barbarian in origin. He was not conversant in the language of the Middle Kingdom and wore clothes of a different fashion. His tongue therefore did not speak the prescribed doctrine of the former Kings, nor did his manner of dress conform to their fashion. He did not recognise the relationship between prince and subject, nor the sentiments of father and son. If he were still alive today and came to our court as emissary by the order of his ruler, your Majesty might condescend to receive him but this should amount to no more than one interview in the Hsüan-chang Hall [where government edicts were issued], one banquet in his honour, one gift of clothing and he would be escorted across the frontier so as to prevent him from misleading the masses.[90]

The same criticisms of foreignness and novelty could have been levied against Manichaeism with greater vehemence since it did not even share the same antiquity as Buddhism. Although Buddhism did not come to China until the first century AD the Buddha was virtually a contemporary of Confucius. Manichaeism, on the other hand, was only five hundred years old and had been in China for about a century. But any attack on Manichaeism or Nestorianism on the grounds of foreignness would implicate Buddhism. As we shall see, when the T'ang court finally ordered the suppression of Manichaeism in 843, the way was paved for a full-scale attack on Buddhism and other foreign cults two years later.

The remainder of the eighth century was a troubled time for the T'ang government. Plagued by factional strife and disastrous frontier wars, the imperial administration was not in a position to rigidly enforce the edict of 732. In 755 occurred the most calamitous event in T'ang history when a powerful military commander by the name of An Lu-shan, who was himself half-Sogdian, rebelled and nearly toppled the central government. He captured both of the capital cities in a lightning campaign and the T'ang court was forced to abandon the north of China and took to the more mountainous regions of west China.[91] As her own armies were in complete disarray, the T'ang government had to turn to the foreign peoples living on China's borders for help. The most powerful of the barbarian tribes then was the Uighur, a branch of the Turks who had gained control of the regions south of Lake Baikal. They responded to the request and attacked the rebels from the rear. Together with the help of Persian refugees and Arab adventurers, the Uighurs successfully put down the rebellion. In 762, a Uighur army liberated the eastern capital of Lo-yang and among those who greeted the victors were Sogdian Manichaean priests.[92] It was in Lo-yang that the Khaghan Mo-yu was converted to Manichaeism and in him the religion found the political support which it had hitherto been denied in China. The story of his conversion is told on the famous trilingual inscription at Karabalghasun on the River Orkhon in which Manichaeism is praised as a civilising influence because it turned the Uighurs from a people which practised 'the abnormal custom of blood sacrifices into a region of vegetarians, from a state which indulged in excessive killing to a nation which exhorts righteousness'.[93] Soon we find Manichaean missionaries in the court of the Khaghan in Karabalghasun, praying for the well-being of their new *defensor fidei* (*d'r'g 'y dyn*) who, along with his retinue, was nor resplendent in titles and honours borrowed from the Chinese.[94]

The conversion of the Khaghan Mo-yu (Bögü Qan) seemed to have been a personal affair and the religion was not received with the same enthusiasm by other Uighur nobles. A hint of serious trouble is discernable from a fragmentary Manichaean text in Turkish, translated from either Sogdian or Chinese. In it the Elect reproached the Khaghan for failing to protect the religion from being attacked by an unnamed Tarqan (minister), probably Tun *mo-ho* who was known to have instigated a coup against Mo-yu in 799.[95] They claimed that the Elect as well as the 'Hearers and Merchants' were being persecuted and killed by the Tarqan wherever they were found. The Khaghan was duly reminded that his kingdom would plunge into ruin if he allowed such sacrilege to continue and that the godly *Mōzak* was most displeased with what he had heard.[96] The Khaghan discussed the matter with the Elect for two days and nights. On the third day he chastised himself. He had been moved by the knowledge

that his soul would not be freed from the body at the moment of death
and would hence be subject to continuous rebirth and redeath unless
he complied with the wishes of the Elect. He went to their assembly
and asked them for forgiveness and promised that he would always
adhere to their advice. Great rejoicing ensued and the Kaghan returned
to the city (Karabalghasun?) with the Manichaean Elect, followed
by cheering crowds. He mounted his throne and issued an edict which
reaffirmed his adherence to Manichaeism.[97]

Whether this document is the Manichaean equivalent of the
Donatio Constantini or a genuine record of a historical event we have
no way of knowing. However one can gain from it a good idea of the
kind of spiritual blackmail which the Elect could use against the
Khaghan in furthering the course of the religion. As Manichaeism was
now the religion of the Uighur Khaghan, the T'ang government had no
alternative but to adopt a more favourable attitude towards it. Both
capital cities soon possessed Manichaean temples which were built
with imperial sanction.[98] The Manichaeans were clearly not content
merely to act as chaplains to the Uighurs. The propagation of their
religion in other parts of China was their foremost ambition. With the
backing of the Uighurs, the Manichaeans were able to secure the
necessary permission from the T'ang government to establish
Manichaean temples in four prefectures in the Yangtze Basin, namely
Ch'ing, Yang, Hung, and Yüeh, in 768.[99] It has been suggested that
missionary motives lay behind these foundations as the prefectures
concerned were not likely to have harboured significant Uighur communities.[100] There might have been Sogdians trading in the Yangtze
Basin in which case we see once more trade going hand in hand with
Manichaean mission, a feature of the religion which goes back to its
Syrian roots. In the same Turkish text concerning the submission of
the Khaghan to the Elect we find the latter pleading the cause of four of
their number in China (*tawɣac*). What their requests are we cannot
make out because of the fragmentary nature of the text but it is
interesting to find the needs of Uighur Manichaean missionaries in
China were not neglected by their co-religionists in the court of the
Khaghan at Karabalghasun.[101]

The texts of the individual edicts on the building of these temples
have not survived but we can be certain that they would have been
couched in obsequious terms praising the Uighurs for the service they
had rendered to the T'ang government and commending them for their
desire to establish Manichaean temples as signs of merit. This we may
infer from an imperial letter of 807, composed by the imperial
censor, the famous poet, Po Chü-i which grants permission to the
Khaghan Ku-tu-lu who requested permission to establish a temple at
the eastern capital of Lo-yang where his predecessor was first

converted to Manichaeism, and another one at the strategic town of T'ai-yüan. The request was deemed 'as a matter which has as its cause the accumulation of merits and the spirit of it is pure and dignified'. Imperial envoys were to be sent to the priests bringing small gifts from the T'ang emperor and a local military official was detailed to look after the priests and to furnish them with temporary shelter.[102]

In allowing the Uighurs to establish Manichaean temples in China, the T'ang government might have hoped that the spread of the religion could be contained, as these temples would soon become centres of expatriate Uighurs and Sogdians. The native population would come to see Manichaeism as a foreign religion like Zoroastrianism which was closely identified with a particular group of aliens. This hope, however, was not to be fulfilled as we possess a story of Buddhist origin which was clearly aimed at warning the faithful against associating themselves with Manichaeism:

Wu K'o-chiu, a man of Yüeh, resided in Ch'ang-an in the fifteenth year of Yüan-ho of the T'ang [820 AD]. He began to practise Manichaeism and his wife Wang also followed his example. She died suddenly after more than a year. Three years later, she appeared to her husband in a dream saying: 'For my perverse belief I have been condemned to become a snake and I am below the *stūpa* at Huang-tzu p'o. I shall die tomorrow at dawn and I wish you would ask monks to go there and recite for me the *Diamond Sūtra* so that I could avoid other forms of suffering'. Wu disbelieved her in his dream and scolded her. She became angry and spat at him. He woke up in fright and his face was unbearably painful. His wife also appeared to his elder brother in a dream, saying, 'Pick some Dragon-tongue herb from the garden which will heal [your brother's] pain immediately when crushed and applied.' His elder brother woke up and ran to get [the herb] to give to him and he was subsequently healed. The next morning both brothers went out together and invited monks to read the *Diamond Sūtra*. Soon a large snake emerged from the *stūpa*. It raised its head and gazed around. It died when the reading of the *sūtra* was ended. K'o-chiu returned [to the fold of] Buddhism and constantly carried with him this [i.e. the *Diamond*] *Sūtra*.[103]

The demise of Uighur military might was as swift and sudden as its rise. In 840, the Uighur empire collapsed in the face of an attack by the Kirghiz in a fratricidal war between the two Turkic peoples and the Uighur Khaghan was killed when Karabalghasun fell to the enemies.[104] The Uighurs had by then incurred much unpopularity in China. As the only effective fighting force at the disposal of the T'ang government they could afford to be arrogant and saw no need to subject themselves to the laws of the land. On one occasion when a Uighur was apprehended by the Chinese authorities for a stabbing incident in the capital city of Ch'ang-an in 775, a Uighur chief burst into the prison and carried off the prisoner after wounding the guards.[105] Such behaviour the Chinese would associate more with conquerors than allies. Chinese annoyance with the Uighurs was manifest in a legislation of 779 which forbade the Uighurs to wear Chinese dress lest they should try to go native and attempt to seduce Chinese women.[106] Uighur Manichaean temples were both a symbol of foreign arrogance and a sore reminder to the Chinese of their military weakness. The T'ang court made no secret of its hope that a supernatural way might be found to remove this national scourge and when in 842 a Buddhist monk called Hsüan-hsüan claimed that he could defeat the Uighurs with a magical sword but was later found to be a fraud, the standing of Buddhism at court took a hard knock.[107] When the tide had turned against the Uighurs in central Asia, thus obviating their usefulness to China, the T'ang government felt the time had come to tighten their grip on the Manichaean communities in China. In 843, an imperial letter, composed by Li Te-yü, an administrator of distinction, informed the new Khaghan that all the Manichaean temples in the Yangtze prefectures would be temporarily closed. In this letter Li made it quite clear to the Khaghan that Manichaeism had once been a proscribed religion and its practice was tolerated only among the Uighurs. Now that the Uighur power had been broken, the temples other than those in the capital cities and Tai-yüan should be closed as the government would not be able to afford them protection against hostile inhabitants of the regions where the temples were sited.

The teaching of Mani was proscribed prior to the T'ien-pao Era [742–56]. Its dissemination has subsequently been permitted because it is practised by the Uighurs. Hence, Manichaean temples were established in Chiang, Huei and several other prefectures. Recently, news has reached us of the collapse of the Uighur Kingdom and because of this, the followers of the sect are apprehensive. Their priests, being foreigners, are bereft of all help and support. To make matters worse for them, the people of Wu and Ch'u [i.e. central and south China] are mean and uncharitable by nature. If a religion loses its credibility, its propagation is unlikely to be successful. Even as great a teacher as Buddha would maintain that a religion should be propagated according to the needs of the times. When there is neither need nor reason to propagate a religion, it will be futile to force it on the masses. We are deeply worried about those foreign priests who are far away from home and wish to see them settled safely. We therefore decree that only the Manichaean temples in the two capital cities and in T'ai-yüan should continue to celebrate the rites of the sect. The other temples in the prefectures of Chiang and Huei should be closed for the time being. Once the conditions of the Uighur homeland seem more settled, we shall revert to the former arrangements.[108]

Not only were the temples in the four prefectures closed indefinitely, the ban was soon extended to the temples in the capital cities and the strategic prefecture of T'ai-yüan. The Minister of Merits (Kung-te-shih), the chief administrator of religious affairs in T'ang China, and his assistants were ordered to take an inventory of the possessions of the temples.[109] This *Valor ecclesiasticus* was the precursor to the full scale proscription of Manichaeism in China and the confiscation of its property. We cannot rule out an economic motive behind this apparently xenophobic measure. Uighur merchants had acquired notoriety as extortionate money lenders. Since in the steppe society of their homeland they could not profitably spend the money they earned from the T'ang in the sale of war horses and exotics, money-lending was an obvious means of recycling their surplus cash. Manichaean temples were very probably centres of credit transactions and banking in the same way that Buddhist temples in the T'ang lent and stored money through the institution commonly known as the 'Inexhaustible Treasure' (*wu-chin tsang*).[110] The late T'ang period witnessed a steady inflation which was exacerbated by a shortage of currency and ready scapegoats are found in the rapacious foreign merchants.[111] Since the edict of prohibition against the Manichaean temples issued in 843 decreed that no one should be allowed to appropriate the property or merchandise of the temples and that anyone caught loitering on their premises would be executed, the government was clearly anxious that it alone should benefit from the spoils of the sequestration.[112] Another edict decreed the burning of Manichaean books and images in the streets and the compulsory wearing of Chinese dress by the Uighurs.[113] The campaign against Manichaeism was further intensified in the late spring of 843. A Japanese Buddhist pilgrim, the famous diarist Ennin, has preserved for us the substance of an edict issued sometime in May:

An imperial edict was issued, ordering the Manichaean priests of the Empire to be killed. Their heads are to be shaved and they are to be dressed in Buddhist robes [kasāya] and are to be killed looking like Buddhist śramana [i.e. monks]. The Manichaean priests are highly respected by the Uighurs.[114]

We are not informed of the full extent of the massacre but according to a Buddhist historian of the Sung period, at least seventy-two women priests perished. Other priests were rounded up and exiled to the border provinces to join up with the remnants of the Uighur tribes but half of them died from the hardships of the journey.[115] The standard dress of Manichaean priests in the east was white robes and they normally did not shave their hair. In ordering the priests to wear Buddhist robes and to have their heads shaved like Buddhist monks before they were executed, the T'ang government was removing their badge of distinction in order to humiliate them.

This attack on Manichaeism coincided with the waning of Buddhist influence at court. The Emperor Wu-tsung (reigned 841–6), an ardent seeker of earthly immortaility, was under the sway of Taoist priests who urged him to suppress their Buddhist rivals. The success of the attack on Manichaean temples had also encouraged scholar-officials like Li Te-yü to clamour for some restrictive measure to be placed on Buddhism. They had seen the profitable side of the suppression of temples and they argued that the returning to lay life of large numbers of monks and nuns would swell the depleted tax registers. In the same way that a census of Manichaean property took place before the suppression of the religion, the T'ang government in the fourth month (April–May) of 845 ordered a census of the Buddhist monastic community. The census revealed a total of 260,000 Buddhist monks and nuns, 4,600 monasteries and 40,000 shrines in China. Armed with these figures, the government ordered all the establishments to be closed except that one tample was to be preserved in each major prefecture while in each of the two capitals, four Buddhist temples were to be permitted, each with thirty monks.[116] The proscription was not aimed at destroying the Buddhist religion in China completely but to restrict its influence drastically. Since Buddhism, the principal foreign religion in China was now under attack, the government felt no compunction to protect minor foreign cults like Zoroastrianism and Nestorianism. About three thousand of their priests were defrocked on the grounds that they were unwilling to adopt Chinese customs.[117]

The events of 842–5 marked the end of a period of two centuries in which China experienced an unprecedented amount of contact with the west. Foreign influences could be felt in T'ang art, music, astrology, botany, and above all in the field of religion. The rebellion of An Lu-shan in 755 was a major turning point as the turmoil and dislocation caused by civil wars which necessitated the presence of large bodies of foreign mercenaries in China gave vent to a rising chorus of anti-foreign sentiments. Although Buddhism would recover some of its lost ground in the Sung, it never regained the zenith of power and influence which it had attained there. Chinese society turned in upon itself as Chinese *literati* endeavoured to revive traditional Confucian scholarship. Thus when Manichaeism re-emerged in south China as a minor heterodox sect, it was to be confronted by scholar-officials who knew little about Buddhism, let alone foreign religions from Iran. Manichaeism came under their censure not because its dualism was heretical but because its organisation and practices threatened the Confucian way of life.

(4) MANICHAEISM IN THE UIGHUR KINGDOMS OF KAN-SU AND TURFAN

The fall of Karabalghasun to the Kirghiz in 840 marked the end of the first Uighur empire. Rather than fleeing *en masse* with the Uighurs, some Manichaean priests remained to propagate their religion among the new conquerors. Rock carvings of Manichaean priests from the banks of the Yenizei show that Sogdian merchant missionaries took the religion deep into Kirghizia.[118] The main part of the Uighur nation moved south from their former power base near Lake Baikal and re-established themselves in the north-western frontier of China, especially in Kan-su and Turfan. Although some of the Uighurs who settled in the Kan-su were Manichaeans, the majority seemed to have been Buddhists. In 998, the Uighur envoy to the Chinese court from Kan-su was a Buddhist monk; previously such posts were the preserve of Manichaeans.[119] The region became a flourishing centre of Buddhism and it was among the thousands of Buddhist texts concealed in a cave temple at Tun-huang that the three extant Manichaean texts in Chinese were found at the beginning of this century.

Manichaeism remained the official religion of the court of the second Uighur empire which was established in the Tarim Basin with its capital city at Qočo (near modern Turfan). The Uighur court and some of its leading nobles lavished patronage on Manichaeism and the cities of Qočo, Tuyuk and Sängim among many others came to possess important Manichaean temples and monasteries. A Chinese visitor to Turkestan in late tenth century, Wang Yen-te, noted that among the many temples there were those of the Manichaeans. The religion, he says, was practised by Persian (i.e. Sogdian) priests and it was castigated as a heresy in Buddhist writings.[120] The Manichaean priests continued to be chaplains to the Uighur Khaghan at Qočo as they once were at Karabalghasun. According to Kardizi, it was customary in the Uighur kingdom for three or four hundred Manichaean priests to gather in the house of a prince to recite the Books of Mani and at the end of the day they would invoke blessings on the ruler before they departed.[121]

Free from persecution and well provided for by royal patronage, Manichaean communities in the Uighur Kingdom became flourishing centres of artistic and economic activities as well as centres for the propagation of the doctrine of Mani. It was from the ruins of these centres, especially one known to scholars as Group K at Qočo (Idiqutsahri) that the second German Turfan expedition (1904–5) under the leadership of Albert von Le Coq, recovered thousands of fragments of beautifully executed Manichaean manuscripts. In one of the rooms of the complex, the archaeologists found themselves ankle deep in layers of manuscripts which had been turned into loess by irrigation water and these manuscripts could not be preserved despite every effort to dry them.[122] The manuscript haul from the entire site was nevertheless enormous and their exquisite artwork and calligraphy attest to a scribal tradition in the Manichaean centres of the highest standard. One of the miniatures recovered from the site shows two rows of Manichaeans scribes studiously copying what must have been Manichaean scriptures. Some of them are pictured as holding their pens ambidextrously, which might have been an artistic motif designed to exalt their diligence and productiveness.[123] The piety with which the monks submitted themselves to scribal duties is also witnessed to by a confessional text in Sogdian in which a monk is required to ask for forgiveness for having neglected his calligraphy, for hating or despising it and for having damaged or injured a brush, a writing board, a piece of silk or paper.[124]

The enormous haul of Manichaean manuscripts, albeit mostly in small fragments, has thrown a great deal of light on the doctrines, practices, ecclesiastical organisation and early history of the eastern Manichaean church. Comprising texts in Middle Persian, Parthian, Sogdian, Uighur, Tocharian and even a small fragment in the rarely attested Bactrian, the Turfan collection, now principally housed in the Deutsche Akademie der Wissenschaften zu Berlin, has also contributed much to our knowledge of these Central Asian languages. On the other hand, as the great majority of these texts are of a theological or liturgical nature, the history of the Manichaean church in the second Uighur empire remains largely concealed from us. One text, though, which is not part of the Berlin collection but was found at Qočo by a Chinese expedition in the 1930s but only recently published, deserves a special mention as it is a royal charter endorsing certain arrangements pertaining to the organisation and economic activities of a group of Manichaean monasteries (m'nyst'n'n) with its principal house at Qočo.[125] That the economic activities of the monasteries required royal approval is ample proof of their importance to the society as a whole. The monasteries owned a substantial amount of land from which they derived both regular supplies of food as well as rent. Some of the land was devoted to viticulture as Turkestan was a main provider of grape-wine for China. Considering the very strict Manichaean prohibition on wine which they regarded as the 'bile of the Prince of Darkness', the cultivation of grapes on Manichaean lands might appear to us to be putting economic motives before theological considerations. Monastic officials were assigned to the management of monastic properties and the text lays down that they were forbidden to use the infertility of the land as an excuse for their bad management. The lands were important as the monasteries derived regular supplies of food stuffs and cloth from them.[126] The importance of the economic activities of the monasteries is reflected in the prominence in the monastic hierarchy of a hitherto unattested office, the controller (Turkish: *is ayγuci*), which was probably held by a lay person.[127] Besides lands, the Manichaean monasteries owned large flocks and enjoyed the service of servants and boy pages as well as bakers, tailors, cooks, carpet-markers and physicians.[128] The text also reveals a draconian scale of penalties for the negligence of duty. For instance an *is ayγuci* who did not manage the monasteries's lands properly and failed to collect his rent efficiently would be punished by three hundred strokes of the rod.[129] Cooks faced the same punishment if the food for the monks was badly prepared.[130]

The level of economic activity centred on the monasteries points to the privileged position which the religion enjoyed as the religion of the court and of some members of the nobility. We may also infer from the great number of donor portraits on the walls of the ruins of the Buddhist temples at Bäzäklik that religious patronage was a common social phenomenon in Turfan.[131] However, the dictum *cuius regio, eius religio* cannot be applied to the Uighur kingdom as the majority of its people were either Buddhists or Nestorians. A still unpublished Manichaean fragment in Turkish recounts the valiant effort of a monk to redecorate a Manichaean temple which had lost its decoration to a three-storeyed Buddhist *vihāra* built under imperial patronage.[131a] By the time of the Mongol conquest of the Tarim Basin in the mid-thirteenth century, Manichaeism was already of little significance in comparison to Buddhism. Even the important Manichaean temple site at Ruin Group K might have come under Buddhist control at the time of the Mongol invasion as mummified corpses of Buddhist monks, violently slain, were found by German archaeologists in one of its rooms.[132] Under the Genghis-Khanate, the majority of the inhabitants of Qočo were either Buddhists or Nestorians. The invaders also introduced Islam, which soon became the predominant religion of this region and has remained so ever since.

CHAPTER VIII

MANI THE BUDDHA OF LIGHT

And again I heard besides this [voice] in the
direction of the south the voice of the Buddha
Enoch ... [Turkish Manichaean fragment T.M.423d]

(1)   THE CHINESE MANICHAEAN TEXTS
FROM TUN-HUANG

The modern study of Manichaeism in China began in earnest only
after the discovery of Manichaean texts in Chinese along with many
thousands of scrolls, mostly containing Buddhist writings, from a
hidden recess in one of the many cave temples in Tun-huang. The
documents were deposited before 1035 when the cave was sealed,
perhaps in order to preserve the scrolls from marauding Tanguts. The
hoard was first discovered in the course of repair work by a Taoist
priest in the early years of this century but it only became widely
known to western scholars through Sir Aurel Stein who paid a short
visit to Tun-huang at the end of his survey of the Han *limes* in Central
Asia, and took a large selection of the scrolls back with him to India.[1]
These documents eventually came into the possession of the British
Museum. The eminent French Sinologist Paul Pelliot also made his
way to Tun-huang in the wake of the news of Stein's discoveries.
Among the many manuscripts he was able to acquire for the
Bibliotheque Nationale of Paris is a small fragment of a Manichaean
text in Chinese which is clearly part of a summary of the rules
governing the organisation of the sect.[2] A much more spectacular
discovery from the point of view of Chinese Manichaean studies is a
long text which contains a treatise on Manichaean cosmogony and its
practical implications on the daily living of the Elect and the Hearers
which was found among the Tun-huang texts not removed by Stein or
Pelliot but transported by Chinese scholars to Peking (hereafter
referred to as *Treatise*). Pelliot, together with another equally eminent
French scholar, Édouard Chavannes, became the first western editors
of this remarkable text which, at the time of discovery, was the
longest genuine Manichaean text in any language, longer than even
the *Confessional for the Hearers* (*X^uāstvānīft*) in Old Turkish which
was found among the Tun-huang texts acquired by Stein.[3]

The discovery of such a lengthy Manichaean work in Chinese surprised many scholars, as few expected the religion to have diffused so far eastwards. Although Chavannes himself had noted the occasional references to a foreign religion called 'Mo-ni' in Chinese sources, he long remained unconvinced that it designated Manichaeism. As late as 1897 he would still write 'Pour ma part, je crois que sous l'expression 'Mo-ni' les Chinois designent les Musulmans'.[4] The same disbelief in the penetration of Manichaeism into China caused Schlegel, the first and so far the only editor of the Chinese version of the famous trilingual Orkhon inscription to mistake Manichaeism, the new religion to which the Uighur Khaghan was converted, for Nestorian Christianity, with disastrous consequences to the accuracy of his translation of the relevant section.[5]

Two more Chinese Manichaean texts were later discovered among the Tun-huang manuscripts now deposited in the British Museum. One is a collection of hymns which contains several praises to Mani and to the deities of the Manichaean pantheon and the saints of the church (hereafter referred to as *Hymnscroll*). The other is a brief summary, a compendium, of the teaching of the sect on such topics as the life of the founder and his writings, the main tenets of the Manichaean religion and the structure of its organisation (hereafter referred to as *Compendium*). The small fragment in Paris brought back by Pelliot is in fact the concluding part of this document.[7]

The three Chinese Manichaean texts are translated in the main from Iranian originals and were not originally composed specifically for a Chinese audience. This is shown by the frequent occurrence of Manichaean terms in transcription which are clearly of Iranian origin.[8] The *Hymnscroll* from Tun-huang includes three short refrains which are phonetically transcribed mainly from Parthian to enable Chinese converts unable to read Iranian languages to join in chanting with their Sogdian priests.[9] The *Hymnscroll* also includes a canto of a hymn-cycle, the original of which has survived in a number of Iranian fragments.[10] There are also Turkish fragments of a later period containing passages on Manichaean cosmogony which are derived from the same Iranian original as the *Treatise*.[11] The translator of the *Hymnscroll*, who styled himself Tao-ming, claims in a postscript that although the texts from which he had made his translation were of diverse origin, his translation was uniformly based on the Sanskrit (*fan*, i.e. Middle Persian and Parthian) and admonishes the learner to study the texts so thoroughly that he will know the right order when they are shown to him.[12] He also exhorts the scribe to collate the texts carefully and arrange them according to established rules. The chanter must also go to the enlightened teacher and 'learn the mistakes and differences' presumably in his pronounciation of the phonetically transcribed refrains.[13] Just to assure the secular authorities that the new religion meant no harm to the Middle Kingdom, the translator of the *Hymnscroll* concludes his postscript with a blatant *captatio benevolentiae* in which he invokes special blessing for the health of the reigning emperor and for the peace of the realm.[14]

The *Compendium* states in its preface that the translation was done by a *Fu-to-tan* (i.e. *episcopus*) under special instruction from the Emperor on the eighth day of the sixth month of the nineteenth year of the period K'ai-yüan (16 July 731) at the College of (the Hall) of Gathered Worthies (*Chi-hsien yüan*).[15] The text in the form which we have it may be a later version of the original translation as it contains a Taoist version of Mani's life in addition to a Buddhicised one. Since Taoism, like Confusianism, was exclusive to China and made no significant impact on the religious life of Central Asia, the Taoist version of Mani's life, therefore, would have meant little to Iranian merchants. We shall return to this Taoist version in due course and it will suffice to say at present that this was probably added to the original translation by some other Manichaean author in the course of the dissemination of the text in T'ang China. That the main part of the *Compendium* is translated from Iranian has never been in doubt. The titles of the Manichaean canon, for instance, as listed in the *Compendium* are given first in Iranian via Chinese transliteration, and then explained in Chinese.[16] In the case of the *Pragmateia*, the Greek form of the original is still easily recognisable as it is *po-chia-ma-ti-yeh* (= Syr.: *prgmty'* and Greek: $\pi\rho\alpha\gamma\mu\alpha\tau\epsilon\acute{\iota}\alpha$) in its transliterated form.[17]

All three of the Chinese Manichaean texts, *viz.* the *Treatise*, the *Hymnscroll* and the *Compendium* contain a significant number of terms which are unmistakably of Buddhist origin. These are Chinese phrases specially coined or adapted for the translation of Buddhist technical terms from Sanskrit or Pali and are rarely encountered in non-Buddhist writings.[18] The *Treatise* itself is cast in the form of a dialogue between Mani and Adda (A-to) with the latter playing the role of the enlightened pupil who asked his master a profound question: 'Is the original nature of the carnal body single or double?' To this Mani, the Envoy of Light (*ming-shih* = Pth. *fryštgrwšn*) prefaced his reply with an often encountered formula in Buddhist sutras:

Good indeed! Good indeed! [= Sanskirt: *sādhu, sādhu*]. In order to benefit the innumerable crowds of living beings, you have addressed to me this query profound and mysterious. You thus show yourself a good friend to all those living beings of the world who have blindly gone astray, and I will now explain the matter to you in detail, so that the net of doubt in which you are ensnared may be broken forever without recall.[19]

This is followed by a detailed account of the creation of the universe from the moment of the rescue of the Primal Man. The shorter hymns in the *Hymnscroll* are composed in the form of Buddhist gāthās. Their strophic rhythm, which makes for easy chanting, is widely used in Buddhist liturgy. When one compares the extant Parthian original of parts of the hymn-cycle of *Huwīdagmān* with the Chinese one can see how the Buddhist style of the Chinese has compelled the translator to pad his translation in order to get four lines of seven characters each. Take for instance verse 22 of *Huwīdagmān* I which is well preserved in both versions:

Parthian:

> Their verdant garlands
>   never fade;
> they are wreathed brightly
>   in numberless colours.[20]

Chinese:

> Floral crowns are verdant, wonderful, dignified and solemn,
> Shining on each other with great vitality, and never fade or fall
> Whilst my carnal tongue wishes to praise, my faculty of
>   thought fails me:
> Immeasurable are the wonderful colours, which never fade or
>   diminish.[21]

The apparent similarities between Manichaean and Buddhist writings in Chinese do not however amount to deliberate disguise. The Manichaean texts contain a host of technical terms like the Five Luminous Limbs, the Call, the Answer, the Column of Light, the Crown-Bearer, the hermaphrodite Messenger, the Custodian of Splendour etc., which are unambiguously Manichaean and have no equivalents in Buddhist parlance.[22] We must bear in mind that the special style of the Chinese Buddhist texts was a language developed for the purpose of translation of western religious writings. The Iranian Manichaean missionaries probably learned their Chinese from polylingual Buddhist monks, hence their choice of Buddhist terminology and literary format is entirely logical. Even the Nestorians who also came to China during the T'ang period from Iran and who had less reason to be interested in Buddhism had one of their texts cast in the form of a Buddhist sūtra.[23] Nor must we forget that the dialogue form of the *Treatise* has parallels in gnostic literature and is particularly well represented in the Coptic Manichaean *Kephalaia* which contains many similar didactic discourses of Mani which were also prompted by intelligent questions from his outstanding pupils.[24] In one instance in the Coptic, the words Mani used in praising his student are strikingly similar to those in the Chinese *Treatise*: 'You have asked intelligently [καλῶς] and I shall clear up your problem for you.'[25] Nor is this the only suggestive similarity between the two bodies of Manichaean texts separated by vast distances of time and geography. There is a passage in the Chinese *Treatise* on the imprisonment of the evil archons which offer strong parallels to the Coptic both in content and in choice of imagery:

Chinese: Therefore, the Pure Wind, the Envoy of Light, took the five classes of demons and the five elements, and combining the powers of these in due relation one to the other, made ten heavens and eight earths of the Universe. Thus, the universe is for the five elements a hospital [a 'clinic'] where they may be cured, and for the demons a prison where they may be kept under restraint.[26]

Coptic: He [sc. the Living Spirit] spread out all the powers of abyss to ten heavens and eight earths, he shut them up into this world [κόσμος] once, he made it a prison too for all the powers of Darkness, it is also a place of purification for the Soul that was swallowed (?) in them.[27]

The two parallel passages, found in texts separated by four centuries and the whole of the Eurasian landmass, testify to the care with which the Manichaeans handled their sacred writings. The Elect were admonished by the *Treatise* not to tamper with the scriptures by inserting or deleting a word let alone, a sentence.[28]

(2)   THE EASTERN TRANSFORMATION
                      OF MANICHAEISM

One would be wrong, though, to assume that the Manichaean missionaries had brought a carbon copy of the religion as we know it in Mesopotamia in China. Their loyalty to the original text of Mani had to be balanced by the need to present the essence of his message in a new cultural context. Manichaeism began life in the cultural milieu of Judaeo-Christianity and its dissemination in the Roman empire was greatly aided by the common Syriac and Christian culture which flourished on both sides of the Roman-Persian frontier. Thus the first Manichaean missionaries to the west could translate Mani's original writings which were rooted in Judaeo-Christianity directly from Aramaic into Greek and from Greek into Coptic and Latin along the same channels which were also utilised by the Christian church for the translation of her own literature. However, as Manichaeism was disseminated in lands east of the Tigris, its missionaries first entered the stronghold of Zoroastrianism and through it into the syncretistic world of Central Asia dominated by shamanism and Mahayana Buddhism. Unlike the expansion of Islam in the seventh century or that of Christianity in more modern times, the diffusion of Manichaeism was not accompanied by any fundamental political or social change to its recipients. On the other hand Christian missionaries in the nineteenth century could graft a Christianity with its western cultural conditioning on to Chinese society, albeit through the medium of the Chinese language, because mission was only part of a major process of social and cultural change. The crossing of the cultural divide between east and west was made easier then because of the adoption of western scientific and philosophical values by a large part of the Chinese intelligentsia which looked to the West for enlightenment and progress. The same advantages were not enjoyed by the Manichaean missionaries who were members of a small and persecuted sect. The need for them to adapt their religion to the cultural conditions of the east was considerably greater than for the nineteenth-century Christian missionaries and their effort in this respect bears some resemblance to the short lived Jesuit mission to China which began in 1582 and was condemned by Clement XI (pope from 1700–21) because of its readiness to accommodate itself to Chinese life and culture.

Since Mani had declared that previous religious leaders like Zoroaster, the Buddha and Jesus had all imparted some aspects of the complete truth which he had received from his divine twin, Manichaean missionaries would see little objection to draw their religion closer to the dominant religions of the land by giving some Manichaean gods the names of the local deities who performed similar functions or occupied similar positions within their own systems. Thus in Manichaean literature in Iranian dialects, a host of Zoroastrian deities were identified with the gods of the Manichaean pantheon, e.g.:

The Father of Greatness (Syr.: *'b' drbwt'*) Zurwān
The Primal Man (Syr.: *'nš' qdmy'*) Ohrmazd
His Five Sons (Syr.: *hmš' 'lh' zywn'*) (A)mahrāspandān (holy immortals)
The Living Spirit (Syr.: *rwḥ ḥy'*) Mihr (i.e. Mithra)
The Third Messenger (Syr.: *'yzgd'*) Nairyōsanha (or Narisah Yazd)
Adam (Syr.: *'dm*) Gayōmard
The Prince of Darkness (Syr.: *mlk hšwk'*) Ahriman
etc.[29]

This process of assimilation began under the guidance of Mani when he presented a summary of his teaching of Shapur I, the *Šābuhragān*, in Middle Persian. It was continued by his disciples as the religion spread eastwards and we can tell from the fact that some Manichaean gods possessed several forms of their names in Iranian texts that this process developed gradually without overall control by the *archeogos* in Babylonia. The Father of Greatness for instance is not always called Zurwan in Middle Persian; he also occurs as Pid ī wuzurgī ('Father of Greatness') which is a more literal translation of his title in Syriac.[30]

The substitution of the names of Manichaean gods and demons by those of local deities inevitably involved the acceptance of some distinguishing features of the latter. A good example of this missionary transformation of Manichaean theology can be seen in the adoption of the Zoroastrian deity Mihr or Mithra. In Middle Persian texts, Mihr was identified with the Living Spirit because of their common function as warrior gods. In Parthian texts however, because of the local emphasis placed on Mihr as a sun-god, he was identified with the Third Messenger whose dwelling is in the sun. Once this identification was made, the function of the Third Messenger as a sun-god significantly increased. Many of the attributes of the sun which we find in a paean to that celestial body in the Coptic Manichaean texts have their closest Parthian parallels in hymns to the Third Messenger, although the Coptic hymn was not directly addressed to him.[31]

In eastern Iran and Central Aisa, Manichaeism flourished alongside Buddhism and the process of assimilation continued apace. We can discern from Manichaean texts in Parthian, Sogdian, Chinese and Turkish a number of technical terms and names of deities which are unmistakably Buddhist in origin. Some Manichaean concepts were also given Buddhist equivalents. The Manichaean concept of Metempsychosis (Gk. & Copt.: μεταγγίσμος) for instance, approximates closely to Buddhist *samsara* ('rebirth and redeath') and in Manichaean Parthian and Chinese texts the respective terms of *zādmurd* and *sheng-ssu* (birth–death) used to translate the Manichaean concept both call to mind the Buddhist equivalent.[32] Similarly, Mani who was naturally exempt from such a process of cyclical rebirth is praised in a Parthian hymn as having entered the state of *parnibrānīg* (= Sanskrit: *parinirvana*, i.e. the state of *nirvāna* achieved by one who will not be reborn) on his martyrdom.[33]

Several Manichaean deities also took on the epithet of Buddha. This is particularly evident in Chinese Manichaean texts as there is no convenient non-Buddhist Chinese word for translating the Iranian term *yazd* ('god'). Thus in a *gatha* to be sung at the end of meals we find a list of some of the principal deities of the Manichaean pantheon, including Jesus, being hailed as Buddhas.[34] The way in which Mani grouped some of the deities into tetrads or pentads also lends itself to Buddhicisation. The Five Limbs (*membra dei*) of the Great Nous (i.e. Reason, Mind, Intelligence, Thought, Understanding) are called Five Great Buddhas of Light in the Chinese *Hymnscroll*.[35] A similar pentad occupies a vital place in Buddhist teaching, namely the Five Dhyāni –

Buddhas or Tathāgathas which are the emanations from the Primal Buddha. In Tibetan Buddhist art they are depicted in a circle or maṇḍala with Vairocana (the pure one) in the centre, Akṣobhya (the immutable one) in the east, Amitābha (the Buddha of infinite light) in the west, Ratnasambhava (the compassionate one) in the south and Amogasiddhi (i.e. Śākyamuni, the final nirvāṇa) in the north. Such a circular depiction is found in a Turkish Manichaean text in which the membra dei are placed on the four points of the compass with Mind (qut) in the centre, and Thought (ög), Intelligence (saqinč), Reason (tuimaq) and Understanding (köngül) seated in south, east, west and north respectively.[36] This arrangement shows that the Manichaean pentad had become firmly identified with the Five Light Realms of the Buddhist Tathāgathas.

On the Upper Indus at Alchi (Ladakh) in West Tibet (Kashmir, India) is located a three storeyed Buddhist temple which exhibits magnificent Buddhist wall paintings of the Tibetan school dating back to the eleven century. Right next to the exist is a depiction of the Five Light Realms of the Tathāgatas in the order of the maṇḍala. This has been generally regarded as a typical, though unusually fine example of Tibeto-Buddhist art.[37] Professor Klimkeit, after a recent visit to the site, has pointed out that there is an exceptional number of cross-symbols in the paintings which are not commonly found in Buddhist art. We know from Central Asian and Chinese Manichaean texts that Vairocana (Chin. Buddh.: pi-lu-she-na, Chin. Manich.: lu-she-na, Turkish: Lusyanta) is identified with the Column of Glory (Pe.: srwš'hr'y), a Manichaean deity of the Third Creation who also signifies Jesus patibilis, the sum total of Light Particles crucified in matter and whose symbol is the Cross of Light. Since Vairocana is the essential body of the Buddha-truth which, like the Light, pervades everywhere, it is a convenient choice for symbolising a gnostic concept which has its origins firmly rooted in apocryphal Christian literature.[38] In the case of the depiction of Aksobyha at Alchi, a Cross of Light has replaced his normal thunderbolt (vajra). Since the latter normally symbolises the Buddha-nature or the vajra (adamant truth) nature which resides in all beings, the substitution is also appropriate. At Alchi the figure of Amitābha, the Buddha of Light, is also accompanied by a white cross and the symbol of the sun. The cross here may represent the Jesus of Light who resides in the moon, hence the juxtaposition of the sun and the cross.[39]

The region of Ladakh came under Manichaean influence through the Uighurs who campaigned there in the eighth/ninth century on behalf of the T'ang government against Tibetan rebels. Although the paintings at the three-storied temple might have been executed by Buddhists their iconography looks back to a period of symbiosis between Manichaeism and Buddhism. A Manichaean could see in them a representation of the five *membra dei* of the Great Nous while a Buddhist would accept them as a more or less traditional depiction of the five Light Realms of the Tathāgatas. In China, the identification of Vairocana as the Manichaean Cross of Light survived as late as the thirteenth century when we find it being ridiculed by a Taoist writer.[40]

A similar example of iconographic borrowing is evident in a small and exquisitely painted miniature from a fragment of a Turfan manuscript. It depicts a Uighur king being blessed by a Manichaean *archegos* whose soul is depicted as an angel and who is labelled as Vahman (i.e. *Nous*). Beside them are four semi-human figures which do not immediately conjure up any Manichaean deities but the miniature itself is undeniably part of a Manichaean manuscript.[41] It has been noted by historians of Indian art that the four figures carry many distinguishing features of four well known Hindu deities and they can be identified as Shiva, Brahma, Vishnu and Ganesha.[42] The first three are worshipped by Buddhists as the *Triratna* (i.e. the Three Precious Ones) and Ganesha, the hinderer, the elephant-god is also known to Buddhism. These Hindu deities therefore might have come to Manichaeism through Buddhism or their use might reflect a certain degree of Hindu influence on the Uighur court at Qočo. Behind these apparent Hindu forms is a clear Manichaean concept, the four attributes of the Father of Light (Divinity, Light, Power and Wisdom) who is called Father of Four Faces in Greek (ὁ τετραπρόσωπος πατήρ) and whose fourfold aspect is worshipped as the Four Kings of Heaven in eastern Manichaeism.[43] Among the items of Manichaean literature seized by Chinese officials in the prefecture of Wen in south China in 1120 is one called *The Portrait of the Four Kings of Heaven* (*Ssu t'ien-wang cheng*).[44] We have no idea was to whether the Chinese version of the 'Four Kings' are depicted as Hindu deities but it is obvious that by depicting these fourfold aspects of the Father of Light as four separate divinities, an important point of Manichaean theology has been preserved. This would have been particularly relevant in China as abstract theological attributes would not have found a ready home in popular religions. The fourfold aspects of the chief deity of the Manichaean godhead would duly become a motto for Manichaeism in south China and they are listed on an extant inscription erected in the fifteenth century in the prefecture of Ch'üan.[45]

(3)   THE BUDDHA OF LIGHT

Nowhere in eastern Manichaean texts is the influence of Buddhism more keenly felt than in the depiction of Mani. We have seen that in

Parthian texts the term *parinirvana* is used to describe his translation into the Realm of Light through his martyrdom. His claim to be the Paraclete is also expressed in a Buddhist manner in that he was regarded as the Maitreya, the Buddha-to-come, the Bodhisattva who will be the next holder of the supreme office of Buddha.[46] In Chinese texts he is called the Envoy of Light which translates his title in Parthian: *fryštgrwsn*, but he is more often referred to as Mani the Buddha of Light (*Mo-ni kuang-fo*).[47] In the West, Mani's credentials as a prophet rested on his claim to a unique revelation which he received in the same manner as St Paul, and his martyrdom gave a Christ-like element to his mission. However, once Mani also came to be regarded as a Buddha, the Christian element in Mani's claim to apostleship also came to be replaced by attributes of Buddhahood. Some eastern Manichaeans, probably Parthians or Sogdians, began to subscribe to a life of Mani based on the life of the Buddha. It is preserved in Chinese translation in the *Compendium* and besides the names of Mani's parents and the date of his birth, the biographical details are almost totally unrelated to those which we can derive from the *Mani-Codex* and other western texts like the *Fihrist* of al-Nadim.

In the 527th year of the era controlled by the twelfth constellation called *mo-hsieh*, Mani, the Buddha of Light was born in the country of Su-lin [i.e. Assuristan] at the royal palace of Pa-ti [i.e. Patīk] by his wife Man-yen [i.e. Maryam, the Chinese literally means 'Full of Beauty'] of the house of Chin-sa-chien [i.e. Kamsaragan]. The [date of] birth [as recorded] in the p'o [sa?]-pi calendar is equivalent to the eighth day of the second month of the thirteenth year of the period Chien-an of emperor Hsien of the [Later] Han dynasty [12 March 208]. [The two systems of time reckoning] wholly [?] corresponding. His mother conceived when the natural endowments had heavenly omens were appropriate and she adhered to the laws of abstinence and strictly purified herself during her pregnancy. She was therefore completely pure [and] he was born from her chest.

He was prominent above all others of his time. His countenance verifies the Nine Tests and his spirit meets the five Natural Auspices as his birth was beyond the ordinary. He was completely provided with the Three Resolves, the Four [types of] Calmness, the Five Truths, and Eight Forms of Fearlessness and all other virtues. His triumphant words came to men from heaven to deliver them from suffering and endow happiness as well as inducing them to the ways of virtue. If this were not so, he would not have been born in a royal palace.

He had great powers of concentration and understood the Way. In elucidating the principles and verifying the fundamentals his wisdom and advice were singularly correct. His bodily condition was exceptionally fine and his perception embraced *ch'ien* and *k'un*, [i.e. Heaven and Earth] and his knowledge penetrated the sun and the moon. He exposed the origins of the Two Principles and demonstrated the diversity of one's nature. He expounded the profound text concerning the Three Epochs. He analysed the association between the primary and the incidental causes. He exterminated what is perverse and protected what is correct. He put an end to muddiness and extolled clarity. His words were simple, his reasoning straight, his actions correct and his testimonies true.[48]

This seems to be the only version of Mani's life which the Chinese Manichaeans possessed. It gives Mani a more distinctly royal parentage than was normally vouchsafed for by Manichaean sources in the West. We know from al-Nadim that Mani's mother was related to the Parthian royal house of the Arsacids but this link was rarely stressed by Manichaeans in the West.[49] To press Mani's royal claims too strongly would have undoubtedly caused embarrassment to those of the sect who lived under the Sassanians in Persia. It would also be a unwelcomed reminder to Manichaeans in Rome of their connection with a hostile power. This tenuous link with royalty however was magnified beyond recognition by the Manichaeans in the East in order to parallel the life of Mani with that of the Buddha whose princely origins were well acknowledged. Mani's birth from his mother's breast because of his purity is also clearly modelled on legends concerning the birth of the Buddha. There is no mention in this account of Mani's life of his receiving blinding revelations from his divine Twin and even none, more remarkably, of his martyrdom which was hailed in the West as his 'crucifixion'. We do find in a later account of the religion by a Chinese writer of the Ming period, Ho Ch'iao-yüan (1558–1632) that Mani suffered martyrdom (miao-tao) in Persia; the exact nature of his death was not, however, elaborated.

On the slopes of Hua-piao Hill about thirty miles south of the modern Chinese city of Ch'üan-chou in the province of Fukien is the only Manichaean building which has survived intact. It is a rustic shrine and in its main hall is a stone statue of Mani as the Buddha of Light. An inscription says that the statue was donated by a local worshipper in 1339.[50] At first glance the image resembles the standard portraits of the Buddha as the figure sits cross-legged on a lotus dressed in a kasāya and is backed by a halo. On closer examination, however, a number of un-Buddhist features are manifest. The Buddha is usually depicted as having downcast eyes and curly hair and as being clean-shaven. The statue of Mani however stares straight at the spectator. His hair is straight and drapes over his shoulders and he is also bearded. He is fleshy-jowled while the facial features of the Buddha are usually more shallow. His eyebrows are arched while those of the Buddha are usually straight. Mani's hands rest on his abdomen with both palms facing upwards while those of the Buddha are usually held up in a symbolic or ritual gesture (mudrā). The head, the body and the hands of the statue of Mani are skilfully carved from stones of different hues to give an overall impression of luminosity.[51] There is no doubt that the shrine is dedicated to the worship of Mani because in the courtyard is an inscription, erected in 1445, exhorting the faithful to remember 'Purity, Light, Power and Wisdom' (i.e. the four attributes of the Father of Light) and 'Mani the Buddha of Light'.[52] Thus, although the statue of Mani, the Buddha of Light, appears Buddhist at first sight, the followers of the sect would have known that the founder of their religion was distinct from Śākyamuni.

(4)   THE TAOICISATION OF MANI

The assimilation of Mani and Buddha took place in Central Asia before Manichaeism was propagated in China. Although we possess no parallels of the Buddicised version of Mani's life in Iranian or Turkish texts we do find in a Turkish Manichaean fragment an extract of the life of Buddha which is paralleled by the legend of Barlaam and Iosaphat, the Christianised version of the life of Buddha in Byzantium.[53] In China, the assimilation of Mani and the Buddha enabled the religion to diffuse in the wake of Buddhist mission. It also prepared the way for the person of Mani to be assimilated to Lao-tzu (fl. sixth century BC), the traditional founder of the school of Taoism in China. To understand how the Manichaeans managed to gain entry into an indigenous religion in China we need to look briefly at the nature of Taoist-Buddhist controversy prior to the arrival of Manichaeism.

Buddhism began to gain ground steadily in China after the end of the first century AD. In the centuries after the collapse of the Han dynasty it was patronised by local rulers, especially those in north China who were of Turkic stock. The Confucianists, the upholders of the state cult of China, saw Buddhist asceticism as basically anti-social and would occasionally advocate governmental suppression of their new rival. The Taoists on the other hand, because of the more eclectic nature of their teaching, attempted to upstage Buddhism by claiming that the Buddha was none other than a reincarnation (avatar) of Lao-tzu, the founder of their school, and that Buddhism was merely a form of Taoism which had developed in foreign lands.

Since the search for the elixir vitae was an important aspect of popular Taoism, it was only logical that some Taoists came to believe that the religion's founder Lao-tzu never died, but left China and went to the Western Heaven (or Regions). The famous Chinese historian of the Han Dynasty, Ssu-ma Ch'ien (?145–?90 BC) says in his Historical Records (Shih-chi) that when Lao-tzu decided to withdraw from the world he went west and 'nobody knows where he died'. This tradition is not much older than Ssu-ma Ch'ien as sources more ancient than the

Shih-chi mention the death of Lao-tzu and indicate the whereabouts of his burial place.[54] The Taoists however asserted that it was to Central Asia and India that Lao-tzu travelled and there he converted a barbarian king to his teaching and thus came to be regarded as the Buddha.

Sometime in the fourth century, a Taoist priest by the name of Wang Fu put flesh and blood to this skeletal story of Lao-tzu's western venture by composing a work entitled *Hua-hu ching* (*Scripture of the Conversion of the Barbarians*) in which he placed Lao-tzu's legendary journey in the setting of what was then known about the Western Regions (i.e. Tibet, India and Turkestan) from contemporary travel accounts of Buddhist pilgrims. Wang's work was an immediate publishing success and became a valuable item in the armoury of the Taoists in their controversy with the Buddhists. Not surprisingly, the Buddhists sought to have it banned and they succeeded in doing so on several occasions when they had the ear of the government.[55] By the eighth century AD the work was due for revision as the reading public had gained much new information on the western regions through the travels of the T'ang pilgrims like the famous Hsüan-tsang, who brought back very detailed accounts of the countries which he had visited in his attempt to procure the original texts of some of the main Buddhist scriptures. The *Scripture of the Conversion of Barbarians* was last proscribed in 668 and again in 705. Although the ban did not last long on both occasions, it was possible that there was a demand for replacement copies as well as a new edition. The version of the *Scripture* which appeared in the eighth century had additional books as well as up-to-date transliteration of western place-names.[56] According to a Buddhist source, Wang Fu's work originally consisted of one book but subsequent versions contain as many as eleven books as it was augmented by later Taoist writers.[57]

No complete version of the *Scripture of the Conversion of Barbarians* has come down to us but it is fortunate for the study of Manichaeism that Pelliot brought back from Tun-huang fragments of the preface and the tenth book of the post ninth-century edition of the work. We can be certain that they are not from the original version of Wang Fu because the fragment containing the preface makes reference to a king of Ta-shih (i.e. Arabia), a country which was unknown to the Chinese until the expansion of Islamic powers in the T'ang period.[58] In chapter one we find the story of Lao-tzu forecasting at the assembly of P'i-mo in 1028 BC his many future manifestations, one of which will take him to the country of Su-lin where he will become Mani. The relevant part of the preface reads:

Then four hundred and fifty or so years after [my last manifestation], I [*sc.* Lao-tzu] shall ride on a vapour of the Tao of natural light. I shall leave the domain of

Truth and Calmness and fly into the precious territory of Hsi-na [? Rome].[59] In the kingdom of Su-lin [i.e. Assuristan] I shall descend into the royal palace and be born as crown-prince. I shall leave my family and enter the Way and be called Mo-mo-ni [i.e. Mar Mani], I shall turn the wheel of the great law [*dharma*] and I shall explain the canonical commandments and regulations and the practice of meditation and knowledge, as well as the doctrines of the Three Epochs and Two Principles. I shall instruct both gods and men and make them realize that the Present Moment reaches up to the Realm of Light and down to the Paths of Darkness. All the beings will thereby be saved.

Five times nine years [i.e. 450 years] after Mani, the metallic vapour (or vital force] will rise and my teaching will prosper. As a sign, holy images of Mani will come spontaneously from the Western Regions to the Middle Continent [i.e. China]. This will be a sign of realisation. The two vapours, yellow and white, will coalesce and the Three Schools [i.e. Confucianism, Taoism and Buddhism] will be united together and return to me. The temples of benevolence and the places of cultivation (will be so numerous) that they will join their beams and link their rafters. The bright and venerable law of the Later Sage will be translated and interpreted. The Taoist masters of the Middle Continent will extensively explain the doctrine of cause and effect [*hetupratyaya*]. They will be the ships of the world and enlarge the scope of the service of the law. All that moves, grows or has life will be saved. This is known as the total absorption of all schools.[60]

The assimilation of Mani to Lao-tzu is of great significance to the subsequent history of Manichaeism in China as it gave the Manichaeans a much needed foothold in the mainstream of Chinese religious life. Did the Manichaeans themselves perpetuate the legend that Mani was one of the many latter-day manifestations of Lao-tzu, or did they gratefully accept what was in essence the anti-Manichaean polemic of the Taoists as a back-handed compliment? Scholarly opinion on this is evenly divided. It has been pointed out that the fragmentary preface of the *Scripture* from Tun-huang carries a different title from that given in the fragment of Book Ten. Whereas the preface is entitled *Lao-tzu hsi-shing hua-hu ching* (*Scripture of the Westward Ascent of Lao-tzu (and his) Conversion of the Barbarians*), the fragment of Book Ten is simply entitled *Lao-tzu hua-hu ching*.[61] Furthermore, the Manichaeans in the Sung dynasty frequently made reference to the *Scripture of the Conversion of Barbarians* to stress their link with Taoism but the relevant passage is rarely attested in other Taoist writings unconnected with Manichaeism.[62] This seems to point to the Manichaeans possessing a special version of the work entitled *Scripture of the Western Ascent of Lao-tzu (and his) Conversion of the Barbarians* which gives the story of Lao-tzu's transformation as Mani in its preface. The Manichaeans might therefore have fabricated the legend themselves and preserved it in a work which could easily be passed off as an important Taoist work when their scriptures were in danger of being confiscated by officials.[63] In the early years of Mongol rule (c. 1291), a Buddhist monk Hsiang-mai wrote a detailed refutation of the *Scripture of the Conversion of Barbarians* in which he cites an edict of 1280 which bans both the *Hua-hu ching* (*Scripture of the Conversion of Barbarians*) by Wang Fu and the *Hsi-shing ching* (*Scripture of the Western Ascent*).[64] We may have here the Taoist and the Manichaean versions of the work listed separately. As we shall see, the Manichaean claim that their religion was handed down by Lao-tzu was also hotly denied by a Taoist writer of the Sung, Po Yu-ch'an (fl. 1215).[65]

Against this view of Manichaean subterfuge we need to bear in mind that the passage we have cited ends on a triumphal note for Lao-tzu rather than for Mani. Moreover, it displays little real knowledge of Manichaeism beyond a few well known phrases like 'Two Principles' and 'Three Moments'. The Manicheans began to use the Lao-tzu story to buttress Mani's claim to a place in Chinese religious life in the T'ang dynasty. The *Compendium* from Tun-huang gives a lengthy citation from the *Scripture* concerning Lao-tzu's reincarnation as Mani as a proof text to substantiate Mani's divine origins. The two accounts sit uncomfortably next to each other as they are at variance on the historical circumstances concerning the birth of Mani. If the Manichaeans had indeed forged the link between Mani and Lao-tzu then they might have made more effort to accommodate it to the Buddhicised version of Mani's birth which was already in circulation. Furthermore, Hsiang-mai in his refutation of the *Scripture* seems to be aware of Lao-tzu's link with Mani and it was unlikely that he went out of his way to find it in a special Manichaean edition of the work.[66] Finally, in the late Sung period (c. 1264) a Confucian *literatus* Huang Ch'en, when confronted by the claim that Mani's link to Lao-tzu was supported by the *Scripture of the Conversion of the Barbarians* actually checked up the reference and found that it was correct.[67]

On balance, the evidence seems to suggest that Mani was made an honorary member of the Taoist pantheon by the Taoists themselves in their endeavour to show that Taoism lay at the root of both Buddhism and Manichaeism. The latter was seen by many as a form of Buddhism in T'ang China and was then a *religio licita*. The Manichaeans, who were always conscious of the foreign origins of their religions, accepted the honorary Chinese citizenship bestowed on Mani with open arms. As the Buddhists became more hostile to Manichaeism because of Mani's claim to be a Buddha, if not *the* Buddha, the Manichaeans strengthened their ties with Taoism. Taoism was less hierarchically structured than Buddhism and placed less emphasis on internal discipline. It therefore provided the Manichaeans with more room for refuge. As we shall see, the Manichaeans in the Sung period would show great ingenuity in preserving the *Scripture of the Conversion of the Barbarians* from confiscation and destruction. They would also register Manichaean temples as Taoist temples in order to acquire the necessary governmental approval. The two versions of Mani's life in the *Compendium* would eventually be harmonised by the Manichaeans in south China, but with greater emphasis given to the Taoist account. (See below, pp. 262–3)

(5)   THE SELF-IDENTITY OF
        CHINESE MANICHAEISM

Of the three western religions which came to China in the T'ang period through contact with Sassanian Persia (viz. Manichaeism, Nestorianism and Zoroastrianism) Manichaeism was the only one which had any real success in establishing a lasting presence in China. Zoroastrianism remained strictly a religion of the foreigners and we rarely hear of it gaining Chinese converts. Nestorianism made some attempt at evangelisation but its success was limited. The surviving Nestorian texts from Tun-huang provide an interesting contrast to those of the Manichaeans. We have already noted that the Nestorians occasionally composed their texts in the form of Buddhist sutras. However, this was virtually their only concession to the religious situation of Central Asia and China. Nestorianism had kept a distinct self-identity in its passage eastwards and we find Nestorians being attacked as an easily identifiable group in a Buddhist sutra in Turkish from Central Asia.[68] In translating their texts into Chinese they judiciously avoided the use of distinctive Buddhist terms although, like the Manichaeans, they occasionally had to use the word *fo* (Buddha) to denote divinity. Otherwise they coined many new terms and phrases to avoid borrowing from Buddhism and their scriptures read surprisingly like translations of Christian texts undertaken by eighteenth- and nineteenth-century western missionaries with local helpers. The missionary record of the Nestorians in China was an unremarkable one. After their priests were expelled along with Zoroastrians and Uighur Manichaeans, the religion was rarely heard of in China. It flourished in Central Asia and made a return to China in the company of the victorious armies of the Mongol Khans in the thirteenth century. After the expulsion of the Mongols in 1367, Nestorian Christianity made a second and more permanent exit from China.[69]

Manichaeism, on the other hand, survived both the explusion of the Uighurs and the Mongols and maintained a presence in south China well into the sixteenth century. This amazing feat of survival owes much to the willingness of its missionaries to cross the cultural gap between Mesopotamia and China by constant adaptation and assimilation. We must not however take this to mean that Manichaeans in T'ang China considered themselves as Buddhists and as Taoists in the Sung. The assimilation of Manichaeism to Buddhism and Taoism was partial or even superficial. Although we find some Manichaean deities being identified with Buddhist divinities and some Manichaean themes expressed in Buddhist terms, in the texts from Tun-huang, their basic teaching is Manichaean. The main theme of the *Treatise* is an account of the deliverance of the primal man and the creation of the world and it has no direct Buddhist parallels. Furthermore, not all the Manichaean deities were given Buddhist titles; a fair number were left in their Iranian forms in transliteration. Terms like *Hu-lu-che-te* (= Pth.: *xrwstg*, i.e. 'Call'), *P'o-lu-huo-te* (= Pth.: *pdw'xtg*, i.e. 'Answer'), *Su-lu-sha-lo-i* (= Pe.: *srwš'hr'y*, i.e. 'the Column of Glory') would have made little sense to Buddhist readers who did not know the meaning of the Iranian words behind the transliterations.[70]

The sect also maintained its self-identity through its veneration of Mani as the Buddha of Light. One can discern from a list of Manichaean works compiled by Confucian officials in 1120 that the Manichaeans in the coastal regions of south China possessed books on distinctly Manichaean topics and one of the them was even called the *Portrait of Jesus the Buddha* (*I-shu fo-cheng*).[71] As late as the sixteenth century, the Manichaeans in the prefecture of Ch'üan still knew that Mani was born in 208 and died in 260. This is only eight years off the mark, as the normally accepted dates of Mani's life are 216–74. The mistake can be explained by a wrong correlation of the Sassanian and the Chinese calendars which the Manichaeans in south China had inherited from the translator of the *Compendium* in the T'ang period.[72] They also knew that the Manichaean canon consisted of seven works and that the religion originated in Assuristan (*Su-lin*) and was propagated in Persia (*Po-ssu*), Rome (*Fu-lin* = Pe.: *hrwm*) and Tochara (*To-hou-lu*) before it came to China. Among the chief deities of the sect were the First Thought (*Hsien-i* = Primal Man) and Jesus (*I-shu*).[73]

By adapting some aspects of their religion to Buddhism and Taoism the Manichaeans had succeeded in narrowing the cultural gap between China and the west. Consequently, Manichaeism was more successfully transplanted onto Chinese soil than Zoroastrianism and Nestorianism which both remained as religions of foreigners throughout their history in China. The missionary achievements of Manichaeism in China cannot of course be compared to that of

Buddhism but it does have the unique distinction of being the only one of the three older western religions from the Middle East to have found a more permanent home in China. Although Islam would later win a more significant number of converts in China than Manichaeism, its success was largely confined to the Turkic peoples of the border regions whose way of life was non-Chinese. Manichaeism, on the other hand, found itself a place of refuge in the main stream of Chinese civilisation and remained part of it for nearly eight hundred years.

CHAPTER IX

THE RELIGION OF LIGHT IN SOUTH CHINA NINTH–SIXTEENTH CENTURIES

The Hui-ch'ang Persecution of Buddhism and other foreign religions was a major watershed in the history of Manichaeism in China. Until then Manichaeism was primiarily a religion of foreigners like Nestorianism and Zoroastrianism although it did have a significantly larger indigenous following than these two other religions from Iran. The expulsion of the foreign Manichaean priests and the public humiliation of those who were probably of Chinese stock put an end to Manichaeism as a *religio licita*. Henceforth, the Manichaeans in China were compelled to sever their ties with foreign merchants and Uighur mercenaries and endeavour to integrate themselves fully into Chinese society. In the subsequent centuries, Manichaeism flourished in the coastal provinces of south China and its Chinese followers had virtually no contact with co-religionists in the Uighur Kingdom of Qočo. That Manichaeism was able to lead an independent existence in south China after the fall of the T'ang and one which long survived the kingdom of Qočo is a fine testimony to its adaptability and the skill of its followers in cloaking the religion with respectability and legality.

(1)   THE FIVE DYNASTIES (907–60)

The T'ang government never fully recovered from the trauma of the rebellion of An Lu-shan. Although the dynasty would continue for another century and a half, its power was a pale shadow compared with the apogee attained by T'ai-tsung in the seventh century. The centralised militia system (*fu-ping*) of the early T'ang which manifested all its shortcomings at the time of the rebellion of An Lu-shan was gradually subverted by ambitious provincial governors who held both civil and military powers. Strife amongst these commanders (*fan-chen*) and between them and the central government became inevitable, further weakening the defences of the empire against barbarian incursions.[1] The period between the T'ang and the Sung dynasties is called the Five Dynasties and Ten Nations, a designation which hides nothing of the turmoil created by a succession of short dynasties and the fragmentation of the empire brought about by foreign invasion.[2]

The political chaos following the fall of the T'ang in the early years of the tenth century probably contributed to the survival of Manichaeism, as successive governments had more urgent matters at hand than to suppress the remnants of a small foreign religion with the Middle Kingdom. It was during this period of anarchy that Manichaeism established itself in the coastal provinces of south China, especially in Fukien. The exact history of how the centre of gravity of the religion migrated from the capital cities, where it was in constant contact with foreign peoples, to the less cosmopolitan south is not entirely clear. We are heavily reliant on the information which Ho Ch'iao-yüan, a sixteenth century *savant*, managed to obtain either from the surviving Manichaeans in the prefecture of Ch'üan or from local records concerning the sect. According to Ho, a *Hu-lu fa-shih* (i.e. *hu-lu-huan* = Pe. *xrwhxw'n*, 'preacher') fled from the persecutions in the capital cities and sought refuge in Fu-t'ang (i.e. Fu-ts'ing), a district of southern Fukien. He attracted a number of disciples and disseminated the religion throughout the province of Fukien. He died in the prefecture of Ch'üan and was buried to the north of the prefecture. He goes on to say that in the Chih-tao period (995–7) under the Sung dynasty, a follower of the sect found a statue of Mani in a soothsayer's shop in the Sung capital of Kai-feng. It was sold to him for 50,000 cash pieces, 'And thus, his [*sc.* Mani's] auspicious image was circulated in the province of Min [i.e. Fukien]'.[3]

The prefecture of Ch'üan (Ch'üan-chou) where the *Hu-lu-huan* ended his day as an itinerant preacher was a major sea port in T'ang times and would remain so until the sixteenth century when the harbour was rendered unusable by the accumulation of silt. It was particularly famous as the main port of call for Arab seafarers of the period of 'Sinbad the Sailor' and was well known in western sources under the name of Zaitun. Marco Polo visited it in 1292 and greatly admired its prosperity and waxed lyrical over the exotic nature of some of the goods which were landed there from the South Seas.[4] There was already a sizeable foreign community in the prefecture under the T'ang, consisting mostly of Jews and Arabs. The cultural diversity of Ch'üan-chou might have afforded some shelter to the refugee Manichaean priest from the north. However, the persecution of foreign religions in the capital cities had unleashed a wave of xenophobia and Canton, also in south China, felt its full impact when rebel troops under the command of Huang Chao came there and massacred 120,000 Muslim, Jewish and Christian merchants with their families.[5] The fact that Manichaeism survived yet another anti-foreign outburst may indicate its success in becoming Sinicised. The *Hu-lu-huan* himself might have been of Chinese stock and his missionary activities were not directed at the foreign community of Ch'üan-chou. In the Sung period few people seemed to know that the Manichaeism which flourished in Fukien was once associated with a detested foreign power.[6] The link was remembered mainly by Buddhist historians who stressed it in order to deflect from Buddhism the charge of being a foreign religion.[7]

Tsan-ning (919–1002), one of the earliest Buddhist historians of the Sung devotes a section of his work the *Compendium of the History of the Buddhist Monks in the Sung* (*Ta Sung seng shih lueh*) to 'Nestorianism and Manichaeism'. In it he gives a brief but confused history of the three western religions from Iran, Nestorianism, Zoroastrianism and Manichaeism. His main aim however was to pin on the Manichaeans the responsibility for popular unrest in the Five Dynasties period. His account of the expulsion of the three religions by the T'ang government in the Hui-chang period is followed by more up to date information:

Nevertheless the roots [of these perverse religions] were not completely eradicated and in due course they spread and became prolific. In the six years of Chen-ming of the [Posterior] Liang Dynasty [i.e. 920 AD] a gang of Manichaeans [Mo-ni] in the prefecture of Ch'en proclaimed Wu I as the Son of Heaven [i.e. emperor]. [The authorities] sent soldiers to quell the rebellion and Wu I was captured alive. His followers were sent in chains to the gate of the palace and decapitated in the public square. The common people of the prefecture of Ch'en had from an early time been accustomed to heterodox practices [*tso-tao*]. They established their own sect based on the teaching of Buddhism which they called the Superior Vehicle. They do not eat meat or drink wine and they mislead the common people by their teaching. [Their behaviour is] disorderly [and their practices are] obscene. They also assemble under the cover of darkness and disperse at dawn. Since the Prefect [Chu] Yu-nang, the Prince of Hui, frequently committed unlawful acts, these villainous brigands increased in number. Repeated expeditions [by government forces] failed to quell [the rebellion] until the last years of the period Chen-ming when it was finally terminated by mass execution.

In the time of Shih Tsin [reigned 936–46] of the Posterior T'ang Dynasty (923–36) a secret reawakening of the rebellion took place. The rebels chose one person as chief and [vowed to] obey him in all things. They also made drawings of the Demon King in a squatting position with the Buddha washing his feet. They declared that Buddhism is the Great Vehicle [*ta-ch'eng*] but theirs is the Superior Vehicle [*shang-shang-ch'eng*]. [In actual fact] their teaching is a shadowy imitation of Buddhism and is what one would call a *Doctrine of Approximation* [*hsiang-ssu tao*]. Some Buddhist monks, driven by cold and famine, joined them from a profit motive. Those who are knowledgeable of such matters will stay away from them as their teaching lures one directly to the Lower Regions. You should be on guard against them.[8]

A fuller account of the rebellion of Wu I is also given in the secular *Dynastic History of the Five Dynasties* which was completed a few years prior to the work of Tsan-ning.[9] Comparison of the two versions shows that Tsan-ning has derived almost all the basic historical facts about the uprising from the secular account except that whereas the secular account claims that the followers of Wu I were a sect of Buddhism, he deflected the charge of sedition from the Buddhists by calling the rebels Manichaeans.[10] Furthermore the rebellion took place in north China at a time when the principal centres of Chinese Manichaeism were in the south. It seems most probable that Manichaeism had by the tenth century acquired a reputation for secrecy and attracted the concomitant allegations of sedition and obscene practices. Thus Tsan-ning found it a ready scapegoat for a charge which was primarily aimed at the more esoteric offshoots of Buddhism. In blaming the rebellions in the prefecture of Ch'en on the Manichaeism, Tsan-ning established a precedent which was later followed by other Buddhist historians of the Sung who saw the Manichaeans as instigators of social unrest in their own times.[10a]

The fall of the T'ang occasioned a new wave of barbarian invasions and some of the new rulers in north China during the Five Dynasties period could not even speak or write Chinese. The Uighurs, now split between two centres round Turfan and Kansu, were able to establish friendly contacts with China and we find Manichaean priests acting once more as their emissaries and gift-bearers to the imperial court.[11] In 929, the court of the posterior T'ang dynasty was informed of the death and burial of a Manichaean priest in the strategically important city of T'ai-yüan. A summary of the relevant memorial is preserved in a Sung encyclopaedia, the *Ts'e-fu yüan-kuei* (*Magic Mirror in the Palace of Books*) and it reads:

On the *kuei-hai* day of the eighth month of the fourth year of the T'ien-ch'eng period of the Posterior T'ang Dynasty [2 October 929], it was reported from the Northern Capital [i.e. T'ai-yüan] that a Manichaean monk was buried. The Manichaean [monk] was a 'Buddhist teacher' [*fo-shih!*] of the Uighurs. It happened [that] Li Yen-t'u the Sub-Prefect [of T'ai-yüan] was the grandson of Li Ssu-chung, who was the prince of the commandery of Huai-hua in the time of the Emperor Wu-tsung [of the T'ang Dynasty, 841-7]. Ssu-chung was originally a Uighur prince with the name of Ohrmuzd [Wu-mu-shih]. After having submitted to [our] state, he was granted both a [Chinese] surname and a personal name. After the great disorders in the territories within the Passes [i.e. Shan-hsi], Yen-t'u and his folks submitted to [Emperor] T'ai-tsu [of the posterior Liang dynasty, 907-15]. He was granted a mansion for his residence and he erected a Manichaean temple beside it for the Manichaean priest to live. It was there that the latter died.[12]

One can deduce from this report that the profession of Manichaeism was permitted to the leaders of refugee Uighurs from the Orkhon who had formally submitted to the Chinese and were officially Sinicised by being granted Chinese names. Nevertheless, the fact that a formal report on the death of a priest was necessary shows that a watchful eye was kept on this liberty which was probably accorded to only a few privileged ex-barbarians. It is unlikely that Manichaean priests who came to China as emissaries of the Uighurs in Kansu or Turfan or those who served the needs of the few exile Uighur communities within China would have been in a position to actively proselytise among the native population. The Uighurs in Kansu were soon converted to Buddhism, while those in Turfan adhered to a mixture of faiths, Manichaeaism, Buddhism and Nestorianism. The whole Tarim Basin would eventually come under the domination of Islam before the end of the twelfth century. Manichaeism soon became extinct in north China, and we hear no more of it after the end of the tenth century.

A different story may be told of Manichaeism in south China where it steadily expanded from its base in Fukien to the nearby provinces. Within Fukien itself the main centres of the sect's activities were the prefectures of Ch'üan, Wen and T'ai. The Manichaeans had already established a reputation in the T'ang for their skills is astrology and sorcery. On at least one occasion Manichaean priests were asked to pray for rain by the T'ang government.[13] In Ho Ch'iao-yüan's time (i.e. sixteenth/seventeenth centuries) the Manichaeans in south China were noted for their skills as sorcerers and they practised their magical acts according to a secret 'Master's Formula' (shih-shih-fa).[14] This seems to have enabled the Manichaeans to integrate themselves into the popular religious scene of the region. An indication of how successfully they had established themselves as sorcerers *extra-ordinaires*, is given by a story of the Five Dynasties period per-served in a collection of fantastic tales called *Chi-shen lu* (Account of the investigation of the spirits) by Hsü Hsüan (917–92). It shows how a Manichaean priest was accredited with exceptional powers in exorcism. The same story which is also found in a larger collection of similar tales, the *T'ai-p'ing kuang-chi* (Extensive Records of the Period of T'ai-ping) is set in Ch'ing-yüan, (i.e. the prefecture of Ch'üan) a known centre of Manichaeism and the burial place of the *Hu-lu fa-shih* who brought the religion to Fukien:

A certain man of Ch'ing-yüan by the name of Yang was Deputy Commander of the Defence Garrison of his commandery. He possessed a large house in the western suburbs [of the commandery]. Early one morning he went to the Prefecture. While he was away, his family was about to eat when a goose carrying paper money came in from the gate and went straight to a chamber off the western gallery. [Someone in] Yang's family said 'This goose must have come from a temple!' They ordered their servant to chase it away. The servant, on entering the room, saw only an old man with hair tied into two tufts and a white beard. All the members of the family ran away in fear. When Yang returned and heard about this he became exceedingly angry and tried to beat it with a stick. The spirit appeared from and disappeared into all four corners in rapid transformations and Yang kept missing it with the stick. Yang became even more angry and said: 'After I have eaten, I shall return to beat it to death'. The spirit bowed, came forward and mouthed an agreement. Yang had two daughters, the elder daughter went to the kitchen to carve meat in preparation for a meal. The meat fell off the chopping board and disappeared. The daughter lashed out with the cleaver in the air in all four directions. Suddenly a large black hairy hand appeared from underneath the chopping board and said: 'Please chop'. The daughter ran away, gasping for breath and subsequently became ill. The younger daughter was fetching salt from a large jar when a monkey suddenly leapt out of the jar and landed on her back. She ran to the front of the hall and there lost it. She too became ill. Thereupon they sent for a shaman to erect an altar to exorcise the spirit. The spirit also erected its own altar and performed its rites so much more zealously than the shaman that the latter was unable to subdue it and left in fear. Shortly afterwards, Yang's two daughters and his wife all died. Later someone who excelled in magic, viz. [a devotee] of the Religion of Light [*Ming-chiao*] was invited to stay overnight with his scriptures. The spirit then spat at Yang, scolded him and left. There upon it disappeared and Yang also died in that year.[15]

(2) MANICHAEAN SCRIPTURES AND THE TAOIST CANON UNDER THE NORTHERN SUNG DYNASTY

More stable political conditions returned to China after the accession of the Sung dynasty in 960. By then Manichaeism, or the Religion of Light (*Ming-chiao*), as it was now more commonly known, had completed its process of Sinicisation and its followers had begun to establish places of worship for the sect in the guise of Taoist temples. One such disguised temple, built in 960s was situated as far north as Ssu-ming, near the modern city of Ning-po on the southern estuary of the Yangtze.[16] Taoism was an eclectic faith which was accustomed to assimilating new ideas. Compared with Buddhism, its various schools manifested a far greater degree of doctrinal diversity and its priestly hierarchy was much less well structured. Hence, it offered Manichaeism ideal cover in a completely Chinese environment and this was further enhanced by the fact that the early Sung emperors were patrons of Taoism and accorded it privileges which one would normally associate with the state cult or Buddhism.

One aspect of the favour shown towards Taoism which was of direct benefit to the Manichaeans in south China was the compilation of a canon of Taoist scriptures at the suggestion of the Emperor Chen-tsung (reigned 998–1022). An earlier attempt to systematically assemble Taoist works had been undertaken in the eighth century, between 713 and 741. A corpus totalling some 3,744 chapters (*chüan*) was produced under the title of *San-tung ch'iung-kang* (*The Precious Index of the Three Caves*). This was largely lost during the political turmoil consequent on the fall of the T'ang. At the beginning of the Sung, the best collection of Taoist scriptures was housed in the new Sung capital of Kai-feng but this was far from complete in comparison to the T'ang collection. The Emperor Chen-tsung who was even-handed in his approach to both Buddhism and Taoism gave orders in 1015 to both the Taoists and the Buddhists to remove works which gave offence to the other religion from their collections.[17] As the Taoist collection was in an incomplete state, the emperor initiated the compilation of a new collection in 1016 to match the Buddhist Canon which had come to comprise some 2,278 titles by the Sung period. The task was entrusted to one of his favourite ministers Wang Ch'in-jo who in turn had the assistance of other ministers, especially that of Chang Chün-fang.

Since Taoist temples all over China housed libraries of some sort, the commissioners had to visit each locality and collect unique titles from them all. The task was completed in 1019 and the resulting corpus was a veritable record of extant Taoist literature. Chang Chün-fang wrote a prefatory work entitled *Seven Slips in a Satchel of Clouds* (*Yün-chi-ch'i ch'ien*) and in it we are told that he travelled extensively in south China where he found Taoist texts which once belonged to the former (i.e. T'ang) Taoist Canon. In Fukien, he acquired 'Taoist works and the scriptures of Mani, the Envoy of Light'.[18]

The Buddhist historian Chih-p'an maintained that the Manichaeans managed to have one of their works included into the Canon by greasing the palms of the commissioners. The work concerned was the *Sūtra of the Two Principles and Three Moments* (*Erh-tsung san-chi ching*).[19] This was one of the most important Manichaean works in China and might have been a Chinese version of the *Šābuhragān* as fragments of this work from Central Asia have the page heading of *dw bwn 'y š'bwhrg'n* (The Two Principles of the *Šābuhragān*).[20] Or it might have been an alternative title of the *Compendium* since it discusses the important Manichaean concept of the Two Principles and Three Moments.[21] The inclusion of a work into the Taoist canon gave it official protection from confiscation and destruction. The effectiveness of this was shown in the absence of the *Sūtra* from a list of Manichaean works labelled as subversive literature by officials in the prefecture of Wen in 1120.[22] In the next year, amidst a vigorous campaign by the government to confiscate the literature of subversive religious sects, a law was issued stressing the fact that the *Sutra of the Two Principles* was not included in the ban.[23] That this was necessary shows that local officials might have been unsure about the exact legal status of the work. This uncertainty is well shown by an incident in the biography of Hung Hao, the father of the famous Sung *literatus* Hung Kua. A few years prior to the outbreak of the Fang La rebellion in 1120, Hung Hao was chief registrar in the prefecture of T'ai, an important centre of Manichaeism in the Sung. A rich local Manichaean by the surname of Li was denounced by an informer who had learned from his daughter that he possessed a copy of the *Sutra of the Two Principles* and that he regularly assembled his neighbours for illegal acts of worship. He was duly arrested and one day, Hung Hao, who was then the acting prefect, overheard the payment of a large bribe by the Li family to secure his release. Hung was bemused as he did not consider the crime to be worthy of such a large bribe. Both Li and the informer were ordered into his presence and questioned in detail. The biography says simply that the case was justly settled, which seems to imply that Hung Hao knew the exact legal status of the *Sūtra* and that the informer's verdict was therefore calumny.[24]

It is possible that the *Scripture of the Conversion of the Barbarians* was retained in the Taoist Canon at the insistence of Wang Ch'in-jo even though it was Chen-tsung's intention that polemical and apocryphal works like it should be removed from both the Taoist and Buddhist canons.[25] The extant copies of Taoist literature no longer contains the *Scripture* nor the *Sutra of the Two Principles* but we must bear in mind that the Sung Taoist Canon which grew to comprise 5,387 *chüan* in its final form in the twelfth century suffered considerable loss when the capital city of Northern Sung fell to the Jurchens in 1126. The collection suffered further losses in the thirteenth century in the hands of the Mongol rulers who favoured Buddhism. The Ming emperors were upholders of Confucianism and they allowed the Taoist Canon to be reconstituted on a much smaller scale. Since the first Ming emperor, Tai-tsu, as we shall see, personally disliked Manichaeism, the chances of any Manichaean texts remaining in the Canon were minimal.[26] At what date the *Scripture of the Conversion of the Barbarians* and the *Sūtra of the Two Principles* were deleted from the Canon we cannot tell. A Buddhist historian of the Southern Sung dynasty, Tsung-chien, in a work published in 1237, cites an undated law which says that those who use the *Sutra of the Two Principles* and other similar 'un-canonical' scriptures to incite the masses should be regarded as guilty of heterodoxy (*tso-tao*).[26a] We possess no other record of such a law from non-Buddhist sources which makes one suspect that Tsung-chien might have re-worded a general proscription of heterodox scriptures to include the *Sūtra of the Two Principles*. Furthermore, the incident of the acceptance of the Manichaean texts into the Taoist Canon was referred to with some pride in 1264 by a superintendent of a Taoist temple which was once a Manichaean meeting place.[27] It seems that the place of the *Sūtra of the Two Principles* in the Canon was a controversial one but since the work was not officially struck off the list in the Sung Dynasty, the Manichaeans made the best use of the seal of approval bestowed upon their principal scripture. A Confucian official, Lu Yu (1125–1210) would later remark that the Manichaeans forged the seals of the commissioners of the Taoist Canon at the end of their texts.[28] Not being a Taoist, Lu Yu might not have been known that Manichaean texts were officially taken into the Canon in the previous century. However, Manichaeans might have also extended the seal of approval unilaterally to some of their other scriptures which were not in the Canon.

(3)   MANICHAEISM AND POPULAR DISSENT IN NORTHERN SUNG

The sedulous efforts of the Manichaeans to practise their religion under the guise of legality received a serious jolt in 1120 when central and south China was convulsed by a wave of popular uprising which the government saw as inspired by heterodox religious groups. A major contributory factor to the unrest was the patronage which the Emperor Hui-tsung (reigned 1101–26) lavished on Taoism. Anxious to strengthen his line of succession he followed the advice of a Taoist priest of the Mao-shan sect to level a hill in the northern sector of the capital city of K'ai-feng as he was told that by doing so the male (*yang*) influence would be improved. The act had the desired effect and Hui-tsung, in an unprecedented show of patronage to Taoism ordered in 1111 the construction of an imperial park on an artificial hill called Ken-yo ('Holy Mount of Steadfastness') which would be replete with every rare tree, plant or rock held to be of magical value. The land-scaping was so designed as to give an exhuberant atmosphere and paradise-like effect. To this end the emperor gave orders to search for rare plants and rocks throughout the provinces and local officials were empowered even to dig up graves and pull down houses in their search of hidden treasure. This soon became licensed profiteering as bribery was probably the only sure way of avoiding the confiscation of treasured belongings and in the case of rare stones, the possible destruction of houses.[29] The transportation of these objects were given higher priority than vital grain supplies. Merchant ships along with their crews were frequently drafted into service and they had to take the more hazardous sea route to Kai-feng if the load was too bulky for the Grand Canal.[30]

Fang La was the owner of a lacquer grove in Ch'ing-ch'i in Cheking, whose livelihood was in danger of being ruined by the imperial confiscations. He was a popular figure in the locality as he was unstinting in his help for those who felt the sharp edge of the government measures. The confiscation and transportarion of rare rocks and plants to the capital were only the latest of an ever-lengthening list of unpopular moves by the government. Hui-tsung had shown little real interest in the affairs of the realm. More gifted in artistic and literary skills than in political acumen, he entrusted the government to self-seeking officials so that he could devote himself to his aesthetic and religious activities. The common peasants were subjected to an ever more burdensome fiscal system as well as onerous forms of *corvée*. Fang La's retinue soon grew to over a thousand men and in the tenth month of the second year of the Hsüan-ho period (October–November 1120) they openly rebelled and slaughtered every local official they could find. Their numbers increased ten-fold within a few days. The central government seriously underestimated the extent of the uprising and no adequate steps to suppress it were taken until several prefectures and sub-prefectures had fallen to be rebels. From its starting point in the prefecture of Mu, the rebellion soon spread westwards and southwards.[31] Fang's 'standard of righteousness' (i.e. his rebel insignia) became the rallying point of dissident groups from other provinces. Among the rebel contingents who joined his ranks was a group led by Lü Shih-nang from Hsien-chü, in the prefecture of T'ai which as we have seen was a known centre of Manichaeism in this period.[32]

The Sung government was in the process of preparing for a campaign against the Khitans who were threathening China's northern frontier when the rebellion broke out. Consequently her army was in a comparative state of readiness and once the gravity of the situation was fully realised, the troops were ordered to march south under the generalship of the eunuch T'ung Kuan. On his arrival at the scene of the rebellion he abolished the imperial order for the confiscation and transporation of rocks and plants and by so doing removed a major grievance which had benefited the cause of the rebels. Fang La's poorly armed forces had relied on their manoeuvrability and guerrilla-style tactics for victory over the troops under the command of local governors but they were no match for the cream of the Sung army in pitched battles. The rebels were repeatedly routed by T'ung Kuan's forces and took refuge in a cave complex deep in the cliffs. Like the followers of Bar Kochba in their uprising against the Romans under Hadrian, Fang La's rebels turned the caves into veritable strongholds.

However one of T'ung's generals systematically scoured the cliffs and the valleys for an access to the stronghold and he finally found the route with the help of a local woman. The rebel redoubt was stormed and Fang La was captured together with his family on 11 May 1121. Remnants of the rebels held out in south China and were not pacified until the summer of 1122.[33]

Fang La's uprising was principally a revolt against corrupt officials and a cumbersome fiscal system which had not been adjusted to suit the needs of new social and economic conditions. Government officials themselves investigating the causes of the revolt in its aftermath were ready to admit that maladministration was principally to blame but they were also eager to stress Fang La's own criminal intentions and his use of sorcery and divination to gain the support of the masses. The official accounts of the rebellion attributed its early success to the unbridled use of spells and incantations by the rebel leaders to whip their poorly-armed followers into a frenzy on the field of battle. One source speaks of the rebels using tall puppets dressed in huge robes which were moved by mechanical devices and children and women with their faces painted as monsters to frighten the soldiers.[34] The officials, being well versed in past history of peasant uprisings saw a strong resemblance between the rebellion of Fang La and that of the so-called Yellow Turbans who brought the government of the Han Dynasty effectively to an end in 189 AD. Their leaders, Chang Chueh and Chang Liang founded the so-called Five Pecks of Rice sect (wu-tu-mi tao) by treating the sick with magical skills and then requiring a contribution of five pecks of rice from their patients. The memory of the Yellow Turbans loomed large in the minds of officials trying to explain the causes of the Fang La rebellion. It was said that the followers of Fang La worshipped facing north because it was in north China that the rebellion of the Yellow Turbans first began.[35]

Even before the outbreak of the Fang La rebellion, officials had begun to keep a closer eye on religious groups like Manichaeism which had flourished on the fringes of Buddhism and Taoism. These sects were often organised into network of cells which were seen by officials as ideal for subversive activities. The widespread use of magical charms, divination and faith healing by the leaders of the sect was seen as a subtle and persuasive means of gaining complete loyalty from their followers. Moreover, these sects were self-help societies in which the mutual aid rendered by their members to each other often helped to offset the effects of repressive government measures. Confucian officials sometimes expressed their admiration for this aspect of sectarianism but they were aware that it would also undermine effective government. They therefore saw clandestine religious groups as potential centres of subversion.[36] As one of them puts it succinctly, the three types of common folk who had a tendency to rebel were those who were starving, those who were simple-minded and hence easily swayed, and those who were conspiratorial. The starving ones could be driven to banditry by force of circumstances but their type of disturbance has no great significance since they are seeking only short-term relief from their immediate plight. Once there are signs of a good harvest, they would hastily return to their farmsteads. The simple-minded folks, on the other hand, are desirous of long-term improvement of their fortunes (fu). To this end they turn to Buddhas and sundry Taoist deities for succour. The conspiratorial-minded could thus gain ascendance over them by becoming leaders of religious societies.[37]

This simplistic view of the relationship between sectarianism and subversion is frequently expressed by officials and the fact that Fang La's followers were armed with magical charms and spells as well as more conventional weapons seemed to support their line of reasoning. Furthermore Fang La was joined by men who were leaders of heterodox religious sects like Lü Shih-nang from the prefecture of T'ai, a fact which points strongly to an important religious element in the revolt.

Confucianism, the state cult of pre-modern China, was essentially a code of ethical behaviour which governs human relationships rather than one's views of the spiritual world. If the argument of the Confucian officials we have cited were followed to its logical conclusion all forms of religion, other than the reverence of one's ancestors which does not entail corporate assembly, were potentially dangerous to the state-politic. However, Taoism and Buddhism which both seek to improve man's condition in this life and hereafter are too well established for any officials, no matter how chauvinistic, to contemplate their wholesale removal. What the government sought to do was to regulate these two religions by bureaucratic means. Thus, monasteries and temples had to be licensed by secular authorities before they could be built or maintained. Similarly men and women desiring to become monks and nuns had to procure certificates of ordination before they could take the tonsure. The formation of Buddhist and Taoist Canons was also intended to limit religious works to an approved corpus. Through these measures, the Confucian state sought to exercise some form of control over the religious life of the common people and a major aim in so doing was to prevent the proliferation of sects and religious societies which could become pockets of protest and subversion. Many of the unauthorised sects met under the cover of darkness and in unregistered meeting places where their members shared in the eating of vegetarian meals, a symbol of their piety. Their secrecy naturally heightened and suspicion that something unethical or subversive took place in such meetings. The officials also found it objectionable that in such meetings the sexes were usually not segregated. A few months prior to the outbreak of the Fang La rebellion an edict was promulgated with relevance to the prefecture of Tsang in the province of Hopei (11 May 1120) expressing officials concern over the frequency of reports of nocturnal un-segregated meetings. The authorities were worried that 'simple-minded people (yu-min)' would be misled by perverse doctrines in such gatherings and would harm 'law abiding citizens (liang-min)'. The local officials were therefore commanded to post bills advertising substantial rewards for informers and to punish the leaders of the sects more severely than was statutory.[38]

The Fang La rebellion gave rise to a flurry of activities by officials against unauthorised religious sects which had flourished when their attitude towards them was more lax. Manichaeism was by no means the most important of these sects now brought under closer scrutiny. Since the end of the T'ang, a number of popular sects had developed out of both Buddhism and Taoism which were not recognized as orthodox by their parent bodies. They were by and large religious associations led by men with little theological training. Their doctrinal outlook was syncretistic and the desire for fusion and conciliation of diverse teachings was often satisfied at the expense of doctrinal purity and clarity. Within these societies, the bond between their members were often very strong as they would normally be each other's sworn brother or sister. This was also frowned upon by Confucian officials not only because of the rebellious potential of such closely knit groups but also because the loyalty shown by their members to each other was seen as incompatible with filial piety, a cardinal virtue of Confucianism. As far as the officals were concerned, the common folks joined these popular sects for their own economic improvement and for the mutual aid which such associations could give to its members in matters of litigation.

The majority of these heterodox sects were Buddhist in origin and their schism and growth bear some resemblance to independent Christian churches in modern Africa in that a major reason for their popularity is their success in assimilating a foreign religion to indigenous cultural and social conditions. The history of Buddhist sectarianism in China is a vast and complex subject but it demands our attention, albeit briefly, because the study of Manichaeism in the Sung period is inextricably bound up with it. To most Confucian officials who were not experts in the various schools of Buddhist teaching, let alone the teaching of Mani, the Religion of Light was one of these many illegal religious societies which held nocturnal meetings in unlicensed 'vegetarian' halls (chai-tang) where they dabbled in magic and other unseemly practices. A few years after the Fang La rebellion, they coined a derogatory phrase to label such groups: 'vegetarian demon worshippers' (ch'ih-ts'ai shih-mo). Since it was a practical rather than doctrinal definition, the Confucian officials could conveniently apply it to a number of sects without detailing their doctrinal particularities but its use immediately obscures for the modern scholar the history of the individual sects.

Of the many sects in the early Sung the oldest was the Maitreya sect (Mi-le chiao-hui) which was founded in the T'ang Dynasty. Maitreya was the future Buddha and it was generally believed that he was living in Tushita heaven waiting for an auspicious moment to return to earth. We have seen how the Manichaeans in central Asia had used this deity to represent Mani's function as the Paraclete promised by Jesus to his disciples.[39] The return of the Maitreya will take place after a period of decay in which the true Way (Dharma) would have prosperity to mankind. Maitreya societies were formed to keep alive this eschatological hope and its utopian appeal was particularly attractive to the uneducated masses in times of widespread social discontent. Not surprisingly, more than one ambitious person had laid claims to Maitreyahood and one of them, Wang Tse, actually started in 1047 a rebellion in Ho-pei and Shan-tung where Maitreya societies were numerous. He seized the prefecture of Pei but the rebellion had no widespread support and it crumbled when government troops recaptured the walled city of the prefecture. The society was officially banned by the Sung and we hear little of it in subsequent centuries. Nevertheless, the concept of a future Buddha remained popular and would later be championed by the White Lotus Society in their rebellion against the Mongols in the fourteenth century.[40]

More recent in origin was the White Cloud Society (Pai-yün chiao-hui) which was founded according to tradition by a monk called Ching-chüeh (1043–1121?) and the sect took its name from the White Cloud chapel in Hang-chou where the society was established in 1108. Ching-chüeh was of the view that the prevailing Ch'an (i.e. Zen) school of Buddhism had preserved the letter of the faith at the expense of real religious experience. His teaching emphasises simple living, good works and mutual help amongst his members. Marriage was forbidden but their meetings were unsegregated, which readily gave rise to accusations of debauchery. The sect gained great popularity in the Chekiang area in the year before the Fang La rebellion. Ching-chüeh himself was exiled to Canton in 1116 but he has officially pardoned shortly before his death in 1121. The date of his pardon seems to indicate that the government saw no immediate link between the White Cloud Society and the Fang La rebellion.

Nevertheless, the sobriquet 'vegetarian demon worshippers' was frequently used to label the sect.[41] For instance in 1198, a memorial was addressed to the throne which expresses concern over the activities of 'vegetarian demon worshippers' in Chekiang. We are told that they masqueraded as Taoists and met in unregistered temples. They built shrines as well as constructing roads and bridges as works of merit. They were a closely knit group and should one of their members be involved in litigation, fellow members would contribute whatever was necessary to bribe the functionaries to obtain a favourable verdict. There were many skilled artisans among their ranks ready to render aid to other members and the sect also held caches of equipment and food. The official saw these activities as signs of the sect preparing to revolt but the uninformed masses, according to the same official, regarded all these as welfare provisions for its members.[42] The real identity of this sect, as revealed to us by the Buddhist historian Chih-p'an who also cited this edict, was the White Cloud Society.[43]

In regions where Manichaeism exercised a strong influence, such as the prefectures of T'ai, Wen and Ming in Che-tung and Fu and Ch'üan in Fukien, the sects labelled as 'vegetarian demon worshippers' were probably mainly Manichaeans. Officials who had always eyed such sects with suspicion were quick to take action against them at the outbreak of the rebellion. The strength of Manichaeism in the prefecture of Wen and the depth of the official's concern about it are well illustrated by a memorial submitted to the throne within a month of the outbreak of the Fang La Rebellion:

[Memorial submitted] on the fourth day of the eleventh month of the second year of the Hsüan-ho reign period [26 November 1120]

The officials say: 'At the prefecture of Wen and other places are recalcitrant persons who proclaim themselves to be the "disciples" [hsing-che = Sanskrit: ācārin] of the Religion of the Light [Ming-chiao].

At present these followers of the Religion of Light set up buildings in the districts and villages of their abode which they called "Vegetarian Halls" (chai-t'ang). In the prefecture of Wen for instance there are some forty such establishments and they are privately built and unlicensed Buddhist temples.

Each year, in the first (lunar) month, and on the day of mi [= Pth. myhr] in their calendar they assemble together the Attendants [of the Law] [shih-(fa)-che], the Hearers [t'ing-che], the Paternal Aunts [ku-p'o], the Vegetarian Sisters [chai-chieh] and others who erect the Platforms of the Tao [tao-cheng = Bēma?] and incite the common folk, both male and female. They assemble at night and disperse at dawn.

The scriptures and the pictures and images of the followers of the Religion of Light have titles such as these:

(1) The Sūtra of exhortation to meditation [Ch'i-ssu ching], (2) The Sūtra of Verification [Cheng-ming ching], (3) The Sūtra of the descent and birth of the

Crown Prince [*T'ai-tzu hsia-sheng ching*], (4) *The Sutra of the Father and the Mother* [*Fu-mu ching*], (5) *The Sūtra (or Book) of Illustrations* [*T'u ching* = Ārdhang], (6) *The Sūtra of the Essay on Causes* [?] [*Wen-yüan ching*], (7) *The Gatha of Seven Moments (or Prayers)* [*Ch'i-shih chieh*], (8) *The Gatha of the Sun* [*Jih-kuang chieh*], (9) *The Gatha of the Moon* [*Yueh-kuang chieh*], (10) *The Essay on the [King of]* [?] *Justice* [*P'ing-wen*], (11) *The Hymn for exhorting [virtuous]* [?] *men* [*Ts'e-han tsan*], (12) *The Hymn for exhorting the Verification* [*Ts'e cheng-ming tsan*], (13) *The Grand Confessional* [*Kuang ta ch'an*], (14) *The Portrait of the Buddha the Wonderful Water* [*Miao-shui fo cheng*], (15) *The Portrait of the Buddha the First Thought* [*Hsien-i fo cheng*], (16) *The Portrait of the Buddha Jesus* [*I-shu fo cheng*], (17) *The Portrait of Good and Evil* [*Shan-o cheng*], (18) *The Portrait of the Prince Royal* [*Tai-tzu cheng*], (19) *The Portrait of the Four Kings of Heaven* [*Ssu t'ien-wang cheng*]. These works and the names of the divinities are not mentioned in the Taoist or Buddhist canons. They are full of false and fantastic sayings and they often cite from texts beginning with [the words] ''Thereupon the Lord of Light . . .'' which are different from Taoist and Buddhist scriptures.

As for the words [for the scriptures] they are hard to recognise and also difficult to pronounce. In short they demonstrate that these are demented and arrogant people who falsely concoct words and terms to deceive and mislead the uninformed masses and usurp the titles of the King of Heaven [*T'ien-wang*] and of the Prince Royal [*T'ai-tzu*].''[43]

To this memorial is appended the following imperial edict:

The imperial rescript received orders the officials of the said localities to make detailed investigations and to pull down the Vegetarian Halls and all other such establishments. The leaders of the offenders will be dealt with in excess of the [penalties laid down in the] established laws. A system of rewards should be rigorously set up to enable informers to come forward. From now on, if a similar situation arises and the officials of the prefectures and sub-prefectures conspire to ignore it they will be regarded as having contravened the imperial rescript. Similarly, should the commissioners fail to be vigilant and should the inspectors fail to investigate and prosecute, they will be similarly punished.[44]

The memorial leaves us in no doubt that the Religion of Light which it condemns was Manichaeism. The spring festival was almost certainly the Feast of the Bēma. The first month in the Chinese lunar calendar normally falls between January and February and we know from Augustine that the Manichaeans celebrated the Feast of the Bēma before Christian Easter.[45] The works listed above contain many easily recognised names of Manichaean deities such as Jesus, the Four Kings of Heaven, the First Thought (Primal Man), the Wonderful Water[46] and the Sun and the Moon. The *Sūtra of Verification* [*Cheng-ming ching*] could well be the *Pragmateia* as the Chinese title given to it in the *Compendium* is *Book of Instruction which Verifies the Past* [*Cheng-ming kuo-ch'ü chiao ching*].[47] Furthermore, the introductory formula 'Thereupon the Lord of Light . . .' is almost identical to one used in the Manichaean *Treatise* from Tun-huang; 'Thereupon the Envoy of Light . . .'[48]

The followers of Fang La did not succeed in capturing the prefecture of Wen and the efforts of the officials there to crack down on the Manichaeans were probably part of a more general attempt to forestall any sympathetic action. In the prefecture of T'ai, the government's position was more precarious. A group of 'vegetarian demon worshippers' led by Lü Shih-nang rose in revolt but they failed to capture the prefecture after three separate attacks. Lü was later captured and beheaded. His action inevitably led to massive retaliation against 'vegetarian demon worshippers' without due regard for their exact connection with Lü's sect. According to the biography of Hung Hao who, as we recall, had earlier dealt with the case of a Manichaean accused of illegally possessing the *Sutra of the Two Principles*, several hundred vegetarian demon worshippers were brought to the Yamen. There the sub-prefect ([hsien]-ch'eng) and the military commander ([hsien]-wei) counselled wholesale beheading. Hung Hao protested against this drastic measure but to no avail. The other two functionaries had their way and were rewarded with promotion. However, within a year, they died in quick succession and it was said that they were killed by the spirits of those whom they had executed.[49]

A much discussed source for our knowledge of the beliefs and practices of the 'vegetarian demon worshippers' is an extract written in 1133 from the collected notes and jottings of a Confucian official called Chuang Ch'o.[50] In it he gives us some unique insights into the organisation of the so-called 'vegetarian demon worshippers' but his account of their beliefs is extremely obscure. Like many other officials he saw them as 'descendants' of the Yellow Turbans and they rose to a man to support the Fang La rebellion. His essay is worth citing in full because of the important place it occupies in any attempt to identify the principal sect or sects behind the official label of 'vegetarian demon worshippers':

The sect of the 'demon worshipping vegetarians [*sic.*]' is strictly prohibited by the laws. Even the family members of the offenders who are not privy to their crime are exiled to distant lands and half of the offender's property would be awarded to the informer and the rest confiscated. Nevertheless the number of followers has increased in recent times. The sect originated in Fukien and spread to the Province of Wen and the two Che Provinces [i.e. eastern and southern Chekiang]. When Fang La rose in rebellion, the followers of the sect incited each other to rebel everywhere.

It is said that their rules prohibit the eating of meat and the drinking of wine. They do not worship spirits or Buddhas or ancestors. Nor do they entertain guests. When [a member of the sect] dies he is buried naked. However the corpse was first laid out fully clothed and capped. Two fellow members of the sect then sit beside the corpse and one of them will ask, 'Did he come with a cap?'. The other will say, 'No, [he did not]'. They then proceed to take off his cap and in similar fashion they remove one by one his other items of clothing, until nothing is left. One of them will then ask: 'What did he wear when he first came?' The other will answer: 'A placenta [i.e. the clothes of the womb]'. They then put the corpse into a cloth sack.

One hears it said that those who join the sect later become rich. These common folk are indeed ignorant for they do not realise that abstaining from wine and meat and lavish feasts and sacrifices and elaborate funerals will enable one to accumulate wealth. There are some who were quite poor when they first joined the sect but other members will help them with contributions. By accumulating these contributions, no matter how small, they can earn a comfortable living. When a member of the sect goes to or passes through another place, fellow members will provide him with board and lodging even if they do not know him. Everything is used by any member with no need for prior permission. They speak of themselves as members of one family and hence they use the term 'an all covering blanket [?]' to entice their followers.

Their leader is called the King Demon [mo-wang] and his assistants are called Demon Fathers [mo-weng] and Demon Mothers [mo-mu]. They all engage in luring people [to join the sect]. On the first and fifteenth of each month, each follower pays forty-nine cash pieces as incense money at the place of the Demon Father. The Demon Mother will then collect all the strings of cash and hands them over to the King Demon from time to time. The amount of money collected each year in this way is not inconsiderable.

The followers of the sect also chant the *Diamond Sūtra* and take from it the verse: 'They who see me [i.e. the Buddha] by visible form are following a perverse way (*hsieh-tao*)'. Hence they worship neither spirits nor buddhas but revere the sun and the moon and regard them as real buddhas. When they interpret the verse: 'The Dharma is even and has no gradations' they would join the word 'no' [through deliberate mispunctuation] to the first part of the verse [i.e. to make it read: 'The Dharma is not even and has gradations']. Such is the way they normally interpret the *sutras*.

The word *mo* [demon] is mispronounced by the common people as *ma* [hemp] and hence their chiefs are called *ma-huang* [yellow hemp] or some other such term with which they substitute the appellation of *mo-wang* [Demon King]. The followers are required to swear solemn oaths at the initiation. Since they regard Chang Chüeh [*fl.* second century AD] as their original founder of the sect, they would not utter the word *chüeh* [horn] even if they are tortured to the point of death. It is said that when Ho Chih-chung was an assiatance magistrate second class of the Prefecture of T'ai, the local authorities had arrested some Demon Worshippers but they were unable to make them confess [their crime] even after detailed examination. Someone reminded them that Ho was a native of Lung-ch'üan commandery in the province of Ch'u where there were many followers of the [demon worshipping] sect and he would be able to determine whether the charge could be substantiated. They therefore asked Ho to investigate the case. Ho placed before them a number of miscellaneous items and asked them if they could name them. He placed a horn in the midst of these items. [The accused] named all of them but they passed over the horn in silence. This was how the case was decided.

Their refusal to pay respects to their ancestors and their practice of naked burial are detrimental to public morals. They also assert that human existence is full of misery. Hence, to terminate it by killing is to relieve misery. This is what they call 'deliverance' and he who 'delivers' many will become a Buddha. Therefore, once their number increases, they will take advantage of political chaos and rise in revolt. Their greatest crime is the pleasure they take in killing. They hate Buddhism in particular because its prohibition of killing is an offence to them.

However, the laws against them are too strict. Every time someone is prosecuted, many others are implicated. When the property of an offender is confiscated and his whole family exiled, the punishment differs little from death. As a result they are united in their effort to resist the authorities. Local officials fear them and dare not press home the charges against them. Thus the proscriptions have the opposite effect of causing their numbers to increase.

My own humble opinion is that the penalties for their crimes should be reduced in severity and the law of confiscation of their property be abolished. However, their leaders should be dealt with severely and in this way they may be subdued.[51]

Chuang Ch'o's description of the vegetarian demon worshippers is redolent with possible references to Manichaeism. Firstly the movement is said to have begun in Fukien and later spread into the prefectures of Wen, T'ai and Yueh. This agrees with what is known of Manichaeism since its diffusion in south China originated in Fukien. Another Confucian source says that the cult of vegetarianism and demon worship could be traced back to one man which can also be seen as a reference to the work of the *Hu-lu fa-shih* in promulgating the religion *ab initio* in south China.[52] Secondly the sun and moon are principal deities of the Manichaean pantheon and they too were worshipped by the 'vegetarian demon worshippers'. Thirdly, the dead members of the sect were stripped naked and then put away in a bag rather than a coffin. The Manichaeans in Central Asia were known not to bury their dead in graves. The term *stupa* in Manichaean usage could well mean a mortuary or an ossuary rather than a Buddhist-style building. A Manichaean parable text in Turkish speaks of a drunken man who entered a *stupa* (Uigur: *supuryan*) and embraced a corpse thinking she was his wife. Whereupon the corpse burst apart gushing puss and blood. The drunk was petrified and fled from the place in disgust.[53] The practice of not burying the dead probably stemmed from the Manichaean belief that the body was a defilement of matter and there was no need therefore to give it an elaborate burial after the soul had actually departed from it. Finally the communal lifestyle of the sect is what one would expect of the Manichaeans since they were not entitled to their own possessions but everything had to be shared.

In the final decade of the thirteenth century, a prefect of T'ai, Li (Shou) Ch'ien composed ten short polemical poems admonishing the local people to refrain from joining the ranks of 'vegetarian demon worshippers'.[54] In one of the poems (Poem 7) he cited the public beheading of Lü Shih-nang which took place some eighty years ago as a warning of what might befall a person who joined them. Although Li does not in his poem give more specifically mention the Religion of Light by name most scholars believe that the sect was his principal target. Among the things he scorned in the poems were the sect's veneration of a 'White Buddha' (pai-fo), the white dress of its members, their use of a *sutra* with a title which is remarkably similar to the *Sutra of the Two Principles*, their vegetarianism, their nocturnal meetings and their use of frankincense. We know from the *Compendium* that the statue of Mani should be clad in a white robe and seated on a white throne.[55] Hence the epithet of the 'White Buddha' is an appropriate description of Mani as the Buddha of Light. The use of frankincense by the Manichaeans is also known to Lu Yu, a Confucian official who had accurate knowledge of the Religion of Light in Fukien. The relevant poems read:

(2)   Meeting at night in white dress to listen to profane teaching
            And fleeing in every direction at day-break;
        These are the hall-marks of the 'outer way' [wai-tao] of the
                    pernicious Demon.
    Joining it will land you in jail and your children will be left uncared for.

(4)   You must not recite the *Sutra of the Dual Principles and
                Two Assemblies*
        The government edicts are manifestly clear on this matter.
    For your crime you will be exiled to a distance of three thousand *li*.
    How will the White Buddha [pai-fo] then be able to rescue you?

(7)   [The district] of Hsien-chü formerly had a hall for the titular saint,
            Which was situated in the village of Pai-ta [White Stupa].
        As many witnessed [there] the beheading of the Chief Vegetarian,
            Nowadays people avoid speaking of Lü Shih-nang.

(9)   Why abstain from the taste of meat and the smell of fish?
            You should adhere to a more common diet.
        At dawn and dusk you must not follow the evil ones
    Who will secretly warm frankincense on golden stoves.[56]

Given the known strength of the Religion of Light in the prefecture of T'ai, the implication that Lü Shih-nang was a Manichaean is an obvious one. Modern scholars have gone a step further to suggest that Fang La himself might have also been influenced by Manichaeism.[57] Ch'uang Ch'o's account states unambiguously that the sect of vegetarian demon worshippers spread from Fukien to Chekiang and Fang La was a native of the prefecture of Mu in western Chekiang. If he too was a Manichaean, then one can easily explain why Lü Shih-nang rose in support of him and also why the officials at the prefecture of Wen singled out the Manichaeans in their memorial of 1120 for special proscription. Furthermore, an official by the name of the Wang Chih, writing towards the end of the twelfth century, mentions the fact that when he was in Kiang-hsi, the province which joins Fukien to the west and Chekiang to the south-west, he witnessed the activities of a sect of 'vegetarian demon worshippers' which was attracting a large number of followers. Among the special terminologies of the sect which he noted are 'Dual cultivation and two assemblies (?)' (*Shuang-hsiu erh-hui*), 'White Buddha' (*Pai-fo*) and 'Diamond Dhyāna' (*Chin-kang ch'an*). As for their scriptures they carry titles such as *Buddha the Master who exposes his heart* (*Fo t'u hsin shih*), *The Buddha who speaks in tears* (*Fo shuo ti-lei*), *The sūtra on the coming to the world of the Major and Minor Enlightened Rulers at the Beginning* (*Ta hsiao ming-wang ch'u-shih k'ai-yüan ching*), *The sermon on the transformation of the entire earth* (*K'ua-ti p'ien-wen*), *The discourse on the reconciliation (of the diverse opinions) on Heaven* (*Ch'i-tien lun*), and the *Chant of the five comings* (*Wu lai ch'u*).[58] An almost identical list of works is also given by the Buddhist historian Tsung-chien in a section of his work which is devoted to the denunciation of Manichaeism.[59] One modern scholar at least has seen in Wang Chih's observations indubitable proof of the extension of Manichaeism from the coastal provinces to the provinces of Chekiang and Chiang-hsi.[60] The religion could therefore have already been established in more inland areas prior to the outbreak of the Fang La rebellion.

The hypothesis that Fang La was influenced to some extent by the teaching of Manichaeism on communal living and that he might even have been a leader of a 'Manichaean' group in his native prefecture is accepted as a proven fact by many modern scholars. In the same way that a syncretistic form of Christianity can be shown to have influenced the T'ai-p'ing rebels of more modern times, Manichaeism is commonly seen as an earlier example of a foreign religion being transformed by the Chinese into a 'rebel ideology'.[61] The term 'vegetarian demon worshippers' (*ch'ih-ts'ai shih-mo*) is generally understood as an official term of opprobrium which was coined solely with the Manichaeans in mind since the word for a demon in Chinese, *mo*, is virtually a homophone of the character Mo in the name of Mani (Mo-ni).[62] It has even been suggested that Manichaeism lent itself to the subversive programme of Fang La because it had long been hostile towards the state and its belief in the polarity of good and evil could be used to justify rebellion.[63]

In recent years, several scholars have independently cautioned against too ready an identification between Fang La and Manichaeism. Our growing body of evidence on Manichaeism in south China has shown that the sect had a strong identity of its own and this is expressed by its adherents to doctrines and ideologies which are unmistakably Manichaean. They worshipped Mani as the Buddha of Light and they had also preserved the four aspects of the Manichaean fourfold Father of Light (i.e. Purity, Light, Divinity and Wisdom) as a kind of motto for the sect. They possessed a corpus of scriptures which were unlike those in the Taoist and Buddhist Canons and they readily resorted to the legend of Lao-tzu's western ascent and his reincarnation as Mani to show that Manichaeism was not a *novum prodigium*. These distinguishing features are almost entirely absent from accounts of 'vegetarian demon worshippers' in more inland regions.[64] The list of so-called Manichaean works given by Wang Chih and Tsung-chien bears no resemblance to the titles of unambiguously Manichaean scriptures listed in the memorial of 1120 submitted by the officials of prefecture of T'ai. Tsung-chien's list is almost identical to that of Wang Chih which suggests that the former is derived from the latter. The Buddhist historians of the Sung were all anxious to disparage the Religion of Light. Its commonly-held association with 'vegetarian demon worshippers' who followed Fang La gave them a ready-made theme for their polemics. Since Wang Chih's essay is a detailed study of how banditry and social unrest were related to 'vegetarian demon worshippers', it would have been an obvious source for Tsung-chien writing about Manichaeism almost a century later. He unhesitatingly incorporated Wang's list of their works unaltered into his own work to show that the Religion of Light was linked to these subversive elements in Chiang-hsi because both groups came under the same censure.

Scholars who argue for Fang La and his supporters as Manichaeans regard Chuang Ch'o's description of the rebels' religious beliefs as sufficient proof of their being Manichaeans. Admittedly, the worship of the sun and the moon strikes one as strongly Manichaean as well as the group's vegetarianism. However Chuang nowhere says in the essay that Fang La's followers called themselves the Religion of Light or the sect of Mo-ni. Moreover, detailed comparison of Ch'uang's description of the beliefs, practices and social composition of Fang La's supporters with what we know of the Manichaeans in the coastal regions reveals a number of significant disparities. Followers of the Religion of Light in Fukien came from a wide social basis. In the thirteenth century they boasted officials, scholars and men of means among their membership.[65] Fang La's followers on the other hand seemed to have come mainly from the lower social classes who joined the sect to seek relief from poverty. Manichaeans were highly reverential to the image of their founder as the Buddha of Light as evidenced by the extant statue in the Manichaean shrine on Hua-p'iao Hill but according to Chuang Ch'o, Fang La's followers were rabid iconoclasts. The strange burial custom of the sect which Ch'uang describes may, as we have seen, stem from a Manichaean belief in the worthlessness of the body but it is equally possible that Fang La's followers avoided elaborate funerals and expensive coffins merely as an expression of their simple lifestyle. The practice of disposing the dead without coffins is not generally observed of Manichaeism in the coastal regions. It is mentioned of them only by the Buddhist historian Tsung-chien, whose account, as we have noted, draws material from sources which may have nothing to do with Manichaeism.[66] Finally, it is very difficult to reconcile what Chuang says of the sect's delight in killing as a means of delivering their victims from pain with the Manichaean aversion of killing. The Manichaean was forbidden to take any form of life, no matter how small or insignificant.[67] In the west, Augustine had to counter the pacifism of Faustus by evoking the concept of the just war,[68] while in China, even as ardent an opponent of Manichaeism as the Buddhist historian Chih-p'an had to admit that the Manichaean prohibition on killing was very strict indeed.[69]

We need also to be cautious about identifying Lü Shih-nang who came to Fang La's support from the prefecture of T'ai too closely with Manichaeism. Although our sources are unequivocal on his being a leader of the 'vegetarian demon worshippers', no contemporary witness states that he was a leader of the Religion of Light. Much of the argument of Lü being a leader of the Manichaeans rests on the one poem by Li Ch'ien which we have cited and the undeniable fact that the prefecture of T'ai was an important centre of Manichaeism in Sung China. However, Li's poems were written some eighty years after the rebellion and like almost all Confucian officials of his time he had no real interest in the doctrinal differences between the different illegal religious societies which he labelled as vegetarian demon worshippers. The term 'White Buddha' which occurs in Poem 4 and which many scholars regard as definitely Manichaean is also found in Wang Chih's essay as a term used by the 'vegetarian demon worshippers' of Kiang-hsi.[70] Li gives the title of the principal scripture of the 'vegetarian demon worshippers' he attacks as *Sutra of the Dual Principles and Two Assemblies (Shuang-tsung erh-hui ching)* which has been seen by many as a corruption for the *Sutra of the Two Principles and Three Moments*.[71] However, in the same essay by

Wang Chih we find 'Dual Cultivation and Two Assemblies' (*Shang-hsiu erh-hui*) being used as a technical phrase by the same sect in Kiang-hsi.[72] Wang also mentions the term 'Diamond Dhyāna' (*Chin-kang ch'an*) and we know from later sources that there was an esoteric Buddhist sect with that title which was popular in Kiang-hsi. Its followers used the *Diamond Sūtra* as their principal scripture and they were regarded by one official as the descendants of the Yellow Turbans because they admired Chuang Chüeh so much so that they would never utter his name in vain.[73] As we have seen, according to Chuang Ch'o, Fang La's followers also read the *Diamond Sutra* and held sacred the memory of Chuang Chüeh, the leader of the Yellow Turbans.[74] Earlier scholars had assumed that the Diamond Dhyāna was a sub-sect of Manichaeism but we now know that it was founded by a Buddhist monk in the prefecture of Liang in the Five Dynasties, and it was popular in Chiang-hsi and Chekiang.[75] The prefecture of T'ai therefore lay within the overlapping spheres of influence of at least two religious societies which were both labelled by officials as 'vegetarian demon worshippers'. One cannot therefore assume without further confirmation that Lü Shih-nang was a leader of the Religion of Light simply because he came from the prefecture of T'ai.

Far from being the instigators or even the enthusiastic supporters of the Fang La rebellion, the Manichaeans in the coastal provinces were more probably its unwitting victims. In the decades prior to the uprising, the sect had sedulously cultivated a semblance of legality and respectability. This was now swept aside as government officials were compelled by the exigencies of the rebellion to take punitive action against all fringe sects which practised vegetarianism and met in secrecy. Inevitably the state itself suffered from the social and economic dislocations caused by the rebellion and troops which would have otherwise taken part in a major offensive against the Jurchens in the northern frontier were dissipated in fighting the rebel forces. The Sung capital was plundered by the Jurchens in 1126 who captured it after a long siege. The imperial park at Ken-yo was destroyed in the fighting. The rare stones which had caused so much protest in their collection were turned into ammunition for the *ballistae* of the invaders.[76]

(4)   MANICHAEISM IN SOUTHERN SUNG

The capture of K'ai-feng by the Jurchens marked the end of the Sung dynasty as the ruling house of a unified China. Hui-tsung had abdicated in 1125 and left the critical state of affairs to his son Ch'in-tsung who could do little to forestall the inevitable collapse of the frontier defences and the decay of an over-burdensome administration. The victorious Jurchens captured both emperors and sent them and the entire royal household to exile in Manchuria. However, they were thwarted in their attempt to extend their conquest beyond the Yangtze. The terrain of south and central China did not facilitate the easy deployment of cavalry and the Jurchens also encountered stiffer resistance the further south they went. The consolidation of their conquests in the north China also demanded their immediate attention. In the absence of a determined effort to subdue the south, the Sung commanders of the unoccupied provinces rallied round one of the sons of Hui-tsung who had avoided capture and declared himself the Emperor Kao-tsung (1127–62). His long reign was devoted to the building up of a centralised government based on the new capital at Hang-chou which he renamed Lin-an ('temporary refuge') to indicate his desire to eventually recover north China from the invaders. The move to the south brought the court closer to the richest and most fertile regions of China and the Sung emperors saw to their fullest exploitation. Although taxes remained high, trade flourished and eventually southern Sung became a more prosperous kingdom than its predecessors who ruled over a unified China. This period saw the full flowering of Confucian scholarship and the corresponding decline of both Taoism and Buddhism in Chinese religious life.

The southward shift of Sung power also brought the government more closely in contact with the main centres of Manichaeism. The new capital is situated in Chekiang which borders Fukien to the north. Moreover, the Fang La rebellion seems to have paved the way for a wave of local uprisings which the government euphemistically referred to as acts of banditry. From 1130 to 1150, our sources mention no less than five separate rebellions in Chiang-nan and Chekiang for which the government held the 'vegetarian demon worshippers' as the principal culprits.[77] The same two decades also saw the formation of the most important religious sect of the Sung period, the White Lotus Society (Pai-lien chiao-hui). Founded as a Buddhist sect in 1133 its teaching emphasises repentance, suppression of desires, vegetarianism and prohibition on the taking of life. It attracted large numbers of followers not only in south China but also in areas occupied by the Jurchens where they formed pockets of patriotic resistance against the barbarian invaders. They would continue this role when China came under the domination of the Mongols and later the Manchus. Despite numerous attempts by the government at suppression, the White Lotus remained an organised society until the early years of the twentieth century.[78]

The scholar-officials of Southern Sung continued to blame sectarianism as a major cause of social unrest and repeatedly appealed to government for repressive legislation. No less than twenty edicts were promulgated between 1132 and 1209.[79] They called for the banning of 'vegetarian demon worshippers' from holding their nocturnal meetings, huge rewards for informers (up to half of the property confiscated from those captured and sentenced), and fearful punishments for the leaders of the sect. The legislators were convinced that the leaders of such sects were perverting the masses with their powers of sorcery and preparing them for revolt. Typical of such legislations is the edict of 25 February 1141:

All 'vegetarian demon worshippers' and those who meet together at night and disperse at dawn to practise and propagate evil teachings shall be strangulated. Those who are their followers shall be exiled to a distance of three thousand *li* [one *li* = ⅓ mile]. Women offenders shall be exiled to a distance of one thousand *li* and kept under supervision. The penalty of those who use conjuring tricks shall be one degree less [than for those above]. They shall be exiled for one thousand *li* and kept under supervision. If the case involves disloyal matters, the punishment shall be by strangulation. All these categories of offenders shall not have their penalties reduced by general pardons. Serious cases should be referred [to higher authorities]. Those [among them] who do not disseminate evil teaching shall be exiled to a distance of three thousand *li*. Permission is given to capture them by force, killing if necessary. Their property shall be used to furnish rewards and the remainder confiscated. Those who are not followers of the sect but have been misled by it shall have their penalties reduced by two degrees if they have not passed on the teaching to others.[80]

Of the many memorials addressed to the Sung emperor on the problem of religious sects, one which has particular significance for the history of Manichaeism was submitted by the scholar-official, Lu Yu (1125–1210). He twice held administrative posts in Fukien (1158 and 1178) and he drew examples from his local situation to support his case. In doing so he tells us much that is interesting about the Religion of Light in south China. The memorial is not dated but most scholars accept a date between 1163–6 for its submission.[81] He saw the sects as a more insidious and permanent problem to public order than natural disasters which had traditionally been held as the primary cause of banditry and unrest. Like most officials he made no attempt to differentiate between the sects and he typecast them all in the mode of the Yellow Turbans and the followers of Fang La:

Since ancient times, the rise or cessation of banditry have been the result of famine caused by floods or drought. Pressed by cold and hunger, men would assemble by a whistle to attack and pillage, but if appropriate steps are taken, they could easily be calmed and pacified and will certainly not become a source of worry to the court. However, perverse people practising demonic sorcery deceive and beguile decent people during times of peace. They form into associations and remain settled, awaiting the right moment to rise. The harm which they cause is harder to fathom.

Your servant humbly thinks that they type of people can be found everywhere. In Huai-nan they are called 'People of Two Knots [?]' [Erh-hui-tzu]. In the two Che they are called the [followers of] the doctrine of Mu-ni. In Chiang-tung, they are called the 'Four Fruits' [Ssu-kuo] and in Chiang-hsi they are called the 'Diamond Dhyāna' [Chin-kang ch'an]. In Fukien they are called followers of the 'Religion of Light' [Ming-chiao] or '[those who observe] the Gati Fast [?]' (Chieh-ti chai) and by various other titles. The Religion of Light is particularly prominent, so much so that it is practised and disseminated by scholars, magistrates and soldiers. Its deity is called the 'Messenger of Light' and it also has names [of deities] like the 'Buddha of Flesh', the 'Buddha of Bones' and the 'Buddha of Blood'. Its followers wear white garments and black caps. They form into associations wherever they are. They possess false scriptures and demonic images and they even go to the extent of engraving print-blocks for the dissemination of their scriptures. They falsely borrowed [the names] of the officials in charge of Taoism [Tao-kuan] like Ch'eng Jo-ch'ing and others of the Cheng-ho period (111–8) as revisers of their texts and [they also named] the Prefect of Fu-chou, Huang Shang as supervisor of the engraving [of the print blocks]. They regard the sacrifices to deceased grandfathers and fathers as an invocation to the [evil] spirits. They abstain completely from food which contains blood. They consider urine as holy water and use it for their ablutions. Their other demonic excesses cannot be easily enumerated. Since they burn frankincense, frankincense has risen in price. Since they eat ground mushrooms and tree fungi, these too have risen in price. Furthermore, because they practise these things together they are like glue and lacquer. If perchance they should stealthily rise [up in revolt] they would make one's heart go cold [with fright]. Chang Chüeh of the Han period, Sun En of the Tsin Dynasty (265–419) and Fang La of more recent times are all men of this sort.[82]

The terms 'Buddha of the flesh', 'Buddha of the bones' and 'Buddha of the blood' may seem strange to scholars of western Manichaeism. They are the Buddhicised nomenclatures of Jesus *patibilis* who in Sogdian is called *Buddha gotra* and we find in the Chinese Manichaean *Hymnscroll* a similar term: 'Jesus of flesh and blood' (Hsueh-ju yi-su).[33] Since Jesus is often given the epithet of 'Buddha' in eastern Manichaean texts, the formation of the terms 'Buddha of the bones' etc. is natural. As for Lu's observation on the use of urine by the Manichaeans as megical or liturgical water we are reminded of a similar accusation made by <Zacharias Mitylene>: 'So I anathema-tise these and I curse as being unclean in their souls and bodies, with the rest of their evils, and, as not suffering their filth to be cleaned in water lest, they say, the water be defiled, but even polluting themselves with their own urine . . .'[84] The principle behind what is being attacked by both Lu Yu and Zacharias is almost certainly the Manichaean avoidance of bathing in running water. Mani himself claimed as we have noted that Elchasaios, the founder of the sect in which he grew up, was once about to wash himself when a spirit appeared to him which rebuked him for defiling the element with his act of ablution. Thereupon Elchasaios refrained from washing in water.[85] The Manichaeans longed instead to be 'washed in the holy waters' which will make them spotless.[86] An almost identical wish is expressed in the Manichaean *Treatise* from Tun-huang where the term 'holy water' is translated as 'magical water' (*fa-shui*).[87] Manichaeans had a reputation in the west for their filthy and unkempt appearance. The accusation by <Zacharias> seems to suggest that urine could be used when washing became unavoidable.[88]

What irked Lu Yu most was the strenuous and often successful efforts of the Manichaeans at winning respectability. He accused them in the memorial of deceitfully placing the names of Taoist commissioners and officials as revisers or printing supervisors of their scriptures to lend them an air of official approval. Of the names he mentioned, we know that Huang Shang was prefect of Fu-chou in the Cheng-ho period (111–18).[89] Taoist works accepted into the canon would have undoubtedly carried colophons with names of officials like Huang. The last time we hear of Manichaean scriptures being accepted into the Canon was 1025. It may be that the Manichaeans in years before the Fang La rebellion were able to persuade the compilers to accept further works when the canon was extended on the grounds that some of their scriptures were already in the Canon. Lu mentions the Manichaeans in a much less condemnatory manner in another context and his account again shows the extent to which the Manichaeans endeavoured to dissociate themselves from accusations of obscenity, demon worship or socially unrespectable activities:

In Fukien there are those who practise heterodoxy who are called the Religion of Light. There are also a large number of scriptures belonging to the Religion of Light. [The followers of the sect] published them by block-printing and they falsely place the names of the functionaries in charge of compiling the Taoist Canon at the end of the texts as their revisors. They burn only frankincense and eat only red mushrooms. Hence, the prices of these commodities have risen considerably. There are the sons of educated families among their ranks and they will say [to you], 'To day I am attending the vegetarian gatherings of the Religion of Light'. I have chided them by saying, 'These are 'demon [worshippers]' why should [someone of your standing] keep such company?' They replied: 'This is not the case. The 'demon [worshippers]' do not segregate men and women but the followers of the Religion of Light ''do not permit men and women to come into contact with each other''. If a [male] follower of the Religion of Light is presented with food prepared by a woman, he will not eat it.' I sometimes manage to procure the scriptures of the Religion of Light for persual. Their contents are boastful and not worth quoting, precisely what one would expect to find in the works of common and vulgar people who practise magic and sorcery. The [followers of the sect] also point at the mansions of distinguished and well educated families and say 'They too are of the Religion of Light'. I find this hard to believe. While reading the *Account of the Investigation of the Spirits*, compiled by the vice-president Hsü [Hsüan], I have come across the sentence, '. . . There was someone skilled in sorcery who was of the Religion of Light'. [See above pp. 224–25]. It is apparent that the Religion of Light is of long standing.[90]

The reply to Lu Yu that the precepts of the Religion of Light do not permit 'men and women to come into contact with each other' is a quotation from the *Book of Rites* (*Li-chi*), the most important Confucian manual on propriety.[91] The charge of promiscuity and obscenity must have been so regularly levelled at the sect by Confucian scholar-officials like Lu Yu that its members were impelled to cite Confucius in their own defence.

The Southern Sung was also the golden age of Chinese Buddhist historiography. As Buddhism was declining in importance it was vital for monk scholars to remind the faithful of the glories of the bygone past and to praise earlier emperors for their patronage in the hope of similar benefits from present day rulers. Chih-p'an, the most important of the Buddhist historians of this period and the author of the monumental *Record of the Lineage of the Buddha and the Patriarchs* (*Fo-tsu tung-chi*) made many disparaging comments on Manichaeism throughout the work. For instance, in discussing the T'ang edict of 732 proscribing the diffusion of Manichaeism, he deeply regretted the fact that the government then did not take more trouble to root it out completely. A partial proscription could never be effective as it would not actually get rid of those who had been perverted by the religion and in due course they would also disseminate it.[92] When he comes to the Sung period, Chih-p'an was ever ready to condemn the subversive tendency of religious societies especially those whom the government denounced as 'vegetarian demon worshippers' in their legislations. In his comments on an edict of 1198, Chih-p'an cites a now lost passage on Manichaeism from a collection of novelettes and short stories entitled the *I-chien chih* by Hung Mai (1123–1202):

The 'vegetarian demon worshippers' are particularly numerous in San-shan [i.e. Fukien]. Their leaders wear purple caps and loose robes and their women wear black caps and white garments. They call themselves the Society of the Religion of Light. The Buddha whom they worship is clad in white and they cite from the scriptures the phrase – 'The White Buddha also called the Lord of the World' as their proof text. They also take from the *Diamond Sutra* the 'First Buddha, Second Buddha, Third, Fourth and Fifth Buddha' [i.e. the list of the five Tathāgathas] for they regard their Buddha as the Fifth Buddha. He is also known as Mo-mo-ni. From the *Scripture of the Conversion of the*

Barbarians they cite the passage: 'I [Lao-tzu] shall ride on a luminous vapour of the way [Tao] and fly into the precious territory of Hsi-na and in the country of Su-lin, I shall be born as crown prince in the imperial palace. I shall leave home to become a monk with the title of Mo-mo-ni,' . . . as proof of his [i.e. Mani's] identity.

Their [principal] sūtra is entitled *Two Principles and Three Moments*. The 'Two Principles' are light and darkness and the 'Three Moments' are past, future and present. When the Taoist Canon was compiled in the time of Ta-chung hsiang-fu reign period [1008–1017] Lin Shih-chiang bribed the chief commissioner to include it in the Canon. It was duly deposited in the Ming-tao temple of the prefecture of Hao.

They also falsely claim that Po Lo-t'ien (i.e. Po Chü-i) has written a poem about them which says:

> I calmly examine the record of Su-lin,
> The doctrine of Mo-ni [i.e. Mani] is amazing,
> The Two Principles display their dignified silence,
> The Five Buddhas accompany the Light,
> The Sun and Moon render their homage,
> The heaven and earth acknowledge their origin.
> In the matter of self-discipline and purification,
> They [i.e. the Manichaeans] do not lag behind the off-spring
> of Śākya [i.e. the Buddhists].

These eight lines of verse they place at the beginning of their scriptures. Those who abide by their ascetic rules eat only one meal which they take in midday. They bury their dead naked and their ritual entails seven sets of [daily] prayers. These are undoubtedly practices which they have inherited from the Yellow Turbans.

Comment: I [Chih-p'an] have gone through the *Ch'ang-ch'ing chi* of Po Lo-t'ien and it does not contain the poem on Su-lin. Since Lo-t'ien was a follower of Buddhism, how could he have written such an impious poem?[93]

The *Ch'ang-ch'ing chi* is the standard collected works of the famous T'ang poet Po Chü-i and the absence of the poem from it is taken as conclusive evidence by Hung Mai of Manichaean subterfuge. Admittedly the poem has no great literary merit but one cannot automatically exclude Po Chü-i from being its author simply on grounds of its style and its exclusion from the *Ch'ang-ch'ing chi*. Before Po died, his collected works stood at seventy-five books containing 3,840 poems but modern editions of the *Ch'ang-ch'ing chi* possess only seventy-one books and 3,670 poems.[94] A possible explanation is that the poem is anonymous and the Manichaeans had attributed it to Po Chü-i because this great T'ang poet had once mentioned them in favourable terms in a letter he wrote to the Uighur Khaghan which is preserved.[95] Or it may be that Po Chü-i in his capacity as imperial censor might have visited the Manichaeans and prefaced one of their scriptures with the poem as a sign of compliment. Like Lu Yu, Chih-p'an was so convinced of the villainous character of the followers of the sect because of their adverse reputation as vegetarian demon worshippers that he was inclined to see every mark of the sect's respectability as a sign of deceit.

Chih-p'an devotes a whole section in the concluding book of his monumental work to the refutation of false doctrines and in it he gives the Manichaeans, the followers of White Lotus and the White Cloud special condemnation.[96] Unlike the Christian church in the later Roman empire, the Buddhist church in Sung China wielded little political influence and did not have the necessary means to take effective action in suppressing these sects. Although Buddhism had undergone a revival in Northern Sung, the memory of the late T'ang persecutions were still fresh and it was important for Buddhist apologists like Chih-p'an to show that Buddhists were law-abiding and useful citizens of the Middle Kingdom. The adverse reputation which the sects had acquired as potential rebels and bandits was a considerable embarrassment to the main stream of Buddhism in China, especially since the White Cloud and the White Lotus societies were avowedly Buddhist in origin and inspiration. Manichaeism came under the same censure as many still considered it an offspring of Buddhism because its chief deity was a 'Buddha of Light' and, like the Buddha, it came from the west.

The evidence we have examined so far is derived principally from the memorials and similar writings of Confucian scholar-officials and from Buddhist historians. A conspicuous gap in our knowledge of Manichaeism in China is the apparent lack of any comments on the sect's activities from Taoist writers. As Manichaeism relied very heavily on its Taoist guise for survival, the absence of Taoist reaction to it has often been taken as a sign of the latter's tolerance necessitated by its own doctrinal diversity and syncretistic nature. It seems however that one Taoist writer at least was anxious to dissociate himself and his schoool from the Religion of Light. Po Yü-ch'an, whose real name was Ko Ch'ang-keng (fl. 1215) was a native of Fukien and in his collected sayings we have the only comment by a Taoist of the Sung period on Manichaeism. I am grateful to Professor P. van der Loon for drawing my attention to this unique passage and for the help he has given me in making the following preliminary translation. To the best of our knowledge it has never before been discussed by modern scholars in relation to the history of Manichaeism in China:

[P'eng] Ssu [a disciple of Po] asked him [i.e. Po Yü-ch'an] saying, 'In the countryside there are many people who are vegetarians and keep fasts as ways of practising the Religion of Light and they say that it exterminates demons. Its followers say: "This is the doctrine handed down by T'ai-shang Lao-chün [i.e. Lao-tzu]." Is this really so?'

He [Po] answered saying, 'In the country of Su-lin [i.e. Assuristan] there was a lay devotee with the title of Mu-che [i.e. Pe. *hmwc'g*]. At first he studied Taoist immortality but did not succeed. Finally he studied the Buddha without accomplishing it. He secluded himself in the Great Naga Hill [Ta Na-chia shan] where he encountered outer ways [*wai-tao*, i.e. heterodoxies] from the Western Heaven [i.e. India]. There was a so-called *P'i-po-chia* [?] Envoy of Light who taught him one form of magic and commanded him to cultivate and practise it. He therefore retained this one doctrine. In actual fact it [i.e. this doctrine] is contrary to reason. Its teaching has one prohibition which says: 'All the great earth, mountains, rivers, plants, trees, water and fire are the *P'i-lu-she-na* [= Sanskrit: *vairocana*] sacred body [*fa-shen* = Sanskrit: *Dharmakaya*]'. Therefore, one dares not trample on them and one does not dare to make a move against them. But although this is so, taking one's stand outside the P'i lu-she-na Buddha Body [*fo-shen* = Sanskrit: *Buddhakāya*], if one holds the eight fasts and pays obeisance to the five directions, this is merely the result of doctrines and prohibitions. There are, in this doctrine, one, the King of Heaven, two, the Envoy of Light, three the spiritual and physical earth [?] [*ling-shang t'u-ti*] which preside over the religion. Its main precept is summarised in eight characters: 'Clear and calm, bright and light; great strength, wisdom and intelligence'. However these eight characters do not come from the mind. Would it be right that people of today should wish to express these eight characters by concentrating one's thought and cultivating their conduct? What is more, they call [their way] the Religion of Light and yet they make themselves blind.[97]

Po's version of how Manichaeism came to China is an interesting parallel to the fictitious life of Mani in the *Acta Archelai* in the west as both accounts try to denigrate Manichaeism by casting aspersions on the credentials of a leading figure in the history of the sect. The passage also contains the only reference to the use of the Buddhist deity Variocana by the Manichaeans outside the documents in Tun-huang. As we have noted in an earlier chapter, Variocana in eastern Manichaeism symbolises the Cross of Light as Variocana in Buddhism is the symbol of light or the essential Buddha-truth which pervades everywhere. We have in fact a Turkish Turfan fragment of either Buddhist or Manichaean origin on Variocana (*Lusyanta*) which contains several verbal echoes to Po's somewhat confused explanation of the Manichaean use of the concept:

And Mayak Dharmadana says the following: 'That Lusyanta-Buddha-being is everything: earth, hills, stones, sand, the water on the beach and the rivers, all the pools, channels and ponds, all trees, all living beings and men. There is no place which is not filled by the Lusyanta-being. If a monk raises his hand against something or reaches out towards something, then he has sinned against the being of Lusyanta-Buddha.[98]

It is remarkable to find an aspect of Manichaean theology which is so central Asian in its origin to have been preserved in south China in the thirteenth century. The motto of eight characters which Po cites are also attested in an inscription outside the extant Manichaean shrine in Hua-piao Hill and as we have already seen they denote the four attributes of the Father of Light, i.e. the Four Kings of Heaven.[99]

The Confucian scholar-officials saw Manichaeism and sects which were similar to it in their secret organisation and strict asceticism as threats to law and order. Few who submitted memorials requesting the imperial authorities for relevant legislation against them bothered to find out about the precise nature of their teaching. Since they were convinced that the leaders of such sects enticed the uninformed masses with irrational and baseless teaching, they saw no serious intellectual threat in the teaching of such sects. Rather it was the organisation of the sects with its elaborate provision for mutual aid among its members which most worried them. Hence we have no Chinese equivalent refutations of Manichaean dualism which are so common in the Patristic Age. When taken out of an administrative context, the Religion of Light could even find admirers among the scholar-officials. We possess an account in Chinese of a correspondence between a Confucian official and a Taoist abbot in which Manichaeism is discussed in favourable and even laudatory terms. Such a positive treatment of the subject would have been unimaginable in the medieval west or in Byzantium.

Huang Chen (1213–80), who recorded the correspondence, was a well known scholar of the late Sung and an ardent follower of the teaching of Chu Hsi (1130–1200) the pre-eminent Confucian scholar of the twelfth century. Sometime before 1264 he received a letter from a friend Chang Hsi-sheng whom he had not seen for nearly twenty years. Chang had become the resident superintendant of a Taoist temple called Ch'ung-shou kung at Ssu-ming near modern Ning-po. In this letter Chang explains to Huang that he had recently extended his abbatial quarters and in so doing he felt that he had forsaken the founding principles of the temple as it was originally founded for the worship of Mani. He asks Huang to make a record of the alterations in the form of a commemorative essay which he would perhaps inscribe and exhibit in his new quarters. In his letter he gives us a detailed account of the transformations which the temple had undergone since 1131 and his own high regard for the principles on which it was founded:

I am not asking you to record my own diligence in making the additions to the building but to record the purpose for which the temple was founded. As my dwelling place is becoming more extended, that which I [or 'it'?] had begun [to observe] is becoming less distinct. This is not what one would call 'examine the past in order to illumine the future'. When my teacher Lao-tzu went to the West, he became Mani-Buddha. His [i.e. Mani's] rules of self-discipline are particularly strict. They allow those who practise it one meal a day and on fast days they have to remain indoors. Their practices are certainly not the same as the rules of purity and tranquility of nowadays.

Although my dwelling place was called a Taoist temple when it was first founded, its real purpose was for the worship of Mani on the grounds that Mani was originally Lao-tzu. In the eleventh month of the first year of Shao-hsing [22 November–21 December 1131], Ch'en Li-cheng, the Grand Master of the Essence of Profusion [Ch'ung-su t'ai-shih] applied for the grant of the present title. It was not until the ninth month of the fourth year of Chia-ting [9 October–6 November 1211] that the priest in charge, Chang Wu-chen, built the Hall of the Three Purities [San-ch'ing-t'ien] . . . [This is followed by a list of additional buildings added to the temple from 1235–64]. I myself arrange for the building of the abbot's room by means of my accumulated insignia and ornaments and for the building of the study-barge [fang-chai] by means of my collected books and musical instruments, I have provided for the building of the kitchen and toilet which are simply furnished out of my own savings. There is therefore no need to record how many people have been involved in this [recent building work] or how much money has been spent on it as I have not relied on anyone's help. It is worth remembering though that one can only make new additions at the expense of the old. A greater degree of physical comfort also means more chance for the heart to grow lax. Mani's rules on asceticism are strict and although they are no longer practised they are still extant and I have made occasional records of them as warning to myself and to posterity. [100]

At the beginning of his letter of Huang, Chang mentions the fact that the temple was about three hundred years old which implies that it was founded in the early years of the Sung dynasty. Its situation at Ssu-ming in Chekiang makes it one of the northernmost known Manichaean sites of this second and southern phase of Manichaeism in China. It was most probably founded as an unregistered Taoist temple and in the decade after the Fang La rebellion it became a proper Taoist temple and acquired a licence. The new buildings added since 1131 had unmistakably Taoist titles but it is worth noting that Mani's rules of asceticism were retained in the temple as a standard of pure living because Mani was an *avatar* of Lao-tzu. This contrasts interestingly with the more scathing remarks of the Taoist Po Yü-ch'an on the relationship between Mani and the founder of Taoism.

Huang was justifiably incredulous. Buddhism and Taoism had always been as irreconcilable as ice and charcoal. Moreover, why should he, a Confucian scholar, be asked to record how Lao-tzu became a Buddha? He wrote back to Chang and asked him for further confirmation on how this transformation happened. In his reply, Chang cited evidence from the writings of Confucianists, Buddhists and Taoists to show that he had the support from all three main schools of philosophical teaching in China. He first cites from the Taoist *Scripture of the Conversion of the Barbarians* on Lao-tzu's visit to Hsia-na where he became a crown prince in Su-lin. This must have been a very common way of proving the link between Mani and Lao-tzu by the Manichaeans. He says that the same passage can also be found in the *Lotus Sutra* but this claim cannot be substantiated by modern editions of this famous Buddhist work. He also gives a line from the poem of Po Chü-i which we have already cited and discussed as proof of Manichaeism from a Buddhist source as Po became a devout Buddhist and a recluse towards the end of his life. Finally he cites a brief reference to the coming of the Uighurs in T'ang China as evidence of the existence of Manichaeism from a Confucian historical source.[101] Huang was impressed by this array of evidence and was even more deeply moved by his friend's desire to perpetuate the memory of Manichaean asceticism. His own verdict was a complete contrast to the derogatory memorials on the activities of the Religion of Light and other 'vegetarian demon worshippers' by scholar-officials like Lu Yu and Chuang Ch'o:

Since the affairs of the world belong to either one of the two extremes, the positive and the negative, good and evil. From the ancient times, those who have established doctrines and handed down admonition have all endeavoured to make men see more clearly what is positive and distinguish it from what is negative, to eschew evil and to cultivate goodness. By this they hope to give succour to human conduct and hence benefit the world. However, when a doctrine has been disseminated for too long, its original principles could become corrupted and confused . . . When Lao-tzu reappeared in the person of Mani, he laid down particularly strict laws about self-discipline. As you have said, the original teachings have suffered little change. You follow a teacher, commit the teaching to memory and disseminate it. Both Taoism and Buddhism must have been like this at the beginning and it comes close to the Confucian principle of 'reverence' [*ch'ing*]. With this one can raise the spiritual forces of the hils and rives as well as extending the knowledge of both priests and laymen! It is through relying on this that 'crystal palaces' [i.e. monasteries] and 'immortal halls' [i.e. Taoist temples] flourish without cease for thousands and ten thousands of years and not only during the present period of restoration.[102]

Huang recorded this correspondence while he was a minor official at the Sung court at Hang-chou. Later when he became a provincial administrator he showed considerable hostility towards subversive sects and might have even persecuted 'vegetarian demon worshippers', among whom were Manichaeans.[103] Even if he did encounter the name Mo-ni it was possible that he would not have realised that the members of the Religion of Light followed the same teaching as that which was admired by his friend Chang Hsi-shang. Chang, though now a Taoist, was a Confucian scholar by training and Huang would have inferred from his friend's social and intellectual background that the teaching of Mani so admired by him was respectable and ethical.

(5)   MANICHAEISM UNDER THE MONGOLS (1280-1368)

The forces of the Sung government which had rarely been successful against the Jurchens were decisively defeated by the Mongols under the brilliant leadership of Mongka and Kublai Khan. Previous barbarian conquerors from central Asia had their advance checked by the more densely populated plains south of the Yangtze where the horsemen from the steppes were at a distinct advantage as the only possible war was one of siege. The generals of Kublai Khan, however, brought in Muslim engineers from Mesopotamia and strongly defended cities soon fell in succession to the invaders, some after long sieges during which great heroism was shown by combatants of both sides. The conquest of south China took more than a decade to accomplish. After the last forces of the Sung were defeated in a naval engagement southwest of Canton in 1280, the Mongols under Kublai Khan had become the first invaders from the steppes of Central Asia to be conquerors of the whole Middle Kingdom.[104]

China was only a part of the vast empire created by the military genius of the sons of Genghis Khan. Chinese society, which had become isolated and inward looking since the end of the T'ang, was suddenly, albeit briefly, exposed to foreign influence. Commerce returned to the Silk Road and the seas between the south China coast and the Persian Gulf teemed with merchant ships. It was via the Silk Road that the two famous Venetian travellers, Marco Polo and his uncle Maffeo came to China. Another intrepid westener, William of Rubruck took the same route to visit the Mongol court at Karakorum. As rulers of one of the largest and most diverse empires the world has ever seen, the Mongols were inclined towards tolerance in the matter of religion. Kublai Khan himself was the son of a Nestorian princess and large numbers of his forces were either Nestorian Christians or Muslims. Once they had become established in China, the Mongols became great patrons of Tibetan Buddhism. Given this religious diversity it is no wonder that Marco Polo gained the impression that 'these Tartars do not care what God is worshipped in their lands. If only they are faithful to the Lord Khan and quite obedient, and give therefore the appointed tribute, and justice is well kept, thou mayest do what pleaseth thee with the soul.'[105]

The Mongols showed little of the same hostility of the Sung

government towards the religious societies at the outset of their rule, and this ignorance of their organised strength would prove to be disastrous in the long run. The White Lotus Society in particular soon became the main focus of national resistance. Although the White Lotus and White Cloud societies were banned in the fourteenth century, we find no repetition of the Sung persecution of 'vegetarian demon worshippers' in south China under the Mongols. In the Yüan code we find only one law which proscribes the secret gathering of those in white dress but we have no evidence to show that even this law was successfully enforced.[106] The Mongols declared that the three main foreign religions now practised in China, Buddhism, Nestorianism and Islam, should be accorded freedom of worship provided that their leaders would register with the Board of Rites (*Li-po*) but failure to do so would be deemed an offence.

The Venetian travellers visited Fukien in 1292 and made stops at both the prefectures of Fu and Ch'üan. At the former, they were approached by a 'wise Saracen' (*sapiens saracenus*) who told them of a sect whose religion no one seemed to recognise as they worshipped neither fire nor Christ, nor Buddha nor Mohammed. Intrigued, the Polos visited one of its meeting places and found its members very reluctant to be interviewed by the Venetians whom they took to be imperial officials. However the Polos managed to break the ice and they were shown some of the wall-paintings and scriptures of the sect. The visitors felt certain that these people were Christians after they had identified one of their books as a psalter.

Marco Polo was a strong supporter of the religious peace which Kublai Khan had innaugurated in China and he therefore urged the members of this so-called Christian sect to send a delegation to the court to procure for themselves the privileges which were granted to the Christians. Two members of the sect duly arrived at the court but a major controversy was soon raging over their exact identity. The head of the Nestorian church who brought the case to the Khan introduced the sect as Christian. However this was contested by the head of the Buddhists who recognised them as idolators who, therefore, should be put under his charge. Kublai Khan grew impatient with the arguments and counter-arguments from both sides and he summoned the delegates before him and personally asked them whether they would like to live under the law of the Christians or the law of the Buddhists. They replied that if it should please the Khan and were not contrary to his majesty, they wished to be classed as Christians as their ancestors had been. Their wish was duly granted.[107]

The prefecture of Fu, as we have seen, was a major centre of Manichaeism under the Sung and most scholars believe that Marco Polo and his uncle had stumbled upon a group of Manichaeans. Their secrecy and their tenuous link with both Christianity and Buddhist all suggest their being Manichaeans. A possible confirmation of this identification is the inscription on a tombstone from the nearby prefecture of Ch'üan which shows that a Nestorian bishop who might have come to China from Samarkand was in charge of Manichaeans and Nestorians in south China:

To the Supervisor of the Christians [Ye-li-ko-wen = Arabic: Rekhabuin]: Manichaeans [Ming-chiao] and Nestorians [Chin-chiao] in the Circuit of Chiang-nan, the Holy Reverend [Ma-li ha-shi-ya = Syriac: mry hsy'], Bishop [A-pi-ssu-ku-pa = Gk: ἐπίσκοπος] Mar Solomon (Ma-li Shi-li-men), Timothy Sauma [Tien-mi-ta Sao-ma] and others have mournfully and respectfully dedicated this tombstone in the second year of Huang-ch'ing, Kuei-ch'ou, on the fifteenth day of the eighth month (5 September 1313).[108]

The discovery of this inscription at the prefecture of Ch'üan, the Zaitun of Marco Polo, once a major port on the south China coast, has led some scholars to think that Manichaeism also came to China by sea. The inscription itself is now housed in a museum devoted to the maritime connections of the prefecture. There are several reasons against such a suggestion. Firstly we have the witness of Ho Ch'iao-yüan that the religion came to Fukien via Central Asia. Secondly the Manichaeans in Fukien used many religious terms which are identical to those used by their co-religionists in north China during the T'ang. If they did come by sea, they might have initiated their own translations. Hence a translation error like the date of Mani's birth and death in the Compendium would not have found its way into Ho's account. Lastly, when maritime trade resumed in earnest between the Persian Gulf and China, the Manichaeans in Mesopotamia were mostly intellectuals, poets and philosophers and not ardent mission-aries in the mode of Adda or Mar Ammo.[109]

It was also during this brief period of eighty eight years of foreign rule in China that the extant Manichaean shrine at Hua-piao Hill in the prefecture of Ch'üan was built.[110] The building dedicated to the worship of Mani the Buddha of Light is almost indistinguishable at first sight from many rustic Buddhist or ancestral shrines. An inscription shows that the statue of Mani in the shrine was donated by a believer in 1339 in the hope that his deceased mother would soon attain nirvāna.[111] This is not the only Manichaean temple in Fukien we know of which has a stone statue of Mani. In the local gazetteer of Fukien (Fu-chien t'ung-chi) is recorded the existence of a Manichaean shrine in the commandery of Fu-ting. We are also told that the statue there was particularly efficacious in effecting answers to prayers.[112] We also know of another Manichaean site in the prefecture of Wen which was the hermitage of a former Confucian scholar. Our source for the existence of this temple with the very suggestive title of 'Hidden

Light' (Ch'ien-kuang-yüan) is an essay by a Confucian scholar called Ch'en Kao (1314–66) written in 1351. His admiration for the resident hermit in that temple was such that like Huang Ch'en he too has given us an unbiased and commendatory account of Manichaeism:

In the commandery of P'ing-yang in the prefecture of Wen is a locality called Yen-t'ing. Bordered by the sea in the east and surrounded by hills on three sides, the plain is shaped like a sieve . . . By taking the path inland, one is soon into the hills and losing sight of the sea. Instead one will find a fertile plain of several hundred *mou* in area. About twenty families live on it and they subsist by farming. This is where the Temple of Hidden Light [*Ch'ien-kuang-yüan*] is situated. It belongs to the Manichaeans who are a type of Buddhists. Tradition has it that their doctrine diffused into the Middle Earth [i.e. China] from Su-lin [i.e. Assuristan]. It has many followers in the region of Ou and Min [i.e. Fukien]. They adhere to very strict rules of discipline and practise vegetarianism zealously. They eat one meal a day and at night they would pray, chant and perform other rites of worship seven times.

On the eastern side of the temple is the residence of the 'Superior Man with the Heart of Stone' [Shih-hsin shang-ren] and his cottage is called West of the Bamboo Grave [Chu-hsi-lou]. It is situated above a stream in the middle of a valley and is well-wooded . . . The stream, rocks, the spray and the mist together make it a delightful spot and it is particularly renowned for its bamboo. The tallness of this plant symbolises purity and frugality and since these are qualities to which philosophers and scholars aspire, they often liken themselves to bamboo . . .

'The Superior Man with the Heart of Stone' was the son of a Confucian family and he was brought up on books concerning the six arts and the various schools of philosophies [i.e. the Confucian classics]. However, he is fond of the simple life and practised a noble form of detachment. Hence he is not corrupted by worldly pleasures and is able to escape into vacuity and free himself from distractions. He practises Manichaeism [*Ming-chiao*] because he can use it to cover up his tracks and to conceal himself. His unwillingness to conform to the rest of the world and his pure living are not inferior to the [noble] qualities which are attributed to bamboo. The cottage was built some years ago and his teacher Te-san was in fact responsible for building it. The real name of 'the Superior Man with the Heart of Stone' is Tao-ch'ien.[113]

Ch'en Kao wrote this essay under the spectre of the religious peace of the Mongol Khan and his admiration for the hermit at P'ing-yang was unfettered by the need to control sectarianism in south China. His remark that Manichaeism has many followers in Fukien is important as it shows that the sect had clearly survived the indiscriminate persecution of 'vegetarian demon worshippers' under the Sung. It also shows that seen on its own, the sect seemed to have enjoyed a high reputation for its asceticism, which casts further doubt on active Manichaean involvement in the sectarian uprisings in the previous two centuries.

(6) THE RELIGION OF LIGHT (MING–CHIAO) AND THE DYNASTY OF LIGHT (MING–CHAO) (1368–c. 1630)

The empire of the Mongols was founded on the military skills which its leaders had acquired in the harsh conditions of the steppes. Soft living, coupled with the burden of administration, soon caused the conquerors of China to lose the fine military edge they had over the Chinese. After the death of Kublai Khan in 1294, the throne in Peking was filled by a succession of Mongol princes who devoted themselves to the civilised pleasures of the wine cup and the harem rather than the saddle. Struggle between the various Turko-Mongol factions in this vast Eurasian empire also weakened the power of the Mongols to hold down an increasingly restive Middle Kingdom. The last Mongol ruler in China, Toghan Temür, was a vacillating person who found delight in the company of his women and Tibetan *lamas* and turned his back to a growing number of nationalist-inspired rebellions which were threatening to wrest south China from his control.

The war of liberation began on the lower Yangtze and the Canton region. It was not a co-ordinated movement but a series of minor rebellions led by local half-patriots and half-bandits. Soon the whole of south China was the scene of strife between the various rebel forces who were more eager to eliminate each other than they were for the final expulsion of the Mongols. Many of these rebel groups had grown out of religious societies and their rallying calls were commonly religious as well as patriotic slogans. Although the White Lotus Society played a prominent rôle in this confused war of liberation, the eventual victor, Chu Yüan-chang, was a leader of a group which had its origins in the Maitreya Society and had the red scarf for its insignia. By 1367 Chu had brought most of South China under his control and the Mongol court, torn apart by conspiracy and factional strife, made no effective attempt at counter-attack. Finally in 1368, he entered Peking and replaced the Yüan dynasty of the Mongols with that of his own, the Dynasty of Light (*Ming-chao*).[114]

Chu was the youngest of the four sons of a poor farmer and for a time he was a novice Buddhist monk. His rise to power was through the help of the Maitreya Society, therefore he knew better than any emperor the potential powers of such religious societies. Once his rule was firmly established, he renewed the proscriptions of the sects in an edict of 1370 which names in particular the White Lotus, the White Cloud and the Religion of Light.

Prohibition of Sorcery and Black Arts Sorcerers who pretend to call down false divinities, write charms, cast spells over water, 'support the phoenix' [i.e.

perform *planchette* writing], invoke the Sages, calling themselves the 'Upright Master', 'Grand Guardian' or 'Mistress', or claim to be members of the Maitreya sect, or the White Lotus sect or the sect of the Venerable [Lord] of Light or the White Cloud sect etc. which indulge in heterodox practices [*tso-tao*] and in distorting the truth [*luan-cheng*], together with those who conceal prints and images of their deities and congregate to burn incense to them and those who meet at night and disperse by dawn and mislead and beguile the masses under false pretences of charity [shall suffer punishment]. Their leaders shall be strangulated and their followers shall receive a hundred strokes of the heavy baton and be exiled to a distance of 3,000 *li*.

Soldiers and civilians who impersonate deities, beat gongs and drums and hold religious processions shall receive a hundred blows of the heavy baton but this should only be meted out to their leaders. Village heads who know of such activities but do not inform the authorities shall receive forty blows of the bamboo cane. However, this proscription does not apply to the spring and autumn sacrifices among the people.[115]

The White Cloud Society had been nominally proscribed since 1306 and the White Lotus Society since 1309.[116] The repetition of the ban against these two sects by Chu was therefore only a renewal of the legal position of these two groups under the Mongols. The Manichaeans on the other hand were under the protection of the laws of the Christians and, as we have seen, the religion had its admirers among scholar-officials. Some extraneous reason had to be given for their proscription and Chu found it in the name of the sect which he said impinged on the title of his reign as they are both named after light [*ming*]. In imperial China it was gross impropriety to use any word which sounded or appeared similar to those used in the names of the ruling emperor or the dynastic title. Thus, the prefecture of Ming in Chekiang was renamed Ning-po to avoid clashing with the dynastic title. To provide the common people with safer alternatives, officials would issue at the beginning of the reign lists of synonyms with different sounds.[117]

Chu Yüan-chang, as we have already mentioned, had formerly been a novice monk and in the chaotic years which marked the end of Mongol rule in China, had joined a rebel group led by Han Shan-tung, whose grandfather was a member of the White Lotus Society. Han Shan-tung himself prophesied that in the midst of the present turmoil an enlightened ruler would appear to prepare for the return of the Maitreya from Tushita Heaven. He proclaimed himself the Major Enlightened Ruler (*Ta ming wang*) but was later killed in battle. His son Han Lin-erh assumed the title of the Minor Enlightened Ruler (*Shiao ming wang*) He in turn was killed by Chu who took over command of the group and eventually gained the throne. It has been pointed out by Wu Han in an influential article pulished in 1940 that the Manichaeans of the Sung, according to the Buddhist historian Tsung-chien, possessed a scripture entitled *The Sūtra on the Coming to the World of the Major and Minor Enlightened Rulers etc*. This had led Wu Han to suggest that Han Lin-erh had borrowed his title from the Manichaeans. Chu Yüan-chang used the symbol of light as title of his dynasty because he too had come under Manichaean influence since the Maitreya Society and the Manichaeans were closely associated.[118]

Wu Han put forward his thesis at a time when the majority of scholars of Chinese Manichaeism accepted the view that Manichaeans were coterminous with the 'vegetarian demon worshippers', as the Buddhist historians of the Sung would have us believe. We have already seen that the title of the sūtra which mentions the Major and Minor Enlightened Rulers occurs in a list of works which were labelled Manichaean by Tsung-chien, but none of the titles correspond with any other known lists of Manichaean works. The list was most probably taken from Wang Chih's essay on the 'vegetarian demon worshippers' in Chekiang, with special reference to the *Diamond Dhyāna*. Furthermore, although we know from Manichaean texts in Central Asia that Mani as the Paraclete was represented by the Maitreya,[119] we have no clear evidence that the Maitreya played a significant role in Chinese Manichaeism. The only tenuous link between the Maitreya Society of Chu and the Religion of Light rests on the title of one scripture from Tsung-chien's list of so-called Manichaean works and once the Manichaean origins of these works is rejected on critical grounds, Wu Han's thesis simply disintegrates.

Our knowledge of the Ming persecutions of Manichaeism besides the edict of 1370 is largely dependent on the account of Ho Ch'iao-yüan on the Manichaean shrine on Hua-piao Hill. The relevant section reads:

When T'ai-tsu of the Ming Dynasty [i.e. Chu Yüan-ch'ang] established his rule, he wanted the common folk to be guided by the Three Religions [i.e. Confucianism, Taoism and Buddhism]. He was further displeased by the fact that [the Manichaeans] in the title of their religion [*Ming-chiao*] usurped his dynastic title [*Ming-chao*] He expelled their followers and destroyed their shrines. The president of the Board of Finance, Yu Hsin, and the president of the Board of Rites, Yang Lung, memorialised the throne to stop [this proscription], and because of this the matter was set aside and dropped. At present (i.e. *c*. 1600) those among the people who follow it practise incantation according to the 'Magic of the Master [of sorcery] [*Shih-shih fa*] but they are not much in evidence.[120]

The extent of the suppression is hard to gauge but we do possess one other piece of evidence which shows that it was carried out in the

prefecture of Wen, and that one of the reasons given for the action was
that the title of the sect was offensive. The source is contained in a
long funerary inscription to a Ming official, Hsiung Ting (1322–76),
composed by Sung Lien (1310–81):

In the Prefecture of Wen there were perverse teachers who were of the Grand
Religion of Light [Ta Ming-chiao]. They built and furnished their shrines and
meeting halls in a rather extravagant manner. Idle folks [lit.: those who
were unemployed] flocked to join it. However, because it was blinding and
misleading the masses, and its title offended [the sanctity] of the dynastic title,
Hsuing memorialised [the throne for permission] to suppress it, to confiscate
its property and to compel its followers to return to the land.[121]

The persecution was later lifted, as we learn from Ho Ch'iao-yüan,
at the intercession of two important ministers. The shrine on Hua-
piao Hill managed to escape destruction and even as late as 1445, its
priests or worshippers erected an inscription exhorting the faithful to
remember 'Purity, Light, Power and Wisdom (i.e. the four attributes
of the Father of Greatness) and Mani and the Buddha of Light'.[122] It
seemed that there were still small pockets of Manichaeism in Min
(Fukien) at the time when Ho Ch'iao-yüan wrote his account of the
shrine on Hua-piao Hill (c. 1600). From them he learned that the
religion originated in Su-lin (i.e. Assuristan) and came to China
through central Asia. Its founder was an *avatar* of Lao-tzu who was
born as a prince of King Pa-ti:

It is said that more than five hundred years after Lao-tzu had entered the
shifting sands of the west, in the Wu-tzu year of the Chien-an period of the
Emperor Hsien of the Han [i.e. 208 AD], he was transformed into a *nai-yün*.
The wife of King Pa-ti, after having eaten it became pregnant. The time having
come, the child came forth through the breast. The *nai-yün* is a pomegranate
from the imperial gardens. The story is similar to that of grasping the pear-tree
and coming forth from the left-side ... He propagated [his religion] in Arabia
[*Ta-shih*], the Roman Empire [*Fu-lin*], Tochariston [*To-hou-lu*] and Persia [*Po-
ssu*]. In the year Ping-ssu of the T'ai-shih period of the emperor Wu of the Tsin
(AD 266) he died in Persia. He entrusted his doctrine to a chief *Mōzak* [Mu-
che].[123]

This version of Mani's life is clearly a reconciliation of the two
contradictory versions of Mani's life given in the *Compendium*.
Historical details like dates and the name and rank of Mani's father are
taken from the Buddhistic version but the story of the birth is set
firmly in the context of the Taoist legend of Mani as an *avatar* of Lao-
tzu. The compiler of this aggregate version also seemed anxious to
show that Mani's birth through his mother's breast, a very Buddhistic
motif, has a Taoist parallel as it is similar to that of the Taoist legend
which says that Lao-tzu was born through left hip of his mother who

grasped a pear tree at the time of his birth. The word for a pear in Chinese is *li* which is also the alleged family name of Lao-tzu.

Ho Ch'iao-yüan informs us that the canon of Manichaean scriptures contained seven works and that two of the principal deities of the sect are Primordial Thought (Sien-yi, i.e. Primal Man) and Jesus (I-ssu). It is also from Ho's account, as we have seen, that we derive the date of the arrival of the first Manichaean *episcopus* (*Fu-to-tan*) at the T'ang court from central Asia and the story of how a *Hu-lu-huan* escaped from the Hui-ch'ang Persecution of the late T'ang and established the religion in Fukien. They even managed to remember that the prefix *mo* in Mani's full name *Mo-mo-ni* means 'great'. Since the character used in Chinese means 'end' or 'small' it will appear to be an extraordinary piece of verbal exegesis to someone who does not know that it is a phonetic transcription for the Syriac honorofic title of 'Lord' (*mr*).[124] The Manichaeans had loyally adhered to a correct interpretation of the title of their founder Mo-mo-ni = Mar Mani (Lord Mani) even though the interpretation makes no philological sense in Chinese. All these incidental but highly accurate details invaribly lead us to conclude that the Manichaeans in south China at this late date (*c.* 1600) still possessed a clear self-identity based on the careful preservation of the history of the sect. Although their knowledge of Mani's life is heavy with local colouring, we can see that they have remained remarkably loyal to the versions current among Chinese Manichaeans in the eighth century. There is nothing in Ho's account to suggest that the Manichaeans in the prefecture of Ch'üan had come under the influence of the White Lotus or the Maitreya societies nor does he give us any reason to suggest that Manichaeism exerted any influence on these two societies. The fact that the Manichaeans were penalised for usurping the dynastic title by calling themselves the Religion of Light was probably nothing more than a sad coincidence.

There were still Manichaeans in Fukien at the time when Ho Ch'iao-yüan compiled his account although he does say that they were not much in evidence. How the sect finally became extinct after having survived in China for eight hundred years is obscure due to our almost complete lack of any reliable information later than Ho's account. The sect faded so completely from memory that Chinese scholars of the Ch'ing Dynasty (1644–1912) regarded the Religion of Light as synonymous with Nestorian Christianity.[125] Even the term 'vegetarian demon worshippers' which is so often encountered in the Sung legislations fell into disuse and a scholar who came across it in his own reading was so baffled by it that he had to delve into the collected works of Lu Yu and a collection of Sung memorials for illumination.[126] Some scholars, like the eminent Ch'ing historian Hu

San-sheng, knew that the Manichaeism of the Uighurs in the T'ang period was not a form of Buddhism, but few scholars would have connected the religion of Mo-ni with the Religion of Light in south China during the Sung period.[127] A notable exception, though, might have been the seventeenth-century scholar T'an Chien who included a piece on Roman Catholicism in his collected essays, *Miscellaneous utensils in a date grove* (*Tsao-lin tsa tsu i chi*), to which he added an appendix on the Religion of Light (*Ming-chiao fu*). However, although the title of the essay and the appendix are given in the list of contents of the work, the texts themselves are missing from the modern reprint versions of this rare work.[128] Had they survived they might have provided us with valuable information on the last phase of Manichaeism in China. It would have been indeed ironical if T'an Chien had viewed Roman Catholicism as a form of 'neo-Manichaeism'.

The shrine on Hua-piao Hill fell into disuse at an unknown date. In 1922 it was renovated and became an adjunct to a Buddhist shrine dedicated to the worship of the 'ancestral teachers of India and China'.[129] The worshippers of the temple most probably thought that the shrine dedicated to Mo-ni was in fact dedicated to Mu-ni (i.e. Śākyamuni, the Buddha). This Buddhist complex later also fell into disuse and disrepair. The Manichaean origins of the annex escaped the notice of the scholars and antiquarians who came to the locality to look for it after Ch'en Yüan had brought to their notice the account of the shrine by Ho Ch'iao-yüan in 1923. It was finally located after much painstaking and systematic searching by a local archaeologist, Wu Wen-liang.[130] It is now preserved as a unique monument to a gnostic world religion which had become so well integrated into Chinese society that few Chinese scholars were aware of its Mesopotamian origins until the Tun-huang discoveries of this century opened a new era in the study of the subject.

LIST OF ABBREVIATIONS

ACO	*Acta Conciliorum Oecumenicorum*, ed. E. Schwartz *et al.* (Strassburg, 1914 ff.)
ADAW	*Abhandlungen der deutschen Akademie der Wissenschaften* (Berlin, 1947 ff.)
Alex. Lyc.	Alexander Lycopolitanus (see Bibliog. I.b.2)
Amm. Marc.	Ammianus Marcellinus (see Bibliog. I.b.3)
AMS	*Acta Martyrum et Sanctorum* ed. P. Bedjan, 7 vols. (Paris, 1890–97)
ANRW	*Aufstieg und Niedergang der römischen Welt*, ed. H. Temporini *et al.* (Berlin, 1872 ff.)
APAW	*Abhandlungen der königlichen preussischen Akademie der Wissenschaften* (Berlin, 1815–1907; philosoph.-hist. Kl., *ibid.*, 1908–49)
Ath.	Athanasius (see Bibliog. I.b.2)
Aug.	Aurelius Augustinus (see Bibliog. I.b.3)
BBB	W. B. Henning, *Ein manichäisches Bet- und Beichtbuch, APAW* 1936, X.
BEFEO	*Bulletin de l'Ecole Française d'Extrême-Orient*
BSO(A)S	*Bulletin of the School of Oriental (and African) Studies*
Catalogue	M. Boyce, *A Catalogue of the Iranian manuscripts in Manichaean Script in the German Turfan collection* (Berlin, 1960)
CCSG	Corpus Christianorum, Series Graeca (Turnhout 1977 ff.)
CCSL	Corpus Christianorum, Series Latina (Turnhout 1967 ff.)
CFHB	Corpus Fontium Historiae Byzantinae (Washington D.C. etc. 1967 ff.)
CJ	*Codex Justinianus* (see Bibliog. I.b.2)
CMC	*Codex Manichaicus Coloniensis* (see Bibliog. I.b.2)
coll.	*Lex Dei sive Mosaicarum et Romanarum legum collatio* (see Bibliog. I.b.3)

CSCO	Corpus Scriptorum Christianorum Orientalium (Paris, Louvain etc. 1903 ff.)
CSEL	Corpus Scriptorum Ecclesiasticorum Latinorum (Vienna, 1866 ff.)
CSHB	Corpus Scriptorum Historiae Byzantinae, 49 vols. (Bonn, 1828–78)
CT	*Codex Theodosianus* (see Bibliog. I.b.2)
Cyr.H.	Cyrillus Hierosolymitanus (see Bibliog. I.b.3)
Cyr.S.	Cyrillus Scythopolitanus (see Bibliog. I.b.3)
Epiph.	Epiphanius Constantensis (see Bibliog. I.b.3)
Eus.	Eusebius Caesariensis (see Bibliog. I.b.3)
FHG	*Fragmenta Historicorum Graecorum*, ed. C. Müller, 5 vols. (Paris, 1841–70).
FIRA	*Fontes Iuris Romani Anteiustiniani*, ed. S. Riccobono *et al.*, 3 vols. (Florence, 1968)
FTTC	*Fo-tsu-t'ung-chi* (see Bibliog. I.c)
GCS	Die griechischen christlichen Schriftsteller der ersten drei Jahrhunderte (Leipzig 1897–1941; Berlin and Leipzig, 1953; Berlin 1954 ff.)
GGM	*Geographici Graeci Minores*, ed. C. Müller, 2 vols. (Paris, 1855 and 1861)
Gnosis III	A. Böhlig and J. P. Asmussen (ed. and trans.), *Die Gnosis III, Der Manichäismus* (Zürich and Munich, 1980)
Hegem.	Hegemonius (see Bibliog. I.b.2)
Hieron.	Hieronymus (see Bibliog. I.b.3)
HJAS	*Harvard Journal of Asiatic Studies*
HO	*Handbuch der Orientalistik* (Leiden and Cologne, 1952 ff.)
Hom.	*Manichäische Homilien*, ed. and trans. H. J. Polotsky (Stuttgart, 1934)
HR ii	F. W. K. Müller, *Handschriften-Reste in Estrangelo-Schrift aus Turfan, Chinesisch-Turkistan II, aus den Anhang zu den APAW*, 1904, pp. 1–117.
Hymn-Cycles	M. Boyce, *Manichaean Hymn-Cycles in Parthian* (London, 1954)
Io.D.	Iohannes Damascenus (see Bibliog. I.b.2)
Iren.	Irenaeus Lugdunensis (see Bibliog. I.b.2)
JRAS	*Journal of the Royal Asiatic Society*
JRS	*Journal of Roman Studies*
Keph.	*Kephalaia*, ed. and trans. H. J. Polotsky *et al.* (Stuttgart, 1940 ff.)
KKZ	M. L. Chaumont, 'L'inscription de Kartir à la

"Ka'bah de Zoroastre" (texte, traduction, commentaire)', *Journal Asiatique*, CCXLVIII (1960) pp. 339–80

KPT W. Sundermann, *Mittelpersische und parthische kosmogonische und Parabeltexte der Manichäer*, Berliner Turfantexte IV (Berlin, 1973)

KSM P. Gignoux, 'L'inscription de Kartīr à Sar Mašhad', *Journal Asiatique*, CCLVI, (1968) pp. 387–418

lib. pontif. *liber pontificalis* (see Bibliog. I.b.3)

Mahrnāmag F. W. K. Müller, *Ein Doppelblatt aus einem manichäischen Hymnenbuch (Mahrnāmag)*, APAW, 1912

Mani-Fund C. Schmidt and H. J. Polotsky, *Ein Mani-Fund in Ägypten*, SPAW, 1933, I, pp. 4–90

Mansi J. D. Mansi, *Sacrorum Conciliorum Nova et Amplissima Collectio*, 31 vols. (Florence, 1759–98)

MGH (Auct. Ant.) *Monumenta Germaniae Historica (Auctores Antiquissimi)*, 15 vols. (Berlin, 1877–1919)

MM i–iii F. C. Andreas and W. B. Henning, *Mitteliranische Manichaica aus Chinesisch-Turkestan* I, SPAW, X, 1932, pp. 175–222; II, *ibid.* 1933, VII, pp. 294–363 and III, *ibid.* 1934, XXVII, pp. 848–912

MMTKGI W. Sundermann, *Mitteliranische manichäische Texte kirchengeschichtlichen Inhalts*, Berliner Turfantexte XI (Berlin, 1981)

MNCHPT *Mo-ni-chiao hsia-pu tsan* (see Bibliog. I.c)

MNKFCFIL *Mo-ni kuang-fo chiao-fa i-lüeh* (see Bibliog. I.c)

MTT P. Zieme, *Manichäisch-türkische Texte*, Berliner Turfantexte V (Berlin, 1975)

MZL O. Klíma, *Manis Zeit und Leben* (Prague, 1962)

NHC, NHL *Nag Hammadi Codices*, cf. *The Nag Hammadi Library in English*, ed. J. M. Robinson (Leiden, 1977)

NT Apoc. (Eng.) E. Hennecke, *New Testament Apocrypha*, ed. W. Schneemelcher, trans. and ed. R. McL. Wilson, 2 vols. (London, 1963–5)

OGIS *Orientis Graeci Inscriptiones Selectae*, ed. W. Dittenberger, 2 vols. (Leipzig, 1903–05)

Or. Origenes (see Bibliog. I.a.2)

PG *Patrologiae cursus completus, series Graeco-Latina*, ed. J. P. Migne, 162 vols. (Paris, 1857–66)

PL *Patrologiae cursus completus, series, Latina*, ed.

J. P. Migne *et al.*, 221 vols. (Paris, 1844–64) and 5 Suppl. (1958–74)

PLRE, I   A. H. M. Jones, J. R. Martindale and J. Morris, *The Prosopography of the Later Roman Empire*, I (Cambridge, 1971)

PO   *Patrologia Orientalis*, ed. R. Graffin and F. Nau (Paris, 1907 ff.)

Pos.   Possidius (see Bibliog. I.b.3)

PS   *Patrologia Syriaca*, 3 vols. (Paris, 1893–1926)

Ps.-Bk.   *A Manichaean Psalm-Book*, I, Pt. 2, ed. and trans. C. R. C. Allberry (Stuttgart, 1938)

PSCTC   *Po-ssu-chiao ts'an-ching* (see Bibliog. I.c)

PW   A. Pauly, *Real-Encyclopädie der classischen Altertumswissenschaft*, ed. G. Wissowa (Stuttgart, 1893 ff.)

Reader   M. Boyce, *A Reader in Manichaean Middle Persian and Parthian*, *Acta Iranica* IX (Tehran-Liège, 1975)

RLByz.   *Reallexikon der Byzantinistik*, ed. P. Wirth (Leiden, 1969 ff.)

SC   Sources Chrétiennes (Paris, 1940 ff.)

SHA   *Scriptores Historiae Augustae* (see Bibliog. I.b.3)

SHYCK   *Sung-hui-yao chi-kao* (see Bibliog. I.c)

ŠKZ   Inscription of Shapur at the Ka'ba of Zoroaster (see Bibliog. I.b.2: *Res Gestae Divi Saporis*)

SPAW   *Sitzungsberichte der preussischen Akademie der Wissenschaften zu Berlin* (Berlin, 1882–1921; philos.-hist. Kl., 1922–49)

T   *Taishō shinshu daizōkyō*, The Tripitaka in Chinese (Tokyo, 1924–9)

Texte   A. Adam, *Texte zum Manichäismus*, *Kleine Texte für Vorelsungen und Übungen*, CLXXV, 2nd edn. (Berlin, 1969)

Thdt.   Theodoretus Cyrrhensis (see Bibliog. I.b.2)

TMC i–iii   A. von Le Coq, *Türkische Manichaica aus Chotscho*, I, *APAW*, 1911; II, *ibid.* 1919 and II, *ibid.* 1922

Traité 1911 and 1913   E. Chavannes and P. Pelliot, 'Un traité manichéen retrouvé en Chine', *Journal Asiatique*, 10ᵉ sér. 18 (1911) pp. 499–617 and *ibid.* 11ᵉ sér., 1 (1913) pp. 99–199 and 261–392

TTT i–v and Index   W. Bang and A. von Gabain, *Türkische Turfantexte* I, *SPAW*, 1929, pp. 241–68; II, *ibid.* 1929, pp. 441–30; III, *ibid.* 1930, pp. 183–211, IV, *ibid.*

1930, pp. 432–50; *V, ibid.* 1931, pp. 323–56,
Analytischer Index, ibid. 1931, pp. 461–517

TTT ix A. von Gabain and W. Winter, *Türkische Turfantexte IX, Ein Hymnus an den Vater Mani auf 'Tocharisch' B mit alttürkischer Übersetzung, ADAW zu Berlin,* 1956, II (Berlin, 1958)

WL i–ii E. Waldschmidt and W. Lentz, *Die Stellung Jesu im Manichäismus, APAW* 1926, 4; *Manichäische Dogmatik aus chinesischen und iranischen Texten,* SPAW 1933, 13, pp. 480–607.

ZDMG *Zeitschrift der deutschen morgenländischen Gesellschaft*

ZNW *Zeitschrift für neutestamentliche Wissenschaft und die Kunde der alteren Kirche*

Zos. Zosimus Historicus (see Bibliog. I.b.2)

ZPE *Zeitschrift für Papyrologie und Epigraphik*

ZRGG *Zeitschrift für Religions-und Geistesgeschichte*

NOTES

NOTES TO CHAPTER I

1. *Cf.* Larsen, 'The tradition of empire', pp. 77–90 and *PW, s.v.* 'Mesopotamien', cols. 1134, l. 51–1140, l. 10 (Schachermeyr).

2. On Alexander in Mesopotamia see esp. Schachermeyr, *Alexander in Babylon, passim,* and Berve, *Alexanderreich,* I, pp. 258–9, 260–63, 292–6.

3. Justinus, XXV, 1, 1. *Cf. PW, s.v.* 'Antiochos I (21) Soter', col. 2453, ll. 19–31 (Wellmann).

4. Appianus, *Syriaca* 58. *Cf.* Hopkins, *Topography,* pp. 149–50 and *PW, s.v.* 'Seleukeia (am Tigris)', cols. 1160, l. 18–1162, l. 26 (Streck).

5. *Cf.* Hopkins, *Topography,* pp. 154–5 and *PW, art.cit.,* cols. 1164, l. 44–1166, l. 38 and 1169, l. 31–1170, l. 35. See also Neusner, *History,* I, pp. 6–10.

6. On this see esp. Neusner, *History,* I, pp. 16–23 and *idem,* 'Political ideology', pp. 40–59.

7. Dura Europos: Welles *et al.* (eds.), *Parchments and Papyri,* docs. 18–20, 22, 24 etc., p. 98 ff. Susa: Welles, *Royal Correspondence,* LXXV, pp. 299–306. Arvōmān: Minns, 'Parchments', pp. 29–30 and Nyberg, 'Pahlavi Documents', p. 209.

8. See, e.g., McDowell, *Coins,* p. 61 ff. See also Welles *et al.* (ed.), *Parchments and Papyri,* doc. 18, 1, p. 100.

9. Crassus: Plutarchus, *Crassus* 14, 4–27, 2, ed. Lindskog and Ziegler, and Dio Cassius, XL, 21–4. Antony: Plutarchus, *Antonius* 38, 2–52, 3, ed. Lindskog and Ziegler.

10. Strabo, *geographia* XVI, 1, 16, Diodorus Siculus, XXXIV, 19 and Plutarchus, *Crassus* 32, 1–6. *Cf.* Debevoisse, *Political History,* p. 22, esp. n. 99.

11. Plutarchus, *Crassus* 33, 1–5, ed. Lindskog and Ziegler.

12. Tacitus, *annales,* VI, 42.

13. *Cf.* Welles, 'Population', p. 274.

14. *Cf.* Chaumont, 'L'Armenie', pp. 101–23, Debevoisse, *Political History,* pp. 175–202 and Dillemann, *Haute Mésop.,* pp. 268–72.

15. Dio Cassius, LXVIII, 17.2 *ad fin.*; Fronto, *principia historiae,* 15; Arrianus, *Parthica,* frags. 41–78, ed. Roos, and Eutropius, VIII, 3, 1–2.

16. *Cf.* Bertinelli, 'I Romani oltre l'Eufrate', pp. 7–22.

17. Dio Cassius, Reliq. LXXI, 2, 3, ed. Boissevain, iii, pp. 247–8 (= Xiph.,

p. 258, l. 31–259, l. 3). *Cf.* Drijvers, 'Hatra etc.' pp. 875–6.

18. Dio Cassius, LXXV, 3, 2, ed. Boissevain, iii, p. 340, ll. 19–21. *Cf. PW, s.v.* 'Nisibis', cols. 737, l. 43–738, l. 14 (Sturm).

19. *Cf.* Welles *et al.* ed., *Parchments and Papyri*, doc. 28, l. 4, p. 146.

20. *Ibid.*, pp. 5–10 and 22–46. See also *idem*, 'Population', pp. 253–4.

21. Dio Cassius, LXXXV, l. 2–4, p. 339, 1–340, 7 and LXXV (Reliq. LXXVI) 9, 1–13, 2, pp. 346, l. 16–350, l. 6, Herodianus, III, 4, 7–5, 2 and 9, 1–12 and *SHA, Severus*, 15–16.

22. Dio Cassius, LXXVII (Reliq. LXXVIII) 18, 1–LXXVIII, 27, 5, pp. 396, l. 28–435, l. 18, Herodianus, IV, 10, 1–15, 9, and *SHA, Ant. Carac.*, 6, 1–7, 2 and *Opelius Macrinus*, 8, 1–2.

23. Ṭabarī/Nöldeke, pp. 3–13. *Cf.* Christensen, *L'Iran*, pp. 84–96.

24. Ṭabarī/Nöldeke, p. 14.

25. [Msiḥa-Zkha, *Chronicon Ecclesiae Arbelae*] 8ᵉ év. Hiran, ll. 34–7, p. 29 (Syr.), ed. Mingana.

26. *Cf.* Fiey, *Jalons*, pp. 40–42, esp. figs. I–III.

27. Dio Cassius, Reliq. LXXI, 2 (= Xiph., p. 259, 2–3), p. 248. *Cf.* Hopkins, *Topography*, p. 161.

28. Ṭabarī/Nöldeke, pp. 15–16. *Cf.* Fiey, *Jalons*, p. 44, fig. III.

29. *Wei-shu*, 102.2271.

30. *Cf.* Frye, *Golden Age*, p. 8.

31. Ṭabarī/Nöldeke, pp. 17–18.

32. Herodianus, VI, 2, 1–3, 7.

33. Dio Cassius, Reliq. LXXX, 4, 1–2, pp. 475, l. 11–476, l. 7.

34. Georgius Syncellus *chron.*, A.M. 5711, p. 674, 3–4 and 5731, p. 681, 6–9, CSHB and Zonaras, *annales* XII, 15, pp. 572, l. 20–571, l. 2, CSHB. See also *SHA, Sev. Alex.*, 50, 1–55, 3.

35. Cf. Oates, 'Three Latin inscriptions', pp. 39–43 and improved texts in Drijvers, 'Hatra etc.', pp. 825–7.

36. Ṭabarī/Nöldeke, pp. 33–40. *Cf.* Drijvers, 'Hatra etc.', pp. 827–88.

37. *CMC* 18, 1–19, 18 (*ZPE* 1975), p. 21.

38. *Keph.* I, p. 7, ll. 23–6, *Hom.* p. 25, ll. 2–6 and *MNKFCFIL*, 1880 b, 14–21.

39. See, e.g. Nadim, *Fihrist*, trans. Dodge, p. 798; Flügel, *Mani*, p. 103. *Cf.* Polotsky, *Abriss*, cols. 244, l. 63–245, l. 5.

40. See esp. *Catalogue*, pp. ix–xxi.

41. See Ch. VIII and Lieu, 'New light' pp. 401–5.

42. *Cf.* Alfaric, 'Un manuscrit', *passim*. Text reproduced in *PL Suppl. 2*, 1378–88.

43. *Cf. Mani-Fund, passim* and Böhlig, *Mysterion*, pp. 182–7.

44. *Cf. Gnosis* III, p. 47.

45. *Cf.* Henning, 'Book of the Giants', *passim*, and Mackenzie, 'Mani's Šābuhragān', I–II.

46. On this still unpublished work see Böhlig, *Mysterion*, pp. 222–7.

47. *haer.* LXVI, 2, 9, GCS XXXVII (Epiph. iii), p. 18, l. 13.

48. *MNKFCFIL* p. 1280 c 28–1281 a 10. *Cf. Traité* 1913, 114–16 [138–40].

49. Theod. b. Kōnī, *Lib. Schol.* XI, pp. 313, l. 10–318, l. 4.

50. *Hom.* CXXIII, ed. and trans. Brière, *PO* XXIX (1961) pp. 152–77. The

relevant parts have been ed. and trans. by Kugener-Cumont, *Recherches* II, pp. 89–150.

51. Ed. and trans. (Latin) by Rahmani, *Studia Syriaca*, IV, *textus*, pp. mḥ-pt, *versio*, pp. 50–67.

52. Theod. b. Kōnī, *Lib. Schol.* XI, p. 313, ll. 14–16.

53. *Hom.* CXXIII p. 152, ll. 15–16, ed. Brière. *Cf.* Thdt., *haer.* I, 26, *PG* 83. 377B.

54. M 176 V 12–13, *HR ii*, pp. 61–2 (= *Reader*, dv, 1, p. 193)

55. *Ps.-Bk*, 191, 11 and <Zach. Mit.> *capita vii c. Manich.* III(59), p. xxxiv. *Cf.* Lieu, 'Byz. Formula', p. 200.

56. Aug., *c. Faust.* XV, 5, CSEL 25/1, p. 425, ll. 16–20. *Cf.* Lieu, *art. cit.*, p. 200.

57. <Zach. Mit.>, *capita vii c. Manich.* III(62), p. xxxiv. *Cf.* Lieu, *art. cit.*, p. 200.

58. Aug., *c. Fel.* I, 18, CSEL 25/2, p. 823, ll. 22–3.

59. *Ps.-Bk.*, p. 9, ll. 12–16, trans. Allberry.

60. Hegem., *Arch.* VII, 3, GCS XVI, p. 10, ll. 6–8 = Epiph., *haer.* LXVI, 25, 5, pp. 54, l. 10–55, l. 2 and Theod. b. Kōnī, *Lib. Schol.* XI, p. 313, ll. 16–17.

61. al-Nadim, *Fihrist*, trans. Dodge, p. 777, Flügel, *Mani*, p. 86.

62. *Hom.* CXXIII, p. 154, ll. 7–18.

63. al-Nadim, *Fihrist*, trans. Dodge, pp. 787–8, Flügel, *Mani*, p. 94.

64. Theod. b. Kōnī, *Lib. Schol.* XI, p. 313, ll. 19–21.

65. *Keph.* VI, p. 30, l. 17–31, l. 2.

66. Theod. b. Kōnī, *Lib. Schol.* XI, p. 313, l. 18. *Cf.* Puech, *Essais*, pp. 128–31.

67. al-Nadim, *Fihrist*, trans. Dodge, p. 778; Flügel, *Mani*, p. 86.

68. Simplicius, *in Epict. encheirid.* 27, p. 72, l. 16, ed. Dübner.

69. *Epistula fundamenti, ap.* Aug., *c. epist. fund.* XV, CSEL 25/1, p. 212, ll. 18–22.

70. al-Nadim, *Fihrist*, trans. Dodge, p. 787; Flügel, *Mani*, p. 94.

71. Sev. Ant., *Hom.* CXXIII, p. 150, ll. 9–10; p. 152, ll. 16–17, 20–23 and p. 163, ll. 6–18, ed. Brière.

72. *Ps.-Bk.* p. 9, ll. 17–21, trans. Allberry.

73. Alex. Lyc., *c. Manich. opinion.* II, p. 5, l. 8, ed. Brinkmann.

74. *Mani-Fund*, p. 78 and Polotsky, *Abriss*, col. 250, ll. 43–7.

75. Sev. Ant., *Hom.* CXXIII, p. 166, ll. 1–3, ed. Brière.

76. Theod. b. Kōnī, *Lib. Schol.* XI, pp. 313, l. 32–314. l. 4.

77. *Ibid.* p. 314, ll. 4–6.

78. *Ibid.*, 7–13.

79. Simplicius, *in Epict. encheirid.* XXVII, p. 70, ll. 42–5. *Cf.* Aug., *c. Faust.* XX, 17, p. 557, ll. 15–18.

80. *Ps.-Bk.* pp. 9, L. 31–10, l. 5, trans. Allberry.

81. *Ibid.*, p. 10, ll. 15–19, trans. *idem.*

82. *PSCTC*, p. 128 l b 3–4, trans. Traité 1911, pp. 514–15 (16–17). See also Thdt., *haer.* I, 26, col. 377C/D and Tit. Bos., *adv.Manich*, I, 17, p. 9, ll. 21–5, ed. Lagarde.

83. Alex. Lyc., *c. Manich. opinion.* XVIII, p. 25, ll. 23–5. *Cf.* Polotsky, *Abriss*, col. 252, l. 27–256, l.6.

84. Trans. Dodge, pp. 779–80; Flügel, *Mani*, p. 88.

85. Theod. b. Kōnī, *Lib. Schol.* XI, p. 314, ll. 14–24. See esp. the textual emendation suggested by Schaeder in Schaeder-Reitzenstein, *Studien*, p. 344, n. 25.

86. Theod. b. Kōnī, *Lib. Schol.* XI, pp. 314, l. 25–315, l. 3.

87. *Cf.* Polotsky, *Abriss*, col. 254, ll. 12–19 and Puech, *Essais*, p. 42.

88. Hegem., *Arch.* VII, 5, pp. 10, l. 11–11, l. 3 (= Epiph., *haer.* LXVI, 25, 7, pp. 55, l. 5–56, l. 5)

89. *Keph.* IX, p. 39, ll. 19–24.

90. Cf. *Ps.-Bk.*, p. 10, ll. 25–9 and *PSCTC*, p. 128l b, ll. 4–6, trans. *Traité* 1911, p. 515 (17). See also Ephraim, *C. haer. ad Hypat.* I, p. 101, ll. 5–17.

91. *Ibid.* p. 11, ll. 8–19. On this see esp. Tardieu, 'Prātā et ad'ur', pp. 340–41.

92. Theod. b. Kōnī, *Lib. Schol.* XI, p. 315, ll. 7–12.

93. Alex. Lyc., *c. Manich. opinion.* III, p. 6, ll. 6–22.

94. Theod. b. Kōnī, *Lib. Schol.* XI, 315, l. 12–317, l. 3. *Cf.* Kugener–Cumont, *Recherches* I, pp. 21–40.

95. Theod. b. Kōnī, *Lib. Schol.* XI, p. 317, ll. 3–6 and Aug., *c. Faust.* XXI, 12, p. 583, ll. 8–14.

96. Ephraim, *c. haer. ad Hypat.*, II, p. 208, ll. 37–8.

97. Theod. b. Kōnī, *Lib. Schol.* XI, p. 316, l. 11.

98. Hegem., *Arch.* VIII, 6, p. 13, ll. 3–8 (= Epiph., *haer.* LXVI, 26, 6–7, p. 60, ll. 2–7) *Cf. Reader*, p. 6.

99. Theod. b. Kōnī, *Lib. Schol.* XI, p. 317, ll. 7–15. See also *Keph.* LV, pp. 133, l. 7–135, l. 26.

100. *PSCTC* 1281 b 23–5, trans. *Traité* 1911, p. 527 [29].

101. *Keph.* LXIV, p. 157, ll. 32–4.

102. Theod. b. Kōnī, *Lib. Schol.* XI, pp. 317, l. 15–318, l. 3, al-Nadim, *Fihrist*, trans Dodge, p. 783 and Flügel, *Mani*, p. 91.

103. al-Nadim, *Fihrist*, trans. Dodge, pp. 784–6; Flügel, *Mani*, pp. 91–3 (see also comm. *ad. loc.*, pp. 263–70).

104. *Cf.* Henning, 'Book of the Giants', pp. 53 and 63–9.

105. *Cf. Mani-Fund* pp. 68–73 and Polotsky, *Abriss*, cols. 256, l. 37–257, l. 13.

106. M299aR5–6, *cf.* Henning, *Henochbuch*, p. 28. See also *idem* ed. 'Book of the Giants' A153–5 (from M101 frag. b, first page) p. 58. *Cf.* Puech, *Essais*, p. 17 and Böhlig, *Mysterion*, p. 207.

107. *Cf.* Schaeder, 'Urform', p. 93, n. 1.

108. *PSCTC*, p. 1282 b 10–17 (I have followed the more accurate reading of the critical edition by Ch'en Yüan, p. 379), trans. *Traité* 1911, p. 546 [48].

109. *Cf.* Puech, *Essais*, pp. 53–5.

110. On the titles of Mani see e.g. *Keph.* IV, p. 25, 11 and M5569R4, *MM iii*, c, p. 860.

111. Simplicius, *in Epict. encheirid.* 27, pp. 70, l. 52–71, l. 2 ed. Dübner.

112. *Ps.-Bk.*, p. 33, ll. 17–23.

113. Aug., *mor. Manich.* VII, 10 and IX, 18, *PL* 32. 1349 and 1353.

114. M32R7, *HR ii*, p. 63 (= *Reader*, bv, 1, p. 125)

115. *mor. Manich.* XV, 36–7, cols. 1360–61.

116. Aug., *haer.*, XLVI (115–17) 11, CCSL XLVI, p. 316.

117. M177R17–24, *HR ii*, p. 89 (= *Reader*, w, 3, p. 8)

118. Aug., *mor. Manich.* XVII, 54–64, cols. 1368–72 and *idem, in Ps. 140*, 12 (6–14); CCSL XL, p. 2034 and M 10 R 10–V 22, *W–L i*, p. 126 (= *Reader*, at, pp. 104–5). *Cf.* Böhlig, 'Lichtkreuz', pp. 485–90, *Reader*, p. 10 and Rose, *Christologie*, pp. 99–103.

119. <Zach. Mit.>, *capita VII c. Manich.* VII (201–4) p. xxxviii, *Cf. Lieu*, 'Byz. formula', pp. 211–12.

120. Aug., *mor. Manich.* XVIII, 65, cols. 1372–3. *Cf.* Puech, *Essais*, p. 67.

121. *Cf.* Lieu, 'Byz. formula', pp. 199–200 for full bibliography. See also Colpe, 'Ethik', p. 408, n. 5.

122. Aug., *haer.* XLVI (22–30), 5, p. 313 and (106–117), 7, p. 316 and *idem, c. Faust*, II, 5, pp. 258, l. 17–259, l. 10.

123. Aug., *in Ps. 140*, XII (24–5), p. 2035.

124. *P. Rylands Gk.* 469, 25–6, p. 42, ed. Roberts, and Hegem., *Arch.* X, 6, pp. 16, l. 4–17, l. 2 (= Epiph., *haer.* LXVI, 28, 7, p. 65, ll. 4–7.)

125. Aug., *haer.* XLVI (62–5), 9, p. 314 (polemical). *Cf.* Puech, *Essais*, pp. 238–41.

126. M8251 (T III D 278 II) R 1–5, *MM ii*, pp. 308–09 (= *Reader*, u. 1, p. 55)

127. *fragmenta Tebestina* II, 2, *PL Suppl.* 2.1380.

128. Aug., *c. Faust.* XXX, 5–6, pp. 752, l. 27–755, l. 7. See also *fragmenta Tebestina* IV, 1, col. 1381. On this see esp. Coyle, *Aug.'s 'De mor. eccl.'*, pp. 414–15 and 427–8.

129. *fragmenta Tebestina* I, 2, col. 1379. *Cf.* Lieu, 'Precept', p. 173.

130. al-Nadim, *Fihrist*, trans. Dodge, pp. 795–6, Flügel, *Mani*, pp. 100–01. *Cf.* Colpe, 'Ethik', pp. 403–4 and Polotsky, *Abriss*, cols. 260, l. 26–261, l. 25.

131. MacKenzie, 'Mani's *Šābuhragān*', pp. 504–20 and al-Nadim, *Fihrist*, trans. Dodge, pp. 782–3 and 796–7, Flügel, *Mani*, pp. 90 and 101–2. *Cf.* Polotsky, *Abriss*, cols. 261, l. 26–262, l. 33.

132. *CMC* 64, 8–15 (*ZPE* 1975), p. 65.

133. *Ibid.* 66, 4–68, 5, pp. 67–9.

134. *in Epict. encheirid.* 27, pp. 71, l. 44–72, l. 16, ed. Dübner. *Cf.* Hadot, 'Widerlegung', pp. 44–54. I have followed Hadot's reading from Vaticanus gr. 2231 (*cf.* p. 46, n. 51a) for p. 71, l. 48 of Dübner's text.

135. See e.g. *Keph.* IV, pp. 25, l. 7–27, l. 31, XXXIX, p. 102, l. 13–104, l. 20, XLVII, pp. 118, l. 13–120, l. 20 and LXIX, pp. 166, l. 31–169, l. 22.

136. Aug. *Conf.* V, x, 18 (20–21), CCSL XXVII, p. 68

NOTES TO CHAPTER II

1. Herodotus III, 158, 2.

2. See e.g. 'A chronicle concerning the Diaodochi', ed. and trans. Smith, *Babyl. Hist. Texts*, p. 137 and p. 144, ll. 29 and 35–6. *Cf.* Pigulevskaja, *Les villes*, pp. 34–5.

3. *Cf.* Segal, 'Jews', pp. 42*–52* and *idem, Edessa*, pp. 41–3.

4. Josephus, *antiquitates Judaicae* XX, 34–53. On the Jewish communities in Babylonia see esp. Neusner, *History*, I, *passim*.

5. I, 3–6.

6. *Doctrina Addai*, p. *h*, 10–11 and *ld*, 16–18, ed. Phillips.

7. Eus., *h.e.* IV, 29, 6–7, GCS IX/1, pp. 392, ll. 1–13. *Cf.* Vööbus, *Hist. Asc.*, I, pp. 39–42.

8. *Cf.* Welles *et al.* ed., *Parchments and Papyri*, doc. 10, pp. 73–4.

9. Eus., *h.e.* I, 13, 1–22, pp. 82, 21–96, 10 and *Doctrina Addai, passim*, ed. Phillips. *Cf.* Bauer, *Rechtgläubigkeit*[2], pp. 1–25 and *NT Apoc. (Eng.)* II, pp. 437–41.

10. *Chronicon Edessenum, praef.*, CSCO I, p. 2, l. 4. *Cf.* Segal, *Edessa*, pp. 24–6.

11. [Msiha-Zkha, *Chronicon Ecclesiae Arbelae*] 1ᵉ év. Pkidha, ll. 1–4, p. 2, ed. Mingana.

12. *Karkā de Bēt Sēlok*, AMS II, p. 512, ll. 14–18, ed. Bedjan. *Cf.* Fiey, 'Vers la réhabilitation', pp. 194–6.

13. *Acta Sancti Maris Apostoli* 29–30, p. 115, ll. 7–11, ed. Abbeloos (= AMS I, p. 86, ll. 8–11). *Cf.* Fiey, *Jalons*, pp. 39–40 and Labourt, *Christianisme*, pp. 11–13.

14. *Cf.* Fiey, *Jalons*, p. 39, n. 40. See also Assfalg, 'Zur Textüberlieferung', pp. 35–6.

15. On Elchasaites in general see esp. Klijn–Reinink, *Patristic Evidence*, pp. 54–67, Daniélou, *Jewish Christianity*, pp. 64–7 and Schoeps, *Theologie*, pp. 325–44.

16. Hipp., *haer.* IX, 13, 1; GCS XXVI, p. 251, 8–13.

17. *Ibid.* IX, 15, 1–6, pp. 253, l. 10–254, l. 15.

18. *Ibid.* IX, 13, 2–3. *Cf.* Epih., *haer.* XIX, 4, 1–2; GCS XXV, p. 221, ll. 6–13.

19. Epiph., *haer.* XIX, 3, 5, p. 220, ll. 13–18.

20. *Ibid.*, XIX, 1, 9 (2, 1), pp. 218, l. 19–219, l. 4.

21. *Cf.* Neusner, *History*, I, pp. 94–9.

22. Hipp., *haer.* IX, 16, 4, p. 255, 1–5.

23. *Ibid.* IX, 14, 1, p. 252, ll. 18–24 and Epiph., *haer.*, XIX, 3, 6, pp. 220, ll. 19–24.

24. Epiph., *haer.* XIX, 3, 7, pp. 220, l. 24–221, l. 5.

25. *Ibid.*, XIX, 4, 1–2, p. 221, ll. 6–13 and Hipp., *haer.* IX, 14, 1, p. 252, ll. 20–25.

26. Epiph., *haer.* LIII, 1, 8, GCS XXI, pp. 315, l. 25–316, l. 3.

27. Or., *hom. in Ps. 82, ap.* Eus., *h.e.*, VI, 38, GCS IX/1, p. 592, ll. 20–22.

28. Eus., *h.e.* VI, 38, p. 592, ll. 13–14.

29. Epiph., *haer.* XIX, 1, 2, p. 217, 20–24.

30. Eus., *h.e.*, IV, 28–9, 1, pp. 388, 17–390, l. 5.

31. al-Nadim, *Fihrist*, trans. Dodge, p. 775, Flügel, *Mani*, p. 84.

32. *CMC* 98, 11, (*ZPE* 1978), p. 119. See comm. *ad loc.*

33. *Lib. Schol.* XI, CSCO LXVI, p. 311, ll 13–19.

34. *Ibid.*, pp. 311, l. 19–313, l. 9. *Cf. Texte*, pp. 76–7.

35. *Fihrist*, trans. Dodge, p. 811. *Cf.* Henrichs, '*CMC* reconsidered', p. 361.

36. *Cf.* Böhlig, 'Synkretismus', pp. 154-5.
37. *Cf.* Widengren, *Mani*, pp. 31-2.
38. See esp. Säve-Söderbergh, *Studies*, pp. 97-164.
39. *Cf.* Henrichs-Koenen 'Mani-Codex', *passim*, esp., pp. 100-105 and 141-60.
40. *Cf.* Böhlig, *Mysterion*, p. 187 and Henrichs-Koenen, 'Mani-Codex', p. 113.
41. On the format and style of the *CMC* see esp. Henrichs, 'Literary criticism', pp. 725-8.
42. *CMC* 94, 10-12 (*ZPE* 1978), p. 115. *Cf.* Rudolph, *Antike Baptisten*, pp. 13-16.
43. *Cf.* Quispel, *Gnostic Studies*, II, p. 232.
44. *CMC* 106, 15-19 (*ZPE* 1981), p. 215.
45. See e.g. *CMC* 6, 7-12, 5 (*ZPE* 1975), pp. 9-15.
46. See e.g. Philo, *quod omnis probus liber sit* XII (76) and *idem*, *hypothetica*, XI, 8. *Cf.* Schürer-Vermes-Millar, *Hist. Jewish People*, II, pp. 562-71.
47. Josephus, *bellum Judaicum* II, 8, 2 (119-20).
48. *CMC* 102, 15-16 (*ZPE* 1981), *Cf.* Henrichs, 'Babylonian Baptists', pp. 48-9.
49. *haer.* XIX, 1, 7, p. 218, ll. 14-15.
50. See above, n. 27.
51. *CMC* 80, 16-18 (*ZPE* 1978), p. 101 and LXXXVII, 16-18, p. 107. *Cf.* Henrichs-Koenen, 'Mani-Codex', p. 135.
52. *Cf.* Henrichs, 'Babylonian Baptists', p. 51.
53. *CMC* 82, 23-83, 19 (*ZPE* 1978), p. 103.
54. *Ibid.* 83, 16-19, p. 103 and 87, 2-6, p. 107. *Cf.* Henrichs, 'Babylonian Baptists', p. 55.
55. *Keph.* VII, *passim*, esp. p. 36, 6-9. Cf. *Mani-Fund*, pp. 64-74 and Henrichs-Koenen, 'Mani-Codex', pp. 183-6.
55a. *CMC* 24, 3-17 (*ZPE* 1975), p. 27.
56. *Cf.* Gruenwald, 'Manichaeism and Judaism', pp. 30-33 and Böhlig, 'Synkretismus', p. 156.
57. *CMC* 48, 16-60, 8 (*ZPE* 1975) pp. 49-61. See comm. *ad loc.*
58. *Keph.* I, pp. 12, ll. 9-14, 30.
59. *Cf.* Milik, *Books of Enoch*, pp. 298-310.
60. *Ibid.* p. 309.
61. *CMC* 9, 12-13 (*ZPE* 1975), p. 11. On the vegetarianism of the community see *ibid.* 102, 14-15 (*ZPE* 1981), p. 211.
62. *Ibid.* 6, 2-8, 14 (*ZPE* 1975), pp. 9-11. *Cf.* Henrichs, 'Thou shalt not kill', pp. 92-5.
63. *Ibid.* 9, 1-10, 14, pp. 11-13.
64. *Ibid.* 73, 8-74, 5 (*ZPE* 1975), pp. 93-5.
65. *Ibid.* 31, 1-2 (*ZPE* 1975), p. 31 and 104, 8-10 (*ZPE* 1981), p. 213. On the term *yḥdy'* see Vööbus, *Hist. Asc.* I, pp. 106-8 and Henrichs, 'Babylonian Baptists', pp. 35-9.
66. *CMC* 20, 11-23, 14 (*ZPE* 1975), pp. 23-5.
67. *Keph.* I. p. 15, ll. 3-20. *Cf.* Puech, *Essais*, pp. 18-19.

68. *CMC* 74, 8–77, 2 (*ZPE* 1978), pp. 95–7.

69. *Ibid.* 80, 18–83, 19, pp. 101–3. *Cf.* Koenen, 'From baptism', pp. 734–49.

70. *Ibid.* 84, 10–17, p. 105.

71. *Ibid.* 85, 4–12, p. 105.

72. *Ibid.* 88, 15–89, 4. p. 109.

73. *Ibid.* 94, 10–97, 17, pp. 115–17.

74. *Ibid.* 99, 12–21 (*ZPE* 1981), p. 207.

75. *Ibid.* 100, 1–101, 3, p. 209.

76. *Ibid.* 103, 1–104, 10, pp. 211–13.

77. *Ibid.* 104, 12–105, 8, p. 213.

78. *Ibid.* 106, 15–22, p. 215. See also 86, 8–87, 8 (*ZPE* 1978), p. 107.

79. *Ibid.* 110, 1–120, 16, pp. 219–29.

80. *Ibid.* 87, 19–21 (*ZPE* 1978), p. 107. *Cf.* Böhlig, 'Synkretismus', p. 158.

81. *Cf.* Harnack, *Geschichte*, I, pp. 191–5 and *idem*, *Marcion*, pp. 20–26 and 1*–27*.

82. Tert., *adv. Marc.* IV, 6, 1, ed. Evans, ii, p. 274. *Cf.* Harnack, *Marcion*, pp. 68–135.

83. *Cf. ibid.*, pp. 165*–7*.

84. *Cf. ibid.*, pp. 65*–124*.

85. *haer.* XLII, 1, 2, GCS XXXI, p. 94, ll. 1–5.

86. *S. Abercii vita* 69, pp. 48, l. 17–49, l. 6, esp. p. 49, ll. 4–6, ed. Nissen.

87. Eus., *m. P.* X, 3, GCS IX/2, p. 931, ll. 7–10. See also *martyrium Pionii* XXI, 5, ed. Musurillo, p. 164, ll. 3–5.

88. *OGIS*, II, 608, pp. 304–5. *Cf.* Harnack, *Marcion*, pp. 263*–6* and *idem*, 'Kircheninschrift', pp. 746–66.

89. Cyrillus H., *catech.* XVI, 26, ed. Reischl and Rupp, II, p. 328.

90. *Vita de Mar Aba*, pp. 211, l. 14–214, l. 9, esp. 213, ll. 16–17, ed. Bedjan.

91. *Narratio de beato Simeone bar Sabba'e*, *PS* I/2, col. 823, 11.

92. M 28 I V i 10–14, *HR ii*, p. 95 (= Boyce, *Reader*, dg, 9, p. 175, see esp. comm. *ad loc.*)

93. *Cf.* Böhlig, *Mysterion*, p. 210 and *idem*, 'Synkretismus', p. 159.

94. See Ch. III.

95. *Cf.* Burkitt, *Religion*, p. 83. See also Schaeder, 'Urform', pp. 73–4.

96. *Cf.* Schoeps, *Theologie*, pp. 179–87 and *Gnosis*, III, p. 28.

97. See e.g. *epistula . . . fundamenti*, *ap.* Aug., *c. ep. fund.* 5, CSEL XXV/1, p. 197, ll. 10–12.

98. *CMC* 99, 9–70, 10 (*ZPE* 1975) pp. 69–71. *Cf.* Böhlig, 'Synkretismus', p. 158.

99. *CMC* 60, 18–61, 22, p. 61.

100. Secundinus, *ep. ad Aug.*, CSEL XXV/2, p. 899, ll. 4–7.

101. On Bardaisan see esp. Harnack, *Geschichte* I, pp. 184–91 and Drijvers, *Bardaisan*, pp. 166–218.

102. *haer.* VII, 31, 1, p. 216, ll. 16–19.

103. *Chronicon Edessenum* 6 (anno 440) and 8 (anno 465), CSCO I, p. 32, ll. 23–5.

104. *Liber Legum Regionum*, *PS* I/2, cols, 536–611, ed. Nau.

105. *Ibid.* 1, col. 536, ll. 11–16.
106. *Ibid.* 2, col. 539, ll. 1–4.
107. *Ibid.* 26, cols. 560, l. 23–562, l. 1.
108. *Ibid.* 9, cols. 547, l. 27–548, l. 6.
109. *Ibid.* 18–22, cols. 564, l. 19–579, l. 17. *Cf.* Drijvers, *Bardaiṣan*, pp. 76–95.
110. *Liber Legum Regionum* 25–46, cols. 583, l. 1–610, l. 23.
111. *S. Abercii vita* 70, p. 49, ll. 16–19, ed. Nissen (meeting with Barchasanes) and 31–9, pp. 23, l. 18–30, l. 2(dialogue with Euxenianos).
112. Epiph., *haer.* LVI, 3, pp. 338, l. 9–339, l. 2.
113. Soz., *h.e.* III, 16, 5, GCS L, p. 128, 15–20. See also Thdt., *haer.* I. 22, *PG* 83.372B/C.
114. *Vita Rabulae*, p. 192, ll. 11–16, ed. Overback. See below Ch. VI, pp. 162–3.
115. Julius Africanus, Κεστοί (Vet. Mathem. Opp., p. 275 *sq.*) cited in Harnack, *Geschichte*, I, p. 184 and *FHG* V, p. 62.
116. *Hymni 56 c. haer.* I, 12, 1–2, CSCO CLXIX, p. 3, ll. 24–5.
117. *Ibid.* I. 17, 1–5, p. 5, ll. 1–5.
118. Moses bar Kepha, *PS* I/2, pp. 513–14 (based on Syr. Ms. Paris 241, fol. 17v). The same text is reproduced with critical notes in Drijvers, *Bardaiṣan*, pp. 98–105.
119. Tert., *adv. Marc.* IV, 11, 8, ed. Evans, ii, p. 308. See also I, 29, 1–7, *ed. cit.*, i, pp. 80–84.
120. *History of the Armenians*, II, 66, trans. Thomson, p. 212.
121. *Vita Rabulae*, p. 193, ll. 1–16, ed. Overbeck.
122. Bardaisan, *Indica*, frag. *ap.* Porphyrius, *de abstinentia* IV, 17–18, pp. 256, l. 1–261, l. 4, ed. Nauck. *Cf.* Sedlar, *India, pp. 174–75.*
123. VI, 10, 1–48, GCS XLIII/1, pp. 335, l. 1–343, l. 15.
124. XIX, 1–29, 2, GCS LI, pp. 270, l. 1–279, 2.
125. Trans. Dodge, p. 806. See also Flügel, *Mani*, p. 162.
126. *Cf.* Segal, *Edessa*, pp. 93–5 and Vööbus, *School of Nisibis*, pp. 7–53.
127. Trans. Dodge, p. 797. See also Flügel, *Mani*, p. 102.
128. Ephraim, *Hymni 56 c. haer.* LVI, 9, 4, p. 211, l. 22. *Cf.* Lieu, 'Byz. Formula', p. 198.
129. *Hymni 56 c. haer.* XXII, 3, 6–7, pp. 79, ll. 5–6.
130. Ephraim, *C. haer. ad Hypat.*, I, p. 122, ll. 26–31. On Bardaiṣan's influence on Mani see esp. Drijvers, 'Mani und Bardaisan', pp. 459–69, Aland 'Mani und Bardesanes', pp. 123–43 and Beck, *Bardaiṣan*, pp. 324–33.
131. On this 'mirage oriental' see esp. Festugière, *La révélation*, I, pp. 19–44.
132. *enneades* II, 9 (33), pp. 203–32, ed. Henry–Schwyzer (*editio minor*).
133. Iren., *haer.* I, 11, 1 (I. 5, ed. Harvey, i, pp. 98–9).
134. *Ibid.*, I, 24, 4, (I, 19, 2, ed. Harvey, i, p. 200). See also Epiph., *haer.* XXIV, 3, 1–5, p. 260, ll. 1–18 and *The Second Treatise of the Great Seth* (*NHC* VII, 2) 56, 6–20, *NHL*, p. 332.
135. Clem., *exc. Thdot.*, LXXVIII, 2, GCS XVII, p. 131, ll. 16–19.
136. Iren., *haer.* I, 6, 2–3 (I, 1, 11, ed. Harvey, I, pp. 54–5).
137. Epiph., *haer* XXXI, 2, 3, p. 384, ll. 9–11. See also Clem., *strom.* VII, xvii, 106, 4, GCS XVII, p. 75, ll. 17–18.

138. Epiph., *haer.* XXXI, 7, 1-2 (pp. 395, 1. 16-396, 1. 7).

139. On Bardaisan's apostasy from Christianity see e.g. Theod. b. Kōnī, *Lib. Schol.* XI, CSCO, XVI, pp. 307, 1. 24-308, 1. 3. On that of Mani see Ch. VI, p. 176.

140. Hipp., *haer.* VI, 29, 2-36, 4, p. 155, 1. 22-166, 1. 14. For another account with major differences of detail see Iren, *haer.*, I, 1, 1-8, 5 (I, 1, 1-1, 18, ed. Harvey, i, pp. 8-80).

141. *Ibid.*, VI, 30, 6, p. 157, 1. 22-158, 1. 1.

142. *Ibid.*, VI, 32, 3, p. 160, 12-15.

143. *Ibid.*, VI, 32, 6, pp. 160, 1. 26-161, 1. 2. The punctuation of this verse is problematical. For a modern study of the Heavenly Christ in the Valentinian system see Rudolph, *Die Gnosis*, pp. 170-72.

144. Iren., *haer.* I, 7, 1 (I, 1, 13, ed. Harvey, i, p. 59).

145. *Cf.* Drijvers, *Bardaisan*, pp. 183-5.

146. *h.e.* IV, 30, 3, p. 392, ll. 23-8.

147. Aphrahates, *Demonstrationes* 9, *PS* I/1, col. 115, ll. 8-12, ed. Parisot.

148. Jul. Imp., *ep. et leges* 115 (424b-425a), pp. 179, 1. 11-180, 1. 10, ed. Bidez-Cumont.

149. Ephraem, *Hymni 56 c. haer.* XXII, 3, 1-3, pp. 78, 1. 26-79, 1. 2.

150. Paulinus, *vita Ambrosii* 22, *PL* 14.34C/D. *Cf.* Homes-Dudden, *Ambrose*, II, pp. 372-92. On the importance of Callinicum, *cf.* Thdt., *h. rel.* XXVI, 16, SC CCLVII, p. 194, ll. 4-6.

151. Ambros., *ep.* 73 (= Maurist 40), 16 (180-89), CSEL LXXXII/3, pp. 63-4.

152. Thdt., *haer.*, *praef.*, PG 83.340A.

153. See e.g. 'The hypostasis of the Archons' (*NHC* II, 4) 85, 7, *NHL*, p. 159. See further, Lieu, 'Byz. Formula', p. 205.

154. 14, p. 254, 1. 1, ed. and trans. MacDermott. *Cf. Gnosis*, III, p. 56.

155. (*NHC* II, 5) 108, 15-110, 1, *NHL*, p. 168. *Cf.* Böhlig, 'Synkretismus', p. 161.

156. (*NHC* II, 2), Logion 77, *NHL*, p. 126.

157. *Acta Ioannis* 98 (13)-101 (15), pp. 199, 1. 20-202, 1. 2, ed. Lipsius-Bonnet, trans. *NT Apoc.* (Eng.), II, pp. 233-4. *Cf.* Böhlig, 'Lichtkreuz', pp. 479-80 and Klimkeit, 'Vairocana', pp. 369-70.

158. CXV, p. 270, ll. 13-23.

159. M299a 5, Henning, *Henochbuch*, p. 28.

160. *vita Plotini*, 16 (1-9), p. 19, ed. Henry-Schwyzer (*editio minor*).

161. 7, p. 235, ll. 17-18, ed. and trans. MacDermott.

162. περί ὀργάνων καὶ καμίνων κ.τ.λ. 6-8, ed. Berthelot-Ruelle, *Collection*, ii, pp. 231, 1. 1-232, 1. 7. *Cf.* Puech, *Essais*, pp. 16-17.

163. Syriac: *AMS* III, pp. 3-175, ed. Bedjan; Greek: *Acta Apostolorum Apocrypha*, 2/2, pp. 299-288. *Cf.* Bornkamm, *Mythos, passim*, and *NT Apoc.* (Eng.), II, pp. 425-42.

164. *ATh* 108-11, *Hymn* 1-57, Syr., pp. 110, 1. 14-113, 1. 6; Gk., pp. 219, 1. 20-222, 1. 13. Trans. of *Hymn* 52-7 by Bevan (*Hymn*, p. 21, slightly altered).

165. *ATh* 111-12, *Hymn* 58-78, Syr. pp. 113, 1. 6-114, 1. 6; Gk., pp. 222, 1. 2-223, 1. 13. Trans. Bevan (*Hymn* p. 29)

166. *Ibid.* 113, *Hymn* 88-9, Syr., p. 114, ll. 14-15; Gk., pp. 224, ll. 1-2.

Trans., Bevan (*Hymn*, p. 29).

167. *Ibid.*, *Hymn*, 95–105, Syr., pp. 114, l. 15–115, l. 10 and Gk., p. 224, ll. 2–20.

168. *Cf.* Bevan, *Hymn*, pp. 2–3, *NT Apoc.*, (Eng.), pp. 433–4 (Bornkamm), *idem*, *Mythos*, pp. 106–11 and Widengren, *Mesopotamian Elements*, pp. 52–73.

168a. See esp. *Ps.-Bk.*, p. 117, ll. 3–31 and p. 216, ll. 1–12. *Cf.* Nagel, *Die Thomaspsalmen*, pp. 98–9. On the influence of the *Hymn* on Manichaean story-telling see e.g. M 46 R 1-V 21, *KPT* (1634–75), 24.1, pp. 84–5, esp. (1659–68), p. 85.

169. *Cf.* Brock, 'Clothing metaphors', pp. 14–21.

170. *Hymni de Nativitate* XXII, 39, 3, trans. Brock, 'Clothing metaphors', p. 18.

171. Agathias, *hist.* II, 26, 3, p. 75, ll. 11–12, ed. Keydell.

172. *CMC* 121, 11–123, 13 (*ZPE* 1982) pp. 13–15.

173. *Ibid.*, 120, 4–129, 17, pp. 17–21. *Cf.* Henrichs, '*CMC* Reconsidered', pp. 341–2.

174. *Ibid.*, 130, 1–135, 6, pp. 23–7.

175. *Keph.* I, p. 15, 25–31. *Cf.* Henrichs, 'Babylonian Baptists', pp. 54–5.

176. *ŠKZ* (Gk.), 4, p. 307, ed. Maricq. *Cf.* Frye, *Heritage*, p. 241.

177. Ṭabarī/Noldeke, p. 17.

178. M48 etc., *cf. MMTKGI* (37–128), 2.2, pp. 20–24.

179. See above, n. 122.

180. *Keph.* I, p. 33, l. 17. *Cf.* Schaeder, 'Der Man. nach neuen Funden', p. 95, n. 1.

181. *Alberuni's India*, trans. Sachau, pp. 54–5.

182. *Cf.* Benz, 'Indische Einflüsse', pp. 175–8 and Sedlar, *India*, pp. 230–31. For a more cautious view see Schaeder, Review of *Mani-Fund*, pp. 340–50.

183. *Hymni 56 c. haer.* III, 7, 3, p. 12, l. 12.

184. *Hymni adversus Julianum* II, 20, 1–3, CSCO CLXXIV, p. 79, ll. 25–8. *Cf.* Beck, *Ephräms Polemik*, p. 25. But see Julianus Imp., *or.* II, 62C–D (III, 11, 10–12, Bidez).

185. See e.g. the very inappropriate borrowings from Buddhist writings in *MNKFCFIL*, p. 1280a 18–21 and b2–7. *Cf.* Haloun–Henning, 'Compendium', pp. 192–4.

186. M4575 R II 1–6, *MMTKGI* (654–9), 4a.1, pp. 56–7.

187. M6040 and M6041, *MMTKGI* (1308–1417), 4b.1–2, pp. 86–8.

187a. See e.g. *Ps.-Bk.*, p. 192, l. 15.

188. See e.g., *Vita S. Simeonis Stylitae Senioris*, Syr., *AMS*, IV, pp. 603, l. 16–604, l. 2.

189. *Cf.* Whitehouse–Williamson, 'Sasanian maritime trade', pp. 42–3.

190. *Cf.* Figulla, 'Manichäer in Indien', pp. 115–16.

191. M47 R 4–V 16, *MMTKGI* (1579–1607), X, pp. 102–3.

192. *Fihrist*, trans. Dodge, p. 776, Flügel, *Mani*, p. 85. *Cf.* Puech, *Le Manichéisme*, pp. 44–6.

193. *Hom.*, p. 48, ll. 7–9.

194. *Keph.* LXXVI, p. 183, ll. 27–9. See below.

195. See e.g., Decret, *Mani*, p. 61 and Seston, 'L'Égypte', p. 364.
196. *ŠKZ* (Gk.), ll. 37–45, pp. 315–19, ed. Maricq. *Cf.* Klíma, *MZL*, pp. 339–41.
196a. *Cf.* Chaumont, 'Conquêtes Sassanides', pp. 701–9.
197. *Cf.* Brown, *Religion*, pp. 99–100.
198. *Cf.* Klíma, *MZL*, pp. 370–87.
199. M 3 V 38–46, Henning, 'Mani's last journey', p. 90 (= *Reader*, n, 3, p. 45).
200. Other examples include Gabriel of Sinjar, Marutha of Maipherqaṭ and 'Aqwālāhā of Karkā de Bēt Selōk (see Ch. III). *Cf.* Murray, *Symbols*, pp. 33–4 and Asmussen, *Christentum*, pp. 8–9.
201. *Keph.* I, pp. 15, l. 33–16, l. 2.
202. Alex. Lyc., *c. Manich. opinion*. II, p. 4, ll. 21–2, ed. Brinkmann.
203. Porphyrius, *vita Plotini*, 3 (17–24), p. 4.

NOTES TO CHAPTER III

1. *ap.* al-Bīrūnī, *Chronology*, trans. Sachau, p. 190.
2. *Keph.* CLIV, cited in *Mani-Fund*, p. 45. Eng. trans. Stevenson, *A New Eusebius*, p. 282. *Cf.* M5794 (T II D 126) I R 6–10, *MM ii*, p. 295 (= *Reader*, a, 1, p. 29).
3. *Keph.* I, pp. 11, l. 35–15, l. 24. *Cf.* Henrichs, 'Babylonian Baptists', pp. 54–5.
4. *Cf.* Schaeder, 'Review of *Mani-Fund*', pp. 351–3.
5. Cited in Christensen, *L'Iran*, pp. 406–7.
6. *Keph.* LXXVII, pp. 188, l. 31–189, l. 11. *Cf.* Altheim, 'Die vier Weltreiche', pp. 115–19.
7. *Liber Legum Regionum* 26 and 31, *PS* I/2, cols. 583–91.
8. Pesiotan was the son of Vistaspa and the priest in charge of Kangdez. In times of trouble he was meant of appear and restore the true faith.
9. Tangri is Old Turkish for 'heaven' or 'God'. *Cf.* Bang–von Gabain, *Analytischer Index zu . . . TTT i–v*, p. 504.
10. *Gannat Bussamē*, the Syriac text of the relevant passage is edited in Bidez–Cumont, *Les mages*, II, p. 115.
11. Schaeder, 'Urform', p. 129, trans. *auct.*
12. *Cf. CMC* 64, l. 3–65, l. 22 (*ZPE* 1975), p. 65. *Cf.* Koenen, 'Augustine', pp. 171–5.
13. al-Nadim, *Fihrist*, trans. Dodge, p. 776, trans. Flügel, p. 85.
14. *Ibid.*, trans. Dodge, pp. 799–80, Flügel, *Mani*, pp. 103–5. See esp. comm. *ad loc.* (pp. 370–81). See also Alfaric, *Les écritures*, II, pp. 115–20.
15. *CMC* 66, 4–7 (*ZPE* 1975), p. 67. *Cf.* Henrichs–Koenen, 'Mani-Codex', pp. 199–202 and *Mani-Fund*, pp. 25–6.
16. Tit. Bos., *adv. Manich.* III, 1 (Gk., p. 97, ll. 15–18; Syr., p. 82, 31–3).
17. *Keph.* I, p. 16, ll. 3–9.
18. al-Bīrūnī, *Chronology*, trans. Sachau, p. 208. See also parallel in *PSCTC*, p. 1284c25–6, trans. *Traité* 1911, p. 576 [78]. *Cf.* Vööbus, *Hist. Asc.*, I, p. 118.

19. *CMC* 93, 14–23 (*ZPE* 1978), p. 113. *Cf.* Henrichs, 'Babylonian Baptists', p. 51.

20. See e.g. *CT* XVI, 5, 40, 7, p. 868 etc. and *SHYCK*, fasc. 165, *hsing-fa* 2.78a/b. *Cf.* Decret, *L'Afrique*, I, pp. 203–5 and Puech, *Essais*, pp. 247–58.

21. M4a I V 13, *HR*, p. 51 (= *Reader*, cv, 21, p. 162). *Cf.* Schaeder, 'Urform', pp. 129–30.

22. *MNKFCFIL*, p. 1280c. *Cf. Traité* 1913, p. 113 [137].

23. *Cf.* Puech, *Essais*, pp. 39–41.

24. Theod. b. Kōnī, *Lib. Schol.* XI, p. 314, l. 22–315, l. 6.

25. *Keph.* LXXXV, p. 209, ll. 12–19. *Cf.* Ries, 'Commandements', pp. 99–100.

26. *PSCTC*, p. 1284b22–4, trans. *Traité* 1911, pp. 572–3 [74–5].

27. 13941 + 14285 V 5, *MMTKGI* (546), 3.1, p. 36.

28. *Historia Karkae de Beth Selok*, *AMS*, II, p. 512, ll. 11–14.

29. M2, [M216a], M1750 + M216c, 13941 + 14285, 18223 + 18222. *Cf.* *MMTKGI*, pp. 17–18, 26–7, and 34–41.

30. M2 R I 1, *MM ii*, p. 301.

31. M1750 + M216c V 8, *MMTKGI* (182), 2.5, p. 26.

32. *Ibid.* R 12, (173), p. 26.

33. *PSCTC*, p. 1281a26–9, trans. *Traité* 1911, pp. 508–9 [10–11].

34. M2 R I 1–4, *MM ii*, p. 301 (= *Reader*, h, 1, p. 39).

35. See Ch. IV.

36. M1750 + M216c V 9–11, *MMTKGI* (183–5), 2.5, p. 26.

37. M2 R I 12–15, *MM ii*, p. 301 (= *Reader*, h, 1, p. 39).

38. *Ibid.* 9–11, p. 301.

39. *Ibid.* 16–21, p. 302 (= *Reader*, h, 2, p. 40).

40. LXXXV [65b13–16], ed. Henry, ii. pp. 9–10.

41. *Cf.* Drijvers, *Bardaisan*, p. 163.

42. *Cf.* Alfaric, *Les écritures*, I, pp. 98–9.

43. Theod. b. Kōnī, *Lib. Schol.* XI, p. 311, l. 18.

44. Hegem., *Arch.* (Lat.), XL, 2, GCS XVI, p. 59, l. 3.

45. *Cf.* Schaeder, 'Urform', pp. 88–9 and Klíma, *MZL*, pp. 263–5.

46. *Cf.* Dupont-Somer, 'Note archéologique', p. 794.

47. Aug., *retr.* I, 21 (22), 1, CSEL XXXVI, p. 100, ll. 8–9 and 11. *Cf.* Châtillon, 'Adimantus', pp. 191–9.

48. Aug., *c. advers. Leg. et Proph.*, II, 42, *PL* 42.666. *Cf.* Decret, *L'Afrique*, I, pp. 174–6 and Frend, 'Gnostic-Manich. tradition', p. 20.

49. On the general principles of Hadrianic defences see *SHA, Hadrianus* 12, 6.

50. *Cf.* Libanius, *or.* XI (Antiochikos), 178, ed. Foerster, i/2, pp. 496, l. 19–497, l. 17, *CT* X, 22, 1, p. 566, ed. Mommsen and Meyer; Malalas, *chron.* XII, p. 307, ll. 20–21, CSHB.

51. *Cf.* Poidebard, *La trace, I, pp.* 23–4, Dillemann, *Haute Mésop.*, pp. 203–4. It is interesting to note that the ownership of a section of the *Strata Diocletiana*, an important part of the limes, was disputed among various Arab tribes in the time of Justinian. *Cf.* Procop., *Pers.* II, 1, ed. Haury, i, p. 149, ll. 4–9.

52. *Cf.* Rostovtzeff, *Dura Europos*, pp. 28–9.

53. Amm. Marc. XVIII, 9, 1, ed. Seyfarth, i, p. 152, ll. 7–11.

54. Pseudo-Josue Stylita, *Historia calamitatum* etc. 90, *ap. Chronicon Pseudo-Dionysianum*, CSCO XCI, pp. 309, ll. 12–22.

55. *ŠKZ* (Gk.), l. 24, p. 313, ed. Maricq.

56. *Ibid.* l. 26, p. 313.

57. *Cf.* Honigmann–Maricq, *Recherches*, pp. 145–9.

58. Procop., *Pers.* II, 5, 1–21, 34, ed. Haury, i, pp. 167, 1–249, l. 7. *Cf.* Theophanes, *chron.* A.M. 6031, p. 218, ll. 18–20 and 6033, pp. 219, ll. 19–222, l. 8 ed. de Boor.

59. Amm. Marc., XIV, 3, 4; i, p. 8, ll. 17–21.

60. Procop., *Pers.* I, 18, 1–3; i, pp. 90, l. 24–91, l. 9.

61. The *Šābuhragān* was not part of the canon of Mani's own writings as stated by al-Nadim. *Cf. Fihrist*, trans. Dodge, p. 798 and Flügel, *Mani*, p. 103.

62. *Cf.* Boyce, *Man. Lit.*, p. 71.

63. The main Iranian fragments are collected in MacKenzie, 'Mani's *Šābuhragān*' I–II. *Cf. Texte*, pp. 5–8 and 112–15 and *Gnosis*, III, pp. 234–9.

64. *Chronique de Séert* II, *PO* 4, p. 221. *Cf.* Chaumont, 'Christianisation', pp. 165–202 and Fiey, 'Les communautés', pp. 282–5.

65. *Cf.* Brock, 'Candida', pp. 167–8.

66. See above, n. 28. *Cf.* Fiey, 'Vers la réhabilitation', pp. 194–6.

67. See below, n. 156.

68. See Ch. IV.

69. Ioannes Ephesi, *Historiae beatorum orientalium*, X, *PO* XVII, pp. 137–58.

70. See Ch. VI.

71. *Cf.* Brown, *Religion*, p. 102.

72. Epiph., *haer.* LXVI, 1, 1, GCS XXXVII (Epiph. iii), pp. 13, l. 21–14, 11.

73. *Cf. MM iii*, p. 865, n. 3 and Henrichs–Koenen, 'Mani-Codex', p. 131, n. 86.

74. Epiph., *haer.* LXVI, 1, 2, p. 14, ll. 2–4.

75. *Cf.* de Stoop, *Essai*, pp. 57–8.

76. *Cf.* Cumont, 'La propagation', p. 39.

76a.Tardieu, 'Vues nouvelles', p. 253.

77. *Cf.* Hiroshi Wada, *Prokops Rätselwort* pp. 23–30 and Herrmann, *Seidenstrassen*, pp. 80–91.

78. *Cf.* Pigulevskaja, *Byzanz . . . nach Indien*, p. 152.

79. *Hou Han-shu* 88. 2919–20.

80. Petr. Pat., frag. 14, *FHG*, IV, p. 189.

81. *Cf.* Altheim–Stiehl, 'Palmyra', pp. 704–09.

82. *expositio* 22, SC CXXIV, p. 156, 4–6.

83. *Ibid.* 6–10.

84. *Cf.* Shiratori Kurakichi, 'Putoremaiosu', p. 46. See also Ptolemaeus, *geog.* I, 11, 3–6, pp. 28–9, ed. Müller; and Amm. Marc., XXIII, 6, 60; i, p. 318, ll. 13–17.

85. 'Cyrillona', *Hymni et sermones*, p. 582. (409–10), trans. Murray, *Symbols*, p. 175.

86. *Keph.* I, p. 11, ll. 18–20. *Cf.* Arnold-Döben, *Bildersprache*, pp. 62–3.

87. Aug., *enarr. in Ps. 140*, 12 (10–15), CCSL XL, p. 2034.

88. Pos., *v. Aug.* 15, p. 74, ll. 10–20, ed. Weisskoten.

89. Theod. b. Kōnī, *Lib. Schol.* XI, p. 311, ll. 24–5.

90. Epiph., *haer.* LXVI, 1, 8–12, pp. 16, l. 4–17, l. 9.

91. *Periplus Maris Erythraei* 18–19, *GGM*, I, pp. 272–3.

92. *Cf.* Whitehouse–Williamson, 'Sasanian maritime trade', pp. 20–49.

93. Procop., *Pers.* I, 20, 12; i, pp. 109, l. 17–110, l. 6.

94. Amm. Marc., XIV, 3, 3; i, p. 8, ll. 16–17. *Cf.* Mommsen, 'Ammians Geographica', pp. 602–36.

95. *Cf.* Reinink, 'Das Land 'Seris'', p. 74.

96. See e.g. Procop., *Pers.* II, 2, 3, p. 151, ll. 10–15. *Cf.* Peeters, *Le trefonds*, pp. 86–7.

97. *Itinerarium Egeriae* XLVII, 3 (13–19), CCSL CLXXV, p. 89.

98. Eus., *h.e.* I, 13, 5, GCS IX/1 (Eus. ii), p. 84, ll. 19–21.

99. Soz., *h.e.* III, 16, 12, GCS L, pp. 127, l. 24–128, l. 3.

100. *Cf. Mani-Fund*, p. 13.

101. *Cf.* Henrichs–Koenen, 'Mani-Codex', pp. 104–5.

102. *Cf. Allberry, Ps.-Bk.*, intro., p. xix. On the question of whether the Coptic texts were translated directly from Syriac or via Greek, see esp. Böhlig, 'Synkretismus', pp. 147–50.

103. Plinius (major), *nat. hist.* V, 88.

104. *Cf.* Will, 'Marchands', pp. 267–77 and Drijvers, 'Hatra etc.', pp. 839–43.

105. Cantineau, *Inventaire*, fasc. 3, no. 19, p. 25, ll. 4–5. *Cf.* Drijvers, 'Hatra etc.', pp. 848–9 and Clermont–Genneau, 'Odeinat', pp. 392–419.

105a. M2 R I 28, *MM ii*, p. 302 (= *Reader*, h, 2, p. 40).

106. 18223 + 18222 (TM 389c) I R 1–13, *MMTKGI* (441–53), 3.3, p. 42.

107. *Cf. Mani-Fund*, p. 28 and Schaeder, 'Review of *Mani-Fund*', p. 344.

108. *Cf.* Geiger, 'Middle Iranian texts', pp. 291–2.

109. *Cf.* Boyce, 'Man. Lit.', p. 67 and Klimkeit, *Art*, pp. 20–21.

110. *Cf.* Lidzbarski, 'Die Herkunft', pp. 1213–22, Rosenthal, *Die Sprache*, pp. 207–11 and Böhlig, 'Synkretismus', pp. 147–8.

111. Alex. Lyc., *c. Manich. opinion.* II, p. 4, ll. 17–19.

112. *Ps.-Bk.*, p. 34, l. 12.

113. *Cf. Mani-Fund*, pp. 14–16.

114. *Cf.* Puech, < 'Les premières missions' >, pp. 80–81.

115. *Cf.* Koenen, 'Manichäische Mission', p. 106.

116. Zos., I, 44, pp. 31, l. 20–32, l. 3, ed. Mendelssohn. See also *SHA, trig. tyr.* 30 2, ed. Hohl, p. 127, ll. 5–11. *Cf.* Tardieu, 'Les Manichéens en Egypte', p. 10.

117. Zos. I, 61, 1, p. 43, ll. 26–8.

118. *Fihrist*, trans. Dodge, p. 799 and Flügel, *Mani*, p. 103.

119. Moses Choren., *Hist. Armen.*, II, 26–33, trans. Thomson, pp. 162–74.

120. *CJ* IV, 63, 4, p. 188.

121. Dio Cassius LXXX, 3, 2–3, ed. Boissevain, iii, p. 475 and Agathanagelos, *Hist. Armen.* 18–24, trans. Thomson, pp. 35–43. *Cf.* Chaumont, 'L'Armenie', pp. 158–62 and *eadem, Recherches*, pp. 25–40.

122. Agathang., *Hist. Armen.* 32–5, pp. 47–51 and Moses Choren., *Hist.*

Armen. II, 71-3, 76-8, pp. 218-20 and 223-5. *Cf.* Chaumont, 'L'Armenie', pp. 165-76 and *eadem, Recherches*, pp. 49-66.

123. Agathang., *Hist. Armen.* 37-47, pp. 53-61 and Moses Choren., *Hist. Armen.* II, 79-82, pp. 226-33. *Cf.* Chaumont, 'L'Armenie', pp. 177-85 and *eadem, Recherches*, pp. 93-111.

124. Pet. Patr., frag. 14, *FHG,* IV, pp. 188-9. *Cf.* Chaumont, *Recherches,* pp. 112-29.

125. Agathang., *Hist Armen.* 804-5, pp. 343-5. *Cf.* Chaumont, *Recherches,*pp. 131-64.

126. TM 389d R 1-V 40, *MMTKGI* (516-97), 3.4, pp. 45-9. *Cf.* Lieu, 'Byz. Formula', p. 195.

127. Trans. Dodge, p. 799, Flügel, *Mani*, p. 103. *Cf.* Klíma, *MZL*, p. 421.

128. *ŠKZ* (Gk.) line 3, ed. Maricq, p. 307. See also p. 336.

129. M216b R 1-V 5, *MMTKGI* (130-45), 2.3, pp. 24-5.

130. M2230 R 5, *MMTKGI* (154), 2.4, p. 25 and U 237 + U 296 (D) R 1-V 13, *MMT* (441-63), 21, p. 51.

131. M18220 R 38-V 3, *MMTKGI* (397-403), 3.2, p. 39. *Cf.* Henning, 'Mitteliranisch', p. 94.

132. *Ibid.* V 3-4 (403-4), p. 39. See also M2 R I 34-II 6, *MM ii*, pp. 302-3 (= *Reader*, h, 3, p. 40).

133. *Cf.* Klíma, *MZL*, pp. 342-3. See also *Reader, loc. cit.*, comm. *ad loc*.

134. M18220 V 34-8, *MMTKGI* (434-8), 3.2, p. 41. *Cf.* Henning, 'Waručān-Šāh', p. 87.

135. M4575 V I 3-9, *MMTKGI* (665-71), 4a.1, p. 57.

136. M5815 II, *MM iii*, b, 166-7, p. 859 (= *Reader*, q, 5, p. 49).

137. *Hom.*, p. 42, ll. 15-30.

138. *Cf.* Frye, 'State and church', p. 326.

139. *KŠM*, 1. 14 (= *KKZ* ll. 9-10), p. 395, ed. Gignoux.

140. *Denkart*, p. 519, ll. 7-8, cited in Boyce, 'Toleranz', p. 331.

141. *Cf.* Klíma, 'Baat', pp. 342-6 and *idem, MZL*, pp. 370-72.

142. M4579 R i 1 - ii 6, *MMTKGI* (975-85), 4a12, p. 70.

143. M6033 I R A3 - C15, Henning, 'Mani's last journey', p. 943 (= *Reader*, k, p. 43).

144. *Hom.*, pp. 45, 1. 9-54, 1. 17. *Cf.* Klíma, *MZL*, pp. 370-87.

145. *Fihrist*, trans. Dodge, p. 802, Flügel, *Mani*, p. 105.

146. *Cf.* Markwart, *Ērānšahr*, p. 81.

147. M5815 II, *MM iii*, b, 210-23, pp. 857-60 (= *Reader*, q. pp. 48-50).

148. *Ibid.* 131-5, p. 858 (= *Reader*, q, 2, p. 49).

149. *Cf. Mani-Fund*, pp. 24-5.

150. See e.g. *Hom.*, pp. 75, 1-85, 1. 30. *Cf.* Vööbus, *Hist. Asc.*, II, p. 68.

151. *Cf. Mani-Fund*, p. 27 and Schaeder, Review, p. 345. On the Lakhmids see Ṭabari/Nöldeke, pp. 78-85.

152. *Cf. Mani-Fund*, p. 29.

153. See Ch. II.

154. *Cf. Mani-Fund*, p. 29.

155. On confusion with Mazdakites see *Chronicon ad Annum Christi 1234 Pertinens*, CSCO LXXXI, pp. 193, 1. 24-194, 1. 11 and Theophanes, *chron.*, A.M. 6016, pp. 169, 1. 27-170, 1. 24, ed. de Boor. On confusion with Ssabians

see e.g. *Chronicon Anonymum*, CSCO I, pp. 33, 14–34, 2 and *Chronicon Pseudo-Dionysianum*, ed. Chabot, *Chronique*, Syr. text, pp. 80, l. 1–82, l. 2. *Cf.* Chwolsohn, *Die Ssabier*, II, p. 497.

156. *Historia Karkae de Beth Selok*, AMS II, pp. 513, l. 10–514, l. 7.
157. *Acta Martyrum Persarum*, Syr.: AMS II, pp. 385, l. 19–386, l. 11; Gk.: X, 52, *PO* II, pp. 511, l. 13–512, l. 7.
158. *Historia Karkae de Beth Selok*, pp. 516, l. 15–517, l. 10. *Cf.* Fiey, 'Vers la réhabilitation', pp. 197 and 209–11.
159. *Cf. Reader*, p. 3 and Colpe, *Der Man.*, p. 235.
160. *Fihrist*, trans. Dodge, pp. 792–3, Flügel, *Mani*, pp. 97–8. *Cf.* Colpe, *op cit.*, pp. 235–6.
161. *Fihrist*, trans. Dodge, p. 794, Flügel, *Mani*, p. 99. *Cf.* Vajda, 'Les Zindîqs', pp. 173–8.
162. *Cf.* Vajda, 'Les Zindîqs', pp. 184–5, Colpe, *diss.cit.*, p. 229 and Decret, *Mani*, pp. 136–41.
163. *Cf.* Colpe, *diss. cit.*, pp. 96–7, 191–220, *idem*, 'Anpassung', pp. 82–91 and *Gnosis*, III, pp. 9–10.
164. *Fihrist*, trans. Dodge, p. 802, Flügel, *Mani*, pp. 105–6.
165. *Fihrist*, trans. Dodge, p. 803, Flügel, *Mani*, p. 106.
166. *Cf.* Henning, 'Neue Materialien', pp. 16–18 and esp., Sundermann, 'Probleme', pp. 305–12.
167. *P. Ryl. Gk.* 469, l. 30, p. 42, ed. Roberts.
168. Alex. Lyc., *c. Manich. opinion.* X, p. 16, ll. 14–19.
169. *Cf. Mani-Fund*, pp. 8–17 and Koenen, 'Zur Herkunft des *CMC*', pp. 240–41.
170. See Ch. IV.
171. *Cf.* Kugener-Cumont, *Recherches*, III, pp. 175–6 and *Textes*, pp. 106–7.
172. *Cf.* Egger, *Forschungen*, II, pp. 52–3, 73 and *idem*, 'Das Mausoleum', p. 796, n. 3. See also Grant, 'Manichees', p. 437.
173. Pall., *h. Laus.* XXXVII, p. 112, ll. 6–12, ed. Butler.
174. XII, pp. 309, l. 19–310, l. 2, CSHB. *Cf.* Christensen, *Kawādh*, pp. 97–8.
175. XVIII, p. 429, ll. 11–12.
176. *lib. pontif.* LXXXIII, 2, ed. Duchesne, i, p. 168, ll. 3–4.
177. *h.Laus.* XIV, p. 37, ll. 12–13.
178. *divers. haer.* LXI (33), 4–5, CSEL XXXVIII, p. 32, ll. 16–21.
179. *Ibid.* LXXXIV (61), 1–2, p. 45, ll. 18–24. On the Five Provinces see Festus, *brev.* VI, p. 50, ll. 5–6, ed. Eadie.
180. On Manichaean fragments in Syriac see Burkitt, *Religion*, pp. 111–19. On Egyptian names in the Psalm-Book see *Ps.-Bk.*, Index C, p. 44*.
181. Epiph., *haer.*, LXVII, 3, 7, GCS XXXVII (Epiph. iii), p. 136, ll. 8–10.
182. XCIV, p. 63, ll. 4–10, ed. Halkin.
183. On the diffusion of Manichaeism in N. Africa see esp. Decret, *L'Afrique*, I, pp. 179–210.
184. The more important citations from these two works are collected in *Texte*, pp. 2–5 and 27–30.
185. Aug., *c. Fel.* I, 14, CSEL XXV/2, p. 817, ll. 17–19 and 27–31. See also

ibid. I, 1, p. 801, ll. 16–26.

186. VII, 7, p. 56, ed. Dobshütz.

187. Aug., *retr.* 21 (22), 1, p. 100, ll. 10–14. *Cf.* <Zach. Mit.>, *capita vii c. Manich.*, II (46–7), CCSG I p. xxxiv.

188. Aug., *conf.* V, iii, 6 (58–61), CCSL XXVII, pp. 59–60.

189. *Ibid.*, V, vi, 11 (41–2), p. 62. On Manichaean scriptures in N. Africa see esp. Decret, *Aspects*, pp. 93–121.

190. *Cf.* Quispel, *Tatian*, pp. 64–5. See also Coyle, *Aug.'s 'De mor. eccl.'*, pp. 148–9.

191. *Ps.-Bk.*, p. 170, ll. 16–26.

192. *Cf.* Nagel, 'Psalmoi', cols. 123–30.

193. *Cf.* Murray, 'Exhortation', pp. 74–7 and *Symbols*, pp. 27–9.

194. *Itinerarium Egeriae, passim*, esp. 18, l. 1–20, l. 2, CCSL CLXXV, pp. 59–62. *Cf.* Segal, *Edessa*, pp. 176–8.

195. Aug., *c. Faust.* XX, 21, CSEL XXV/1, p. 561, ll. 18–20.

196. *Cf.* Hunt, *Holy Land Pilgrimage*, pp. 63–4 and *PW*, *s.v.* 'Xenodochium' (O. Hiltbrunner), cols 1492, l. 52–1493, l. 35 and 1494, l. 45 *ad fin.*

197. *Cf.* Alfaric, 'Un manuscrit', pp. 62–3 (see under *fragmenta Tebestina*), and Decret, *L'Afrqiue*, I, pp. 201–2. On Tabessa as a stopping place for pilgrims see Diehl, *L'Afrique Byz.*, pp. 430–31.

NOTES TO CHAPTER IV

1. *coll.* xv, 3, *FIRA* II pp. 580–81. On this edict see esp. Stade, *Diokletian*, pp. 83–92 Volterra, 'La costituzione', *passim*, Kaden, 'Die Edikte', pp. 56–7, Chadwick, 'Relativity', *passim*, and Decret, *L'Afrique* I, pp. 162–73. On the date of the edict see esp. Thomas, 'Revolt of L. Domitius Domitianus', pp. 261–2, Barnes, 'Imperial victories', pp. 174–93 and *PLRE*, I, pp. 473–4.

2. See Ch. II, n. 175. On the campaigns of Shapur I, see Honigmann–Maricq, *Recherches*, pp. 111–49.

3. *coll.* xv, 3, 1, p. 580.

4. *Ibid.* 4, pp. 580–81.

5. *Ibid.* 5, p. 581.

6. *Ibid.* 6–8, p. 581 and Eus., *h.e.* VIII, 13, 5, *ed. cit.*, p. 772, ll. 16–19. *Cf.* Garnsey, *Social Status*, pp. 103–52 and 222–3.

7. Baynes, review of Stade, *op. cit.*, p. 124.

8. Festus, *brev.* 25, pp. 65, l. 17–66, l. 5, ed. Eadie.

9. *Cf.* Chadwick, 'Relativity', pp. 144–5 and Decret, *L'Afrique* I, pp. 162–5.

10. *Cf.* Frend, *Martyrdom*, pp. 109–11.

11. See e.g. Just. *apol.* I, 66, *PG* 6.429A, Gr. Naz., *or.* 39 (*in sancta lumina*), *PG* 36.340B and Firm., *de err.* V, 2, CSEL II, pp. 81, l. 29–82, l. 4. These can be found in Cumont, *Textes et monuments*, II, pp. 14–20.

12. *coll.* XV, 3, 1, and 5, pp. 78, 580–81.

13. Paulus, *sententiae*, V, 21, 2. *FIRA* II, pp. 406–7. *Cf.* Volterra, *art. cit.*, p. 48.

14. LII, 36, 1-2, ed. Boissevain, ii, p. 407, ll. 2-11. *Cf.* Volterra, *art. cit.*, p. 47.

15. *coll.* xv, 3, 2, p. 580.

16. *Ibid. 4, p. 581. Cf. coll.* VI, 4, 1, 4 (on incest), p. 560. On Diocletian's preference for 'Roman' customs see Stade, *Diokletian*, p. 78, Mitteis, *Reichsrecht*, p. 514 and Gaudemet, *La formation de droit seculier*, p. 121, n. 1.

17. See e.g. Van Sickle, 'Conservative influence', pp. 51-8.

18. Lact., *de mort. persec.* 7, 1-5, CSEL XXVII, pp. 179, l. 25-180, l. 20.

19. *Cf.* Stade, *Diokletian*, pp. 92-4.

20. See Ch. II, n. 176. It seems, however, that philosophers, especially those of Syrian origin, had less difficulty in travelling to India via Persia in the fourth century. Witness the peregrinations of Metrodorus which became *causa belli* between Rome and Persia. *Cf.* Amm. Marc. XXV, 4, 23 and Cedrenus, *hist. comp.* 1516, pp. 516 l. 12-517, l. 11 CSHB = *PG* 121.561B-C.

21. *Cf.* Gordon, 'Franz Cumont', pp. 215-58, esp. 243-8 and Hinnells, 'Iranian background', pp. 242-50.

22. *Cf.* Honigmann, *Die Ostgrenze*, pp. 5-8.

23. *CJ* IV, 63, 4, p. 188, ed. Krueger. On espionage by merchants *cf.* Procop., *Pers.* I, 21, 11-12, ed. Haury, i, p. 111, ll. 20-26.

24. p. *lz*, 2-5, ed. Phillips.

25. *Cf.* van der Lof, 'Mani', pp. 77-80.

26. *Historia beatorum orientalium* X, (Simeon the Persian Debater). PO XVII, pp. 138-9. See also Segal, *Edessa*, pp. 93-5.

27. *Synodicon orientale*, ed. Chabot, p. 567, ll. 18-23 (Syr).

28. *Leges novellae Valentiniani III*, 8, ed. Mommsen and Meyer, *Theodosiani Libri XVI*, II, p. 103.

29. See below Ch. V, n. 154.

30. *Cf.* Kugener-Cumont, *Recherches* III, pp. 175-6.

31. *haer.* LXVI, 42, 2, p. 79, ll. 1-4.

32. *ep. ad Alexandrinum*, *ap.* Epiph., *haer.* LXIX, p. 158, ll. 12-13.

33. XV, 13, 1-2, ed. Seyfarth, i, p. 68, ll. 4-10. *Cf.* Dölger, 'Konstantin . . . und der Manichäismus', pp. 304-7.

34. Amm. Marc. XXX, 10, 3, ed. Seyfarth, ii, p. 157, ll. 21-3. *Cf.* Brown, *Religion*, p. 109.

36. Ath., *fug.* VI, 5, p. 72, ll. 10-13, ed. Opitz and *h. Ar.*, LIX, 1, p. 216, ll. 11-13, ed. *idem*.

37. Soc., *h.e.* II, 28, 6, ed. Hussey, i, p. 271 and Thdt., *h.e.* II, 13, 6, GCS XLIV, p. 216, ll. 2-6.

38. *Cf.* sources cited in *PLRE*, I, pp. 812-13 and *PW*, *s.v.* 'Sebastianus', col. 954, ll. 2-46. See esp. Eunapius, frag. 47, *FHG*, IV, pp. 34-5.

39. Aug., *conf.* III, x, 18 (10-13), p. 37, *idem, mor. Manich.* XV, 36, cols. 1360-61, Thdt., *haer.* I, 26, col. 380c and <Zach. Mit> *capita VII c. Manich.*, VII (187-8) p. xxxviii.

40. *Cf.* Ath., *h, Ar.* LIX, 1-61, 3, pp. 216, l. 23-217, l. 20, ed. Optiz.

41. On the date of the letter see *P. Rylands Greek* 469, III p. 38.

42. *P. Rylands Gk.* 469, ll. 12-21, p. 42.

43. *Ibid.* ll. 25-9, p. 42.

44. *Ibid.* ll. 29-35, p. 42.

45. *Cf.* Ries, 'Introduction (2)', pp. 395-8, Quasten, *Patrology*, III, pp. 397-8 and Harnack, *Geschichte*, II, pp. 540-41.

46. Hegem., *Arch.* (Lat.) V, 1-13, 4, GCS XVI, pp. 5, l. 25-22, l. 15-Epiph., *haer.* LXVI, 6, 1-11, pp. 25, ll. 14-27, XVI, 7, 5, p. 28, ll. 15-20 and 25, 2-31, l. 5, pp. 53, l. 19-72, l. 8.

47. Hegem., *Arch.* (Lat.), pp. 1-100.

48. *Cf.* Crum, 'Eusebius', pp. 76-7 and Polotsky, 'Koptische Zitate', pp. 18-20. See also *TTT ii*, pp. 429-30.

49. See e.g. Theod. b. Kōnī, *Lib. Schol.* XI, pp. 311, l. 19-313, l. 9, *Chronicon Maroniticum*, CSCO I, pp. 58, l. 21-60, l. 9 and Michael the Syrian, *Chronicon*, ed. Chabot, iv, pp. 116, left col. 36-118, left col. 7.

50. *de vir. illus.* LXXII, *PL* 23. 719.

51. The Greek origins of some of the names in the Syriac versions like b'dws (Bados), sqwntyws (Scythianus) and trwbntws (Terebinthus) are particularly apparent. *Cf.* Theod. b. Kōnī, *Lib. Schol.* XI, p. 311, ll. 20-21 and 312, l. 5.

52. Epiph., *haer*, LXVI, 2, 3-4, p. 17, ll. 16-22, *Cf.* Iren., *haer.* I, 23, 2 (I, 16, 2, ed. Harvey, I. p. 191) and Epiph., *haer.* XXI, 2, 2, GCS 25, p. 239, ll. 19-21. On this see esp. Klíma, *MZL* pp. 223-31.

53. Hegem., *Arch.* (Lat.) XLII, 1-44, 2, pp. 90, l. 8-92, l. 25.

54. *Ibid.* XLIV, 3-9, pp. 92, l. 25-93, l. 25.

55. *Acta S. Marcelli Papae et Mart.*, in *Acta Sanctorum* 16 Jan., pp. 5-9, *Cf.* Dufourcq, *Étude*, I, pp. 341-2 and IV, pp. 366-7.

56. Hegem., *Arch.* XLIV, 7, p. 93, ll. 17-20.

57. *Ibid.* XLIV, 9-XLV, 7, pp. 93, l. 26-94, l. 32.

58. *Ibid.*, XLV, 8, pp. 94, l. 32-95, l. 2 and IV, 1, p. 4, ll. 20-25. On the problem of locating the city of Carchar, see esp. Kessler, *Mani*, pp. 89-97 (largely discredited) and Fiey, *Assyrie Chrétienne*, III, pp. 152-5, who argues for Carrhae. We must, however, bear in mind that Carrhae was noted for its lack of a strong Christian preserve well into the fifth century. *Cf.* Thdt., *h.e.* III, 26, 1-2, p. 205, ll. 4-11 and *Itinerarium Egeriae* XX, 8 (49-56), CCSL CLXXV, p. 63.

59. Hegem., *Arch.* (Lat.), IV, 2-14, 3, pp. 4, l. 25-23, l. 1.

60. *Ibid.* XIV, 6-46, pp. 23, l. 11-95, l. 20.

61. Soc., *h.e.* I, 22, 1-14, ed. Hussey, i, pp. 124, l. 15-129, l. 20. *Cf.* Thdt., *haer.* I, 26.

62. See above n. 46 and Filastrius, *divers. haer. lib.* XXXIII (61) 1-4, CSEL XXXVIII, p. 32, ll. 6-20.

64. *Cf.* Traube, 'Vorbemerkung', pp. 534-7 and Ries, 'Introduction' (2), p. 397.

65. Cyr. H., *catech.* VI, 20-35, ed. Reischl-Rupp, I, pp. 182-206.

66. *Ibid.* VI, 36, p. 206. *Cf.* Lieu, 'Byz. Formula', p. 153.

67. See e.g. Julianus Imp., *ep. et leg.* 44 (= Aug., *c. litt. Petil.* II, 97, CSEL LII, p. 142, ll. 2-6); pp. 50, l. 36-51, l. 3 and XLVI (404B/C), p. 52, ll. 18-24, ed. Bidez-Cumont.

68. *Ibid.* 60, pp. 68, l. 20-69, l. 3.

69. See Ch. I, n. 124.

70. Julianus Imp., *ep. et leg.* 114 (437B), p. 117, ll. 13–18. *Cf.* Soz., *h.e.* v, 15, 11–12, GCS 50, p. 215, ll. 7–16.

71. *Cf. PW. s.v.* 'Titus v. Bostra' (Casey), cols. 1586, l. 63–1587, l. 9.

72. *Cf. ibid.* cols. 1588, l. 35–1590, l. 9; Sickenberger, *Titus von Bostra,* 1–16, 111–18 and 253–9 and Quasten, *Patrology,* III, pp. 359–61.

73. *Cf.* Nagel, 'Neues griechischer Material', pp. 297–348. See also *idem, Die antimanich. Schriften* (Habilitationschrift), pp. 6–12.

74. Tit. Bost., *adv. Manich.* (Gk.) II, 13–24, pp. 32, l. 5–42, l. 30.

75. Amm. Marc. XXV, 7, 9–11; i, pp. 370, l. 23–371, l. 12.

76. On the three seiges see Theophanes, *chron.* A.M. 5829, 5838 and 5841, pp. 34, l. 32–35, l. 7, p. 38, ll. 9–11 and pp. 39, l. 13–40, l. 13, ed. de Boor. See also Zonaras XIII, 7, 1 for a detailed account of the first siege.

77. Thdt., *h. rel.* II, 11–12, SC CCXXXIV, pp. 184–8,. See also *Historia Sancti Ephraemi,* 6, cols. 16–19, ed. Lamy.

78. *Ibid.* 9–42, cols. 23–89.

79. *Ibid.* 30, col. 63.

80. p. *lh,* ll. 5–8, ed. Phillips.

81. XXII, 5, 3–7, p. 79, ll. 22–7.

82. On the recovery of the text from the underwritings of a palimpsest, see Burkitt, *Religion,* pp. 13–14.

83. Ephraim, *C. haer. ad Hypat.,* I, pp. 98, l. 9–99, l. 42. *Cf.* Beck, *Ephräms Polemik,* p. 75.

84. Ephraim, *C. haer. ad Hypat.,* I, p. 128, ll. 3–6.

85. *Ibid.* I, 15, 20–26. *Cf.* Beck, *Ephräms Polemik,* p. 7.

85a. Soz., *h.e.* III, 16, 7, GCS, L, p. 129, ll. 1–9. *Cf. Historia Sancti Ephraemi* 31–2, cols. 63–9, ed. Lamy.

86. Aug. *retr.* I, 18 (20), 1, CSEL. XXXVI, p. 96, ll. 11–14.

87. *Hym. 56 c. haer.* II, 1, p. 5, ll. 16–21. *Cf.* Beck, *Ephräms Polemik,* p. 2.

88. *haer.* LXVI, 1, 4, p. 15, ll. 1–2.

89. *haer.* XLVI, 1 (2–5), pp. 312–13.

90. *Cf. CMC* 66, 4, p. 67 and *Hom.* p. 7, l. 4.

91. Ephraim, *Hym. 56 c. haer.,* LVI, 9, p. 211, ll. 19–24. *Cf.* Beck, *Ephräms Polemik,* p. 6.

92. *Hym. 56 c. haer.* L, 5, pp. 194, l. 24–195, l. 1. *Cf.* Beck, *op. cit.,* pp. 7–8.

93. *Hym. 56 c. haer.* LV, 14, p. 14, ll. 18–23.

94. *ep.* 1253, ed. Foerster, xi, p. 329. *Cf.* Bang, 'Aus Manis Briefen', p. 66 n. 1.

95. *Cf.* Seeck, *Die Briefe des Libanius,* pp. 244–5.

96. *Cf.* Matthews, 'Symmachus', pp. 175–95.

97. See esp. *ep.* 1251 (on Jews, addressed to Sebastianus), ed. Foerster, xi, p. 327, ll. 12–24 and *idem, or.* XXX ('Pro Templis'), ed. *idem,* iii, pp. 87–118.

98. *h.e.* III, 5, pp. 46, l. 23–47, l. 8.

99. Photius, *bibliotheca* 85 (65b, 8–10), ed. Henry, ii, p. 85. *Cf.* Thdt., *haer.* I, 26, col. 382B.

100. *Ibid.* 179 (125a, 15–16), p. 187. *Cf.* Brillet, 'Agapius', cols. 902–3, *NT Apoc.* (Eng.), II, p. 180 and Obolensky, *Bogomils,* pp. 25–6.

101. *bibliotheca* 179 (124a, 16-23), p. 184.

102. *Cf. Long Abjuration Formula, PG* 1.1468A4 and B10; Peter. Sic., *hist. Manich.* LXVII, p. 31, l. 28, ed. Astruc *et al.* and Photius, *narratio* L, p. 137, l. 17, ed. *idem*.

103. *bibliotheca* 85 (125a, 25-28).

104. *Ibid.* (124a, 24-39) pp. 184-5.

105. *Ibid.* (124b, 35-7) p. 186. *Cf.* Hegem., *Arch.* VIII, 7, p. 13, ll. 11-12 (= Epiph., *haer.* LXVI 26, 8, p. 60, l. 10). On this see, *Mani-Fund*, p. 67.

106. *bibliotheca* 85 (124a, 25-125a, 9) pp. 185-6.

107. <Zach. Mit.>, *capita vii c. Manich.* II (47-8), p. xxxiv and Tim. Cpol., *haer. PG* 86.21C5.

108. *bibliotheca* 179 (124a, 36-b25), pp. 184-5.

109. *Ibid.* (124a, 21-3).

110. Aug., *conf.,* VII, ix, 13 (1-8) p. 101, xx, 26 (1-9) p. 109 etc.; *idem, c. acad.* I, 4, CSEL LXIII, pp. 5, l. 26-6, l. 17. *Cf.* Brown, *Augustine*, pp. 89-91.

111. See e.g. *Theosophia Tubingensis* 1, p. 95, ll. 1-8. *Cf.* Buresch, *Klaros*, pp. 44-7 and 50-51 and Lewy, *Chaldaean Oracles*, pp. 5-10. On Aristocritus, see p. 16, n. 41.

112. *Captia vii c. Manich.* VII (221-33) p. xxxix.

113. *Cf.* Brinkmann, 'Aristokritos', pp. 278-80.

114. Zosimus Panopolitanus περὶ ὀργάνων καί καμίνων IX, ed. Berthelot-Ruelle, *Collection*, II, p. 232. ll. 13-17.

115. *Cf.* Festugière, 'La révélation', I, p. 271, n. 7, and Reitzenstein, *Poimandres*, pp. 105-6, n. 10.

116. Or., *Cels.* VI, 80, GCS III, p. 151, ll. 22-5.

117. *Keph.* LXIX, pp. 166, l. 34-169, l. 22.

118. Procopius, *anecdota* XXII, 25, ed. Haury, iii/1, p. 138, ll. 13-17.

119. *coll.* XV, 3, 5, p. 581.

120. *Ibid.* XV, 2, 1, p. 579.

121. See e.g. Iohannes Scylitzes, *synopsis historiarum*, CFHB V, p. 92.

122. Lact., *de mort. persec.* X, 1-2, CSEL XXVII, p. 184, ll. 6-12. *Cf.* Frend, *Martyrdom*, p. 489.

123. *CT* XVI, 10, 1, p. 897, ed. Mommsen.

124. *Ibid.* XVI, 10, 5, p. 898. *Cf.* Noethlichs, *Massnahmen*, p. 57.

125. On this see esp. Brown, *Religion*, pp. 119-46 and Barb, 'The survival', pp. 100-25.

126. Ll. 33-5, p. 42.

127. See e.g. *P. Oslo* 1, l. 323 (= *Papyri Graecae Magicae*, II, ed. Preizendanz, rev. Henrichs, p. 174).

128. *haer.* XXVI, 4, 8, GCS XXV (Epiph., i) p. 281, ll. 13-17.

129. See e.g. Amm. Marc. XXXI, 14, 5, ii, p. 195, 10-16.

130. See esp. the material from Amm. Marc. collected together in Funke, 'Majestäts', *passim*.

131. Amm. Marc. XXIX, 2, 9.

132. *Cf.* Macmullen, *Enemies*, p. 131.

133. Amm. Marc. XXIX, 1, 32, ii, p. 101, ll. 9-15; *cf.* Funke, *art. cit.*, p. 167.

134. *CT* XVI, 5, 3, p. 855. *Cf.* Noethlics, *Massnahmen*, p. 81; Kaden, 'Die

Edikte', p. 58, Funke, 'Majestäts', p. 88 and Decret, *L'Afrique*, l, pp. 212-13.

135. Soc. *h.e.* V, 2, 1, ed. Hussey, ii, pp. 574, l. 30-575, 37 and Soz., *h.e.*, VII, 1, 3, GCS, p. 302, ll. 13-15. *Cf.* Kaden, 'Die Edikte', p. 67.

136. *CT* XVI, 5, 5, p. 856. *Cf.* Homes-Dudden, *Ambrose*, I, pp. 191-2.

137. Soz., *h.e.* VII, 4, 3, p. 305, ll. 3-8. *Cf.* King, *Theodosius*, pp. 23-4.

138. *CT* XVI, 1, 2, p. 833.

139. Soc., *h.e.* V, 7, 4-8, ed. Hussey, ii, pp. 582-3 (14-32), Soz., *h.e.* VII, 5, 5-7, pp. 306, l. 21-307, l. 8.

140. *CT* XVI, 5, 6, pp. 856-7.

141. *Ibid.* XVI, 5, 7, pr., p. 857. *Cf.* Kaden, 'Die Edikte', pp. 60-61 and King, *Theodosius*, pp. 51-2.

142. *Cf.* Kaser, D *röm. Privatrecht* I, pp. 682-5 and Mommsen, *Röm. Strafrecht*, pp. 603-4.

143. *CT* XVI, 5, 7, 1, pp. 857, l. 11-858, l. 2.

144. *CT* I, 1, 3, p. 27.

145. *CT* XVI, 5, 7, 1, p. 858, l. 2. *Cf. Rescriptum Constantini de quadraginta annorum praescriptione*, l. 23-5, *FIRA* I, p. 465.

146. *CT* XVI, 5, 7, 3, p. 858, ll. 5-13.

147. *Ibid.* XVI, 7, 1, p. 884.

148. *Ibid.* XVI, 7, 3, pp. 884-5.

149. *Cf.* Baus, *Handbook*, I, pp. 236-7 and Brown, *Religion*, p. 112.

150. *Long Abjuration Formula*, *PG* 1.1469D (= Adam, *Texte*, 64, p. 103). *Cf.* de Stoop, *Essai*, p. 46 and Decret, *Aspects*, p. 333.

151. Greg. Nyss., *ep. can.* (can. 1-2), *PG* 45.2256.

152. *CT* XVI, 5, 9, 1, p. 858, ll. 11-13.

153. *Cf.* Plinius Secundus, *ep.* X, 97, 2. *Cf.* Sherwin-White, *Letters*, p. 712.

154. *CT* X, 10, 1 and 2, p. 540.

155. Under the High Empire, informers could hope to gain a quarter of the victim's confiscated property in the event of a successful prosecution. *Cf.* Tacitus, *annales* IV, 20.

156. *CT*, *Gesta Senatus* 5, p. 2, l. 49.

157. *CT* IX, 16, 1, p. 459, ll. 9-10.

158. Greg. Turon., *Mirac.* II, 4, *PL* 71.804, cited in Homes-Dudden, *Ambrose* I, p. 1.

159. Sulp. Sev., *chron.* II, 51, 2-3, CSEL I, p. 104, ll. 5-11 and Pacatus, *panegyricus Theodosio dictus* XXIX, 3, ed. Galletier, iii, p. 96, ll. 1-13. *Cf.* Giradet, 'Trier 385', pp. 587-603.

160. 'Collectio Avellana', *ep.* 40, 3-4 CSEL XXXV/1, p. 91, ll. 14-27.

161. *haer.* LXI (33) 5, CSEL XXXVIII, p. 32, ll. 20-21. See also *ibid.* LXXXIV (56), 1, p. 45, ll. 18-22.

162. *haer.* LXX, 1 (1-5), p. 333 and 2 (26-30), p. 334.

163. *Cf.* Babut, *Priscillian*, pp. 2-4 and 253-90; Chadwick, *Priscillian*, pp. 62-99 and *PW* (Suppl. XIV), *s.v.* 'Priscillianus', cols. 523, l. 55-526, l. 44 (Vollmann).

164. See e.g. Priscillianus, *tract.* VI, CSEL XVIII, pp. 75, l. 18-76, l. 5 and 77, l. 24-78, l. 3 and *trac.* X, p. 93, ll. 1-4 and 93, l. 16, *Cf.* Babut, *Priscillien*, pp. 253-63 and Gasparro, 'Des influences', pp. 321-2.

165. Turribius Asturicensis, *ep. ad Idacium et Ceporium* 5, *PL* 54.694 and Orosius, *commonitorium*, CSEL XVIII, p. 154, ll. 4–5. *Cf. NT Apoc*, I, p. 265-7.

166. Priscillianus, *tract.* III, pp. 44–56. *Cf.* Gasparro, 'Des influences', pp. 323-5.

167. Aug., *c. Faust.* XXX, 4, p. 751, l. 24–752, l. 5 and XII, 79, pp. 681, l. 11–682. l. 1. *Cf.* Nagel, 'Apostelakten', pp. 174–82.

168. Priscillianus, *tract.* II, pp. 40, l. 27–41, l. 2. *Cf.* Babut, *Priscillien*, pp. 147–57 and esp. Giradet, *Trier 385*, pp. 581–5.

169. Priscillianus, *tract.* I, p. 22, 13–17. *Cf.* de Stoop, *Essai*, pp. 91–2.

170. Priscilliànus, *tract.* I, p. 17, ll. 29–30.

171. Theod. b. Kōnī, *Lib. Schol.* XI, p. 317, 9–15.

172. Priscillianus, *tract.* I, p. 22, l. 19–23, l. 4.

173. Sulp. Sev., *chron.* II, 48, 4–6, p. 101, ll. 20–30.

174. *Ibib.*, II, 49, 5–8, p. 102, ll. 13–24; *idem, vita S. Martini*, XX, 1, CSEL I, pp. 128, l. 23–129, l. 7 and *idem, dial.* II (III), 11, 10–11, CSEL I, pp. 209, l. 21–210, l. 3. *Cf.* Homes-Dudden, *Ambrose*, I, p. 232 and Chadwick, *Priscillian*, pp. 144–5.

175. Sulp. Sev., *chron.* II, L, 8, p. 103, ll. 25–31.

176. Priscillianus, *ep. (frag.), ap.* Orosius, *commonitorium* pp. 153, l. 11–154, l. 5. *Cf.* Aug., *haer* LXX, 1 (13–19). On this see esp. Chadwick, *Priscillian*, p. 192.

177. *Keph.* LXIX, pp. 166, l. 34–169, l. 22. *Cf.* Stegemann, 'Zu Kap. 69 der Keph.', pp. 214–23.

NOTES TO CHAPTER V

1. Aug., *conf.* III, vi, 10 (1–9), CCSL XXVII, p. 31.

2. On Augustine as a Manichaean Hearer see esp. Decret, *Aspects*, pp. 27–38, Brown, *Augustine*, pp. 40–114, Pelligrino, *Les Confessions*, pp. 83–144, Courcelle, *Recherches*, pp. 60–92, Alfaric, *L'Evolution*, pp. 79–225 and Coyle, *Aug.'s 'De mor. eccl.'*, pp. 50–57.

3. Aug., *conf.* III, v, 9 (5–10), pp. 30–31. *Cf.* Hieron., *ep.* 22, 30, 2, CSEL LIV, pp. 189, l. 17–190, l. 1.

4. Aug., *conf.* IV, ix, 13 (11–12), p. 47.

5. *Ibid.*, III, x, 18 (5–9), p. 37. *Cf. Keph.* LXXXI, pp. 193, l. 24–197, l. 34.

6. Aug., *util. cred.*, I, 2, CSEL XXV/1, p. 4, ll. 14–19.

7. *Idem, beat. vit.* I, 4, CSEL LXIII, p. 91, ll. 19–22.

8. *c. Manich. opinion.* 5, p. 8, ll. 11–20, ed. Brinkmann.

9. M2 R I 20–26, *MM ii*, p. 302, *cf. MMTKGI*, p. 17. See also M216c V 8–13, *MMTKGI* (181–7), 2.5, p. 26.

10. Aug., *util. cred.* I, 2, pp. 4, l. 28–5, l. 1 and 5, ll. 11–16.

11. *Ibid.* VII, 20, p. 24, ll. 20–23. On the personality and other biographical details of Faustus see Decret, *Aspects*, pp. 51–70, Brückner, *Faustus*, pp. 1–18 and Monceaux, *Faustus*, pp. 1–14.

12. The fragments are collected in Monceaux, *Faustus*, pp. 45–111. On the problem of reconstituting the *'Apologia'* of Faustus see esp. Decret,

Aspects, pp. 64–7.

13. See Ch. VI, n. 18.

14. Aug., *c. Faust.* VIII, 1, pp. 305, l. 20–306, l. 5. On the Manichaean criticism of the Old Testament see esp. Alfaric, *L'Evolution*, pp. 174–92 and Decret, *Aspects*, pp. 123–49.

15. Aug., *c. Fuast.* I, 2, p. 252, ll. 1–3. *Cf.* Lieu, 'Byz. Formula', p. 194 and Brückner, *Faustus*, pp. 42–3, n. 2.

16. Aug., *c. Faust.* XXII, 5, pp. 594, l. 8–5 as, l. 21.

17. *Ibid.*, X, 1, p. 310, ll. 18–20.

18. *Ibid.* XXXII, 1, pp. 760, l. 24–761, l. 3. See also XXII, 2, p. 592, ll. 9–19.

19. *Ibid.*, VI, 1, p. 284, ll. 12–19.

20. *Ibid.*, XIX, 3, p. 498, ll. 21–2. On Seth in Manichaeism see *Ps.-Bk.*, p. 142, ll. 4–9 and *Hom.* p. 61, l. 23 and 68, ll. 17–19. *Cf.* Klijn, *Seth*, pp. 48–117, esp. 109.

21. *Cf.* Milik, *Books of Enoch*, pp. 298–317.

22. Aug., *c. Faust.* XII, 1, p. 329, ll. 3–4.

23. *Ibid.* XIII, 1, pp. 378, l. 28–379, l. 6.

24. *Ibid.* XIV, 1, p. 403, ll. 17–22.

25. *Ibid.* XVII, 1, p. 483, l. 17–484, l. 2.

26. *Ibid.* XXXIII, 3, p. 788, ll. 10–23.

27. *Ibid.* XVII, 1, p. 483, ll. 20–24.

28. On the pagan background of Nebridius and Honoratus see Aug., *conf.* IX, iii, 6 (22–3), p. 136 and *idem*, *util. cred.* I, 2, p. 5, ll. 7–11. *Cf.* Decret, *L'Afrique*, I, pp. 368–9 and 371–2.

29. Aug., *c. Faust.* XIX, 5, p. 501, ll. 1–17. *Cf.* Alfaric, *L'Évolution*, pp. 169–73.

30. *Cf.* Geffcken, *Komposition*, pp. 38–46 and *NT Apoc.* (Eng.), II, pp. 707–9.

31. *v. Porph.* LXXXV, 3–6, pp. 66–7, ed. Grégoire-Kugener.

32. *C. haer. ad Hypat.*, II, p. 208, ll. 21–9, trans. Mitchell; *ibid.*, p. xcviii.

33. Alex. Lyc., *c. Manich. opinion.* II, p. 5, ll. 2–8.

34. *Ibid.* VII, pp. 11, ll. 10–24 and 9, p. 15, ll. 2–8.

35. 51, p. 200, ll. 15–17, ed. Griffiths.

36. *Cf.* Troje, 'Zum begriff', pp. 98–102.

37. *c. Manich. opinion.* 5, p. 8, ll. 5–11. *Cf.* Reitzenstein, 'Alexander', pp. 196–8 and *idem*, 'Eine wertlose u. eine wertvolle Überlieferung', pp. 43–4.

38. Alex. Lyc., *c. Manich. opinion.* 10, p. 16, ll. 9–24.

39. *C. haer. ad Hypat.*, II, p. 210, ll. 8–23, trans. Mitchell, p. xcix.

40. *Corpus Hermeticum, Poimandres* IV, 3–4, ed. Nock and Festugière, i, p. 50, ll. 2–13.

41. Zosimus Panopolitanus, τὸ πρῶτον βιβλίον τῆς τελευταίας ἀποχῆς, 8, ed. Berthelot-Ruelle, *Collection des anciens alchemistes grecs*, ii, p. 245, ll. 6–7.

42. See esp. Libanius, or. XXX 'Pro Templis', ed. Foerster, iii, pp. 87–118 and Julianus Imp., *ep. et leges* 89b (Ad Theodorum sacerdotem de sacerdotibus), (288a–305d), pp. 128–46, ed. Bidez-Cumont. *Cf.* Geffcken, *Ausgang*, pp. 90–141.

43. *Cf. Reader.* p. 10 and Lieu, 'Byz. formula', pp. 206–8.

44. *Cf. W.-L.i*, pp. 36-7 and Rose, *Christologie*, pp. 66-76.

45. *Cf. Ps.-Bk.*, p. 121, l. 23.

46. Aug., *c. Faust.* XXXII, 7, p. 766, ll. 20-24.

47. *Ibid.*, XX, 2, p. 536, ll. 19-21.

48. Aug., *nat. bon.* 44, p. 881, ll. 1-5. See also sources cited in Decret, *Aspects*, p. 285, n. 1.

49. *Ps.-Bk.*, p. 54, ll. 19-30, trans. Allberry.

50. Aug., *c. Faust.* XX, 11, p. 550, ll. 14-19. *Cf.* Coyle, *Aug.'s 'De mor. eccl'.*, pp. 44-5.

51. *de fide c. Manich.* XXVIII, CSEL XXV/2, p. 964, ll. 7-10.

52. Aug., *conf.* III, xi, l. 19-xii, l. 21, pp. 37-9.

53. *Cf.* <Zach. Mit.> *capita vii c. Manich.* 4 (24-31), p. xxxvi.

54. Aug., *c. Faust.* XXIII, 1-3, pp. 707, l. 6-709, l. 27.

55. *Cf. NT Apoc.* (Eng.), I, pp. 370-88.

56. Aug., *c. Faust.* XXIII, 4, pp. 709, l. 28-710, l. 9.

57. *Ibid.* XXVI, 1-2, pp. 728, l. 13-730, l. 14.

58. *Ibid.* XXVI, 2, p. 730, ll. 17-18. *Cf.* Brückner, *Faustus*, pp. 59-60.

59. Aug., *c. Faust.* XXVI, 1, pp. 737, l. 27-738, l. 2.

60. *Ibid.* XXIX, 1, p. 744, ll. 1-5.

61. *Ibid.* XVI, 26, p. 470, ll. 22-4; reading *dicat* for *dicam*. *Cf.* Evans, *Augustine*, pp. 75-6.

62. On the Gnostic-Manichaean use of this verse se e.g. Ir., *haer.* III, 7, 1 ed. Harvey, ii, pp. 25-6, Hegem., *Arch.* XV, p. 24, ll. 22-30 and *Ps.-Bk*, p. 172, ll. 26-7.

63. Aug., *c. Faust.* XXI, 2, pp. 569, l. 19-570, l. 3. *Cf.* Decret, *Aspects*, p. 200, n. 5.

64. *Idem, util. cred.* I, 2, p. 4, ll. 21-2.

65. *Idem, de duab. anim.* 11, CSEL XXV/1, pp. 65, l. 19-66, l. 11.

66. *Idem, beat. vit.*, I, 4, p. 91, ll. 22-4.

67. *Idem, util. cred.* II, 4, p. 6, ll. 21-9.

68. *Ibid.* III, 5, pp. 7, l. 26-8, l. 6.

69. Secundinus, *ad Sanctum Augustinum ep.*, CSEL XXV/2, pp. 893, l. 6-895, l. 25.

70. *Ibid.*, pp. 896, l. 12-897, l. 6.

71. *Ibid.*, p. 899, ll. 4-7. *Cf.* Decret, *L'Afrique*, I, pp. 145-50 and Courcelle, *Recherches*, pp. 236-8. See also Aug., *retr.* II, 36, CSEL XXXVI, p. 143, ll. 5-18.

72. Aug., *de duab. anim.* XI, p. 65, ll. 21-3.

73. *Ibid.*, *conf.* IV, iii, l. 13-ix, l. 14, pp. 46-7.

74. *Cf.* Decret, *L'Afrique*, I, pp. 360 (Cornelius), 368-9 (Honoratus), 371-2 (Nebridius) and 373-4 (Romanianus).

75. Aug., *c. acad.* II, 2, 3, CSEL LXIII, p. 25, ll. 9-11.

76. *Idem*, conf. IV, viii, 13 (9-24), p. 47.

77. *Idem, c. Fort.* I, 3, CSEL XXV/1, pp. 84, l. 26-85, l. 3.

78. *Cf.* de Menasce, 'Augustin Manichéen', pp. 88-93 and Murray, *Symbols*, pp. 27-9.

79. *Cf.* Ries, 'Une version liturgique', pp. 41-49 and Decret, *L'Afrique*, II, pp. 87-8, n. 2.

80. Aug., *c. Faust.* XV, 5-6, pp. 425, ll. 4-6, 426, 7-12 and 428, ll. 5-16.

Cf. Brückner, *Faustus*, pp. 77-8 and Jackson, *Researches*, pp. 300-301.
   81. *Ps.-Bk.*, p. 136, ll. 13a-17a, 29-38 and 43-9. *Cf.* Puech, *Essais*, pp. 210-11.
   82. *Ps.-Bk.*, p. 2, ll. 6-20. See also *ibid.*, p. 138, ll. 28-55.
   83. Aug., *c. epist. fund.* 8, CSEL XXV/1, pp. 202, l. 7-203, l. 4. *Cf.* Allberry, 'Bema-Fest', pp. 2-3 and Ries, 'La fête de Bêma,' pp. 218-23.
   84. I, 1, ed. Alfaric, 'Manuscrit', pp. 64-5 (= *PL Suppl.* 2.1379).
   85. Aug., *conf.* IV, iv, 1 (9-11), p. 40.
   86. *Ibid.* (11-12), p. 40.
   87. *PL* 73.945. *Cf.* de Stoop, *Essai*, pp. 78-9.
   88. Aug., *mor. Manich.* XX, 74, *PL* 32.1376-7. See also *idem, c. Faust.* V, 5, p. 277, ll. 21-6.
   89. *Idem, conf.* III, xii, 21 (13-15), p. 39. *Cf. CMC* 123, 4-11 (*ZPE* 1982), p. 15.
   90. *Idem, conf.* V, x, 18-19 (1-34), pp. 67-8.
   91. *Ibid.* V, ix, 16 (16-18), p. 66. Cornelius, on the other hand, was baptised when he fell into a severe illness. *Cf.* Aug., *ep.* 259, 3, CSEL LVII, p. 613, ll. 6-7.
   92. Aug., *conf.* V, xiii, 23 (1-6), p. 70.
   93. See above note 88.
   94. Aug. *conf.* IV, i, 1 (4-5), p. 40 and III, i, 1 (2-3), p. 27.
   95. *Idem, mor. Manich.* XIX, 72, col. 1375. *Cf.* Decret, *L'Afrique*, I, pp. 212-15.
   96. *Idem, conf.* VI, xiv, 24 (9-11), p. 89. *Cf.* Brown, *Augustine*, p. 90 and 117.
   97. *Idem, mor. Manich.* XIX, 72, col. 1375.
   98. *Ibid.* XIX, 69 and 72, cold. 1374-5.
   99. *Idem, c. Faust.* XXIII, 1, p. 707, ll. 6-7 and *conf.* V, vi, 11 (28-31), p. 60. *Cf.* Pellegrino, *Les Confessions*, p. 128-30.
   100. Aug., *c. litt. Petil.* III, 25, 30, CSEL LII, p. 185, ll. 14-28. *Cf.* Frend, 'Manichaeism', pp. 859-66 and Courcelle, *Recherches*, pp. 238-45.
   101. Aug., *c. Faust.* V, 8, p. 280, ll. 19-22. *Cf.* Mommsen, *Röm. Strafrecht*, p. 600 and Brown, *Augustine*, p. 325.
   102. Hydatius, *chron.* 14 (Olymp. CCLXXXI B), SC 218, p. 108. *Cf.* Decret, *L'Afrique*, II, p. 165, n. 44.
   103. *C. haer. ad Hypat.*, I, p. 127, ll. 7-11, trans. Mitchell, p. xciii.
   104. Coptic: *Hom.*, p. 25, l. 5; Chin.: *MNKFCFIL*, p. 1280b22; Pth.: M 35 V 3-18; Henning, 'Book of the Giants', pp. 71-2. *Cf. Catalogue*, p. 4.
   105. M 216c + M1750 R 12, *MMTKGI* (173), 2.5, p. 26 and M2 R II 7, *MMii*, p. 303.
   106. M 5815 II R I (134-6), *MM iii*, p. 858.
   107. Firdausi, *Shâhnâmeh*, cited in Kessler, *Mani*, p. 375.
   108. Mirxond, cited in Klimkeit, *Art*, p. 18.
   109. Bayānu 'l-Adyān, cited in Haloun-Henning, 'Compendium', p. 210.
   110. M 801 33-4 (524-30), *BBB*, pp. 33-4.
   111. Ibrāhīm al-Sindi, *ap* Al-Gāhit, cited in Klimkeit, *Art*, p. 21.
   112. Aug., *c. Faust.* XIII, 6 and 18, pp. 384, ll. 11-14 and 400, ll. 10-13.
   113. Aug., *conf.* III, xii, 21 (13-17), p. 39.

114. *Cf.* Henrichs-Koenen, 'Mani-Codex', pp. 100-103.

115. Aug., *c. epist. fund.* XXI, pp. 218, l. 22-219, l. 2.

116. Libanius, *or.* I, 43 and 98, ed. Foerster, i/1, p. 105, ll. 5-13 and p. 131, ll. 7-13.

117. Aug., *conf.* IV, ii, 3 (16-20), p. 41.

118. *Ibid.* IV, iii, 4 (1-15), p. 41 and V, iii, 6 (58-61), pp. 59-60.

119. *Keph.* LXIX, pp. 166, l. 19-169, l. 22. On the interest of the Manichaeans in astrology see also Marutha Maipherkatensis, *Trac. de Haer.*, p. *q*, ll. 6-7. ed. Rahmani. On the other hand, the Manichaeans were expressly forbidden to dabble in the black arts. See, e.g., *Hom.*, p. 30, l. 3, $X^u\bar{a}stv\bar{a}n\bar{i}ft$ VI B, 108-9, ed. Asmussen, p. 173 and al-Nadim, *Fihrist*, trans. Dodge, p. 789, Flügel, *Mani* p. 96. *Cf.* Colpe, *Der Man.* (Phil. Diss.), pp. 109-10 and *idem*, 'Die Formulierung', p. 410.

120. *Cf.* Gombrich, *Precept and Practice*, pp. 146-7.

121. Marc. Diac., *v. Porph.* 85, p. 67, ll. 16-19.

122. Aug., *conf.* V, iii, 6 (64-6), p. 60.

123. Alex. Lyc., *c. Manich. opinion.* XXII, p. 30, ll. 5-13, ed. Brinkmann.

124. *Cf.* Stegemann, 'Zu Kap. 69 der *Keph.*', pp. 218-19.

125. *Keph.* LXIX, p. 167, ll. 22-3. *Cf.* Stegemann, *art. cit., p. 217.*

126. *Keph.* LXIX, pp. 168, l. 17-169, l. 8. *Cf.* Stegemann, *art. cit.*, p. 221.

127. *Keph.* LXIX, pp. 168, l. 26-169, l. 8.

128. *Cf.* Stegemann, *art. cit.*, pp. 221-2 and Widengren, *Mani*, pp. 73-5.

129. Aug., *mor. eccl.* I, 2, *PL* 32.1311. On Manichaean asceticism see esp. Vööbus, *Hist. Asc.*, I, pp. 114-30 and Coyle, *Aug.'s De mor. eccl.*, pp. 194-201.

130. *Ps.-Bk.*, p. 175, ll. 12-30.

131. Aug., *c. Faust.* V, 1, p. 271, ll. 8-24. *Cf.* Schaeder, 'Urform', pp. 132-4 and Böhlig, *Die Bibel bei den Manich.* (Inaug. Diss.), pp. 21-21a.

132. *C. haer. ad Hypat.*, I, p. 184, ll. 28-32, trans. Mitchell, p. cxix. *Cf.* Beck, *Ephräms Polemik*, p. 24.

133. *Hymni 56 c. haer.* XXIII, 7, 5-10, CSCO CLXIX, p. 88, ll. 21-6. *Cf.* Vööbus, *Hist. Asc.*, I, p. 163.

134. *Hymni 56 c. haer.* I, 12, 3-4, pp. 3, l. 26-4, l. 1.

135. *Ibid.* L, 8, 4-6, p. 185, ll. 17-19.

136. Eutychius, *Annales*, ed. Cheikho, CSCO L, p. 148, 2 ff. *Cf.* Colpe, *Der Man.* (Phil. Diss.), pp. 224-5. See also Schaeder, 'Review of *Mani-Fund*', p. 342. I am grateful to Mrs (Dr.) S. and Dr G. Stroumsa for an English translation of this important passage from the Arabic.

137. *P. Ryl. Gk.* 469, p. 42, l. 12-13, ed. Roberts.

138. Didym., *comm. in Eccles.* 9, 9a (274, 18-275, 2), pp. 8-10, ed. Grünewald.

139. *CMC* 89, 9 (*ZPE* 1978), p. 109. See esp. comm. *ad loc.* (pp. 168-9).

140. *Cf.* Koenen, 'Manichaische Mission', pp. 99-105.

141. Ath., *v. Anton.* 68, *PG* 26.940B.

142. Epiph., *haer.* 67, GCS XXXVII (Epiph. iii), pp. 132-40. See also *Acta SS. Macariorum Aegyptii et Alexandrini*, *PG* 34.214B/C.

143. *Cf. NHL* (Eng.), ed. Robinson, p. 406.

144. See e.g. Petr. Sic., *hist. Manich.* LXVII, p. 31, ll. 27-8, ed. Astruc *et*

al. and Photius, *narr.* 50, p. 137, ll. 15–16, ed. *idem.* See other sources cited in Lieu, 'Byz. Formula', p. 197. See also Wisse, 'Gnosticism', p. 439.

145. *Annales*, p. 146, l. 20 ff. *Cf.* Colpe, *Der Man.* (Phil. Diss.), p. 224. See above, note 126.

146. *Cf.* Stroumsa, 'Monachisme', p. 187.

147. Aug., *conf.* VI, xii, 21 (3–7), p. 87.

148. *Idem, ep.* 259, 3, p. 613, ll. 3–8.

149. *Idem, conf.* V, x, 18 (6–12), p. 67.

150. *Ibid.*, VIII, vi, 15 (43–86), pp. 122–3.

151. Hieron. *ep.* 127, 5, 1, CSEL LVI, pp. 149, l. 5–150, l. 21.

152. *Ibid.* 108, 4, 1, CSEL LV, p. 309, ll. 12–20.

153. *Ibid.* XXII, 13, 3–5, p. 161, ll. 4–6.

154. *in ep. ad Tim. ii* 3, 6–7, 2, CSEL LXXXI/3, pp. 311, l. 27–312, l. 24.

155. Hieron., *adv. Jovin.* I, 40, *PL* 23.280.

156. *Ibid.*, I, 3–5, cols. 222–8. See esp. 227C/D.

157. Ambros., *ep.* 15 (42), 12 (120–25), CSEL LXXXII, pp. 309–10.

158. *Ibid.* 13 (129–36), p. 310. On Jovinian see esp. Homes-Dudden, *Ambrose* II, pp. 393–8.

159. Aug., *c. Fort.* 21, p. 103, ll. 13–16.

160. *Ibid. conf.* VII, v, 7 (21–9), p. 96.

161. See esp. *Keph.* VI, pp. 30, l. 17–34, l. 12. *Cf.* Puech, *Essais*, pp. 106–9. Mani did, however, affirm that evil did not come from God even if he did not discuss the problem of theodicy on a philosophical level. *Cf. Keph.* CXII, p. 267, ll. 11–18.

162. Aug., *util. cred.*, XVIII, 36, p. 46, ll. 17–18.

163. Tit. Bos., *adv. Manich.* 2, 4–24, (Gk.) pp. 27, l. 20–42, l. 30.

164. M 183 I R 1–12, *KPT* (1174–87), 11, p. 62.

165. Aug., *in Joh. Evang. tract.* I, 14 (5–22), CCSL CXXIV, p. 8.

166. Tert., *adv. Marc.* II, 4, 1–8, 3, pp. 95–111, ed. Evans.

167. Ps.-Victoriunus, *Liber ad Justinum Manichaeum*, PL 8.999–1010. *Cf.* Monceaux, *Histoire*, III, p. 399.

168. Aug., *conf.* V, xi, 21 (4–11), p. 69.

169. *Ibid.* VII, ii, 3 (1–6), p. 93.

170. *Ibid.* V, xiii, 23–VI, i, 1, pp. 63–74.

171. *Ibid.* VII, ix, 13–xvii, 23, pp. 98–107 and *beat.vit.* I, 4, *PL* 32.961.

172. Aug., *conf.* VIII, vi, 14–xii, 30, pp. 121–32 and *mor. eccl.* XXXIII, 70, *PL* 32. 1339–40. *Cf.* Courcelle, *Recherches*, pp. 227–9 and Coyle, *Aug.'s 'De mor. eccl.'*, pp. 193–240.

NOTES TO CHAPTER VI

1. Aug., *retr.* I, 15 (16), 1, CSEL XXXVI, p. 82, l. 6. *Cf.* Decret, *Aspects*, pp. 39–50.

2. Poss., *v. Aug.*, 6, pp. 50, ll. 12–15, ed. Weisskoten.

3. Aug., *c. Fort.*, prol., CSEL XXV/1, p. 83, ll. 3–6, *idem, retr.* I, 15 (16), p. 82, ll. 4–8 and Poss., *v. Aug.* 6, pp. 50, l. 27–52, l. 1.

4. Aug., *c. Fort.* I, 1–3, pp. 84, l. 7–86, l. 2.

5. See e.g., *ibid.* I, 8, p. 88, ll. 11–12; 10, p. 89, ll. 7–8.

6. *Ibid.* I 7, p. 87, ll. 7–18, II, 23, p. 108, ll. 4–5; 26, p. 109, ll. 2–3; 30, p. 110, ll. 19–20 etc.

7. *Idem, retr.* I, 15 (16) 1, p. 83, ll. 13–14.

8. Marc. Diac., *v. Porph.* 85 (1–7), pp. 66–7, ed. Grégoire–Kugener.

9. Soz., *h.e.* V, 3, 6–7, GCS L, p. 196, ll. 4–14.

10. Marc. Diac., *v. Porph.* 87–91, pp. 68–71. *Cf.* Burkitt, *Religion,* pp.7–11.

11. Cyr. S., *v. Euthym.* 12, pp. 22, l. 11–23, l. 3, ed. Schwartz.

12. *CT* XVI, 5, 11, p. 859.

13. *historia monachorum in Aegypto* X, 30–35 (190–225), pp. 87–9, ed. Festugière. *Cf.* Rufinus, *historia monachorum* 9, *PL* 21.426C–27B.

14. 'Enaniso' monachus, *Paradisum Patrum,* ed. Budge, ii, Syr. text, p. 416, l. 9.

15. *CT* XVI, 5, 35, p. 866.

16. Aug., *c. Fel.* I, 12, CSEL XXV/2, p. 815, ll. 17–22. On the background to the debate see esp. Decret, *Aspects,* pp. 71–89.

17. Aug., *ep.* 79, CSEL XXXIV, pp. 345, l. 11–346, l. 22.

18. *Idem, c. Fel.* I, 12, p. 815, ll. 18–20.

19. *Ibid.* I, 12, pp. 814, l. 29–815, l. 2.

20. *Ibid.* I, 19–20, p. 826, ll. 1–8 and II, 1, p. 828, ll. 11–13.

21. *Ibid.,* p. 828, ll. 14–19.

22. *Ibid.,* I, 12, p. 813, ll. 14–16.

23. *Ibid.,* II, 9, p. 838, ll. 26–9.

24. *Ibid.,* II, 14, pp. 843, ll. 8–844, l. 6.

25. *Ibid.,* II, 22, p. 852, ll. 18–26. *Cf.* Lieu, 'Byz. formula', p. 154.

26. *v. Aug.* 16. pp. 76, l. 25–78, l. 2.

27. CSEL XXV/2, pp. 979–82. *Cf.* Ries, 'Introduction (2)', p. 408.

28. *Const. Sirm.* 12, p. 917, ed. Mommsen and Meyer (*cf. CT*).

28a. Aug., *haer.* XLVI, 9 (67–80), p. 315.

29. *Ibid.* (81–3), p. 315.

30. Ps.-Aug., *commonitorium, prol.,* p. 979, ll. 5–11.

31. *Ibid.* 10, p. 982, ll. 11–19. *Cf.* Lieu, 'Byz. formula', pp. 217–18 and Brown, *Religion,* p. 111.

32. *Cf.* Brown, *Religion,* p. 312.

33. Text in Mai, *Nova Patrum Bibliotheca,* I, pp. 282–3 (= *PL Suppl.* 2.1389). *Cf.* Lieu and Lieu, 'Felix', pp. 173–6.

34. *vita Rabulae,* pp. 192, l. 3–194, l. 2, ed. Overbeck. *Cf.* Blum, *Rabbula,* pp. 96–101, Segal, *Edessa,* pp. 91–2 and Bauer, *Rechtgläubigkeit²,* pp. 31–2. See also the more emphatic entry on Rabbula's role as an agent of the imperial authorities in the suppression of the Jews (or Audians?) in Edessa in *Chronicon Edessenum* LI, CSCO I, p. 6, ll. 21–5.

35. Ibas Edessenus, *ep. ad Marim Persam,* in *ACO* II, 1, 3, p. 33 [392], l. 26. *Cf.* Lieu, 'Holy Men', pp. 118–9.

36. *CT* XVI, 5, 3, p. 855.

37. *Ibid.* XVI, 5, 40, 7, p. 868.

38. For Egypt see e.g. *P. Oslo* 111 (235) cited in MacMullen, 'Imperial Bureaucrats', p. 310 and for Africa see Haywood, 'Africa', in Frank, *Economic Survey,* IV, p. 115 and 118.

39. Aug., *ep.* 236, CSEL XLIV, pp. 523, l. 21–525, l. 4. *Cf.* Decret, *L'Afrique*, I pp. 376–7.

40. Vict. Vit., *hist. pers.* 3, 10–11, CSEL VII, pp. 76, l. 14–77, l. 4. This is modelled on *CT* XVI, 5, 52, pp. 872–3. *Cf.* Tengstrom, *Donatisten*, pp. 27–30.

40a. Vict. Vit., *hist. pers.* 2, 1–2 , p. 24, ll. 7–14.

41. Gregorius II Papa, *ep.* 7, *PL* 89.502.

42. al-Nadim, *Fihrist*, trans. Dodge, p. 793, *Flügel*, Mani, pp. 98–100. *Cf.* Decret, *L'Afrique*, I, pp. 232–53.

43. *lib. pontif.* XXXIII, 2, ed. Duchesne, i, p. 168, ll. 3–4.

44. *Ibid.*, XL, 3; i, p. 216, ll. 4–8.

45. *Ibid.* XLI, 2, p. 218, ll. 2–5.

46. *CT* XVI, 5, 62, p. 877.

47. Leo M., tract. XVI, 4 (79–99), CCSL CXXXVIII, p. 64. *Cf.* Jalland, *Leo*, pp. 43–50, van der Lof, 'Man. Verbeugungen', pp. 156–60, Lauras, 'Saint Leon', pp. 203–9 and Decret, *L'Afrique*, I, p. 230 and II, pp. 183–4, n. 139.

48. *Leges Novellae Valentiniani* 18, pp. 103–5, see esp. prol., p. 104, ll. 5–7.

49. Leo M., *tract.* IX, 4 (97–101), p. 37.

50. *Idem, ep.* 7, *PL* 54.620B–22A and *ep.* 8, cols. 622B–24A (= *Leges Novellae Valentiniani* 18, pp. 103–5).

51. Leo M., *tract.* XLII, 5 (196–205) CCSL CXXXVIIIA, pp. 247–8.

52. Prosper, *chron.* 1350 (*sub anno* 443), p. 479, *MGH* (Auct. Ant.).

53. Thdt., *ep.* 113, SC CXI, p. 58, ll. 12–15.

54. Hydatius, *chron.* (Olymp. CCCVIB) 130 and 138, pp. 140–42 (= Vollman, *Studien*, Q 46 and 49, p. 64).

55. *CT* XVI, 2, 23, p. 842. *Cf.* Ensslin, 'Valentinianus III', pp. 373–8.

56. *Constitutiones Sirmondianae* 6, pp. 911–12.

57. *ep.* 15, praef. 10 (43–8), ed. Vollmann, *Studien*, p. 124.

58. *Cf.* Brown, *Religion*, p. 316 and Conrat, *Römisches Recht*, p. 803.

59. *lib. pontif.* LI, ed. Duchesne, i, p. 255, ll. 2–3.

60. *Ibid.* LIII, 5, p. 261, ll. 8–9.

61. *Ibid.* LIX, 9, pp. 270, l. 20–271, l. 1.

62. *Libellus appellationis Eutychis ad Papem Leonem, ACO* II, 2, 1, p. 34, ll. 20–25.

63. See e.g. Severus Antiochenus, *Ep. tom. vi* V, 6, ed. Brooks, i/2, p. 358, ll. 7–8.

64. Zach. Mit., *h.e.* 15, 16, CSCO LXXXIV, p. 128, ll. 15–17.

65. *Hom.* CXXIII, PO XXIX, pp. 148 (652)–188 (692).

66. *Acta Concilii Constantinopoli anno 536 sub Mena* IV, *PO* II, p. 349, ll. 5–11.

67. Evag., *h.e.* III, 32, p. 130, ll. 10–12, ed. Bidez–Parmentier. See also Zach. Mit., *h.e.* VII, 7, CSCO LXXXIII, p. 40, ll. 6–7 and Theophanes, *chron.* A.M. 5983, p. 136, ll. 13–16 and 5999, pp. 149, l. 28–150, l. 1.

68. *CJ* I, 5, 11, p. 53. *Cf.* Jarry, *Hérésies*, pp. 335–6.

69. <Zach. Mit.>, *capita vii c. Manich.* IV–V (107–35) p. xxxvi.

70. Ps.-Acacius, *ep. ad Petrum (Fullonem) episc. Ant., ACO* III, p. 18, ll. 14–18.

71. *Frag. ep. ad. Addam, ap.* Eust. Mon., *ep., PG* 86.904A (= *Texte*, p. 33).

72. *Frag. ep. ad. Scythianum*, *ap.* Eust. Mon., *ep.* col. 903B.

73. Justn., *monoph.* 89–92, pp. 38, l. 30–40, l. 2, ed. Schwartz; rev. Amelotti, and Eulogius, *ap.* Photius, *bibl.* 230 (273a41–68) ed. Henry, v, pp. 26–7.

74. Aug., *c. Jul. op. impf.* III, 166, *PL* 45.1316.

75. *Ibid.* III, cols. 1318–27 (= *Texte*, pp. 31–2). *Cf.* Aalders, 'L'Épitre', pp. 245–9.

76. *Cf.* Brown, *Augustine*, p. 370. See also Alfaric, *Les écritures*, II, p. 74.

77. *CJ* I, 5, 12, 2–3, p. 53. *Cf.* Theophanes, *chron.* A.M. 6016, p. 171, ll. 2–3.

78. Zach. Mit., *adv. Manich. (Antirrēsis)*, prol., pp. γ'–δ', ed. Demetrakopoulos.

79. *Cf.* Honigmann, 'Zacharias of Mitylene', p. 200.

80. *disp. Phot.*, *PG* 88.529A–551C. *Cf.* Mercati, 'Per la vita', pp. 184–7, 198–203 and Ries, 'Introduction (2)', p. 400 and Jarry, *Hérésies*, pp. 210–12 and 331–9.

81. Paul. Pers., *inst.*, pp. 467, l. 11–468, l. 4, ed. Kihn.

82. *Ibid.* pp. 468, ll. 11–12.

83. Mansi, ix, col. 199.

84. [*Chronicon Ecclesiae Arbelae*] 20ᵉ év. Hnana, 48–9, p. 75. *Cf.* Vööbus, *Hist. Sch. Nisbis*, pp. 170–72.

85. Barhebraeus, *Chron. Eccl.* III, ed. Abbeloos and Lamy, i, col. 79. For *Pauli Persae Logica* see Land, *Anecdota Syriaca*, IV, pp. 1–30.

86. *Catalogus Librorum omnium ecclesiasticorum* 65, ed. Assemani, *Bibl. Or.* III/1, pp. 87–8.

87. *Cf.* Vööbus, *Hist. Sch. Nisibis*, pp. 171–2.

88. Agathias, *hist.*, II, 31, 4, p. 81, ll. 15–16, ed. Keydell. *Cf.* Guillaumont, 'Justinien', pp. 47–50.

89. *disp. Phot.* I, *PG*, 88.529A–540B. *Cf.* Mercati, 'Per la vita', pp. 184–7 and 193–4.

90. *Ibid.* cols. 529A–832B.

91. *Ibid.* 532B–33A.

92. *Ibid.* 533A–36A.

93. *Ibid.* 533D–35B. *Cf.* Mercati, 'Per la vita', pp. 201–2.

94. *disp. Phot.* II–III, cols. 540B–52C.

95. *chron.* XVII, p. 423, ll. 16–18, CSHB.

95a. John of Nikiu, *Chronicle* XC, 55, trans. Charles, p. 139.

96. *Chron. Eccl.*, i, cols. 219–21.

97. *Long Abjuration Formula*, *PG* 1.1469C. *Cf.* Lieu, 'Byz. formula', p. 214.

98. *CJ* I, 5, 15, p. 55. ed. Krueger.

99. *Ibid.* I, 5, 16, pp. 55–6.

100. *Ibid.* I, 5, 18, 13, p. 58 and I, 5, 12, 22, p. 55.

101. *Ibid.* I, 5, 18, 12, p. 58.

102. Aug., *in evang. Joh.* XL, 7, cited in Brown, *Religion*, p. 114.

103. Ioh. Caes., *adv. Manich. Hom.* i–ii, CCSG I, pp. 85–105; Ioh. D., *Man.* I–II, See esp. Richard's comments in CCSG I, p. xlv.

104. See e.g. Petr. Sic. *hist. Manich.* 48–77, pp. 23, l. 28–35, l. 22, ed. Astruc *et al.*; Photius, *narr.* 38–53, pp. 131, l. 30–139, l. 15, ed. *idem*, and

Nicetas, *adv. Man.* 1, pp. 110–11, ed. Mai.
105. See Ch. IX.
106. *Cf.* Garsoïan, *Paulician Heresy*, pp. 189–203.
107. See Ch. III.
108. *Cf.* Garsoïan, *Paulician Heresy*, pp. 196–7.
109. See e.g. Ioh. D., *haer.* 101, *PG* 94.763A–65A.
110. *Cf.* Kaser, *Das röm Privatrecht*, II, p. 83.
111. See e.g. Michael Syrus, *chron.*, VI, 10, pp. 117, col. 1, ll. 35–118, col. 3, l. 7. See also *Chronicon Maroniticum*, CSCO I, pp. 59, ll. 24–60, l. 9. *Cf.* Bauer, *Rechtgläubigkeit²*, p. 44.
112. Ed. Scheltama, Ser. B, ii, p. 1268, schol. 3. *Cf.* Georg. Mon. et Presb., *de haer. ad Epiph.* I, 1–2, p. 350, ll. 5–21, ed. Richard; Georg. Mon., *chron.* XLIII, ed. de Boor, ii, pp. 467, l. 20–470, l. 9 and *Suidae Lexicon*, *s.v.* Μάνης, ed. Adler, iii, pp. 318, l. 14–319, l. 18.
113. Seven out of the eleven laws in *Basilica* I, 1 are repetitions of Justinianic laws against Manichaeans. *Cf.* Kaden, 'Die Edikte', p. 66.
114. VI, 11, 7–8, p. 768, ed. Juristic Faculty of the Univ. of Thessaloniki.
115. *Ibid.* VI, 11, 8, p. 768.
116. *Ibid.* VI, 11, 6.
117. *Cf.* Avi-Yonah, *Geschichte*, p. 254 and Frend, *Monophysite Movement*, pp. 304–7.
118. *Cf.* Scharf, *Byz. Jewry*, pp. 31–3.
119. E.g. Leo VI (886–912), *cf.* Scharf, *Byz. Jewry*, pp. 93–4.
120. Mommsen, *Röm. Strafrecht*, p. 123.
121. *Cf.* Lear, *Treason*, p. 72.

NOTES TO CHAPTER VII

1. On Bagard see Bailey, *Zoroastrian Problems*, p. 67.
2. M2 R II 16–V II 27, *MM ii*, pp. 303–5 (= *Reader*, h, 4–9, pp. 40–42).
3. *MMTKGI* (99–123) 2.2, pp. 22–3. *Cf.* Sundermann, 'Lebensbesch-reibungen', p. 130.
4. See Ch. III.
5. M1 166–9, *Mahrnamag*, p. 16 (= *Reader*, s, 1, p. f2).
6. M801a 214–67, *BBB* pp. 24–5 (= *Reader*, cu, 22–6, pp. 156–7).
7. Arrianus, *anabasis* III, 18, 4–19, 3.
8. Henning, 'Mitteliranisch', p. 54.
9. *Cf.* Livšic, *Sogdijskie Dokumenty s Gory Mug*, II, R 2–3, p. 94.
10. *Cf.* Dubs, *History of the Former Han Dynasty*, II, pp. 132–5, On the location of Ta-yüan see Pulleyblank, *Chinese and Indo-Europeans*, p. 31.
11. *Cf.* Henning, 'Sogdian Ancient Letters', P. 607.
12. *Ibid.*, p. 605.
13. *Wei-shu* 102.2270.
14. *Cf.* Maenchen-Helfen, 'Pseudo-Huns', pp. 101–6.
15. Amm. Marc. XIX, 1, 17; i, p. 156, l. 12. *Cf.* Enoki Kazuo, 'Sogudeiana to Kyōdo', pp. 757–80.
16. Proc., *Pers.* I, 4, 14–16, ed. Haury, i, pp. 16, l. 14–17, l. 10.

17. Frye, *Heritage*, pp. 226-7. See also Miyakawa–Kollautz 'Abdelai', *RL Byz*, Ser. A. 1, cols. 88-126.

18. *Cf.* Hsia Nai, 'Ho-pei Ting-hsien t'a-chi', pp. 267-70, Göbl, *Dokumente*, II, pp. 112-25. and Chang Hsing-liang, *Chung-hsi chiao-tung* IV, pp. 60-61.

19. *Wei-shu, loc. cit.*

20. *Sung-shu* 95.2357-58.

21. Hsia Nai, 'Tsung-shu', pp. 91-110.

22. *Cf.* Chung Hsing-liang, *Chung-hsi chiao-tung*, IV, pp. 60-61.

23. Nei mung-ku wen-wu kung-tso-tui, 'Huo-ho-hao-te', pp. 182-3.

24. *Cf.* Harmatta, 'Oldest Evidence', pp. 650-84.

25. *Kao-seng chuan* I, 6, p. 325a.

26. *Cf.* Asmussen, *X^uāstvānīft*, pp. 141-3.

27. *Cf.* Wright, 'Fo-t'u-têng', pp. 22-3.

28. *Cf.* Kljastornyi and Livšic, 'Sogdian inscription', p. 79.

29. *T'ung-tien* 193.1039b. On Wei Chich's mission to the west, see *Sui-shu* 83.1841.

30. On Manichaean Bactrian, see Boyce, 'Manichaean Literature', p. 68. On Manichaean texts in Tocharian, see von Gabain–Winter, *TTT* ix, p. 8.

31. *Cf.* Frye, *Golden Age*, p. 43.

32. *Ta T'ang Ta tz'u-en ssu San-tsang fa-shih chüan*, p.227e.

33. *Cf.* Frumkin, *Archaeology*, p. 52 and Zürcher, 'Yueh-chih', pp. 346-90.

34. M48 and M5815 in particular contain a large number of Buddhist terms. See the general remarks in Markwart, *Wehrot*, p. 95.

35. *Cf.* Frye, 'Significance', p. 37-8.

36. *Kao-seng chuan*, I, 3, p. 323a, *Cf.* Ikemoto Jushin, 'Amita', pp. 443-56, esp. 446.

37. *Cf.* Lang, 'St Euthymius', pp. 306-25 and Asmussen, 'Vermittler', pp. 14-21.

38. *Ta T'ang hsi-yü chi* 11.938a. *Cf. Traité* 1913, p. 150 [174].

39. Theophanes, *chron.* AM 6103, p. 299, ll. 31-2, 6105, p. 300, ll. 20-27, 6106, pp. 300, l. 30-301, l. 5, 6107-8, p. 301, ll. 9-19. See also *Chronicon Anonymum*, CSCO 1, pp. 25, ll. 1-7.

40. Menander Protector, *ap.* Constantine Porphyrogenitus, *Excerpta de legationibus gentium* 7 (frag. 18) p. 450, ll. 3-10, ed. de Boor. *Cf.* Hannested, 'Les rélations', pp. 421-56 and Chavannes, *Documents*, pp. 233-5.

41. *Cf.* Schaeder, 'Der Manichäismus und sein Weg nach Osten', p. 251 and Pigulevskaja, *Byzanz*, p. 164.

42. 150, ed. Adler, ii, p. 319, ll. 2-23.

43. *Alexiados* VIII, 4, 2, ed. Leib, ii, p. 136, l. 18.

44. *Ibid.* V, 8, 2, p. 33, l. 15. *Cf.* Moravisik, *Byzantinoturcica* II, p. 181.

45. Menander Protector, 7, pp. 450, l. 15-451, l. 26, ed. de Boor.

46. *Ibid.* 7-8 (frags. 18 and 21) pp. 451, l. 26-453, l. 22. *Cf.* Pigulevskaja, *Byzanz*, p. 116.

47. *hist.* VII, 9, 1-12, pp. 260, l. 25-262, l. 14. ed. de Boor. *Cf.* Haussig, 'Theophylacts Exkurs', pp. 285-6 and 387-99 and Boodberg, 'Marginalia', pp. 223-4.

48. *Cf.* Hsia Nai, 'Hsien-yang ti', pp. 135–42.
49. *Cf.* Franke, *Geschichte*, II, pp. 355, l. 29–365, l. 19.
50. *Chiu T'ang-shu* 198.5312–13.
51. *Hsin T'ang-shu* 2218.6251–52.
52. *Cf.* Schafer, 'Iranian merchants', pp. 407–9.
53. *Cf.* Sundermann and Thilo, 'Grabinschrift', p. 439.
54. *Fihrist*, trans. Dodge, pp. 802–3; Flügel, *Mani*, pp. 105–6.
55. *Cf.* Boulnois, *La route de soïe*, pp. 97–9.
56. *Cf.* Spuler, 'Die Uiguren', p. 153.
57. *Fihrist*, trans. Dodge, pp. 802–3; Flügel, *Mani*, p. 106.
58. *Cf.* Frumkin, *Archaeology*, pp. 79–80.
59. *Cf.* Frye, 'Tarxun', p. 107.
60. *Sui-shu* 67.1582. *Cf.* Liu Mau-tsai, *Nachrichten*, p. 87.
61. *Cf.* Henning, 'Magical texts', p. 49 and *idem*, *Sogdica*, pp. 12–14.
62. al-Nadim, *Fihrist*, trans. Dodge, p. 794, Flügel, Mani, p. 99. *Cf.* Maenchen-Helfen, 'Manichaeans in Siberia', pp. 321–6.
64. M6 R1 20–24, *MM iii*, e, pp. 865–6 (= *Reader*, ch, 1, pp. 139–40).
65. *Cf.* Reichelt, *Die soghdischen Handschriften*, II, pp. 33–5.
66. *Cf.* Henning, 'Neue Materialien', pp. 11–12.
67. *Ts'e-fu yüan-kuei* 971.4b–5a. *Cf. Traité* 1913, pp. 152–3 [126–77] and Henning, 'Argi', p. 570.
68. A good example of a multilingual interpreter of Sogdian origin is An Lu-shan, the famous rebel of the T'ang dynasty. *Cf.* Pulleyblank, *Background*, p. 106 and de Rotours, *Histoire*, p. 11.
69. *Cf.* Pelliot, 'Les influences iraniennes', pp. 102–5.
70. *Cf. idem*, 'La "Cha tcheou tou fou t'ou king"' p. 123.
71. *Min-shu* 7.32a. *Cf.* Pelliot, 'Traditions', p. 199 (trans p. 203).
72. *Fo-tsu t'ung-chi* 54.474c. *Cf. Traité* 1913 pp. 150–51 [174–5].
73. *Cf. Traité* 1913, pp. 378–81 [340–43]. *Cf.* Maenchen-Halfen, 'Manichaeans in Siberia', p. 322.
74. *Min-shu* 7.32a. *Cf.* Pelliot, 'Traditions', p. 200 (trans. pp. 203–4).
75. *Cf.* Weinstein, 'Imperial Patronage', pp. 297–9.
76. *Cf.* Ch'en, *Buddhism*, p. 222.
77. *Chiu T'ang-shu* 8.9b and *Ts'e-fu yüan-kuei* 986.19a. *Cf.* Pulleyblank, 'Sogdian colony', p. 336.
78. *Cf.* Haloun–Henning, 'Compendium', p. 188, n. 3.
79. *T'ung-tien* 40.229c, trans. *Traité* 1913, p. 154 [178].
80. *Ch'ao-yeh ch'ien-tsai* 3.34 trans. Eichhorn, 'Materialien', p. 536.
81. *Cf.* Müller, 'Kalenderausdrücke', pp. 458–65.
82. *Cf. Traité* 1913 pp. 171–2 [195–6] and *SHYCK*, *hsing-fa* 2.19b, trans. Forte, 'Deux études', p. 234.
83. A facsimile reproduction of the work can be found in Pelliot–Haneda (eds.), *Tun-huang i-shu*, I.
84. See e.g. *Sui-shu* 7.14 and *Wei-shu* 13.338. *Cf.* Ch'en Yüan, 'Huo-shen chiao', pp. 29–30 and Eichhorn, 'Materialien', p. 533.
85. *Cf.* Sundermann–Thilo, 'Grabinschrift', p. 430.
86. *T'ang hui-yao* 49.864 (edict of 638). *Cf.* Lo Hsiang-lin, *T'ang Yüan erh-tai chih Ching-chiao*, pp. 12–13.

87. T'ang hui-yao 49.864 (edict of 745).

88. See esp. texts collected in Lo Hsiang-lin, op.cit., pp. 193–224.

89. al-Nadim, Fihrist, trans. Dodge, pp. 836–7.

90. Chiu T'ang-shu 160.4200. Cf. de Groot, Sectarianism, p. 55.

91. Cf. Franke, Geschichte, II, p. 458, ll. 8–11 and de Rotours, Histoire, pp. 285–94.

92. Cf. Traité 1913, pp. 189–90 [213–14].

93. The Inscription of Karabalghasun, l. 10 in Schlegel, Die chinesische Inschrift, pp. 60–63 (Manichaeism was wrongly identified as Nestorianism in the commentary) and Traité 1913, p. 194 [218].

94. T II D 135, cited in Müller, 'Der Hofstaat', pp. 208–9.

95. Cf. Tasaka Kōdō, 'Uiguru', pp. 228–31 and MacKerras, Uighur Empire, pp. 152–3.

96. TM 276a 2–27, TTT ii, p. 414. Cf. Klimkeit, 'Manichaean Kingship', pp. 22–3. I am extremely grateful to Prof. Klimkeit for an English translation of this Turkish fragment.

97. TM 276a 27–96, TTT ii, pp. 414–18.

98. FTTC 54.474c.

99. Ibid. 40.378c, trans. Traité, 1913 p. 262 [224].

100. Cf. Ch'en Yüan, 'Mo-ni-chiao', p. 215 [343].

101. TM 276a13, TTT ii, p. 414.

102. Po-shih ch'ang-ching chi 59.35a–36a, trans. Traité 1913, pp. 277–9 [239–41]. Cf. Zieme, 'Die Uiguren', pp. 285–7 and Moses, 'T'ang Tribute Relations', pp. 61–89.

103. T'ai-p'ing kuang-chi 107.727. On the Pao-ying chi which was the source of this story see Uchiyama Chinari, Zui-Tō shōsetsu kenkyū, pp. 81–2 and 85–109 and esp. 167–78.

104. Cf. Franke, Geschichte, II, 493, 25–495, 44 and Traité 1913, pp. 285–7 [247–9].

105. Chiu T'ang-shu 145.5207. Cf. MacKerras, Uighur Empire, p. 86.

106. Tzu-chih t'ung-chien 225.7265.

107. Cf. Ch'en, Buddhism, pp. 227–8.

108. Hui-ch'ang i-p'in chi 5.4a, trans. Traité 1913, pp. 293–5 [255–7]. See also Ch'uen T'ang-wen 701.56–7a.

109. T'ang hui-yao 49.864, trans. Traité 1913, pp. 296–8 [258–60].

110. Cf. Gernet, Les aspects économiques, passim and Ch'en, Buddhism, pp. 264–7.

111. Cf. Twitchett, Financial Adminstration, p. 296, n. 53.

112. Chiu T'ang-shu 217B.6133, trans. Traité 1913, pp. 298–300 [260–62].

113. Hsin T'ang-shu 18A.594, trans. Traité 1913, pp. 298 [260].

114. Nittō gūho junrei gyōki no kenkyū, iii, p. 491, ed. Ono Katsutoshi, trans. Reischauer, Ennin's Travels, p. 232.

115. FTTC 42.385c, trans. Traité 1913, pp. 301–2 [263–4].

116. Chiu T'ang-shu 18A.605 and FTTC 42.386a. Cf. Ch'en, 'Hui-ch'ang Persecution', pp. 67–109.

117. Chiu T'ang-shu 18A.605–6. Cf. Lo Hsiang-lin, T'ang Yüan erh-tai, p. 19.

118. *Cf.* Maenchen-Helfen, 'Manichaeans in Siberia', pp. 324–5.

119. *Cf.* Pinks, *Die Uiguren von Kan-chou*, p. 114.

120. *Hiu-chu ch'ien-lu* 4, cited in *Traité* 1913, pp. 308–9 [270–71].

121. *Cf.* Markwart, *Osteuropäische und ostasiatische Streifzüge*, pp. 90–95. See also von Gabain, *Das Leben*, pp. 71–2.

122. *Cf. Catalogue*, p. xiv.

123. *Cf.* le Coq, *Die Buddhistische Spätantike*, II, plate 8b/b and pp. 56–7, and Klimkeit, *Art*, fig. 26 and p. 38.

124. M801 33–4 (524–30), *BBB*, pp. 33–4. *Cf.* Vööbus, *Hist. Asc.* I, p. 130.

125. *Tsung* 8782T, 82, *cf.* Keng Shih-min, 'Hui-heh-wen', pp. 502–5.

126. *Cf.* Zieme, 'Ein uigurischer Text', pp. 332–6 and Lieu, 'Precept', pp. 165–8. On the cultivation of vine see 1. 11 of the Turkish text. *Cf.* Lieu, *art. cit.*, p. 168.

127. Ll. 1–43, pp. 505–7.

128. *Cf.* Zieme, 'Ein uigurischer Text', p. 333 and Lieu, 'Precept', p. 166.

129. *Cf.* Lieu, *art. cit.*, pp. 170–71.

130. *Tsung* 8782T, 82, ll. 97–9, Keng Shih-min, 'Hui-heh-wen', p. 505.

131. *Ibid.*, l. 119, p. 505.

131a. M112 V 9–21. I owe my knowledge of this text entirely to Professor Klimkeit who is in the process of publishing it in collaboration with Mr Keng Shih-min.

132. *Cf.* Klimkeit, *Art*, figs. 12–13a/c and p. 30.

133. *Cf. Catalogue*, p. xv.

NOTES TO CHAPTER VIII

1. *Cf.* Stein, *Serindia*, II, pp. 819–24 and *idem*, *Ruins*, I, pp. 159–219.

2. *MNKFCFIL*, pp. 1280c12–1281a11, trans. *Traité* 1913, pp. 105–16 [129–40].

3. *PSCTC*, pp. 1281a16–1286a29, trans. *Traité* 1911, pp. 508–90 [12–94].

4. *Cf.* Chavannes, 'Le Nestorianisme', pp. 76 and 85.

5. *Cf.* Schlegel, *Die chinesische Inschrift*, pp. 43–69.

6. *MNCHPT*, pp. 1279c17–1281a11, trans. Tsui-chi, 'The Lower Section', pp. 174–219.

7. *MNKFCFIL*, pp. 1279c17–1280c12, trans. Haloun–Henning, 'Compendium', pp. 184–212.

8. See e.g. *Traité* 1911, p. 509 [13], n. 3, 521 [23], n. 2 etc.

9. *MNCHPT* 1–5, p. 1270b24–9, 154–8, p. 1274a4–9 and 176–83, p. 1274b12–23. *Cf.* W-L i, pp. 80–92 and *Gnosis*, III, pp. 290–91. See also Yoshida, 'Manichaean Aramaic', pp. 327–28 which shows that the second of these hymns is diglottal, i.e. Aramaic and Parthian.

10. *MNCHPT* 261–338, p. 1276a28–1278a9. *Cf. Huwıdagmān* I, *Hymn-Cycles*, pp. 66–77.

11. The relevant fragments are collected in *TMC iii*, pp. 15–22.

12. *MNCHPT* 417 (postscript), p. 1279c2, trans. p. 215. See also trans. p. 216, n. 9.

13. *Ibid.* 417-19, p. 1279c3-5, trans. p. 215.

14. *Ibid.* 415-11, p. 1279c8-9, trans. p. 215.

15. *MNKFCFIL*, p. 1279c17-18, trans. Haloun-Henning, 'Compendium', p. 188.

16. *Ibid.* p. 1280b14-21, trans. pp. 194-5.

17. *Ibid.* p. 1280b19, trans. p. 195.

18. See e.g. *Traité* 1911, p. 515 [19], n. 2; p. 533 [37], n. 3; *W-L* i, p. 98, n. 10; p. 101, n. 3, p. 105, n. 4; Haloun-Henning, 'Compendium', p. 189, n. 4, n. 9 etc.

19. *PSCTC*, p. 1281a23-9, trans. *Traité* 1911, pp. 508-10 [12-14].

20. *Huwīdagmān* I, 22 (= M93 I R), trans. *Hymn Cycles*, p. 69.

21. *MNCHPT* 283, p. 1276c14-15, trans. Tsui Chi, 'The Lower Section', p. 201 (revised).

22. For discussion see esp. *Traité* 1911, pp. 508-72 [12-76] (notes) and *W-L* ii, pp. 495-545.

23. See e.g. *Chih-hsüan an-lo ching*, ed. and comm. Saeki Yoshiro, *Keikyō*, pp. 710-36.

24. See e.g. *Keph.* IX, pp. 37, 1. 31-38, 1. 4 and LV, p. 133, 11. 7-20. *Cf.* Böhlig, *Mysterion*, pp. 228-44 and *Gnosis* III, pp. 54-70. For a useful selection of Manichaean didactic literature see *ibid.* pp. 157-88. On the gnostic use of the dialogue see Hoffmann, *Der Dialog*, pp. 105-8.

25. *Keph.* LXXXVI, pp. 213, 1. 16-216, 1. 30. See esp. pp. 214, 1. 31-215, 1. 1.

26. *PSCTC*, p. 1281b5-7, trans. *Traité* 1911, pp. 514-1/ [18-19].

27. *Ps.-Bk.*, p. 10, 11. 25-9. *Cf.* Lieu, 'New light', pp. 407-9.

28. *PSCTC*, p. 1285a21, trans. *Traité* 1911, p. 579 [83].

29. See esp. Sundermann, 'Namen', p. 101 (3/1-20).

30. *Ibid.* p. 99 (2/1).

31. *Cf.* Boyce, 'Mithra', *passim* and Sundermann, 'Some remarks', *passim*.

32. See e.g. M5815 I V II (96-7), *MM iii, p. 856* (= *Reader*, r, p. 52) and *MNCHPT* 52, p. 1271c3, trans. Tsui Chi, 'The Lower Section', p. 80. *Cf.* Klimkeit, *Stupa*, pp. 229-33.

33. See e.g. M8171 VII (37-45) *MM iii*, pp. 868-9 (= *Reader*, cg, p. 139).

34. *MNCHPT* 169-71, p. 1274a27-b4, trans. Tsui Chi, 'The Lower Section', p. 191. See also *W-L* ii, p. 12 and comm. *ad loc.*

35. See e.g. *MNCHPT* 236, p. 1275c8, trans. Tsui Chi, 'The Lower Section', p. 196. *Cf.* Klimkeit, 'Vairocana', pp. 368-9.

36. T I D 20 V 6-11 (191-6), *MTT*, p. 32. *Cf.* Klimkeit, 'Vairocana', pp. 369-70.

37. *Cf.* Snellgrove-Skorupski, *Ladakh*, pp. xii, 10 and 56.

38. *Cf.* Klimkeit, 'Vairocana', pp. 370-72, and *idem*, 'Kreuzessymbol', pp. 112-15. See also Böhlig, 'Lichtkreuz', pp. 478-91.

39. *Cf.* Klimkeit, 'Vairocana', pp. 376-8 and *idem*, 'Art', *pp. 32-3*.

40. See Ch. IX, n. 97.

41. *Cf.* von Le Coq, *Die buddhistische Spätantike* II, pl.8a/a and pp. 51-2.

42. *Cf.* Klimkeit, 'Hindu deities', pp. 181-2.

43. *Cf.* von Le Coq, *Die buddhistische Spätantike*, II, p. 57, n. 2,

Klimkeit, 'Hindu deities', pp. 188-9 and *idem, Art*, pp. 34-5. The Greek term is found in <Zach. Mit.>, *capita vii c. Manich.* III (59), p. xxxiv.

44. *SHYCK*, fasc. 165, *hsing-fa* 2.78b6, trans. Forte, 'Deux etudes', p. 250. For a different interpretation of the term see Liu Ts'un-yan, 'Traces', p. 35.

45. Wu Wen-liang, *Ch'üan-chou*, p. 44. *Cf. PSCTC* p. 1283a15-17, trans. *Traité* 1911, p. 556 [60]. See Ch. IX.

46. M42 V I (64), *MM iii.* p. 880. See also TM 161 V 9, *MTT* (294), p. 40 and comm. *ad loc. Cf.* Klimkeit, 'Stupa', p. 232.

47. *MNKFCFIL*, p. 1279c20, trans. Haloun–Henning, 'Compendium', p. 189. *Cf.* Ishida Mikinosuke, 'Tonkō hakken', pp. 160-62.

48. *MNKFCFIL*, p. 1280a, trans. Haloun-Henning, 'Compendium', pp. 190-91 (revised).

49. *Cf.* al-Nadim, *Fihrist*, trans. Dodge, p. 723, Flügel, *Mani* p. 85. See also *Gnosis*, III, p. 77. *Cf.* Lieu, 'Byz. Formula', pp. 196-7 and Klíma, *MZL*, pp. 281-4.

50. Wu Wen-liang, *Ch'üan-chou*, p. 44, trans. Lieu, 'Nestorians', p. 82.

51. *Cf. Ch'üan-chou ming-sheng kuo-chi*, pp. 55-6.

52. See above, note 45.

53. T II D 173e R 1 – V 16, ed. and trans. von Le Coq, 'Manuskriptfragment', pp. 1208-11, revised by Bang, 'Erzähler', p. 9. *Cf.* Lang, *Wisdom*, pp. 27-9 and Lieu, 'Holy Men', pp. 114-5.

54. *Shih-chi* 63.2141. *Cf.* Zürcher, *Buddhist Conquest*, I, pp. 290-91 and Seidel, *La Divinisation*, pp. 105-10.

55. *Cf.* Ch'en, *Buddhism*, pp. 184-6, Zürcher, *op. cit.*, pp. 288-30 and Eichhorn, *Die Religionen*, pp. 191-2.

56. *FTTC* 36.339c-40a. *Cf.* Ch'en Yüan, 'Mo-ni-chiao', pp. 215-16 [344-5].

57. *FTTC* 36.340a/b.

58. *Cf.* Ch'en Yüan, 'Mo-ni-chiao', p. 216 [344].

59. On *Hsi-na* = Rome *cf. Traité* 1913, pp. 121-2 [145-6].

60. *Lao-tzu hsi-hsing hua-hu ching*, p. 1267b19-cl. *Cf. Traité* 1913, pp. 120-26 [144-50].

61. *Cf.* Fukui Kōjun, *Dōkyō*, pp. 267-8.

62. *Ibid.* pp. 268-72.

63. On the survival of Manichaean scriptures in Sung see Ch. IX.

64. *Pien-wei lu* 2.764b4-5 (= *Fo-tsu li-tai t'ung-tsai* 22.719a27).

65. See Ch. IX.

66. *Pien-wei lu* 2.759b7-8 and 761b17-19 (= *Fo-tsu li-tai t'ung tsai* 22.716c29a-b and 718c26a-27a). The second reference is based on *Lao-tzu hsi-shing hua-hu ching*, p. 1267a25-8. *Cf.* Ch'en Yüan, 'Mo-ni-chiao', p. 217 [346].

67. *Huang-shih jih-chao* 86.9a/b. *Cf.* Kubo Noritada, 'Sōdai', pp. 367-8. See Ch. IX.

68. *Cf.* Tezcan, *Insadi Sūtra* (1019 ff.), p. 70ff. I do not agree with the editor that the group under attack were Manichaeans. The leader of the group had the very Nestorian ecclesiastical title of *Mari hasia (Syr.: mry hsy')*.

69. *Cf.* Saeki Yoshiro, *Keikyō*, pp. 530-70 and Eichhorn, *Die Religionen*, pp. 319-21.

70. *PSCTC p. 1281b13-14. Cf. W-L ii*, p. 514.

71. *SHYCK*, fasc. 165 *hsing-fa* 2.78b5, trans. Forte, 'Deux études', p. 250.

72. *Min-shu* 7.31b6, trans. Pelliot, 'Les traditions', p. 201 and Lieu, 'Nestorians', p. 87. The error is derived from *MNKFCFIL*, p. 1280a6, trans. Haloun–Henning, 'Compendium' p. 191. See esp. Henning's note on the dates on p. 198.

73. *Min-shu* 7.32a1-6, trans. Pelliot, 'Les traditions', p. 199 and Lieu, 'Nestorians', p. 87.

NOTES TO CHAPTER IX

1. *Cf.* Wang Shu-nan, *T'ang-tai fan-chen, passim.* See esp. pp. 141-246. See also Franke, *Geschichte*, IV, pp. 11, 1. 34-12, 1. 32 and Wang Gung-wu,*Structure of Power*, pp. 7-46.

2. *Cf.* Franke, *Geschichte*, IV, pp. 10-124.

3. *Min-shu* 7.32a-b. *Cf.* Pelliot, 'Les traditions', pp. 205-6.

4. *Il Milione*, ed. Moule and Pelliot, p. lv. *Cf.* Lieu, 'Nestorians', pp. 71-2.

5. Abu Said Hassan, cited in Levy, *Huang Chao*, p. 117.

6. *Cf. Huang-shih jih-ch'ao* 86.9a-b. See also *SHYCK*, fasc. 165, *hsing-fa* 2.78b.

7. See e.g. *FTTC* 40.374c and 54.474c. On Buddhist historians of the Sung in general see Jan Yün-hua, 'Buddhist historiography', pp. 362-72.

8. Chüan hsia.253c.

9. *Chiu Wu-tai shih* 10.144. *Cf. Traité* 1913, pp. 320-24 [282-6], Shigematsu Toshiake, 'Tō-sō jidai', pp. 106-10 and Lieu, 'Polemics', p. 139.

10. See e.g. *FTTC* 39.370a, 48.430c-431a and 50.475a.

11. *Ts'e-fu yüan-kuei* 976.20a. *Cf.* Ch'en Yüan, 'Mo-ni-chiao', p. 223 [353-4].

12. *Ts'e-fu yüan-kuei* 976.18b-19a. *Cf.* Hamilton, *Les Ouïghours*, p. 69. I have followed the punctuation of Ch'en Yüan, 'Mo-ni-chiao', p. 223 [353].

13. *T'ang hui-yao* 49.864. *Cf. Traité* 1913, pp. 263-4 [225-6].

14. *Min-shu* 7.32b. *Cf.* Pelliot 'Les traditions', p. 207.

15. *Chi-shen lüeh* 3.4a-b. *Cf. T'ai-p'ing kuang-chi* 355.2812.

16. *Huang shih jih-ch'ao* 86.7b. *Cf.* Mou Jun-sun, 'Sung-tai', p. 143 [97].

17. *Cf.* Eichhorn, *Die Religionen*, pp. 284-7, *Traité* 1913, pp. 325-6 [287-8], Shigematsu Toshiake, 'Tō-Sō jidai', p. 108 and Yoshioka Yoshitoyo, *Dōkyō keiten*, p. 148.

18. *Yün-chi ch'i-ch'ien*, preface 1a-2a. *Cf. Traité* 1913, pp. 326-7 [288-9]. See also Liu Ts'un-yan, 'Compilation', pp. 112-13 and Kubo Noritada, 'Sōdai', pp. 364-6.

19. *FTTC* 48.431a. *Cf. Traité* 1913, p. 336 [298].

20. M477 I etc. *Cf.* MacKenzie, 'Mani's *Šābuhragān*', p. 509 and Alfaric, *Les écritures*, II, pp. 49-54.

21. *MNKFCFIL* pp. 1280a-81a.

22. See below, n. 43.

23. *SHYCK*, fasc. 166, hsing-fa 2.83a-b. *Cf.* Mou Jun-sun, 'Sung-tai', pp. 126-30 [78-83].

24. *P'an-chou wen-chi* 74.1a-b. *Cf.* Mou Jun-sun, 'Sung-tai', pp. 127-8

[81] and 132–3 [86–7].

25. *Cf.* Mou Jun-sun, 'Sung-tai', pp. 128–9 [81–2].

26. *Cf.* Eichhorn, *Die Religionen*, p. 339.

26a. *Shih-men cheng t'ung* 4.412Ab.

27. *Huang-shih jih-chao* 86.9b. *Cf.* Fukui Kojun, *Dōkyō* pp. 270–71.

28. *Wei-nan wen-chi* 5.8a. See below, n. 82.

29. *Jung-chai i-shih*, ap. *Ch'ing-ch'i k'ou-kuei* 6b. On the transportation of plants and stones see esp. Eichhorn, *Die Religionen*, and Kao Yu-kung, 'Fang La Rebellion', pp. 41–4. On the political and economic background of the rebellion, see esp. *ibid.*, pp. 38–41 and 44–52 and Chikusa Masaaki, 'Hō Rō (Fang La) no ran', pp. 470–75.

30. *Jung-chai i-shih*, ap. *Ch'ing-ch'i k'ou-kuei*, 5a, trans. Kao Yu-kung, 'Source material', pp. 218–19.

31. *Po-che pien* 5.1b. trans. Kao Yu-kung, 'Source material', pp. 212–12.

32. *Ibid.* 5.3b, *trans. cit.*, pp. 214–15. *Cf.* Chikusa Masaaki, 'Hō Rō (Fang La) no ran', pp. 466–9.

33. *Ibid.* 5.4a–b, *trans. cit.*, pp. 215–16 and *Sung-shih* 48.13660. *Cf.* Kao Yu-kung, 'Fang La rebellion', pp. 35–8.

34. *Sung-shih* 468.13659. See also *SHYCK*, fasc. 176, *p'ing 10.18b.*

35. *Chi-lei pien*, chung. 9b. *Cf. Po-che pien* 5.4b.

36. See e.g. *Kao-feng wen-chi* 2.22a/b and *Chien-yen i-lai hsi-nien yao-lu* 76.1249.

37. *Hsüeh-shan chi* 3.25–26. *Cf.* Chikusa Masaaki, '*Kitsusaijima*', p. 257.

38. *SHYCK*, fasc. 165, *hsing-fa* 2.15a/b.

39. See Ch. VIII.

40. *Cf.* Ch'en, *Buddhism*, pp. 427–9, Wu Han, 'Ming-chiao', pp. 69–73 [258–61] and Shigematsu Toshiake, 'Tō-Sō jidai no Mirokukyō', pp. 68–103, esp. p. 88ff.

41. *FTTC* 54.474c–75a. *Cf.* Overmyer, 'White Cloud sect', pp. 620–34.

42. *SHYCK*, fasc. 166, *hsing-fa* 2.130a/b.

43. *Shih-men cheng-tung* 4.413Aa/b. See also *FTTC* 54.475a. *Cf.* Chikusa Masaaki, '*Kitsusaijima*', pp. 253–6.

44. *SHYCK*, fasc. 165, *hsing-fa* 2.78a–79b. *Cf.* Forte, 'Deux études', pp. 227–53.

45. See Ch. V.

46. See esp. Forte, 'Deux études', pp. 244–6.

47. *Cf. ibid.* pp. 239–40. See also Mou Jun-sun, 'Sung-tai', p. 135 [88]. For the fullChinese title of the *Pragmateia* see *MNKFCFIL*, p. 128Ob19.

48. *Cf. PSCTC*, p. 1281a26.

49. *P'an-chou wen-chi*, 74.1b. *Cf.* Mou Jun-sun, 'Sung-tai', p. 133 [86] and Chikusa Masaaki, 'Hō-Rō (Fang La) no ran', p. 467.

50. *Cf.* Hervouet (ed.), *Sung Bibliography*, *s.v.* '*Ch'ing-ch'i k'ou-kuei*' pp. 92–93 (MacKnight).

51. *Chi-lei-pien*, chung, 9a–10a. *Cf.* Shih, 'Rebel ideologies', pp. 74–5, Kao Yu-kung, 'Source Material', pp. 223–5, Bauer, *China*, pp. 311–23, esp. 312–13. See also Shigematsu Toshiake, 'Tō-Sō jidai', pp. 114–16.

52. *Kao-feng wen-chi* 2.22a6–7.

53. *Cf.* Klimkeit, 'Stupa', p. 235. See also *MNCHPT*, 98, p. 1272c8.

54. On Li (Shou) Ch'ien see *Chia-t'ing ch'ih-cheng chih* 9.22a/b. *Cf.* Mou Jun-sun, 'Sung-tai', p. 139 [93] and Wang Kuo-wei, 'Mo-ni-chiao', p. 33b.

55. *MNKFCFIL*, p. 128Ob11.

56. *Chia-t'ing ch'ih-cheng chih* 37.20b10–21a1, 21a4–5, 21a10–21b1 and 21b4–5. The translations here replace those in Lieu, 'Polemics', pp. 153–7, 160 and 162.

57. See esp. Kao Yu-kung, 'Fang La rebellion', pp. 33–4 and 57–61.

58. *Hsüeh-shan chi* 3.26. *Cf.* Chikusa Masaaki, '*Kitsusaijima*', p. 257.

59. *Shih-men cheng-t'ung* 4.412Aa. *Cf. FTTC* 48.431a, trans., *Traité*, 1913, pp. 353–7[315–20].

60. *Cf.* Kao Yu-kung, 'Fang La rebellion', p. 53.

61. *Ibid.* p. 53. See also Shigematsu Toshiake, 'Tō-Sō jidai', pp. 110–38 and Yuji Muramatsu, 'Chinese rebel ideologies', pp. 247–8.

62. *Cf.* Ch'en Yüan, 'Mo-ni-chiao', p. 230 [364] and Shigematsu Toshiake, 'To-So jidai', pp. 110–111.

63. *Cf.* Kao Yu-kung, 'Fang La rebellion', p. 53.

64. *Cf.* Chikusa Masaaki, '*Kitsusaijima*', pp. 240–44.

65. See below, n. 90.

66. *Shih-men cheng t'ung* 4.412Aa-Ba, trans., *Traité* 1913 [pp. 345–6] (The translation is found only in the monograph reprint version of the work).

67. Aug., *c. Faust.* XXII 74–6, pp. 671, l. 24–76, l. 6.

68. *Xᵘāstvānīft* V A/B (80–85), p. 172, ed. Asmussen.

69. *FTTC* 39.370a, trans. *Traité* 1913, p. 361 [323].

70. *Hsüeh-shan chi* 3.26, l. 13.

71. See esp. Mou Jun-sun, 'Sung-tai', p. 139 [93].

72. *Hsüeh-shan chi* 3.26, l. 13. *Cf.* Chikusa Masaaki, '*Kitsusaijima*', p. 343.

73. *Chi-lei pien*, chung, 9b, trans. Kao Yu-kung, 'Source material', p. 225.

74. *Ibid.* 9b, *trans. cit.*, pp. 224–5.

75. See esp. Chikusa Masaaki, '*Kitsusaijima*', pp. 243–4.

76. *Cf.* Eichhorn, *Die Religionen*, p. 284.

77. *Cf.* Shigematsu Toshiake, 'Tō-Sō jidai', pp. 118–29 and Chikusa Masaaki, '*Kitsusaijima*', pp. 247–8.

78. See esp. Ch'en, *Buddhism*, pp. 451–2.

79. *SHYCK*, fasc. 165–6, *hsing-fa* 2.52b–136b. *Cf.* Mou Jun-sun, '*Sung-tai*', pp. 135–42 [89–96].

80. *SHYCK*, fasc. 166, *hsing-fa* 2.122a/b.

81. *Cf. Traité* 1913, pp. 343–4 [305–6].

82. *Wei-nan wen-chi* 5.7b–8b. *Cf. Traité* 1913, pp. 344–51 [306–13].

83. T I Da R 13, Henning, *Sogdica*, p. 64. *Cf. MNCHPT* 254, p. 1276a14. On this see Puech, *Essais*, pp. 161–2.

84. <Zach. Mit.>, *capita vii c. Manich.* VII (199–204) p. xxxviii. *Cf.* Lieu, 'Byz. formula', p. 212.

85. *CMC* 94, 10–95,17 (*ZPE* 1978), pp. 114–15. See esp. comm. *ad loc.*, pp. 185–8.

86. *Ps.-Bk.*, p. 59, ll. 26–7.

87. *PSCTC*, p. 1286a11–12. *Cf. Traité* 1913, p. 349 [311], n. 2.

88. *Cf.* Vööbus, *Hist. Asc.*, I, p. 123.

89. On Huang Shang see Ch'ang Pi-te *et al.*, ed., *Sung-jen ch'uan-chi*, V, p. 2867.

90. *Lao-hsüeh yen pi-chi 10.2a*. *Cf. Traité* 1913, pp. 343–5 [301–5].

91. *Li-chi chu-shu* 2.22a.

92. *FTTC* 40.374c. *Cf.* Ch'en Yüan, 'Mo-ni-chiao', pp. 228–9 [361–2].

93. *Ap. FTTC* 48.431a/b. *Cf. Traité* 1913, pp. 330–39 [292–301].

94. *Cf.* Hiraoka Takeo, 'Haku-shi bunshū', p. 273.

95. *Po-shih ch'ang-ch'ing chi* 59.35a–36a. *Cf. Traité* 1913, pp. 276–9 [238–41].

96. *FTTC* 54.474b–75a.

97. *Hai-ch'iung Po-chen-jen yü-lu* l. 11a–12a.

98. T I D 200, *TTT* v, pp. 334–5. *Cf.* Klimkeit, 'Vairocana', pp. 357–99 and Zieme, 'Uigurische Steuerbefreiungsurkunden', p. 242, n. 46.

99. *Cf.* Wu Wen-liang, *Ch'üan-chou*, p. 44.

100. *Huang-shih jih-chao* 86.8a/b. The translation here replaces that in Lieu, 'Lapsed Manichaean's Correspondence', pp. 402–3.

101. *Ibid.* 86.9a/b.

102. *Ibid.* 86.9b/c. *Cf.* Kubo Noritada, 'Sōdai ni okeru', pp. 366–70.

103. *Sung-shih* 438.12993–3.

104. *Cf.* Grousset, *Empire*, pp. 282–4 and 86–8.

105. Marco Polo, *Il Milione* XXI, p. 14, ed. Benedetto.

106. *Yüan-shih* 105.1684.

107. Marco Polo, *Il Milione* (Manuscript Z), ed. Moule and Pelliot, ii, pp. liii–liv. *Cf.* Olschki, 'Manichaeism', pp. 2–21 and Lieu, 'Nestorians', pp. 76–9.

108. Wu Wen-liang, *Ch'üan-chou*, p. 46. *Cf.* Murayama, 'Grabinschrift', pp. 397–8, Enoki, 'Nestorian Christianism' (sic.), p. 62, Goodrich, 'Recent Discoveries', Hsia Nai, 'Liang-chung wen-tzu', pp. 59–63 and Lieu, 'Nestorians', p. 73.

109. *Cf.* Lieu, 'Nestorians', p. 75. For an opposite view see Chiang Wei-chi, 'Ch'üan-chou', pp. 77–82. On the wrong date of Mani's birth see *Min-shu* 7.31b, trans. Pelliot, 'Les traditions,' p. 201 *Cf. MNKFCFIL*, p. 1280a6.

110. *Min-shu* 7.31b. *Cf.* Pelliot, 'Les traditions', p. 200.

111. *Cf.* Wu Wen-liang, *Ch'üan-chou*, p. 44 and *Ch'üan-chou ming-sheng kuo-chi*, p. 56.

112. *Fu-chien t'ung-chi* 47.4b. *Cf.* Schafer, *Empire of Min*, p. 102.

113. *Pu-hsi-chou-yü chi* 12.14b–15b.

114. *Cf.* Grousset, *Empire*, pp. 320–25.

115. *Ming lü chi-chieh fu li* 11.9b–10a, trans. *Traité* 1913, pp. 367–8 [329–30].

116. *Cf.* Ch'en, *Buddhism*, p. 430 and Eichhorn, *Die Religionen*, pp. 322–3.

117. *Min-shu* 7.32b, trans. Pelliot, 'Les traditions', p. 206. On the change of Ming-chou, see Wu Han, *Chu Yüan-chang*, p. 107. On the provision of lists of alternatives to dynastic title see Niida Naboru, *Chūgoku hoseī shi*, IV, pp. 458–60.

118. *Cf.* Wu Han, 'Ming-chiao', pp. 49–81 [259–70] and *idem*, *Chu Yüan-chang*, pp. 105–8.

119. *Cf.* M42 V I (64), *MM iii*, p. 880 and TM 161 V 9, *MTT* (294), p. 40.
120. *Min-shu* 7.32b, trans. Pelliot, 'Les traditions', pp. 206–7.
121. *Chih-yüan hsü-chi*, in *Sung Wen-hsien kung ch'üan-chi* 31.5a. *Cf.* Wu Han, 'Ming-chiao', p. 78 [268].
122. *Cf.* Wu Wen-liang, *Ch'üan-chou*, p. 44.
123. *Min-shu* 7.31b, trans. Pelliot, 'Les traditions', pp. 201–2.
124. *Ibid.*, 7.32a, *trans. cit.*, p. 204.
125. *Cf.* Saeki Yoshiro, *Keikyō*, Appendix, pp. 181–5.
126. *Shih-chia-chai yang-hsin-lu* 8.185–7.
127. *Cf.* Ch'en Yüan, 'Mo-ni-chiao', p. 226 [356].
128. Reprinted in *Pi-chi hsiao-shuo ta-kuan*, Series 22, vi, p. 3316 (table of contents).
129. *Cf.* Ch'üan-chou ming-sheng kuo-chi, p. 55.
130. *Cf.* Wu Wen-liang, *Chüan-chou*, pp. 44–5.

BIBLIOGRAPHY OF
WORKS CITED

(See also works cited in List of Abbreviations)

I. PRIMARY SOURCES

(a) **Syriac**

(Aba), see Mar Aba I, Catholicos.
'Abdiso' Bar Berika, *Carmen Ebedjesu* . . . *continens Catalogum Librorum omnium Ecclesiasticorm*, ed.J. S. Assemanus, *Bibliotheca Orientalis* III/1 (Rome, 1728) pp. 1–362.
[Addai apost.], *Doctrina Addai*, ed. G. Phillips (London, 1876).
'Anân-Ishô', see 'Enaniso' monachus.
Aphrahates, *Demonstrationes*, ed. I. Parisot, *PS* I (1894) and II (1907) cols. 1–489.
(Arbela) See under [Msiha-Zkha].
Bardaisan, school of, *Liber Legum Regionum*, ed. F. Nau, *PS* II, cols. 426–601.
Barhebraeus (Gregorius Abul-l-Farag) *Chronicon Ecclesiasticum*, ed. J. B. Abbeloos and T. J. Lamy, 2 vols. (Louvain, 1872–7).
Chronicon anonymum ad annum 1234 pertinens, ed. J.B. Chabot, CSCO LXXXI (1920) and LXXXII (1916).
Chronicon anonymum (nestorianum), ed. I. Guidi, CSCO I, *Chronica Minora* (1903) pp. 13–32.
'Cyrillona', *Hymni et Sermones*, ed. G. Bickell, 'Die Gedichte des Cyrillonas', *ZDMG* 27 (1873) pp. 556–98.
[Dionysius e Tellmahre], *Chronicon Pseudo-Dionysianum*, ed. J. B. Chabot, CSCO XCI (1927)and CIV (1933).
(Edessa), *Chronicon Edessenum*, ed. I. Guidi, CSCO I, *Chronica Minora* (1903) pp. 1–13.
'Enaniso' monachus, *Paradisum Patrum*, ed. E. A. Wallis Budge, *The Book of Paradise etc.*, 2 vols. (London, 1904).
Ephraem, *Contra haereses ad Hypatium* et *Contra haereses ad Domnum*, Discourse I: ed.J. J. Overbeck, *S. Ephraem Syri, Rabulae, Balaei etc.* (Oxford, 1865) pp. 21–58; the rest: C. W. Mitchell *et al.* ed., *S. Ephraim's Prose Refutations of Mani, Marcion and Bardaisan*, 2 vols. (London, 1912–21).
Hymni contra Julianum, ed. E. Beck. CSCO CLXXIV (Louvain, 1957).

(Ephraem), *Historia Sancti Ephraemi*, ed. T. J. Lamy, *Sancti Ephraem(i) Syri hymni et sermones* II (Mechliniae, 1886) cols. 3–89.

— *Hymni 56 contra haereses*, ed. E. Beck, CSCO CLXIX (1957).

Ioannes Ephesi, *Historiae beatorum orientalium*, ed. E. W. Brooks, *Lives of Eastern Saints*, PO XVII (1923) pp. 1–307, XVIII (1924) pp. 311–496 and XIX (1925) pp. 499–631.

[Iosue Stylita], see under [Dionysius e Tellmahre].

(Karkā de Bēt Selōk), *Historia Karkae de Beth Selok*, ed. P. Bedjan, *AMS* II (1891) pp. 507–35.

(Mani), *Fragmenta Manichaica Syriaca, Cf.* F. Burkitt, *The Religion of the Manichees* (Cambridge,1925) pp. 111–19.

(Mar Aba I, Catholicos), *Vita*, ed. P. Bedjan, *Histoire de Jabalaha et de trois autres Patriarches* (Paris, 1895), pp. 206–87.

(Mari), *Acta Sancti Maris Apostoli*, ed. J. B. Abbeloos, *Analecta Bollandiana* IV (1885) pp. 50–131.

(Maronite), *Chronicon Maroniticum*, ed. E. W. Brooks, CSCO III, *Chronica Minora* (1903) pp. 43–74.

(Martyres Persarum), *Acta Martyrum Persarum*, ed. P. Bedjan, *AMS* II (1891) pp. 351–96.

Marutha Maipherkatensis, *Tractatus de Haeresibus*, ed. I. Rahmani, *Studia Syriaca* IV, Documenta de antiquis haeresibus (Beirut, 1909) pp. *sh-qg.*

Michael Syrus, *Historia Ecclesiastica*, ed. and trans. J. B. Chabot, *Chronique de Michel le Syrien, Patriarche Jacobite d'Antioche*, 4 vols. (Paris, 1899–1910).

[Msiha-Zkha (?), *Chronicon Ecclesiae Arbelae*], ed. A. Mingana, *Sources syriaques* I (Leipzig, 1907) pp. 1–75.

Paulus Persa, *Logica*, ed. J. P. N. Land, *Anecdota Syriaca* IV (Leiden, 1875) pp. 1–32.

(Rabbula), *Vita*, ed. Overbeck, *op. cit.* (see under Ephraem) pp. 159–209.

Severus Antiochenus, *Epistularum selectarum tomus sextus*, ed. E. W. Brooks, *The Sixth Book of the Select Letters of Severus of Antioch*, 2 vols. (London, 1902–4).

— *Homilia CXXIII*, ed. M. Brière, *Les Homiliae Cathédrales de Sévère d'Antioche*, PO XXIX (1961) pp. 124–88 (trans. of Jacob of Edessa), ed. Rahmani, *op. cit.* (see under Marutha) pp. *mh-pt* (trans. of Paul of Callinicum).

(Simeon Bar Sabba'e), *Narratio de beato Simeone Bar Sabba'e*, ed. O. Kmosko, PS II (1907) cols. 779–960.

(Simeon Stylita senior), *Vita*, ed. P. Bedjan, *AMS* IV (1894) pp. 507–644.

Synodicon orientale où recueil de synodes nestoriennes, ed. J. B. Chabot (Paris, 1902).

Theodorus bar Kōnī, *Liber Scholiorum*, ed. A. Scher, CSCO LV (1910) and LXIX (1912).

(Thomas apost.), *Acta Thomae*, ed. P. Bedjan, *AMS* III (1892) pp. 1–175.

Titus Bostrensis, *Titi Bostreni contra manichaeos libri quatuor syriace*, ed. P. A. de Lagarde (Berlin, 1859).

Zacharias Mitylenensis Rhetor, *Historia Eccelsiastica*, ed. E. W. Brooks, CSCO LXXXIII-IV (1919–21).

(b) **Greek and Latin**

1. *Inscriptions and papyri*
(excluding whole works)

Papyri Magicae Graecae, ed. K. Preizendanz and rev. A. Henrichs, 2 vols. (Stuttgart, 1974).

P. Rylands Greek 469, ed. and trans. C. H. Roberts, *Catalogue of the Greek and Latin Papyri* in the John Rylands Library of Manchester, III (Manchester, 1938), pp. 38–46.

Welles, C. B. *et al.*, ed. *The Excavations at Dura-Europos*, Final Report V, *The Parchments and Papyri* (New Haven, 1959).

__ *Royal Correspondence in the Hellenistic Period* (New Haven, 1934).

2. *Individual works: Greek*
(including works extant only in Latin translation)

(Abercius), *S. Abercii vita*, ed. T. Nissen (Leipzig, 1912).

__ *Abercii titulus sepulcralis*, ed. W. Lüdtke and T. Nissen (Leipzig, 1910).

(Abjuration formula, the longer Greek), *Quo modo haeresim suam scriptis oporteat anathematizare eos qui e Manichaeis accedunt ad sanctam Dei catholicam et apostolicam Ecclesiam*, PG 1.1461–71.

(Abjuration formula, the Shorter Greek), *Qualiter oporteat a Manichaeorum haeresi ad sanctam Dei Ecclesiam accedentes scriptis (errorem) abjurare*, PG 100.1217–25.

Ps. Acacius, *epistula ad Petrum Fullonem*, ACO III, pp. 18–19.

Acta Concilii Constantinopoli anno 536 sub Mena, ed. M. A. Kugener, 'Textes grecs relatifs à Sévère, (I) Actes du councile de Constantinople de 536', PO II (1904), pp. 336–61.

Acta Ioannis, see (Ioannes apost.).

Acta Thomae, see (Thomas apost.).

Agathias Myrinaeus, *historiarum libri quinque*, ed. R. Keydell, CFHB II (Berlin, 1967).

Alexander Lycopolitanus, *contra Manichaei opiniones disputatio*, ed. A. Brinkmann (Leipzing,1895).

Anna Comnena, *Alexiados*, ed. B. Leib, *Alexiade*, 3 vols. (Paris, 1937–45).

Appianus, *Syriaca*, ed. P. Viereck and A. G. Roos, *Appiani historia romana* I (Leipzig, 1962) pp. 352–418.

Arrianus, *Alexandri anabasis*, ed. A. G. Roos and rev. P. Wirth, *Flavii Arriani quae exstant omnia* I (Leipzig, 1967).

__ *Parthica*, ed. *idem, ibid.* II (1968) pp. 224–52.

Athanasius, *(fug.) apologia de fuga sua*, ed. H. G. Opitz, *Athanasius Werke* II,1 (Berlin,1935–41) pp. 68–86.

__ *(h.Ar.) historia Arianorum, ibid.*, pp. 183–230.

__ *vita Antonii*, PG 26.837–976.

(*Basilica*), *Basiclicorum libri LX*, ed. H. J. Scheltema *et al.* (Groningen, 1953 ff.).

Cedrenus, Georgius, *historiarum compendium*, ed. I. Bekker, 2 vols., CSHB (1838–9) (= PG 121–2).

Clemens Alexandrinus, *excerpta Theodoti*, ed. O. Stählin, GCS XVII (Leipzig, 1909) pp. 103–33.

__ *stromateis*, ed. *idem*, GCS XV (Leipzig, 1939) and XVII (1909) pp. 3–102.

Ps. Clemens (Romanus), *recognitiones*, ed. B. Rhem and F. Paschke, GCS LI (Berlin, 1965).

Codex Manichaicus Coloniensis, ed. A. Henrichs and L. Koenen, *ZPE* XIX (1975) pp. 1–85, XXXII (1978), pp. 87–199, XLIV (1981), pp. 201–318 and XLVIII (1982), pp. 1–59.

Constantinus I Imperator (*Rescriptum Constantini de quadraginta annorum praescriptione*), ed. S. Riccobono, *FIRA* I (1968) pp. 465–6.

Corpus Hermeticum, ed. A. D. Nock and trans. A. J. Festugière, 4 vols. (Paris, 1945–54).

Cyrillus Hierosolymitanus, *catecheses*, ed. W. K. Reischl and J. Rupp, 2 vols. (Munich, 1848).

Cyrillus Scythopolitanus, *vita Euthymii*, ed. E. Schwartz, *Kyrillos von Skythopolis*, TU LXIX/2 (Leipzig, 1939) pp. 3–84.

Didymus Alexandrinus, *commentarii in Ecclesiasten* (in chartis papyraceis Turanis) ed. G. Binder, M. Grönewald *et al.* (Bonn, 1969 ff.).

Dio Cassius (Cassius Dio Cocceianus) *historiae romanae*, ed. U. P. Boissevain, 4 vols. (Berlin,1895–1931).

Diodorus Siculus, *bibliotheca historica*, ed. F. Vogel *et al.* 5 vols. (Leipzig, 1888–1906).

Ecloga, ed. C. A. Spuller, *L'Eclogue des Isauriens* (Crenautzi, 1929).

Epiphanius, *de haeresibus* (*Panarion*), ed. K. Holl, GCS XXV, XXXI and XXXVII (Leipzig,1915–33).

Eunapius Sardianus, *fragmenta*, *FHG* IV, pp. 7–56.

Eusebius Caesariensis, *historia ecclesiastica*, ed. E. Schwartz, GCS IX/1–3 (Leipzig, 1903–9).

__ *de martyribus Palestinae*, ed. *idem*, ibid. IX/2, pp. 907–45.

__ *praeparatio evangelica*, ed. K. Mras, GCS XLIII/1–2, (Berlin, 1954–6).

Eustathius Monachus, see under [Manes].

Georgius Monachus, *chronicon*, ed. C. de Boor and rev. P. Wirth, 2 vols. (Leipzig, 1978).

Georgius Monachus et Presbyter, *de haeresibus ad Epiphanium*, ed. M. Richard, 'Le traité de George hiéromoine sur les hérésies', *Revue des études byzantines* XXVIII (1970), pp. 239–69.

Georgius Syncellus, *chronographia*, ed. G. Dindorf, 2 vols. CSHB (Bonn, 1829).

Gregorius Nyssenus, *epistula canonica ad Leontium*, PG 45.221–36.

Harmenopoulos, Constantine, *Hexabiblos* (publication of the Department of Law and Economics of the University of Thessaloniki, 1952).

Hegemonius, *Acta Archelai*, ed. C. H. Beeson, GCS XVI (Leipzig, 1906).

Herodianus, ed. C. R. Whittaker, 2 vols. (London and Camb., Mass., 1969–70).

Herodotus, *historiae*, ed. C. Hude, 2 vols. (Oxford, 1927).

Hippolytus, *refutatio omnium haeresium*, ed. P. Wendland, GCS XXVI (Leipzig, 1916).

historia monachorum in Aegypto, ed. A. J. Festugière (Brussels, 1961).

Ibas Edessenus, *epistula ad Marim Persam*, *ACO* II, 1, 3, pp. 32–4.

(Ioannes apost.), *Acta Ioannis*, ed. M. Bonnet, *Acta Apostolorum Apocrypha*, II/1 (Leipzig, 1897) pp. 151–216.

Ioannes Caesariensis, *adversus Manichaeos homiliae ii*, ed. M. Richard, CCSG I (1977) pp. 85–105.

Ioannes Damascenus, *dialogus contra Manichaeos*, *PG* 94.1505–84.

Iohannes (Orthodoxus), *disputatio cum Manichaeo*, ed. M. Richard, CCSG I (1977) pp. 109–28.

Iohannes Scylitzes, *synopsis historiarum*, ed. J. Thurn, CFHB V (Berlin, 1973).

Irenaeus Lugdunensis, *adversus haereses*, ed. W. W. Harvey, 2 vols. (Cambridge, 1857).

Josephus, *antiquitates Judaicae*, ed. H. St. S. Thackeray *et al.*, 7 vols. (London, New York and Camb., Mass., 1930–81).

__ *bellum Judaicum*, ed. H. St. J. Thackeray, 2 vols. (London and New York, 1927–8).

Julianus Imperator, *epistulae et leges*, ed. J. Bidez and F. Cumont, *Iuliani imperatoris epistulae et leges* (Paris, 1922).

__ *orationes*, ed. J. Bidez, *L'Empereur Julien, oeuvres complète*, I/1 (Paris, 1932).

Justinianus Imperator, *contra Monophysitas*, ed. E. Schwartz, *Drei dogmatische Schriften Iustinians* (*Legum Iustiniani Imperatoris vocabularium*, Subsidia II, ed. M. Amelotti *et al.* (Milan, 1973).

Libanius, *epistulae*, ed. R. Foerster, *Libanii opera*, X–XI (Leipzig, 1921).

__ *orationes*, ed. *idem, ibid.* I–IV (Leipzig, 1903–8).

Libellus appellationis Eutychis ad Papam Leonem, *ACO* II, 2, 1, pp. 33–4.

Malalas, Iohannes, *chronographia*, ed. L. Dindorf, CSHB (1831).

[Manes], *fragmentum epistulae ad Addam*, *ap.* Eustathius Monachus, *epistulae*, *PG* 86.904A.

__ *fragmentum epistulae ad Scythianum, ap. ibid.*, col. 903B.

Marcus Diaconus, *vita Porphyrii Gazensis*, ed. H. Grégoire and M. A. Kugener, *Marc le Diacre, Vie de Porphyre* (Paris, 1930).

martyrum Pionii, ed. H. Musurillo, *The Acts of the Christian Martyrs* (Oxford, 1972) pp. 136–66.

martyrum Persarum Acta, ed. H. Delehaye, 'Les versions grecques des Actes des martyrs Persans sous Sapor II', *PO* II (1907) pp. 405–560.

Menander Protector, *ap.* Constantine Porphyrogenitus, *Excerpta de legationibus gentium*, in *Excerpta historica iussu imp. Constantini Porphyrogeniti confecta* I, ed. C. de Boor (Berlin, 1903) pp. 170–221 and 442–77.

Nicetas Choniatae, *thesaurus orthodoxae fidei*, excerpt on Manichaeism edited in A. Mai, *Nova Patrum Bibliotheca*, IV/2 (Rom, 1847) pp. 110–11.

Origenes, *contra Celsum*, ed. P. Koetschau, GCS II–III (Leipzig, 1899).

(Pachomius), *vita prima Sancti Pachomii*, ed. P. Halkin, *Sancti Pachomii vitae Graecae* (Brussels, 1932) pp. 1–96.

Palladius, *historia Lausiaca*, ed. C. H. Butler, Text and Studies VI/2 (Cambridge, 1904).

Paulus Persa, *disputatio cum Manichaeo*, *PG* 88.529–52.

__ *instituta regularia divinae legis* (Latine), ed. H. Kihn, *Theodor von Mop-*

suestia und Junilius Africanus als Exegeten (Freiburg, 1880) pp. 465–528.

Periplus maris Erythraei, ed. C. Müller, *GGM* I (1855) pp. 257–305.

Petrus Patricius, *fragmenta, FHG* IV (1870) pp. 181–91.

Petrus Siculus, *historia Manichaeorum*, ed. Ch. Astruc *et al.*, 'Les sources grecques pour l'histoire des Pauliciens d'Asie Mineure', *Travaux et Memoires*, IV (1970) pp. 7–67.

Philo Judaeus, *hypothetica (apologia pro Iudaeis)* ed. F. H. Colson, *Philo* IX (London and Camb., Mass., 1941) pp. 10–100.

__ *quod omnis probus liber sit, ibid.*, pp. 414–42.

Philostorgius, *historia ecclesiastica*, ed. J. Bidez and rev. F. Winkelmann, GCS (Berlin,1972).

Photius, *bibliotheca*, ed. P. Henry, 8 vols. (Paris, 1959–77).

__ *narratio de Manichaeis recens repullulantibus*, ed. Astruc *et al.*, (see under Petrus Siculus) pp. 99–179.

Plotinus, *enneades*, ed. P. Henry and H.-R. Schwyzer, *Plotini opera, editio minor*, 3 vols. (Oxford, 1964–82).

Plutarchus, *de Iside et Osiride*, ed. J. Gwynn Griffiths (Cardiff, 1970).

__ *vitae parallelae*, ed. C. Lindskog and K. Ziegler, 4 vols. (Leipzig, 1957–80).

Porphyrius, *de abstinentia*, ed. A. Nauck (Leipzig, 1886).

__ *vita Plotini*, ed. Henry and Schwyzer (see under Plotinus) I, pp. 1–38.

Procopius, *anecdota*, ed. J. Haury, *Procopii Caesariensis opera omnia* III (Leipzig, 1906).

__ *(Pers.) de bello Persico*, ed. *idem, ibid.* I (1905) pp. 4–304.

Ptolemaeus, *geographia*, ed. C. Müller, I, 2 parts (Paris, 1883–91).

Res Gestae Divi Saporis (Greek text), ed. A. Maricq, *Syria* XXXV (1958) pp. 245–60.

Serapion Thmuitanus, *contra Manichaeos*, ed. R. P. Casey, *Serapion of Thmuis against the Manichees, Harvard Theological Studies* XV, (Camb., Mass., 1931).

Simplicius, *in Epictetum encheiridion*, ed. F. Dübner, post *Theophrasti Characteres, Scriptorum Graecorum Bibliotheca* X (Paris, 1840).

Socrates, *historia ecclesiastica*, ed. R. Hussey, 3 vols. (Oxford, 1853).

Sozomenus, *historia ecclesiastica*, ed. J. Bidez and rev. G. C. Hansen, GCS L (Berlin,1960).

Strabo, *geographia*, ed. A. Meineke, 3 vols. (Leipzig, 1866–77).

Suidae Lexicon, ed. Adler, 5 vols, (Leipzig, 1928–38).

Theodoretus, *epistulae*, ed. Y. Azema, SC XL, XCVIII and CXI (Paris, 1955–65).

__ *haereticarum fabularum compendium, PG* 83.336–65.

__ *historia ecclesiastica*, ed. L. Parmentier and F. Scheidweiler, GCS XLIV (Berlin, 1954).

__ *(h. rel.) historia religiosa*, ed. P. Canivet and A. Leroy-Molinghen, SC CCXXXIV and CCLVII (Paris, 1977–9).

Theophanes Confessor, *chronographia*, ed. C. de Boor, 2 vols. (Leipzig, 1883–5).

Theophylactus Simoccata, *historiae*, ed. *idem* and rev. P. Wirth (Leipzig, 1972).

'*Theosophia Tubingensis*', ed. K. Buresch, *Klaros* (Leipzig, 1889) pp. 95–126.

(Thomas apost.) *Acta Thomae*, ed. M. Bonnet, *Acta Apostolorum Apocrypha*, II/2 (Leipzig, 1903) pp. 99–291.

Timotheus Presbyter Constantinopolitanus, *de iis qui ad ecclesiam accedunt*, *PG* 86.12–74.

Titus Bostrensis, *adversus Manichaeos* I–III, 7, ed. P. A. de Lagarde, *Titi Bostreni quae ex opere contra Manichaeos edito in codice Hamburgensis servata sunt* (Berlin, 1859); III, 7–29, ed. P. Nagel, 'Neues griechisches Material zu Titus von Bostra' in H. Ibscher (ed.), *Studia Byzantina*, Folge II (Berlin, 1973) pp. 285–350.

vita prima Sancti Pachomii, see under (Pachomius).

Zacharias Mitylenensis Rhetor, *adversus Manichaeos (Antirrēsis)*, ed. A. K. Demetrakopoulos, *Bibliotheca Ecclesiastica* I (Leipzig, 1886) pp. 1–18.

<Zacharias Mitylenensis>, *capita vii contra Manichaeos*, ed. M. Richard, CCSG I (1977) pp. xxxiii–xxxix.

Zonaras, *annales*, ed. M. Pinder, 3 vols. CSHB (Bonn, 1841–97).

Zosimus Historicus, *historia nova*, ed. L. Mendelssohn (Leipzig, 1887).

Zosimus Panopolitanus, περὶ ὀργάνων καί καμίνων, ed. M. Berthelot and M. Ch.-Em. Ruelle, *Collection des anciens alchemistes grecs* II (Paris, 1888) pp. 228–35.

__ τὸ πρῶτον βιβλίον τῆς τελευταίας ἀποχῆς, ibid. pp. 239–46.

3. *Individual works: Latin*

'Ambrosiaster', *in epistulam ad Timotheum secundam*, ed. H. I. Vogels, CSEL LXXXI/3 (1963).

Ambrosius, *epistulae*, ed. O. Faller and M. Zelzer, CSEL LXXXII/1-3 (1968–82).

Ammianus Marcellinus, *res gestae*, ed. W. Seyfarth, 2 vols. (Leipzig, 1978).

Augustinus, (*c. acad.*) *contra academicos*, ed. P. Knöll, CSEL LXIII (1922) pp. 3–81.

__ (*c. Adim.*) *contra Adimantum*, ed. J. Zycha, CSEL XXV/1 (1891) pp. 115–90.

__ (*c. adv. Leg. et Proph.*) *contra adversarium Legis et Prophetarum*, PL 42.603–66.

__ (*de duab. anim.*) *de duabus animabus*, ed. J. Zycha, CSEL XXV/1, pp. 3–48.

__ (*beat. vit.*) *de beata vita*, ed. P. Knöll, CSEL LXIII, pp. 89–116.

__ (*conf.*) *confessiones*, ed. L. Verheijen, CCSL XXVII (1981).

__ (*ep.*) *epistulae*, ed. A. Goldbacher and J. Divjak, CSEL XXXIV/1-2, XLIV, LVII, LVIII and LXXXVI (1895–1981).

__ (*c. ep. fund.*) *contra epistulam Manichaei quam vocant 'fundamenti'*, ed. J. Zycha, CSEL XXV/1, pp. 193–248.

__ (*in evang. Ioh.*) *in Iohannis Evangelium tractatus cxxiv*, ed. D. R. Willems, CCSL XXXVI (1954).

__ (*c. Faust.*) *contra Faustum*, ed. J. Zycha, CSEL XXV/1, pp. 251–797.

__ (*c. Fel.*) *contra Felicem*, ed. *idem*, CSEL XXV/2 (1892) pp. 801–52.

__ (*c. Fort.*) *contra Fortunatum*, ed. *idem*, CSEL XXV/1, pp. 83–112.

__ (*haer.*) *de haeresibus*, ed. R. Vander Plaetses and C. Beukers, CCSL XLVI (1969) pp. 283–345.

__ (*c. Iul. op. impf.*) *contra secundam Iuliani responsionem opus imperfectum*, PL 45.1049–1608.

__ (mor. eccl. et mor. manich.) de moribus Ecclesiae Catholicae et de moribus Manichaeorum, PL 32.1309-78.

__ (nat. bon.) de natura boni, ed. J. Zycha, CSEL XXV/1, pp. 855-89.

__ (c. litt. Petil.) contra litteras Petiliani, ed. M. Petchenig, CSEL LII (1909).

__ (enarr. in Ps.) enarrationes in Psalmos, ed. E. Dekkers and J. Fraipont, CCSL XXXVIII-XL (1956).

__ (retr.) retractationes, ed. P. Knöll, CSEL XXXVI (1902).

__ (c. Secund.) contra Secundium, ed. J. Zycha, CSEL XXV/2 (1892) pp. 905-47.

__ (until. cred.) de utilitate credendi, ed. idem, CSEL XXV/1, pp. 3-48.

Ps.-Augustinus, commonitorium cuomodo agendum sit cum Manichaeis, qui confitentur privatem huius nefandi erroris, ed. idem, CSEL XXV/2, pp. 979-82.

Codex Justinianus, ed. P. Kreuger, Corpus Iuris Civilis II, (Berlin, 1929).

Codex Theodosianus, ed. T. Mommsen and E. Meyer, Theodosiani libri XVI, (Berlin, 1905).

collatio: Lex Dei sive Mosaicarum et Romanarum legum collatio, ed. J. Baviera, FIRA II, pp. 544-89.

'Collectio Avellana', ed. O. Guenther, Epistulae imperatorum pontificum aliorum, CSEL XXXV (1895).

Constitutiones Sirmondianae, ed. Mommsen and Meyer in Codex Theodosianus I/2.

Decretum Gelasianum, ed. E. von Dobschütz, TU XXXVIII/4 (Leipzig, 1912).

Egeria, Itinerarium, ed. A Franceschini and R. Weber, CCSL CLXXV (1958) pp. 28-103.

Eutropius, breviarium ab urbe condita, ed. C. Santini (Leipzig, 1979).

Evodius, de fide contra Manichaeos, ed. J. Zycha, CSEL XXV/2, ,pp. 951-75.

Expositio totius mundi et gentium, ed. J. Rougé, SC CXXIV (Paris, 1966).

Festus, breviarium, ed. J. W. Eadie (London, 1967).

Filastrius, diversarum haereseon liber, ed. F. Marx, CSEL XXXVIII (1898).

Fragmenta Tebestina, ed. and trans. P. Alfaric, 'Un manuscrit manichéen', Revue d'Histoire de Littérature Religieuses, N.S. VI (1920) pp. 62-98. Text reproduced in PL Suppl. 2.1378-88.

Fronto, principia historiae, ed. C. R. Haines, The Correspondence of Marcus Cornelius Fronto II (London and New York, 1920) pp. 198-218.

Gregorius II Papa, epistulae et canones, PL 89.453-534.

Hieronymus, epistulae, ed. I. Hilberg, CSEL LIV-LVI (1910-18).

__ adversus Iovinianum, PL 23.211-338.

__ de viris illustribus, ibid., cols. 603-759.

Hydatius, chronicon, ed. A. Tranoy, SC 218-19 (1974).

Justinus, epitoma historiarum, ed. O. Seel (Stuttgart, 1972).

Lactantius, de mortibus persecutorum, ed. S. Brandt and G. Laubmann, CSEL XXVII/2 (1897) pp. 171-238.

Leges novellae Theodosii II, ed. Mommsen and Meyer in Codex Theodosianus II, pp. 3-68.

Leges novellae Valentiniani, ibid. pp. 68-154.

Leo Magnus, epistulae, PL 54.593-1218.

__ epistula XV, ed. Vollmann (see Bibliog. II. a) pp. 122-38.

— *tractatus septem et nonaginta*, ed. A. Chavasse, CCSL CXXXVIII–CXXXVIIIA (1973).
liber pontificalis, ed. L. Duchesne, 3 vols. (Paris, 1886–92).
(Marcellus Papa), *Acta S. Marcelli Papae et martyris*, ed. J. Bollandus, *Acta Sanctorum*, 16 January (Antwerp, 1643) pp. 5–9.
Orosius, *commonitorium de errore Priscillianistarum et Origenistarum*, ed. G. Schepss, CSEL XVIII (1889) pp. 151–7.
Pacatus, *Panegyricus Theodosio dictus*, ed. E. Galletier, *Panégyriques Latins* III (Paris, 1955) pp. 68–114.
Paulinus, *vita Ambrosii*, PL 14.29–50.
Paulus, *sententiae*, ed. J. Baviera *et al.*, *FIRA* II, pp. 317–418.
Plinius Secundus (major), *naturalis historiae*, ed. H. Rackham *et al.*, 10 vols. (London and Camb., Mass., 1938–78).
Plinius Secundus (minor), *epistulae*, ed. R. A. B. Mynors (Oxford, 1963).
Polo, Marco, *Il Milione*, ed. L. F. Benedetto (Florence, 1928).
— *ibid.* (Edition of Manuscript Z), ed. A. C. Moule and P. Pelliot, *Marco Polo, The Description of the World* II (London, 1938).
Possidius, *vita S. Augustini*, ed. H. T. Weisskotten (New Jersey, 1919).
Priscillianus, *tractatus*, ed. G. Schepss, CSEL XVIII (1889) pp. 3–106.
Prosper Aquitanus, *epitoma chronicorum*, ed. T. Mommsen, *MGH, Auct. Ant.*, *Chronica Minora* I (Berlin, 1892) pp. 385–485.
Prosperi anathematismata, PL 45.23–30.
Rufinus, *historia monachorum*, PL 21.391–462.
Scriptores Historiae Augustae, ed. K. Hohl, 2 vols. (Leipzig, 1927–45).
Secundinus, *epistula ad Augustinum*, ed. J. Zycha, CSEL XXV/2, pp. 893–901.
Sulpitius Severus, *chronicorum libri II*, ed. C. Halm, CSEL I (1886) pp. 3–105.
— *vita Martini Turonensis*, *ibid.*, pp. 109–37.
— *dialogorum libri ii*, *ibid.*, pp. 152–216.
Tacitus, *annales*, ed. C. D. Fisher (Oxford, 1906).
Tertullianus, *adversus Marcionem*, ed. E. Evans, 2 vols. (Oxford, 1972).
Turribius episcopus Asturicensis, *epistula ad Idacium et Ceponium*, PL 54.693–95.
Victor Vitensis, *historia persecutionis Africanae provinciae*, ed. M. Petschenig, CSEL VII (1881).
Ps.-Victorinus, *ad Justinum Manichaeum*, PL 8.999–1010.

(c.) Chinese

Ch'ao-yeh ch'ien tsai 朝野僉載, 6 ch. (*c.* 720) compiled by Chang Cho 張鷟, in *Ts'ung-chu chi-ch'eng*.
Chi-lei pien 雞筋編, 3 ch. (1133) by Chuang Ch'o 莊綽 (*c.* 1090–*c.* 1150), in *Sung Yüan jen shuo-pu shu* (Shanghai, 1919).
Chi-shen lu 稽神錄, 6 ch. compiled by Hsü Hsüan 徐鉉 (917–92) with Shih-i 拾遺, 1 ch. and Pu-i 補遺, 1 ch., in *Sung Yüan jen shuo-pu shu* (Shanghai, 1919).
Chia-t'ing chi'ih-ch'eng-chih 嘉定赤城志, 40 ch. (1223) compiled by Ch'en Ch'i-ch'ing 陳耆卿, in *T'ai-chou ts'ung-shu* 台州叢書
Chih-yüan pien-wei lu 至元辨偽錄, 5 ch., ed. Hsiang-mai 祥邁, T 2116, LII, PP. 751b–80a.

Chih-yüan hsü-chi 芝園續集, 4 ch., ed. in *Sung Wen-hsien kung ch'üan-chi* 宋文憲公全集, 52 ch., by Sung Lien 宋濂 (1310-81) in *Ssü-pu pei-yao*.

Ch'ing-ch'i k'ou-kuei 青溪寇軌, 1 ch. (1132) attributed to Fang Shao 方勺 in *Chin-hua ts'ung-shu* 金華叢書, fasc. 84, 1a-10a.

Ch'ing-yüan tiao-fa shih-lei 慶元條法事類, 80 ch. (*c.* 1200) compiled by Hsieh Shen-fu 謝深甫 and others, ed. Nakajima Satoshi 中嶋敏, *Koten kenkyukai sōsho* (Tokyo, 1968).

Chien-yen i-lai hsi-nien yao-lu 建炎以來繫年要錄, 200 ch., compiled by Li Hsin-ch'uan 李心傳 (1166-1243), Chung-hua shu-chü edition (Peking, 1956).

Chiu T'ang-shu 舊唐書, 200 ch., compiled by Liu Hsü 劉昫 (887-946), Chung-hua shu-chü edition (Peking, 1975).

Chiu Wu-tai shih 舊五代史, 150 ch., compiled by Hsieh Chü-chêng 薛居正 (912-81) and others, Chung-hua shu-chü edition (Peking, 1976).

Ch'üan T'ang wen (see *Chin-ting ch'üan T'ang wen*).

[*Chin-ting*] *Ch'üan T'ang wen* 欽定全唐文, 1000 ch., compiled by Tung Kao 董誥 (1740-1818) Hua-wen shu-chü edition 華文書局 (Taipei, 1965) (photographic reprint of the 1814 edition).

Fo-tsu li-tai t'ung-tsai 佛祖歷代通載, 22 ch. (1341) compiled by Nien-chang 念常, *T* 2036, XLIX, pp. 129a-475c.

Fo-tsu t'ung-chi 佛祖統記, 54 ch. (1265) compiled by Chih-p'an 志磐, *T* 2039, XLIX, pp. 129a-475c.

Fu-chien t'ung-chih 福建通志, ed. Ch'en shou-ch'i 陳壽祺 (Fukien, 1867).

Hai-ch'ing Po-chen-jen yü-lu 海瓊白珍人語錄 by Po Yü-ch'an 白玉蟾, compiled by Hiseh Hsien-tao 謝顯道 in *Tao-tsang* 道藏, fasc. 1016.

Hou Han-shu 後漢書, 90 ch., compiled by Fan Yeh 范曄 (398-445), Chung-hua shu-chü edition (Peking, 1973).

Hsin T'ang-shu 新唐書, 225 ch., compiled by Ou-yang Hsiu 歐陽修 (1007-72) and others, Chung-hua shu-chü edition.

Hsüeh-shan chi 雪山集, 16 ch., by Wang Chih 王質 (1135-89), in *Ts'ung-shu chi ch'eng*.

Huang-shih jih-ch'ao 黃氏日抄, 97 ch., by Huang Chen 黃震 (1213-80) in *Ssu-k'u ch'üan-shu chen-pen ch'u-chi* (1934-5, repr. Taipei, 1969). Also consulted is the edition of Wang Pei-o, 汪佩鍔 (1767).

Hui-ch'ang i-p'in chi 會昌一品集, 36 ch., by Li Te-yü 李德裕 (787-849), in *Ssu-k'u ch'üan-shu chen-pen ch'u-chi.*

Ju T'ang ch'iu-fa hsün-li hsing-chi 入唐求法巡禮行記, see below *Nittō gūho junrei gyōki no kenkyū.*

Jung-chai i-shih 容齋逸史 (*see under Ch'ing-ch'i kuo-kuei*).

Kao-feng wen-chi 高峯文集, 12 ch., compiled by Liao Kang 廖剛 (1071-1143), in *Ssu-k'u ch'üan-shu chen-pen ch'u-chi.*

Kao-seng chuan 高僧傳, 14 ch. (519), compiled by Hui-chao 慧皎, *T* 2059, L, pp. 322c-423a.

Lao-hsüeh yen pi-chi 老學庵筆記, 10 ch., by Lu Yu 陸遊 (1125-1210) in *Sung Yüan jen shou-pu-shu* (Shanghai, 1920).

Lao-tzu hsi-hsing hua-hu ching 老子西昇化胡經, see next item.

Lao-tzu hua-hu ching 老子化胡經, fragments ed. in *T* 2139, LIV, pp. 1266a-1270b.

Li-chi chu-shu 禮記注疏, 63 ch., in *Shih-shan ching chu-shu fu chiao-k'an chi*

十三經注疏坿校勘記, ed. Jüan Yüan 阮元 (1815) in *Ssu-pu pei-yao*.

Meng-tzu 孟子, ed. and trans. James Legge, *The Works of Mencius, The Chinese Classics*, II, second edition (Oxford, 1893).

Min shu 閩書, 154 fasc. (1629) compiled by Ho Ch'iao-yüan 何喬遠, edition of 1629.

Ming lü chi-chieh fu li 明律集解附例, see below *Ta Ming lü chi-chieh fu li*.

Mo-ni chiao hsia-pu tsan 摩尼敎下部讚 (*Hymnscroll*) T 2140, LIV, pp. 1270b21–1279c10. Eng. trans. Tsui Chi, 'Mo-ni chiao hsia-pu tsan, the Lower (Second?) Section of the Manichaean hymns', BSOAS, XI, (1943) pp. 174–219.

Mo-ni kuang-fu chiao-fa i-lüeh 摩尼光佛敎法儀略 (*Compendium*), T 2141A, LIV, pp. 1279c17–1281a11. Eng. trans. of pp. 1279c17–1280c12: G. Haloun and W. B. Henning, 'The Compendium of the Doctrines and Styles of the teaching of Mani, the Buddha of Light', *Asia Major*, N.S., III (1952) pp. 184–212. French trans. of pp. 1280c12–1281a11, *Traité* 1913, pp. 107–16.

Nittō gūho junrei gyōki no kenkyū 入唐求法巡禮行記の硏究, ed. by Ono Katsutoshi 小野勝年 (Tokyo, 1968).

P'an-chou wen-chi 盤州文集, 80 ch., by Hung Kua 洪适 (1117–84), with Fu-lu 附錄, 1, ch. and Shih-i 拾遺, 1 ch., in *Ssu-pu ts'ung-k'an*.

Pien-wei lu (see *Chih-yüan pien-wei lu*).

Po-che pien 泊宅編, 10 ch., by Fang Shao 方勺 (1066–after 1141) in *Chin-hua ts'ung-shu*.

Po-shih ch'ang-ch'ing chi 白氏長慶集, 70 ch., by Po Chü-i 白居易 (772–846) in *Ssu-pu ts'ung-k'an*.

Po-ssu chiao ts'an-ching 波斯敎殘經 (*Treatise*) T 2141B, LIV, pp. 1281a16–1286a29. French trans, *Traité* 1911, pp. 499–617. See also the edition by Ch'en Yüan at the end of the reprint version of his article (i.e. pp. 375–92) cited in Bibliography II.b.

Pu-hsi-chou-yü chi 不繫舟漁集, 16 ch., by Ch'en Kao 陳高 (1314–66) in *Ching-hsiang-lou ts'ung-shu* 敬鄉樓叢書.

Shih chi 史記, 130 ch., compiled by Ssu-ma chien 司馬遷 (c. 145–86 BC) Chung-hua shu-chü edition (Peking, 1959).

Shih-chia chai-yang hsin lu 十駕齋養新錄, 20 ch., by Ch'ien Ta-hsin 錢大昕 (1729–1809), Shang-wu yin-shu kuan edition (Shanghai, 1957).

Shih-men cheng-t'ung 釋門正統, 8 ch. (1237), comilation begun by Wu K'o-chi 吳克己 (d. 1208) and completed by Tsung-chien 宗鑑. *Hsü tsang-ching* 續藏經, second series, B, 3.5, pp. 357Aa–463Ab.

Sui shu 隋書, 85 ch., compiled by Wei Ch'eng 魏徵 (580–643), Chung-hua shu-chü edition (Peking, 1973).

Sung hui-yao chi-kao 宋會要輯稿, 200 fasc., compiled by Hsü Sung 徐松 (1781–1848) and others (Shanghai, 1936).

Sung shih 宋史, 496 ch., compiled by T'o T'o 脫脫 (1575–1620) and others, Chung-hua shu-chü edition.

Sung shu 宋書, 100 ch., compiled by Shen Yüeh 沈約 (441–513), Chung-hua shu-chü edition (Peking, 1974).

Sung ta chao-ling chi 宋大詔令集, 240 ch., edition of Chung-hua shu-chü (Peking, 1962).

Ta Ming lü chi-chieh fu li 大明律集解附例, 30 ch., in *Ming-tai shih-chi hui k'an* (Taipei, 1970).

Ta Sung seng shih lüeh 大宋僧史略, 3 ch. (c. 999), compiled by Tsan-ning 贊寧, T 2126, LIV, pp. 235a–55b.

Ta T'ang hsi-yü chi 大唐西域記, 52 ch. (646) by Hsüan-tsang 玄奘, T 2053, L, pp. 221b–280a.

Ta T'ang Ta tz'u-en ssu San-tsang fa-shih chüan 大唐大慈恩寺三藏法師傳, 10 ch., compiled by Hui-li 慧立, T 2053, L, pp. 221b–280a.

T'ai-p'ing kuang-chi 太平廣記, 500 ch. (978), compiled by Li Fang 李昉, Jen-min wen-hsüeh ch'u-p'an she edition (Peking, 1959).

T'ang hui-yao 唐會要, 100 ch., compiled by Wang Po 王溥 (922–82), Kuo-hsüeh chi-pen ts'ung-shu edition (Shanghai, 1935).

T'ang lü shu-i 唐律疏義, 30 ch. (653) compiled by Chang-sun Wu-chi 長孫無忌, in *Ts'ung-shu chi-ch'eng*.

Ts'e-fu yüan-kuei 册府元龜, 1000 ch., compiled by Wang Ch'in-jo 王欽若 (d. 1025) and Yang I 楊億 (974–1020), edition of Li Ssu-ching 李嗣京 (1642).

Tsao-lin tsa tsu i chi 棗林雜俎義集 8 ch., ed. T'an Ch'ien 談遷 (1594–1658) in *Pi-chi hsiao-shuo ta-kuan* 筆記小說大觀 Series 22, VI (Taipei, 1981).

Tun-huang i-shu 燉煌遺書 edited by P. Pelliot and Haneda Toru 羽田亨, I (Shanghai, 1926).

T'ung-tien 通典, 200 ch. (801) by Tu Yu 杜佑, in *Shih t'ung* 十通 (Shanghai, 1936).

Tzu-chih t'ung-chien 資治通鑑, 294 ch. (1084) compiled by Ssu-ma Kuang 司馬光 and others, Ku-chi ch'u-pan she edition (Shanghai, 1956).

Wei-nan wen-chi 渭南文集, 50 ch. by Lu Yu 陸遊 (1125–1210) in *Lu Fang-weng ch'üan-chi* 陸放翁全集, in *Ssu-pu pei-yao*.

Wei shu 魏書, 114 ch., compiled by Wei Su 魏收 (506–72), Chung-hua shu-chü edition (Peking, 1974).

Yüan shih 元史, 210 ch., compiled by Sung Lien 宋濂 (1310–81), Chung-hua shu-chü edition (Peking, 1976).

Yün-chi ch'i-ch'ien 雲笈七籤, 122 ch. (1019) compiled by Chang Chün-fang 張君房, in *Ssu-pu ts'ung kan*.

II. SECONDARY WORKS

(a) In western languages

Aalders, G. J. D., 'L'épître à Menoch attribuée à Mani', *Vigiliae Christianae*, XIV (1960), pp. 245–9.

Agathanagelos, *History of the Armenians*, ed. and trans. R. W. Thomson (Albany, 1976).

Aland, B., 'Mani und Bardesanes – Zur Entstehung des manichäischen Systems', in A. Dietrich (1975) pp. 123–43.

__ ed., *Gnosis. Festschrift für Hans Jonas* (Göttingen, 1978).

Alfaric, P., *Les écritures manichéennes*, 2 vols. (Paris, 1918–9).

__ *L'Évolution intellectuelle de S. Augustin* (Paris, 1918).

Allberry, C. R. C., 'Das manichäische Bema-Fest', ZNW XXXVII (1938), pp. 2–10.

Altheim, F., 'Die vier Weltreiche in der manichäischen *Kephalaia*', in P. Nagel ed., *Probleme der Koptischen Literatur* (Halle, 1968) pp. 115–19.

Altheim, F. and R. Stiehl. 'Palmyra und die Seidenstrasse', in Altheim and Stiehl (eds.) (1970), pp. 704–9.

__ eds., *Geschichte Mittelasiens im Altertum* (Berlin, 1970).

Arnold-Döben, V., *Die Bildersprache des Manichäismus* (Köln, 1978).

Asmussen, Jes P., 'Das Christentum in Iran und sein Verhältnis zum Zoroastrismus', *Studia Theologica*, XVI (1962), pp. 1–24.

__ *X^uāstvānīft. Studies in Manichaeism* (Copenhagen, 1965).

__ 'Der Manichäismus als Vermittler literarischen Gutes', *Temenos*, II (1966), pp. 14–21.

__ *Manichaean Literature* (New York, 1975).

Assfalg J., 'Zur Textüberlieferung der Chronik von Arbela, Beobachtungen zum Ms. or. fol. 3126', *Oriens Christianus*, L (1960), pp. 19–36.

Avi-Yonah, M., *Geschichte der Juden im Zeitalter des Talmud* (Berlin, 1962).

Babut, E.-Ch., *Priscillien et le priscillianisme* (Paris, 1909).

Bailey, H. W., *Zoroastrian Problems in the Ninth-century Books* (Oxford, 1943).

Bang, W., 'Aus Manis Briefen' in *Aus den Forschungsarbeiten der Mitglieder des ungarischen Instituts in Berlin dem Andenken Robert Graggers gewidmet* (Berlin, 1927).

__ 'Manichäische Erzähler', *Le Muséon*, XLIV (1931) pp. 1–36

Barb, A. A., 'The survival of magical arts', in A. D. Momigliano (ed.), *The Conflict between Paganism and Christianity in the Fourth Century* (Oxford, 1963) pp. 100–125.

Barnes, T. D., 'Imperial victories', *The Phoenix*, XXX/2 (1976), pp. 174–93.

Bauer, Walter, *Rechtgläubigkeit und Ketzerei im ältesten Christentum*, 2nd ed. mit einem Nachtrag von G. Strecker (Tübingen, 1964).

Bauer, Wolfgang, *China und die Hoffnung auf Glück* (Munich, 1971).

Baus, K., *Handbook of Christianity* (Eng. edition, London, 1965).

Baynes, N. H. review of K. Stade (see below), *JRS* XVII (1927), pp. 123–4

Beck, E., *Ephräms Polemik gegen Mani und die Manichäer*, CSCO CCCXCI, (Subs. 55, Louvain, 1978).

__ 'Bardaiṣan und seine Schule bei Ephräm', *Le Museon* XCI (1978), pp. 271–333.

Beck, H.-G., *Kirche und theologische Literatur im byzantinischen Reich* (Munich, 1959).

Benz, E., 'Indische Einflüsse auf die frühchristliche Theologie', *Abhandlungen der Akademie der Wissenschaften und der Literatur in Mainz*, Nr. 3 (Wiesbaden, 1951).

Bertinelli, M. G. A., 'I Romani oltre l'Eufrate nel II secolo d.C.', *ANRW* IX/1 (Berlin, 1976), pp. 3–45.

Berve, H., *Das Alexanderreich auf prosopographischer Grundlage*, 2 vols. (Munich, 1926).

Bevan, A. A., *The Hymn of the Soul contained in the Syriac Acts of Thomas, Texts and Studies*, V, ed. J. A. Robinson (Cambridge, 1899).

Bidez, J., and F. Cumont, *Les Mages Hellenisés*, 2 vols. (Paris, 1938) al-Bīrūnī, *Chronology of the Ancient Nations*, trans. E. Sachau (London, 1879).

__ *Alberuni's India*, trans. E. Sachau, 2 vols. (London, 1888).

Blum, G. G. *Rabbula von Edessa*, CSCO CCC (Subs. 49, Louvain, 1969).

Böhlig, A., 'Zur Vorstellung vom Lichtkreuz in Gnostizismus und Manichäismus', in B. Aland (ed.) (1918), pp. 473–91.

__ 'Der Synkretismus des Mani', in Dietrich (ed.) (1975), pp. 144–69.

__ *Mysterion und Wahrheit. Gesammelte Beiträge zur spätantiken Religionsgeschichte* (Leiden, 1968), pp. 202–21.

__ *Die Bibel bei den Manichäern* (Theol. Diss., Münster, 1947, unpublished).

Boodberg, P. A., 'Marginalia to the histories of the northern dynasties, I, Theophylactus Simocatta on China', *HJAS* III (1938), pp. 223–43.

Bornkamm, G., *Mythos und Legende in den apokryphen Thomas-Akten*, Forschungen zur Rel. und Lit. d. Alten und Neuen Test. XLIX, N.F. 31 (Göttingen, 1933).

Boulnois, L., *La route de soie* (Paris, 1963).

Boyce, M., 'The Manichaean literature in Middle Iranian', *HO*, IV, 2, 1 (Leiden, 1968), pp. 67–76.

__ 'Toleranz und Intoleranz im Zoroastrismus', *Saeculum*, XXI (1970), pp. 325–47.

Brillet, G., 'Agapius', *Dictionnaire d'histoire et de géographie ecclesiastiques*, I (Paris, 1912), cols. 902–3.

Brinkmann, A., 'Die Theosophie des Aristokritos', *Rheinisches Museum für Philologie*, N.F. 51 (1896), pp. 273–80.

Brock, S. P., 'A martyr at the Sasanid court under Vahran II, Candida', *Analecta Bollandiana*, XCVI (1978), pp. 167–81.

__ 'Clothing metaphors as a means of theological expression in Syriac tradition', in M. Schmidt and C. F. Geyer (eds.), *Typus, Symbol, Allegorie bei den östlichen Vätern und ihren Parallelen im Mittelalter* (Regensburg, 1981), pp. 11–40.

Brown, P. R. L., *Augustine of Hippo – a Biography* (London, 1967).

__ *Religion and Society in the Age of St Augustine* (London, 1972).

Bruce Codex (*Codex Brucianus*), *The Books of Jeu and the Untitled Text in the Bruce Codex*, ed. C. Schmidt and trans. V. MacDermot (Leiden, 1978).

Brückner, A., *Faustus von Mileve* (Basel, 1901).

Burkitt, F. C., *The Religion of the Manichees* (Cambridge, 1925).

Cameron, A., 'Agathias on the Sassanians' *Dumbarton Oaks Papers*, XXIII (1969), pp. 69–183.

Cantineau, J., *Inventaire des inscriptions de Palmyre*, fasc. 3, La Grand Colonnade (Beirut, 1930).

Chadwick, H., *Priscillian of Avila* (Oxford, 1976).

__ 'The relativity of moral codes: Rome and Persia in late antiquity', *Early Christian Literature and the Classical Intellectual Tradition*, ed., W. R. Schoedel and R. L. Wilken (Paris, 1978), pp. 135–53.

Chastagnol, A., *La préfecture urbaine sous le Bas-Empire* (Paris, 1960).

Châtillon, F., 'Adimantus Manichaei discipulus', *Revue de Moyen Age Latin*, X (1954), pp. 191–203.

Chaumont, M.-L., 'Conquêtes Sassanides et propagande Mazdéenne (IIIème

Siècle)', Historia, XXII (1973), pp. 664-709.

___ 'Les Sassanides et la Christianisation de l'Empire iranien au IIIème siècle de notre ère', Revue de l'Histoire des Religions, CLXV (1964), pp. 165-202.

___ Recherches sur l'histoire d'Arménie (Paris, 1969).

___ 'L'Arménie entre Rome et l'Iran, I', ANRW IX/1 (Berlin, 1976) pp. 72-194

Chavannes, E., 'Le Nestorianisme et l'inscription de Kara-Balgassoun', Journal Asiatique, 9e ser, IX (Jan-Feb. 1897), pp. 43-85.

___ Documents sur les Tou-kie (Turcs) occidentaux (Paris, 1941).

Ch'en, K., Buddhism in China, A Historical Survey (New Jersey, 1964).

___ 'The Hui-chang persecution of Buddhism', HJAS, XIX (1956), pp. 67-109.

Christensen, A., L'Iran sous les Sassanides (Copenhagen, 1936).

___ Le règne du roi Kawādh I et le communisme mazdakite (Copenhagen 1925).

Chwolsohn, D., Die Ssabier und der Ssabismus, 2 vols. (St Petersburg, 1856).

Clark, L. V., 'The Manichaean Turkic Pothi-Book', Altorientalische Forschungen IX (1982), pp. 145-218

Clermont-Genneau, M., 'Odeinat et Vaballat, rois de Palmyre et leur titre romain de Corrector', Revue Biblique XXIX (1920) pp. 382-419.

Colpe, C., Die religionsgeschichtliche Schule (Göttingen, 1961).

___ Der Manichäismus in der arabischen Überlieferung, Dissertation zur Erlangung des Doktorgrades der Philosophischen Fakultät der Georg-August-Universität zu Göttingen 1954, unpublished.

___ 'Anpassung des Manichäismus an den Islam', ZDMG CIX (1959), pp. 82-91.

___ 'Die Formulierung der Ethik in arabischen Manichäer-Gemeinden', in Ex Orbe Religionum, I (Leiden, 1972) pp. 401-12.

Conrat, M., Römisches Recht im fränkischen Reich (Leipzig, 1913).

Coq, A. v. Le, Die buddhistische Spätantike II, Die manichäischen Miniaturen (Berlin, 1923).

___ 'Ein christliches und ein manichäisches Manuskriptfragment in türkischer Sprache aus Turfan', Sitzungsberichte der königlichen preussischen Akademie der Wissenschaften, 1909, pp. 1202-18.

Courcelle, P., Recherches sur les 'Confessions' de S. Augustin (Paris, 1950).

Coyle, J. K., Augustine's 'De Moribus ecclesiae catholicae' (Fribourg, 1978).

Crum, W.E., 'Eusebius and Coptic church historians', Proceedings of the Society of Biblical Archaeology, Feb. 1907, pp. 76-7.

Cumont, F., 'La propagation du manichéisme dans l'Empire romain', Revue d'Histoire et de Littérature Religeuse, N.S. I (1910), pp. 31-43.

___ Textes et monuments figures relatifs aux mystères de Mithra, 2 vols. (Brussels, 1896).

___ and M. Kugener, Recherches sur le manichéisme, 2 vols. (Brussels, 1908-19).

Daniélou, J., The Theology of Jewish Christianity, trans. and ed. J. A. Baker (London, 1964).

Daniels, C. M., 'The role of the Roman army in the spread and practice of Mithraism', in Mithraic Studies, ed. J. R. Hinnells, II (Manchester, 1975), pp. 249-79.

Debevoisse, N. C., A Political History of Parthia (Chicago, 1938).

Decret, F., *Aspects du manichéisme dans l'Afrique romaine* (Paris, 1970).

___ *Mani et la tradition manichéenne* (Paris, 1974).

___ *L'Afrique manichéenne, Étude historique et doctrinale*, 2 vols. (Paris, 1978.)

___ 'Les conséquences sur le christianisme en Perse de l'affrontement des empires romain et sassanide de Shapur Ier à Yazdgard Ier', *Recherches Augustiniennes*, XIV (1979) pp. 91–152.

Dietrich, A., ed., *Synkretismus im syrisch-persischen Kulturgebiet* (Göttingen, 1975).

Dillemann, L., *Haute Mésopotamie orientale et pays adjacents* (Paris, 1962).

Dölger, F., 'Konstantin der Grosse und der Manichäismus, Sonne und Christus in Manichäismus', *Antike und Christentum. Kultur und religionsgeschichtliche Studien* (Münster, 1931), pp. 310–14.

Drijvers, H., *Bardaiṣan of Edessa* (Assen, 1966).

___ 'Mani und Bardaiṣan', in *Mélanges d'Histoire des religions offerts à Henri-Charles Peuch* (Paris, 1975), pp. 459–69.

___ 'Hatra, Palmyra und Edessa', *ANRW* VIII (Berlin, 1978) pp. 799–906.

Dubs, H. H., *The History of the Former Han Dynasty*, II (Baltimore, 1941).

Dufourcq, *Étude sur les Gesta martyrum romains*, 4 vols. (Paris, 1900–07)

Dupont-Somer, A., 'Note archaeologique sur le proverbe evangelique "Mettre la lampe sous le boisseau",' in *Mélanges syriens offerts à M. R. Dussaud*, II (Paris, 1939), pp. 789–94.

Egger, R., *Forschungen in Salona*, 2 vols. (Vienna, 1926).

___ 'Das Mausoleum von Marusinae und seine Herkunft' in *Römische Antike und frühes Christentum*, 2 vols. (Klagenfurt, 1962).

Eichhorn, W., 'Materialien zum Auftreten iranischer Kulte in China', *Die Welt des Orients*, II (1959), pp. 531–41.

___ *Die Religionen Chinas* (Stuttgart, 1973).

Enoki, Kazuo, 'Nestorian Christianism [sic] in medieval times accordingg to recent historical and archaeological researches', *L'Oriente Cristiano*, Accademia dei Lincei, anno 361, quaderno 62 (Rome, 1964), pp. 45–77.

Ensslin, W., 'Valentinianus III, Novellen XVII und XVIII von 445. Ein Beitrag zur Stellung von Staat und Kirche', *Zeitschrift der Savigny-Stiftung für Rechtsgeschichte*, Rom. Abt., LVII (1937), pp. 373–8.

Evans, G. R., *Augustine on Evil* (Cambridge, 1982).

Festugière, A.-J., *La révélation d'Hermès Trismégiste*, 4 vols., II (Paris, 1944).

Ficker, G., 'Eine Sammlung von Abschwörungsformeln', *Zeitschrift für Kirchengeschichte*, XXVIII (1906), pp. 443–64.

Fiey, J. M., 'Les communautés syriaques en Iran', *Acta Iranica*, III (1974), pp. 279–97.

___ 'Vers la réhabilitation de l'Histoire de Karka d'Bét Slôh', *Analecta Bollandiana*, LXXXII (1964), pp. 189–222.

___ *Assyrie Chrétienne*, III (Beirut, 1968).

___ *Jalons pour une histoire de l'église en Iraq*, CSCO CCCX (Subs. 36, Louvain, 1970).

Figulla, H., 'Manichäer in Indien und das Zeitalter des tamulischen Dichters Māṇikkavācagar', *Archiv Orientalni*, XVII (1938), pp. 112–22.

Flügel, G., *Mani. Seine Lehre und seine Schriften* (Leipzig, 1862).

Forte, A., 'Deux études sur le manichéisme chinois', T'oung Pao LIX (1972) pp. 220-53.

Frank, T. (ed.), An Economic Survey of Ancient Rome, 5 vols. and Index (Baltimore, 1933-40).

Franke, H., Sung Biographies, 4 vols. (Wiesbaden, 1976).

Franke, O., Geschichte des Chinesischen Reiches, 5 vols. (Berlin, 1930-52).

Frend, W. H. C., 'The Gnostic-Manichaean tradition in Roman North Africa'. Journal of Ecclesiastical History, IV (1953), pp. 13-26.

__ The Donatist Church, a Movement of Protest in N. Africa, 2nd ed. (Oxford, 1971).

__ Martyrdom and Persecution in the Early Church (Oxford, 1965).

__ The Rise of the Monophysite Movement (Cambridge, 1972).

__ 'Manichaeism in the struggle between Saint Augustine and Petilian of Constantine', Augustine Magister II (Paris, 1954), pp. 859-66

Frumkin, G., Archaeology in Soviet Central Asia, HO VIII (Leiden/Kölin, 1970).

Frye, R. N., The Golden Age of Persia (London, 1975).

__ The Heritage of Persia (London, 1976)

__ 'Notes on the early Sassanian state and church', in Studi Orientalistici in onore di Giorgio Levi della Vida, I (Rome, 1956), pp. 314-35.

__ 'The significance of Greek and Kushan archaeology in the history of Central Asia', Journal of Asian History (Wiesbaden) I (1967) pp. 33-44.

__ 'Tarxun-Türxun and Central Asian history', HJAS, XIV (1951), pp. 105-29.

Funke, H., 'Majestäts- und Magierprozesse bei Ammianus Marcellinus', Jahrbuch für Antike und Christentum, X (1967) pp. 145-75.

Gabain, A. von, Das uigurische Königreich von Chotscho 850-1250, 2 vols. (Wiesbaden, 1973).

Gagé, J., La montée des Sassanides et l'heure de Palmyre (Paris, 1964).

Garnsey, P. D. A., Social Status and Legal Privilege in the Roman Empire (Oxford, 1970).

Garsoïan, N. G., The Paulician Heresy: a Study of the Origin and Development of Paulicianism in Armenia and the Eastern Provinces of the Byzantine Empire (The Hague, 1967).

Gasparro, G. S., 'Sur l'histoire des influences du Gnosticisme' in Aland (ed.) (1978), pp. 316-50.

Gaudemet, J., La formation du driot seculier et du droit de l'église aux IVe et V^e siecles (Paris, 1958).

Geffcken, J., Komposition und Entstehungzeit der Oracula Sibyllina, TU XXIII/1 (Leipzig, 1902).

__ Der Ausgang der griechisch-römischen Heidentums (Heidlberg, 1920).

Geiger, B., 'The Middle Iranian texts' in The Excavations at Dura Europos, Final Report VIII: Pt. 1. The Synagoue (New Haven, 1956) pp. 283-317.

Gernet, J., Les aspects économiques du Bouddhisme dans la société chinoise du Ve au Xe siècle, (Hanoi, 1956).

Giradet, K., 'Trier 385, der Prozess gegen die Priscillianer', Chiron IV (1974), pp. 577-608.

Göbl, R., Dokumente zur Geschichte der iranischen Hunnen in Bactrien und Indien, II (Wiesbaden, 1967).

Gombrich, R., *Precept and Practice: Traditional Buddhism in the Rural Highlands of Ceylon* (Oxford, 1971).

Goodrich, L. C., 'Recent discoveries at Zaitun' *Journal of the American Oriental Soceity*, LXXVII (1957), pp. 160–5.

__ *et al.* (ed.), *Dictionary of Ming Biography, 1368–1644*, I (New York, 1976).

Gordon, R. L., 'Franz Cumont and the doctrines of Mithraism', in J. R. Hinnells (ed.), *Mithraic Studies*, I (Manchester, 1975), pp. 215–58.

Grant, R. M., 'Manichees and Christians in the third and fourth centuries', in *Ex Orbe Religionum*, I (Leiden, 1972), pp. 430–39.

Groot, J. J. M. de, *Sectarianism and Religious Persecution in China*, 2 vols. (Amsterdam, 1903).

Grousset, R., *The Empire of the Steppes*, trans. N. Walford (New Jersey, 1970).

Gruenwald, I., 'Manichaeism and Judaism in light of the Cologne Mani Codex', *ZPE* L (1983), pp. 29–43.

Guillaumont, A., 'Justinien et l'Eglise de Perse', *Dumbarton Oaks Papers*, XXIII (1969), pp. 41–66.

Hadot, I., 'Die Widerlegung des Manichäismus im Epictetkommentar des Simplikios', *Archiv für Geschichte der Philosophie*, LI (1969), pp. 31–57.

Haloun-Henning, 'Compendium': See under *Mo-ni kuang-fo chiao-fa i-lüeh* in Bibliography I.(c).

Hamilton, J. R., *Les Ouïghours à l'époque des cinq dynastries d'après les documents chinois* (Paris, 1955).

Hannested, K., 'Les rélations de Byzance avec la Transcaucasie et l'Asie Centrale aux 5ᵉ et 6ᵉ siècles', *Byzantion*, XXV–XXVII (1955–7), pp. 421–56.

Harmatta, J., 'The oldest evidence for silk-trade between China and India', in Altheim and Stiehl (ed.) (1970), pp. 650–84.

Harnack, A., *Die Geschichte der altchristlichen Literatur bis Eusebius*, 3 vols. (Leipzig, 1893–1904).

__ 'Die älteste Kircheninschrift', *SPAW* (1915), pp. 746–66.

__ *Marcion, Das Evangelium vom fremden Gott*, TU XLV (Leipzig, 1921).

Haussig, H. W., 'Theophylacts Exkurs über die skythischen Völker', *Byzantion*, XXIII (1953), pp. 275–462.

Henning, W. B., 'Argi and the "Tocharians" ', *BSOS* IX/3 (1938), pp. 545–71.

__ 'Mani's last journey', *BSOAS* X/4 (1942), pp. 941–53.

__ 'Waručān-Šāh', *Journal of the Greater India Society*, XI/2 (July 1944), pp. 85–90.

__ 'The date of the Sogdian Ancient Letters', *BSOAS* XII (1948), pp. 601–15.

__ 'Mitteliranisch', *HO* I, 4, 1 (Leiden/Köln, 1958), pp. 20–130.

__ 'Neue Materialien zur Geschichte des Manichäismus', *ZDMG* XC (1936), pp. 1–18.

__ *Sogdica*, James Forlong Fund Prize Publications, XXI, (London, 1940).

__ 'Two Manichaean magical texts with an excursus on the Parthian ending -ēndēh', *BSOAS* XII/1 (1947), pp. 39–66.

__ 'A fragment of the Manichaean hymn-cycle in Old Turkish', *Asia Major*, N.S. VII (1959), pp. 122–4.

__ 'The Book of the Giants', *BSOAS* XI, 1 (1943) pp. 52–74.

__ *Ein manichäisches Henochbuch*, *SPAW* V (1934), pp. 27–35.

Henrichs, A., 'Mani and the Babylonian Baptists: a historial confrontation'

Harvard Studies in Classical Philology, LXXVII (1973), pp. 23–59. [= Henrichs, 'Babylonian Baptists']

__ ''Thou shalt not kill a tree': Greek, Manichaean and Indian tales', *Bulletin of the American Society of Papyrologists*, XVI, 1–2 (1979), pp. 85–108.

__ 'The Cologne Mani Codex reconsidered', *HSCP* LXXXIII (1979), pp. 339–67.

__ and L. Koenen, 'Ein griechischer Mani-Codex (P. Coln. inv. nr. 4780)', *ZPE* V/2 (1970), pp. 97–216. [= Henrichs-Koenen, 'Mani-Codex']

__ 'Literary criticism of the Mani Codex' in Layton (ed.) (1981), pp. 724–33.

Herrmann, A., *Die alten Seidenstrassen zwischen China und Syrien* (Berlin, 1910).

Hervouet, E.(ed.), *A Sung Bibliography* (Hong Kong, 1978).

Hinnells, J. R., 'The Iranian background of Mithraic iconography', *Acta Iranica*, I (1974), pp. 242–50.

Hoffman, M., *Der Dialog bei den christlichen Schriftstellern der ersten vier Jahrhunderte*, TU XCI (Berlin, 1966).

Homes-Dudden, F., *The Life and Times of St. Ambrose*, 2 vols. (Oxford, 1935).

Honigmann, E., *Die Ostgrenze des byzantinischen Reiches* (Brussels, 1961).

__ 'Zacharias of Mitylene', in *Patristic Studies*, Studi e Testi CLXXIII (1953), pp. 914–204.

__ and A. Maricq, *Recherches sur les Res Gestae Divi Saporis* (Brussels, 1952).

Hopkins, C., *The Topography and Architecture of Seleucia on the Tigris* (Ann Arbor, 1972).

Hunt, D., *Holy Land Pilgrimage in the Later Roman Empire* (Oxford, 1982).

(*Insadi-Sūtra*), S. Tezcan, *Das uigurische Insadi-Sūtra*, Berliner Turfantexte III (Berlin, 1974).

Jackson, A. V. W., *Researches into Manichaeism with special reference to Turfan Fragments* (New York, 1932).

Jalland, T., *The Life and Times of St Leo the Great* (London, 1941).

Jan Yün-hua, 'Buddhist historiography in Sung China', *ZDMG* CXIV (1964) pp. 360–81.

Jarry, J., *Hérésies et factions dans l'empire byzantin du IVe au VIIe siècle* (Cairo, 1968).

John of Nikiu, *The Chronicle of John, Bishop of Nikiu*, trans. R. H. Charles (London, 1916).

Jushin Ikemoto, 'Amita' in *Encyclopaedia of Buddhism*, ed. G. P. Malasekera (Ceylon, 1961), pp. 443–56.

Kaden, E. H., 'Die Edikte gegen die Manichäer von Diokletian bis Justinian', *Festschrift Hans Lewald* (Basel, 1953), pp. 55–68.

Kao Yu-kung, 'A study of the Fang La rebellion', *Harvard Journal of Astiatic Studies*, XXIV (1962–3), pp. 17–63.

__ 'Source material on the Fang La rebellion', *HJAS* XXVI (1966), pp. 211–40 = Kao Yu-kung, 'Source material'.

Kaser, M., *Das römische Privatrecht*, 2 vols., I, 2nd edn. (Munich, 1971), II (1969).

Kessler, K., *Mani. Forschungen über die manichäische Religion*, I (Berlin, 1889).

King, N. Q., *The Emperor Theodosius and the Establishment of Christianity* (London, 1961).

Klijn, A. F. J., *Seth in Jewish, Christian and Gnostic Literature* (Leiden, 1979).

___ and G. J. Reinink, *Patristic Evidence for Jewish Christian Sects* (Leiden, 1973).

Klíma, O., 'Baat the Manichee', *Archiv Orientalní* XXVI (1958), pp. 342–6.

___ *Manis Zeit und Leben* (Prague, 1962). [= Klíma, MZL]

Klimkeit, H. J., 'Manichäische und buddhistische Beichtformeln aus Turfan', *ZRGG*, XXIX/3 (1977), pp. 193–228.

___ 'Vairocana und das Lichtkreuz. Manichäische Elemente in der Kunst von Alchi (West Tibet)', *Zentralasiatische Studien*, XIII (1979), pp. 357–98.

___ 'Stūpa and Parinirvāṇa as Manichaean motifs', in A. L. Dallapiccola (ed.), *The Stūpa* (Weisbaden, 1980), pp. 229–37.

___ 'Hindu deities in Manichaean art', *Zentralasiatische Studien*, XIV (1980) 179–99.

___ *Manichaean art and calligraphy, Iconography of Religions* XX (Brill, 1982). [= Klimkeit, Art]

___ 'Das Kreuzessymbol in der zentralasiatischen Religionsbegegnung', *ZRGG* XXXI/1 (1979) pp. 99–115.

___ 'Der Buddha Henoch: Qumran und Turfan', *ZRGG* XXXII/4 (1980) pp. 367–76.

___ 'Manichaean kingship: gnosis at home in the world', *Numen* XXIX (1982), pp. 17–32.

Kljaštornyi, S. G. and V. A. Livsic, 'The Sogdian inscription of Bugut revised' *Acta Orientalia . . . Hungaricae*, XXVII (1972) pp. 69–102.

Köbert, R., 'Ein zum Abfall gezwungener Manichäer muss Ameisen töten', *Orientalia* XXXVIII (1969), pp. 128–30.

Koenen, L., 'Zur Herkunft des Kölner Mani-Codex', *ZPE* XI (1973), pp. 240–41.

___ 'Augustine and Manichaeism in the light of the Cologne Mani Codex', *Illinois Classical Studies*, III (1978), pp. 154–95.

___ 'Form baptism to the gnosis of Manichaeism' in Layton (ed.), (1981), pp. 734–56.

___ 'Manichäische Mission und Klöster in Ägypten', in *Das römisch-byzantinische Ägypten* (*Aegyptiaca Treverensia*, Mainz am Rhein, 1983), pp. 93–108.

Labourt, J., *Le christianisme dans l'Empire perse* (Paris, 1904).

Land, D. M. 'St Euthymius the Georgian and the Barlaam and Josaphat Romance', *BSOAS*, XVII/2 (1965), pp. 306–25.

___ *The Wisdom of Balahvar* (London, 1957).

Larsen, M. T., 'The tradition of empire in Mesopotamia', in *idem* (ed.) *Mesopotamia 7, Power and Propaganda* (Copenhagen, 1979), pp. 75–103.

Lauras, A., 'Saint Léon le Grand et le Manichéisme romain', *Studia Patristica* XI, Tu 108 (Berlin 1972), pp. 203–9.

Layton, B. (ed.), *The Rediscovery of Gnosticism*, II, *Sethian Gnosticism* (Leiden, 1981).

Lear, F. S., 'The idea of majesty in Roman political thought', in *idem, Treason in Roman and Germanic Law* (Austin, Texas, 1965), pp. 49–72.

Levy, H. S., *The Biography of Huang Chao (Los Angeles, 1955)*.

Lewy, H., *Chaldaean Oracles and Theurgy*, new edn., ed. M. Tardieu (Paris, 1978).

Lidzbarski, M., 'Die Herkunft der manichäischen Schrift', *SPAW*, 1916, pp. 1213-22.

Liebeschuetz, J. H. W. G., *Antioch: City and Administration in the Later Roman Empire* (Oxford, 1972).

Lieu, J. M. and S. N. C., '*Felix Conversus ex Manichaeis*' a case of mistaken identity', *Journal of Theological Studies* XXIII/1 (1981) pp. 173-6.

Lieu, S. N. C., 'A lapsed Chinese Manichaean's correspondence with a Confucian official in the late Sung dynasty (1264): a study of the *Ch'ung-shou-kung chi* by Huang Chen', *Bulletin of the John Rylands University Library of Manchester* LIX/2 (spring 1977), pp. 397-425.

__ 'Polemics against Manichaeism as a subversive cult in Sung China', *ibid.*, LXII (autumn 1979), pp. 151-67.

__ 'Nestorians and Manichaeans on the South China coast', *Vigiliae Christianae* XXXIV (1980), pp. 71-88.

__ 'Precept and practice in Manichaean monasticism', *Journal of Theological Studies* XXXII/1 (1981) pp. 153-73.

__ *The Religion of Light: an Introduction to the History of Manichaeism in China* (Hong Kong, 1979).

__ 'An early Byzantine formula for the renunciation of Manichaeism, the *Capita VII contra Manichaeos* of < Zacharias of Mitylene >', *Jahrbuch für Antike und Christentum*, XXVI (1983), pp. 152-218.

__ 'New light on Manichaeism in China' to appear in *Papers in Honour of Prof. Mary Boyce*, pp. 401-19.

__ *The Diffusion and Persecution of Manichaeism in Rome and China – a Comparative Study* (D. Phil. Diss. Oxford, 1981, unpublished).

__ 'The Holy Men and their biographers in Early Byzantium and Medieval China', in A. Moffatt ed., *Maistor: Classical, Byzantine and Renaissance Studies for Robert Browning* (Canberra, 1984) pp. 113-47.

Liu Mau-t'sai, *Die chinesischen Nachrichten zur Geschichte der Ost-Türken*, 2 vols. (Wiesbaden, 1958).

Liu Ts'un-yan, 'The compilation and historical value of the *Tao-tsang*', in *Essays on the Sources for Chinese History*, ed. D. Leslie *et. al.*, Canberra, 1973) pp. 104-19.

__ 'Traces of Zoroastrian and Manichaean activities in pre-T'ang China', in *idem, Selected Papers from the Hall of Harmonious Winds* (Leiden, 1976), pp. 2-55.

Livšic, V. A., *Sogdijskie Documenty s Gory Mug*, Part II (Moscow, 1962).

McDowell, R. H., *Coins from Seleucia on the Tigris* (Ann Arbor, 1935).

MacKenzie, D. N., 'Mani's Šābuhragān', *BSOAS*, XLII/3 (1979), pp. 500-534.

__ 'Mani's Šābuhragān – II', *ibid.* XLII/3 (1980), pp. 288-310.

MacKerras, C., *The Uighur Empire* (Canberra, 1972).

McKnight, B., *Village and Bureaucracy in Southern Sung China* (Chicago, 1971).

Macmullen, R., *Enemies of the Roman Order (Cambridge, Mass., 1967)*.

__ 'Imperial bureaucrats in the Roman provinces', *Harvard Studies in Classical*

Philology, LVIII (1964), pp. 305-16.

Maenchen-Helfen, O., 'Pseudo-Huns', *Central Asiatic Journal*, I (1955), 101-6.

__ 'Manichaeans in Siberia', in *Semitic and Oriental Studies presented to William Popper*, University of California Publications in Semitic Philology, XI (1951) pp. 311-26.

Markwart, J., *Ērānšahr nach der Geographie des Ps. Moses Xorenac'i*, *Abhandlungen der königlichen Gesellschaft der Wissenschaften zu Göttingen*, Phil.-Hist. Klasse, N.S. III/2 (1901).

__ *Wehrot und Arang*, ed. H. H. Schaeder (Leiden, 1938).

__ *Osteuropäische und ostasiatische Streifzüge* (Leipzig, 1903).

Matthews, J. F., 'Symmachus and the Oriental cults', *JRS* LXII (1973), pp. 175-95.

Menasce, P. J. de, 'Augustin manichéen', in *Freundesgabe für Ernst Robert Curtius zum 14 April 1956* (Berne, 1956), pp. 79-83.

Mercati, G., 'Per la vita e gli scritti di ''Paulo il Persiano''. Appunti da una disputa di religione sotto Giustine e Giustiniano',*Studi e Testi* V (Rome, 1901), pp. 180-206.

Milik, J. T., *The Books of Enoch, Aramaic Fragments of Qumrân Cave 4* (Oxford, 1976).

Millar, F. G. B., 'Paul of Samosata, Zenobia and Aurelian: the church, local culture and political allegiance in third-century Syria', *JRS*, LXI (1971), pp. 1-17.

Mitteis, L., *Reichsrecht und Volksrecht in den östlichen Provinzien des römischen Kaiserreichs (Leipzig, 1981)*.

Miyakawa, H. and A. Kollautz, 'Abdelai' in *Reallexikon der Byzantinistik* ed. P. Wirth, Ser.A., I (Amsterdam, 1969, in progress), cols. 88-126.

Mommsen, T., 'Ammians Geographica', *Hermes*, XVI (1881), pp. 602-36.

__ *Römisches Strafrecht*, 2nd edn. (Leipzig, 1899).

Monceaux, P., *Histoire littéraire de l'Afrique chrétienne*, 7 vols. (Paris, 1901-23).

__ *Le manichéen Faustus de Milev, restitution de ses capitula* (Paris, 1924).

Moravisik, G., *Byzantinoturcica*, 2 vols. (Berlin, 1958).

Morony, G., *Transition and Continuity in Seventh Century Iraq* (Diss. U.C.L.A., 1972, University Mircrofilms 72-25816).

Moses Chorenats'i, *History of the Armenians*, trans. R. W. Thomson (Camb., Mass., 1978).

Moses, L. W., 'T'ang tribute relations with the Upper Asian barbarians' in J. C. Perry and B. L. Smith (eds.), *Essays on T'ang Society* (Leiden, 1976) pp. 61-89.

Müller, F. W. K., 'Die ''persischen'' Kalenderausdrücke im chinesischen Tripitaka', *SPAW* (1907), pp. 458-65.

__ 'Der Hofstaat eines Uiguren-Königs', *Festschrift Vilhelm Thomsen* (Leipzig, 1912) pp. 207-13.

Muramatsu, Yuji, 'Some themes in Chinese rebel ideologies', in A. F. Wright (ed.), *The Confucian Persuasion*, (Stanford, 1960), pp. 243-56.

Murayama, S., 'Eine nestorianische Grabinschrift in türkischer Sprache aus Zaiton', *Ural-Altaische Jahrbücher*, XXLV (1964) pp. 394-6.

Murray, R., 'The exhortation to candidates for ascetical vows at baptism in the

ancient Syrian Church', *New Testament Studies*, XXI (1974–5), pp. 59–80.
__ *Symbols of Church and Kingdom* (Cambridge, 1975).
al-Nadim, *The Fihrist of al-Nadim*, trans. B. Dodge, 2 vols. (New York, 1970).
Nagel, P., 'Die Psalmoi Sarakōtōn des manichäischen Psalmbuches', *Orientalische Literaturzeitung*, LXII (1967), cols. 123–30.
__ 'Die apokryphen Apostelakten des 2. und 3. Jh. in der manichäischen Literatur', in K. W. Tröger (ed.), *Gnosis und Neues Testament* (Gütersloh, 1973) pp. 149–82.
__ *Die antimanichäischen Schriften des Titus von Bostra* (Habilitationschrift Halle/Wittenburg, 1967, unpublished).
__ *Die Thomaspsalmen des Koptisch-manichäischen Psalmenbuches* (Leipzig, 1980).
Neusner, J., *A History of the Jews in Babylonia*, 5 vols. (Leiden, 1969–70).
__ 'Parthian political ideology', *Iranica Antiqua* III/1 (1963) pp. 40–59.
Noethlichs, K.-L., *Die gesetzgeberischen Massnahmen der christlichen Kaiser des vierten Jahrhunderts gegen Häretiker, Heiden und Juden* (Diss., Köln, 1971).
Nyberg, H. S., 'The Pahlavi documents from Avroman', *Le Monde Oriental*, XVII (1923) pp. 182–230.
Oates, D., 'Note on three Latin inscriptions at Hatra', *Sumer*, XI (1955), pp. 39–43.
Obolensky, D., *The Bogomils: A Study in Balkan Neo-Manichaeism* (Cambridge, 1948).
Olschki, L., 'Manichaeism Buddhism and Christianity in Marco Polo's China', *Zeitschrift der schweizerischen Gesellschaft für Asienkunde*, V, Pt. 1/2 (1951), 1–21.
Overymyer, D., *Folk Buddhist Religion, Dissenting Sects in Late Traditional China* (Camb., Mass., 1976).
__ 'The White Cloud sect in Sung and Yüan China', *HJAS* XLII/2 (1982), pp. 615–42.
Peeters, P., *Le tréfonds oriental de l'hagiographie byzantine*, *Subsidia Hagiographica*, XXVI (Brussels, 1950).
Pellegrino, M., *Les Confessions de Saint Augustin: Guide de lecture* (Paris, 1960).
Pelliot , P., 'Le Mo-ni et le Houa-hou-king', *BEFEO*, III (1903), pp. 318–27.
__ *Notes on Marco Polo*, ed. L. Hambis, II, (Paris 1963).
__ 'Les traditions manichéennes au Foukien', *T'oung Pao*, XXII (1923) pp. 193–208.
__ 'Les influences iraniennes en Asie Centrale et en Extrême-Orient', *Revue d'Histoire et de Litterature Religieuses*, N.S. III (1912), pp. 97–119.
__ 'Le "Cha-tcheou-tou-fou-t'ou-king" et la colonie sogdienne de la religion du Lob Nor', *Journal Asiatique*, 2 ser., VII (Jan–Feb., 1916), pp. 111–23.
__ review of E. Chavannes, *Les pays d'Occident d'après les Wei-lio*, *BEFEO*, VI (1906), pp. 361–400.
Pétrement, S., *Le Dualisme chez Platon, les gnostiques et les manichéens* (Paris, 1947).
Piganiol, A., *L'Empire Chrétien (Paris, 1947).*
Pigulevskaja, N., *Les villes de l'état iranien aux époques parthe et sassanide*

(Paris/The Hague, 1963).

__ *Byzanz auf den Wegen nach Indien, Berliner Byzantinische Arbeiten*, XXXVI (Berlin, 1970).

Pinks, E., *Die Uiguren von Kan-chou in der frühen Sung-Zeit* (Wiesbaden, 1968).

Poidebard, A., *La trace de Rome dans le désert Syrie*, 2 vols. (Paris, 1934).

Polotsky, J. H., 'Koptische Zitate aus den Acta Archelai', *Le Muséon*, XLVI (1932), pp. 18–20.

__ *Abriss des manichäischen Systems* (Stuttgart, 1934 = *PW* Suppl. VI, 1935, cols. 241–72.)

Puech, H.-Ch., *Le Manichéisme. Son fondateur – sa doctrine* (Paris, 1949).

__ 'Dates manichéennes dans les chroniques syriaques', *Melanges Syriens offerts a M. R. Dussaud*, II (Paris, 1939), pp. 593–607.

__ *Sur le Manichéisme et autres essais* (Paris, 1979) [= Puech, *Essais*.]

__ <'Les premières missions manichéennes dans l'Inde et en Egypte'>, *Annuaire de l'École pratique des Hautes études*, V^c section, 80–81 (1973–4), pp. 327–9.

Pulleyblank, E. G., 'Chinese and Indo-Europeans', *JRAS* (1966), pp. 9–39.

__ *Background to the Rebellion of An Lu-shan* (Oxford, 1955).

__ 'A Sogdian colony in Inner Mongolia', *T'oung Pao*, XLI (1952), pp. 317–56.

Quasten, J., *Patrology*, III (Washington DC, 1960).

Quispel, G., 'Mani The Apostle of Christ', in *idem*, *Gnostic Studies*, II (Amsterdam, 1975) pp. 230–7.

__ *Tatian and the Gospel of Thomas* (Leiden, 1975).

Reichelt, H., *Die sogdischen Handschriften des Britischen Museums*, II, *Die nichtbuddhistischen Texte* (Heidelberg, 1931).

Reinink, G. J., 'Das Land ''Seris'' (Sir) und das Volk der Serer in jüdischen und christlichen Traditionen', *Journal for the Study of Judaism*, VI/1 (June 1965) pp. 72–85.

Reischauer, E. O. *Ennin's Travels in T'ang China* (New York, 1955).

Reitzenstein, R., 'Eine wertlose und eine wertvolle Überlieferung über den Manichäismus', *Nachrichten von der Gesellschaft der Wissenschaften zu Göttingen*, (1931), pp. 28–58.

__ 'Alexander von Lycopolis', *Philologus*, LXXXVI/2 (1931), pp. 185–98.

__ *Poimandres* (Leipzig, 1904).

__ and H. H. Schaeder, *Studien zum antiken Synkretismus* (Leipzig, 1926).

Ries, J., 'Introduction aux études manichéennes: Quatre siécles de recherches', *Ephemerides Theologicae Lovanienses*, XXXIII (1957), pp. 453–82 and XXXV (1959) pp. 362–409.

__ 'La fête de Bêma dans l'Église de Mani', *Revue des études Augustiniennes*, XXII (1976), pp. 218–33.

__ 'Commandements de la justice et vie missionaire dans l'Église de Mani', in *Gnosis and Gnosticism*, ed. M. Krause (Leiden, 1977), pp. 93–106.

__ 'Une version liturgique copte de l' ''Epistola Fundamenti'' réfutée par saint Augustin?', *Studia Patristica*, XI, TU 108 (Berlin, 1972) pp. 41–9.

Rose, E., *Die manichäische Christologie*, *Studies in Oriental Religions*, V (Wiesbaden, 1979).

Rosenthal F., *Die aramäistische Forschung seit Theodor Nöldeke's Veroffentli-*

chungen (Leiden, 1939).

— *Die Sprache der Palmyrenischen Inschriften und ihrer Stellung innerhalb das Aramäischen, Mitteilungen der Vorderasiatisch-Aegyptischen Gesellschaft*, XLI, 1 (Leipzig, 1936).

Rotours, R. de, *Histoire de Ngan Lou-chen* (Paris, 1962).

Rudolph, K., *Die Gnosis* (Göttingen, 1977).

— *Antike Baptisten, Sitzungsberichte der sächsischen Akademie der Wissenschaften zu Leipzig*, Phil.-hist. Klasse, CXXI/4 (Berlin, 1981).

Runciman, S., *The Medieval Manichee* (Cambridge, 1948).

Sahas, D. J., *John of Damascus on Islam – the 'heresy of the Ishmaelites'* (Leiden, 1972).

Säve-Söderbergh, T., *Studies in the Coptic Manichaean Psalmbook* (Upsala, 1949)

Schachermeyr, F., *Alexander in Babylon und die Reichsordnung nach seinem Tode, Sitzungsberichte der österreichischen Akademie der Wissenschaften*, CCLXVIII (Vienna, 1970).

Schaeder, H. H. 'Urform und Fortbildungen des manichäischen Systems', *Vorträge der Bibliothek Warburg, 1924–5* (Leipzig, 1927), pp. 65–157.

— *Iranica, Abhandlungen der Gesellschaft der Wissenschaften zu Göttingen* Phil.-hist. Klasse Folge 3, Nr. 10, (Berlin, 1934).

— 'Der Manichäismus nach neuen Funden und Forschungen', *Morgenland*, XXVIII (1936), pp. 80–109.

— Review of C. Schmidt and H. J. Polotsky, *Ein Mani-Fund in Ägypten, Gnomon* IX (July 1933), pp. 337–362.

— 'Der Manichäismus und sein Weg nach Osten', *Glaube und Geschichte – Festschrift für F. Gogarten* (Giessen, 1948), pp. 236–54.

Schafer, E., *The Golden Peaches of Samarkand: A Study of T'ang Exotics* (Los Angeles, 1962).

— 'Iranian merchants in T'ang dynasty tales', in *Semitic and Oriental Studies Presented in William Popper, University of California Publications in Semitic Philology*, XI (1951), pp. 403–22.

— *The Empire of Min* (Vermont, 1954).

Scharf, A., *Byzantine Jewry* (London, 1971).

Schlegel, G., *Die Chinesische Inschrift auf dem uigurischen Denkmal in Kara Balgassun* (Helsingfors, 1896).

Schmidt, C. and H. J. Polotsky, 'Ein Mani-Fund in Ägypten. Originalschriften des Mani und seiner Schüler', *SPAW*, Phil.-Hist. Klasse, I, (1933), 4–90.

Schoeps, H., *Theologie und Geschichte des Judenchristentums* (Tübingen, 1949).

Schürer, E., *The History of the Jewish People in the Age of Jesus Christ*, rev. and ed. G. Vermes and F. Millar, II (Edinburgh, 1979).

Sedlar, J., *India and the Hellenic World* (New York, 1980).

Seeck, O., *Die Briefe des Libanius zeitlich geordnet* (Leipzig, 1906).

(Séert), A. Sher, *Histoire nestorienne inédite* (Chronique de Séert). *PO* IV (1908), pp. 211–313; V (1909) pp. 217–344; VII (1910), pp. 93–203 and XIII (1919) pp. 433–640

Segal, J. B., *Edessa, the Blesed City* (Oxford, 1970).

— 'The Jews of North Mesopotamia', in J. M. Grintz and J. Liver (ed.), *Sepher*

Segal(Jerusalem, 1964) pp. 32–63.

Seidel, Anna K., La divinisation de Lao Tseu dans le Taoisme des Han (Paris, 1969).

Seston, W., 'L'Égypte manichéenne', Chronique d'Égypte, XIV (1939), pp. 362–72.

___ Dioclétien et la tétrarchie (Paris, 1949).

Sherwin-Shite, A. N., The Letters of Pliny (Oxford, 1966).

Shih, V. Y. C., 'Some Chinese rebel ideologies', T'oung Pao XLIV (1956) pp. 150–226.

Sickenberger, J., Titus von Bostra, Studien zu dessen Lukashomilien, TU XXI/1 (Leipzig, 1901).

Smith, S., Babylonian Historical Texts (London, 1924).

Snellgrove, L. and T. Skorupski, The Cultural Heritage of Ladakh I, Central Ladakh(Worminster, 1977).

Spuler, B., 'Die Uiguren, die Sogd(i)er und der Manichäismus', HO I, 5, 5 (Leiden/Köln, 1966), pp. 148–62.

Stade, K., Der Politiker Diokletian und die letzte grosse Christenverfolgung (Wiesbaden, 1926).

Starcky, J., Palmyre (Paris, 1952).

Stark, J. K., Personal Names in Palmyrene Inscriptions (Oxford, 1971).

Stegemann, V., 'Zu Kapitel 69 der Kephalaia des Mani', ZNW, XXXVII (1938) pp. 214–23

Stein, A., Ruins of Desert Cathay, 2 vols. (London, 1912).

___ Serindia, 2 vols. (Oxford, 1921).

Stevenson, J., A New Eusebius (London, 1968).

Stoop, E. de, Essai sur la diffusion du manichéisme dans l'empire romain (Ghent, 1909).

Stroumsa, G., 'Monachisme et Marranisme chez les Manichéens d'Égypte', Numen, XXIX/2 (1982), pp. 184–201.

Sundermann, W., 'Iranische Lebensbeschreibungen Manis', Acta Orientalia, XXVI (Copenhagen, 1974) pp. 129–45.

___ 'Namen von Göttern, Dämonen und Menschen in iranischen Versionen des manichäischen Mythos', Altorientalische Forschungen, VI (Berlin, 1979), pp. 95–133.

___ 'Some remarks on Mithra in the Manichaean pantheon', Études mithraiques = Acta Iranica XVII (Tehran–Liège, 1978), pp. 485–99.

___ 'Christliche Evangelientexte in der Überlieferung der iranisch-manichäischen Literatur', Mitteilungen des Instituts für Orientforschung, XIV (1968), pp. 386–405.

___, 'Probleme der Interpretation manichäisch–soghdischer Briefe' Acta Antiqua . . . Hungaricae XXVIII (1983) pp. 289–316.

___ and W. Thilo, 'Zur mittelpersisch-chinesischen Grabinschrift aus Xi'an (Volksrepublik China)', Mitteilungen des Instituts für Orientforchung, XI (1966), pp. 437–50.

al-Ṭabarī (Muḥammad b. Ǧarīr), Geschichte der Perser und Araber zur Zeit der Sasaniden, trans. T. Nöldeke (Leiden, 1879).

Tardieu, M., 'Vues nouvelles sur le manichéisme africain?', Revue des Études Augustiniennes, LXXXI (1979) pp. 249–55.

___ 'Prātā et ad'ur chez les manichéens', *ZDMG* CXXX (1980) pp. 340–41.

___ 'Les manichéens en Égypte' *Bulletin de la Société Francaise d'Égyptologie*, XCIV (1982) pp. 5–19.

Tengstrom, E., *Donatisten und Katholiken* (Gothenburg, 1964).

Tezcan, see under (Insadi-Sūtra).

Thomas, J. D., 'The date of the the revolt of L. Domitius Domitianus', *ZPE*, XXII (1976), pp. 253–279.

Traube, L., '*Acta Archelai*. Vorbemerkung zu einer neuen Ausgabe', *Sitzungsberichte der königlichen bayerischen Akademie der Wissenschaften zu München*, Phil.-Hist. Klasse (1903), pp. 533–49.

Trietinger, O., *Die oströmische Kaiser- und Reichsidee* (Darmstadt, 1956).

Troje, L., *Die Dreizehn und die Zwölf im Traktat Pelliot* (Leipzig, 1925).

___ 'Zum Begriff ἄτακτος κίνησις bei Platon und Mani', *Museum Helveticum*, V (1948), pp. 95–115.

Tsui Chi, 'The Lower Section', see under *Mo-ni chiao hsia-pu tsan* in Bibliography I.(c).

Twitchett, D.C., *Financial Administration in T'ang China* (Cambridge, 1970).

___ (ed.), *The Cambridge History of China*, III, Pt. 1 (Cambridge, 1979).

Vajda, G., 'Les Zîndiqs en pays d'Islam au début de la période abbaside', *Revisita degli Studi Orientali*, XVII (1937–8), pp. 173–229.

Van der Lof, L. J., 'Mani as the danger from Persia in the Roman empire', *Augustiniana*, XXIV (1974), pp. 75–84.

___ 'Manichäische Verbeugungen der Sonne auf dem Vorderplatze der Sankt Peterskirche in Rom?' *Numen*, XVI/2 (1969) pp. 156–60.

Van Sickle, C. E., 'Conservative influence in the reign of Diocletian', *Classical Philology*, XXVII (1932), pp. 51–8.

Vasiliev, A. A., *Justin the First* (Camb., Mass., 1950).

Vollmann, B., *Studien zum Priscillianismus* (St. Ottilien, 1965).

Volterra, E., 'La costituzione di Diocleziano e Massiminiano contro i Manichaei', *Persia e il mondo grecoromano*, Accademia dei Lincei, anno 363, quaderno 76 (1966), pp. 27–50.

Vööbus, A., *A History of Asceticism in the Syrian Orient*, 2 vols., CSCO CLXXXIV (Subs. 14) and CXCVII (Subs. 17) (Louvain, 1958–60).

___ *History of the School of Nisibis*, CSCO CCLXVI, (Subs. 26 Louvain, 1965).

___ *Literary, Critical and Historical Studies in Ephrem the Syrian* (Stockholm, 1958).

Wada Hiroshi, *Prokops Rätselwort Serinda und die Verpflanzung des Seidenbaus von China nach dem oströmischen Reich* (Köln, 1970).

Wang, Gung-wu, *The Structure of Power in North China during the Five Dynasties* (Kuala Lumpur, 1963).

Weinstein, S., 'Imperial patronage in T'ang Buddhism', in *Perspectives on the T'ang*, ed. A. Wright and D. C. Twitchett (New Haven, 1973) pp. 265–302.

Welles, C. B., 'The population of Roman Dura', in *Studies . . . in honour of A. C. Johnson* (New Jersey, 1951) pp. 251–74.

___ See also works listed in Bibliography I.b.1.

Whitehouse, D. and A. Williamson, 'Sasanian maritime trade' *Iran*, XI (1973) pp. 29–49.

Widengren, G., *Mesopotamian Elements in Manichaeism*, Uppsala

Universitets Arsskrift, III 1946 (Uppsala and Leipzig, 1946).

___ Mani und der Manichäismus (Stuttgart, 1961).

Wiessner, G., Zur Märtyrerüberlieferung aus der Christenverfolgung Shapurs II (Göttingen, 1967).

Will, E., 'Marchands et chefs de caravanes à Palmyre' Syria, XXXIV (1957) pp. 267-77.

Williams, E. T., 'Witchcraft in the Chinese penal code', Journal of the North China Branch of the Royal Asiatic Society, XXXVII (1907) pp. 61-96.

Wright, A. F., 'Fo-t'u t'êng 佛圖澄-a Biography', HJAS XI (1948), pp. 321-71.

Yoshida, Yutaka, 'Manichaean Aramaic in the Chinese Hymnscroll', BSOAS XLVI/2 (1983) pp. 326-31.

Zieme, P., 'Die Uiguren und ihre Beziehungen zu China', Central Asiatic Journal, XVII (1973) pp. 281-93.

___ 'Ein uigurischer Text über die Wirtschaft manichäischer Klöster im uigurischen Reich', Researches in Altaic Languages, ed. L. Ligetti (Budapest, 1975).

___ 'Uigurische Steuerbefreiungsurkunden für buddhistische Klöster', Altorientalische Forschungen VIII (1981), pp. 237-63.

Zürcher, E., 'The Yüeh-chih and Kaniṣka in Chinese sources', in H. L. Basham (ed.), Papers on the Date of Kaniṣka (Leiden, 1968), pp. 346-90.

___ The Buddhist Conquest of China, 2 vols. (Leiden, 1959).

(b) **In Chinese and Japanese**

Chang Hsing-lang 張星烺, Chung-hsi chiao-t'ung shih-liao hui pien 中西交通史料滙編, IV (Taipei, 1962).

Ch'ang Pi-te 昌彼得 and others (eds.), Sung-jen ch'uan-chi tzu-liao so-yin 宋人傳記資料索引, 6 vols. (Taipei, 1976).

Ch'en Yüan 陳垣, 'Mo-ni-chiao ju Chung-kuo k'ao' 摩尼教入中國考, Kuo-hsüen chi-k'an 國學季刊 I/2 (1923) pp. 203-39. [Reprinted with additional material in Ch'en Yüan hsüeh-hsü lun-wen chih 陳垣學術論文集, I (Peking, 1980) pp. 329-74.]

Chiang Wei-chi 蔣爲璣 'Ch'üan-chou Mo-ni-chiao ch'u-t'an' 泉州摩尼教初探 Shih-chiai tsung-chiao yen-chiu 世界宗教研究 1983, Pt. 3, pp. 77-82.

Chikusa Masaaki 竺沙雅章, 'Kitsusaijima (Ch'ih-ts'ai shih-mo) ni tsuite' 喫菜事魔 について, in Aoyama hakushi koki kinen Sōdaishi ronsō 青山博士古稀紀念宋代史論叢 (Tokyo, 1974) pp. 239-62.

___ 'Hō Rō (Fang La) no ran to Kitsusaijima (Ch'ih-ts'ai shih-mo)' 方臘の亂と 喫菜事魔, Tōyōshi kenkyū 東洋史研究, XXXII, 4 (1973-4) pp. 455-77.

Chu Jui-hsi 朱瑞熙, 'Lun Fang La chih yü Mo-ni chiao ti kuan-hsi' 論方臘之與摩尼教的關係, Li-shih yen-chiu 歷史研究, 1979, Pt. 9, pp. 69-84.

Ch'üan-chou ming-sheng kuo-chi 泉州名勝古迹, compiled by a committee (Fukien, 1980).

Enoki Kazuo 榎一雄 'Sogudeiana to Kyōdo' リグディアナと匈奴, Pt. 3, Shigaku zasshi 史學雜誌 LXIV (1955) pp. 757-80.

Fang Hao 方豪, Chung-hsi chiao-t'ung shih 中西交通史, II (Taipei, 1960).

Fang Ch'ing-ying 方慶英, 'Pai-lien chiao ti yüan-liu chi ch'i ho Mo-ni chiao ti kuan-hsi'   白蓮教的源流及其和摩尼敎的關係, *Li-shih chiao-hsüeh wen-t'i* 歷史敎學問題, V (1959) pp. 34-8.

Fukui Kōjun 福井康順, *Dōkyō no kisoteki kenkyū* 道教の基礎的研究 (Tokyo, 1958).

Hiraoka Takeo 平岡武夫, 'Haku-shi bunshū no seiritsu' 白氏文集の成立 in *Tōhō Gakkai sōritsu jugo shūnen kinen, Tōhō-gaku ronshū* 東方學會創立 五十週年記念東方學論集 (Tokyo, 1962) pp. 260-75.

Hsia Nai 夏鼐, 'Ho-pei Ting-hsien t'a-chi she-li-han chung Po-ssu Sa-san ch'ao yin-pi'   河北定縣塔基舍利函中波斯薩珊朝銀幣, *K'ao-ku* 考古, 1966, Pt. 5, pp. 91-110.

___ 'Tsung-shu Chung-kuo ch'u-t'u ti Po-ssu Sa-san ch'ao yin-pi' 綜述中國 出土的波斯薩珊朝銀幣, *K'ao-ku hsüeh-pao*, XL (1974) pp. 91-110.

___ 'Hsien-yang ti Chang-wan Sui-mu ch'u-t'u ti Tung Lo-ma chin-pi' 咸陽底張灣隋墓出土的東羅馬金幣, in *K'ao-ku hsüeh lun-wen chi* 考古學 論文集 (Peking, 1961) pp. 135-42.

___ 'Liang-chung wen-tzu ho-pi ti Ch'üan-chou Yeh-li-k'o-wen (Ching-chiao) mu-pei' 兩種文字合璧的泉州也里可溫（景教）墓碑 *Kao-kuo* 1981, Pt. 1, pp. 59-62.

Ishida Mikinosuke 石田幹之助, 'Tonkō hakken *Manikō Bokkyō Hogiryakugi*' ni mietaru nisan no gengo ni tsuite 敦煌發見「摩尼光佛敎法儀略」に見えたる 二三の言語に就いて in *Shiratori-hakase kanreki-kinen tōyōshi ronsō* 白鳥博 士還曆記念東洋史論叢 (Tokyo, 1925) pp. 157-72.

Keng Shih-min 耿世民 'Hui-heh-wen Mo-ni-chiao ssu-yüan wen-shu ch'u-shih' 回鶻文摩尼敎寺院文書初釋 *K'ao-ku hsueh-pao* 考古學報 LI (1978), Pt. 4, pp. 497-516.

Kubo Noritada 窪德忠, 'Sōdai ni okeru dōkyō to Manikyō' 宋代における 道教とマニ教, *Wada hakushi koki kinen tōyōshi ronsō* 和田博士古稀紀念 東洋史論叢 (Tokyo, 1961) pp. 361-71.

Lin Wu-shu 林悟殊, 'Tun-huang pen *Mo-ni kuang-fo chiao-fa i-lüeh* ti ch'an-sheng' 敦煌本「摩尼光佛敎法儀略」的產生, *Shih-chiai tsung-chiao yen-chiu* 1983, Pt. 3, pp. 71-6.

Lo Hsiang-lin 羅香林, *T'ang Yüan erh-tai chih ching-chiao* 唐元二代之景教 (Hong Kong, 1966)

Mou Jun-sun 毛潤孫, 'Sung-tai Mo-ni chiao' 宋代摩尼教, *Fu-jen hsüeh-chih* 輔仁學誌, VII, Pts. 1 and 2 (1938), pp. 125-46, Reprinted in *Sung-shih yen-chiu chi* 宋史研究集, I (Taipei, 1958) pp. 79-100.

Nei-mung-ku wen-wu kung-tso-tui, Nei-mung ku po-wu-kuan 內蒙古 文物工作隊,   內蒙古博物舘, 'Huo-ho- hao-te shih fu-chin ch'u-t'u ti wai-kuo chin-yin-pi'   呼和浩特市附近出土的外國金銀幣, *K'ao-ku* 1975, Pt. 3, pp. 182-5.

Niida Noboru 仁井田陞, *Chūgoku hōsei shi kenkyū* 中國法制史研究, IV (Tokyo, 1964).

Saeki Yoshiro 佐伯好郎, *Keikyō no kenkyū* 景教の研究 (Tokyo, 1935).

Shigematsu Toshiake (Shunsho) 重松俊章, 'Tō Sō jidai no Manikyō to Makyō mondai' 唐宋時代の末尼敎と魔敎問題, *Shien* 史淵, XII (1936) pp. 85-143.

___ 'Tō Sō jidai no Mirokukyō-hi' 唐宋時代の彌勒敎匪, *ibid*. III (1931), pp. 68-103.

Shiratori Kurakichi 白鳥吉庫, 'Putoremaiosu ni mietaru Sorei tsukaro ni tsuite' プトレマイオスに見えたる葱嶺通過路に就いて, in *Seiiki shi kenkyū* 西域史研究, II (Tokyo, 1941) pp. 1-63.

Tasaka Kōdō 田坂興道 'Uiguru ni okeru Manikyō hakugai undō' 回訖に於ける 摩尼教迫害運動 *Tōhō Gakuho* (Tokyo) 東洋學報 XI/1 (1940) pp. 223-32.

Uchiyama Chinari 内山知也, *Zui Tō shōsetsu kenkyū* 隋唐小説研究, (Tokyo, 1977).

Wang Kuo-wei 王國維 'Mo-ni-chiao liu-hsing Chung-kuo kao' 摩尼教 流行中國考 in *idem, Kuan-t'ang pieh-chi hou-pien* 觀堂別集後篇 (n.d.) fasc. 1.24a-35b.

Wang Shu-nan 王壽南, *T'ang-tai fan-chen yü chung-yang kuan-hsi chih yen-chiu* 唐代藩鎮與中史關係之研究, (Taipei, 1970)

Wu Han 吳晗, 'Ming-chiao yü ta Ming ti-kuo' 明教與大明帝國, *Ch'ing-hua hsüeh-pao* 清華學報, XIII (1941) pp. 49-85, reprinted in the author's *Tu shih cha-chi* 讀史劄記 (Peking, 1956) pp. 235-70.

__ *Chu Yüan-chang chuan* 朱元璋傳 (Peking, 1944).

Wu Wen-liang 吳文良, *Ch'üan-chou tsung-chiao shih-k'o* 泉州宗教石刻 (Peking, 1957).

Yoshioka Yoshitoyo 吉岡義豐, *Dokyo keiten shiron* 道教經典史論 (Tokyo, 1955).

III. ADDENDA

The following works are relevant to the aspects of Manichaeism covered by the present study but they became available to me only after I had completed the text of the book.

Arrigoni, E., *Manicheismo Mazdakismo e confessione dell' eresiarca romano-Persiano Bundos*, Collezione Sebastiani (Milan, 1982).

Birley, A.R. 'Magnus Maximus and the persecution of heresy', *Bulletin of the John Rylands University Library of Manchester* LXVI/1 (autumn 1983), 13-43.

Klimkeit, H. J., 'Christians, Buddhists and Manichaeans in Central Asia', in *Buddhist-Christian Studies*, 1, 1981, S. 46-50.

__ 'Der Stifter im Lande der Seidenstrassen: Bemerkungen zur buddhistischen Laienfrömmigkeit', *ZRGG* XXXV (1983) pp. 289-308.

__ 'Das manichäische Königtum in Zentralasien', in *Documenta Barbarorum*, Festschrift für Walther Heissig zum 70. Geburtstag (Veröffentlichungen der Societas Uralo-Altaica, XVIII, Wiesbaden 1983) pp. 225-44.

__ 'Das Pferd Kaṇthaka – Symbol buddhistischer Erzähl- und Kunstelemente im zentralasiatischen Manichäismus', in *Aus dem Osten des Alexanderreichs*, Festschrift für Klaus Fischer, ed. J. Ozols and V. Thewalt. (Köln 1984) pp. 91-97.

__ and H. Schmidt-Glintzer: 'Die türkischen Parallelen zum chinesisch-manichäischen Traktat', *Zentralasiatische Studien* XVII (1984) pp. 82-117.

Merklebach, R., 'Manichaica (1-3)', *ZPE* LVI (1984) 45-54.

__ 'Manichaica (4)', *ZPE* LVII (1984) 73-7.

Rochow, I, 'Zum Fortleben des Manichäismus in Byzantinischen Reich nach

Justinian I', Byzantinoslavica XL (1979) 13–21.

G. Stroumsa, 'König und Schwein: Zur Struktur des manichäischen Dualismus', in Gnosis und Politik, ed. J. Taubes (Paderborn, 1984) 141–53.

W. Sundermann, 'Ein weiteres Fragment aus Manis Gigantentuch', Orientalia J. Duchesne-Guillemin emerito oblata (= Acta Iranica XXIII, 2nd Ser. IX, 1984) 491–505.

___, 'Der chinesische Traité Manichéen und der parthische Sermon vom Lichtnous', Altorientalische Forschungen X/2 (1983) 231–42.

___, 'Die Prosaliteratur der iranischen Manichäer', Orientalia Lovaniensia Analecta XVI (1984) 227–41.

Tardieu, M., Le Manichéisme ('Que Sais-je?' MCMXL, Paris, 1981)

___, P. Gignoux et al., 'Manichéisme' (review article), Abstracta Iranica (= Studia Iranica Suppl.) I (1978) 17–22, II (1979) 16–23, III (1980) 129–40, IV (1981) 100–7, V (1982) 142–51, VI (1983) 109–14.

Yarshater, E., The Cambridge History of Iran III, 2 pts, The Seleucid, Parthian and Sasanian Periods (Cambridge, 1983).

INDEX AND GLOSSARY